THE
DOLPHIN
READER

THE
DOLPHIN
READER

FIFTH EDITION

DOUGLAS HUNT
University of Missouri

CAROLYN PERRY
Westminster College

HOUGHTON MIFFLIN COMPANY   BOSTON   NEW YORK

Senior Sponsoring Editor: Dean Johnson
Associate Editor: Bruce Cantley
Senior Project Editor: Janet Young
Editorial Assistant: Nasya Laymon
Senior Production/Design Coordinator: Jill Haber
Manufacturing Manager: Florence Cadran
Senior Marketing Manager: Nancy Lyman

COVER DESIGNER: Harold Burch, Harold Burch Design, New York City
COVER IMAGES: Top: ©1990 Graham Monro—Photonica; bottom: ©1996 Jane Vollers—Photonica

Printed in the U.S.A.

Library of Congress Catalog Card Number: 98-72045

ISBN: 0-395-90353-X

7 8 9-DOC-05 04 03 02

CONTENTS

Note: An asterisk denotes fiction, poem, or drama. Annotated Contents may be found in the Overviews that begin each unit.

PREFACE

Just as a physician's first responsibility is "to do no harm," a reviser's first responsibility may be to avoid throwing the baby out with the bath water. Let's begin, therefore, by mentioning two features that have remained constant from the first edition of *The Dolphin Reader* to the present edition. The first is *connectedness*. The readings cluster around questions central to the lives of students and central to the disciplines they study:

> How are we initiated into our culture?
> How do we define what is masculine and what is feminine?
> How does the community we live in shape our individual identities?
> How do we deal with social differences within the community?
> Do we view ourselves as a part of nature or apart from nature?
> How is our identity affected by the way we get and spend money?
> How do the media shape our perceptions of life?
> What is the difference between mere learning and real understanding?

Though each of the eight units in this edition "specializes" in one of these questions, each question is such a powerful magnet for ideas that, as one user reports, they saturate the book and create crossovers: Randall Jarrell's "A Sad Heart at the Supermarket" is placed in "Media," but it would be equally at home in "Work and the Economy" or in "Understanding." Carol Bly's "Growing Up Expressive" could contribute to *any* unit in the book. All this is to say that we took our questions seriously, knowing that each would lead eventually to all and that a ball put up by one essay would land resoundingly in several other essays.

The second baby in the bath water is *variety in tone and style*. If every edition of *The Dolphin Reader* has taken ideas seriously, every edition has likewise avoided the stuffiness of some "great ideas" readers by balancing major essays with others that are shorter, lighter, more contemporary, and (frankly) more transient. We think that the major essays are crucial: they contain what Malcolm X called "intellectual vitamins," and no student should leave college without learning to deal with a "hard" reading. But, as Samuel Johnson once said, every reader eventually wants to escape the schoolmaster and turn to a friend. The shorter and lighter essays deal with the central ideas in forms that many students are more likely to warm to and perhaps more likely to emulate.

We have retained three innovations from more recent editions: poetry, paper topics, and style lessons. Users (some of them poets) tell us that the addition of a poem to each unit has provided spice and fresh insight. The paper topics collected in Appendix A and revised to reflect our new readings have been used "as is" or modified by instructors who report that they have provoked some good student essays. Appendix B contains a sampler of eighteen style lessons drawn from essays in the text. These lessons may provide students with an opportunity to imitate the author's way of styling a sentence or dovetailing a paragraph or managing some of the other technical skills that might otherwise go unnoticed and unused. In the *Instructor's Resource Manual,* instructors will find additional style lessons to accompany most of the essays in the reader.

Users of the fourth edition will find that twenty-eight of the eighty-six selections in the fifth edition are new and that the book contains two new units: "Initiation" and "Work and the Economy." In general, the changes are intended to sharpen the book's usefulness in helping students think about social forces that shape their identities. "Initiation" brings students face to face with some of the most common experiences of growing up, but at the same time it gives them tools to analyze such experiences from the perspectives of sociology or anthropology, religious studies or literary studies. "Work and the Economy" combines reflections about day-to-day life on the job with discussions of the larger philosophical questions raised by our often frenetic getting and spending.

The *Instructor's Resource Manual* is certainly one of the most thorough available, containing "work-ups" of each reading, including background for the instructor, style lessons, questions for class discussion or writing, and a teacher-to-teacher discussion of how these questions may play out in class. For several of the "work-ups" in the *Instructor's Resource Manual,* we thank Melody Richardson Daily. For excellent research and editing help, we thank Rachel Palencia.

Thanks go also to our supportive editors at Houghton Mifflin, especially to Dean Johnson, whose steady hand on the tiller reassured us. We are indebted to dozens of teachers who have made suggestions in person, by phone, and by mail, and especially to the following colleagues for their reviews:

Franklin Case, Eastern Michigan University
Patrick Dolan, Arapahoe Community College, CO
Robert Dornsife, Creighton University, NE
Patricia A. Malinowski, Finger Lakes Community College, NY
Eric Nelson, Georgia Southern University
Linda Quinlan-Rus, Roberts Wesleyan College, NY
Carl Silvio, West Virginia University
Robert P. Sowada, Mesa State College, CO

D.H.

C.P.

THE
DOLPHIN
READER

A clear example of the relation between generalization and specification comes from Nazi Germany, where Hitler's propaganda machine made sweeping statements about the superiority of the Aryan race and the threat posed to it by Jews and Judaism. The reaction of many intelligent and well-educated Germans was to examine the logic of these claims. For every generalization, they reasoned, there ought to be specification. To justify the generalization that the Jews were conspiring to undermine the Aryan race, the Nazis should offer specific evidence, specific examples. A historian tells me that the call for "specification" (in German, *Spezifizierung*) became so closely identified with resistance to the Nazi "big lie" that Hitler's agents would sit in bars, restaurants, and other public places, listening for the word *Spezifizierung* and prepared to arrest and interrogate those who said it too loudly or too often. That no questionable generalization should stand without adequate specification is one of the rules of the road in the logical level of an essay.

When the generalization is new or controversial, logical people will usually want the writer to provide several examples. Take, for example, the way historian Daniel Boorstin supports his generalization that technology has produced a "removal of distinctions" in our ordinary experience:

> One of the consequences of our success in technology, of our wealth, of our energy and our imagination, has been the removal of distinctions, not just between people but between everything and everything else, between every place and every other place, between every time and every other time. For example, television removes the distinction between being here and being there. And the same kind of process, of thinning out, of removing distinctions, has appeared in one area after another of our lives.
>
> For instance, in the seasons. One of the great unheralded achievements of American civilization was the rise of transportation and refrigeration, the development of techniques of canning and preserving meat, vegetables, and fruits in such a way that it became possible to enjoy strawberries in winter, to enjoy fresh meat at seasons when the meat was not slaughtered, to thin out the difference between the diet of winter and the diet of summer.[1]

Boorstin's essay goes on to talk about central heating and air conditioning (which thin the distinction between summer and winter), plate glass windows (which lessen the difference between indoors and outdoors), and easy-to-use cameras (which mix the past into the present). The generalization that technology "thins" our experience by removing distinctions may never have occurred to us before, but Boorstin's specification makes it relatively clear and convincing.

---

1. "Technology and Democracy," *Democracy and Its Discontents* (New York, 1974), pp. 103–104.

Of course, *disputing* generalizations is as much a logical action as *proposing* them. Couldn't we write a short essay challenging Boorstin's generalization by offering a few counter-examples of our own? We could point out that when a family flies from Minneapolis to southern Florida for a midwinter vacation, the contrast between winter and summer is not diminished for them, but sharpened. Or we could argue that in our own experience, sitting snug by a window during a thunderstorm doesn't diminish our awareness of the difference between being outdoors and indoors, but heightens it.

That Boorstin's generalization can be disputed does not weaken his essay; in fact it adds spice. Readers are more likely to be engaged by the logic of the essay if there is a real chance of dispute, a real need to show a connection between generalization and specifics. Offer the generalization that "Goldfish are easy pets to keep" and few readers will wait, breathless, to hear the predictable specifics about water temperature, food, and aeration.

Much more, of course, could be said about the logical aspect of writing, but for now we can conclude that it involves making connections between generalizations and specific cases. The writer who offers a sweeping generalization without specifics has done nothing at the logical level; the writer who offers a list of details unconnected to any general idea has done nothing. We should also say, however, that the logical level of an essay is not the only one; in some fine essays, it is far from the most important. Developing the logical level alone is acting as if we were severed heads, kept alive by tubes and machines and interacting with society only by analyzing data. The essayist remembers that we are alive from the neck down and that we have an almost inexhaustible interest in the lives of those around us.

Let's leave the logic behind for now and move to the social level of our lives and of the essay. I'll begin indelicately by putting you in my shoes on the day I composed this page, and putting those shoes into a stall in the men's rest room of the public library. To our left is another stall, occupied by a man wearing a pair of brown Kangaroos who is puffing noisily as he hauls himself to his feet and slowly walks out. As he opens the stall door, we hear him say, "They ought to make these stalls wider; you can hardly turn around in there." Into the newly vacated stall walks a pair of Adidas, and as the outer door closes behind the Kangaroos, the man in the Adidas says, apparently to us, "That guy ought to lose some weight."

The scene reminds us that humans are a gossipy, judgmental race, always ready to give and take opinions about the proper management of society ("*They* ought to make these stalls wider") or about the proper management of the individual life ("*That guy* ought to lose some weight"). As Aristotle said, we are all creatures of the *polis* (the community), and one of our life's great projects is to contribute to the community's consensus on what behavior is good or bad, noble or base, cool or uncool. You may remember reading a children's magazine that contained a comic strip called "Gufus and Gallant." Week after week, the cartoonist would produce a scenario in which Gufus would show us how not to behave and Gallant would behave with a shining nobility. From childhood forward, we think incessantly about what behavior is Gufus and what is Gallant.

Among the earliest surviving essays are thirty short sketches by Theophrastus, Aristotle's pupil. These "characters" as he called them, explore the social side of life as directly as "Gufus and Gallant" did. Here, for instance, is a Gufus piece usually called "The Faultfinder":

> Faultfinding is being unreasonably critical of your portion in life. For example, a friend sends over a serving of the main dinner course with his compliments: the faultfinder is the kind who says to the messenger, "You can go tell your master I said that he didn't want me to have a taste of his soup and his third-rate wine—that's why he wouldn't give me a dinner invitation." And even while his mistress is kissing him he will complain, "I wonder if you really love me the way you say you do." He gets angry at the weather, too, not because it rained but because it didn't rain soon enough.
>
> If he comes on a wallet in the street, his comment is "Always this—never a real find!" Let him get a slave at bargain prices, moreover, after begging and pleading, and what does he say but, "I really wonder if the fellow can be in sound shape, seeing that he was so cheap." Or supposing somebody announces, "You've got a baby boy!" He meets this good news with: "You might as well have told me half my estate's down the drain—that's what it really means." What's more, he can win a case with every single ballot in his favor; he will still claim that his lawyer passed over a lot of sound arguments. And when friends have raised a loan to help him out and one of them asks him, "Aren't you pleased?" his answer is "How can I be, when I have to pay everybody back and then act grateful besides?"

This essay makes the modest logical claim that there exists in society (or at least there existed in ancient Athens) a recognizable category of people who can be called faultfinders. The point, however, is less to show that the group exists than to remind us that we don't want to belong to it. For a day or two after reading "The Faultfinder," we may be less likely to complain about the food someone cooks for us, less likely to be critical of the present a friend gives us.

As "The Faultfinder" reminds us, the social level of our thinking inevitably involves matters of style, tone, and sensitivity. Consider this passage about Dick Cavett in Naomi Wolf's essay "The Rites of Sisterhood."[2] Cavett, a talk-show host known for his intelligence and his lib-

2. *Next: Young American Writers on the New Generation.* Ed. Eric Liv (New York, 1984), p. 188.

eral views, was the commencement speaker when Wolf graduated from Yale.

> Cavett took the microphone and seemed visibly to pale at the sight of two thousand female about-to-be Yale graduates. "When I was an undergraduate," he said, "there were no women here. The women went to Vassar. At Vassar," he said, "they had nude photographs taken of the women to check their posture in gym class. One year some of the photos were stolen, and they showed up for sale in New Haven's red-light district." His punch line? "The photos found no buyers."

Even this short passage should give you some sense of Wolf's reaction to Cavett's speech, but the statements that follow do much more to develop the social level of Wolf's essay:

> I will never forget that moment. There were our parents and grandparents, many of whom had come long distances at great expense to be with us on our special day. There were we, silent in our black gowns, our tassels, our new shoes. We did not break the silence with boos or hisses, out of respect for our families who had given so much to make that day a success; and they in turn kept silent out of the same concern for us.

Wolf's objection is not to Cavett's logic, but to his behavior. Wolf couldn't convince us by logical argument to favor respect over disrespect, fair play over bias, sensitivity over insensitivity. She presumably doesn't *need* to convince us. She needs only to show us that Cavett's speech was disrespectful, unfair, and insensitive. This showing isn't an open-and-shut business, of course; we can imagine another writer setting out to show that Cavett's speech wasn't as boorish as Wolf makes it out to be, and that Wolf is herself being disrespectful, unfair, and insensitive. The debate about such matters is one way that the community and the nation gradually form and change their shared values.

Since we are thinking now as essayists, it is worth noting that Wolf criticizes Cavett for the words he chose to write and read on a particular occasion for a particular audience. We may accept her criticism or not, but since essays inevitably have a social dimension, their tone *is* a serious issue. Some writers swagger or whine, insult or patronize, and yet somehow expect that the reader will listen with patience and respect. They ought to make those essays wider; you can hardly turn around in there.

Our educational system does less to alert us to the visceral (bodily) level of writing than to the logical or social levels, perhaps because teachers tend to see the body as a natural enemy. Let me introduce the visceral level by telling you about my baby daughter Kate and her first word, *kitty.* She learned the word early because her baby sitter Nancy used to lure a neighbor's cat onto the porch on summer days to pet it. After winter set in, we would show Kate a photograph and ask her where the kitty was, and she would smile, coo, and wiggle all over as she pointed to the cat and said "kitty." For her, the word must have been the key that unlocked a number of bodily experiences. It probably summoned up memories of summer days on the porch, the silky feel of the fur, the purring, the comfort of being held on Nancy's lap. As the rhetorician Kenneth Burke put it, the word "glowed" for her; it had emotional and physical associations no dictionary maker records. She reacted to these associations as a whole creature, not merely as a logical or social being.

This creaturely reaction to words, phrases, and images may become dulled as we grow older—it may be overlayered by the development of our logical and social responses to what we read—but it never goes away. My reaction to words like *lake, sandpaper,* and *baby* is not as dramatic as Kate's response to *kitty* (I can read them and sit still), but it is not different in kind. And, of course, it is not just words, but phrases and whole sentences that may have a bodily impact on us. The other day, in the midst of an abstract discussion of social policy, I heard one speaker quote the Buddhist proverb, "You can't water a tree by watering each individual leaf." The escape from this dry discussion of hard issues to the familiar and tangible world of trees and water had great appeal to me, for reasons my body probably understood better than my mind ever will.

The writer of a scientific paper or a mathematical proof may ignore the body's "reasoning," but the skillful writer of essays doesn't. Take, for example, the first sentence of George Orwell's "Marrakech": "As the corpse went past, the flies left the restaurant table in a cloud and rushed after it, but they came back a few minutes later." The sentence might have no effect on an android with a stainless steel gut, but it is enough to make a human's skin crawl. It probably *does* make our skins crawl, as a clever physiologist with a galvanometer might demonstrate. Or consider this paragraph from Carol Bly's "Getting Tired":

> The second day I was promoted from elevating corncobs at the corn pile to actual plowing. Hour after hour I sat up there on the old Alice, as she was called (an Allis-Chalmer WC that looked rusted from the Flood). You have to sit twisted part way around, checking that the plowshares are scouring clean, turning over and dropping the dead crop and soil, not clogging. For the first two hours I was very political. I thought about what would be good for American farming—stronger marketing organizations, or maybe a law like the Norwegian Odal law, preventing the breaking up of small farms or selling them to business interests. Then the sun got high, and each time I reached the headlands area at the field's end I dumped off something else, now my cap, next my jacket, finally my sweater.

Few of us, these days, have plowed with an open tractor, but our muscles have probably been in the twisted posture Bly describes, and we probably remember stripping off layers of clothing on days that start out cold and then heat with the rising sun. These bodily memories are evoked, however briefly, as we read. Those who have been around farms may associate Bly's language—*plowshares, scouring, headlands*—with the sights and sounds and solid objects they remember, objects that carry with them memories and emotions, pleasant or unpleasant. Writing that points us to objects and sensations—to tastes, textures, smells, temperatures, sounds, colors, shapes, motions—will ordinarily involve us more deeply than writing that is merely logical or merely social.

I don't want to leave the impression that our visceral responses depend entirely on the relation between words and past physical experience. Language is also, itself, a *present* physical experience. Perhaps half a dozen times in the last decade I have passed through a room where Martin Luther King, Jr.'s "I Have a Dream" speech was playing on radio or television. It has always stopped me cold. Listen to the following passage, a series of sentences that are rhythmically perfect in themselves and that are joined rhythmically by the repetition of "I have a dream":

> I say to you today, my friends, that in spite of the difficulties and frustrations of the moment I still have a dream tonight. It is a dream deeply rooted in the American dream.
>
> I have a dream that one day this nation will rise up and live out the true meaning of its creed: "We hold those truths to be self-evident, that all men are created equal."
>
> I have a dream that one day on the red hills of Georgia the sons of former slaves and the sons of former slaveowners will be able to sit down together at the table of brotherhood.
>
> I have a dream that one day even the state of Mississippi, a desert state sweltering with the heat of injustice and oppression, will be transformed into an oasis of freedom and justice.
>
> I have a dream that my four little children will one day live in a nation where they will not be judged by the color of their skin but by the content of their character.

Listen to the beat of the *k* sounds in the last sentence (*color, skin, content, character*) and think how much would be lost if King had said, "where they will be judged by their character, rather than their skin tone." The speech moves us partly because of the way the language moves. Essays are not speeches, but when we read closely we register the sounds in our mental ear and even (researchers tell us) subconsciously form them with our vocal cords. Rhythm, assonance, alliteration, onomatopoeia—the whole palette of verbal sound effects—create visceral responses.

*   *   *

What difference does it make if we read essays with increased consciousness that they work on three levels? If my experience is typical, we begin to *see* essays more clearly, to become more consciously aware of what essayists have accomplished. When I graduated from high school as part of a post-*Sputnik*, scientifically oriented generation of students, I was fixated on the logical level of writing and simply missed the other two in most of what I read. I was like an artist attempting to see all objects as balls, and so dismissing cones, cylinders, and cubes as balls that failed the test of roundness. Eventually I broadened my range and learned to recognize that writing could be excellent because it engaged us socially and viscerally. And eventually I learned to recognize a type of excellence I had not suspected, the excellence of balance achieved when an essay works on all three levels and so appeals to mind, body, and character at once.

Have we exhausted the truth about the essay when we recognize that it has three levels? Certainly not. The harder we look, the more levels we are likely to see: four, six, ten, who can say? The well-written essay, like a ray of clear light, contains a whole spectrum of colors. The important thing is to recognize both its complexity and its unity.

THE THREE LEVELS AND REVISION

Being aware as we write that an essay can develop at three levels is both a blessing and a challenge. It is a blessing because it gives us three channels through which to reach the reader. It is a challenge because we must now

1. Think what the subject means logically. (How can its details be connected to generalizations or generalizations to details?)
2. Think what the subject means socially. (How can it be related to a standard for admirable or dishonorable behavior?)
3. Think what the subject means viscerally. (How can it be connected to the senses and the emotions that are evoked by the senses?)

The struggle to work at three levels is part of the hidden drama behind drafting and revision.

Those who have written very little are generally surprised at the amount of revision experienced writers do. The economist John Kenneth Galbraith, equally famous for the subtlety of his theories and for the clarity of his prose, put it this way:

> There may be inspired writers for whom the first draft is just right. But anyone who is not certifiably a Milton had better assume that the first draft is a very primitive thing. The reason is simple: writing is very difficult work. . . . Thinking, as Voltaire avowed, is also a very tedious process

which men and women will do anything to avoid. So all first drafts are deeply flawed by the need to combine composition with thought. Each later one is less demanding in this regard; hence the writing can be better.

Galbraith tells us that on bad days he writes so poorly that "no fewer than five revisions are required. However, when I'm greatly inspired, only four are needed before, as I've often said, I put in that note of spontaneity which even my meanest critics concede."[3]

Great writers rarely preserve the four or five (or more) drafts that led them to a finished product. By good fortune, however, we do have access to six drafts of a *New Yorker* "comment" by E. B. White, one of the best American essayists of this century. In this section we will take a short tour through three of White's drafts, watching the way that he develops the logical, social, and visceral levels. I am not, of course, saying that White wrote with these levels consciously in his mind (any more than a bicyclist consciously thinks about balance, velocity, and centrifugal force as she rounds a corner), but I think we can see their presence in the decisions White makes.

First, a word about the nature of the writing and the writer. "Comments" are unsigned essays in miniature; in *The New Yorker* they have traditionally been written using the "editorial *we*," a practice that irritated White because it tends to make the writer sound like a Siamese twin. White began writing comments in 1927, and so had more than forty years of experience with them by 1969, when the magazine asked him to comment on *Apollo 11*'s landing on the moon.

The deadline pressure on White was more intense than usual. Neil Armstrong took his historic "small step" to the lunar surface at 10:56 P.M. on July 20, and the television broadcast of the moon walk lasted until 1:00 A.M., White, who lived on a farm in Maine, had to cable his comment to New York in time for it to go to press at noon.

The visceral level, for this writer and this subject, posed a problem. White's best writing generally evoked the places and activities he loved best—ball games, circuses, zoos, farming, camping, canoeing. He was by disposition and habit an outdoorsman, capable of describing barns, pigs, and spiders affectionately (as you will know if you have read *Charlotte's Web*) and passionate about the sights, sounds, and smells of sailing. A few years before he wrote the moon-landing comment, he wrote these sentences in "The Sea and the Wind That Blows":

> My first encounter with the sea was a case of hate at first sight. I was taken, at the age of four, to a bathing beach in New Rochelle. Everything about the experience frightened and repelled me: the taste of salt in my mouth, the foul chill of the wooden bathhouse, the littered sand, the stench of the tide flats. I came away hating and fearing the sea. Later, I found that what I had hated and feared, I now feared and loved.

3. "Writing, Typing, and Economics," *The Atlantic Monthly* (March 1978), p. 103.

In the wide outdoors world, White could certainly find the keys that unlock visceral responses, the connections between the senses and the emotions. Now, however, he was being asked to write about what is to the senses a much narrower world—the images and sounds produced by his television set. This situation presented him with a handicap that, as we will see, he had difficulty overcoming.

The logical level presented White with another sort of difficulty. Here there was generalization to connect the event with, but the nature of the connection wasn't clear. World War II had convinced White that in a world of electronic communication, long-range bombers, and nuclear weaponry, nationalism was irrational and dangerous.

> Whether we wish it or not, we may soon have to make a clear choice between the special nation to which we pledge our allegiance and the broad humanity of which we are born a part. The choice is implicit in the world to come. We have a little time in which we can make that choice intelligently. Failing that, the choice will be made for us in the confusion of war, from which the world will emerge unified—the unity of total desolation.

Logic taught White that nationalism was a thing of the past, and (as we will see) this generalization shaped his view of the particular event he witnessed.

At the social level, the moon landing presented White the familiar struggle between pride and modesty, between boasting about our accomplishments and keeping them in perspective. In this struggle, White consistently favored modesty. Much of the humor in his writing comes from his tendency to find himself slightly ridiculous, and many of his essays aim to "keep Man in a mood of decent humility," particularly when people are crowing about their conquest of nature. "I am pessimistic about the human race," he once said, "because it is too ingenious for its own good. Our approach to nature is to beat it into submission." To the degree that the moon landing became an occasion for crowing and strutting, therefore, it went against the grain of White's character.

If we look at White's very rough first draft, we can see his struggle to make one coherent statement that combines his visceral, logical, and social responses to the event.

> Planning a trip to the moon differs in no essential respect from planning a trip to the beach. You have to decide what to take along, what to leave behind. Should the thermos jug go? The child's rubber horse? The dill pickles? These are the sometimes fateful decisions on which the success or failure of the whole outing turns. Something goes along that spoils everything because it is always in the way. Something gets left behind that is desperately needed for comfort or safety. The men who had to decide what to take along to the moon must have pondered long and hard, drawn up many a list. We're not sure they planned well, when they in-

cluded the little telescoped flagpole and the American flag, artificially stiffened so that it would fly to the breeze that didn't blow. As we watched the Stars and Stripes planted on the surface of the moon, we experienced the same sensations of pride that must have filled the hearts of millions of Americans. But the emotion soon turned to
This was our great chance, and we muffed it. The men who stepped out onto the surface of the moon are in a class by themselves—pioneers of what is universal. They saw the earth whole—just as it is, a round ball in   But they colored the moon red, white, and blue— good colors all—but out of place in that setting. The moon still influences the tides, and the tides lap on every shore, right around the globe. The moon still belongs to lovers, and lovers are everywhere—not just in America. What a pity we couldn't have planted some emblem that precisely expressed this unique, this incredible occasion, even if it were nothing more than a white banner, with the legend: "At last!"

White clearly didn't intend this to be a final draft: he twice began sentences that he couldn't end. *What* exactly did our emotions turn to? A round ball in *what*? Having no adequate answers, he left spaces and went on. His aim was to discover the general shape of the comment, to see what he had to say.

I mentioned before that the subject was difficult for White because it offered so little visceral interest, and he knew that he needed to engage his own senses and emotions if he wanted to engage his readers'. In this draft, you can see the attempts to overcome the difficulty. One comes directly from the television screen: "the American flag, artificially stiffened so that it would fly to the breeze that didn't blow." Here is a visual image most of White's readers would have remembered, one that jars us a little by reminding us that there is no *air* up there. Another attempt is the analogy with the beach trip. This analogy gives White access to objects and sense impressions: a Thermos jug (with its suggestion of hot liquid), a rubber horse (an interesting item for those who think about the feel of it), and dill pickles (a pungent taste). The third attempt is the mention of the moon's effects here on earth, on the tides and on lovers. Here we have some footholds for visceral reactions.

Of course, the flag is related to White's key logical concern: the outdated nature of nationalism. The astronauts are "pioneers of what is universal"; they can see "the earth whole"; they are standing on the moon, creator of tides that "lap on every shore." In this draft, White wants us to see that for them to plant a *national* flag is a case of invoking antiquated patriotism in an international age.

The most serious difficulty in the draft is social. White is clearly uneasy about the amount of boasting and strutting associated with the moon landing, but he can't seem to find the right alternative posture. The opening sentences seem determined to take the whole occasion lightly. Later, he criticizes the planners harshly: "We're not sure they planned well. . . . This was our great chance, and we muffed it." In these passages he sounds like Theophrastus' faultfinder. On the other hand, he sometimes bends over backward to sound like a patriot and enthusiast: "As we watched the Stars and Stripes planted on the surface of the moon, we experienced the same sensations of pride that must have filled the hearts of millions of Americans. . . . red, white, and blue—good colors all. . . . this unique, this incredible occasion." It would be hard for readers to trust (or even understand) a man who seems to have three sides to his mouth and seems to talk out of all three in a single paragraph.

The changes White made in the next two drafts show him working at the social level, trying to find the proper tone. Since some of the changes are slight, we'll find them easier to detect if we look at drafts one and three side by side, section by section. The first section in both drafts presents the analogy to the beach trip.

DRAFT ONE	DRAFT THREE
Planning a trip to the moon differs in no essential respect from planning a trip to the beach. You have to decide what to take along, what to leave behind. Should the thermos jug go? The child's rubber horse? The dill pickles? These are the sometimes fateful decisions on which the success or failure of the whole outing turns. Something goes along that spoils everything because it is always in the way. Something gets left behind that is desperately needed for comfort or safety. The men who had to decide what to take along to the moon must have pondered long and hard, drawn up many a list.	Planning a trip to the moon differs in no essential respect from planning a trip to the beach. You have to decide what to take along, what to leave behind. Should the thermos jug go? The child's rubber horse? The dill pickles? These are the sometimes fateful decisions on which the success or failure of the whole outing turns. Something goes along that spoils everything because it is always in the way; something gets left behind that is desperately needed for comfort or for safety. The men who drew up the moon list for the astronauts planned long and hard and well. (Should the vacuum cleaner go to suck up moondust?)

"Do not adjust your set," as they say on television. The two columns are nearly identical until we get to the last sentence or two. There we get some changes that soften White's scolding tone. Now the planners don't just work "long" and "hard"; they work "well." The parenthetical sentence about the vacuum cleaner is apparently intended as an example of the sort of planning they did well, though it seems a lame joke. (In draft two it had been lamer still: "Should they take along a vacuum cleaner to suck up moondust and save the world?") Notice, too, that White separates the astronauts from the planners. This distinction will be useful to him as he continues to rewrite and rethink.

In the middle section, the complaint about the presence of the flag, the drafts differ more sharply.

DRAFT ONE	DRAFT THREE
We're not sure they planned well, when they included the little telescoped flagpole and the American flag, artificially stiffened so that it would fly to the breeze that didn't blow. As we watched the Stars and Stripes planted on the surface of the moon, we experienced the same sensations of pride that must have filled the hearts of millions of Americans. But the emotion soon turned to This was our great chance, and we muffed it. The men who stepped out onto the surface of the moon are in a class by themselves—pioneers of what is universal. They saw the earth whole—just as it is, a round ball in But they colored the moon red, white, and blue—good colors all—but out of place in that setting.	Among the items they sent along, of course, was the little jointed flag that could be stiffened to the breeze that did not blow. (It is traditional for explorers to plant the flag.) Yet the two men who stepped out on the surface of the moon were in a class by themselves and should have been equipped accordingly; they were of the new breed of men, those who had seen the earth whole. When, following instructions, they colored the moon red, white, and blue, they were fumbling with the past—or so it seemed to us who watched, trembling with awe and admiration and pride. This was the last chapter in the long book of nationalism, one that could well have been omitted.

Most of the changes affect White's tone, bringing out a less cantankerous, more sympathetic side of his character. In the first draft, White directly challenged NASA's decision to plant the flag ("We're not sure they planned well"). Now he is understanding: the planners send along the flag "of course," since it is "traditional" for explorers to plant one. White has been more generous toward the astronauts, especially. In draft one, they were lumped with the planners who had "muffed" our "great chance." Anyone who has played baseball knows the sting of being told that you have "muffed it." In draft three, they are "following instructions" and "fumbling with the past" (a ball too large for anyone to catch neatly). Notice that in the last sentence of this section, White states his logical point more clearly than ever before: "This was the last chapter in the long book of nationalism, one that could well have been omitted." The relation between White's logical position and his social posture is now considerably clearer. This draft says, "Look, I am convinced that nationalism is outdated, and I don't intend to hide my conviction, but I don't intend to be a spoilsport either. It was a shining moment, and I felt its wonder, though I wish we could have used it for a better purpose."

The final section in both drafts reminds us that the moon is international property and argues that the right "flag" to plant would have been one that represented the entire world. White has reworked the passage considerably by the time he gets to draft three.

DRAFT ONE	DRAFT THREE
The moon still influences the tides, and the tides lap on every shore, right around the globe. The moon still belongs to lovers, and lovers are everywhere—not just in America. What a pity we couldn't have planted some emblem that precisely expressed this unique, this incredible occasion, even if it were nothing more than a white banner, with the legend: "At last!"	But the moon still holds the key to madness, which is universal, still controls the tides that lap on shores everywhere, and guards lovers that kiss in every land, under no banner but the sky. What a pity we couldn't have forsworn our little Iwo Jima scene and planted instead a banner acceptable to all—a simple white handkerchief, perhaps, symbol of the common cold, which, like the moon, affects us all.

Partly because of the forceful verbs, the first sentence in the new draft has more visceral effect than the old version:

> But the moon
>   still *holds* the key to madness,
>   which is universal,
>   still *controls* the tides that lap on shores everywhere,
>   and *guards* lovers that kiss in every land,
>   under no banner but the sky.

The moon sounds like a strong ruler here, stronger than any mere superpower. A more dramatic change happens in the final sentence of the new draft. By mentioning Iwo Jima, White conjures up memories of the most famous photograph of World War II, an object that "glows" with associations. And in contrast to this image of embattled marines planting a flag on a conquered hilltop, White offers a white handkerchief, "symbol of the common cold, which . . . affects us all." Again we have an object that "glows" with visceral associations, but very different ones. Rather than encouraging stiff-necked pride, the handkerchief "keeps Man in a mood of decent humility." White has brought the visceral level and the social level together.

By common standards, this third draft seems a finished product; White telegraphed it to *The New Yorker,* but when the heat of composition began to cool, he saw there was more work to be done at both the social and logical levels. By beginning with the beach comparison and ending with the handkerchief, White had trivialized the moon landing, and he now saw that this trivializing was unfair and shoddy. By hinging his essay on the generalization that nationalism was out of date, he had demanded that his readers accept an enormous assumption without any reasoning or evidence. Time was very short, but White took the paragraph through three more drafts before telegraphing *The New Yorker* that the comment was "no good as is" and offering to dictate over the phone "a shorter one on the same theme but different in tone." Here, for comparison, are draft three and draft six, the one that appeared on page one of the magazine:

DRAFT THREE

Planning a trip to the moon differs in no essential respect from planning a trip to the beach. You have to decide what to take along, what to leave behind. Should the thermos jug go? The child's rubber horse? The dill pickles? These are the sometimes fateful decisions on which the success or failure of the whole outing turns. Something goes along that spoils everything because it is always in the way; something gets left behind that is desperately needed for comfort or for safety. The men who drew up the moon list for the astronauts planned long and hard and well. (Should the vacuum cleaner go to suck up moondust?)

Among the items they sent along, of course, was the little jointed flag that could be stiffened to the breeze that did not blow. (It is traditional for explorers to plant the flag.) Yet the two men who stepped out on the surface of the moon

DRAFT SIX

The moon, it turns out, is a great place for men. One-sixth gravity must be a lot of fun, and when Armstrong and Aldrin went into their bouncy little dance, like two happy children, it was a moment not only of triumph, but of gaiety.

The moon, on the other hand, is a poor place for flags. Ours looked stiff and awkward, try-

were in a class by themselves and should have been equipped accordingly; they were of the new breed of men, those who had seen the earth whole. When, following instructions, they colored the moon red, white, and blue, they were fumbling with the past—or so it seemed to us who watched, trembling with awe and admiration and pride. This was the last chapter in the long book of nationalism, one that could well have been omitted.

ing to float on the breeze that does not blow. (There must be a lesson here somewhere.) It is traditional, of course, for explorers to plant the flag, but it struck us, as we watched with awe and admiration and pride, that our two fellows were universal men, not national men, and should have been equipped accordingly.

But the moon still holds the key to madness, which is universal, still controls the tides that lap on shores everywhere, and guards lovers that kiss in every land, under no banner but the sky. What a pity we couldn't have forsworn our little Iwo Jima scene and planted instead a banner acceptable to all—a simple white handkerchief, perhaps, symbol of the common cold, which, like the moon, affects us all.

Like every great river and every great sea, the moon belongs to none and belongs to all. It still holds the key to madness, still controls the tides that lap on shores everywhere, still guards the lovers that kiss in every land under no banner but the sky. What a pity in our moment of triumph we couldn't have forsworn the familiar Iwo Jima scene and planted instead a device acceptable to all: a limp white handkerchief, perhaps, symbol of the common cold, which, like the moon, affects us all, unites us all.

What has happened here? Socially, White has stopped being a killjoy, stopped being the one person at the party who intends to spend the evening complaining. Once he gets the chip off his shoulder, he is able to recall a detail that appeals to all of us on the visceral level—the "bouncy little dance" of the astronauts.

He is also able to clarify and strengthen his logical point. Rather than insist on the controversial generalization that nationalism is anachronistic, he builds on the widely acceptable generalization that some things belong to all humankind: "Like every great river and every great sea, the moon belongs to none and belongs to all." If the high seas are regarded as beyond nationalism, how much more so the moon, which "still holds the key to madness, still controls the tides that lap on shores everywhere"? And with the little addition of "unites us all" at the very end, White brings the three dimensions of the essay together. The visceral things that affect us all—tides, kisses, the common cold, the moon—also unite us all, as logic should tell us; as social creatures we should behave accordingly. No flags for the moon, no sniping in the essay. White has come to terms with his subject.

You will find many more changes in White's drafts than I have mentioned: of the 305 words in the first draft, only 15 remain to the end, a survival rate lower than we find in most airline crashes. But the small changes in the essay are less important than the changes of mind that go with them. An essay is not just a finished product. For the writer, it is a process that leads to changes, not only on paper, but in the logical, social, and visceral levels of the self.

Our word *essay*, any dictionary will tell you, is derived from the French word *essai*, "a trial, an attempt, a test." The attempt begins with the blank page and ends when the writer declares some draft final. In this sense, we don't see a living essay in a book, any more than we see a living butterfly in the collector's case. To read well, we have to bring the essay back to life. We have to enter the writer's mind far enough to understand what his or her "attempt" was and against what resistances it made its way forward. Even if we finally disagree with the writer, we should use our intelligence and imagination to see the distance traveled since the page was blank.

As writers, we travel the same road in the other direction. Faced with the blank sheet, we must feel the pull of the completed essay, which is partly the pull of all the essays we have read, understood, and admired. When E. B. White was nearly fifty, his brother gave him a box of white typing paper. Writing back his thanks, White said, "I'm glad to report that even now, at this late day, a blank sheet of paper holds the greatest excitement there is for me—more promising than a silver cloud, prettier than a little red wagon. It holds all the hope there is, all fears." To learn what our own blank sheets may hold is one of the reasons to read.

INITIATION

We find ourselves growing up in a grown-up world.

Overview

One way or another, we all grow up. Often this transition from childhood to adulthood is marked by rites of passage, such as graduation or marriage, that help us to see ourselves as adults. Sometimes the transition involves our acceptance into a specific group: our First Communion or bar mitzvah, initiation into Eagle Scouts or into a sorority. For many of us, something as simple as living away from home for the first time "initiates" us into the adult world. Indeed, sometimes "initiation" simply refers to the turning points in our lives that force us to shed some of our innocence and become acquainted with the world of experience. Our literature and culture are filled with images of these types of experiences: from *Lord of the Flies* to *Animal House,* from debutante balls to vision quests. Yet our culture has also been confronted with the anti-initiate—one who either scorns the whole notion of adulthood, or, seeing little reason to enter its world, graduates from college and moves back home. In fact, judging from the number of Internet sites devoted to the cause, many people today are worried about the lack of significant rites of passage in American culture. In an age when religious ceremonies are on the decline, when it is more cool to join a gang than the Kiwanis Club, when marriage is more of a lifestyle option than a sacred institution, perhaps it is time to re-evaluate initiation and rites of passage in our culture. From a wide range of perspectives, the writers in this unit will help us do just that.

ALICE MUNRO   Circle of Prayer   98

It was like a religious ceremony. The girls behaved as if they'd been told what to do, as if this was what was always done on such occasions. They sang, they wept, they dropped their jewellery. The sense of ritual made every one of them graceful.

ALBERT GOLDBARTH   26   113

Once,
at thirteen, I came unto my manhood
under wool and silver.

Cub-Pilot

Mark Twain (1835–1910), also known by his real name, Samuel Langhorne Clemens, spent his childhood on the Mississippi River in Hannibal, Missouri. Leaving school early, Twain learned the printing trade, began writing for newspapers, and finally fulfilled his childhood dream when he became a Mississippi steamboat pilot in the years just before the Civil War. He often wrote about his experiences: piloting on the river in *Life on the Mississippi* (1883), traveling in Europe in *The Innocents Abroad* (1869), and exploring America in *Roughing It* (1872). All of these books contain as much social commentary as autobiography. After his death, hundreds of additional pages of autobiography were discovered and published in various forms; the most complete is *The Autobiography of Mark Twain* (1959). A master storyteller, as every reader of *Tom Sawyer* (1876) and *Huckleberry Finn* (1884) knows, Twain was at the same time a relentless satirist. "Cub-Pilot" is taken from two early chapters of *Life on the Mississippi* that describe young Sam Clemens's longing to become a pilot and his scheme for fulfilling this ambition. Like Rigoberta Menchú ("Life in the *Altiplano*"), Twain describes initiation through hard work—and the mixed feelings the process evokes.

When I was a boy, there was but one permanent ambition among   1
my comrades in our village[1] on the west bank of the Mississippi River. That was, to be a steamboatman. We had transient ambitions of other sorts, but they were only transient. When a circus came and went, it left us all burning to become clowns; the first negro minstrel show that ever came to our section left us all suffering to try that kind of life; now and then we had a hope that, if we lived and were good, God would permit us to be pirates. These ambitions faded out, each in its turn; but the ambition to be a steamboatman always remained.

Once a day a cheap, gaudy packet arrived upward from St. Louis,   2
and another downward from Keokuk. Before these events, the day was glorious with expectancy; after them, the day was a dead and empty thing. Not only the boys, but the whole village, felt this. After all these years I can picture that old time to myself now, just as it was then: the white town drowsing in the sunshine of a summer's morning; the streets empty, or pretty nearly so; one or two clerks sitting in front of the Water Street stores, with their splint-bottomed chairs tilted back against the walls, chins on breasts, hats slouched over their faces, asleep—with single-shavings enough around to show what broke them down; a sow and a litter of pigs loafing along the sidewalk, doing

1. our village: Hannibal, Missouri.

a good business in watermelon rinds and seeds; two or three lonely little freight piles scattered about the "levee"; a pile of "skids" on the
slope of the stone-paved wharf, and the fragrant town drunkard asleep
in the shadow of them; two or three wood flats at the head of the
wharf, but nobody to listen to the peaceful lapping of the wavelets
against them; the great Mississippi, the majestic, the magnificent Mississippi, rolling its mile-wide tide along, shining in the sun; the dense
forest away on the other side; the "point" above the town, and the
"point" below, bounding the river-glimpse and turning it into a sort of
sea, and withal a very still and brilliant and lonely one. Presently a film
of dark smoke appears above one of those remote "points": instantly a
negro drayman, famous for his quick eye and prodigious voice, lifts up
the cry, "S-t-e-a-m-boat a-comin'!" and the scene changes! The town
drunkard stirs, the clerks wake up, a furious clatter of drays follows,
every house and store pours out a human contribution, and all in a
twinkling the dead town is alive and moving. Drays, carts, men, boys,
all go hurrying from many quarters to a common center, the wharf.
Assembled here, the people fasten their eyes upon the coming boat as
upon a wonder they are seeing for the first time. And the boat *is* rather
a handsome sight, too. She is long and sharp and trim and pretty; she
has two tall, fancy-topped chimneys, with a gilded device of some kind
swung between them; a fanciful pilot-house, all glass and "gingerbread," perched on top of the "texas" deck behind them; the paddle-
boxes are gorgeous with a picture or with gilded rays above the boat's
name; the boiler-deck, the hurricane-deck, and the texas deck are
fenced and ornamented with clean white railings; there is a flag gal-
lantly flying from the jack-staff; the furnace doors are open and the
fires glaring bravely; the upper decks are black with passengers; the
captain stands by the big bell, calm, imposing, the envy of all; great
volumes of the blackest smoke are rolling and tumbling out of the
chimneys—a husbanded grandeur created with a bit of pitch-pine just
before arriving at a town; the crew are grouped on the forecastle; the
broad stage is run far out over the port bow, and an envied deck-hand
stands picturesquely on the end of it with a coil of rope in his hand; the
pent steam is screaming through the gauge-cocks; the captain lifts his
hand, a bell rings, the wheels stop; then they turn back, churning the
water to foam, and the steamer is at rest. Then such a scramble as
there is to get aboard, and to get ashore, and to take in freight and to
discharge freight, all at one and the same time; and such a yelling and
cursing as the mates facilitate it all with! Ten minutes later the steamer
is under way again, with no flag on the jack-staff and no black smoke
issuing from the chimneys. After ten more minutes the town is dead
again, and the town drunkard asleep by the skids once more.

My father was a justice of the peace, and I supposed he possessed ₃
the power of life and death over all men, and could hang anybody that
offended him. This was distinction enough for me as a general thing;

but the desire to be a steamboatman kept intruding, nevertheless. I
first wanted to be a cabin-boy, so that I could come out with a white
apron on and shake a table-cloth over the side, where all my old comrades could see me; later I thought I would rather be the deck-hand
who stood on the end of the stage-plank with the coil of rope in his
hand, because he was particularly conspicuous. But these were only
day-dreams—they were too heavenly to be contemplated as real possibilities. By and by one of our boys went away. He was not heard of for
a long time. At last he turned up as apprentice engineer or "striker" on
a steamboat. This thing shook the bottom out of all my Sunday-school
teachings. That boy had been notoriously worldly, and I just the reverse; yet he was exalted to this eminence, and I left in obscurity and
misery. There was nothing generous about this fellow in his greatness.
He would always manage to have a rusty bolt to scrub while his boat
tarried at our town, and he would sit on the inside guard and scrub it,
where we all could see him and envy him and loathe him. And whenever his boat was laid up he would come home and swell around the
town in his blackest and greasiest clothes, so that nobody could help
remembering that he was a steamboatman; and he used all sorts of
steamboat technicalities in his talk, as if he were so used to them that
he forgot common people could not understand them. He would speak
of the "labboard" side of a horse in an easy, natural way that would
make one wish he was dead. And he was always talking about "St.
Looy" like an old citizen; he would refer casually to occasions when he
was "coming down Fourth Street," or when he was "passing by the
Planter's House," or when there was a fire and he took a turn on the
brakes of "the Old Big Missouri"; and then he would go on and lie
about how many towns the size of ours were burned down there that
day. Two or three of the boys had long been persons of consideration
among us because they had been to St. Louis once and had a vague
general knowledge of its wonders, but the day of their glory was over
now. They lapsed into a humble silence, and learned to disappear
when the ruthless "cub"-engineer approached. This fellow had money,
too, and hair-oil. Also an ignorant silver watch and a showy brass
watch-chain. He wore a leather belt and used no suspenders. If ever a
youth was cordially admired and hated by his comrades, this one was.
No girl could withstand his charms. He "cut out" every boy in the village. When his boat blew up at last, it diffused a tranquil contentment
among us such as we had not known for months. But when he came
home the next week, alive, renowned, and appeared in church all battered up and bandaged, a shining hero, stared at and wondered over
by everybody, it seemed to us that the partiality of Providence for an
undeserving reptile had reached a point where it was open to criticism.

This creature's career could produce but one result, and it speedily   4
followed. Boy after boy managed to get on the river. The minister's son
became an engineer. The doctor's and the postmaster's sons became

"mud clerks"; the wholesale liquor dealer's son became a barkeeper on a boat; four sons of the chief merchant, and two sons of the county judge, became pilots. Pilot was the grandest position of all. The pilot, even in those days of trivial wages, had a princely salary—from a hundred and fifty to two hundred and fifty dollars a month, and no board to pay. Two months of his wages would pay a preacher's salary for a year. Now some of us were left disconsolate. We could not get on the river—at least our parents would not let us.

So, by and by, I ran away. I said I would never come home again ₅ till I was a pilot and could come in glory.

.   .   .

The *Paul Jones*² was now bound for St. Louis. I planned a siege ₆ against my pilot, and at the end of three hard days he surrendered. He agreed to teach me the Mississippi River from New Orleans to St. Louis for five hundred dollars, payable out of the first wages I should receive after graduating. I entered upon the small enterprise of "learning" twelve or thirteen hundred miles of the great Mississippi River with the easy confidence of my time of life. If I had really known what I was about to require of my faculties, I should not have had the courage to begin. I supposed that all a pilot had to do was to keep his boat in the river, and I did not consider that that could be much of a trick, since it was so wide.

The boat backed out from New Orleans at four in the afternoon, ₇ and it was "our watch" until eight. Mr. Bixby, my chief, "straightened her up," plowed her along past the sterns of the other boats that lay at the Levee, and then said, "Here, take her; shave those steamships as close as you'd peel an apple." I took the wheel, and my heartbeat fluttered up into the hundreds; for it seemed to me that we were about to scrape the side off every ship in the line, we were so close. I held my breath and began to claw the boat away from the danger; and I had my own opinion of the pilot who had known no better than to get us into such peril, but I was too wise to express it. In half a minute I had a wide margin of safety intervening between the *Paul Jones* and the ships; and within ten seconds more I was set aside in disgrace, and Mr. Bixby was going into danger again and flaying me alive with abuse of my cowardice. I was stung, but I was obliged to admire the easy confidence with which my chief loafed from side to side of his wheel, and trimmed the ships so closely that disaster seemed ceaselessly imminent. When he had cooled a little he told me that the easy water was

2. Before his money ran out, Twain had been a paying passenger on the *Paul Jones* to New Orleans and had had an opportunity to befriend one of the ship's pilots.

close ashore and the current outside, and therefore we must hug the bank, up-stream, to get the benefit of the former, and stay well out, down-stream, to take advantage of the latter. In my own mind I resolved to be a down-stream pilot and leave the up-streaming to people dead to prudence.

Now and then Mr. Bixby called my attention to certain things. 8 Said he, "This is Six-Mile Point." I assented. It was pleasant enough information, but I could not see the bearing of it. I was not conscious that it was a matter of any interest to me. Another time he said, "This is Nine-Mile Point." Later he said, "This is Twelve-Mile Point." They were all about level with the water's edge; they all looked about alike to me; they were monotonously unpicturesque. I hoped Mr. Bixby would change the subject. But no; he would crowd up around a point, hugging the shore with affection, and then say: "The slack water ends here, abreast this bunch of China trees; now we cross over." So he crossed over. He gave me the wheel once or twice, but I had no luck. I either came near chipping off the edge of a sugar-plantation, or I yawed too far from shore, and so dropped back into disgrace again and got abuse.

The watch was ended at last, and we took supper and went to bed. 9 At midnight the glare of a lantern shone in my eyes, and the night watchman said:

"Come, turn out!"   10

And then he left. I could not understand this extraordinary proce- 11 dure; so I presently gave up trying to, and dozed off to sleep. Pretty soon the watchman was back again, and this time he was gruff. I was annoyed. I said:

"What do you want to come bothering around here in the middle 12 of the night for? Now, as like as not, I'll not get to sleep again to-night."

The watchman said: 13

"Well, if this ain't good, I'm blessed."   14

The "off-watch" was just turning in, and I heard some brutal 15 laughter from them, and such remarks as "Hello, watchman! ain't the new cub turned out yet? He's delicate, likely. Give him some sugar in a rag, and send for the chambermaid to sing 'Rock-a-by Baby,' to him."

About this time Mr. Bixby appeared on the scene. Something like 16 a minute later I was climbing the pilot-house steps with some of my clothes on and the rest in my arms. Mr. Bixby was close behind, commenting. Here was something fresh—this thing of getting up in the middle of the night to go to work. It was a detail in piloting that had never occurred to me at all. I knew that boats ran all night, but somehow I had never happened to reflect that somebody had to get up out of a warm bed to run them. I began to fear that piloting was not quite so romantic as I had imagined it was; there was something very real and worklike about this new phase of it.

It was a rather dingy night, although a fair number of stars were out. The big mate was at the wheel, and he had the old tub pointed at a star and was holding her straight up the middle of the river. The shores on either hand were not much more than half a mile apart, but they seemed wonderfully far away and ever so vague and indistinct. The mate said: 17

"We've got to land at Jones's plantation, sir." 18

The vengeful spirit in me exulted. I said to myself, "I wish you joy of your job, Mr. Bixby; you'll have a good time finding Mr. Jones's plantation such a night as this; and I hope you never *will* find it as long as you live." 19

Mr. Bixby said to the mate: 20

"Upper end of the plantation, or the lower?" 21

"Upper." 22

"I can't do it. The stumps there are out of water at this stage. It's no great distance to the lower, and you'll have to get along with that." 23

"All right, sir. If Jones don't like it, he'll have to lump it, I reckon." 24

And then the mate left. My exultation began to cool and my wonder to come up. Here was a man who not only proposed to find this plantation on such a night, but to find either end of it you preferred. I dreadfully wanted to ask a question, but I was carrying about as many short answers as my cargo-room would admit of, so I held my peace. All I desired to ask Mr. Bixby was the simple question whether he was ass enough to really imagine he was going to find that plantation on a night when all plantations were exactly alike and all of the same color. But I held in. I used to have fine inspirations of prudence in those days. 25

Mr. Bixby made for the shore and soon was scraping it, just the same as if it had been daylight. And not only that, but singing: 26

"Father in heaven, the day is declining," etc.

It seemed to me that I had put my life in the keeping of a peculiarly reckless outcast. Presently he turned on me and said:

"What's the name of the first point above New Orleans?" 27

I was gratified to be able to answer promptly, and I did. I said I didn't know. 28

"Don't *know?*" 29

This manner jolted me. I was down at the foot again, in a moment. But I had to say just what I had said before. 30

"Well, you're a smart one!" said Mr. Bixby. "What's the name of the *next* point?" 31

Once more I didn't know. 32

"Well, this beats anything. Tell me the name of *any* point or place I told you." 33

I studied awhile and decided that I couldn't. 34

"Look here! What do you start out from, above Twelve-Mile Point,   35
to cross over?"

"I—I—don't know."   36

"You—you—don't know?" mimicking my drawling manner of   37
speech. "What *do* you know?"

"I—I—nothing, for certain."   38

"By the great Cæsar's ghost, I believe you! You're the stupidest   39
dunderhead I ever saw or ever heard of, so help me Moses! The idea of
you being a pilot—*you!* Why, you don't know enough to pilot a cow
down a lane."

Oh, but his wrath was up! He was a nervous man, and he shuffled   40
from one side of his wheel to the other as if the floor was hot. He
would boil awhile to himself, and then overflow and scald me again.

"Look here! What do you suppose I told you the names of those   41
points for?"

I tremblingly considered a moment, and then the devil of tempta-   42
tion provoked me to say:

"Well to—to—be entertaining, I thought."   43

This was a red rag to the bull. He raged and stormed so (he was   44
crossing the river at the time) that I judged it made him blind, because
he ran over the steering-oar of a trading-scow. Of course the traders
sent up a volley of red-hot profanity. Never was a man so grateful as
Mr. Bixby was; because he was brimful, and here were subjects who
could *talk back.* He threw open a window, thrust his head out, and such
an irruption followed as I never had heard before. The fainter and farther away the scowmen's curses drifted, the higher Mr. Bixby lifted his
voice and the weightier his adjectives grew. When he closed the window he was empty. You could have drawn a seine through his system
and not caught curses enough to disturb your mother with. Presently
he said to me in the gentlest way:

"My boy, you must get a little memorandum-book; and every time   45
I tell you a thing, put it down right away. There's only one way to be a
pilot, and that is to get this entire river by heart. You have to know it
just like A B C."

That was a dismal revelation to me; for my memory was never   46
loaded with anything but blank cartridges. However, I did not feel discouraged long. I judged that it was best to make some allowances, for
doubtless Mr. Bixby was "stretching." Presently he pulled a rope and
struck a few strokes on the big bell. The stars were all gone now, and
the night was as black as ink. I could hear the wheels churn along the
bank, but I was not entirely certain that I could see the shore. The
voice of the invisible watchman called up from the hurricane-deck:

"What's this, sir?"   47

"Jones's plantation."   48

I said to myself, "I wish I might venture to offer a small bet that it   49
isn't." But I did not chirp. I only waited to see. Mr. Bixby handled the
engine-bells, and in due time the boat's nose came to the land, a torch
glowed from the forecastle, a man skipped ashore, a darky's voice on
the bank said: "Gimme de k'yarpet-bag, Mass' Jones," and the next
moment we were standing up the river again, all serene. I reflected
deeply awhile, and then said—but not aloud—"Well, the finding of
that plantation was the luckiest accident that ever happened; but it
couldn't happen again in a hundred years." And I fully believed it *was*
an accident, too.

By the time we had gone seven or eight hundred miles up the   50
river, I had learned to be a tolerably plucky up-stream steersman, in
daylight; and before we reached St. Louis I had made a trifle of
progress in night work, but only a trifle. I had a note-book that fairly
bristled with the names of towns, "points," bars, islands, bends,
reaches, etc.; but the information was to be found only in the notebook—none of it was in my head. It made my heart ache to think I had
only got half of the river set down; for as our watch was four hours off
and four hours on, day and night, there was a long four-hour gap in
my book for every time I had slept since the voyage began.

My chief was presently hired to go on a big New Orleans boat, and   51
I packed my satchel and went with him. She was a grand affair. When
I stood in her pilot-house I was so far above the water that I seemed
perched on a mountain; and her decks stretched so far away, fore
and aft, below me, that I wondered how I could ever have considered
the little *Paul Jones* a large craft. There were other differences, too.
The *Paul-Jones's* pilot-house was a cheap, dingy, battered rattletrap,
cramped for room; but here was a sumptuous glass temple; room
enough to have a dance in; showy red and gold window-curtains; an
imposing sofa; leather cushions and a back to the high bench where
visiting pilots sit, to spin yarns and "look at the river"; bright, fanciful
"cuspidores," instead of a broad wooden box filled with sawdust; nice
new oilcloth on the floor; a hospitable big stove for winter; a wheel as
high as my head, costly with inlaid work; a wire tiller-rope; bright
brass knobs for the bells; and a tidy, white-aproned, black "texas-
tender," to bring up tarts and ices and coffee during mid-watch, day
and night. Now this was "something like"; and so I began to take heart
once more to believe that piloting was a romantic sort of occupation
after all. The moment we were under way I began to prowl about the
great steamer and fill myself with joy. She was as clean and as dainty
as a drawing-room; when I looked down her long, gilded saloon, it
was like gazing through a splendid tunnel; she had an oil-picture, by
some gifted sign-painter, on every stateroom door; she glittered with
no end of prism-fringed chandeliers; the clerk's office was elegant, the

bar was marvelous, and the barkeeper had been barbered and upholstered at incredible cost. The boiler-deck (*i. e.,* the second story of the
boat, so to speak) was as spacious as a church, it seemed to me; so with
the forecastle; and there was no pitiful handful of deck-hands, firemen, and roustabouts down there, but a whole battalion of men. The
fires were fiercely glaring from a long row of furnaces, and over them
were eight huge boilers! This was unutterable pomp. The mighty engines—but enough of this. I had never felt so fine before. And when I
found that the regiment of natty servants respectfully "sir'd" me, my
satisfaction was complete.

RIGOBERTA MENCHÚ

Life in the Altiplano

Rigoberta Menchú (1959–) was born in the village of Chimel,
Guatemala, a community continuing to live in the tradition of the
Maya-Quiché culture. As a young woman, she worked in the fields
and later as a domestic employee. Menchú's early life was marked by
poverty, oppression, and tragedy. Two of her brothers died in infancy
of malnutrition, and another was burned alive when the Quiché attempted to fight the government takeover of their land. Later, her
mother was tortured to death and her father murdered. Because of
her unflinching commitment to her people, Menchú assumed the role
of organizer; self-educated, she proved an intelligent and inspiring
leader. Her work to promote human rights and peace earned her the
Nobel Peace Prize in 1992; she was the youngest person to have received the award. Menchú's story is found in *I, Rigoberta Menchú: An
Indian Woman* (1983), which she told to a transcriber, Elisabeth Burgos-
Debray. She continues to write, primarily poetry, is the personal adviser
to the general director of UNESCO, and presides over the Indigenous
Initiative for Peace. This chapter from *I, Rigoberta Menchú* illustrates the
difficult life the indigenous people of Guatemala have endured. A useful companion essay is Mary McCarthy's "Names," for though Mc-
Carthy experienced none of Menchú's physical hardships, she faced a
similar initiation into a world governed by other people's expectations.

Back in the *Altiplano,*[1] we all set to work with our hoes. I remember from the age of nine going off to the fields with my hoe to help my

1. *Altiplano:* high plateau or plain.

father. I was like a boy, chopping wood with an axe, or with a machete. There was very little water near our village. We had to walk about four kilometres[2] to fetch our water, and that added to our work a lot. But we were happy because that was the time of year we sowed our bit of maize and it was sometimes enough for us to live on. At times, we managed to scrape a living in the *Altiplano* and didn't go down to the *fincas*.[3] When the fields were full of plants and we had a bit of maize and a few *tortillas*, we were very happy up there. The land was fertile and I remember my mother giving us different types of beans like *ayote, chilacayote,* and others that grew up there. But we didn't eat a lot of beans because most of what my mother grew was taken to market to buy soap, or some chile. That's what we ate—chile. And if we wanted to, we could pick plants in the fields. So, with chile, plants, and *tortillas*, we ate very well. That was our menu most of the time.

It's not the custom among our people to use a mill to grind the maize to make dough. We use a grinding stone; that is, an ancient stone passed down from our ancestors. We don't use ovens either. We only use wood fires to cook our *tortillas*. First we get up at three in the morning and start grinding and washing the *nixtamal*,[4] turning it into dough by using the grinding stone. We all have different chores in the morning. Some of us wash the *nixtamal,* others make the fire to heat water for the coffee or whatever. In our house there were a lot of us— my elder sister, my mother, myself, and my sister-in-law, my elder brother's wife. So there were four women working in the house. Each of us had her job to do and we all had to get up at a certain time, our time was three in the morning. The men get up at that time too because they have to sharpen their hoes, machetes and axes before going off to work. So they get up at the same time. There are no lights in our village so at night we see by the light of *ocotes.* An *ocote* is a piece cut from a pine tree. It lights up immediately as if petrol had been poured on it. It burns easily. You can light it with matches and it flames up. That's what we use for light to move about the house. It burns slowly and if you put a bunch of *ocote* somewhere, it lights everything up. 2

Whoever gets up first, lights the fire. She makes the fire, gets the wood hot and prepares everything for making *tortillas*. She heats the water. The one who gets up next washes the *nixtamal* outside, and the third one up washes the grinding stone, gets the water ready and prepares everything needed for grinding the maize. In our house, I made the food for the dogs. My father had a lot of dogs because of the 3

2. four kilometres: about 2½ miles.
3. *fincas:* farms or ranches.
4. *nixtamal:* grain.

animals which came down from the mountain. These dogs guarded
our animals. It was my job to make food for them. Their food was
the hard core of the maize, the cob. We had a little place just outside
the house, a sort of little hollow, where we'd throw the cob when
we'd taken the grains of corn off. With time, the cobs rot and go soft,
and are cooked with lime. Then it's all ground up for the dogs' food.
Lime makes our dogs strong, otherwise they'd all die. They don't eat
our food which is maize, but, sometimes, when there's no maize, we
eat the dogs' food.[5] We make it into *tortillas*, just as we do with the
maize dough. Anyway, it was my job to make the dogs' food. I'd get
up, wash the stone and things I needed and start grinding the dogs'
food. I started doing this when I was seven. When the fire is made and
the *nixtamal* washed, everyone starts grinding. One person grinds the
maize, another grinds it a second time with a stone to make it finer,
and another makes it into little balls for the *tortilla*. When that's all
ready, we all start making *tortillas*. We have a flat earthenware pan big
enough to hold all the *tortillas*. Then the men—my brothers and my father—all come and get their *tortillas* from the pan and start eating. In
the mornings, we sometimes drink coffee or sometimes only water.
We usually make *pinol*, that is, maize toasted and ground. This is drunk
instead of coffee because coffee is too expensive for my parents to buy.
Sometimes my parents haven't enough money for *panela* either, we
don't use sugar but *panela* which comes straight from the sugar cane.
When there's no panela in the house, we can't drink *pinol* or coffee. So
we drink water. In the mornings, we usually have a big plate of chile,
and all of us have a good meal of *tortilla* and chile before going off to
work. Our dogs are used to being with people, they enjoy the natural
world as well and like going off to work with the men. So we have to
feed the dogs before the workers leave, as the dogs always go with
them. If the men are going to work a long way off, we have to make
tortillas for them to take with them, but if they're working nearby, one
of the women stays at home and makes the midday meal for them.

Our men usually leave around five or half past every morning.
They go and tend the maize or cultivate the ground. Some of the
women go with them because we sow the beans and, when the plant
starts sprouting, we stick in little branches for it to wind itself around,
so that it doesn't damage the maize. So, yes, at times we're working
alongside the men all day. What we used to do, was that my sister-in-
law stayed at home because she had a baby. She stayed at home,
looked after the animals, made the food and brought it to us at midday.

---

5. It often happened that we had no maize and my brothers and sisters and I, even
when we were ill, had to eat the dog's food. [author's note]

She'd bring *atol, tortillas,* and if she saw anything she could use in the fields, she'd prepare that too and bring it along for us to eat. *Atol* is the maize dough. We use it for a drink, as refreshment. It's dissolved in water, boiled, and it thickens, according to how you want to drink it. Of course, sometimes we take it in turns to stay home because my sister-in-law grew up on the *fincas* and in the *Altiplano* too, so she gets bored in the house because the food only takes a minute to make and the rest of the time she has to herself. She uses the time to do a lot of weaving. She makes mats, cloth, *huipiles,*[6] blouses, or other things like that. But she often gets bored and wants to work in the fields, even though she's carrying her baby on her back. So we take it in turns, my sister, my mother and I.

In our village we have the habit of talking very loudly because   5
we haven't really any close neighbours. When the workers leave in the morning, they call out to all their neighbours because the neighbours' maize fields are all near each other, so they all go together. We all get together like one family. Our maize fields aren't in the village itself. They're a short distance away, towards the mountain, so we call all our neighbours and we all go together—twenty or thirty people going off to work together with our dogs. We eat at midday or whenever we feel hungry. We usually go home again at six in the evening. Six o'clock is when our men come home, hungry and thirsty, and the woman who stays at home has to make food again. That's when we do all the extra chores in the house. The men tie up the dogs in the *corrales* where the animals are and the women fetch water to wash the *nixtamal* and washing pots, chop wood, and prepare the torches for the night. We prepare all our things for the next day to save time in the morning. When night falls, we're still working. Afterwards, we sing a bit; songs we Indians have in our own language. I don't know how, but my brothers got hold of an accordion, and we'd sing until our parents told us off because we were very tired and they sent us to bed. We usually go to bed at ten or half past because we have to get up so early and since our house is very small, when one person gets up, we all have to get up.

Our house measures about eight *varas.*[7] It's not made of wood but   6
of cane; straight sticks of it we find in the fields and fasten together with *agave*[8] fibres. Any tree will do to make a house, but (I think this is part of our culture) only if it's cut at full moon. We say the wood lasts longer if it's cut when the moon is young. When we build a house, we

---

6. *huipiles:* embroidered smocks.
7. eight *varas:* about 22 feet.
8. *agave:* aloe.

make the roof from a sort of palm tree found near the foot of the mountains. We call it *pamac*. For us, the most elegant houses are made with cane leaves, because you have to go a long way to get them. You have to have men to go and get them to make the house. We were poor and had neither money to buy cane leaves nor anyone to go and get them. They're only found down in the *fincas* on the coast and they're very expensive. The landowners charge by the bunch— seventy-five centavos[9] the bunch—and it takes fifty bunches for a house. We didn't have the means to buy cane leaves, so what we did was go to the mountains and collect this leaf called *pamac*. The mature leaves last about two years and after that you have to start again. So we all went to cut the mature leaves. Between us—men, women and children—we could build a house in fifteen days. We had a very big family, and we were able to use sticks, although many people used maize stalks. After the maize is harvested, people cut the stalks and use them for walls. But our house was made of sticks of cane: that lasts longer. The houses are not very high because, if there's a lot of wind, it can lift the house and carry it all away. That's why we make them small and put sticks all round. The sticks are stuck in the ground and tied together with *agave* fibres. There are no nails in our houses—you won't find a single nail. Even the roof props, the corners, or anything supporting the house, comes from trees.

We all sleep in there together. The house has two floors; one above, where the corn cobs are stored (we call it the *tapanco*) and another below where we all live. But at the times of the year when there's no maize, many of us go up and sleep in the *tapanco*. When the cobs are stored there, we have to sleep on the ground floor. We don't usually have beds with mattresses or anything like that. We just have our own few clothes and we're used to being cold, because the roof doesn't give much protection. The wind comes in as if we were out on the mountain. As for sex, that's something we Indians know about because most of the family sees everything that goes on. Couples sleep together but don't have a separate place for themselves. Even the children realize most of the time, but sometimes they don't, because I think married couples don't have enough time to enjoy their life together and, anyway, we're all in there together. Of course, when we sleep, we sleep like logs, we're so tired. We often get home so tired we don't want to eat anything, or do anything. We just want to sleep. So we sleep. Perhaps that's when the others take the opportunity to have sexual relations, but there's hardly any room. Often just the children go down to the *finca* and the parents stay at home and look after the

9. centavos: cents.

animals. That's when they have a bit more time to themselves. But most of the time my father goes to one *finca* and my mother takes the children to another *finca* so they're apart for three months. Or we all go together to one *finca* but there it's even worse for sleeping than at home, because we're with people we don't even know and there are hundreds of people and animals sleeping together. It is really difficult there. We're piled up in one place, almost on top of one another. I'm sure the children notice a lot of things. In our case, all the brothers and sisters in our family slept together in one row. My older brother, who'd been married for some time, slept with his *compañera*,[10] but the ones who weren't married (my other two older brothers, my sister, myself, and my three younger brothers who were alive then) we all slept together in a row. We put all the women's *cortes*[11] together and used them for blankets. My parents slept in another corner quite near us. We each had a mat to sleep on and a little cover over us. We slept in the same clothes we worked in. That's why society rejects us. Me, I felt this rejection very personally, deep inside me. They say we Indians are dirty, but it's our circumstances which force us to be like that. For example, if we have time, we go to the river every week, every Sunday, and wash our clothes. The clothes have to last us all week because we haven't any other time for washing and we haven't any soap either. That's how it is. We sleep in our clothes, we get up next day, we tidy ourselves up a bit and off to work, just like that.

My tenth birthday was celebrated in the same way as all our people. I was up in the *Altiplano*. It might not have been the exact date of my birth because I was in the *finca* at the time, but when we went back up to the *Altiplano*, that was when we celebrated my birthday. My parents called me to them and explained what an adult's life is like. I didn't really need them to explain because it was the life I'd seen and lived with my mother; so it was really only a show of accepting what parents tell us. 8

My elder brothers were present and my sister who's now married. But my younger brothers were not. I'm the sixth in the family, with three brothers after me, but they weren't present because it's a ceremony in which my parents tell me about the new life I'm about to start. They told me I would have many ambitions but I wouldn't have the opportunity to realize them. They said my life wouldn't change, it would go on the same—work, poverty, suffering. At the same time, my parents thanked me for the contribution I'd made through my work, for having earned for all of us. Then they told me a bit about being a woman; that I would soon have my period and that was when 9

10. *compañera:* companion; wife.
11. *cortes:* material used to make clothing.

a woman could start having children. They said that would happen one day, and for that they asked me to become closer to my mother so I could ask her everything. My mother would be by my side all this time in case I had any doubts or felt alone. They talked about the experiences with my elder brothers and sisters. My elder sister, who was already grown up (she'd be about twenty-four, I think) told me about when she was young: when she was ten, twelve, thirteen, fifteen. My father said that sometimes she didn't do things as she should but that that wasn't right: we should not stop doing good things but accept life as it is. We shouldn't become bitter or look for diversions or escape outside the laws of our parents. All this helps you to be a girl who is respected by the community. My father explained the importance of our example and the example of every one of our neighbours' children. We know that not just one pair of eyes is watching us, but the eyes of the whole community are on us. It's not a case of giving things up. We have a lot of freedom, but, at the same time, within that freedom we must respect ourselves.

Well, my mother, father, and all my brother and sisters, gave me their experiences. Suddenly they treated me like an adult. My father said, "You have a lot of responsibility; you have many duties to fulfill in our community as an adult. From now on you must contribute to the common good." Then they made me repeat the promises my parents had made for me when I was born; when I was accepted into the community; when they said I belonged to the community and would have to serve it when I grew up. They said they'd made these promises and now it was up to me to keep them, because now I had to participate in the community as one more member of it. In those days, there was already the mixture of our culture with the Catholic religion, let's say Catholic customs. So my duty was to promise to serve the community and I looked for ways in which I could work for the community. When you reach the age of ten, your family and the whole community holds a meeting. It's very important. There's a ceremony as if we were praying to God. The discussion is very important because, as I said, it initiated me into adult life. Not the life of a young girl but adult life with all its responsibilities. I'm no longer a child, I become a woman. So in front of my parents, in front of my brothers and sisters, I promised to do many things for the community. That's when I started to take over some of my father's duties: that is, praying in our neighbours' houses like my father does. Whenever there's a meeting, it's always my father who speaks, and he coordinates a lot of things in the community. I felt responsible for many things and my mother let us into many secrets, telling us to try and do things the way she had. It was then, I remember, I became a catechist, and began working with the children both in the community and down in the *finca*, since, when

some of the community go to the *finca*, others stay in the *Altiplano*
looking after our animals, or whatever, so we don't have to take them
with us to the coast.

MARY McCARTHY

Names

Mary McCarthy (1912–1989) grew up in Seattle and Minneapolis,
raised by her relatives and in parochial boarding schools after being
orphaned at six. She recounts her early life in *Memories of a Catholic
Girlhood* (1957), from which "Names" is taken. McCarthy graduated
from Vassar in 1933 and began writing book reviews for *The New Republic* and *The Nation,* making a reputation for herself because of her
unflinching frankness. Known also for her keen political and social
criticism, McCarthy established her literary career with a collection of
satiric short stories, *The Company She Keeps* (1942). She taught at Sarah
Lawrence College and Bard College during the 1940s, but, urged to
continue writing by her second husband, critic Edmund Wilson, Mc-
Carthy also worked as an editor and drama critic for *Partisan Review.*
McCarthy later published an autobiographical novel, *The Group*
(1963), as well as several volumes of nonfiction, including *Vietnam*
(1967), *The Writing on the Wall* (1970), and *How I Grew* (1987). Mc-
Carthy spent the final years of her life teaching at Bard, attaining the
Stevenson Chair in Literature in 1986. Like Nathan McCall's "Makes
Me Wanna Holler," the memoir demonstrates a young person's strug-
gle against becoming what other people perceive him or her to be.

Anna Lyons, Mary Louise Lyons, Mary von Phul, Emilie von Phul,   1
Eugenia McLellan, Marjorie McPhail, Marie-Louise L'Abbé, Mary
Danz, Julia Dodge, Mary Fordyce Blake, Janet Preston—these were
the names (I can still tell them over like a rosary) of some of the older
girls in the convent: the Virtues and Graces. The virtuous ones wore
wide blue or green moire good-conduct ribbons, bandoleer-style,
across their blue serge uniforms; the beautiful ones wore rouge and
powder or at least were reputed to do so. Our class, the eighth grade,
wore pink ribbons (I never got one myself) and had names like Patricia
("Pat") Sullivan, Eileen Donohoe, and Joan Kane. We were inelegant
even in this respect; the best name we could show, among us, was
Phyllis ("Phil") Chatham, who boasted that her father's name, Ralph,
was pronounced "Rafe" as in England.

Names had a great importance for us in the convent, and foreign   2
names, French, German, or plain English (which, to us, were foreign,

because of their Protestant sound), bloomed like prize roses among a collection of spuds. Irish names were too common in the school to have any prestige either as surnames (Gallagher, Sheehan, Finn, Sullivan, McCarthy) or as Christian names (Kathleen, Eileen). Anything exotic had value: an "olive" complexion, for example. The pet girl of the convent was a fragile Jewish girl named Susie Lowenstein, who had pale red-gold hair and an exquisite retroussé nose, which, if we had had it, might have been called "pug." We liked her name too and the name of a child in the primary grades: Abbie Stuart Baillargeon. My favorite name, on the whole, though, was Emilie von Phul (pronounced "Pool"); her oldest sister, recently graduated, was called Celeste. Another name that appealed to me was Genevieve Albers, Saint Genevieve being the patron saint of Paris who turned back Attila from the gates of the city.

All these names reflected the still-pioneer character of the Pacific Northwest. I had never heard their like in the parochial school in Minneapolis, where "foreign" extraction, in any case, was something to be ashamed of, the whole drive being toward Americanization of first name and surname alike. The exceptions to this were the Irish, who could vaunt such names as Catherine O'Dea and the name of my second cousin, Mary Catherine Anne Rose Violet McCarthy, while an unfortunate German boy named Manfred was made to suffer for his. But that was Minneapolis. In Seattle, and especially in the convent of the Ladies of the Sacred Heart, foreign names suggested not immigration but emigration—distinguished exile. Minneapolis was a granary; Seattle was a port, which had attracted a veritable Foreign Legion of adventurers—soldiers of fortune, younger sons, gamblers, traders, drawn by the fortunes to be made in virgin timber and shipping and by the Alaska gold rush. Wars and revolutions had sent the defeated out to Puget Sound, to start a new life; the latest had been the Russian Revolution, which had shipped us, via Harbin, a Russian colony, complete with restaurant, on Queen Anne Hill. The English names in the convent, when they did not testify to direct English origin, as in the case of "Rafe" Chatham, had come to us from the South and represented a kind of internal exile; such girls as Mary Fordyce Blake and Mary McQueen Street (a class ahead of me; her sister was named Francesca) bore their double-barreled first names like titles of aristocracy from the ante-bellum South. Not all our girls, by any means, were Catholic; some of the very prettiest ones—Julia Dodge and Janet Preston, if I remember rightly—were Protestants. The nuns had taught us to behave with social courtesy to these strangers in our midst, and the whole effect was of some superior hostel for refugees of all the lost causes of the past hundred years. Money could not count for much in such an atmosphere; the fathers and grandfathers of many of our "best" girls were ruined men.

Names, often, were freakish in the Pacific Northwest, particularly   4
girls' names. In the Episcopal boarding school I went to later, in
Tacoma, there was a girl called De Vere Utter, and there was a girl
called Rocena and another called Hermoine. Was Rocena a mistake for
Rowena and Hermoine for Hermione? And was Vere, as we called her,
Lady Clara Vere de Vere? Probably. You do not hear names like those
often, in any case, east of the Cascade Mountains; they belong to the
frontier, where books and libraries were few and memory seems to
have been oral, as in the time of Homer.

Names have more significance for Catholics than they do for other   5
people; Christian names are chosen for the spiritual qualities of the
saints they are taken from; Protestants used to name their children out
of the Old Testament and now they name them out of novels and
plays, whose heroes and heroines are perhaps the new patron saints of
a secular age. But with Catholics it is different. The saint a child is
named for is supposed to serve, literally, as a model or pattern to imitate; your name is your fortune and it tells you what you are or must
be. Catholic children ponder their names for a mystic meaning, like
birthstones; my own, I learned, besides belonging to the Virgin and
Saint Mary of Egypt, originally meant "bitter" or "star of the sea." My
second name, Therese, could dedicate me either to Saint Theresa or to
the saint called the Little Flower, Soeur Thérèse of Lisieux, on whom
God was supposed to have descended in the form of a shower of roses.
At Confirmation, I had added a third name (for Catholics then rename
themselves, as most nuns do, yet another time, when they take orders); on the advice of a nun, I had taken "Clementina," after Saint
Clement, an early pope—a step I soon regretted on account of "My
Darling Clementine" and her number nine shoes. By the time I was in
the convent, I would no longer tell anyone what my Confirmation
name was. The name I had nearly picked was "Agnes," after a little
Roman virgin martyr, always shown with a lamb, because of her purity. But Agnes would have been just as bad, I recognized in Forest
Ridge Convent—not only because of the possibility of "Aggie," but because it was subtly, indefinably *wrong*, in itself. Agnes would have
made me look like an ass.

The fear of appearing ridiculous first entered my life, as a govern-   6
ing motive, during my second year in the convent. Up to then, a desire
for prominence had decided many of my actions and, in fact, still persisted. But in the eighth grade, I became aware of mockery and perceived that I could not seek prominence without attracting laughter.
Other people could, but I couldn't. This laughter was proceeding, not
from my classmates, but from the girls of the class just above me, in
particular from two boon companions, Elinor Heffernan and Mary
Harty, a clownish pair—oddly assorted in size and shape, as teams of
clowns generally are, one short, plump, and baby-faced, the other tall,

lean, and owlish—who entertained the high-school department by calling attention to the oddities of the younger girls. Nearly every school has such a pair of satirists, whose marks are generally low and who are tolerated just because of their laziness and non-conformity; one of them (in this case, Mary Harty, the plump one) usually appears to be half asleep. Because of their low standing, their indifference to appearances, the sad state of their uniforms, their clowning is taken to be harmless, which, on the whole, it is, their object being not to wound but to divert; such girls are bored in school. We in the eighth grade sat directly in front of the two wits in study hall, so that they had us under close observation; yet at first I was not afraid of them, wanting, if anything, to identify myself with their laughter, to be initiated into the joke. One of their specialties was giving people nicknames, and it was considered an honor to be the first in the eighth grade to be let in by Elinor and Mary on their latest invention. This often happened to me; they would tell me, on the playground, and I would tell the others. As their intermediary, I felt myself almost their friend and it did not occur to me that I might be next on their list.

I had achieved prominence not long before by publicly losing my faith and regaining it at the end of a retreat. I believe Elinor and Mary questioned me about this on the playground, during recess, and listened with serious, respectful faces while I told them about my conversations with the Jesuits. Those serious faces ought to have been an omen, but if the two girls used what I had revealed to make fun of me, it must have been behind my back. I never heard any more of it, and yet just at this time I began to feel something, like a cold breath on the nape of my neck, that made me wonder whether the new position I had won for myself in the convent was as secure as I imagined. I would turn around in study hall and find the two girls looking at me with speculation in their eyes.

It was just at this time, too, that I found myself in a perfectly absurd situation, a very private one, which made me live, from month to month, in horror of discovery. I had waked up one morning, in my convent room, to find a few small spots of blood on my sheet; I had somehow scratched a trifling cut on one of my legs and opened it during the night. I wondered what to do about this, for the nuns were fussy about bedmaking, as they were about our white collars and cuffs, and if we had an inspection those spots might count against me. It was best, I decided, to ask the nun on dormitory duty, tall, stout Mother Slattery, for a clean bottom sheet, even though she might scold me for having scratched my leg in my sleep and order me to cut my toenails. You never know what you might be blamed for. But Mother Slattery, when she bustled in to look at the sheet, did not scold me at all; indeed, she hardly seemed to be listening as I explained to her about the cut. She told me to sit down: she would be back in a minute. "You can be excused from athletics today," she added, closing the door. As I waited, I considered this remark, which seemed to me strangely munificent, in view of the unimportance of the cut. In a moment, she returned, but without the sheet. Instead, she produced out of her big pocket a sort of cloth girdle and a peculiar flannel object which I first took to be a bandage, and I began to protest that I did not need or want a bandage; all I needed was a bottom sheet. "The sheet can wait," said Mother Slattery, succinctly, handing me two large safety pins. It was the pins that abruptly enlightened me; I saw Mother Slattery's mistake, even as she was instructing me as to how this flannel article, which I now understood to be a sanitary napkin, was to be put on.

"Oh, no, Mother," I said, feeling somewhat embarrassed. "You don't understand. It's just a little cut, on my leg." But Mother, again, was not listening; she appeared to have grown deaf, as the nuns had a habit of doing when what you were saying did not fit in with their ideas. And now that I knew what was in her mind, I was conscious of a funny constraint; I did not feel it proper to name a natural process, in so many words, to a nun. It was like trying not to think of their going to the bathroom or trying not to see the straggling iron-grey hair coming out of their coifs (the common notion that they shaved their heads was false). On the whole, it seemed better just to show her my cut. But when I offered to do so and unfastened my black stocking, she only glanced at my leg, cursorily. "That's only a scratch, dear," she said. "Now hurry up and put this on or you'll be late for chapel. Have you any pain?" "No, no, Mother!" I cried, "You don't understand!" "Yes, yes, I understand," she replied soothingly, "and you will too, a little later. Mother Superior will tell you about it some time during the morning. There's nothing to be afraid of. You have become a woman."

"I know all about that," I persisted. "Mother, please listen. I just cut my leg. On the athletic field. Yesterday afternoon." But the more excited I grew, the more soothing, and yet firm, Mother Slattery became. There seemed to be nothing for it but to give up and do as I was bid. I was in the grip of a higher authority, which almost had the power to persuade me that it was right and I was wrong. But of course I was not wrong; that would have been too good to be true. While Mother Slattery waited, just outside my door, I miserably donned the equipment she had given me, for there was no place to hide it, on account of drawer inspection. She led me down the hall to where there was a chute and explained how I was to dispose of the flannel thing, by dropping it down the chute into the laundry. (The convent arrangements were old-fashioned, dating back, no doubt, to the days of Louis Philippe.)

The Mother Superior, Madame MacIllvra, was a sensible woman, and all through my early morning class, I was on pins and needles, chafing for the promised interview with her which I trusted would clear things up. *"Ma Mère,"* I would begin, "Mother Slattery thinks . . ." Then I would tell her about the cut and the athletic field. But precisely the same impasse confronted me when I was summoned to her office at recess-time. *I* talked about my cut, and *she* talked about becoming a woman. It was rather like a round, in which she was singing "Scotland's burning, Scotland's burning," and I was singing "Pour on water, pour on water." Neither of us could hear the other, or, rather, I could hear her, but she could not hear me. Owing to our different positions in the convent, she was free to interrupt me, whereas I was expected to remain silent until she had finished speaking. When I kept breaking in, she hushed me, gently, and took me to her lap. Exactly like Mother Slattery, she attributed all my references to the cut to a blind fear of this new, unexpected reality that had supposedly entered my life. Many young girls, she reassured me, were frightened if they had not been prepared. "And you, Mary, have lost your dear mother, who could have made this easier for you." Rocked on Madame MacIllvra's lap, I felt paralysis overtake me and I lay, mutely listening, against her bosom, my face being tickled by her white, starched, fluted wimple, while she explained to me how babies were born, all of which I had heard before.

There was no use fighting the convent. I had to pretend to have become a woman, just as, not long before, I had had to pretend to get my faith back—for the sake of peace. This pretense was decidedly awkward. For fear of being found out by the lay sisters downstairs in the laundry (no doubt an imaginary contingency, but the convent was so very thorough), I reopened the cut on my leg, so as to draw a little blood to stain the napkins, which were issued me regularly, not only on this occasion, but every twenty-eight days thereafter. Eventually, I abandoned this bloodletting, for fear of lockjaw, and trusted to fate. Yet I was in awful dread of detection; my only hope, as I saw it, was either to be released from the convent or to become a woman in reality, which might take a year, at least, since I was only twelve. Getting out of athletics once a month was not sufficient compensation for the farce I was going through. It was not my fault; they had forced me into it; nevertheless, it was I who would look silly—worse than silly; half mad—if the truth ever came to light.

I was burdened with this guilt and shame when the nickname finally found me out. "Found me out," in a general sense, for no one ever did learn the particular secret I bore about with me, pinned to the linen band. "We've got a name for you," Elinor and Mary called out to me, one day on the playground. "What is it?" I asked, half hoping, half fearing, since not all their sobriquets were unfavorable. "Cye," they answered, looking at each other and laughing, "'Si'?" I repeated, supposing that it was based on Simple Simon. Did they regard me as a hick? "C.Y.E.," they elucidated, spelling it out in chorus. "The letters stand for something. Can you guess?" I could not and I cannot now. The closest I could come to it in the convent was "Clean Your Ears." Perhaps that was it, though in later life I have wondered whether it did not stand, simply, for "Clever Young Egg" or "Champion Young Eccentric." But in the convent I was certain that it stood for something horrible, something even worse than dirty ears (as far as I knew, my ears were clean), something I could never guess because it represented some aspect of myself that the world could see and I couldn't, like a sign pinned on my back. Everyone in the convent must have known what the letters stood for, but no one would tell me. Elinor and Mary had made them promise. It was like halitosis; not even my best friend, my deskmate, Louise, would tell me, no matter how much I pleaded. Yet everyone assured me that it was "very good," that is, very apt. And it made everyone laugh.

This name reduced all my pretensions and solidified my sense of *wrongness*. Just as I felt I was beginning to belong to the convent, it turned me into an outsider, since I was the only pupil who was not in the know. I liked the convent, but it did not like me, as people say of certain foods that disagree with them. By this, I do not mean that I was actively unpopular, either with the pupils or with the nuns. The Mother Superior cried when I left and predicted that I would be a novelist, which surprised me. And I had finally made friends; even Emilie von Phul smiled upon me softly out of her bright blue eyes from the far end of the study hall. It was just that I did not fit into the convent pattern; the simplest thing I did, like asking for a clean sheet, entrapped me in consequences that I never could have predicted. I was not bad; I did not consciously break the rules; and yet I could never, not even for a week, get a pink ribbon, and this was something I could not understand, because I was trying as hard as I could. It was the same case as with the hated name; the nuns, evidently, saw something about me that was invisible to me.

The oddest part was all that pretending. There I was, a walking mass of lies, pretending to be a Catholic and going to confession while really I had lost my faith, and pretending to have monthly periods by cutting myself with nail scissors; yet all this had come about without my volition and even contrary to it. But the basest pretense I was driven to was the acceptance of the nickname. Yet what else could I do? In the convent, I could not live it down. To all those girls, I had become "Cye McCarthy." That was who I was. That was how I had to identify myself when telephoning my friends during vacations to ask them to the movies: "Hello, this is Cye." I loathed myself when I said it, and yet I succumbed to the name totally, making myself over into a sort of hearty to go with it—the kind of girl I hated. "Cye" was my new patron saint. This false personality stuck to me, like the name, when I entered public high school, the next fall, as a freshman, having finally persuaded my grandparents to take me out of the convent, although they could never get to the bottom of my reasons, since, as I admitted, the nuns were kind, and I had made many nice new friends. What I wanted was a fresh start, a chance to begin life over again, but the first thing I heard in the corridors of the public high school was that name called out to me, like the warmest of welcomes: "Hi, there, Si!" That was the way they thought it was spelled. But this time I was resolute. After the first weeks, I dropped the hearties who called me "Si" and I never heard it again. I got my own name back and sloughed off Clementina and even Therese—the names that did not seem to me any more to be mine but to have been imposed on me by others. And I preferred to think that Mary meant "bitter" rather than "star of the sea."

NATHAN McCALL

Makes Me Wanna Holler

Nathan McCall's (1955–) autobiographical best-seller *Makes Me Wanna Holler: A Young Black Man in America* (1994) details his violent and criminal youth in Portsmouth, Virginia. In 1975, while on probation for attempted murder, McCall held up a McDonald's and received a twelve-year prison sentence. Although he served only three years of his term, it was in jail that he began to turn away from crime and find hope in intellectual and spiritual pursuits. After his release, McCall went on to graduate with a B.A. from Norfolk State University and work as a reporter for the *Virginia Pilot/Ledger Star.* In 1989 he took a job at the *Washington Post,* for which he continues to write today. McCall's recent book *What's Going On: Personal Essays* (1997), addresses white American history and attitudes, the black middle class, and gangsta rap. The film rights to *Makes Me Wanna Holler* have been bought by Columbia Pictures. The following excerpts have been taken from chapters in the book. Writers interested in the importance of mentors or the community in the initiation process may wish to study both McCall's essay and Maya Angelou's "Graduation."

There were moments in that jail when the confinement and heat   1
nearly drove me mad. At those times, I desperately needed to take my thoughts beyond the concrete and steel. When I felt restless tension rising, I'd try anything to calm it. I'd slap-box with other inmates until I got exhausted, or play chess until my mind shut down. When all else failed, I'd pace the cellblock perimeter like a caged lion. Sometimes, other inmates fighting the temptation to give in to madness joined me,

and we'd pace together, round and round, and talk for hours about anything that got our minds off our misery.

I eventually found a better way to relieve the boredom. I noticed that some inmates broke the monotony by volunteering for certain jobs in the jail. Some mopped the halls, and others worked in the dispensary or the kitchen. When the inmate librarian was released from jail, I asked for and was given his job. I began distributing books on the sixth floor as part of a service provided by the Norfolk Public Library. A couple of times a week, I pushed a cart to each cellblock and let inmates choose books and place orders for literature not on the cart. I enjoyed the library work. It gave me a chance to get out into the halls and walk around, and to stick my face to the screens on the floor windows and inhale fresh air.

Beyond the short stories I'd read in high school, I hadn't done much reading. Naturally, while working for the library, I leafed through more books than I normally would have. One day, shortly after starting the job, I picked up a book featuring a black man's picture on the cover. It was titled *Native Son,* and the author was Richard Wright.[1] I leafed through a few pages in the front of the book, and couldn't put it down. The story was about a confused, angry young black man named Bigger Thomas, whose racial fears lead him to accidentally suffocate a white woman. In doing so, he delivers himself into the hands of the very people he despises and fears.

I identified strongly with Bigger and the book's narrative. He was twenty, the same age as me. He felt the things I felt, and, like me, he wound up in prison. The book's portrait of Bigger captured all those conflicting feelings—restless anger, hopelessness, a tough facade among blacks and a deep-seated fear of whites—that I'd sensed in myself but was unable to express. Often, during my teenage years, I'd felt like Bigger—headed down a road toward a destruction I couldn't ward off, beaten by forces so large and amorphous that I had no idea how to fight back. I was surprised that somebody had written a book that so closely reflected my experiences and feelings.

I read that book every day, and continued reading by the dim light of the hall lamps at night, while everyone slept. On that early morning when I finished reading *Native Son,* which ends with Bigger waiting to go to the electric chair, I broke down and sobbed like a baby. There is one passage that so closely described how I felt that it stunned me. It is a passage where a lawyer is talking to Bigger, who has given up hope and is waiting to die:

> You're trying to believe in yourself. And every time you try to find a way to live, your own mind stands in the way. You know why that is? It's because others have said you were bad and they made you live in bad con-

---

1. Wright's classic protest novel was published in 1940.

ditions. When a man hears that over and over and looks about him and sees that life is bad, he begins to doubt his own mind. His feelings drag him forward and his mind, full of what others say about him, tells him to go back. The job in getting people to fight and have faith is in making them believe in what life has made them feel, making them feel that their feelings are as good as others'.

After reading that, I sat up in my bunk, buried my face in my hands, and wept uncontrollably. I cried so much that I felt relieved. It was like I had been carrying those feelings and holding in my pain for years, keeping it pushed into the back of my mind somewhere.   6

I was unaccustomed to dealing with such deep feelings. Occasionally, I'd opened up to Liz,[2] but not a lot. I was messed up inside, empty and afraid, just like Bigger. *Native Son* confirmed for me that my fears *weren't* imagined and that there were rational reasons why I'd been hurting inside.   7

I developed through my encounter with Richard Wright a fascination with the power of words. It blew my mind to think that somebody could take words that described exactly how I felt and put them together in a story like that. Most of the books I'd been given in school were about white folks' experiences and feelings. I spent all that time learning about damned white folks, like my reality didn't exist and wasn't valid to the rest of the world. In school, the only time we'd really focused on the lives of black people was during Black History Week, which they set aside for us to learn the same old tired stories about Booker T. Washington and a few other noteworthy, dead black folks I couldn't relate to. But in *Native Son* I found a book written about a plain, everyday brother like myself. That turned me on in a big way and inspired me to look for more books like that.   8

Before long, I was reading every chance I got, trying to more fully understand why my life and the lives of friends had been so contained and predictable, and why prison—literally—had become a rite of passage for so many of us. I found books that took me places I'd never dreamed I could travel to and exposed me to a range of realities that seemed as vast as the universe itself.   9

Once, after reading a book of poems by Gwendolyn Brooks,[3] I wrote to her, not really expecting to receive a reply. She wrote me back and sent me an inspirational paperback of hers titled *Aloneness*. I was thrilled that a well-known black writer like her had taken the time to respond to me.   10

I was most attracted to black classics, such as Malcolm X's autobiography. Malcolm's tale helped me understand the devastating effects of self-hatred and introduced me to a universal principle: that if you   11

2. Liz: McCall's ex-fiancée and the mother of his son.
3. Pulitzer Prize–winning poet and novelist Gwendolyn Brooks (1917–) published *Aloneness* in 1971.

change your self-perception, and you can change your behavior. I concluded that if Malcolm X, who had also gone to prison, could pull his
life out of the toilet, then maybe I could, too.

Up to that point, I'd often wanted to think of myself as a baad nig-   12
ger, and as a result, I'd tried to act like one. After reading about Malcolm X, I worked to get rid of that notion and replace it with a positive
image of what I wanted to become. I walked around silently repeating
to myself, "You are an intelligent-thinking human being; you are an
intelligent-thinking human being . . . ," hoping that it would sink in
and help me begin to change the way I viewed myself.

Malcolm X made his conversion through Islam. I'd seen Muslims   13
selling newspapers and bean pies on the streets, but I didn't know anything about their religion. I was drawn to Christianity, mostly because
it was familiar. I hadn't spent much time in church. It seemed that all
they did in churches I'd been to was learn how to justify suffering at
the hands of white folks. But now there were Christian ministers active at the jail, and I became interested. They came around about once
a week and talked to inmates through the bars, prayed with them and
read Scripture. I started talking with them about God and about life in
general.

It wasn't hard to accept the possibility that there was a higher force   14
watching over me. When I looked back at my life, I concluded that
there had been far too many close calls—times when I could have
offed somebody or gotten killed myself—for me to believe I had survived solely on luck. I wondered, *Why didn't that bullet strike Plaz in the
heart when I shot him? Why didn't I pull the trigger on that McDonald's manager when he tried to get away? And why wasn't I on the corner the night my
stick partners were shot?* Unable to come up with rational answers to
those questions, I reasoned that God must have been pulling for me.

My interest in spiritual things also came from a need to reach out   15
at my most powerless point and tap into a higher power, something
beyond me and, at the same time, within me. I longed for a sense of
wholeness that I had never known but sensed I was entitled to. I set
out to learn more about my spiritual self, and I began exploring the
Bible with other inmates who held Bible studies some nights in the
cellblock.

At some point, I also got a library copy of the book—*As a Man   16
Thinketh*[4]—that Reverend Ellis had given me in college. I immediately
understood what he had been trying to get across: that thinking
should be an *active* process that, when cultivated, can change a person's behavior, circumstances, and, ultimately, his fate.

When I first started reading, studying, and reflecting on the infor-   17
mation I got from books, I had no idea where it all might lead. Really,

4. *As a Man Thinketh* was written by James Allen (1864–1912).

it didn't matter. I was hungry for change and so excited by the sense of awakening I glimpsed on the horizon that the only thing that mattered was that I had made a start. I often recited the Scripture that Reverend Ellis had given me to read before I was sentenced: "Everything works together for the good of those that love God, for those who are called according to His purpose."[5] *If that's true,* I thought, *maybe I can get something positive out of this time in prison.* It sure didn't seem like it. But it made me feel better just thinking it might be possible.

. . .

In a way, Jim[6] was also similar to Mo Battle, my mentor in the 18 Norfolk jail. When he saw young guys with potential come out of the Receiving Unit, he'd take the time to school them about anything he could. He'd pull them aside and tell them the dos and don'ts of prison life so the wolves couldn't get to them. The wolves resented Jim because of that, but none made a move to do anything about it.

It amazed me to see how much the so-called tough cats respected 19 Jim. Whenever he was around, they cursed less and toned down their macho posturing, as if he were an authority figure or a revered elder. Initially, that kind of deference, which bordered on fear, puzzled me, because Jim didn't carry himself like a knockout artist or anything. Brown-skinned and medium-built, he always dressed neat and spoke softly. He was clean-shaven, and he constantly carried books and newspapers tucked under his arms.

Eventually, I figured out that the characteristics that made him so 20 widely respected had little to do with how he looked; instead, it was his manly demeanor. Ever since I could recall, I and everybody else I knew had associated manhood with physical dominance and conquest of someone else. Watching Jim, I realized we'd gone about it all wrong. Jim didn't have to make a rep for himself as a thumper. He could whip a man with his sharp mind and choice words far more thoroughly than with his fists. The wolves feared his kind of ass-whipping much more than a physical beating, so they kept their distance.

I decided that this was the kind of respect I wanted to command, 21 and I noticed other guys who without being fully aware wanted to be like Jim, too. They strutted on the yard, looking super-macho, like killers, but acted differently in private. In those moments when they weren't profiling with their buddies, some of my tough-acting homies would stop by my perch on the yard or in my cell and ask, "What you reading'?" I sensed they wanted to improve themselves but didn't

5. "Everything . . . purpose": Romans 8:28.
6. Jim was an inmate at Southampton prison, to which McCall was transferred after serving time in Norfolk prison.

want their other homies to see them, because self-improvement wasn't a macho thing. Pearly Blue was one of them. He sometimes tried to draw me into deep private discussions about God and reality while sticking to the tough street vernacular that helped him maintain his macho facade.

As I learned more about misguided ideas about manhood, I experimented with some of those macho dudes: Whenever I passed them, I looked into their eyes to see what was there. A few had that cold-blooded, killer look about them, but in the eyes of most of them I saw something I hadn't noticed before: fear.

Even in Big Earl. Big Earl was one of the brawniest, most outwardly fearless cats in the place. He was tall and jet-black, his muscles rippled through his T-shirt, and his thighs were so massive that all his pants fit too tight. Big Earl, who was thirtyish, was from a small, off-brand town in rural Virginia, but he didn't need homies to back him up. He walked around the yard, talking loud and intimidating other inmates like he owned the place.

One day, while walking down the long sidewalk on my way to the cafeteria, I spotted Big Earl pimping toward me. (He never said anything to me, Jim, or some of the others who were part of our progressive group.) As he approached, I fixed my eyes on his and kept them locked there. When we got closer, I kept my eyes fastened to his, not in a hostile gaze, but in an expression of serene self-assurance. Initially, he tried to meet my gaze. Then he turned his eyes away and looked toward the ground. I smiled to myself. I would have never been able to back down Big Earl in a rumble, but I had certainly backed him down with my mind.

Several times after that brief, silent encounter, I caught Big Earl watching me curiously. He never said anything. He just watched and turned away whenever he realized I'd caught him staring. I sensed he knew I'd figured that he wasn't as confident of his manhood as he pretended to be, and he felt naked, exposed.

I practiced the piercing eye contact with other guys like Earl and realized that few of the seriously baad cats could meet my gaze. That helped me see my homies and the other toughs at Southampton as they were (and as I had been): streetwise, pseudo baad-asses who were really frightened boys, bluffing, trying to mask their fear of the world behind muscular frames.

·   ·   ·

On the day I went before the parole board, I was so nervous I was nearly paralyzed. I was scared that I'd get in there, get asked a question, and choke. I was scared that when it was time for me to speak, all my suffering would come to the surface and all my emotions would bum-rush my throat, and nothing would come out. So I did deep-breathing exercises and prayed for the best.

I waited in a hallway with about six other dudes who were going before the board that day. All of us looked alike. We looked like choir-boys sitting out there. We were spit-shined and scrubbed and lotioned down to the max. We all had our hair cut short. We had our shirts buttoned to the very top, and we were so quiet you could hear the roaches walking across the shiny floor.

But appearances didn't seem to sway the board. When dudes came out after meeting with the board, they were red-eyed and withdrawn. I asked one guy how he thought things had gone for him. He looked at me, shook his head slowly, and said, "It looks bad for the home team."

When my name was called, I went in and took a seat before the board members—several white men and a black woman—who sat behind a long table. It was a stern-faced, tight-butt bunch. No-nonsense all the way. They asked a few questions about my crime, my family, that sort of thing. Then, after several other minor questions, came the biggie: "So, Mr. McCall, what do you plan to do to better yourself if you get out, and what arrangements have you made to carry out those plans?"

If a cat hasn't given serious consideration to his future, really thought it out, that's the question that cold-cocks him. That's the one that renews his lease for another year. If he's wasted his time and neglected to improve himself, he can't answer that question convincingly. He's down for the count. TKO.[7] With the parole board, you've got to come strong or not at all, because they've heard all the bullshit they care to hear, and they can smell it a mile away.

I knew all that going in. I knew I couldn't go in there half-stepping. I was prepared. My future? Shit, I had thought about it, prayed about it, and dreamed about it the entire time I was down. I had thought a helluva lot about my future—enough to know that I might not *have* a future if I didn't get sprung that first time up. When they hit me with the question, they hit the right person that time, because I was ready.

I rapped. I rapped *hard*. I rapped harder than I'd ever rapped in my life. I took all the skills I'd picked up rapping with those penitentiary philosophers out on the yard and threw the whole handful at the parole board. I told them all I'd done to improve myself in the nearly three years that I'd been locked up, and shared my plans to go home to my family and to enroll at Norfolk State. I told them that robbing that hamburger joint was the stupidest thing I could have done, and that I'd spent a lot of time thinking about that and other mistakes I'd made

7. TKO: technical knockout, a boxing term.

in my life. The bottom line was, I came straight from the heart. I came from so deep within the heart that I surprised myself. But I meant every word I said. I was changed. I knew it, and I wanted to make sure they knew it.

I'll bet those white folks on that parole board were glad when I fi-   34
nally finished talking. I'll bet they thought I'd never shut up. I'll bet that when I finished and left that room, they burst out laughing and said, "Damn! We need to hurry up and let this nigger out. This dude wants *badly* to get out of here."

But they didn't come off like that. They were very professional.   35
When I finished talking, one of the parole board members said, "Thank you, Mr. McCall. The board will take into consideration all that you have said. You will be notified within the next month of our decision." They sent me on my way without a hint of the verdict.

· · ·

Waiting for an answer was like waiting to be sentenced all over   36
again. Those few weeks were as hard on me as the entire three years had been. I nagged my institutional counselor constantly to see if a response had come. He got mad at me for nagging him, and I got mad at him for getting mad at me. If he had been an inmate and not a counselor, we would have come to blows, because I was uptight as hell and I already had a full head of steam.

When my letter from the board finally arrived, I took it to my   37
bunk and sat down alone. I looked at the letter in the sealed envelope a long time before even attempting to open it. I needed a drink, but since there were no bars open in the penitentiary, I had to face it straight. I gave myself a long talking-to before opening it: *Keep cool. You've done the best you could do. You've given it your best shot and programmed hard. Stay strong, no matter what happens.*

Then I opened the letter and I could hardly believe it. For a long   38
while, I just sat there, staring at the words, reading the letter over and over, making sure I'd gotten it right. I thought, *I made parole. I made it. I'm getting out. They're gonna let me go. I can go home. Soon. I made it. I can't believe it. I made it. I made parole!*

· · ·

I remember clearly that snowy February day in 1978 when I was released from the joint. My homies gathered on the sidewalk that morning and watched me leave. As I climbed into the car and my mother drove off, I cast a long, hard look at the prison, and tears began streaming uncontrollably down my face. I felt a strange mixture of pain and pride. I was mostly proud that I had survived, and I told myself, then and there, *I can do ANYTHING*.

Although it had been the most tragic event in my life, prison—with all its sickness and suffering—had also been my most instructional challenge. It forced me to go deep, real deep, within and tap a well I didn't even know I had. Through that painful trip, I'd found meaning. No longer was life a thing of bewilderment. No longer did I feel like a cosmic freak, a black intruder in a world not created for me and my people. No longer were my angry feelings about the vast white world simply vague, invalid impulses dangling on the edge of my mind. I knew the reasons for those feelings now. I understood them better, and, most important, I could express them precisely as they arose. I knew that there was purpose and design in creation and that my life was somehow part of that grand scheme. I had just as much right to be alive and happy as anybody else, and I wasn't going to let anybody, especially not white folks, make me feel otherwise. 39

MAYA ANGELOU

Graduation

Maya Angelou (1929–), poet, dancer, actress, civil rights organizer, film director, and now Reynolds Professor of American Studies at Wake Forest University, is best known for her five volumes of autobiography, beginning with *I Know Why the Caged Bird Sings* (1970). This book chronicles Angelou's childhood in the rigidly segregated town of Stamps, Arkansas. There she was raised by her grandmother, known to her as Momma, who owned a store and a large amount of land, much of which she rented to whites. Despite her grandmother's prominence in the black community of Stamps, Angelou's early years were marred by poverty, discrimination, and abuse, all of which she presents with frankness and honesty when she writes about her life. These hardships gave her a sharp sense of everyone's struggle to become adult with pride and dignity: "Most people don't grow up," she once said. "It's too damn difficult." "Graduation," a chapter from *I Know Why the Caged Bird Sings*, describes a milestone most students remember well from their own lives. Writers interested in making meaning of their graduation experiences may find inspiration in Angelou's essay, as well as in Steven Foster's sociological study of the ceremony, "Bunny Bashing into Manhood."

The children in Stamps trembled visibly with anticipation. Some 1 adults were excited too, but to be certain the whole young population had come down with graduation epidemic. Large classes were grad-uating from both the grammar school and the high school. Even those who were years removed from their own day of glorious release were anxious to help with preparations as a kind of dry run. The ju-nior students who were moving into the vacating classes' chairs were tradition-bound to show their talents for leadership and management. They strutted through the school and around the campus exerting pressure on the lower grades. Their authority was so new that occa-sionally if they pressed a little too hard it had to be overlooked. After all, next term was coming, and it never hurt a sixth grader to have a play sister in the eighth grade, or a tenth-year student to be able to call a twelfth grader Bubba. So all was endured in a spirit of shared under-standing. But the graduating classes themselves were the nobility. Like travelers with exotic destinations on their minds, the graduates were remarkably forgetful. They came to school without their books, or tablets or even pencils. Volunteers fell over themselves to secure re-placements for the missing equipment. When accepted, the willing workers might or might not be thanked, and it was of no importance to the pregraduation rites. Even teachers were respectful of the now quiet and aging seniors, and tended to speak to them, if not as equals, as beings only slightly lower than themselves. After tests were re-turned and grades given, the student body, which acted like an ex-tended family, knew who did well, who excelled, and what piteous ones had failed.

Unlike the white high school, Lafayette County Training School 2 distinguished itself by having neither lawn, nor hedges, nor tennis court, nor climbing ivy. Its two buildings (main classrooms, the grade school and home economics) were set on a dirt hill with no fence to limit either its boundaries or those of bordering farms. There was a large expanse to the left of the school which was used alternately as a baseball diamond or a basketball court. Rusty hoops on the swaying poles represented the permanent recreational equipment, although bats and balls could be borrowed from the P.E. teacher if the borrower was qualified and if the diamond wasn't occupied.

Over this rocky area relieved by a few shady tall persimmon trees 3 the graduating class walked. The girls often held hands and no longer bothered to speak to the lower students. There was a sadness about them, as if this old world was not their home and they were bound for higher ground. The boys, on the other hand, had become more friendly, more outgoing. A decided change from the closed attitude they projected while studying for finals. Now they seemed not ready to give up the old school, the familiar paths and classrooms. Only a small percentage would be continuing on to college—one of the South's A & M (agricultural and mechanical) schools, which trained Negro youths to be carpenters, farmers, handymen, masons, maids, cooks and baby nurses. Their future rode heavily on their shoulders, and blinded them to the collective joy that had pervaded the lives of the boys and girls in the grammar school graduating class.

Parents who could afford it had ordered new shoes and ready-made clothes for themselves from Sears and Roebuck or Montgomery Ward. They also engaged the best seamstresses to make the floating graduating dresses and to cut down secondhand pants which would be pressed to a military slickness for the important event.

Oh, it was important, all right. Whitefolks would attend the ceremony, and two or three would speak of God and home, and the Southern way of life, and Mrs. Parsons, the principal's wife, would play the graduation march while the lower-grade graduates paraded down the aisles and took their seats below the platform. The high school seniors would wait in empty classrooms to make their dramatic entrance.

In the Store I was the person of the moment. The birthday girl. The center. Bailey[1] had graduated the year before, although to do so he had had to forfeit all pleasures to make up for his time lost in Baton Rouge.

My class was wearing butter-yellow piqué dresses, and Momma launched out on mine. She smocked the yoke into tiny crisscrossing puckers, then shirred the rest of the bodice. Her dark fingers ducked in and out of the lemony cloth as she embroidered raised daisies around the hem. Before she considered herself finished she had added a crocheted cuff on the puff sleeves, and a pointy crocheted collar.

I was going to be lovely. A walking model of all the various styles of fine hand sewing and it didn't worry me that I was only twelve years old and merely graduating from the eighth grade. Besides, many teachers in Arkansas Negro schools had only that diploma and were licensed to impart wisdom.

The days had become longer and more noticeable. The faded beige of former times had been replaced with strong and sure colors. I began to see my classmates' clothes, their skin tones, and the dust that waved off pussy willows. Clouds that lazed across the sky were objects of great concern to me. Their shiftier shapes might have held a message that in my new happiness and with a little bit of time I'd soon decipher. During that period I looked at the arch of heaven so religiously my neck kept a steady ache. I had taken to smiling more often, and my jaws hurt from the unaccustomed activity. Between the two physical sore spots, I suppose I could have been uncomfortable, but that was not the case. As a member of the winning team (the graduating class of 1940) I had outdistanced unpleasant sensations by miles. I was headed for the freedom of open fields.

1. Bailey: Angelou's brother.

Youth and social approval allied themselves with me and we tram-   10
meled memories of slights and insults. The wind of our swift passage
remodeled my features. Lost tears were pounded to mud and then to
dust. Years of withdrawal were brushed aside and left behind, as hanging ropes of parasitic moss.

My work alone had awarded me a top place and I was going to be   11
one of the first called in the graduating ceremonies. On the classroom
blackboard, as well as on the bulletin board in the auditorium, there
were blue stars and white stars and red stars. No absences, no tardi-
nesses, and my academic work was among the best of the year. I could
say the preamble to the Constitution even faster than Bailey. We timed
ourselves often: "WethepeopleoftheUnitedStatesinordertoformamore-
perfectunion . . ." I had memorized the Presidents of the United States
from Washington to Roosevelt in chronological as well as alphabetical
order.

My hair pleased me too. Gradually, the black mass had lengthened   12
and thickened, so that it kept at last to its braided pattern, and I didn't
have to yank my scalp off when I tried to comb it.

Louise[2] and I had rehearsed the exercises until we tired out our-   13
selves. Henry Reed was class valedictorian. He was a small, very black
boy with hooded eyes, a long, broad nose and an oddly shaped head. I
had admired him for years because each term he and I vied for the best
grades in our class. Most often he bested me, but instead of being disappointed I was pleased that we shared top places between us. Like
many Southern Black children, he lived with his grandmother, who
was as strict as Momma and as kind as she knew how to be. He was
courteous, respectful and soft-spoken to elders, but on the playground
he chose to play the roughest games. I admired him. Anyone, I reckoned, sufficiently afraid or sufficiently dull could be polite. But to be
able to operate at a top level with both adults and children was admirable.

His valedictory speech was entitled "To Be or Not to Be." The rigid   14
tenth-grade teacher had helped him write it. He'd been working on
the dramatic stresses for months.

The weeks until graduation were filled with heady activities. A   15
group of small children were to be presented in a play about buttercups and daisies and bunny rabbits. They could be heard throughout
the building practicing their hops and their little songs that sounded
like silver bells. The older girls (nongraduates, of course) were assigned
the task of making refreshments for the night's festivities. A tangy
scent of ginger, cinnamon, nutmeg and chocolate wafted around the
home economics building as the budding cooks made samples for themselves and their teachers.

2. Louise: Angelou's friend.

In every corner of the workshop, axes and saws split fresh timber   16
as the workshop boys made sets and stage scenery. Only the graduates
were left out of the general bustle. We were free to sit in the library at
the back of the building or look in quite detachedly, naturally, on the
measures being taken for our event.

Even the minister preached on graduation the Sunday before. His   17
subject was, "Let your light so shine that men will see your good works
and praise your Father, Who is in Heaven." Although the sermon was
purported to be addressed to us, he used the occasion to speak to back-
sliders, gamblers and general ne'er-do-wells. But since he had called
our names at the beginning of the service we were mollified.

Among Negroes the tradition was to give presents to children   18
going only from one grade to another. How much more important this
was when the person was graduating at the top of the class. Uncle
Willie and Momma had sent away for a Mickey Mouse watch like Bailey's. Louise gave me four embroidered handkerchiefs. (I gave her
three crocheted doilies.) Mrs. Sneed, the minister's wife, made me an
underskirt to wear for graduation, and nearly every customer gave me
a nickel or maybe even a dime with the instruction "Keep on moving
to higher ground," or some such encouragement.

Amazingly the great day finally dawned and I was out of bed before   19
I knew it. I threw open the back door to see it more clearly, but
Momma said, "Sister, come away from that door and put your robe on."

I hoped the memory of that morning would never leave me. Sun-   20
light was itself still young, and the day had none of the insistence maturity would bring it in a few hours. In my robe and barefoot in the
backyard, under cover of going to see about my new beans, I gave myself up to the gentle warmth and thanked God that no matter what
evil I had done in my life He had allowed me to live to see this day.
Somewhere in my fatalism I had expected to die, accidentally, and
never have the chance to walk up the stairs in the auditorium and
gracefully receive my hard-earned diploma. Out of God's merciful
bosom I had won reprieve.

Bailey came out in his robe and gave me a box wrapped in Christ-   21
mas paper. He said he had saved his money for months to pay for it. It
felt like a box of chocolates, but I knew Bailey wouldn't save money to
buy candy when we had all we could want under our noses.

He was as proud of the gift as I. It was a soft-leather-bound copy of   22
a collection of poems by Edgar Allan Poe, or, as Bailey and I called him,
"Eap." I turned to "Annabel Lee" and we walked up and down the garden rows, the cool dirt between our toes, reciting the beautifully sad
lines.

Momma made a Sunday breakfast although it was only Friday.   23
After we finished the blessing, I opened my eyes to find the watch on
my plate. It was a dream of a day. Everything went smoothly and to

my credit. I didn't have to be reminded or scolded for anything. Near evening I was too jittery to attend to chores, so Bailey volunteered to do all before his bath.

Days before, we had made a sign for the Store, and as we turned out the lights Momma hung the cardboard over the doorknob. It read clearly: CLOSED. GRADUATION.   24

My dress fitted perfectly and everyone said that I looked like a sunbeam in it. On the hill, going toward the school, Bailey walked behind with Uncle Willie, who muttered, "Go on, Ju." He wanted him to walk ahead with us because it embarrassed him to have to walk so slowly. Bailey said he'd let the ladies walk together, and the men would bring up the rear. We all laughed, nicely.   25

Little children dashed by out of the dark like fireflies. Their crepe-paper dresses and butterfly wings were not made for running and we heard more than one rip, dryly, and the regretful "uh uh" that followed.   26

The school blazed without gaiety. The windows seemed cold and unfriendly from the lower hill. A sense of ill-fated timing crept over me, and if Momma hadn't reached for my hand I would have drifted back to Bailey and Uncle Willie, and possibly beyond. She made a few slow jokes about my feet getting cold, and tugged me along to the now-strange building.   27

Around the front steps, assurance came back. There were my fellow "greats," the graduating class. Hair brushed back, legs oiled, new dresses and pressed pleats, fresh pocket handkerchiefs and little handbags, all homesewn. Oh, we were up to snuff, all right. I joined my comrades and didn't even see my family go in to find seats in the crowded auditorium.   28

The school band struck up a march and all classes filed in as had been rehearsed. We stood in front of our seats, as assigned, and on a signal from the choir director, we sat. No sooner had this been accomplished than the band started to play the national anthem. We rose again and sang the song, after which we recited the pledge of allegiance. We remained standing for a brief minute before the choir director and the principal signaled to us, rather desperately I thought, to take our seats. The command was so unusual that our carefully rehearsed and smooth-running machine was thrown off. For a full minute we fumbled for our chairs and bumped into each other awkwardly. Habits change or solidify under pressure, so in our state of nervous tension we had been ready to follow our usual assembly pattern: the American national anthem, then the pledge of allegiance, then the song every Black person I knew called the Negro National Anthem. All done in the same key, with the same passion and most often standing on the same foot.   29

Finding my seat at last, I was overcome with a presentiment of worse things to come. Something unrehearsed, unplanned, was going   30 to happen, and we were going to be made to look bad. I distinctly remember being explicit in the choice of pronoun. It was "we," the graduating class, the unit, that concerned me then.

The principal welcomed "parents and friends" and asked the Baptist minister to lead us in prayer. His invocation was brief and punchy, and for a second I thought we were getting back on the high road to right action. When the principal came back to the dais, however, his voice had changed. Sounds always affected me profoundly and the principal's voice was one of my favorites. During assembly it melted and lowed weakly into the audience. It had not been in my plan to listen to him, but my curiosity was piqued and I straightened up to give him my attention. 31

He was talking about Booker T. Washington, our "late great leader," who said we can be as close as the fingers on the hand, etc. . . . Then he said a few vague things about friendship and the friendship of kindly people to those less fortunate than themselves. With that his voice nearly faded, thin, away. Like a river diminishing to a stream and then to a trickle. But he cleared his throat and said, "Our speaker tonight, who is also our friend, came from Texarkana to deliver the commencement address, but due to the irregularity of the train's schedule, he's going to, as they say 'speak and run.'" He said that we understood and wanted the man to know that we were most grateful for the time he was able to give us and then something about how we were willing always to adjust to another's program, and without more ado—"I give you Mr. Edward Donleavy." 32

Not one but two white men came through the door offstage. The shorter one walked to the speaker's platform, and the tall one moved over to the center seat and sat down. But that was our principal's seat, and already occupied. The dislodged gentleman bounced around for a long breath or two before the Baptist minister gave him his chair, then with more dignity than the situation deserved, the minister walked off the stage. 33

Donleavy looked at the audience once (on reflection, I'm sure that he wanted only to reassure himself that we were really there), adjusted his glasses and began to read from a sheaf of papers. 34

He was glad "to be here and to see the work going on just as it was in the other schools." 35

At the first "Amen" from the audience I willed the offender to immediate death by choking on the word. But Amens and Yes, sir's began to fall around the room like rain through a ragged umbrella. 36

He told us of the wonderful changes we children in Stamps had in store. The Central School (naturally, the white school was Central) had already been granted improvements that would be in use in the fall. A well-known artist was coming from Little Rock to teach art to them. They were going to have the newest microscopes and chemistry 37 equipment for their laboratory. Mr. Donleavy didn't leave us long in the dark over who made these improvements available to Central High. Nor were we to be ignored in the general betterment scheme he had in mind.

He said that he had pointed out to people at a very high level that one of the first-line football tacklers at Arkansas Agricultural and Mechanical College had graduated from good old Lafayette County Training School. Here fewer Amen's were heard. Those few that did break through lay dully in the air with the heaviness of habit. 38

He went on to praise us. He went on to say how he had bragged that "one of the best basketball players at Fisk sank his first ball right here at Lafayette County Training School." 39

The white kids were going to have a chance to become Galileos and Madame Curies and Edisons and Gauguins, and our boys (girls weren't even in on it) would try to be Jesse Owenses and Joe Louises. 40

Owens and the Brown Bomber were great heroes in our world, but what school official in the whitegoddom of Little Rock had the right to decide that those two men must be our only heroes? Who decided that for Henry Reed to become a scientist he had to work like George Washington Carver, as a bootblack, to buy a lousy microscope? Bailey was obviously always going to be too small to be an athlete, so which concrete angel glued to what country seat had decided that if my brother wanted to become a lawyer he had to first pay penance for his skin by picking cotton and hoeing corn and studying correspondence books at night for twenty years? 41

The man's dead words fell like bricks around the auditorium and too many settled in my belly. Constrained by hard-learned manners I couldn't look behind me, but to my left and right the proud graduating class of 1940 had dropped their heads. Every girl in my row had found something new to do with her handkerchief. Some folded the tiny squares into love knots, some into triangles, but most were wadding them, then pressing them flat on their yellow laps. 42

On the dais, the ancient tragedy was being replayed. Professor Parsons sat, a sculptor's reject, rigid. His large, heavy body seemed devoid of will or willingness, and his eyes said he was no longer with us. The other teachers examined the flag (which was draped stage right) or their notes, or the windows which opened on our now-famous playing diamond. 43

Graduation, the hush-hush magic time of frills and gifts and congratulations and diplomas, was finished for me before my name was called. The accomplishment was nothing. The meticulous maps, drawn in three colors of ink, learning and spelling decasyllabic words, memorizing the whole of *The Rape of Lucrece*[3]—it was for nothing. Donleavy had exposed us. 44

---

3. *The Rape of Lucrece:* a long narrative poem by Shakespeare.

We were maids and farmers, handymen and washerwomen, and anything higher that we aspired to was farcical and presumptuous. 45

Then I wished that Gabriel Prosser and Nat Turner[4] had killed all whitefolks in their beds and that Abraham Lincoln had been assassinated before the signing of the Emancipation Proclamation, and that Harriet Tubman[5] had been killed by that blow on her head and Christopher Columbus had drowned in the *Santa María*. 46

It was awful to be Negro and have no control over my life. It was brutal to be young and already trained to sit quietly and listen to charges brought against my color with no chance of defense. We should all be dead. I thought I should like to see us all dead, one on top of the other. A pyramid of flesh with the whitefolks on the bottom, as the broad base, then the Indians with their silly tomahawks and teepees and wigwams and treaties, the Negroes with their mops and recipes and cotton sacks and spirituals sticking out of their mouths. The Dutch children should all stumble in their wooden shoes and break their necks. The French should choke to death on the Louisiana Purchase (1803) while silkworms ate all the Chinese with their stupid pigtails. As a species, we were an abomination. All of us. 47

Donleavy was running for election, and assured our parents that if he won we could count on having the only colored paved playing field in that part of Arkansas. Also—he never looked up to acknowledge the grunts of acceptance—also, we were bound to get some new equipment for the home economics building and the workshop. 48

He finished, and since there was no need to give any more than the most perfunctory thank-you's, he nodded to the men on the stage, and the tall white man who was never introduced joined him at the door. They left with the attitude that now they were off to something really important. (The graduation ceremonies at Lafayette County Training School had been a mere preliminary.) 49

The ugliness they left was palpable. An uninvited guest who wouldn't leave. The choir was summoned and sang a modern arrangement of "Onward, Christian Soldiers," with new words pertaining to graduates seeking their place in the world. But it didn't work. Elouise, the daughter of the Baptist minister, recited "Invictus,"[6] and I could have cried at the impertinence of "I am the master of my fate, I am the captain of my soul." 50

My name had lost its ring of familiarity and I had to be nudged to go and receive my diploma. All my preparations had fled. I neither marched up to the stage like a conquering Amazon, nor did I look in 51

4. Gabriel Prosser (1776–1800) led the Virginia slave rebellion of 1800; Nat Turner (1800–1831), the rebellion of 1830.
5. Harriet Tubman (1821–1913), an escaped slave and abolitionist, became legendary for her work with the Underground Railroad.
6. "Invictus": an inspirational poem by English author and editor William Ernest Henley (1849–1903).

the audience for Bailey's nod of approval. Marguerite Johnson, I heard
the name again, my honors were read, there were noises in the audience of appreciation, and I took my place on the stage as rehearsed.

I thought about colors I hated: ecru, puce, lavender, beige and black.   52

There was shuffling and rustling around me, then Henry Reed was   53
giving his valedictory address, "To Be or Not to Be." Hadn't he heard
the whitefolks? We couldn't *be,* so the question was a waste of time.
Henry's voice came out clear and strong. I feared to look at him.
Hadn't he got the message? There was no "nobler in the mind" for
Negroes because the world didn't think we had minds, and they let
us know it. "Outrageous fortune"? Now, that was a joke. When the
ceremony was over I had to tell Henry Reed some things. That is, if I
still cared. Not "rub," Henry, "erase." "Ah, there's the erase." Us.

Henry had been a good student in elocution. His voice rose on   54
tides of promise and fell on waves of warnings. The English teacher
had helped him to create a sermon winging through Hamlet's solilo-
quy. To be a man, a doer, a builder, a leader, or to be a tool, an un-
funny joke, a crusher of funky toadstools. I marveled that Henry could
go through with the speech as if we had a choice.

I had been listening and silently rebutting each sentence with my   55
eyes closed; then there was a hush, which in an audience warns that
something unplanned is happening. I looked up and saw Henry Reed,
the conservative, the proper, the A student, turn his back to the audience and turn to us (the proud graduating class of 1940) and sing,
nearly speaking,

> *"Lift ev'ry voice and sing*
> *Till earth and heaven ring*
> *Ring with the harmonies of Liberty . . ."*

It was the poem written by James Weldon Johnson.[7] It was the music
composed by J. Rosamond Johnson.[8] It was the Negro national anthem. Out of habit we were singing it.

Our mothers and fathers stood in the dark hall and joined the   56
hymn of encouragement. A kindergarten teacher led the small children onto the stage and the buttercups and daisies and bunny rabbits
marked time and tried to follow:

> *"Stony the road we trod*
> *Bitter the chastening rod*
> *Felt in the days when hope, unborn, had died.*
> *Yet with a steady beat*

7. James Weldon Johnson (1871–1938): author, social reformer, and leader of the
Harlem Renaissance.
8. J. Rosamond Johnson (1873–1954): American composer and singer, brother of
James Weldon Johnson.

Have not our weary feet
Come to the place for which our fathers sighed?"

Every child I knew had learned that song with his ABC's and along 57
with "Jesus Loves Me This I Know." But I personally had never heard
it before. Never heard the words, despite the thousands of times I had
sung them. Never thought they had anything to do with me.

On the other hand, the words of Patrick Henry had made such an 58
impression on me that I had been able to stretch myself tall and trembling and say, "I know not what course others may take, but as for me,
give me liberty or give me death."

And now I heard, really for the first time: 59

"We have come over a way that with tears
has been watered,
We have come, treading our path through
the blood of the slaughtered."

While echoes of the song shivered in the air, Henry Reed bowed 60
his head, said "Thank you," and returned to his place in the line. The
tears that slipped down many faces were not wiped away in shame.

We were on top again. As always, again. We survived. The depths 61
had been icy and dark, but now a bright sun spoke to our souls. I was
no longer simply a member of the proud graduating class of 1940; I
was a proud member of the wonderful, beautiful Negro race.

Oh, Black known and unknown poets, how often have your auc- 62
tioned pains sustained us? Who will compute the lonely nights made
less lonely by your songs, or by the empty pots made less tragic by
your tales?

If we were a people much given to revealing secrets, we might 63
raise monuments and sacrifice to the memories of our poets, but slavery cured us of that weakness. It may be enough, however, to have it
said that we survive in exact relationship to the dedication of our poets
(include preachers, musicians and blues singers).

STEVEN FOSTER

Bunny Bashing into Manhood

Steven Foster (1938–), prompted by his desire to reintroduce ancient
rites of passage into modern culture, quit teaching at San Francisco
State University in 1971 in order to spend a year alone in the Great
Basin deserts. A few years later he married Meredith Little, and together they founded Rites of Passage, Inc., a school that conducts

wilderness passage rites for people of all ages. Foster and Little almost always write together and have published several books, including *The Book of the Vision Quest: Personal Transformation in the Wilderness* (1980), *The Trail Ahead: A Course Book for Graduating Seniors* (1983), *Betwixt and Between: Patterns of Masculine and Feminine Initiation* (with Louise Carus Mahdi, 1987), and *Wilderness Questing and the Four Shields of Human Nature* (1996).

"Bunny Bashing into Manhood" was included in *Crossroads: The Quest for Contemporary Rites of Passage* (1996) edited by Louise Carus Mahdi. The essay's analysis of graduation rituals in light of ancient rites of passage provides a framework through which students may view their own graduation experiences. A useful companion essay is Naomi Wolf's "Promiscuities," for Wolf shares Foster's view that contemporary culture not only stands in the way of meaningful rites of passage for young people, but also sends harmful messages about what it means to grow up.

> When I was a child, I spake as a child, I understood as a child, I thought as a child; but when I became a man, I put away childish things.
>
> I CORINTHIANS 13:11

Bend City exists in one of the most beautiful places on earth. Travelers through these parts have often likened it to Nepal, Tibet, or the Andes. Gargantuan mountains rise to heights two miles above sea level on both sides of the valley. A few miles east of town, the tule-green Inyo River runs south through big sage-rabbitbrush flats to the reservoir, where the valley narrows to a few miles across, the Range of Light to the west, the Dwelling-Place-of-the-Great-Spirit Mountains to the east. Green veins of trees line the river and the numerous creeks that flow out of the mountains.

The region in and around Bend City offers unparalleled outdoor recreation, tourism, and "unconfined wilderness solitude." There's cross-country skiing in the winter, trout fishing (rainbow, German brown, Eastern brook, cutthroat, and golden) in the summer, hunting (elk, deer, game birds) in the fall, backpacking, hiking, rock hounding, fossil hunting, four-wheeling, mountain and rock climbing, hang gliding, photography, prospecting, nature watching—all year round. Less than an hour away you can visit with bristlecone pines, the oldest living things on earth. Two hours away and you can play in Funeral Valley, Termination Valley, Inconsolable Valley, Panamint Valley, Lost Valley, Deep Springs Valley, the Blanco Mountains . . . I could go on.[1] With its unique combination of desert and alpine mountains, of lowest

---

1. Place and personal names are generally fictitious. [author's note]

and highest, hottest and coldest, the regions adjacent to Bend City are like no others on the continent.

Since they are in such proximity to such beauty and wonder, you might think the people of Bend City would be self-sufficient, independent, adventuresome noble savages, lovers and preservers of the wilderness. But that is an urbanized notion. Anyone familiar with the rural American West knows that there is little correlation between imagined romantic notions of the noble savage living close to nature and the genuine article—the American "redneck." Not that all the citizens of Bend City are rednecks. If we could flush all the citizens out of their holes we'd probably find a fairly wide variety of cultural types, including many with convictions and values that run counter to the prevailing redneck, small-town attitudes. But most of us with notions opposite to the stampede usually prefer to keep a low profile. The rock standing too high in the middle of the rapids runs the risk of being overturned. Better for us opposition to practice guerrilla warfare, and to pick our shots.

Bend City is "California redneck"—as opposed to "Arkansas redneck," "Idaho redneck," or "Southern redneck." And being as how it is only a little over half a day from the Los Angeles area, Bend City contains a distinct subspecies of "California redneck." *Redneckus Californium Bend Citii* is unique in that it includes "redskin rednecks" (redneck Paiutes) as well as white ones. To a certain extent, the two types overlap—that is, they are often seen together, as in the little Bend City High School, with its student body of eighty-three. After high school, redskin redneck and paleface redneck cultures seem to diverge, although many of the symbols and badges are still held in common. It's often difficult to tell whose four-wheel drives, guns, and clothes are whose.

The high school is the most advantageous place to study the Bend City redneck. The male and female adults have freshly hardened into their roles. In high school the most exaggerated tendencies of redneckism can be seen at their innocent, irrational best. Cars, sex, alcohol (the redneck drug of preference), firearms, parties, anti-intellectualism, racism, follow-like-sheep-to-the-right politics, and all kinds of "macho" poses are informal signs of redneck coming-of-age behavior. I'm reminded of the kid who came to the prom wearing the T-shirt that read, "Nuke 'Em Until They Glow." He was showing signs of being grown-up. He was taking a political stand.

These kids grow up surrounded by some of the most beautiful mountains on earth. Every morning they can get up with sunrise and see the radiant eastern face of the Range of Light. Every sunset they can watch the Dwelling-Place-of-the-Great-Spirit Mountains glow like the coals of a dying fire. Whatever horizon they peer into greets their eyes with beauty, vastness, sublimity. Shadowy distances beckon to be explored, wondered at, known. Peaks beg to be scaled, rivers and lakes to be fished, back country to be traveled, animals to be tracked, specimens to be taken. The challenge is there. Now bring on our adventuresome young to accept the challenge of the land.

The truth is, the vast majority of the kids in Bend City High School aren't interested in the land. Their preoccupations are primarily social. Girlfriends, boyfriends, gaining acceptance, doing the right things, wearing the right clothes, telling the right jokes, seeing the right movies, listening to the right music, partying with the right people (sound familiar?) are the aspects of life that concern them. The natural world (and school as well) is but a backdrop to the all-important social drama—or an enormous receptacle into which unwanted items can be dropped and forgotten. This lack of interest is evidenced by the comparative few who graduate and pursue college studies or skilled professions related to the care and preservation of the natural world. On the other hand, high-school graduates often wind up working for Water and Power, Caltrans, the county, the tourist industry, or a local mine or ranch.

To a certain extent, our redneck teenage culture is aware of the land, and the kids do venture out into it. Down to the river to tan and swim in the summer, four-wheeling it on (or off) outlying roads, fishing with a couple of buddies, deer and dove hunting, partying all night up some dirt road above town, skiing up in Mammoth in the winter, parking and smooching along some country lane. Invariably, the motivation of getting into the land is social and recreational. Who wants to go hiking just to be hiking, or bird-watching, or tracking, backpacking, sleeping on the ground looking up at the stars? They do not go out there just to be going out there.

The infinite number of hiding places in the hills make for much outdoor drinking. One reason why there are such concentrations of beer cans and liquor bottles and other trash associated with drinking in outlying areas around town is because the high-school kids don't want to be caught drinking by the Sheriff. The best way to party freely is to drive to some semi-remote place seldom visited by the fuzz and drink there, making sure every bottle and can has been thrown from their car before they drive back to town. It would be very difficult indeed to persuade these kids to accept the challenge of their land. They have already voted. Their social-drinking rites of passage take precedence over pride and respect in the appearance of their incomparably precious home country.

One good reason why I've been interested in the local passage rites into adulthood is because my son Christian recently graduated from Bend City High School. I wanted to know what social mechanisms had been built into the redneck culture to bring him safe and sanely to

7

8

9

10

Margin notes:

point: culture is about finding the mainstream as opposed to self-identity

use surrounding for social use not individual?

manhood. Surely, I reasoned, any manhood passage rites, redneck or not, would have to include, or take place in, the natural environment. Surely it would include culture-wise teaching about the need to maintain, sustain, and protect, our natural resources, if only as a matter of survival. I'm not referring to all the informal, and often illegal, things the kids were doing in order to prove they were grown-up. I was interested in the formal means by which the Bend City culture effected the passage of boys into men—or if *any* means existed.

With the help of Chris, who was willing to be open with me, I kept 11 abreast of what Bend City High School was doing to help him formally mark his passage into manhood. In his senior year there were various school dances, including Homecoming. There was participation in varsity athletics—basketball, football, and baseball. There was a series of classes on human sexuality. There was a "mock trial" contest, a spelling bee, an inter-school math competition, an Armed Services recruiting day, and a senior-class fundraiser (selling worms to fishermen on opening day). There was an ostentatiously expensive prom, an academic/athletic-achievement awards banquet, an SAT testing day, and a senior sneak. These manhood-marking events and services culminated in the passage rites of "Graduation," which included "commencement exercises" in the afternoon and a nonalcoholic all-night party later that night. Other than things the kids did on their own (like getting a job), this was the sum total of the formal rites of passage provided by Bend City, California. Note that they are not much different from those in most of the rural communities in America.

"Wait!" you say. "That's not enough. How can a boy become a man 12 just by doing such paltry things?" Perhaps you are one of those who wonder, where's the risk? Where's the perilous passage that *proves* the boy has become the man? The more you think about it, the more ridiculous it seems. "Look," you say. "What about those mountains surrounding Bend City? What about that desert out there? What are you doing about that? Surely, a proper challenge could be found, one that truly tests the mettle of a young man and helps him to truly understand his place on and relationship to the Mother Earth."

I agree, and I don't want to disillusion you further, but there's 13 more. There are also the "informal" rites which, by their occurrence through the years, have become secretly formal. I'm referring to certain clandestine activities such as playing hooky, mild acts of vandalism, secret stag parties with showings of X-rated videos, and the subject at hand: "bunny bashing."

What is bunny bashing? Perhaps we should take it as it came in the chronology of Chris' graduation day, sandwiched between the commencement exercise in the afternoon and the all-night party late that night. These three events roughly formed a tripartite sequence or process reminiscent of Arnold van Gennep's classic definition of the three phases of a rite of life-transition: severance, threshold, and incorporation.[2] Of course, Bend City school administrators never intended Graduation Day's events to be measured by an anthropological ruler. Largely ignorant of *rites de passage,* these dignitaries planned only two ceremonies. The middle or "threshold" ceremony, bunny bashing, was less legitimate and performed in semi-secrecy.

SEVERANCE

Traditional passage rites into adulthood begin with a kind of ending. The child is leaving home, school, and the haunts of innocence. He is saying goodbye to his parents, for henceforth he will live as a man among men. Because the cord attaching him to all he knows as security is being cut, the man-child is afraid. He faces an unknown ordeal, some kind of encounter with real or imagined death, at the conclusion of which the mantle of manhood will be placed upon him. But for now he is a trembling child, awed by the enormity of the challenge of the future: 14

> "Father, Oh father! I hear weeping. Is it my mother I leave in grief?"
> "Have courage, my son . . . In your mother's womb you were conceived. From an individual human womb you were born to an individual human life. It was necessary, it was good. But individual human life is not sufficient to itself. It depends upon and is a part of all life. So now another umbilical cord must be broken—that which binds you to your mother's affections, that which binds you to the individual human life she gave you. . . . Now you belong to your greater mother. And you return to her womb to emerge once again, as a man who knows himself not as an individual but a unit of his tribe and a part of all life which ever surrounds him."[3]

Nice sentiments, but hardly appropriate at the Bend City High School commencement ceremony. Mother may be weeping because Johnny's getting older, but she's certainly not saying goodbye to him. In fact, before she could let him go he had to promise that he would clean up his room tomorrow morning, and he had to stand there and listen to his father lecture about how not to abuse the family car. And if Johnny's afraid about anything, it has to do with whether or not the cummerbund is snug enough or the pants long enough to cover his   15

2. Arnold van Gennep, *The Rites of Passage,* translated by Monika Vizedom and Gabrielle Caffee (Chicago: University of Chicago Press, 1960). [author's note]
3. Frank Waters, *The Man Who Killed the Deer* (New York: Ballentine, 1972). [author's note]

sweat socks. Otherwise, he doesn't appear to be too apprehensive. The severest test of manhood he will face will be when he has to march in rhythm to "Pomp and Circumstance," take a precarious seat on the riser, and walk across the stage without tripping to receive the hand-shake and diploma.

The long-awaited June day arrived. But the weather refused to co-operate. Huge multi-layered clouds settled darkly into the valley, fu-eled by gale-force western winds. Scattered rain began to fall. It was as though Mother Nature was trying to say, "Look at me you fools! I mock your feeble ceremonies!" Plans to hold the shindig outside in the open air (surely in one of the most beautiful commencement settings on earth) were scuttled hastily. Chairs, risers, and props were moved inside the gymnasium, where the friends and relatives gathered to watch the graduates march down the aisle, robed in gowns of green and gold (the school colors).

Smirking self-consciously, tassels swaying awkwardly from mor-tarboards, the candidates took their places on the risers facing the au-dience. The school band played a number, a local reverend made an invocation, the valedictorian (Chris' ex-girlfriend) and the salutatorian (who happened to be Chris), gave nostalgic, inspiring speeches. I was proud of my son's speech, especially when he mentioned the need for humans to live in harmony with their environment, the only time during the entire proceedings when the subject was actually broached. Then the graduates of '89 were introduced to the audience. Great show was made of the switching of tassels, of mortarboards tossed in the air, of the graduates marching triumphantly back through the au-dience, bravely, innocently unaware of the enormity of the burdens of the adult world which they had just inherited.

Who was kidding whom? How could they be expected to under-stand that they had just formally severed from childhood? They weren't going anywhere, at least for a while. In the early hours of the next morning, exhausted and sleepless from the all-night party, they would straggle back to their homes, back into the womb of childhood, back into the routines of parent vs. adolescent, back to the same living situation they were supposed to leave, a situation that taunted them with the fear that they were neither strong, intelligent, nor resourceful enough to leave. They were, in fact, not expected to depart. They were to remain on the runway. They could rev up their engines and taxi around, but they couldn't take off. Full freedom wouldn't come until they were twenty-one, three years from then.

Despite the fact that the ceremony was one big empty promise, there was hardly a dry eye in the crowd. Though the commencement exercise had been almost completely devoid of experiential content that meaningfully formalized the act of severance, the audience, Indian and white, had been deeply moved anyway. It wouldn't have mattered if the graduates had run around in diapers. The tears would have flowed. Nostalgia and family pride would have brightened the air. I remember thinking how much more meaningful—in an unsentimental way—the ceremony would have been if it had been held outside, in the full fury of the storm. No such luck.

I stood with Meredith and Selene and watched Chris and his class- 20 mates march out of the gym. I too felt the tugging of pride at my breast. At least the ceremony gave me a chance to feel that. Did this moment of fatherly pride make up for all the trauma, conflict, pain, and despair involved in the fathering of this young man? Certainly not. Had the ceremony proved to me that my son was ready for manhood, that I'd done a good, or at least serviceable job, in fathering him? Certainly not. Had Chris been challenged by a rite of passage that had truly confirmed his mettle as a man? Certainly not. How well both Chris and I knew that his "commencement" had been incomplete, that the boy had been officially stamped "man" when, in fact, he'd done hardly anything to officially demonstrate his manhood. The speech— yes, that was important. And brave words were one thing. Deeds were another.

I stood and watched and wondered if I'd fathered him well 21 enough. He'd had a difficult time growing through adolescence in this little redneck town. At age fourteen he'd left his mother, who was living in Santa Cruz, to come and live with me. Sub-species *Californium radicalis* mingled with *Bend City Redneckus*, but not without a few volatile reactions. He'd had to earn his place. His father's values had differed vastly from the values of his male peers, and from the values of many adult males whose professional task had been to instruct, coach, and otherwise prepare him to put on the Bend City redneck mantle of manhood. I had a seemingly endless anxiety list. Maybe I'd failed him in one way or another. I hadn't been accessible enough. I hadn't encouraged him enough. I hadn't been interested enough in his problems. I hadn't gone off with him on enough father-son trips. I hadn't been a good role model. . . . Any father is familiar with the routine.

Consequently, I was surprised and pleased when, after the hand- 22 shaking and hugging were over, Chris came up and told me he was coming home. He'd decided not to go bunny bashing with his friends. He'd mess around at home for a few hours, then take off for the all-night party. "Chris is bugging out!" yelled Hank Williams, one of Chris' closest friends, from across the crowded commons. "I am not!" yelled Chris. "I'm tired. I've had about four hours of sleep in the last two days." Mark Talbot, a clean-cut kid headed for the Marines came run-

[handwritten marginalia:] graduation : a public association w/ the right of passage. Author showing its actual insignificance

[handwritten marginalia:] put actions to words

ning over. "O.K. then. If you're not going you owe me some money." Reluctantly, Chris handed over his share of the bunny bash. A lot of the guys were going. They'd been planning it for a long time.

BUNNY BASHING

In anthropological terms, bunny bashing is an informal, semi-[23] taboo, puberty threshold rite performed in a "wild area" outside the security circle of the rural village. It carries the implied sanction of the Bend City male "elders." Although bunny bashing seems to be rooted in old Paiute rabbit hunting rituals, it is not exclusively Indian. A significant number of white adolescents willingly participate. The perennial celebration of the rite is insured by the fact that many of the young men who bunny bash never leave town or the reservation. A sizeable and growing number of bunny bashing initiates, going back some twenty years, guarantees that next year's crop of male graduates will also be bunny bashers. Bunny bashing exists because the adult male "elders" of Bend City are ignorant of any other way, and are secretly proud that the young guys are doin' it the way they did.

If, in Bend City High School graduation rites, the commencement [24] exercise marks the severance phase, then the bunny bash marks the threshold, or liminal phase.[4] The boy-who-is-becoming-a-man leaves his mother and the maternal nest and ventures into the wild, unknown, sacred world of bunny bashing. He experiences what it means to be a male adult in Bend City.

Sacred Symbols:
—Booze (usually beer)
—a dangerous firearm (preferably a shotgun)
—four-wheel-drive pickup (if you can get one)
—KC spotlights and good shocks

Sacred Arena:
—Alkali flats and sage-rabbitbrush fields east of town, down by the river

Sacred Ritual:
—Get drunk, pile into trucks, drive off-road into dark night, hop sagebrush, giggle and scream like maniacs, flush jackrabbit, freeze it in the lights, blaze away with guns, tear rabbit apart with gunfire. Bash not successful if corpse is recognizable as

4. For explorations of the threshold rites of America and other cultures, see Victor Turner, *A Forest of Symbols* (Ithaca, N.Y.: Cornell University Press, 1967); Ray Raphael, *The Men from the Boys* (Lincoln: Nebraska University Press, 1988); and *Betwixt and Between: Patterns of Masculine and Feminine Initiation,* edited by Louise Mahdi with Steven Foster and Meredith Little (LaSalle, Ill.: Open Court, 1987). [author's note]

jackrabbit. Having murdered, return home, rest, dress up, and leave at ten for all-night party.

The entire rite is illegal, of course. Underage boys are drinking and 25 driving and playing with firearms. In a more ethical sense, they are murdering Mother Nature's innocent creatures and transgressing the Law of Nature (killing for sport). Why, then, should such a meaningless, violent, repugnant, irresponsible ritual exist, especially at a time when graduating senior boys might be expected to exhibit signs of maturity?

The first and most obvious answer is that such a ceremony exists 26 because it has the tacit approval of the small town, male-dominated culture and is assented to by the male-dominated women. "Boys will be boys. Hell, they ain't doin' anything I didn't do when I was a kid. No real harm done. A few flea-bitten rabbits, a few torn-up bushes. They're just havin' some innocent fun." Indeed, many of the bunny bashers borrow their fathers' guns.

But the fact that bunny bashing is nurtured by contemporary 27 Bend City male values doesn't ultimately explain its existence. Given all the other possible alternatives open to them, considering the close proximity of a wilderness that can be truly dangerous, why this *particular* ceremony on this *particular* night? Why even think of doing such a thing? Why didn't they climb a mountain, swim a river, walk a mile blindfolded, or do something pseudo-dangerous, like hunting a mountain lion or capturing a live rattlesnake?

The Jungian psychologist might postulate that the boys' collective 28 unconscious recognized the need for a liminal experience otherwise absent from the pomp and circumstance of graduation day, that the boys were acting out unconscious, ancestral urges to confront shadows and monsters and prove themselves as men. To that end, they went out into the darkness of night like Jason and the Argonauts[5] into the unknown, to heroically flush out the terrible fire breathing dragon and do battle. So far so good. But now the allegory breaks down. The Bend City Argonauts possessed weapons and tools that were all-powerful, and their sacred quarry was not the terrible, fire-breathing dragon but the meek, shrub-nibbling jackrabbit whose only means of defense was to run away and hide.

For some reason, our young heros became the very fire-breathing 29 dragon they sought, the very evil power they wanted to eliminate. Their quarry didn't stand a chance. And their story didn't turn out right. They didn't get very far before they turned back. They never honorably faced the monster. They never earned the golden fleece. Their odyssey into manhood was aborted. They prematurely shot their

5. In this heroic quest from Greek mythology, Jason led the Argonauts to capture the Golden Fleece and so became king of Corinth.

[handwritten margin notes:]
parents support this rite of passage into manhood

What is the monster? Childhood?

wad into the body of a completely helpless creature. The journey into manhood became anti-heroic and sadistic. Violence was committed against the heart of Nature. And the boys returned as boys.

The redneck male mentality finds nothing but humor in this story. "Hell, boys is boys. They were jest out on a lark. They gotta let off steam somehow. Jest be glad they took it out on a jackrabbit." The boys would agree. "We didn't mean no harm. We was havin' fun." 30

But one wonders, given the Bend City mentality, if something else besides "havin' fun" was going on in the psyches of these young men raised in the rain shadow of the Range of Light. "Boys is boys," yes. But when do they become men? And what makes a man? Is it possible that these boys were also attempting in some obscure way to prove themselves as men? That in a psychological sense they went into the darkness of themselves to hunt down the scared, confused, helpless rabbit (the little boy) of themselves? That they sacrificed the sacred, innocent, helpless one so that the deadly, dangerous, all-powerful tool-wielding "man" could live? 31

If so, the folly of their actions is apparent. It's the folly of the "macho" psychology of the redneck male —to suppose that with a gun he can destroy the rabbit of fear within himself. Again and again the rabbit will reappear. Again and again the rabbit will have to be sacrificed in order for the man to maintain his image of himself as a man. The more this happens, the more he will look like an eternal adolescent trying to prove he is a man. 32

Although the Bend City senior boys are to be commended for wanting to add a threshold component to their rites of graduation, they were wide of the mark if they meant to confirm their manhood. If the proof of a man is his ability to endure certain trials, hardships, or states of consciousness, none of these are contained in bunny bashing. The all-important conditions of solitude and exposure to natural forces are missing. The boys did not go out alone, as did the traditional vision-questing Indian boy, to a fateful rendezvous with their greater Mother. Instead they hunted in a pack, giggling, egging each other on. It was all a big joke, and the biggest joke was on the jackrabbit. Peer pressure allowed little space for a single boy to develop a sense of who he was apart from the others. The constraint was to belong, to be accepted, to evade self-discovery. 33

Fasting, or "going without," an almost universal taboo in traditional rites of passage, was also missing from the bunny bash. The boys transgressed the ancient taboos of abstinence by filling themselves with beer. In this case the sacred drug, beer served as an anodyne to the exercise of personal conscience. They would forget such social strictures as "Thou shalt not kill," or "If you drink, don't drive." Beer, a social drug, also served to short-circuit any respect they might have had for nature as manifestation of "Spirit" or God. It was a drunken 34 lark, and they got to play with men's toys—the trucks with the big engines, the dangerous guns, the still-forbidden (until the age of twenty-one) can of beer. The traditional solitude and empty belly of the vulnerable initiate instead had become a social lark, a "boys will be boys," an expression of savage glee culminating in a technologically aided murder.

"Murder?" yells the outraged Bend City father. "What do we have here, another one of them tree huggers? Those boys didn't murder anythin' but a dumb little jackrabbit." Well if it isn't the murder of a jackrabbit soul, what is it? Let's look at it from another perspective. Take the guns, spotlights, and big trucks away from the boys. What do they have left? Two good hands and feet. O.K.? Tell them if they want to eat they have to go out into the sagebrush flats down by the river, on a moonless night, and hunt a jackrabbit with their bare hands. Have each of them go alone. No flashlight, no lantern, no knife, no dogs. Bare hands. You think your boys would take you up on this? You don't even know how to do it. God knows what might be out there—rattlesnakes, mountain lions, jackrabbits with huge teeth and claws. Strip your boys down to their bare hands, and they'll be happy to stay home with mama. Put a steering wheel, a can of beer, and a shotgun in their hands and they'll bravely go into the night and murder a deadly leaf-chomper.

Murder? Yes. The traditional Indian vision-quest cry, "Have mercy on me that my people may live" has been changed to "Show no mercy to innocent creatures." The first cry comes from a young man who knows his place on the earth. The second cry comes from a boy who has no idea of his place on the earth, and who, with a gun in his hand, thinks he is God.

Informal rites such as bunny bashing will continue to exist and/or come into being wherever communities, institutions, families, and elders fail to provide adequate, meaningful rites of passage into adulthood. The boys (and the girls) will take it upon themselves to fashion their own rites. Because they lack the wisdom of true manhood, and have little idea of what actually makes a man (thanks to the inadequacy of cultural and media definitions), they will invent grotesque parodies, twisted psychodramas, dangerous and self-destructive scenarios (operating in packs or groups, like the Bend City boys), that sidestep or mock the major issues facing them as boys who are trying to be men in modern America.

THE ALL-NIGHT PARTY

First the ending, the severance from home and family—the commencement exercise. Next, the sacred threshold experience in a wilderness place, the trial of the boy to test his mettle as an adult—the bunny bash. Finally, the beginning of a new life, incorporation of the candidate into adulthood—the all-night party.

Traditionally, an incorporation ceremony might involve the elders, 39 parents, and relatives—or at least the elders. They would sit in council as the candidate recounted how the story of the threshold hero reflected his "medicine power" or giftedness, and revealed the man and his life path. Then there would be a celebration, a party, a feast that honored the "graduate" and accorded him every right and privilege due a full grown man.

The Bend City "all-night party" bears little resemblance to the tra- 40 ditional incorporation ceremonies. Conceived mainly as an alternative to more potentially dangerous activities such as unchaperoned keggers (beer busts), tailgate parties, or other booze/dope fortified blasts, the all-nighter is mainly distinctive as a mean of controlling a potentially dangerous situation. We don't want them to hurt themselves, do we? They're not truly men and women anyway. So let's get them all into one place and out of trouble. Let's keep them away from the dangerous adult world of alcohol, sex, cars, and freedom with responsibility. But we'll tease them a little. We'll let them have a party without a curfew.

hypocritical actions of parents

By 9:30 that evening, the skies above the Inyo Valley had cleared. 41 The moon rose into a crystal sky spangled with stars untold billions of years old. The Range of Light, still streaked with patches of snow at the higher elevations, glowed palely in the moonlight. Aspen Mountain, an old, old spirit, glowered down on our little town, and on the tiny ant-lights attached to cars headed north and south on the highway. Did Aspen Mountain care about human coming-of-age rituals in Bend City? Did Aspen Mountain care that the night was cool, but not cold, that the live music was good, the food was great, and the dancing was hot? Did Aspen Mountain care that the boys left the forbidden bloodlust of the bunny bash and presented themselves at the party, welldressed, clean-cut, and drunk?

Old Aspen Mountain saw everything, heard everything, felt every- 42 thing, probably knew everything. But I don't think he cared that the party was successful, that not a single teenager died that night, that by 4:00 that morning most of Bend City's newest "men" and "women" had gone home to their mamas and daddies. Human time must unfold incredibly fast before the eyes of Old Aspen Mountain. He hasn't had much time to develop any empathy for the ephemeral humans, who have been part of his awareness for less than an instant. By human time, the night passed hour by hour. By Aspen Mountain time, it was already over. The sun was already bathing the Range of Light with rose petals. Graduation day was history.

We didn't see Chris until 11:00 that morning. He shuffled into the 43 living room looking worn and slightly hung over, mumbling a good morning. How'd the party go? "Uh, O.K." Did you have a good time? "Uh huh." Did you dance your ass off? "Uh, kind of." Who'd you dance with? "Uh, several girls." Well, welcome to the world of adulthood. "Thanks. Aren't the Lakers and the Pistons on T.V.?" The new graduate hardly seemed different from how he'd been hundreds of other mornings. We hadn't changed much either. Before the day was over, we'd probably get on him for not doing this or that, and he'd be mad at us for reminding him.

Nevertheless, Chris' chances for attaining manhood were better than for most of his ex-classmates. For one thing, he wasn't a bunny basher. His dragons were not jackrabbits. They'd scorched his hide a few times. He had a realistic idea of what he was up against. He'd never entirely bought the redneck macho line on what constitutes a man. He wanted to get out of town. He didn't want to fall into the Bend City going-nowhere alcoholic swamp that characterized much of young unmarried life in the valley. He'd had his fill of country-western music. He knew there had to be a cultural big-sky country out there somewhere. Two months later, he was gone. Now he's a student at Sonoma State University. We hardly hear from him anymore. He's groping his way toward manhood through jobs, girlfriends, examinations, cars, and the like.

Chris went off to find wider cultural horizons. He left behind the deep valley, the highest mountains. They couldn't hold him because Bend City couldn't hold him. He'd had enough of redneck ways, he said, "enough to last me the rest of my life." Funny, I used to get so upset with him because it seemed more important to him to be with his friends than to find out what was in the wild, beautiful, man-making desert kingdom called the Inyo-Mojave. I despaired that my fascination with the natural world would ever rub off on him. He seemed impervious to the call of the wild, a thoroughly domesticated couch potato. I was wrong. Within six months of leaving home, he'd found a place to live away from campus, out in the country. His house mates were laid back, organic, environmentalist types actively involved in a variety of earth-oriented causes.

And what happened to the bunny bashers? Graduation day came and went. Summer officially began. The boys had become men without the right to drink. What could they show as proof that they had attained the state of manhood? A high-school diploma? A class ring? A tassel hanging from the rearview mirror? A watch from Grandpa Earl? A new car from the folks? A few of the boys received scholarships—invaluable opportunities to sever—from the Armed Forces, lured by the promise of learning a trade and free college tuition, and wound up in Kuwait. A couple went to junior colleges. A couple more went into vocational training (truck-driving school and heavy-equipment repair).

Most of the Indians and a fair number of the whites stayed right here, though employment opportunities were almost nil.

I see a few of Chris' old friends around town now and then. We wave at each other but rarely talk. I guess I always thought they were O.K., as small town kids go, though I might not choose to be super friendly just for Chris' and oldtime's sake. Some of them drive around town flaunting their official redneck badges: the cap, the gun rack, the Chevy pickup, the KC lights, the Warn hubs, the Desert Duelers, the Boom Box. I wonder what rites have these seemingly grown boys undergone recently to demonstrate, not only to the waiting world, but to themselves, that they are responsible, self-reliant, in control, able to go without, sexually balanced, spiritually aware, racially tolerant, humanitarian, and earth-mindful gentlemen of feeling, thought, emotion, and vision? What wilderness rites of passage could boys of this redneck mettle endure? How about three days and nights alone, without food, gun, ghetto blaster, dog, flashlight, or tent, on a bluff overlooking Baker Creek, where the cougar comes down every night to drink? Or how about a walking journey from Bend City all the way to Funeral Valley with a pack on the back, camping out, moving from spring to spring?

I feel like grabbing one of them, saying, "Hey Paul! How about a real wilderness challenge, a rite of passage worthy of a man? Let's go up on Black Mountain and I'll show you a couple things you can do to prove you have some of the real stuff."

But I know it wouldn't work. The essence of the redneck male is the little boy's fear of nature and her kind. If you take away that fear, you take away his reason to wield guns, bash cougars, and intimidate the environment. You take away his need to blast to smithereens the numbed, innocent jackrabbit hiding in the wasteland of himself. Paul's little boy's fears are too great. It would be too easy for him to relegate my challenge to the category marked REALLY WEIRD. Besides, he's a hometown boy, right? He grew up surrounded by the wilderness. He knows what's goin' on out there. He doesn't need to know more. He went to school: he dissected a frog; he graduated; he got his diploma; he danced at the all-night party. He passed the bunny-bashing test. Wasn't that proof enough that he was man?

NAOMI WOLF

Promiscuities: The Secret Struggle Toward Womanhood

Naomi Wolf (1962–), born in San Francisco, has become a leading spokesperson for the latest wave of feminism. Wolf gives credit to her grandmother, a professor and a first-generation feminist, for shaping her thinking as a young girl. Growing up in the midst of progressive ideas, however, did not save Wolf from the pressures of femininity: Although she always thought of herself as a feminist, Wolf nearly died of anorexia as a teenager. After graduating from Yale in 1984, Wolf went to Oxford University as a Rhodes scholar, and there her thesis on the ideals of beauty in nineteenth- and twentieth-century writing paved the way for her first book, the controversial *The Beauty Myth: How Images of Beauty Are Used Against Women* (1990). Wolf argues that as long as Western thought continues to impose standards of beauty on women that force them to put looks before health and self-esteem, women will not attain political power equal to that of men. Wolf has since published three more books, *Fire with Fire: The New Female Power and How It Will Change the Twenty-first Century* (1983), *Promiscuities: The Secret Struggle Toward Womanhood* (1996), and *Power Feminism: How to Love the Women's Movement Again* (1997). Her poetry has twice won the Academy of American Poets' prize. In 1993 she married magazine editor David Shipley; they have one child, a daughter. In her spare time, Wolf enjoys in-line skating and country music.

The following excerpts from *Promiscuities* highlight Wolf's proposal to assist adolescent girls in their search for womanhood. She is describing both the problem she sees and the solution she advocates. Readers may also find in the essay answers to questions Robert Bly raises in "A World of Half-Adults."

"THIRD BASE: IDENTITY"

He and I could have been a poster couple for the liberal ideal of responsible teen sexuality—and, paradoxically, this was reflected in the lack of drama and meaning that I felt crossing this threshold. Conscientious students who were mapping out our college applications and scheduling our after-school jobs to save up for tuition, we were the sort of kids who Planned Ahead. But even the preparations for losing one's virginity felt barren of larger social significance.

When Martin and I went together to a clinic to arrange for contraception some weeks before the actual deed, no experience could have been flatter. He waited, reading old copies of *Scientific American*, while I

was fitted for a diaphragm ("the method with one of the highest effectiveness levels if we are very careful, and the fewest risks to you," Martin had explained after looking it up). The offices were full of high
school couples. If the management intended the mood to be welcoming to adolescents, they had done an excellent job. Cartoon strips
about contraception were displayed in several rooms. The staff members were straight-talking, and they did not patronize. The young,
bearded doctor who fitted me treated it all as if he were explaining to
me a terrific new piece of equipment for some hearty activity such as
camping or rock climbing.

In terms of the mechanics of servicing teenage desire safely in a   3
secular, materialistic society, the experience was impeccable. The technology worked and was either cheap or free. But when we walked
out, I still felt there was something important missing. It was weird to
have these adults just hand you the keys to the kingdom, ask, "Any
questions?" wave, and return to their paperwork. They did not even
have us wait until we could show we had learned something concrete—until we could answer some of their questions. It was easier
than getting your learner's permit to drive a car. Now, giving us a
moral context was not their job. They had enough to handle, and they
were doing so valiantly. Indeed, their work seems in retrospect like
one of the few backstops we encountered to society's abdication of us
within our sexuality. But from visiting the clinic in the absence of any
other adults giving us a moral framework in which to learn about sexuality, the message we got was: "You can be adults without trying. The
only meaning this has is the meaning you give it." There was a sense, I
recall in retrospect, that the adults who were the gatekeepers to society had once again failed to initiate us in any way.

For not at the clinic, at school, in our synagogue, or anywhere in   4
pop culture did this message come through clearly to us: sexual activity comes with responsibilities that are deeper than personal. If our
parents did say this, it was scarcely reinforced outside the home. No
one said, at the clinic, "You must use this diaphragm or this condom,
not only because that is how you will avoid the personal disaster of
unwanted pregnancy but because if you have sex without using protection you are doing something antisocial and morally objectionable.
If you, boy or girl, initiate a pregnancy out of carelessness, that is
dumb, regrettable behavior." Nothing morally significant about the
transfer of power from adults to teenagers was represented in that
technology. It was like going to the vet: as if we were being processed
not on a social but on an animal level.

.   .   .

Unsurprisingly, the more forbidden women are to own their sexu-   5
ality lest they become "sluts," the more inclined they are to project an

out-of-control sexuality onto men. The more a woman's "appropriate" sexual persona is defined as being for others, the more the demon lover stands in her mind as promising a sexuality that can be, subversively, for herself.

"FOURTH BASE: HOW TO MAKE A WOMAN"

Losing our virginity was supposed to pass for attaining sexual maturity. But it was too easy, what we did, and it didn't matter enough to satisfy us more than physically. The end of our virginity passed unmarked, neither mourned nor celebrated: the worldview we inherited told us that what we gained by becoming fully sexual was infinitely valuable and what we lost by leaving behind our virgin state was less than negligible. In other cultures I have looked at, older women, who upheld the values of femaleness, decided when a girl could join them in womanhood. Their decision was based on whether the girl had attained the level of wisdom and self-discipline that would benefit her, her family, and the society. Those older women alone, through their deliberations, had the power to bestow womanhood on the initiates.   6

In our culture, men were deciding for us if we were women. Heck: *teenage boys* were deciding for us if we were women.   7

Instead we should be telling girls what they already know but rarely see affirmed: that the lives they lead inside their own self-contained bodies, the skills they attain through their own concentration and rigor, and the unique phase in their lives during which they may explore boys and eroticism at their own pace—these are magical. And they constitute the entrance point to a life cycle of a sexuality that should be held sacred.   8

·   ·   ·

"THE TIME AND THE PLACE: 1996"

If one is allowed to grow up being proud of one's sexual womanhood as it develops day by day, one may acquire that "sureness" that Margaret Mead[1] spoke of, and be far less susceptible to the blandishment of industries or ideologies that promise to bestow a sexual womanhood, as well as being less susceptible to the pressures in the marketplace that stand ready to stigmatize women for any hint of their sexuality.   9

---

1. Margaret Mead (1901–1978) was an American anthropologist whose classic *Coming of Age in Samoa* (1928) describes adolescent girls in a largely noncompetitive and permissive culture.

Obviously, girls need better rites of passage in our culture. Such 10
rituals, we have seen, require rigor, separation from males and from
the daily environment, and the exchange of privileged information. It
is important, in such rituals, for grown women outside the family to do
the initiating. I'd like to propose that groups of friends with children
sign one another up, upon the birth of a daughter, for the responsibility of becoming part of small groups—Womanhood Guides. Instead or
in addition to the familiar role of godparent, someone who signs on for
such a task will join with a few other women, and a small cohort of
girls, in the girls' thirteenth year, for a retreat into the wilderness—
something as simple as a trip to a state park, organized through the
schools, church groups, or through individual family groups. There,
amid stories, songs, and hikes the older women would pass on to the
younger everything they have learned about womanhood, and answer
every single question the girls want to ask—questions that will be far
more trusting and substantive than those asked in the constrained,
public environment of a sex education class. The older women can certainly, depending on the religious and cultural sensitivities of the
group, show the girls birth control devices and explain how they work.
They would explain a sexual ethic that, as women initiates, the girls
would be asked to commit to—an ethic that might include committing
never to do anything one does not fully consent to do; never to use sex
to get something (love, status, money) that one should seek in other
ways; never to have sex without consciousness—not to use drugs or
alcohol to mask one's sexual intention and responsibility; to practice
saying what one wants; to practice saying what one doesn't want; to
seek conscientiously, with every means at one's disposal, to avoid having to undergo an abortion or to bring into the world a child one is not
ready to parent; never to degrade or violate one's own sexuality, or
tolerate others' degrading or violating it. But their most important
task—one that the culture would value these women for undertaking—would be to explain to the girls, in clear, compassionate terms,
just how to explore female sexual desire in such a way as to postpone
intercourse until they are really, truly, feeling safe, sensually aware,
and ready; until, that is, whether the marker is their eighteenth birthday or their engagement or their marriage, they feel ready to undertake such a profound step not as curious, passionate, half certain girls,
but as *empowered, self-knowing, mature women.* When the retreat is over
and the girls have proven to the older women that they have mastered
some of the skills and knowledge of womanhood—the rudiments of
taking care of themselves professionally and sexually, and understanding what it means to take care of children—they return to their neighborhoods and a great big party is thrown to welcome them back and
celebrate their changed status.

In addition to the sexual education, a family's friends can commit 11 to being part of a wisdom initiation: transmitting their professional skills to the girl whom they are assigned to guide. I have, for instance, such a commitment of exchange from the scientist parents of a two-year-old girl; as my daughter grows up, they have agreed to teach her about earth sciences, show her experiments, and explain to her the jobs that one can do in that field—something in which I have no expertise—and I in turn have committed to working with their daughter on writing. In this way, through these commitments of mentoring exchanges, girls feel specially valued not only by their families but by the extended community—the locus of the initiation tension, and the possibilities of what they might love and become good at expands, and these skills are undertaken at the special time when they begin to cross the border into womanhood. "Privilege knowledge" associated with becoming women need not be sexual; through adolescent exchange relationships, that hunger for a special women's wisdom is filled.

ROBERT BLY

A World of Half-Adults

Robert Bly (1926–) was born in Minnesota and educated at St. Olaf College, Harvard, and the University of Iowa. After living for several years in New York City, Bly returned with his family to a farm in Moose Lake, Minnesota, where he still lives today. His several volumes of poetry include *Silence in the Snowy Fields* (1962) and *Loving a Woman in Two Worlds* (1987); in 1968 he received the National Book Award for *The Light Around the Body* (1967). Bly is perhaps best known, though, not for poetry but for his 1990 best-seller *Iron John: A Book about Men*, which argues that contemporary men are out of touch with their masculinity. For ten years before this publication, Bly had been leading seminars for men in which he taught poetry, ancient rituals, and myths along with ideas about initiation. Often called the wild man leader and guru of the men's movement, he has sparked controversy and confrontation with feminists. Consequently, in 1994 Bly produced the video *Men & Women: Talking Together* with Deborah Tannen (see p. 144). A prolific poet, editor, and translator, Bly's most recent books include *What Have I Ever Lost by Dying* (1993) and *The Sibling Society* (1996).

This excerpt from *The Sibling Society* was published in the *Utne Reader* (May/June 1996). Bly emphasizes how far removed we are from the world of Mark Twain ("Cub-Pilot") or Rigoberta Menchú ("Life in the *Altiplano*"), and his point of view plays well against that of the narrator in Peter Cameron's "Homework."

It's the worst of times; it's the best of times. That's how we feel as ₁
we navigate from a paternal society, now discredited, to a society in
which impulse is given its way. People don't bother to grow up, and
we are all fish swimming in a tank of half-adults. The rule is: Where
repression was before, fantasy will now be; we human beings limp
along, running after our own fantasy. We can never catch up, and so
we defeat ourselves by the simplest possible means: speed. Everywhere we go there's a crowd, and the people all look alike.

We begin to live a lateral life, catch glimpses out of the corners of ₂
our eyes, keep the TV set at eye level, watch the scores move horizontally across the screen.

We see what's coming out the sideview mirror. It seems like inti- ₃
macy; maybe not intimacy as much as proximity; maybe not proximity
as much as sameness. Americans who are 20 years old see others who
look like them in Bosnia, Greece, China, France, Brazil, Germany, and
Russia, wearing the same jeans, listening to the same music, speaking
a universal language that computer literacy demands. Sometimes they
feel more vitally connected to siblings elsewhere than to family members in the next room.

When we see the millions like ourselves all over the world, our ₄
eyes meet uniformity, resemblance, likeness, rather than distinction
and differences. Hope rises immediately for the long-desired possibility
of community. And yet it would be foolish to overlook the serious implications of this glance to the side, this tilt of the head. "Mass society,
with its demand for work without responsibility, creates a gigantic
army of rival siblings," in German psychoanalyst Alexander Mitscher-
lich's words.

Commercial pressures push us backward, toward adolescence, to- ₅
ward childhood. With no effective rituals of initiation, and no real way
to know when our slow progress toward adulthood has reached its
goal, young men and women in our culture go around in circles. Those
who should be adults find it difficult or impossible to offer help to
those behind. That pressure seems even more intense than it was in
the 1960s, when the cry "Turn on, tune in, drop out" was so popular.
Observers describe many contemporaries as "children with children of
their own."

"People look younger all the time." Photographs of men and ₆
women a hundred years ago—immigrants, for example—show a certain set of the mouth and jaws that says, "We're adults. There's nothing we can do about it."

By contrast, the face of Marilyn Monroe, of Kevin Costner, or of ₇
the ordinary person we see on the street says, "I'm a child. There's
nothing I can do about it."

People watching Ken Burns' *History of Baseball* remarked that faces ₈
of fans even in the 1920s looked more mature than faces of fans now.

Looking at those old photos, one sees men and women who knew how to have fun, but they had one foot in Necessity. Walk down a European street these days and you will see that American faces stand out for their youthful and naive look. Some who are 50 look 30. Part of this phenomenon is good nutrition and exercise, but part of it is that we are losing our ability to mature.

Perhaps one-third of our society has developed these new sibling qualities. The rest of us are walking in that direction. When we all arrive there may be no public schools at all, nor past paradigms, because only people one's own age will be worth listening to. 9

We know that the paternal society had an elaborate and internally consistent form with authoritative father reflected upward to the strong community leader and beyond him to the father god up among the stars, which were also arranged in hierarchical levels, called "the seven heavens." Children imitated adults and were often far too respectful for their own good to authorities of all kinds. However, they learned in school the adult ways of talking, writing, and thinking. For some, the home was safe, and the two-parent balance gave them maximum possibility for growth; for others, the home was a horror of beatings, humiliation, and sexual abuse, and school was the only safe place. The teaching at home and in school encouraged religion, memorization, ethics, and discipline, but resolutely kept hidden the historical brutalities of the system. 10

Our succeeding sibling society, in a relatively brief time, has taught itself to be internally consistent in a fairly thorough way. The teaching is that no one is superior to anyone else: high culture is to be destroyed, and business leaders look sideways to the other business leaders. The sibling society prizes a state of half-adulthood in which repression, discipline, and the Indo-European, Islamic, Hebraic impulse-control system are jettisoned. The parents regress to become more like children, and the children, through abandonment, are forced to become adults too soon, and never quite make it. There's an impulse to set children adrift on their own. The old (in the form of crones, elders, ancestors, grandmothers and grandfathers) are thrown away and the young (in the form of street children in South America, or latchkey children in the suburbs of this country, or poor children in the inner city) are thrown away. 11

When I first began to write about this subject, I found it hard to understand why a society run by adolescents should show so much disregard for children who are, in the mass, worse off under Bill Clinton than they were under Theodore Roosevelt or Warren Harding. And yet, in an actual family, adolescents do not pay much attention to the little ones or to the very old. Newt Gingrich's Contract with America is adolescent. 12

The deepening rage of the unparented is becoming a mark of the   13
sibling society. Of course, some children in our society feel well par-
ented, and there is much adequate parenting; but there is also a new
rage. A man said to me, "Having made it to the one-parent family, we
are now on our way toward the zero-parent family." The actual wages
of working-class and middle-class parents have fallen significantly since
1972, so that often both parents work, one parent the day shift, another
at night; family meals, talks, reading together no longer take place.

What the young need—stability, presence, attention, advice, good   14
psychic food, unpolluted stories—is exactly what the sibling society
won't give them. As we look at the crumbling schools, the failure to
protect students from guns, the cutting of funds for Head Start and
breakfasts for poor children, cutting of music and art lessons, the enormous increase in numbers of children living in poverty, the poor pre-
natal care for some, we have to wonder whether there might not be a
genuine anger against children in the sibling society.

If we think of catching these changes in story form, "Jack and the   15
Beanstalk" immediately comes to mind. There a fatherless boy, Jack,
living alone with his mother, climbs the stalk and finds himself in danger of being eaten by a cruel and enormous giant. Jack, from his hiding
place in the kitchen, "was astonished to see how much the giant devoured, and thought he would never have done eating and drinking."
That's the way the rest of the world thinks of the United States.

More specifically, the boy, as helpless and vulnerable as the young   16
ones are today, finds himself faced with an enemy much stronger than
he is. We could say that the giant represents the current emphasis on
greed, violent movies, and pornographic advertising. The giant is television. It eats up more and more of childhood each year. In the original story Jack learns to steal back some of his family treasures—the
gold and silver coins, the divine hen, the golden harp—from the giant.
But we have not gotten to that part of the story in our time. We have
no idea how to steal back "gold" from the giant. Rather than keeping
the children hidden, the adults in the sibling society call the giant over
to the cabinet where the children are hidden, open the door and say,
"Here they are!" In the sibling society Jack gets eaten alive.

Television is the thalidomide of the 1990s. In 1995 American   17
children spent about one-third of their waking hours out of school
watching television. The National Assessment of Educational Progress
reported that only 5 percent of high school graduates could make their
way through college-level literature. A recent 1,200-subject study,
supported by the National Institute of Mental Health and guided by
Mihaly Csikszentmihalyi and Robert Kuby, found that more skill and
concentration were needed to eat a meal than to watch television, and

the watching left people passive, yet tense, and it left them unable to concentrate.

Television provides a garbage dump of obsessive sexual material   18 inappropriate to the child's age, minute description of brutalities, wars, and tortures all over the world: an avalanche of specialized information that stuns the brain. Even lyrics of songs come too fast for the brain to hear.

Grade school teachers report that in recent years they have had to   19 repeat instructions over and over, or look each child in the face and give instructions separately, which interrupts class work. We know that the sort of music children hear much of—characterized by a heavy beat—is processed mainly by the right brain, which hears the tune as a whole and doesn't see its parts or question it. The brain goes into an alpha state, which rules out active thinking or learning.

American movies in the late 1950s vividly brought forward an old   20 theme of adolescence: the impulse not to defend common projects, common stories, common values. James Dean and Marlon Brando played the roles of young men who demonstrated this rebellion, and the theme began to have an edge on it. "What are you rebelling against?" a Brando character is asked. "What do you have?" is the witty reply.

Human beings often struggle to preserve a given cultural group   21 through the stories it holds in common, its remembered history of fragments of it, and certain agreed-on values and courtesies. A gathering of novels, plays, poems, and songs—these days wrongly called "the canon," more properly "the common stories"—held middle-aged people, elders, and the very young together.

That most adolescents these days reject the common stories is no   22 surprise. More often than not, they reject them without having read or heard them. When adolescence lasted only three or four years, the youths' refusal to support the commonly agreed on novels and poems did not affect the long-range commitment of the group to this reservoir; but now, as American adolescence stretches from age 15 or so all the way to 35, those 20 years of sullen silence or active rejection of any commonality, in literature or otherwise, can have devastating results. One can say that colleges and universities are precisely where the gifts of the past are meant to be studied and absorbed, yet those very places are where the current damage to the common reservoir is taking place. Men and women in their 20s take teaching jobs, and if they are still adolescent in their 30s, their hostility to the group's literature and to the group itself becomes palpable.

We know it is essential to open the cabinet of common stories to   23 include literature from other cultures besides the European, and to include much more women's literature than the old reservoir held. That is long overdue. But inclusion, one could say, is a job for adults. When the adolescent gets hold of it, a deep-lying impulse comes into play, and it says, "I'm taking care of people my age, and that's it! My needs are important, and if the group doesn't survive, it doesn't deserve to."

What is asked of adults now is that they stop going *forward,* to re- 24 tirement, to Costa Rica, to fortune, and turn to face the young siblings and the adolescents—the thousands of young siblings we see around us. Many of these siblings are remarkable and seem to have a kind of emotional knowledge that is far older than they are. Some have sharper intuitions into human motives and people's relationships with each other than any of us had at that age. Some who expect to die early—as many do—see with a brilliant clarity into the dramas taking place all around them.

One can imagine a field with the adolescents on one side of a line 25 drawn on the earth and adults on the other side looking into their eyes. The adult in our time is asked to reach his or her hand across the line and pull the youth into adulthood. That means of course that the adults will have to decide what genuine adulthood is. If the adults do not turn and walk up to this line and help pull the adolescents over, the adolescents will stay exactly where they are for another 20 or 30 years. If we don't turn to face the young ones, their detachment machines, which are louder and more persistent than ours, will say, "I am not a part of this family," and they will kill any relationship with their parents. The parents have to know that.

During the paternal society, there were "representatives" of the 26 adult community: highly respected grade school and high school teachers, strong personalities of novels and epics, admired presidents and senators, Eleanor Roosevelts and Madame Curies, priests untouched by scandal, older men and women in each community, both visible and capable of renunciation, who drew young people over the line by their very example. But envy and the habit of ingratitude have ended all that.

The hope lies in the longing we have to be adults. If we take an in- 27 terest in younger ones by helping them find a mentor, by bringing them along to adult activities, by giving attention to young ones who aren't in our family at all, then our own feeling of being adult will be augmented, and adulthood might again appear to be a desirable state for many young ones.

In the sibling society, as a result of the enormous power of the lev- 28 eling process, few adults remain publicly visible as models. Because they are invisible, the very idea of the adult has fallen into confusion. As ordinary adults, we have to ask ourselves, in a way that people 200 years ago did not, what an adult is. I have to ask myself what I have found out in my intermittent, poem-ridden attempts to become an adult. Someone who has succeeded better than I could name more qualities of the adult than I will, but I will list a few.

I would say that an adult is a person not governed by what we have called pre-Oedipal wishes, the demands for immediate pleasure, comfort, and excitement. The adult quality that has been hardest to understand for me, as a greedy person, is renunciation. Moreover, an adult is able to organize the random emotions and events of his or her life into a memory, a rough meaning, a story. **29**

It is an adult perception to understand that the world belongs primarily to the dead, and we only rent it from them for a little while. The idea that each of us has the right to change everything is a deep insult to them. **30**

The true adult is the one who has been able to preserve his or her intensities, including those intensities proper to his or her generation and creativity, so that he or she has something with which to meet the intensities of the adolescent. We could say that an adult becomes an elder when he not only preserves his intensities but adds more. In the words of the Persian poet Ansari, an adult is a person who goes out into the world and "gathers jewels of feeling for others." **31**

The hope lies in our longing to be adults, and the longing for the young ones, if they knew what an honorable adulthood is, to become adults as well. It's as if all this has to be newly invented, and the adults then have to imagine as well what and elder is, what the elder's responsibilities are, what it takes for an adult to become a genuine elder. **32**

I will end with a Norwegian story. A man walking through the forest and in danger of dying from cold sees at last a house with smoke rising from the chimney. He sees a 30-year-old man chopping wood and says to him, "Pardon me, but I am a traveler who has been walking all day. Would it be possible for me to stay overnight in your house?" The man says, "It's all right with me, but I am not the father of the house. You'll have to ask my father." He sees a 70-year-old man standing just inside the door, and the man says, "Pardon me, but I am a traveler and have been walking all day. Would it be possible to stay overnight in your house?" The old man says, "It's all right with me, but I am not the father of this house. You'll have to ask my father, who is sitting at the table." He says to this man, who looks about a hundred years old, "Pardon me, but I am a traveler who has been walking all day. Would it be possible for me to stay overnight in your house?" The hundred-year-old says, "It's all right with me, but I am not the father of this house. You'll have to ask my father." And he gestures toward the fireplace. He sees a very old man sitting in a chair near the fire. He goes up to him and says, "I am a traveler, and I have been walking all day. Would it be possible for me to stay overnight in your house?" In a **33** hoarse voice this old man says, "It's all right with me, but I am not the father of the house. You'll have to ask my father." The traveler glances at the boxed-in bed, and he sees a very, very old man who seems no more than four feet tall lying in the bed. He raises his voice and says to him, "Pardon me, I am a traveler, and I have been walking all day. Would it be possible for me to stay overnight in your house?" The little man in the bed says in a weak voice, "It's all right with me, but I am not the father of this house. You'll have to ask my father." Suddenly the traveler sees a cradle standing at the foot of the bed. In it, there is a very, very little man, hardly the size of a baby, lying curled in the cradle. The man says, "Pardon me, but I am a traveler. I have been walking all day. Would it be possible for me to stay at your house tonight?" In a voice so faint it can hardly be heard, the man in the cradle says, "It's all right with me, but I am not the father of this house. You'll have to ask my father." As the traveler lifts his eyes, he sees an old hunting horn hanging on the wall, made from a sheep's horn, curved like the new moon. He stands and walks over to it, and there he sees a tiny old man no more than six inches long with his head on a tiny pillow and a tiny wisp of white hair. The traveler says, "Pardon me, I am a traveler, and I have been walking all day. Would it be possible for me to stay overnight in your house?" He puts his ear down close to the hunting horn, and the oldest man says, "Yes."

We know there is a Seventh Mother of the House, who is also very small. Perhaps she is far inside the womb, or sitting in the innermost cell of our body, and she gives us permission to live, to be born, to have joy. Her contribution is life. The contribution of the Seventh Father is a house. Together they grant permission from the universe for civilization. 34

PETER CAMERON

Homework

Peter Cameron (1959–) grew up in Pompton Plains, New Jersey. After graduating from Hamilton College in 1982, he began writing while doing clerical work for St. Martin's Press and for New York City's Trust for Public Land. His early stories were an instant success, particularly "Homework," which was included in *Prize Stories: O. Henry Awards* for 1985. By 1986, Cameron had published his first collection of stories, *One Way or Another*. One critic remarked that these stories reflect a sense of anger directed at families that, "rather than providing havens, are themselves the fulcrums of the most sweeping upheavals." While an assistant professor at Oberlin College in 1987, Cameron worked on his first novel, *Leap Year*, which was published in 1989 and depicts a year in the life of young New Yorkers. His second collection of short stories, *Far Flung* (1991), continues to explore the difficulty, particularly for young people, of connecting emotionally with others, and his second novel, *The Weekend* (1994), has been compared to the works of E. M. Forster and Virginia Woolf. In 1997 Cameron published both a new novel, *Andorra,* and a collection of new and previously collected stories, *The Half You Don't Know.*

"Homework," like many of Cameron's other stories, depicts a young man "indelicately balanced between adolescence and adult-hood." Apparently unable to find a meaningful way to grow up, the narrator searches for a metaphor to explain his baffling state of being. A useful companion piece is Albert Goldbarth's poem "26," which views with ambivalence an age-old ritual designed to give adolescence meaning.

My dog, Keds, was sitting outside of the A. & P. last Thursday   1
when he got smashed by some kid pushing a shopping cart. At first we thought he just had a broken leg, but later we found out he was bleeding inside. Every time he opened his mouth, blood would seep out like dull red words in a bad silent dream.

Every night before my sister goes to her job she washes her hair in   2
the kitchen sink with beer and mayonnaise and eggs. Sometimes I sit at the table and watch the mixture dribble down her white back. She boils a pot of water on the stove at the same time; when she is finished with her hair, she steams her face. She wants so badly to be beautiful.

I am trying to solve complicated algebraic problems I have set for   3
myself. Since I started cutting school last Friday, the one thing I miss is homework. Find the value for *n*. Will it be a whole number? It is never a whole number. It is always a fraction.

"Will you get me a towel?" my sister asks. She turns her face to-   4
ward me and clutches her hair to the top of her head. The sprayer hose slithers into its hole next to the faucet.

I hand her a dish towel. "No," she says. "A bath towel. Don't be   5
stupid."

In the bathroom, my mother is watering her plants. She has   6
arranged them in the tub and turned the shower on. She sits on the toilet lid and watches. It smells like outdoors in the bathroom.

I hand my sister the towel and watch her wrap it round her head.   7
She takes the cover off the pot of boiling water and drops lemon slices in. Then she lowers her face into the steam.

This is the problem I have set for myself: 8

$$\frac{245\ (n + 17)}{34} = 396\ (n - 45)$$

$n =$

Wednesday, I stand outside the high-school gym doors. Inside, students are lined up doing calisthenics. It's snowing, and prematurely dark, and I can watch without being seen. 9

"Well," my father says when I get home. He is standing in the garage testing the automatic door. Every time a plane flies overhead, the door opens or closes, so my father is trying to fix it. "Have you changed your mind about school?" he asks me. 10

I lock my bicycle to a pole. This infuriates my father, who doesn't believe in locking things up in his own house. He pretends not to notice. I wipe the thin stripe of snow off the fenders with my middle finger. It is hard to ride a bike in the snow. This afternoon on my way home from the high school I fell off, and I lay in the snowy road with my bike on top of me. It felt warm. 11

"We're going to get another dog," my father says. 12

"It's not that," I say. I wish everyone would stop talking about dogs. I can't tell how sad I really am about Keds versus how sad I am in general. If I don't keep these things separate, I feel as if I'm betraying Keds. 13

"Then what is it?" my father says. 14

"It's nothing," I say. 15

My father nods. He is very good about bringing things up and then letting them drop. A lot gets dropped. He presses the button on the automatic control. The door slides down its oiled tracks and falls shut. It's dark in the garage. My father presses the button again and the door opens, and we both look outside at the snow falling in the driveway, as if in those few seconds the world might have changed. 16

My mother has forgotten to call me for dinner, and when I confront her with this she tells me that she did, but that I was sleeping. She is loading the dishwasher. My sister is standing at the counter, listening, and separating eggs for her shampoo. 17

"What can I get you?" my mother asks. "Would you like a meatloaf sandwich?" 18

"No," I say. I open the refrigerator and survey its illuminated contents. "Could I have some scrambled eggs?" 19

"O.K.," says my mother. She comes and stands beside me and puts her hand on top of mine on the door handle. There are no eggs in the refrigerator. "Oh," my mother says; then, "Julie?" 20

"What?" my sister says. 21

"Did you take the last eggs?" 22

"I guess so," my sister says. "I don't know." 23

"Forget it," I say. "I won't have eggs." 24

"No," my mother says. "Julie doesn't need them in her shampoo. That's not what I bought them for." 25

"I do," my sister says. "It's a formula. It doesn't work without the eggs. I need the protein." 26

"I don't want eggs," I say. "I don't want anything." I go into my bedroom. 27

My mother comes in and stands looking out the window. The 28
snow has turned to rain. "You're not the only one who is unhappy
about this," she says.

"About what?" I say. I am sitting on my unmade bed. If I pick up 29
my room, my mother will make my bed: that's the deal. I didn't pick
up my room this morning.

"About Keds," she says. "I'm unhappy too. But it doesn't stop me 30
from going to school."

"You don't go to school," I say. 31

"You know what I mean," my mother says. She turns around and 32
looks at my room, and begins to pick things off the floor.

"Don't do that," I say. "Stop." 33

My mother drops the dirty clothes in an exaggerated gesture of de- 34
feat. She almost—almost—throws them on the floor. The way she
holds her hands accentuates their emptiness. "If you're not going to go
to school," she says, "the least you can do is clean your room."

In the algebra word problems, a boat sails down a river while a 35
jeep drives along the bank. Which will reach the capital first? If a plane
flies at a certain speed from Boulder to Oklahoma City and then at a
different speed from Oklahoma City to Detroit, how many cups of coffee can the stewardess serve, assuming she is unable to serve during
the first and last ten minutes of each flight? How many times can a
man ride the elevator to the top of the Empire State Building while his
wife climbs the stairs, given that the woman travels one stair slower
each flight? And if the man jumps up while the elevator is going
down, which is moving—the man, the woman, the elevator, or the
snow falling outside?

The next Monday I get up and make preparations for going to 36
school. I can tell at the breakfast table that my mother is afraid to acknowledge them for fear it won't be true. I haven't gotten up before
ten o'clock in a week. My mother makes me French toast. I sit at the
table and write the note excusing me for my absence. I am eighteen,
an adult, and thus able to excuse myself from school. This is what my
note says:

> DEAR MR. KELLY [my homeroom teacher]:
>   Please excuse my absence February 17–24. I was unhappy and did not
> feel able to attend school.
>
> > Sincerely,
> > MICHAEL PECHETTI

This is the exact format my mother used when she wrote my 37
notes, only she always said, "Michael was home with a sore throat," or
"Michael was home with a bad cold." The colds that prevented me
from going to school were always bad colds.

My mother watches me write the note but doesn't ask to see it. I 38
leave it on the kitchen table when I go to the bathroom, and when I
come back to get it I know she has read it. She is washing the bowl she
dipped the French toast into. Before, she would let Keds lick it clean.
He liked eggs.

In Spanish class we are seeing a film on flamenco dancers. The 39
screen wouldn't pull down, so it is being projected on the blackboard,
which is green and cloudy with erased chalk. It looks a little as if the
women are sick, and dancing in Heaven. Suddenly the little phone on
the wall buzzes.

Mrs. Smitts, the teacher, gets up to answer it, and then walks over 40
to me. She puts her hand on my shoulder and leans her face close to
mine. It is dark in the room. "Miguel," Mrs. Smitts whispers, *"Tienes
que ir a la oficina de* guidance."

"What?" I say. 41

She leans closer, and her hair blocks the dancers. Despite the click- 42
ing castanets and the roomful of students, there is something intimate
about this moment. *"Tienes que ir a la oficina de* guidance," she repeats
slowly. Then, "You must go to the guidance office. Now. *Vaya."*

My guidance counsellor, Mrs. Dietrich, used to be a history 43
teacher, but she couldn't take it anymore, so she was moved into guidance. On her immaculate desk is a calendar blotter with "LUNCH" written across the middle of every box, including Saturday and Sunday.
The only other things on the desk are an empty photo cube and my
letter to Mr. Kelly. I sit down, and she shows me the letter as if I
haven't yet read it. I reread it.

"Did you write this?" she asks. 44

I nod affirmatively. I can tell Mrs. Dietrich is especially nervous 45
about this interview. Our meetings are always charged with tension.
At the last one, when I was selecting my second-semester courses, she
started to laugh hysterically when I said I wanted to take Boys' Home
Ec. Now every time I see her in the halls she stops me and asks me
how I'm doing in Boys' Home Ec. It's the only course of mine she remembers.

I hand the note back to her and say, "I wrote it this morning," as if 46
this clarified things.

"This morning?" 47

"At breakfast," I say. 48

"Do you think this is an acceptable excuse?" Mrs. Dietrich asks. 49
"For missing more than a week of school?"

"I'm sure it isn't," I say. 50

"Then why did you write it?" 51

Because it is the truth, I start to say. It is. But somehow I know 52
that saying this will make me more unhappy. It might make me cry.
"I've been doing algebra at home," I say.

"That's fine," Mrs. Dietrich says, "but it's not the point. The point 53
is, to graduate you have to attend school for a hundred and eighty
days, or have legitimate excuses for the days you've missed. That's the
point. Do you want to graduate?"

"Yes," I say. 54

"Of course you do," Mrs. Dietrich says. 55

She crumples my note and tries to throw it into the wastepaper 56
basket but misses. We both look for a second at the note lying on the
floor, and then I get up and throw it away. The only other thing in her
wastepaper basket is a banana peel. I can picture her eating a banana
in her tiny office. This, too, makes me sad.

"Sit down," Mrs. Dietrich says. 57

I sit down. 58

"I understand your dog died. Do you want to talk about that?" 59

"No," I say. 60

"Is that what you're so unhappy about?" she says. "Or is there 61
something else?"

I almost mention the banana peel in her wastebasket, but I don't. 62
"No," I say. "It's just my dog."

Mrs. Dietrich thinks for a moment. I can tell she is embarrassed to 63
be talking about a dead dog. She would be more comfortable if it were
a parent or a sibling.

"I don't want to talk about it," I repeat. 64

She opens her desk drawer and takes out a pad of hall passes. She 65
begins to write one out for me. She has beautiful handwriting. I think
of her learning to write beautifully as a child and then growing up to
be a guidance counsellor, and this makes me unhappy.

"Mr. Neuman is willing to overlook this matter," she says. Mr. 66
Neuman is the principal. "Of course, you will have to make up all the
work you've missed. Can you do that?"

"Yes," I say. 67

Mrs. Dietrich tears the pass from the pad and hands it to me. Our 68
hands touch. "You'll get over this," she says. "Believe me, you will."

My sister works until midnight at the Photo-Matica. It's a tiny 69
booth in the middle of the A. & P. parking lot. People drive up and
leave their film and come back the next day for pictures. My sister
wears a uniform that makes her look like a counterperson in a fast-
food restaurant. Sometimes at night when I'm sick of being at home I
walk downtown and sit in the booth with her.

There's a machine in the booth that looks like a printing press, 70
only snapshots ride down a conveyor belt and fall into a bin and then
disappear. The machine gives the illusion that your photographs are
being developed on the spot. It's a fake. The same fifty photographs
roll through over and over, and my sister says nobody notices, because

everyone in town is taking the same pictures. She opens up the envelopes and looks at them.

Before I go into the booth, I buy cigarettes in the A. & P. It is open   71
twenty-four hours a day, and I love it late at night. It is big and bright
and empty. The checkout girl sits on her counter swinging her legs.
The Muzak plays, "If Ever I Would Leave You." Before I buy the cigarettes, I walk up and down the aisles. Everything looks good to eat,
and the things that aren't edible look good in their own way. The de-
tergent aisle is colorful and clean-smelling.

My sister is listening to the radio and polishing her nails when I get   72
to the booth. It is almost time to close.

"I hear you went to school today," she says.   73

"Yeah."   74

"How was it?" she asks. She looks at her nails, which are so long   75
it's frightening.

"It was O.K.," I say. "We made chili dogs in Home Ec."   76

"So are you over it all?"   77

I look at the pictures riding down the conveyor belt. I know the   78
order practically by heart: graduation, graduation, birthday, mountains, baby, baby, new car, bride, bride and groom, house . . . "I guess
so," I say.

"Good," says my sister. "It was getting to be a little much." She puts   79
her tiny brush back in the bottle, capping it. She shows me her nails.
They're an odd brown shade. "Cinnamon," she says. "It's an earth
color." She looks out at the parking lot. A boy is collecting the abandoned shopping carts, forming a long silver train, which he noses back
toward the store. I can tell he is singing by the way his mouth moves.

"That's where we found Keds," my sister says, pointing to the Sal-   80
vation Army bin.

When I went out to buy cigarettes, Keds would follow me. I hung   81
out down here at night before he died. I was unhappy then, too. That's
what no one understands. I named him Keds because he was all white
with big black feet and it looked as if he had high-top sneakers on. My
mother wanted to name him Bootie. Bootie is a cat's name. It's a dumb
name for a dog.

"It's a good thing you weren't here when we found him," my sis-   82
ter says. "You would have gone crazy."

I'm not really listening. It's all nonsense. I'm working on a new   83
problem: Find the value for n such that n plus everything else in your
life makes you feel all right. What would n equal? Solve for n.

ALICE MUNRO

Circle of Prayer

Alice Munro (1931–) is a Canadian-born writer who began producing stories at age twelve while growing up on her father's fox farm. Re-creating the world of her childhood, Munro's works often examine the lives of women in small-town Ontario. She began writing short stories partly because raising three children left her too little time to undertake a novel but also because the short story genre allows her to present "intense, but not connected, moments of experience." Her works include *Lives of Girls and Women* (1971), *Something I've Been Meaning to Tell You* (1974), *The Beggar Maid* (1984), and *The Progress of Love* (1986). Her eighth book of short stories, *Open Secrets,* was published in 1994. Winner of three Canadian Governor General's Awards, Munro is also popular in the United States, where she is a frequent contributor to such magazines as *The New Yorker* and *The Atlantic Monthly.* Munro continues to live near her childhood home in Ontario, where, in addition to writing, she has recently taken up an amateur acting career. "Circle of Prayer" was included in *The Progress of Love*. In the way in which the story demonstrates the impulse of unguided teenage girls toward ritual, it complements Naomi Wolf's "Promiscuities: The Secret Struggle Toward Womanhood."

1 Trudy threw a jug across the room. It didn't reach the opposite wall; it didn't hurt anybody, it didn't even break.

2 This was the jug without a handle—cement-colored with brown streaks on it, rough as sandpaper to the touch—that Dan made the winter he took pottery classes. He made six little handleless cups to go with it. The jug and the cups were supposed to be for sake, but the local liquor store doesn't carry sake. Once, they brought some home from a trip, but they didn't really like it. So the jug Dan made sits on the highest open shelf in the kitchen, and a few odd items of value are kept in it. Trudy's wedding ring and her engagement ring, the medal Robin won for all-round excellence in Grade 8, a long, two-strand necklace of jet beads that belonged to Dan's mother and was willed to Robin. Trudy won't let her wear it yet.

3 Trudy came home from work a little after midnight; she entered the house in the dark. Just the little stove light was on—she and Robin always left that on for each other. Trudy didn't need any other light. She climbed up on a chair without even letting go of her bag, got down the jug, and fished around inside it.

4 It was gone. Of course. She had known it would be gone.

5 She went through the dark house to Robin's room, still with her bag over her arm, the jug in her hand. She turned on the overhead

light. Robin groaned and turned over, pulled the pillow over her head. Shamming.

"Your grandmother's necklace," Trudy said. "Why did you do that? Are you insane?" 6

Robin shammed a sleepy groan. All the clothes she owned, it seemed, old and new and clean and dirty, were scattered on the floor, on the chair, the desk, the dresser, even on the bed itself. On the wall was a huge poster showing a hippopotamus, with the words underneath "Why Was I Born So Beautiful?" And another poster showing Terry Fox running along a rainy highway, with a whole cavalcade of cars behind him. Dirty glasses, empty yogurt containers, school notes, a Tampax still in its wrapper, the stuffed snake and tiger Robin had had since before she went to school, a collage of pictures of her cat Sausage, who had been run over two years ago. Red and blue ribbons that she had won for jumping, or running, or throwing basketballs. 7

"You answer me!" said Trudy. "You tell me why you did it!" 8

She threw the jug. But it was heavier than she'd thought, or else at the very moment of throwing it she lost conviction, because it didn't hit the wall; it fell on the rug beside the dresser and rolled on the floor, undamaged. 9

You threw a jug at me that time. You could have killed me. 10
Not at you. I didn't throw it at you. 11
You could have killed me. 12

Proof that Robin was shamming: She started up in a fright, but it wasn't the blank fright of somebody who'd been asleep. She looked scared, but underneath that childish, scared look was another look— stubborn, calculating, disdainful. 13

"It was so beautiful. And it was valuable. It belonged to your grandmother." 14

"I thought it belonged to me," said Robin. 15

"That girl wasn't even your friend. Christ, you didn't have a good word to say for her this morning." 16

"You don't know who is my friend!" Robin's face flushed a bright pink and her eyes filled with tears, but her scornful, stubborn expression didn't change. "I knew her. I talked to her. So get out!" 17

Trudy works at the Home for Mentally Handicapped Adults. Few people call it that. Older people in town still say "the Misses Weir's house," and a number of others, including Robin—and, presumably, most of those her age—call it the Half-Wit House. 18

The house has a ramp now for wheelchairs, because some of the mentally handicapped may be physically handicapped as well, and it has a swimming pool in the back yard, which caused a certain amount of discussion when it was installed at taxpayers' expense. Otherwise 19 the house looks pretty much the way it always did—the white wooden walls, the dark-green curlicues on the gables, the steep roof and dark screened side porch, and the deep lawn in front shaded by soft maple trees.

This month, Trudy works the four-to-midnight shift. Yesterday afternoon, she parked her car in front and walked up the drive thinking how nice the house looked, peaceful as in the days of the Misses Weir, who must have served iced tea and read library books, or played croquet, whatever people did then. 20

Always some piece of news, some wrangle or excitement, once you get inside. The men came to fix the pool but they didn't fix it. They went away again. It isn't fixed yet. 21

"We don't get no use of it, soon summer be over," Josephine said. 22

"It's not even the middle of June, you're saying summer'll be over," Kelvin said. "You think before you talk. Did you hear about the young girl that was killed out in the country?" he said to Trudy. 23

Trudy had started to mix two batches of frozen lemonade, one pink and one plain. When he said that, she smashed the spoon down on the frozen chunk so hard that some of the liquid spilled over. 24

"How, Kelvin?" 25

She was afraid she would hear that a girl was dragged off a country road, raped in the woods, strangled, beaten, left there. Robin goes running along the country roads in her white shorts and T-shirt, a headband on her flying hair. Robin's hair is golden; her legs and arms are golden. Her cheeks and limbs are downy, not shiny—you wouldn't be surprised to see a cloud of pollen delicately floating and settling behind her when she runs. Cars hoot at her and she isn't bothered. Foul threats are yelled at her, and she yells foul threats back. 26

"Driving a truck," Kelvin said. 27

Trudy's heart eased. Robin doesn't know how to drive yet. 28

"Fourteen years old, she didn't know how to drive," Kelvin said. "She got in the truck, and the first thing you know, she ran it into a tree. Where was her parents? That's what I'd like to know. They weren't watching out for her. She got in the truck when she didn't know how to drive and ran it into a tree. Fourteen. That's too young." 29

Kelvin goes uptown by himself; he hears all the news. He is fifty-two years old, still slim and boyish-looking, well-shaved, with soft, short, clean dark hair. He goes to the barbershop every day, because he can't quite manage to shave himself. Epilepsy, then surgery, an infected boneflap, many more operations, a permanent mild difficulty with feet and fingers, a gentle head fog. The fog doesn't obscure facts, just motives. Perhaps he shouldn't be in the Home at all, but where else? Anyway, he likes it. He says he likes it. He tells the others they shouldn't complain; they should be more careful, they should behave themselves. He picks up the soft-drink cans and beer bottles that peo- 30 ple have thrown into the front yard—though of course it isn't his job to do that.

When Janet came in just before midnight to relieve Trudy, she had the same story to tell.

"I guess you heard about that fifteen-year-old girl?"

When Janet starts telling you something like this, she always starts off with "I guess you heard." *I guess you heard Wilma and Ted are breaking up,* she says. *I guess you heard Alvin Stead had a heart attack.*

"Kelvin told me," Trudy said. "Only he said she was fourteen."

"Fifteen," Janet said. "She must've been in Robin's class at school. She didn't know how to drive. She didn't even get out of the lane."

"Was she drunk?" said Trudy. Robin won't go near alcohol, or dope, or cigarettes, or even coffee, she's so fanatical about what she puts into her body.

"I don't think so. Stoned, maybe. It was early in the evening. She was home with her sister. Their parents were out. Her sister's boy-friend came over—it was his truck, and he either gave her the keys to the truck or she took them. You hear different versions. You hear that they sent her out for something, they wanted to get rid of her, and you hear she just took the keys and went. Anyway, she ran it right into a tree in the lane."

"Jesus," said Trudy.

"I know. It's so idiotic. It's getting so you hate to think about your kids growing up. Did everybody take their medication okay? What's Kelvin watching?"

Kelvin was still up, sitting in the living room watching TV.

"It's somebody being interviewed. He wrote a book about schizo-phrenics," Trudy told Janet.

Anything he comes across about mental problems, Kelvin has to watch, or try to read.

"I think it depresses him, the more he watches that kind of thing," Janet said. "Do you know I found out today I have to make five hun-dred roses out of pink Kleenex for my niece Laurel's wedding? For the car. She said I promised I'd make the roses for the car. Well, I didn't. I don't remember promising a thing. Are you going to come over and help me?"

"Sure," said Trudy.

"I guess the real reason I want him to get off the schizophrenics is I want to watch the old *Dallas,*" said Janet. She and Trudy disagree about this. Trudy can't stand to watch those old reruns of *Dallas,* to see the characters, with their younger, plumper faces, going through tribulations and bound up in romantic complications they and the au-dience have now forgotten all about. That's what's so hilarious, Janet says; it's so unbelievable it's wonderful. All that happens and they just forget about it and go on. But to Trudy it doesn't seem so unbelievable that the characters would go from one thing to the next thing—forgetful, hopeful, photogenic, forever changing their clothes. That it's not so unbelievable is the thing she really can't stand.

Robin, the next morning, said, "Oh, probably. All those people she hung around with drink. They party all the time. They're self-destructive. It's her own fault. Even if her sister told her to go, she didn't have to go. She didn't have to be so stupid." 46

"What was her name?" Trudy said. 47

"Tracy Lee," said Robin with distaste. She stepped on the pedal of the garbage tin, lifted rather than lowered the container of yogurt she had just emptied, and dropped it in. She was wearing bikini underpants and a T-shirt that said "If I Want to Listen to an Asshole, I'll Fart." 48

"That shirt still bothers me," Trudy said. "Some things are disgusting but funny, and some things are more disgusting than funny." 49

"What's the problem?" said Robin. "I sleep alone." 50

Trudy sat outside, in her wrapper, drinking coffee while the day got hot. There is a little brick-paved space by the side door that she and Dan always called the patio. She sat there. This is a solar-heated house, with big panels of glass in the south-sloping roof—the oddest-looking house in town. It's odd inside, too, with the open shelves in the kitchen instead of cupboards, and the living room up some stairs, looking out over the fields at the back. She and Dan, for a joke, gave parts of it the most conventional, suburban-sounding names—the patio, the powder room, the master bedroom. Dan always had to joke about the way he was living. He built the house himself—Trudy did a lot of the painting and staining—and it was a success. Rain didn't leak in around the panels, and part of the house's heat really did come from the sun. Most people who have the ideas, or ideals, that Dan has aren't very practical. They can't fix things or make things; they don't understand wiring or carpentry, or whatever it is they need to understand. Dan is good at everything—at gardening, cutting wood, building a house. He is especially good at repairing motors. He used to travel around getting jobs as an auto mechanic, a small-engines repairman. That's how he ended up here. He came here to visit Marlene, got a job as a mechanic, became a working partner in an auto-repair business, and before he knew it—married to Trudy, not Marlene—he was a small-town businessman, a member of the Kinsmen. All without shaving off his nineteen-sixties beard or trimming his hair any more than he wanted to. The town was too small and Dan was too smart for that to be necessary. 51

Now Dan lives in a townhouse in Richmond Hill with a girl named Genevieve. She is studying law. She was married when she was very young, and has three little children. Dan met her three years ago when 52 her camper broke down a few miles outside of town. He told Trudy about her that night. The rented camper, the three little children hardly more than babies, the lively little divorced mother with her hair in pigtails. Her bravery, her poverty, her plans to enter law school. If the camper hadn't been easily fixed, he was going to invite her and her children to spend the night. She was on her way to her parents' summer place at Pointe au Baril.

"Then she can't be all that poor," Trudy said.

"You can be poor and have rich parents," Dan said.

"No, you can't."

Last summer, Robin went to Richmond Hill for a month's visit. She came home early. She said it was a madhouse. The oldest child has to go to a special reading clinic, the middle one wets the bed. Genevieve spends all her time in the law library, studying. No wonder. Dan shops for bargains, cooks, looks after the children, grows vegetables, drives a taxi on Saturdays and Sundays. He wants to set up a motorcycle-repair business in the garage, but he can't get a permit; the neighbors are against it.

He told Robin he was happy. Never happier, he said. Robin came home firmly grownup — severe, sarcastic, determined. She had some slight, steady grudge she hadn't had before. Trudy couldn't worm it out of her, couldn't tease it out of her; the time when she could do that was over.

Robin came home at noon and changed her clothes. She put on a light, flowered cotton blouse and ironed a pale-blue cotton skirt. She said that some of the girls from the class might be going around to the funeral home after school.

"I forgot you had that skirt," said Trudy. If she thought that was going to start a conversation, she was mistaken.

The first time Trudy met Dan, she was drunk. She was nineteen years old, tall and skinny (she still is), with a wild head of curly black hair (it is cropped short now and showing the gray as black hair does). She was very tanned, wearing jeans and a tie-dyed T-shirt. No brassière and no need. This was in Muskoka in August, at a hotel bar where they had a band. She was camping with girlfriends. He was there with his fiancée, Marlene. He had taken Marlene home to meet his mother, who lived in Muskoka on an island in an empty hotel. When Trudy was nineteen, he was twenty-eight. She danced around by herself, giddy and drunk, in front of the table where he sat with Marlene, a meek-looking blonde with a big pink shelf of bosom all embroidered in little fake pearls. Trudy just danced in front of him until he got up and joined her. At the end of the dance, he asked her name, and took her back and introduced her to Marlene.

"This is Judy," he said. Trudy collapsed, laughing, into the chair ₆₁ beside Marlene's. Dan took Marlene up to dance. Trudy finished off Marlene's beer and went looking for her friends.

"How do you do?" she said to them. "I'm Judy!" ₆₂

He caught up with her at the door of the bar. He had ditched Mar- ₆₃ lene when he saw Trudy leaving. A man who could change course quickly, see the possibilities, flare up with new enthusiasm. He told people later that he was in love with Trudy before he even knew her real name. But he told Trudy that he cried when he and Marlene were parting.

"I have feelings," he said. "I'm not ashamed to show them." ₆₄

Trudy had no feelings for Marlene at all. Marlene was over ₆₅ thirty—what could she expect? Marlene still lives in town, works at the Hydro office, is not married. When Trudy and Dan were having one of their conversations about Genevieve, Trudy said, "Marlene must be thinking I got what's coming to me."

Dan said he had heard that Marlene had joined the Fellowship of ₆₆ Bible Christians. The women weren't allowed makeup and had to wear a kind of bonnet to church on Sundays.

"She won't be able to have a thought in her head but forgiving," ₆₇ Dan said.

Trudy said, "I bet." ₆₈

This is what happened at the funeral home, as Trudy got the story ₆₉ from both Kelvin and Janet.

The girls from Tracy Lee's class all showed up together after school. ₇₀ This was during what was called the visitation, when the family waited beside Tracy Lee's open casket to receive friends. Her parents were there, her married brother and his wife, her sister, and even her sister's boyfriend who owned the truck. They stood in a row and people lined up to say a few words to them. A lot of people came. They always do, in a case like this. Tracy Lee's grandmother was at the end of the row in a brocade-covered chair. She wasn't able to stand up for very long.

All the chairs at the funeral home are upholstered in this white- ₇₁ and-gold brocade. The curtains are the same, the wallpaper almost matches. There are little wall-bracket lights behind heavy pink glass. Trudy has been there several times and knows what it's like. But Robin and most of these girls had never been inside the place before. They didn't know what to expect. Some of them began to cry as soon as they got inside the door.

The curtains were closed. Soft music was playing—not exactly ₇₂ church music but it sounded like it. Tracy Lee's coffin was white with gold trim, matching all the brocade and the wallpaper. It had a lining of pleated pink satin. A pink satin pillow. Tracy Lee had not a mark on her face. She was not made up quite as usual, because the undertaker had done it. But she was wearing her favorite earrings, turquoise-colored triangles and yellow crescents, two to each ear. (Some people thought that was in bad taste.) On the part of the coffin that covered her from the waist down, there was a big heart-shaped pillow of pink roses.

The girls lined up to speak to the family. They shook hands, they 73
said sorry-for-your-loss, just the way everybody else did. When they got through that, when all of them had let the grandmother squash their cool hands between her warm, swollen, freckled ones, they lined up again, in a straggling sort of way, and began to go past the coffin. Many were crying now, shivering. What could you expect? Young girls.

But they began to sing as they went past. With difficulty at first, 74
shyly, but with growing confidence in their sad, sweet voices, they sang:

"Now, while the blossom still clings to the vine,
I'll taste your strawberries, I'll drink your sweet wine—"

They had planned the whole thing, of course, beforehand; they 75
had got that song off a record. They believed that it was an old hymn.

So they filed past, singing, looking down at Tracy Lee, and it was 76
noticed that they were dropping things into the coffin. They were slipping the rings off their fingers and the bracelets from their arms, and taking the earrings out of their ears. They were undoing necklaces, and bowing to pull chains and long strands of beads over their heads. Everybody gave something. All this jewellery went flashing and sparkling down on the dead girl, to lie beside her in her coffin. One girl pulled the bright combs out of her hair, let those go.

And nobody made a move to stop it. How could anyone interrupt? 77
It was like a religious ceremony. The girls behaved as if they'd been told what to do, as if this was what was always done on such occasions. They sang, they wept, they dropped their jewellery. The sense of ritual made every one of them graceful.

The family wouldn't stop it. They thought it was beautiful. 78

"It was like church," Tracy Lee's mother said, and her grand- 79
mother said, "All those lovely young girls loved Tracy Lee. If they wanted to give their jewellery to show how they loved her, that's their business. It's not anybody else's business. I thought it was beautiful."

Tracy Lee's sister broke down and cried. It was the first time she 80
had done so.

Dan said, "This is a test of love." 81

Of Trudy's love, he meant. Trudy started singing, "Please release 82
me, let me go—"

She clapped a hand to her chest, danced in swoops around the 83
room, singing. Dan was near laughing, near crying. He couldn't help it; he came and hugged her and they danced together, staggering. They were fairly drunk. All that June (it was two years ago), they were

drinking gin, in between and during their scenes. They were drinking, weeping, arguing, explaining, and Trudy had to keep running to the liquor store. Yet she can't remember ever feeling really drunk or having a hangover. Except that she felt so tired all the time, as if she had logs chained to her ankles.

She kept joking. She called Genevieve "Jenny the Feeb."   84

"This is just like wanting to give up the business and become a pot-   85
ter," she said. "Maybe you should have done that. I wasn't really against it. You gave up on it. And when you wanted to go to Peru. We could still do that."

"All those things were just straws in the wind," Dan said.   86

"I should have known when you started watching the Ombuds-   87
man on TV," Trudy said. "It was the legal angle, wasn't it? You were never so interested in that kind of thing before."

"This will open life up for you, too," Dan said. "You can be more   88
than just my wife."

"Sure. I think I'll be a brain surgeon."   89

"You're very smart. You're a wonderful woman. You're brave."   90

"Sure you're not talking about Jenny the Feeb?"   91

"No, you. You, Trudy. I still love you. You can't understand that I   92
still love you."

Not for years had he had so much to say about how he loved her.   93
He loved her skinny bones, her curly hair, her roughening skin, her way of coming into a room with a stride that shook the windows, her jokes, her clowning, her tough talk. He loved her mind and her soul. He always would. But the part of his life that had been bound up with hers was over.

"That is just talk. That is talking like an idiot!" Trudy said. "Robin, 94
go back to bed!" For Robin in her skimpy nightgown was standing at the top of the steps.

"I can hear you yelling and screaming," Robin said.   95

"We weren't yelling and screaming," Trudy said. "We're trying to   96
talk about something private."

"What?"   97

"I told you, it's something private."   98

When Robin sulked off to bed, Dan said, "I think we should tell her.   99
It's better for kids to know. Genevieve doesn't have any secrets from her kids. Josie's only five, and she came into the bedroom one afternoon—"

Then Trudy started yelling and screaming. She clawed through   100
a cushion cover. "You stop telling me about your sweet fucking Genevieve and her sweet fucking bedroom and her asshole kids—you shut up, don't tell me anymore! You're just a big dribbling mouth without any brains. I don't care what you do, just shut up!"

Dan left. He packed a suitcase; he went off to Richmond Hill. He   101
was back in five days. Just outside of town, he had stopped the car to

pick Trudy a bouquet of wildflowers. He told her he was back for good, it was over.

"You don't say?" said Trudy.

But she put the flowers in water. Dusty pink milkweed flowers that smelled like face powder, black-eyed Susans, wild sweet peas, and orange lilies that must have got loose from old disappeared gardens.

"So you couldn't stand the pace?" she said.

"I knew you wouldn't fall all over me," Dan said. "You wouldn't be you if you did. And what I came back to is you."

She went to the liquor store, and this time bought champagne. For a month—it was still summer—they were back together being happy. She never really found out what had happened at Genevieve's house. Dan said he'd been having a middle-aged fit, that was all. He'd come to his senses. His life was here, with her and Robin.

"You're talking like a marriage-advice column," Trudy said.

"Okay. Forget the whole thing."

"We better," she said. She could imagine the kids, the confusion, the friends—old boyfriends, maybe—that he hadn't been prepared for. Jokes and opinions that he couldn't understand. That was possible. The music he liked, the way he talked—even his hair and his beard— might be out of style.

They went on family drives, picnics. They lay out in the grass behind the house at night, looking at the stars. The stars were a new interest of Dan's; he got a map. They hugged and kissed each other frequently and tried out some new things—or things they hadn't done for a long time—when they made love.

At this time, the road in front of the house was being paved. They'd built their house on a hillside at the edge of town, past the other houses, but trucks were using this street quite a bit now, avoiding the main streets, so the town was paving it. Trudy got so used to the noise and constant vibration she said she could feel herself jiggling all night, even when everything was quiet. Work started at seven in the morning. They woke up at the bottom of a river of noise. Dan dragged himself out of bed then, losing the hour of sleep that he loved best. There was a smell of diesel fuel in the air.

She woke up one night to find him not in bed. She listened to hear noises in the kitchen or the bathroom, but she couldn't. She got up and walked through the house. There were no lights on. She found him sitting outside, just outside the door, not having a drink or a glass of milk or a coffee, sitting with his back to the street.

Trudy looked out at the torn-up earth and the huge stalled machinery. "Isn't the quiet lovely?" she said.

He didn't say anything.

Oh. Oh.

She realized what she'd been thinking when she found his side of the bed empty and couldn't hear him anywhere in the house. Not that he'd left her, but that he'd done worse. Done away with himself. With all their happiness and hugging and kissing and stars and picnics, she could think that.

"You can't forget her," she said. "You love her."   117

"I don't know what to do."   118

She was glad just to hear him speak. She said, "You'll have to go   119
and try again."

"There's no guarantee I can stay," he said. "I can't ask you to stand   120
by."

"No," said Trudy. "If you go, that's it."   121

"If I go, that's it."   122

He seemed paralyzed. She felt that he might just sit there, repeat- 123
ing what she said, never be able to move or speak for himself again.

"If you feel like this, that's all there is to it," she said. "You don't   124
have to choose. You're already gone."

That worked. He stood up stiffly, came over, and put his arms   125
around her. He stroked her back.

"Come back to bed," he said. "We can rest for a little while yet."   126

"No. You've got to be gone when Robin wakes up. If we go back to   127
bed, it'll just start all over again."

She made him a thermos of coffee. He packed the bag he had   128
taken with him before. All Trudy's movements seemed skillful and
perfect, as they never were, usually. She felt serene. She felt as if they
were an old couple, moving in harmony, in wordless love, past injury,
past forgiving. Their goodbye was hardly a ripple. She went outside
with him. It was between four-thirty and five o'clock; the sky was beginning to lighten and the birds to wake, everything was drenched in
dew. There stood the big harmless machinery, stranded in the ruts of
the road.

"Good thing it isn't last night—you couldn't have got out," she   129
said. She meant that the road hadn't been navigable. It was just yesterday that they had graded a narrow track for local traffic.

"Good thing," he said.   130

Goodbye.   131

"All I want is to know why you did it. Did you just do it for show? 132
Like your father—for show? It's not the necklace so much. But it was
a beautiful thing—I love jet beads. It was the only thing we had of
your grandmother's. It was your right, but you have no right to take
me by surprise like that. I deserve an explanation. I always loved jet
beads. Why?"

"I blame the family," Janet says. "It was up to them to stop it.   133
Some of the stuff was just plastic—those junk earrings and bracelets—
but what Robin threw in, that was a crime. And she wasn't the only
one. There were birthstone rings and gold chains. Somebody said a di-

amond cluster ring, but I don't know if I believe that. They said the girl inherited it, like Robin. You didn't ever have it evaluated, did you?"

"I don't know if jet is worth anything," Trudy says.   134

They are sitting in Janet's front room, making roses out of pink   135
Kleenex.

"It's just stupid," Trudy says.   136

"Well. There is one thing you could do," says Janet. "I don't hardly   137
know how to mention it."

"What?"   138

"Pray."   139

Trudy'd had the feeling, from Janet's tone, that she was going to   140
tell her something serious and unpleasant, something about herself—
Trudy—that was affecting her life and that everybody knew except
her. Now she wants to laugh, after bracing herself. She doesn't know
what to say.

"You don't pray, do you?" Janet says.   141

"I haven't got anything against it," Trudy says. "I wasn't brought   142
up to be religious."

"It's not strictly speaking religious," Janet says. "I mean, it's not   143
connected with any church. This is just some of us that pray. I can't tell
you the names of anybody in it, but most of them you know. It's supposed to be secret. It's called the Circle of Prayer."

"Like at high school," Trudy says. "At high school there were se-   144
cret societies, and you weren't supposed to tell who was in them. Only
I wasn't."

"I was in everything going." Janet sighs. "This is actually more on   145
the serious side. Though some people in it don't take it seriously
enough, I don't think. Some people, they'll pray that they'll find a
parking spot, or they'll pray they get good weather for their holidays.
That isn't what it's for. But that's just individual praying. What the Circle is really about is, you phone up somebody that is in it and tell them
what it is you're worried about, or upset about, and ask them to pray
for you. And they do. And they phone one other person that's in the
Circle, and they phone another and it goes all around, and we pray for
one person, all together."

Trudy throws a rose away. "That's botched. Is it all women?"   146

"There isn't any rule it has to be. But it is, yes. Men would be too   147
embarrassed. I was embarrassed at first. Only the first person you
phone knows your name, who it is that's being prayed for, but in a
town like this nearly everybody can guess. But if we started gossiping
and ratting on each other it wouldn't work, and everybody knows
that. So we don't. And it does work."

"Like how?" Trudy says.   148

"Well, one girl banged up her car. She did eight hundred dollars'   149
damage, and it was kind of a tricky situation, where she wasn't sure
her insurance would cover it, and neither was her husband—he was

raging mad—but we all prayed, and the insurance came through without a hitch. That's only one example."

"There wouldn't be much point in praying to get the necklace back when it's in the coffin and the funeral's this morning," Trudy says.

"It's not up to you to say that. You don't say what's possible or impossible. You just ask for what you want. Because it says in the Bible, 'Ask and it shall be given.' How can you be helped if you won't ask? You can't, that's for sure. What about when Dan left—what if you'd prayed then? I wasn't in the Circle then, or I would have said something to you. Even if I knew you'd resist it, I would have said something. A lot of people resist. Now, even—it doesn't sound too great with that girl, but how do you know, maybe even now it might work? It might not be too late."

"All right," says Trudy, in a hard, cheerful voice. "All right." She pushes all the floppy flowers off her lap. "I'll just get down on my knees right now and pray that I get Dan back. I'll pray that I get the necklace back and I get Dan back, and why do I have to stop there? I can pray that Tracy Lee never died. I can pray that she comes back to life. Why didn't her mother ever think of that?"

Good news. The swimming pool is fixed. They'll be able to fill it tomorrow. But Kelvin is depressed. Early this afternoon—partly to keep them from bothering the men who were working on the pool—he took Marie and Josephine uptown. He let them get ice-cream cones. He told them to pay attention and eat the ice cream up quickly, because the sun was hot and it would melt. They licked at their cones now and then, as if they had all day. Ice cream was soon dribbling down their chins and down their arms. Kelvin had grabbed a handful of paper napkins, but he couldn't wipe it up fast enough. They were a mess. A spectacle. They didn't care. Kelvin told them they weren't so pretty that they could afford to look like that.

"Some people don't like the look of us anyway," he said. "Some people don't even think we should be allowed uptown. People just get used to seeing us and not staring at us like freaks and you make a mess and spoil it."

They laughed at him. He could have cowed Marie if he had her alone, but not when she was with Josephine. Josephine was one who needed some old-fashioned discipline, in Kelvin's opinion. Kelvin had been in places where people didn't get away with anything like they got away with here. He didn't agree with hitting. He had seen plenty of it done, but he didn't agree with it, even on the hand. But a person like Josephine could be shut up in her room. She could be made to sit in a corner, she could be put on bread and water, and it would do a lot of good. All Marie needed was a talking-to—she had a weak personality. But Josephine was a devil.

"I'll talk to both of them," Trudy says. "I'll tell them to say they're   156
sorry."

"I want for them to *be* sorry," Kelvin says. "I don't care if they say   157
they are. I'm not taking them ever again."

Later, when all the others are in bed, Trudy gets him to sit down to   158
play cards with her on the screened veranda. They play Crazy Eights.
Kelvin says that's all he can manage tonight; his head is sore.

Uptown, a man said to him, "Hey, which one of them two is your   159
girlfriend?"

"Stupid," Trudy says. "He was a stupid jerk."   160

The man talking to the first man said, "Which one you going to   161
marry?"

"They don't know you, Kelvin. They're just stupid."   162

But they did know him. One was Reg Hooper, one was Bud   163
DeLisle. Bud DeLisle that sold real estate. They knew him. They had
talked to him in the barbershop; they called him Kelvin. "Hey, Kelvin,
which one you going to marry?"

"Nerds," says Trudy. "That's what Robin would say."   164

"You think they're your friend, but they're not," says Kelvin.   165
"How many times I see that happen."

Trudy goes to the kitchen to put on coffee. She wants to have fresh   166
coffee to offer Janet when she comes in. She apologized this morning,
and Janet said all right, I know you're upset. It really is all right. Sometimes you think they're your friend, and they are.

She looks at all the mugs hanging on their hooks. She and Janet   167
shopped all over to find them. A mug with each one's name. Marie,
Josephine, Arthur, Kelvin, Shirley, George, Dorinda. You'd think
Dorinda would be the hardest name to find, but actually the hardest
was Shirley. Even the people who can't read have learned to recognize
their own mugs, by color and pattern.

One day, two new mugs appeared, bought by Kelvin. One said   168
Trudy, the other Janet.

"I'm not going to be too overjoyed seeing my name in that lineup,"   169
Janet said. "But I wouldn't hurt his feelings for a million dollars."

For a honeymoon, Dan took Trudy to the island on the lake where   170
his mother's hotel was. The hotel was closed down, but his mother still
lived there. Dan's father was dead, and she lived there alone. She took
a boat with an outboard motor across the water to get her groceries.
She sometimes made a mistake and called Trudy Marlene.

The hotel wasn't much. It was a white wooden box in a clearing by   171
the shore. Some little boxes of cabins were stuck behind it. Dan and
Trudy stayed in one of the cabins. Every cabin had a wood stove. Dan
built a fire at night to take off the chill. But the blankets were damp
and heavy when he and Trudy woke up in the morning.

Dan caught fish and cooked them. He and Trudy climbed the big   172
rock behind the cabins and picked blueberries. He asked her if she
knew how to make a piecrust, and she didn't. So he showed her,
rolling out the dough with a whiskey bottle.

In the morning there was a mist over the lake, just as you see in   173
the movies or in a painting.

One afternoon, Dan stayed out longer than usual, fishing. Trudy   174
kept busy for a while in the kitchen, rubbing the dust off things, washing some jars. It was the oldest, darkest kitchen she had ever seen,
with wooden racks for the dinner plates to dry in. She went outside
and climbed the rock by herself, thinking she would pick some blueberries. But it was already dark under the trees; the evergreens made
it dark, and she didn't like the idea of wild animals. She sat on the
rock looking down on the roof of the hotel, the old dead leaves and
broken shingles. She heard a piano being played. She scrambled down
the rock and followed the music around to the front of the building.
She walked along the front veranda and stopped at a window, looking
into the room that used to be the lounge. The room with the blackened stone fireplace, the lumpy leather chairs, the horrible mounted
fish.

Dan's mother was there, playing the piano. A tall, straight-backed   175
old woman, with her gray-black hair twisted into such a tiny knot. She
sat and played the piano, without any lights on, in the half-dark, half-
bare room.

Dan had said that his mother came from a rich family. She had   176
taken piano lessons, dancing lessons; she had gone around the world
when she was a young girl. There was a picture of her on a camel. But
she wasn't playing a classical piece, the sort of thing you'd expect her
to have learned. She was playing "It's Three O'Clock in the Morning."
When she got to the end, she started in again. Maybe it was a special
favorite of hers, something she had danced to in the old days. Or
maybe she wasn't satisfied yet that she had got it right.

Why does Trudy now remember this moment? She sees her young   177
self looking in the window at the old woman playing the piano. The
dim room, with its oversize beams and fireplace and the lonely leather
chairs. The clattering, faltering, persistent piano music. Trudy remembers that so clearly and it seems she stood outside her own body,
which ached then from the punishing pleasures of love. She stood outside her own happiness in a tide of sadness. And the opposite thing
happened the morning Dan left. Then she stood outside her own unhappiness in a tide of what seemed unreasonably like love. But it was
the same thing, really, when you got outside. What are those times
that stand out, clear patches in your life—what do they have to do
with it? They aren't exactly promises. Breathing spaces. Isn't that all?

*   *   *

She goes into the front hall and listens for any noise from upstairs.   178
All quiet there, all medicated.   179

The phone rings right beside her head.   180
"Are you still there?" Robin says. "You're not gone?"   181
"I'm still here."   182
"Can I run over and ride back with you? I didn't do my run earlier   183
because it was so hot."

You threw the jug. You could have killed me.   184
Yes.   185

Kelvin, waiting at the card table, under the light, looks bleached   186
and old. There's a pool of light whitening his brown hair. His face sags,
waiting. He looks old, sunk into himself, wrapped in a thick bewilderment, nearly lost to her.
"Kelvin, do you pray?" says Trudy. She didn't know she was going   187
to ask him that. "I mean, it's none of my business. But, like for anything specific?"
He's got an answer for her, which is rather surprising. He pulls his   188
face up, as if he might have felt the tug he needed to bring him to the
surface.
"If I was smart enough to know what to pray for," he says, "then I   189
wouldn't have to."
He smiles at her, with some oblique notion of conspiracy, offering   190
his halfway joke. It's not meant as comfort, particularly. Yet it radiates—what he said, the way he said it, just the fact that he's there
again, radiates, expands the way some silliness can, when you're very
tired. In this way, when she was young, and high, a person or a moment could become a lily floating on the cloudy river water, perfect
and familiar.

ALBERT GOLDBARTH

26

Albert Goldbarth (1948–) was born in Chicago, received his B.A.
from the University of Illinois, Chicago Circle (1969), and his M.F.A.
from the University of Iowa (1971). The following year, he won the
Theodore Roethke Prize for poetry. A prolific writer, Goldbarth soon
published his *Opticks* (1974) and *Comings Back* (1976). He received

three fellowships (1974, 1979, and 1986) from the National Endowment for the Arts and a Guggenheim Fellowship. His more recent
books include *The Gods* (1993), *Ancient Music: A Poetry Sequence* (1995),
and *Marriage and Other Science Fiction* (1995). In 1992 Goldbarth, with
Jane Smiley (see p. 438), won a National Book Critics Circle Award.
The poem "26" was published in *A Lineage of Ragpickers, Songpluckers,
Elegiasts and Jewelers: Selected Poems of Jewish Family Life, 1973–1995*
(1996). Commenting on the use of formal ritual in initiation, the
poem complements Steven Foster's analysis of informal ritual in
"Bunny Bashing into Manhood."

This was the prayershawl:[1] *two huge, golden tassels*   1
of sun draped over my shoulders. I walked

a hill, after rain, from the breaking of clouds as
from the splitting of fresh loaves ending a fast,

a ritual expectation streamed. If a pointing of light   5
in the stilled world showed a leaf

to be bipinnate, wasn't this an open
hymnal? This was the yarmulke:[2] *black*

hair weighted with water, which, no less
than silk, indicated Presence. Once,   10

at thirteen, I came unto my manhood
under wool and silver. Mitzvah:[3] *luck. And*

now, having tried to be that man, with the litany
of crystals of salt, with the psalm of crystals of sugar,

at the doubling of my years, this was my more   15
naked rite of passage. Not that I said

more, but that I said it more lucid, or
thought so, and sang a long, low note

to the carrying further of air
we call Sky, and asked not for acceptance   20

1. prayershawl: Also called a *tallith* or *tallis,* a prayer shawl is worn by adult males during morning prayer. It is a four-cornered garment, usually made of wool, with fringes
knotted on the corners in accordance with biblical law.
2. *yarmulke:* a skullcap worn by Jewish males during prayer and worn all the time by
observant Jews.
3. *Mitzvah:* Literally, the word *mitzvah* means "commandment" (either positive or negative), but it also can mean "good deed."

in the sanctum of my heritage, but
for the understanding to breathe air where it thinned

at the borders of settlement. A fish leapt
out of the waters becomes a dead fish

or a man. This was the   25
text of the sermon, called The

Lost Tribe.[4] *And at each*
multiple of thirteen,[5] *let me say it.*

4. Lost Tribe: Ten Hebrew tribes inhabiting the northern kingdom of Israel were taken into captivity by Sargon II, king of Assyria 721–705 B.C. They were believed never to have returned to their lands.
5. The bar mitzvah ceremony occurs when a Jewish male is thirteen years old, and it signals his coming into adulthood.

FEMININITY AND MASCULINITY

We find ourselves confronting a fork in the road.

Overview

Even in our time, when the roles of men and women are defined with a flexibility that would have astonished our ancestors, sexual identity provides one of the great forks in the road of everyone's life. We may no longer see men as strong oaks and women as clinging vines, men as brutes and women as sweet civilizers. Nonetheless, we grow up with strong signals about what our society considers feminine (or effeminate) and what it considers masculine (or mannish). In schoolyards you can still hear children repeat the rhyme that little girls are made of "sugar and spice and everything nice" and boys are made of "nails and snails and puppy-dog tails." Most men can remember being told that some kind of behavior might be acceptable in a *girl*, but not in a boy, and most women can remember getting the mirror image of the same talk. How do such messages affect our view of ourselves? That is the underlying question of this unit.

Once upon a time, a Baby named X was born. It was named X so that nobody could tell whether it was a boy or a girl.

Its parents could tell, of course, but they couldn't tell anybody else. They couldn't even tell Baby X—at least not until much, much later.

You who come of a younger and happier generation may not have heard of her—you may not know what I mean by the Angel in the House. I will describe her as shortly as I can. She was intensely sympathetic. She was immensely charming. She was utterly unselfish. She excelled in the difficult arts of family life.

For each of us getting our hair pressed is an important ritual. It is not a sign of our longing to be white. It is not a sign of our quest to be beautiful. We are girls. It is a sign of our desire to be women.

Looking down, I recognize my mother's body, my grandmother's body, my great-grandmother's body. Flawed but familiar. Living and dying at the same time. There is some comfort—even grace—in synchrony, in being the daughter of a mother and the mother of a daughter.

Gender markers pick up extra meanings that reflect common associations
with the female gender: not quite serious, often sexual. . . . I asked myself
what style we women could have adopted that would have been unmarked,
like the men's. The answer was none. There is no unmarked woman.

The lore of sports may be all that some fathers have to pass down to their
sons in place of lore about hunting animals, planting seeds, killing enemies,
or placating the gods. Instead of telling him how to shoot a buffalo, the father whispers in the son's ear how to shoot a lay-up.

The instant Grady shot from the pool, shaking water from his orange hair,
freckled shoulders shining, my attraction to members of my own sex became a matter I could no longer suppress or rationalize.

It was "masculine" to think the blots looked like man-made objects, and
"feminine" to think they looked like natural objects. It was masculine to
think they looked like things capable of causing harm, and feminine to
think of innocent things.

I can, through the force of my imagination, draw on the woman in me, but
I will always be—in my mind's eye and in my metaphysics—a man. And
there's not a blessed thing wrong with that.

. . . most males rarely prepare food for others, and when they do, they have
their one specialty dish (spaghetti, in my case) that they prepare maybe twice
a year in a very elaborate production, for which they expect to be praised as
if they had developed, right there in the kitchen, a cure for heart disease.

He tore out a reed, the great god Pan . . .
And hacked and hewed as a great god can,
With his hard bleak steel at the patient reed,
Till there was not a sign of the leaf indeed
    To prove it fresh from the river.

X

Lois Gould (1938?–), a full-time writer of journalism, fiction, and social commentary, has devoted much of her career to writing about gender issues. As executive editor and columnist for *Ladies' Home Journal* and a contributor to *The New York Times* "Hers" column, Gould has made her opinions, often controversial, known to a wide audience. Because of her iconoclastic handling of women's issues, Gould has been labeled an antifeminist by feminists and an archfeminist by antifeminists. Some critics labeled her first novel, *Such Good Friends* (1970), pornographic, while others praised its impact on the women's movement; one commentator called it an "important, awful, believable book." *A Sea-Change* (1976), an allegory in which a woman becomes a man ("exploitee-turning-exploiter," as one reviewer said), was no less controversial. Other novels include *La Presidenta* (1981), *Medusa's Gift* (1991), and *No Brakes: A Novel* (1997).

"X," first published in *Ms.* magazine in 1972, was later expanded into Gould's third novel, *X: A Fabulous Child's Story* (1978), a controversial book praised for its insight into gender stereotyping. The story may encourage some readers to compare gender stereotyping of the 1970s with that found today, other readers to challenge the suggestion that it is "best to be an X," and still others to experiment with making their points by creating a fairy tale. Like Dave Barry ("Lost in the Kitchen"), Gould provides a model for using humor to express serious thought.

1   Once upon a time, a Baby named X was born. It was named X so that nobody could tell whether it was a boy or a girl.

2   Its parents could tell, of course, but they couldn't tell anybody else. They couldn't even tell Baby X—at least not until much, much later.

3   You see, it was all part of a very important Secret Scientific Xperiment, known officially as Project Baby X.

4   This Xperiment was going to cost Xactly 23 billion dollars and 72 cents. Which might seem like a lot for one Baby, even if it was an important Secret Scientific Xperimental Baby.

5   But when you remember the cost of strained carrots, stuffed bunnies, booster shots, 28 shiny quarters from the tooth fairy . . . you begin to see how it adds up.

6   Long before Baby X was born, the smartest scientists had to work out the secret details of the Xperiment, and to write the *Official Instruction Manual,* in secret code, for Baby X's parents, whoever they were.

7   These parents had to be selected very carefully. Thousands of people volunteered to take thousands of tests, with thousands of tricky questions.

Almost everybody failed because, it turned out, almost everybody   8
wanted a boy or a girl, and not a Baby X at all.

Also, almost everybody thought a Baby X would be more trouble   9
than a boy or a girl. (They were right, too.)

There were families with grandparents named Milton and Agatha,   10
who wanted the baby named Milton or Agatha instead of X, even if it
was an X.

There were aunts who wanted to knit tiny dresses and uncles who   11
wanted to send tiny baseball mitts.

Worst of all, there were families with other children who couldn't   12
be trusted to keep a Secret. Not if they knew the Secret was worth 23
billion dollars and 72 cents—and all you had to do was take one little
peek at Baby X in the bathtub to know what it was.

Finally, the scientists found the Joneses, who really wanted to   13
raise an X more than any other kind of baby—no matter how much
trouble it was.

The Joneses promised to take turns holding X, feeding X, and   14
singing X to sleep.

And they promised never to hire any baby-sitters. The scientists   15
knew that a baby-sitter would probably peek at X in the bathtub, too.

The day the Joneses brought their baby home, lots of friends and   16
relatives came to see it. And the first thing they asked was what kind
of a baby X was.

When the Joneses said, "It's an X!" nobody knew what to say.   17

They couldn't say, "Look at her cute little dimples!"   18

On the other hand, they couldn't say, "Look at his husky little bi-   19
ceps!"

And they didn't feel right about saying just plain "kitchy-coo."   20

The relatives all felt embarrassed about having an X in the family.   21

"People will think there's something wrong with it!" they whis-   22
pered.

"Nonsense!" the Joneses said cheerfully. "What could possibly be   23
wrong with this perfectly adorable X?"

Clearly, nothing at all was wrong. Nevertheless, the cousins who   24
had sent a tiny football helmet would not come and visit any more.
And the neighbors who sent a pink-flowered romper suit pulled their
shades down when the Joneses passed their house.

The *Official Instruction Manual* had warned the new parents that   25
this would happen, so they didn't fret about it. Besides, they were too
busy learning how to bring up Baby X.

Ms. and Mr. Jones had to be Xtra careful. If they kept bouncing it   26
up in the air and saying how *strong* and *active* it was, they'd be treating
it more like a boy than an X. But if all they did was cuddle it and kiss it
and tell it how *sweet* and *dainty* it was, they'd be treating it more like a
girl than an X.

On page 1654 of the *Official Instruction Manual,* the scientists pre-   27
scribed: "plenty of bouncing and plenty of cuddling, *both.* X ought to be
strong and sweet and active. Forget about *dainty* altogether."

There were other problems, too. Toys, for instance. And clothes.   28
On his first shopping trip, Mr. Jones told the store clerk, "I need some
things for a new baby." The clerk smiled and said, "Well, now, is it a
boy or a girl?" "It's an X," Mr. Jones said, smiling back. But the clerk
got all red in the face and said huffily, "In *that* case, I'm afraid I can't
help you, sir."

Mr. Jones wandered the aisles trying to find what X needed. But   29
everything was in sections marked BOYS or GIRLS: "Boys' Pajamas"
and "Girls' Underwear" and "Boys' Fire Engines" and "Girls Housekeeping Sets." Mr. Jones went home without buying anything for X.

That night he and Ms. Jones consulted 2326 of the *Official Instruc-*   30
tion Manual. It said firmly: "Buy plenty of everything!"

So they bought all kinds of toys. A boy doll that made pee-pee and   31
cried "Pa-Pa." And a girl doll that talked in three languages and said, "I
am the Pres-i-dent of Gen-er-al Mo-tors."

They bought a storybook about a brave princess who rescued a   32
handsome prince from his tower, and another one about a sister and
brother who grew up to be a baseball star and a ballet star, and you
had to guess which.

The head scientists of Project Baby X checked all their purchases   33
and told them to keep up the good work. They also reminded the
Joneses to see page 4629 of the *Manual,* where it said, "Never make
Baby X feel *embarrassed* or *ashamed* about what it wants to play with.
And if X gets dirty climbing rocks, never say, 'Nice little Xes don't get
dirty climbing rocks.'"

Likewise, it said, "If X falls down and cries, never say, 'Brave little   34
Xes don't cry.' Because, of course, nice little Xes *do* get dirty, and brave
little Xes *do* cry. No matter how dirty X gets, or how hard it cries, don't
worry. It's all part of the Xperiment."

Whenever the Joneses pushed Baby X's stroller in the park, smil-   35
ing strangers would come over and coo: "Is that a boy or a girl?" The
Joneses would smile back and say, "It's an X." The strangers would
stop smiling then and often snarl something nasty—as if the Joneses
had said something nasty to *them.*

Once a little girl grabbed X's shovel in the sandbox, and zonked X   36
on the head with it. "Now, now, Tracy," the mother began to scold, "little girls mustn't hit little—" and she turned to ask X, "Are you a little
boy or a little girl, dear?"

Mr. Jones, who was sitting near the sandbox, held his breath and   37
crossed his fingers.

X smiled politely, even though X's head had never been zonked so   38
hard in its life. "I'm a little X," said X.

"You're a *what?*" the lady exclaimed angrily. "You're a little b-r-a-t, you mean!"   39

"But little girls mustn't hit little Xes, either!" said X, retrieving the shovel with another polite smile. "What good's hitting, anyway?"   40

X's father finally X-haled, uncrossed his fingers, and grinned.   41

And at their next secret Project Baby X meeting, the scientists grinned, too. Baby X was doing fine.   42

But then it was time for X to start school. The Joneses were really worried about this, because school was even more full of rules for boys and girls, and there were no rules for Xes.   43

Teachers would tell boys to form a line, and girls to form another.   44

There would be boys' games and girls' games, and boys' secrets and girls' secrets.   45

The school library would have a list of recommended books for girls, and a different list for boys.   46

There would even be a bathroom marked BOYS and another one marked GIRLS.   47

Pretty soon boys and girls would hardly talk to each other. What would happen to poor little X?   48

The Joneses spent weeks consulting their *Instruction Manual.*   49

There were 249 and one-half pages of advice under "First Day of School." Then they were all summoned to an Urgent Xtra Special Conference with the smart scientists of Project Baby X.   50

The scientists had to make sure that X's mother had taught X how to throw and catch a ball properly, and that X's father had been sure to teach X what to serve at a doll's tea party.   51

X had to know how to shoot marbles and jump rope and, most of all, what to say when the Other Children asked whether X was a Boy or a Girl.   52

Finally, X was ready.   53

X's teacher had promised that the class could line up alphabetically, instead of forming separate lines for boys and girls. And X had permission to use the principal's bathroom, because it wasn't marked anything except BATHROOM. But nobody could help X with the biggest problem of all—Other Children.   54

Nobody in X's class had ever known an X. Nobody had even heard grown-ups say, "Some of my best friends are Xes."   55

What would other children think? Would they make Xist jokes? Or would they make friends?   56

You couldn't tell what X was by its clothes. Overalls don't even button right to left, like girls' clothes, or left to right, like boys' clothes.   57

And did X have a girl's short haircut or a boy's long haircut?   58

As for the games X liked, either X played ball very well for a girl, or else played house very well for a boy.   59

The children tried to find out by asking X tricky questions, like, 60
"Who's your favorite sports star?" X had two favorite sports stars: a girl
jockey named Robyn Smith and a boy archery champion named Robin
Hood.

Then they asked, "What's your favorite TV show?" And X said: 61
"Lassie," which stars a girl dog played by a boy dog.

When X said its favorite toy was a doll, everyone decided that X 62
must be a girl. But then X said the doll was really a robot, and that X
had computerized it, and that it was programmed to bake fudge and
then clean up the kitchen.

After X told them that, they gave up guessing what X was. All they 63
knew was they'd sure like to see X's doll.

After school, X wanted to play with the other children. "How 64
about shooting baskets in the gym?" X asked the girls. But all they did
was make faces and giggle behind X's back.

"Boy, is *he* weird," whispered Jim to Joe. 65

"How about weaving some baskets in the arts and crafts room?" X 66
asked the boys. But they all made faces and giggled behind X's back, too.

"Boy, is *she* weird," whispered Susie to Peggy. 67

That night, Ms. and Mr. Jones asked X how things had gone at 68
school. X tried to smile, but there were two big tears in its eyes. "The
lessons are okay," X began, "but . . ."

"But?" said Ms. Jones. 69

"The Other Children hate me," X whispered. 70

"Hate you?" said Mr. Jones. 71

X nodded, which made the two big tears roll down and splash on 72
its overalls.

Once more, the Joneses reached for their *Instructional Manual*. 73
Under "Other Children," it said:

"What did you Xpect? Other Children have to obey silly boy-girl 74
rules, because their parents taught them to. Lucky X—you don't have
rules at all! All you have to do is be yourself.

"P.S. We're not saying it'll be easy." 75

X liked being itself. But X cried a lot that night. So X's father held 76
X tight, and cried a little, too. X's mother cheered them up with an
Xciting story about an enchanted prince called Sleeping Handsome,
who woke up when Princess Charming kissed him.

The next morning, they all felt much better, and little X went back 77
to school with a brave smile and a clean pair of red and white checked
overalls.

There was a seven-letter-word spelling bee in class that day. And a 78
seven-lap boys' relay race in the gym. And a seven-layer-cake baking
contest in the girls' kitchen corner.

X won the spelling bee. X also won the relay race. 79

And X almost won the baking contest, Xcept it forgot to light the oven. (Remember, nobody's perfect.)

One of the Other Children noticed something else, too. He said: "X doesn't care about winning. X just thinks it's fun playing boys' stuff *and* girls' stuff."

"Come to think of it," said another one of the Other Children, "X is having twice as much fun as we are!"

After school that day, the girl who beat X in the baking contest gave X a big slice of her winning cake.

And the boy X beat in the relay race asked X to race him home.

From then on, some really funny things began to happen.

Susie, who sat next to X, refused to wear pink dresses to school any more. She wanted red and white checked overalls—just like X's.

Overalls, she told her parents, were better for climbing monkey bars.

Then Jim, the class football nut, started wheeling his little sister's doll carriage around the football field.

He'd put on his entire football uniform, except for the helmet.

Then he'd put the helmet *in* the carriage, lovingly tucked under an old set of shoulder pads.

Then he'd jog around the field, pushing the carriage and singing "Rockabye Baby" to his helmet.

He said X did the same thing, so it must be okay. After all, X was now the team's star quarterback.

Susie's parents were horrified by her behavior, and Jim's parents were worried sick about his.

But the worst came when the twins, Joe and Peggy, decided to share everything with each other.

Peggy used Joe's hockey skates, and his microscope, and took half his newspaper route.

Joe used Peggy's needlepoint kit, and her cookbooks, and took two of her three baby-sitting jobs.

Peggy ran the lawn mower, and Joe ran the vacuum cleaner.

Their parents weren't one bit pleased with Peggy's science experiments, or with Joe's terrific needlepoint pillows.

They didn't care that Peggy mowed the lawn better, and that Joe vacuumed the carpet better.

In fact, they were furious. It's all that little X's fault, they agreed. X doesn't know what it is, or what it's supposed to be! So X wants to mix everybody *else* up, too!

Peggy and Joe were forbidden to play with X any more. So was Susie, and then Jim, and then *all* the Other Children.

But it was too late: the Other Children stayed mixed-up and happy and free, and refused to go back to the way they'd been before X.

Finally, the parents held an emergency meeting to discuss "The X Problem."

They sent a report to the principal stating that X was a "bad influ- 104
ence," and demanding immediate action.

The Joneses, they said, should be *forced* to tell whether X was a boy 105
or a girl. And X should be *forced* to behave like whichever it was.

If the Joneses refused to tell, the parents said, then X must take an 106
Xamination. An Impartial Team of Xperts would Xtract the secret.
Then X would start obeying all the old rules. Or else.

And if X turned out to be some kind of mixed-up misfit, then X 107
must be Xpelled from school. Immediately! So that no little Xes would
ever come to school again.

The principal was very upset. X, a bad influence? A mixed-up mis- 108
fit? But X was a Xcellent student! X set a fine Xample! X was Xtraordi-
nary!

X was president of the student council. X had won first prize in the 109
art show, honorable mention in the science fair, and six events on field
day, including the potato race.

Nevertheless, insisted the parents, X is a Problem Child. X is the 110
Biggest Problem Child we have ever seen!

So the principal reluctantly notified X's parents and the Joneses re- 111
ported this to the Project X scientists, who referred them to page 85769
of the *Instructional Manual.* "Sooner or later," it said, "X will have to be
Xamined by an Impartial Team of Xperts.

"This may be the only way any of us will know for sure whether X 112
is mixed up—or everyone else is."

At Xactly 9 o'clock the next day, X reported to the school health 113
office. The principal, along with a committee from the Parents' Association, X's teacher, X's classmates, and Ms. and Mr. Jones, waited in the
hall outside.

Inside, the Xperts had set up their famous testing machine: the Su- 114
perpsychiamedicosocioculturometer.

Nobody knew Xactly how the machine worked, but everybody 115
knew that this examination would reveal Xactly what everyone wanted
to know about X, but were afraid to ask.

It was terribly quiet in the hall. Almost spooky. They could hear 116
very strange noises from the room.

There were buzzes. 117

And a beep or two. 118

And several bells. 119

An occasional light flashed under the door. Was it an X ray? 120

Through it all, you could hear the Xperts' voices, asking questions, 121
and X's voice, answering answers.

I wouldn't like to be in X's overalls right now, the children thought. 122

At last, the door opened. Everyone crowded around to hear the re- 123
sults. X didn't look any different; in fact, X was smiling. But the Im-

partial Team of Xperts looked terrible. They looked as if they were crying!

"What happened?" everyone began shouting. 124

"*Sssh,*" ssshed the principal. "The Xperts are trying to speak." 125

Wiping his eyes and clearing his throat, one Xpert began: "In our opinion," he whispered—you could tell he must be very upset—"in our opinion, young X here—" 126

"Yes? Yes?" shouted a parent. 127

"Young X," said the other Xpert, frowning, "is just about the *least* mixed-up child we've ever Xamined!" Behind the closed door, the Superpsychiamedicosocioculturometer made a noise like a contented hum. 128

"Yay for X!" yelled one of the children. And then the others began yelling, too. Clapping and cheering and jumping up and down. 129

"*SSSH!*" SSShed the principal, but nobody did. 130

The Parents' Committee was angry and bewildered. How *could* X have passed the whole Xamination? 131

Didn't X have an *identity* problem? Wasn't X mixed up at *all?* Wasn't X any kind of a misfit? 132

How could it *not* be, when it didn't even *know* what it was? 133

"Don't you see?" asked the Xperts. "X isn't one bit mixed up! As for being a misfit—ridiculous! X knows perfectly well what it is! Don't you, X?" The Xperts winked. X winked back. 134

"But what *is* X?" shrieked Peggy and Joe's parents. "*We* still want to know what it is!" 135

"Ah, yes," said the Xperts, winking again. "Well, don't worry. You'll all know one of these days. And you won't need us to tell you." 136

"What? What do they mean?" Jim's parents grumbled suspiciously. 137

Susie and Peggy and Joe all answered at once. "They mean that by the time it matters which sex X is, it won't be a secret any more!" 138

With that, the Xperts reached out to hug Ms. and Mr. Jones. "If we ever have an X of our own," they whispered, "we sure hope you'll lend us your instructional manual." 139

Needless to say, the Joneses were very happy. The Project Baby X scientists were rather pleased, too. So were Susie, Jim, Peggy, Joe, and all the Other Children. Even the parents promised not to make any trouble. 140

Later that day, all X's friends put on their red and white checked overalls and went over to see X. 141

They found X in the backyard, playing with a very tiny baby that none of them had ever seen before. 142

The baby was wearing very tiny red and white checked overalls. 143

"How do you like our new baby?" X asked the Other Children proudly. 144

"It's got cute dimples," said Jim. "It's got husky biceps, too," said   145
Susie.

"What kind of baby is it?" asked Joe and Peggy.   146

X frowned at them. "Can't you tell?" Then X broke into a big, mis-   147
chievous grin. *"It's a Y!"*

VIRGINIA WOOLF

Professions for Women

Virginia Woolf (1882–1941), the daughter of a distinguished Victorian biographer, was denied formal education because women could
not take degrees from British universities until 1920. Nonetheless,
she became one of the first women in British history to be a literary
professional, supporting herself by writing and by operating (with her
husband, Leonard) a successful publishing firm, the Hogarth Press.
The disadvantages under which she labored were considerable, and
they showed her that English women, however they might be pam-
pered and honored, were a political underclass. Out of this awareness
grew *A Room of One's Own* (1929), a book based on addresses given to
women's societies in 1928.

"Professions for Women" was a talk delivered to the Women's
Service League in 1931. Using the image of the Victorian "angel in
the house," Woolf describes the psychological barriers women must
overcome to succeed in professions commonly dominated by men. A
useful companion essay is Deborah Tannen's "Every Choice a Woman
Makes Sends a Message," which suggests that, nearly seventy years
later, habits of mind continue to hinder the struggle for equality.

When your secretary invited me to come here, she told me that   1
your Society is concerned with the employment of women and she
suggested that I might tell you something about my own professional
experiences. It is true I am a woman; it is true I am employed; but
what professional experiences have I had? It is difficult to say. My profession is literature; and in that profession there are fewer experiences
for women than in any other, with the exception of the stage—fewer,
I mean, that are peculiar to women. For the road was cut many years
ago—by Fanny Burney, by Aphra Behn, by Harriet Martineau, by Jane
Austen, by George Eliot—many famous women, and many more unknown and forgotten, have been before me, making the path smooth,
and regulating my steps. Thus, when I came to write, there were very

few material obstacles in my way. Writing was a reputable and harmless occupation. The family peace was not broken by the scratching of a pen. No demand was made upon the family purse. For ten and sixpence one can buy paper enough to write all the plays of Shakespeare—if one has a mind that way. Pianos and models, Paris, Vienna and Berlin, masters and mistresses, are not needed by a writer. The cheapness of writing paper is, of course, the reason why women have succeeded as writers before they have succeeded in the other professions.

But to tell you my story—it is a simple one. You have only got to   2
figure to yourselves a girl in a bedroom with a pen in her hand. She had only to move that pen from left to right—from ten o'clock to one. Then it occurred to her to do what is simple and cheap enough after all—to slip a few of those pages into an envelope, fix a penny stamp in the corner, and drop the envelope into the red box at the corner. It was thus that I became a journalist; and my effort was rewarded on the first day of the following month—a very glorious day it was for me—by a letter from an editor containing a cheque for one pound ten shillings and sixpence. But to show you how little I deserve to be called a professional woman, how little I know of the struggles and difficulties of such lives, I have to admit that instead of spending that sum upon bread and butter, rent, shoes and stockings, or butcher's bills, I went out and bought a cat—a beautiful cat, a Persian cat, which very soon involved me in bitter disputes with my neighbours.

What could be easier than to write articles and to buy Persian cats   3
with the profits? But wait a moment. Articles have to be about something. Mine, I seem to remember, was about a novel by a famous man. And while I was writing this review, I discovered that if I were going to review books I should need to do battle with a certain phantom. And the phantom was a woman, and when I came to know her better I called her after the heroine of a famous poem, The Angel in the House. It was she who used to come between me and my paper when I was writing reviews. It was she who bothered me and wasted my time and so tormented me that at last I killed her. You who come of a younger and happier generation may not have heard of her—you may not know what I mean by the Angel in the House. I will describe her as shortly as I can. She was intensely sympathetic. She was immensely charming. She was utterly unselfish. She excelled in the difficult arts of family life. She sacrificed herself daily. If there was a chicken, she took the leg; if there was a draught she sat in it—in short she was so constituted that she never had a mind or a wish of her own, but preferred to sympathize always with the minds and wishes of others. Above all—I need not say it—she was pure. Her purity was supposed to be her chief beauty—her blushes, her great grace. In those days—

the last of Queen Victoria—every house had its Angel. And when I came to write I encountered her with the very first words. The shadow of her wings fell on my page; I heard the rustling of her skirts in the room. Directly, that is to say, I took my pen in hand to review that novel by a famous man, she slipped behind me and whispered: "My dear, you are a young woman. You are writing about a book that has been written by a man. Be sympathetic; be tender; flatter; deceive; use all the arts and wiles of our sex. Never let anybody guess that you have a mind of your own. Above all, be pure." And she made as if to guide my pen. I now record the one act for which I take some credit to myself, though the credit rightly belongs to some excellent ancestors of mine who left me a certain sum of money—shall we say five hundred pounds a year?—so that it was not necessary for me to depend solely on charm for my living. I turned upon her and caught her by the throat. I did my best to kill her. My excuse, if I were to be had up in a court of law, would be that I acted in self-defence. Had I not killed her she would have killed me. She would have plucked the heart out of my writing. For, as I found, directly I put pen to paper, you cannot review even a novel without having a mind of your own, without expressing what you think to be the truth about human relations, morality, sex. And all these questions, according to the Angel in the House, cannot be dealt with freely and openly by women; they must charm, they must conciliate, they must—to put it bluntly—tell lies if they are to succeed. Thus, whenever I felt the shadow of her wing or the radiance of her halo upon my page, I took up the inkpot and flung it at her. She died hard. Her fictitious nature was of great assistance to her. It is far harder to kill a phantom than a reality. She was always creeping back when I thought I had despatched her. Though I flatter myself that I killed her in the end, the struggle was severe; it took much time that had better have been spent upon learning Greek grammar; or in roaming the world in search of adventures. But it was a real experience; it was an experience that was bound to befall all women writers at that time. Killing the Angel in the House was part of the occupation of a woman writer.

But to continue my story. The Angel was dead; what then remained? You may say that what remained was a simple and common object—a young woman in a bedroom with an inkpot. In other words, now that she had rid herself of falsehood, that young woman had only to be herself. Ah, but what is "herself"? I mean, what is a woman? I assure you, I do not know. I do not believe that you know. I do not believe that anybody can know until she has expressed herself in all the arts and professions open to human skill. That indeed is one of the reasons why I have come here—out of respect for you, who are in process of showing us by your experiments what a woman is, who are in

⁴

process of providing us, by your failures and successes, with that extremely important piece of information.

But to continue the story of my professional experiences. I made one pound ten and six by my first review; and I bought a Persian cat with the proceeds. Then I grew ambitious. A Persian cat is all very well, I said; but a Persian cat is not enough. I must have a motor car. And it was thus that I became a novelist—for it is a very strange thing that people will give you a motor car if you will tell them a story. It is a still stranger thing that there is nothing so delightful in the world as telling stories. It is far pleasanter than writing reviews of famous novels. And yet, if I am to obey your secretary and tell you my professional experiences as a novelist, I must tell you about a very strange experience that befell me as a novelist. And to understand it you must try first to imagine a novelist's state of mind. I hope I am not giving away professional secrets if I say that a novelist's chief desire is to be as unconscious as possible. He has to induce in himself a state of perpetual lethargy. He wants life to proceed with the utmost quiet and regularity. He wants to see the same faces, to read the same books, to do the same things day after day, month after month, while he is writing, so that nothing may break the illusion in which he is living—so that nothing may disturb or disquiet the mysterious nosings about, feelings round, darts, dashes and sudden discoveries of that very shy and illusive spirit, the imagination. I suspect that this state is the same both for men and women. Be that as it may, I want you to imagine me writing a novel in a state of trance. I want you to figure to yourselves a girl sitting with a pen in her hand, which for minutes, and indeed for hours, she never dips into the inkpot. The image that comes to my mind when I think of this girl is the image of a fisherman lying sunk in dreams on the verge of a deep lake with a rod held out over the water. She was letting her imagination sweep unchecked round every rock and cranny of the world that lies submerged in the depths of our unconscious being. Now came the experience, the experience that I believe to be far commoner with women writers than with men. The line raced through the girl's fingers. Her imagination had rushed away. It had sought the pools, the depths, the dark places where the largest fish slumber. And then there was a smash. There was an explosion. There was foam and confusion. The imagination had dashed itself against something hard. The girl was roused from her dream. She was indeed in a state of the most acute and difficult distress. To speak without figure she had thought of something, something about the body, about the passions which it was unfitting for her as a woman to say. Men, her reason told her, would be shocked. The consciousness of what men will say of a woman who speaks the truth about her passions had roused her from her artist's state of unconsciousness. She could write no more. The trance was over. Her imagination could work no longer. This I believe to be a very common experience with women writers—they are impeded by the extreme conventionality of the other sex. For though men sensibly allow themselves great freedom in these respects, I doubt that they realize or can control the extreme severity with which they condemn such freedom in women.

These then were two very genuine experiences of my own. These were two of the adventures of my professional life. The first—killing the Angel in the House—I think I solved. She died. But the second, telling the truth about my own experiences as a body, I do not think I solved. I doubt that any woman has solved it yet. The obstacles against her are still immensely powerful—and yet they are very difficult to define. Outwardly, what is simpler than to write books? Outwardly, what obstacles are there for a woman rather than for a man? Inwardly, I think, the case is very different; she has still many ghosts to fight, many prejudices to overcome. Indeed it will be a long time still, I think, before a woman can sit down to write a book without finding a phantom to be slain, a rock to be dashed against. And if this is so in literature, the freest of all professions for women, how is it in the new professions which you are now for the first time entering?

Those are the questions that I should like, had I time, to ask you. And indeed, if I have laid stress upon these professional experiences of mine, it is because I believe that they are, though in different forms, yours also. Even when the path is nominally open—when there is nothing to prevent a woman from being a doctor, a lawyer, a civil servant—there are many phantoms and obstacles, as I believe, looming in her way. To discuss and define them is I think of great value and importance, for thus only can the labour be shared, the difficulties be solved. But besides this, it is necessary also to discuss the ends and the aims for which we are fighting, for which we are doing battle with these formidable obstacles. Those aims cannot be taken for granted; they must be perpetually questioned and examined. The whole position as I see it—here in this hall surrounded by women practising for the first time in history I know not how many different professions—is one of extraordinary interest and importance. You have won rooms of your own in the house hitherto exclusively owned by men. You are able, though not without great labour and effort, to pay the rent. You are earning your five hundred pounds a year. But this freedom is only a beginning; the room is your own, but it is still bare. It has to be furnished; it has to be decorated; it has to be shared. How are you going to furnish it, how are you going to decorate it? With whom are you going to share it, and upon what terms? These, I think, are questions of the utmost importance and interest. For the first time in history you are able to ask them; for the first time you are able to decide for yourselves what the answers should be. Willingly would I stay and discuss those questions and answers—but not tonight. My time is up; and I must cease.

Bone Black: Memories of Girlhood

bell hooks (1952–), born Gloria Watkins, grew up in a small town in Kentucky. She graduated from Stanford University and went on to teach at Oberlin College and Yale University and become a leading scholar in the field of feminist and cultural studies. She is now Distinguished Professor of English at City College in New York. Hooks began writing *Ain't I a Woman: black women and feminism* when she was an undergraduate at Stanford, but she did not publish it until 1989. Her next several books were academic: *Feminist Theory: from margin to center* (1984), *Yearning: Race, Gender, and Cultural Politics* (1990), and *Teaching to Transgress: Education as the Practice of Freedom* (1994). Also interested in film study and art, hooks has published books on each, including *Art on My Mind: Visual Politics* (1995) and *Reel to Real: Race, Sex, and Class at the Movies* (1996). She established herself as a poet years earlier with *And There We Slept: Poems* (1978) and is also known for her creative writing. Recently hooks published two memoirs, *Bone Black: memories of girlhood* (1996) and *Wounds of Passion: A Writing Life* (1997).

Bone Black tells the story of growing up black in the South during the 1950s, and it is a model of writing memoir with a specific social context. Although hooks grew up rejecting many of her family's traditions, she expresses a deep emotional connection to her mother, grandmother, and sisters. This excerpt, therefore, links naturally to Jennifer Brice's "My Mother's Body."

Bone Black: memories of girlhood is not an ordinary tale. It is the story   1 of girlhood rebellion, of my struggle to create self and identity distinct from and yet inclusive of the world around me. Writing imagistically, I seek to conjure a rich magical world of southern black culture that was sometimes paradisical and at other times terrifying. While the narratives of family life I share can be easily labeled dysfunctional, significantly that fact will never alter the magic and mystery that was present—all that was deeply life sustaining and life affirming. The beauty lies in the way it all comes together exposing and revealing the inner life of a girl inventing herself—creating the foundation of selfhood and identity that will ultimately lead to the fulfillment of her true destiny—becoming a writer.

Nowadays, more than ever before, feminist thinkers are writing ²
about the significance of girlhood as a time when females feel free and
powerful. Our bodies do not yet distinguish themselves as definitively
from those of boys. And our energies are just as intense if not more so.
Not enough is known about the experience of black girls in our society.
Indeed, one of my favorite novels in the whole world is Toni Morrison's *The Bluest Eye*.[1] When the book was first published she explained
that it was her desire to write about "the people who in all literature
were always peripheral—little black girls who were props, background;
those people were never center stage and those people were me." I
was still in my teens when I read this book. It shook me to the very
roots of my being. There in this fictional narrative were fragments of
my story—my girlhood. Always an obsessive reader, I had felt this
lack. To see this period of our life given serious recognition was awesomely affirming. My life was never going to be the same after reading
this book. It wasn't simply that Morrison focused on black girls but
that she gave us girls confronting issues of class, race, identity, girls
who were struggling to confront and cope with pain. And most of all
she gave us black girls who were critical thinkers, theorizing their
lives, telling the story, and by so doing making themselves subjects of
history.

Many feminist thinkers writing and talking about girlhood right ³
now like to suggest that black girls have better self-esteem than their
white counterparts. The measurement of this difference is often that
black girls are more assertive, speak more, appear more confident. Yet
in traditional southern-based black life, it was and is expected of girls
to be articulate, to hold ourselves with dignity. Our parents and teachers were always urging us to stand up right and speak clearly. These
traits were meant to uplift the race. They were not necessarily traits associated with building female self-esteem. An outspoken girl might
still feel that she was worthless because her skin was not light enough
or her hair the right texture. These are the variables that white researchers often do not consider when they measure the self-esteem of
black females with a yardstick that was designed based on values
emerging from white experience. White girls of all classes are often encouraged to be silent. But to see the opposite in different ethnic groups
as a sign of female empowerment is to miss the reality that the cultural
codes of that group may dictate a quite different standard by which female self-esteem is measured. To understand the complexity of black
girlhood we need more work that documents that reality in all its variations and diversity. Certainly, class shapes the nature of our childhood
experiences. Undoubtedly, black girls raised in materially privileged

---

1. Toni Morrison: (1931–), author of several novels since *The Bluest Eye* (1969), and
winner of the Nobel Prize for literature in 1993.

families have different notions of self-esteem from peers growing up poor and/or destitute. It's vital then that we hear about our diverse experience. There is no one story of black girlhood.

·   ·   ·

Good hair—that's the expression. We all know it, begin to hear it when we are small children. When we are sitting between the legs of mothers and sisters getting our hair combed. Good hair is hair that is not kinky, hair that does not feel like balls of steel wool, hair that does not take hours to comb, hair that does not need tons of grease to untangle, hair that is long. Real good hair is straight hair, hair like white folk's hair. Yet no one says so. No one says Your hair is so nice, so beautiful because it is like white folk's hair. We pretend that the standards we measure our beauty by are our own invention—that it is questions of time and money that lead us to make distinctions between good hair and bad hair. I know from birth that I am lucky, lucky to have hair at all for I was bald for two years, then lucky finally to have thin, almost straight hair, hair that does not need to be hot-combed.   4

We are six girls who live in a house together. We have different textures of hair, short, long, thick, thin. We do not appreciate these differences. We do not celebrate the variety that is ourselves. We do not run our fingers through each other's dry hair after it is washed. We sit in the kitchen and wait our turn for the hot comb, wait to sit in the chair by the stove, smelling grease, feeling the heat warm our scalp like a sticky hot summer sun.   5

For each of us getting our hair pressed is an important ritual. It is not a sign of our longing to be white. It is not a sign of our quest to be beautiful. We are girls. It is a sign of our desire to be women. It is a gesture that says we are approaching womanhood—a rite of passage. Before we reach the appropriate age we wear braids and plaits that are symbols of our innocence, our youth, our childhood. Then we are comforted by the parting hands that comb and braid, comforted by the intimacy and bliss. There is a deeper intimacy in the kitchen on Saturday when hair is pressed, when fish is fried, when sodas are passed around, when soul music drifts over the talk. We are women together. This is our ritual and our time. It is a time without men. It is a time when we work to meet each other's needs, to make each other beautiful in whatever way we can. It is a time of laughter and mellow talk. Sometimes it is an occasion for tears and sorrow. Mama is angry, sick of it all, pulling the hair too tight, using too much grease, burning one ear and then the next.   6

At first I cannot participate in the ritual. I have good hair that does not need pressing. Without the hot comb I remain a child, one of the uninitiated. I plead, I beg, I cry for my turn. They tell me once you start you will be sorry. You will wish you had never straightened your hair.   7

They do not understand that it is not the straightening I seek but the chance to belong, to be one in this world of women. It is finally my turn. I am happy. Happy even though my thin hair straightened looks like black thread, has no body, stands in the air like ends of barbed wire; happy even though the sweet smell of unpressed hair is gone forever. Secretly I had hoped that the hot comb would transform me, turn the thin good hair into thick nappy hair, the kind of hair I like and long for, the kind you can do anything with, wear in all kinds of styles. I am bitterly disappointed in the new look.

Later, a senior in high school, I want to wear a natural, an Afro. I want never to get my hair pressed again. It is no longer a rite of passage, a chance to be intimate in the world of women. The intimacy masks betrayal. Together we change ourselves. The closeness is an embrace before parting, a gesture of farewell to love and one another. 8

JENNIFER BRICE

My Mother's Body

Jennifer Brice (1963–) was born in Fairbanks, Alaska, and has spent most of her life there. After graduating from Smith College, she began her writing career composing obituaries for a Fairbanks newspaper. Five years later she entered graduate school in creative writing at the University of Alaska. To complete a collection of essays for her M.A. thesis, Brice spent several years traveling through the Alaskan interior with a photographer, interviewing families on remote home sites. The hybrid documentary photography, reportage, and memoir, which became *The Last Settlers* (1998), looks at the arbitrary nature of the borders between nature and civilization. Brice divides her time between writing and raising her three young daughters, trying to fit in as much skiing and solitude as possible between the two.

"My Mother's Body" was published in the Sierra Club's *American Nature Writing* (1994). In writing the essay, Brice explains, she came to see that "generations of women are connected by having wrestled with the same issues." The essay invites writers, both female and male, to look for such connections in their own lives. A fine companion essay—because it explores connections between parents and children, the mind and the body, and life and death—is Scott Russell Sanders's "Reasons of the Body."

Winter solstice. Festive and frail like the orange globe of a Chinese lantern, the sun hangs on the horizon where it seems to absorb rather than radiate heat. Outside the window of the spare bedroom in my mother's house, where I dress for my sister's wedding, ice fog wisps 1 around the frost-filigreed branches of birch trees, and glittering snow carapaces the ground. With a lamp at my back, the window is a mirror into which I lean, struggling with the old-fashioned clasp on my pearl necklace. I see my reflection—a slender, dark-haired woman in green velvet—and next to it, my sister-in-law, eight months pregnant. She tugs the lace bertha of the bridesmaid's dress up over her shoulders and steps back, cradling her ponderous belly in both hands. "I was crazy to say yes when Hannah asked me to be in this wedding," she says. "I look obscene." I tell her she's beautiful and mean it, but she shrugs. Then I turn sideways to the window and slide flattened hands over my collarbones, breasts, stomach, hips. My fingers meet at the center of my body where they probe gently for something smaller than the mole above my right breast, something more mysterious than the black spots on the sun. I have never been good at secrets. "Can you see my baby yet?" I ask.

The wedding is by candlelight in the same log-cabin Episcopal 2 church where my husband and I made our vows eighteen months earlier. It was June then, summer solstice, and the church doors were flung open. Baskets of roses and peonies flanked the steps to the nave. Purcell's trumpet voluntary shattered dust motes hanging in shafts of sunlight. Tonight, however, the earth pitches away from the sun. After the service the guests shrug into furs and parkas against the thirty-five-below night. After the church empties out, the wedding photographer shapes my family into a V headed by Helenka, my grandmother, in her sequined evening gown and fluffy bedroom slippers. The slippers catch me unawares. They remind me how everything living is dying: this is likely to be Grandma's last wedding.

When my grandfather died in 1987, he left her eighty acres, a 3 farm, and a construction business. Grandma hired a landscaper to fill in the swimming pool with dirt and she planted a rose garden there with as many bushes as grandchildren. Greenhouse owners laughed at her. "You might as well try growing cacti in Antarctica," they said. But Grandma fertilizes her rose bushes with backbone. They bloom only for her. Whenever one of her grandchildren is ill, she sends a crystal bowl of fragrant roses instead of chicken soup. In the winter when her bushes sleep, their colors tumble off her tongue, incantatory, like Abraham's[1] descendants in the book of Genesis: Sterling Silver, Sunflare, Summer Fashion, Summer Sunshine, Allspice, American Pride, Touch of Class, Tropicana, Mr. Lincoln, Legend, Prince Charles, Fountain Square, White Lightning, Double Delight, Sheer Bliss, and Peace. "Jennifer's color is American Beauty," she declared once. Deeper than pink and shallower than red, it is a rare shade. I see it in the northern lights that stain the sky on my sister's wedding night.

---

1. Abraham: traditional progenitor of the Hebrew people.

Surrounded by her children and grandchildren, Helenka perches   4
like a plump, bright-eyed chickadee on a barstool in the old-timey saloon the bride and groom rented for their reception. I tell my grandmother I'm pregnant. She has a knack for planting familiar words in
unfamiliar gardens, so I'm not surprised when she says, serenely, "I
loved making my babies." The way she uses "make" emphasizes the
"-creation" end of "procreation," as though a baby were a bowl crafted
from clay on a pottery wheel and glazed for strength and beauty, or a
seed pressed into the womb of the earth and nourished with food and
water until it is strong enough to bend in the wind. I've never been
good with my hands, never thrown a pot, never painted a still life with
fruit, never even grown a Mother's Day geranium from a seed planted
in a Styrofoam cup. But my body is making a baby.

Vernal equinox. The myth of Demeter and Persephone[2] was at the   5
heart of The Eleusinian Mysteries, the rites of spiritual renewal celebrated in Greece for more than 2,000 years. The myth encompasses
the cycle of the seasons, death and reincarnation, rending and healing,
loss and joy, but it centers on the relationship between mother and
daughter. Adrienne Rich, in *Of Woman Born*, writes extensively about
the relevance of the myth to modern mother-daughter bonds. In my
own life, the biggest complication in my relationship with my mother
has always been my relationship with my grandmother, who, seren-
dipitously, is the mother of my father. In *Our Mothers/Our Selves*, Nancy
Friday says every household reverberates with the voices of three
women: mother, daughter, and grandmother. My mother's voice was
reverent when she unveiled the mysteries of cycles, Kotex and garter
belts. Everything was in place, waiting in the special drawer in the
bathroom for the special moment when I shed the chrysalis of childhood. I got my first period on a trip with my grandmother. When I told
her in the airport, she asked, offhandedly, "Do you need anything?"
Yes, I told her, everything. She bought me a box of OB tampons, and
nothing more was ever said.

Spring is late this year. Torn between mother and lover, Per-   6
sephone tarries in the Underworld. Jealous Demeter stirs up blizzards
in May. No one is able to coax Helenka's rose bushes, dull green sticks
brandishing thorns, into bloom. Melting snow and mud puddles paint
a landscape in charcoal grays and dingy browns on the day of her funeral. I wear pearls again, and my first maternity dress. Last week in
the ultrasound lab at the hospital I watched my healthy baby girl som-
ersault in her amniotic sac of fluid and blood. Now it is early morning

2. In Greek mythology, after being abducted by Hades, Persephone became both queen
of the underworld and goddess of vegetation; her release from the underworld each
spring to spend several months with her mother, Demeter, is reflected in the cycle of the
seasons.

and the family has gathered, some seventy-strong, to pray with Episcopal restraint and to spread Grandma's ashes over the farm. With our coffee and croissants we mill about as helplessly as geese without a leader. I want to writhe on the wet grass and gouge at the soil. Today, my baby's cells multiply by the million; my grandmother's ashes fertilize her rose bushes. In *The Lives of a Cell,* Lewis Thomas writes: "Everything that comes alive seems to be in trade for something that dies, cell for cell. There might be some comfort in . . . synchrony." There may be some comfort in synchrony, but it is not great.

I never thought of my mother as beautiful. Evenings when I was   7
growing up, I used to nudge open the bathroom door and roost on the edge of her tub, soaking my feet in the steaming, scented water. "Tell me about your day," Mom would say. As we talked, I studied surreptitiously the landscape of her body. Blue-black varicose veins, like tangled rivers and their tributaries, roped their way up to the sparse triangle between her legs. Scarlet moles punctuated a stomach puckered and seamed by surgeries, including the hysterectomy that had proscribed her motherhood. One side of her belly was firm as a ripe pomegranate; the other hemisphere, molded by scar tissue, collapsed in folds of flab. Illness and childbirth had buffeted her body in ways that I, with the vanity of youth, vowed they would never touch me.

Pregnant, I find myself back on the edge of my mother's bathtub   8
where I now study the landscape of possibility while we design flower gardens in our heads. "You know the gravel pit off Peger Road?" she asks. "I saw wild iris growing there last week." For us, garden talk is a code: "Plant perennials instead of annuals so you won't have to work so hard next summer, with the baby." The only roses in my mother's garden are portulaca, moss roses, whose silver-dollar-size blooms quilt the sandy soil of her wildflower garden in pastel patches. From Memorial Day until Labor Day, Mom lets spiders spin webs in her basement and dust bunnies collect under the beds. Wearing a terry-cloth sun suit, she kneels outside in the dirt from eight in the morning until seven at night, digging troughs in the topsoil, planting seeds one at a time, sprinkling mounds with fertilized rainwater. She weeds a little every day and coaxes more blooms by snipping off deadheads. By the time July rolls around, the plants are so profuse it can be difficult to find my mother in her garden. Fiddlehead ferns, delphinium, tiger lilies, snapdragons, geraniums, daisies, begonias, pansies, lobelia, Johnny-jump-ups, creeping Jenny, forget-me-nots, lettuce, tomatoes, peas, carrots, radishes, squash and pumpkins: my mother's garden is both hymn to the regenerative power of earth and drunken orgy under the midnight sun.

Summer solstice. Two years ago Mom flew to Anchorage for what   9
the doctors expected to be routine gallbladder surgery. Instead she developed complications and nearly died. Her garden withered while she

lay in a hospital bed on life-support machines. Watching my mother weaken and realizing she might die kindled a deep existential fear in me. I was working in Fairbanks from Monday through Friday and flying to Anchorage on the weekends; for the first time in my life, I was afraid of dying in a plane crash. Strangely, I felt safe on takeoff and landing, but once airborne, I dreaded elements beyond human control—turbulence, wind shear, electrical storms—that might tear the jet apart in mid-air. I left the pressurized cabin of the jet for the silent, gray, temperature-controlled corridors of Humana Hospital. The tinted windows in my mother's room watered down harsh sunlight and drained the landscape of color. Mom shrunk daily into a chaos of plastic umbilical cords. Intellectually, I knew it was the natural order of things for my mother to die before me. But not in her 50s, not before she taught me how to be a mother, not until I had come to terms with the fact of my own mortality. My mother's illness taught me this: my strongest identification is not as someone's friend, sister, granddaughter or wife but as my mother's daughter. She is my road map; without her, I would be completely lost.

Mom is nearly her old self again now. Working in her garden,   10
squeezing dirt between her fingers, she grows stronger daily. Unlike her, I lack the patience to let things grow. I over-fertilize in a fit of solicitousness or forget to weed in a fit of laziness. This summer of my pregnancy, for the first time in my life, I crave the physicality of gardening. Mornings Mom and I visit local greenhouses. She discourages me from temperamental species; I yearn toward hothouse roses. Every afternoon I lug baskets onto the back porch, fill them with dirt, dig shallow holes with a trowel or my fingers, pop the seedlings out of their six-packs, and set them in their new nests. Mosquitos buzz around my head. Hugely pregnant in a denim jumper, I make trip after trip to the kitchen sink for jugs of water mixed with pink fish fertilizer. The front yard is a typical Alaska lawn, which is to say no lawn at all, just a few spruce trees, willow bushes, a delphinium here and there, and a ground covering of ferns, wild roses and cranberry bushes. If I cannot have long-stemmed roses then I want wildness. I strew wildflower seeds everywhere. By mid-summer, daisies overflow a rusting wheelbarrow, impatiens spring from the hollows of rotting stumps, and nasturtiums cascade off the roof of the doghouse. One of the reasons I never liked gardening before was the waste: all that money and energy expended on something that was going to die anyway. Recently a couple of friends stopped by on bicycles and stayed to help me plant a lilac bush. Afterward, over ice cream, one of them asked, "How can you justify bringing a child into this over-populated world full of wars and famine and acid rain and ozone holes?" I replied, "Because I still hope." Lewis Thomas finds comfort, not despair, in the knowledge that everything living is also dying. Cultivating a garden that will

surely die in September can be seen as an act of senseless futility or one of consummate hope. So can having a baby. After all, everything dying is also living.

On the Fourth of July, friends invite Craig and me to float the Chena River with them. The river is a shallow, slow-moving artery that winds through town, binding three-story houses with gazebos to houses with chain-link fences and yapping dogs to houses that are really lean-tos. A radio announcer says it's 75 degrees but a cooling breeze riffles the leaves of birch trees on shore. We paddle the stretch of water below the city power plant because the water there never freezes in winter, not even at 50 below. Now we rest our paddles on our knees and float, trading insults and banter between canoes. I gasp when the first bucket of river water slaps me in the back of the head. I see the second bucket coming and lean to the right. Quicker than re-gret, the canoe spills all 165 pounds of me into the river. Panicked, I grab for the overturned boat, but my lifejacket rides up over my belly, hampers my arms. Lisa mimics me—"The baby, oh God, the baby"—and, laughing, my friends tug me ashore like a harpooned whale.   11

Back on the river, I think about how this baby fills up space inside me that used to be wilderness unexplored by anyone, least of all me. Hugh Brody, the anthropologist and author, has spoken of finding the center at the edge, in the most remote hut in the most remote village in the most remote region of the country farthest from home. I have found certain truths at the edge but, for me, the center is at the center: in my family, in my flower boxes, in my womb. For the rest of the af-ternoon I ride in the middle of the canoe with hands cupped over the mound of my tummy.   12

My due date is still six weeks away, but I feel like one of those an-cient stone fertility figures whose images flashed on the screen of the darkened art history auditorium during college. I drive the half-mile to my mother's house instead of walking. She lays down her trowel and fixes us sandwiches of turkey breast, garden lettuce and tomatoes. Afterward we work on Sunday's *New York Times* crossword puzzle. Deeply afraid of giving birth, I yearn for the only solace my mother cannot—or will not—give. Casually, while she looks up a four-letter word for an African gazelle, I ask about labor. She tells me stories about water breaking in the middle of the night, evenly spaced con-tractions, the urge to push, a swaddled baby drowsing in her arms. She never uses the word "pain." During our Lamaze class, my husband and I watched three films of women having babies: an "easy" labor, an "av-erage" labor, and a "hard" labor. One friend says it's like bad menstrual cramps. Another friend, the one who cuts my hair, laid down her scis-sors when I told her I was pregnant. She spun my chair around until her face was right up against mine, and she placed a hand on either side of my head to hold it still. Then she said: "Don't let anyone ever tell you having a baby doesn't hurt. There is no worse pain in the   13 world." What I want to ask my mother is this: how bad is the pain when a woman's lips turn white? But she will not look in my eyes. My mother knows. My garden grows. There is mystery as well as synchrony. Some comfort.

The first contraction tears through me at midnight on August 14 thirty-first. It feels less like a menstrual cramp than a hot poker. Earlier, I had made a pact with my doctor to try to get by without drugs. Now I want a talisman against pain. My mother walks into the hospital room at 7:30 in the morning, pale but crisp in a madras jumpsuit, carrying a pile of books and newspapers against her chest. Insulation against my wildness, her helplessness. For a while we tell jokes between contractions. My mother and Craig take turns walking the corridors with me, pushing the IV tree with its bag of sap-like fluid. Only water and electrolytes at this point, but the doctor predicts a long, exhausting labor, and she wants to be able to administer drugs quickly, if necessary. We stop in front of the nursery windows. I look at the newborns and think, "Soon. Soon." My water has not yet broken. The nurse swabs the inside of my cervix and looks at the cells under a microscope. If the sac of amniotic fluid has broken, she would see a fern-like pattern. "No ferns," she tells me, shaking her head.

My contractions are severe but irregular. The doctor uses an in- 15 strument like a crochet hook to reach inside me and puncture the bag of waters. It feels as though someone broke a ten-gallon hot water bottle over my stomach. The distance between pains narrows a little, but daylight is waning outside my window. On the doctor's orders, the nurse adds pitocin, a labor-intensifying drug, to my IV line. Within minutes, my body travels to a place inhabited by insatiable pain, a place where language can never go, a place where I am no longer someone's daughter and not yet someone's mother. The nurse grabs the backs of my hands, spreads my fingers in front of my clenched eyelids. "Jennifer, listen to me. *Listen* to me. Open your eyes. Don't go inside the pain. You'll only make it worse." What is she talking about? There is no inside or outside to this pain. The plate tectonics of childbirth remold the peaks and valleys of my body. The bones of my mother's hand feel as frail as a fledgling's skeleton. It is extraordinary to me that the process of bringing forth life should bring women to the brink of death. For a baby, the violent, bruising passage through the birth canal must be like expulsion from paradise. Before, amniotic bliss; after, cold and hunger and hands. As the mother's pain ends, the daughter's begins.

Autumnal equinox. Last night, the temperature dipped below 16 freezing. In Alaska, the cusp seasons of spring and fall can be figments of the calendar's imagination. So reluctant to be dragged from the earth's womb last spring, Persephone seems eager to return this fall. The birch trees have barely begun to shed their chattering leaves when the first snow falls in big, wet clumps. In a defiant blaze of color, the blossoms in my garden faced death, their stems and leaves collapsing around them like tattered seaweed. Turbulent post-partum depression runs in my family but still it blindsides me. Grief for my grandmother, who will never name a rose for my daughter, Kinzea Grace, is a sub-terranean place into which I burrow every night. My mother probably will not live to see another generation grow up. As for me, creating life has forced me to confront my own mortality as never before. In the Es-kimo culture, babies were traditionally granted the same title and respect as a recently deceased elder. I could find comfort in calling Kinzea "Grandmother."

I left the hospital after the baby was born without seeing her 17 naked. I was so tired, the nurses so smoothly efficient. Now, as she wriggles and coos in the bathtub, I study her body for the first time: the parallel lines beneath her lips, the pearls of dirt that collect under her chin, her nearly invisible nipples, bracelets of fat at wrists and an-kles, a tulip-shaped birthmark on her left buttock, the arch of a tiny foot. Her fifth toes are shriveled like mine, with nails the size of carrot seeds. Our feet foretell a time when the descendants of homo sapiens will balance on eight toes instead of ten.

I sit behind Kinzea in the tub, cradling her body between thighs 18 gone flaccid from lack of exercise. My belly slides back and forth in the moving water like a Jell-O mold at a church picnic. Violet stretch marks form a complex root system spreading upward from the fork of my legs where the baby's head rests. My breasts are laden with milk. Looking down, I recognize my mother's body, my grandmother's body, my great-grandmother's body. Flawed but familiar. Living and dying at the same time. There is some comfort—even grace—in synchrony, in being the daughter of a mother and the mother of a daughter. Some-where, I read that a child needs the care of someone for whom she is a miracle. Mother love, I think, is born of wonder at that miracle.

DEBORAH TANNEN

Every Choice a Woman Makes Sends a Message

Deborah Tannen (1945–) is Professor of Linguistics at Georgetown University and an internationally known scholar in the field of soci-olinguistics. In 1986 she published *You Just Don't Understand: Women and Men in Conversation,* which became an instant best-seller and was on *The New York Times* Best Seller list for over four years. Since that time she has written several books on communication, particularly between women and men. *Gender and Discourse* (1994) contains several of her essays on the effect of language on male/female relationships and provides the scholarly backdrop for Tannen's *You Just Don't Understand*. She applies her theories to the workplace in *Talking 9 to 5: How Women's and Men's Conversational Styles Affect Who Gets Heard, Who Gets Credit, and What Gets Done* (1994). In 1998 she published *The Argument Culture: Moving from Debate to Dialogue*.

"Every Choice a Woman Makes Sends a Message" was published in the June 20, 1998, issue of *The New York Times Magazine*. Filled with example after example of how women are perceived in our culture, the essay demonstrates the power of illustration to support a thesis. A useful companion essay is Bernard Cooper's "A Clack of Tiny Sparks," in which the junior-high world Cooper describes is rife with confusing and conflicting messages, this time about what it means to be gay.

Some years ago I was at a small working conference of four 1
women and eight men. Instead of concentrating on the discussion I found myself looking at the three other women at the table, thinking how each had a different style and how each style was coherent.

One woman had dark brown hair in a classic style, a cross between 2
Cleopatra and Plain Jane. The severity of her straight hair was softened by wavy bangs and ends that turned under. Because she was beautiful, the effect was more Cleopatra than plain.

The second woman was older, full of dignity and composure. Her 3
hair was cut in a fashionable style that left her with only one eye, thanks to a side part that let a curtain of hair fall across half her face. As she looked down to read her prepared paper, the hair robbed her of bifocal vision and created a barrier between her and the listeners.

The third woman's hair was wild, a frosted blond avalanche falling 4
over and beyond her shoulders. When she spoke she frequently tossed her head, calling attention to her hair and away from her lecture.

Then there was makeup. The first woman wore facial cover that 5
made her skin smooth and pale, a black line under each eye and mascara that darkened already dark lashes. The second wore only a light gloss on her lips and a hint of shadow on her eyes. The third had blue bands under her eyes, dark blue shadow, mascara, bright red lipstick and rouge; her fingernails flashed red.

I considered the clothes each woman had worn during the three 6
days of the conference: In the first case, man-tailored suits in primary colors with solid-color blouses. In the second, casual but stylish black T-shirts, a floppy collarless jacket and baggy slacks or a skirt in neutral colors. The third wore a sexy jump suit; tight sleeveless jersey and tight yellow slacks; a dress with gaping armholes and an indulged tendency to fall off one shoulder.

Shoes? No. 1 wore string sandals with medium heels; No. 2, sensi- 7 ble, comfortable walking shoes; No. 3, pumps with spike heels. You can fill in the jewelry, scarves, shawls, sweaters—or lack of them.

As I amused myself finding coherence in these styles, I suddenly wondered why I was scrutinizing only the women. I scanned the eight men at the table. And then I knew why I wasn't studying them. The men's styles were unmarked. 8

The term "marked" is a staple of linguistic theory. It refers to the way language alters the base meaning of a word by adding a linguistic particle that has no meaning on its own. The unmarked form of a word carries the meaning that goes without saying—what you think of when you're not thinking anything special. 9

The unmarked tense of verbs in English is the present—for example, *visit.* To indicate past, you mark the verb by adding *ed* to yield *visited.* For future, you add a word: *will visit.* Nouns are presumed to be singular until marked for plural, typically by adding *s* or *es,* so *visit* becomes *visits* and *dish* becomes *dishes.* 10

The unmarked forms of most English words also convey "male." Being male is the unmarked case. Endings like *ess* and *ette* mark words as "female." Unfortunately, they also tend to mark them for frivolousness. Would you feel safe entrusting your life to a doctorette? Alfre Woodard, who was an Oscar nominee for best supporting actress, says she identifies herself as an actor because "actresses worry about eyelashes and cellulite, and women who are actors worry about the characters we are playing." Gender markers pick up extra meanings that reflect common associations with the female gender: not quite serious, often sexual. 11

Each of the women at the conference had to make decisions about hair, clothing, makeup and accessories, and each decision carried meaning. Every style available to us was marked. The men in our group had made decisions, too, but the range from which they chose was incomparably narrower. Men can choose styles that are marked, but they don't have to, and in this group none did. Unlike the women, they had the option of being unmarked. 12

Take the men's hair styles. There was no marine crew cut or oily longish hair falling into eyes, no asymmetrical, two-tiered construction to swirl over a bald top. One man was unabashedly bald; the others had hair of standard length, parted on one side, in natural shades of brown or gray or graying. Their hair obstructed no views, left little to toss or push back or run fingers through and, consequently, needed and attracted no attention. A few men had beards. In a business setting, beards might be marked. In this academic gathering, they weren't. 13

There could have been a cowboy shirt with string tie or a three-piece suit or a necklaced hippie in jeans. But there wasn't. All eight 14 men wore brown or blue slacks and nondescript shirts of light colors. No man wore sandals or boots; their shoes were dark, closed, comfortable and flat. In short, unmarked.

Although no man wore makeup, you couldn't say the men didn't wear makeup in the sense that you could say a woman didn't wear makeup. For men, no makeup is unmarked.   15

I asked myself what style we women could have adopted that would have been unmarked, like the men's. The answer was none. There is no unmarked woman.   16

There is no woman's hair style that can be called standard, that says nothing about her. The range of women's hair styles is staggering, but a woman whose hair has no particular style is perceived as not caring about how she looks, which can disqualify her for many positions, and will subtly diminish her as a person in the eyes of some.   17

Women must choose between attractive shoes and comfortable shoes. When our group made an unexpected trek, the woman who wore flat, laced shoes arrived first. Last to arrive was the woman in spike heels, shoes in hand and a handful of men around her.   18

If a woman's clothing is tight or revealing (in other words, sexy), it sends a message—an intended one of wanting to be attractive, but also a possibly unintended one of availability. If her clothes are not sexy, that too sends a message, lent meaning by the knowledge that they could have been. There are thousands of cosmetic products from which women can choose and myriad ways of applying them. Yet no makeup at all is anything but unmarked. Some men see it as a hostile refusal to please them.   19

Women can't even fill out a form without telling stories about themselves. Most forms give four titles to choose from. "Mr." carries no meaning other than that the respondent is male. But a woman who checks "Mrs." or "Miss" communicates not only whether she has been married but also whether she has conservative tastes in forms of address—and probably other conservative values as well. Checking "Ms." declines to let on about marriage (checking "Mr." declines nothing since nothing was asked), but it also marks her as either liberated or rebellious, depending on the observer's attitudes and assumptions.   20

I sometimes try to duck these variously marked choices by giving my title as "Dr."—and in so doing risk marking myself as either uppity (hence sarcastic responses like "Excuse me!") or an overachiever (hence reactions of congratulatory surprise like "Good for you!")   21

All married women's surnames are marked. If a woman takes her husband's name, she announces to the world that she is married and has traditional values. To some it will indicate that she is less herself, more identified by her husband's identity. If she does not take her husband's name, this too is marked, seen as worthy of comment: she has *done* something; she has "kept her own name." A man is never said to   22 have "kept his own name" because it never occurs to anyone that he might have given it up. For him using his own name is unmarked.

A married woman who wants to have her cake and eat it too may use her surname plus his, with or without a hyphen. But this too announces her marital status and often results in a tongue-tying string. In a list (Harvey O'Donovan, Jonathan Feldman, Stephanie Woodbury McGillicutty), the woman's multiple name stands out. It is marked.   23

I have never been inclined toward biological explanations of gender differences in language, but I was intrigued to see Ralph Fasold bring biological phenomena to bear on the question of linguistic marking in his book "The Sociolinguistics of Language." Fasold stresses that language and culture are particularly unfair in treating women as the marked case because biologically it is the male that is marked. While two X chromosomes make a female, two Y chromosomes make nothing. Like the linguistic markers *s, es* or *ess,* the Y chromosome doesn't "mean" anything unless it is attached to a root form—an X chromosome.   24

Developing this idea elsewhere, Fasold points out that girls are born with fully female bodies, while boys are born with modified female bodies. He invites men who doubt this to lift up their shirts and contemplate why they have nipples.   25

In his book, Fasold notes "a wide range of facts which demonstrates that female is the unmarked sex." For example, he observes that there are a few species that produce only females, like the whiptail lizard. Thanks to parthenogenesis, they have no trouble having as many daughters as they like. There are no species, however, that produce only males. This is no surprise, since any such species would become extinct in its first generation.   26

Fasold is also intrigued by species that produce individuals not involved in reproduction, like honeybees and leaf-cutter ants. Reproduction is handled by the queen and a relatively few males; the workers are sterile females. "Since they do not reproduce," Fasold says, "there is no reason for them to be one sex or the other, so they default, so to speak, to female."   27

Fasold ends his discussion of these matters by pointing out that if language reflected biology, grammar books would direct us to use "she" to include males and females and "he" only for specifically male referents. But they don't. They tell us that "he" means "he or she," and that "she" is used only if the referent is specifically female. This use of "he" as the sex-indefinite pronoun is an innovation introduced into English by grammarians in the 18th and 19th centuries, according to Peter Mühlhäusler and Rom Harré in "Pronouns and People." From at least about 1500, the correct sex-indefinite pronoun was "they," as it still is in casual spoken English. In other words, the female was declared by grammarians to be the marked case.   28

Writing this article may mark me not as a writer, not as a linguist, 29
not as an analyst of human behavior, but as a feminist—which will
have positive or negative, but in any case powerful, connotations for
readers. Yet I doubt that anyone reading Ralph Fasold's book would
put that label on him.

I discovered the markedness inherent in the very topic of gender 30
after writing a book on differences in conversational style based on geographical region, ethnicity, class, age and gender. When I was interviewed, the vast majority of journalists wanted to talk about the
differences between women and men. While I thought I was simply
describing what I observed—something I had learned to do as a researcher—merely mentioning women and men marked me as a feminist for some.

When I wrote a book devoted to gender differences in ways of 31
speaking, I sent the manuscript to five male colleagues, asking them to
alert me to any interpretation, phrasing or wording that might seem
unfairly negative toward men. Even so, when the book came out, I encountered responses like that of the television talk show host who,
after interviewing me, turned to the audience and asked if they thought
I was male-bashing.

Leaping upon a poor fellow who affably nodded in agreement, she 32
made him stand and asked, "Did what she said accurately describe
you?" "Oh, yes," he answered. "That's me exactly." "And what she said
about women—does that sound like your wife?" "Oh yes," he responded. "That's her exactly." "Then why do you think she's male-
bashing?" He answered, with disarming honesty, "Because she's a
woman and she's saying things about men."

To say anything about women and men without marking oneself 33
as either feminist or anti-feminist, male-basher or apologist for men
seems as impossible for a woman as trying to get dressed in the morning without inviting interpretations of her character.

Sitting at the conference table musing on these matters, I felt sad 34
to think that we women didn't have the freedom to be unmarked that
the men sitting next to us had. Some days you just want to get dressed
and go about your business. But if you're a woman, you can't, because
there is no unmarked woman.

SCOTT RUSSELL SANDERS

Reasons of the Body

Scott Russell Sanders (1945–), a native of Tennessee, received his Ph.D. from Cambridge University and is currently a professor of English at Indiana University. Although he has written in a variety of genres, including science fiction, folktales, children's stories, and historical novels, he has concentrated in recent years on essays and autobiography. Sanders is well acquainted with the rugged side of American culture, which he explores in *Wilderness Plots: Tales About the Settlement of the American Land* (1983) and in *Paradise of Bombs* (1987), a collection of personal essays about violence in contemporary culture. Recent essays are collected in *Staying Put: Making a Home in a Restless World* (1993) and *Writing from the Center* (1996). His most recent work, *Meeting Trees* (1997), brings together two of Sanders's greatest interests: nature and the interaction between father and son.

"Reasons of the Body" was published in *Georgia Review* in 1990 and collected in *Secrets of the Universe* (1991), Sanders's recollections of his Midwestern childhood. The essay obviously invites writers to explore the lessons they learned from involvement (or lack of involvement) in sports. It connects well with two other explorations of masculinity, Noel Perrin's "The Androgynous Man" and Michael Norman's "Against Androgyny."

My son has never met a sport he did not like. I have met a few that left an ugly tingle—boxing and rodeo and pistol shooting, among others—but, then, I have been meeting them for forty-four years, Jesse only for twelve. Our ages are relevant to the discussion, because, on the hill of the sporting life, Jesse is midway up the slope and climbing rapidly, while I am over the crest and digging in my heels as I slip down. 1

"You still get around pretty well for an old guy," he told me last night after we had played catch in the park. 2

The catch we play has changed subtly in recent months, a change that dramatizes a shift in the force field binding father and son. Early on, when I was a decade younger and Jesse a toddler, I was the agile one, leaping to snare his wild throws. The ball we tossed in those days was rubbery and light, a bubble of air as big around as a soup bowl, easy for small hands to grab. By the time he started school, we were using a tennis ball, then we graduated to a softball, then to gloves and a baseball. His repertoire of catches and throws increased along with his vocabulary. 3

Over the years, as Jesse put on inches and pounds and grace, I still had to be careful how far and hard I threw, to avoid bruising his ribs or his pride. But this spring, when we began limbering up our arms, his 4 throws came whistling at me with a force that hurt my hand, and he caught effortlessly anything I could hurl back at him. It was as though the food he wolfed down all winter had turned into spring steel. I no longer needed to hold back. Now Jesse is the one, when he is feeling charitable, who pulls his pitches.

Yesterday in the park, he was feeling frisky rather than charitable. We looped the ball lazily back and forth awhile. Then he started backing away, backing away, until my shoulder twinged from the length of throws. Unsatisfied, he yelled, "Make me run for it!" So I flung the ball high and deep, low and wide, driving him over the grass, yet he loped easily wherever it flew, gathered it in, then whipped it back to me with stinging speed.

"Come on," he yelled, "put it where I can't reach it." I tried, ignoring the ache in my arm, and still he ran under the ball. He might have been gliding on a cushion of air, he moved so lightly. I was feeling heavy, and felt heavier by the minute as his return throws, grown suddenly and unaccountably wild, forced me to hustle back and forth, jump and dive.

"Hey," I yelled, waving my glove at him, "look where I'm standing!"

"Standing is right," he yelled back. "Let's see those legs move!" His next throw sailed over my head, and the ones after that sailed farther still, now left now right, out of my range, until I gave up even trying for them, and the ball thudded accusingly to the ground. By the time we quit, I was sucking air, my knees were stiffening, and a fire was blazing in my arm. Jesse trotted up, his T-shirt dry, his breathing casual. This was the moment he chose to clap me on the back and say, "You still get around pretty well for an old guy."

It was a line I might have delivered, as a cocky teenager, to my own father. He would have laughed, and then challenged me to a round of golf or a bout of arm-wrestling, contests he could still easily have won.

Whatever else these games may be, they are always contests. For many a boy, a playing field, court, or gym is the first arena in which he can outstrip his old man. For me, the arena was a concrete driveway, where I played basketball against my father, shooting at a rusty hoop that was mounted over the garage. He had taught me how to dribble, how to time my jump, how to follow through on my shots. To begin with, I could barely heave the ball to the basket, and he would applaud if I so much as banged the rim. I banged away, year by year, my bones lengthening, muscles thickening. I shuffled over the concrete to the jazz of birdsong and the opera of thunderstorms. I practiced fervently, as though my life depended on putting the ball through the hoop, practiced when the driveway was dusted with pollen and when it was drifted with snow. From first light to twilight, while the chimney swifts spiraled out to feed on mosquitoes and the mosquitoes fed on me, I kept shooting, hour after hour. Many of those hours, Father was tin-

kering in the garage, which reverberated with the slap of my feet and
the slam of the ball. There came a day when I realized that I could out-
leap him, outhustle and outshoot him. I began to notice his terrible
breathing—terrible because I had not realized he could run short of air.
I had not realized he could run short of anything. When he bent over
and grabbed his knees, huffing, "You're too much for me," I felt at
once triumphant and dismayed.

I still have to hold back when playing basketball with Jesse. But   11
the day will come, and soon, when he'll grow taller and stronger, and
he will be the one to show mercy. The only dessert I will be able to eat,
if I am to avoid growing fat, will be humble pie. Even now my shots
appear old-fashioned to him, as my father's arching two-handed
heaves seemed antique to me. "Show me some of those Neanderthal
moves," Jesse cries, as we shoot around at a basket in the park, "Show
me how they did it in the Stone Age!" I do show him, clowning and
hot-dogging, wishing by turns to amuse and impress him. As I fake
and spin, I am simultaneously father and son, playing games forward
and backward in time.

The game of catch, like other sports where body faces body, is a di-   12
alogue carried on with muscle and bone. One body speaks by throwing
a ball or a punch, by lunging with a foil, smashing a backhand, sinking
a putt, rolling a strike, kicking a shot toward the corner of the net; the
other replies by swinging, leaping, dodging, tackling, parrying, balancing. As in lovemaking, this exchange may be a struggle for power or a
sharing of pleasure. The call and response may be in the spirit of an-
tiphonal singing, a making of music that neither person could have
achieved alone, or it may be in the spirit of insults bellowed across a
table.

When a father and son play sports, especially a game the son has   13
learned from the father, every motive from bitter rivalry to mutual delight may enter in. At first eagerly, then grudgingly, and at last unconsciously, the son watches how his father grips the ball, handles the
glove, swings the bat. In just the same way, the son has watched how
the father swings a hammer, how the father walks, jokes, digs, starts a
car, gentles a horse, pays a bill, shakes hands, shaves. There is a season
in one's growing up, beginning at about the age Jesse is now, when a
son comes to feel his old man's example as a smothering weight. You
must shrug free of it, or die. And so, if your father carries himself soldier straight, you begin to slouch; if he strides along with a swagger,
you slink; if he talks in joshing Mississippi accents to anybody with
ears, you shun strangers and swallow your drawl. With luck and time,
you may come to accept that you bear in your own voice overtones of
your father's. You may come to rejoice that your own least motion—
kissing a baby or opening a jar—is informed by memories of how your

father would have done it. Between the early delight and the late reconciliation, however, you must pass through that season of rivalry, the
son striving to undo or outdo his father's example, the father chewing
on the bitter rind of rejection.

Why do I speak only of boys and men? Because, while there are   14
females aplenty who relish any sport you can name, I have never
shared a roof with one. In her seventies, my mother still dances and
swims, even leads classes in aerobics, but she's never had much use for
games played with balls, and neither has my wife Ruth or our daughter. When Ruth was a child, a bout of rheumatic fever confined her to
bed and then to a wheelchair for several years. Until she was old
enough for university, a heart rendered tricky by the illness kept her
from doing anything that would raise her pulse, and by then she had
invested her energies elsewhere, in music and science. To this day,
Ruth sees no point in moving faster than a walk, or in defying gravity
with exuberant leaps, or in puzzling over the trajectory of a ball.

And what of our firstborn, sprightly Eva? Surely I could have   15
brought her up to become a partner for catch? Let me assure you that
I tried. I put a sponge ball in her crib, as Father had put a baseball in
mine. (I was gong to follow tradition exactly and teethe her on a baseball, but Ruth, sensible of a baby's delicacy, said nothing doing.) From
the moment in the hospital when the nurse handed me Eva, a quivering bundle, ours to keep, I coached my spunky girl, I coaxed and ex-
horted her, but she would not be persuaded that throwing or shooting
or kicking a ball was a sensible way to spend an hour or an afternoon.
After seventeen years of all the encouragement that love can buy, the
one sport she will deign to play with me is volleyball, in which she
hurtles over the grass, leaping and cavorting, as only a dancer could.

A gymnast and ballerina, Eva has always been on good terms with   16
her body, and yet, along with her mother and my mother, she rolls her
eyes when Jesse and I begin rummaging in the battered box on the
porch for a baseball, basketball, or soccer ball. "So Dad," she calls, "it's
off to recover past glories, is it? You show 'em, tiger. But don't break
any bones."

Eva's amusement has made the opinion of the women in my life   17
unanimous. Their baffled indulgence, bordering at times on mockery,
has given to sports a tang of the mildly illicit.

Like many other women (not all, not all), those in my family take   18
even less interest in talking about sports than in playing them. They
pride themselves on being above such idle gab. They shake their heads
when my son and I check the scores in the newspaper. They are astounded that we can spend longer rehashing a game than we spent in
playing it. When Jesse and I compare aches after a session on field or
court, the women observe mildly that it sounds as though we had

been mugged. Surely we would not inflict such damage on ourselves? Perhaps we have gotten banged up from wrestling bears? We kid along and say, "Yes, we ran into the Chicago Bears," and my daughter or mother or wife will reply, "You mean the hockey team?"

In many households and offices, gossip about games and athletes   19
breaks down along gender lines, the men indulging in it and the women scoffing. Those on each side of the line may exaggerate their feelings, the men pumping up their enthusiasm, the women their in-difference, until sport becomes a male mystery. No locker room, no sweat lodge is needed to shut women out; mere talk will do it. Men are capable of muttering about wins and losses, batting averages and slam dunks, until the flowers on the wallpaper begin to wilt and every woman in the vicinity begins to yearn for a supply of gags. A woman friend of mine, an executive in a computing firm, has been driven in self-defense to scan the headlines of the sports pages before going to work, so that she can toss out references to the day's contests and stars, like chunks of meat, to feed the appetites of her male colleagues. After gnawing on this bait, the men may consent to speak with her of things more in keeping with her taste, such as books, birds, and the human condition.

My daughter has never allowed me to buy her a single item of   20
sports paraphernalia. My son, on the other hand, has never declined such an offer. Day and night, visions of athletic gear dance in his head. With religious zeal, he pores over magazine ads for sneakers, examin-ing the stripes and insignia as if they were hieroglyphs of ultimate truth. Between us, Jesse and I are responsible for the hoard of equip-ment on our back porch, which contains at present the following items: one bicycle helmet and two bicycles; a volleyball set, badminton set, and a bag of golf clubs; three racquets for tennis, two for squash, one for paddle ball; roller skates and ice skates, together with a pair of hockey sticks; goalie gloves, batting gloves, three baseball gloves and one catcher's mitt; numerous yo-yos; ten pairs of cleated or waffle-soled shoes; a drying rack festooned with shorts and socks and shirts and sweatsuits; and a cardboard box heaped with (I counted) forty-nine balls, including those for all the sports implicated above, as well as for ping-pong, lacrosse, juggling, and jacks.

Excavated by some future archaeologist, this porch full of gear   21
would tell as much about how we passed our lives as would the shells and seeds and bones of a kitchen midden. An excavation of the word *sport* also yields evidence of breaks, bruises, and ambiguities. A sport is a game, an orderly zone marked off from the prevailing disorder, but it can also be a mutation, a violation of rules. To be good at sports is to be a winner, and yet a good sport is one who loses amiably, a bad sport one who kicks and screams at every setback. A flashy dresser might be

called a sport, and so might a gambler, an idler, an easygoing companion, one who dines high on the hog of pleasure. But the same label may be attached to one who is the butt of jokes, a laughingstock, a goat. As a verb, to sport can be to wear jewelry or clothes in a showy manner, to poke fun, to trifle, to roll promiscuously in the hay. It is a word spiced with unsavory meanings, rather tacky and cheap, with hints of brothels, speakeasies, and malodorous dives. And yet it bears also the wholesome flavor of fairness, vigor, and ease.

The lore of sports may be all that some fathers have to pass down   22
to their sons in place of lore about hunting animals, planting seeds, killing enemies, or placating the gods. Instead of telling him how to shoot a buffalo, the father whispers in the son's ear how to shoot a lay-up. Instead of consulting the stars or the entrails of birds, father and son consult the smudged print of newspapers to see how their chosen spirits are faring. They fiddle with the dials of radios, hoping to catch the oracular murmur of a distant game. The father recounts heroic deeds, not from the field of battle, but from the field of play. The seasons about which he speaks lead not to harvests but to championships. No longer intimate with the wilderness, no longer familiar even with the tamed land of farms, we create artificial landscapes bounded by lines of paint or lime. Within those boundaries, as within the frame of a chessboard or painting, the life achieves a memorable, seductive clarity. The lore of sports is a step down from that of nature, perhaps even a tragic step, but it is lore nonetheless, with its own demigods and demons, magic and myths.

The sporting legends I carry from my father are private rather than   23
public. I am haunted by scenes that no journalist recorded, no camera filmed. Father is playing a solo round of golf, for example, early one morning in April. The fairways glisten with dew. Crows rasp and fluster in the pines that border the course. Father lofts a shot toward a par-three hole, and the white ball arcs over the pond, over the sand trap, over the shaggy apron of grass onto the green, where it bounces, settles down, then rolls toward the flag, rolls unerringly, inevitably, until it falls with a scarcely audible click into the hole. The only eyes within sight besides his own are the crows'. For once, the ball had obeyed him perfectly, harmonizing wind and gravity and the revolution of the spheres, one shot has gone where all are meant to go, and there is nobody else to watch. He stands on the tee, gazing at the distant hole, knowing what he has done and that he will never do it again. The privacy of this moment appeals to me more than all the clamor and fame of a shot heard round the world.

Here is another story I live by: The man who will become my fa-   24
ther is twenty-two, a catcher for a bush-league baseball team in Tennessee. He will never make it to the majors, but on weekends he earns

a few dollars for squatting behind the plate and nailing runners foolish enough to try stealing second base. From all those bus rides, all those red-dirt diamonds, the event he will describe for his son with deepest emotion is an exhibition game. Father's team of whites, most of them fresh from two-mule farms, is playing a touring black team, a rare event for that day and place. To make it even rarer, and the sides fairer, the coaches agree to mix the teams. And so my father, son of a Mississippi cotton farmer, bruised with racial notions that will take a lifetime to heal, crouches behind the plate and for nine innings catches fastballs and curves, change-ups and screwballs from a whirling, muttering wizard of the Negro Baseball League, one Leroy Robert Paige, known to the world as Satchel. Afterward, Satchel Paige tells the farm boy, "You catch a good game," and the farm boy answers, "You've got the stuff, mister." And for the rest of my father's life, this man's pitching serves as a measure of mastery.

And here is a third myth I carry: One evening when the boy who will become my father is eighteen, he walks into the Black Cat Saloon in Tupelo, Mississippi. He is looking for a fight. Weary of plowing, sick of red dirt, baffled by his own turbulent energy, he often picks fights. This evening the man he picks on is a stranger who occupies a nearby stool at the bar, a husky man in his thirties, wearing a snap-brim hat, dark suit with wide lapels, narrow tie, and infuriatingly white shirt. The stranger is slow to anger. The red-headed Sanders boy keeps at him, keeps at him, mocking the Yankee accent, the hat worn indoors, the monkey suit, the starched shirt, until at last the man stands up and backs away from the bar, fists raised. The Sanders boy lands three punches, he remembers that much, but the next thing he remembers is waking up on the sidewalk, the stranger bending over him to ask if he is all right, and to ask, besides, if he would like a boxing scholarship to Mississippi State. The man is headed there to become the new coach. The boy who will become my father goes to Mississippi State for two years, loses some bouts and wins more, then quits to pursue a Golden Gloves title, and when he fails at that he keeps on fighting in bars and streets, and at last he quits boxing, his nose broken so many times there is no bone left in it, only a bulb of flesh which a boy sitting in his lap will later squeeze and mash like dough. From all those bouts, the one he will describe to his son with the greatest passion is that brawl from the Black Cat Saloon, when the stranger in the white shirt, a good judge of fighters, found him worthy.

Father tried, with scant success, to make a boxer of me. Not for a career in the ring, he explained, but for defense against the roughs and rowdies who would cross my path in life. If I ran into a mean customer, I told him, I could always get off the path. No, Father said, a man never backs away. A man stands his ground and fights. This advice ran against my grain, which inclined toward quickness of wits rather than fists, yet for years I strove to become the tough guy he envisioned. Without looking for fights, I stumbled into them at every turn, in schoolyard and backyard and in the shadows of barns. Even at my most belligerent, I still tried cajolery and oratory first. Only when that failed did I dig in my heels and start swinging. I gave bruises and received them, gave and received bloody noses, leading with my left, as Father had taught me, protecting my head with forearms, keeping my thumbs outside my balled fists to avoid breaking them when I landed a punch.

Some bullies saw my feistiness as a red flag. One boy who kept 27 hounding me was Olaf Magnuson, a neighbor whose surname I would later translate with my primitive Latin as Son of Big. The name was appropriate, for Olaf was two years older and a foot taller and forty pounds heavier than I was. He pestered me, cursed me, irked and insulted me. When I stood my ground, he pounded me into it. One evening in my twelfth summer, after I had staggered home several times from these frays bloodied and bowed, Father decided it was time for serious boxing lessons. We would train for two months, he told me, then challenge Olaf Magnuson to a fight, complete with gloves and ropes and bell. This did not sound like a healthy idea to me; but Father insisted. "Do you want to keep getting pushed around," he demanded, "or are you going to lick the tar out of him?"

Every day for two months I ran, skipped rope, did chin-ups and 28 push-ups. Father hung his old punching bag from a rafter in the basement, and I flailed at it until my arms filled with sand. He wrapped an old mattress around a tree and told me to imagine Olaf Magnuson's belly as I pounded the cotton ticking. I sparred with my grizzly old man, who showed me how to jab and hook, duck and weave, how to keep my balance and work out of corners. Even though his feet had slowed, his hands were still so quick that I sometimes dropped my own gloves to watch him, dazzled. "Keep up those dukes," he warned. "Never lower your guard." For two months I trained as though I had a boxer's heart.

Father issued our challenge by way of Olaf Magnuson's father, a 29 strapping man with a voice like a roar in a barrel. "Hell yes, my boy'll fight," the elder Magnuson boomed.

On the morning appointed for our bout, Father strung rope from 30 tree to tree in the yard, fashioning a ring that was shaped like a lozenge. My mother, who had been kept in the dark about the grudge match until that morning, raised Cain for a while; failing to make us see what fools we were, disgusted with the ways of men, she drove off to buy groceries. My sister carried word through the neighborhood, and within minutes a gaggle of kids and a scattering of bemused adults pressed against the ropes.

"You're going to make that lunkhead bawl in front of the whole   31
world," Father told me in the kitchen while lacing my gloves. "You're
going to make him call for his mama. Before you're done with him, he's
going to swallow so many teeth that he'll never mess with you again."

So long as Father was talking, I believed him. I was a mean hom-   32
bre. I was bad news, one fist of iron and the other one steel. When he
finished his pep talk, however, and we stepped out into the sunshine,
and I saw the crowd buzzing against the ropes, and I spied enormous
Olaf slouching from his own kitchen door, my confidence hissed away
like water on a hot griddle. In the seconds it took me to reach the ring,
I ceased to feel like the bringer of bad news and began to feel like the
imminent victim. I danced in my corner, eyeing Olaf. His torso, hulk-
ing above jeans and clodhopper boots, made my own scrawny frame
look like a preliminary sketch for a body. I glanced down at my ropy
arms, at my twiggy legs exposed below red gym shorts, at my high-
topped basketball shoes, at the grass.

"He'll be slow," Father growled in my ear, "slow and clumsy. Keep   33
moving. Bob and weave. Give him that left jab, watch for an opening,
and then *bam*, unload with the right."

Not trusting my voice, I nodded, and kept shuffling my sneakers to   34
hide the shivers.

Father put his palms to my cheeks and drew my face close to his   35
and looked hard at me. Above that smushed, boneless nose, his brown
eyes were as dark and shiny as those of a deer. "You okay, big guy?" he
asked. "You ready for this?" I nodded again. "Then go get him," he
said, turning me around and giving me a light shove toward the center
of the ring.

I met Olaf there for instructions from the referee, a welder who   36
lived down the road from us, a wiry man with scorched forearms who
had just fixed our trailer hitch. I lifted my eye reluctantly from Olaf's
boots, along the trunks of his jean-clad legs, over the expanse of
brawny chest and palooka jaw to his ice-blue eyes. They seemed less
angry than amused.

A cowbell clattered. Olaf and I touched gloves, backed apart and   37
lifted our mitts. The crowd sizzled against the ropes. Blood banged in
my ears, yet I could hear Father yelling. I hear him still. And in memory I follow his advice. I bob, I weave, I guard my face with curled
gloves, I feint and jab within the roped diamond, I begin to believe in
myself, I circle my lummoxy rival and pepper him with punches, I feel
a grin rising to my lips, and then Olaf tires of the game and rears back
and knocks me flat. He also knocks me out. He also breaks my nose,
which will remain crooked forever after.

That ended my boxing career. Olaf quit bullying me, perhaps be-   38
cause my blackout had given him a scare, perhaps because he had
proved whatever he needed to prove. What I had shown my father

was less clear. He may have seen weakness, may have seen a doomed and reckless bravery, may have seen a clown's pratfall. In any case, he never again urged me to clear the path with my fists.

And I have not offered boxing lessons to my son. Instead, I offered him the story of my defeat. When Jesse would still fit in my lap, I cuddled him there and told him of my fight with Olaf, and he ran his delicate finger against the crook in my nose, as I had fingered the boneless pulp of Father's nose. I told Jesse about learning to play catch, the ball passing back and forth like a thread between my father and me, stitching us together. I told him about the one time one of my pitches sailed over Father's head and shattered the windshield of our 1956 Ford, a car just three days old, and Father only shook his head and said, "Shoot, boy, you get that fastball down, and the batters won't see a thing but smoke." And I told Jesse about sitting on a feather tick in a Mississippi farmhouse, wedged between my father and grandfather, shaking with their excitement while before us on a tiny black-and-white television two boxers slammed and hugged each other. Cradling my boy, I felt how difficult it is for men to embrace without the liquor of violence, the tonic of pain.

Why do we play these games so avidly? All sports, viewed dispassionately, are dumb. The rules are arbitrary, the behaviors absurd. For boxing and running, perhaps, you could figure out evolutionary advantages. But what earthly use is it to become expert at swatting a ball with a length of wood or at lugging an inflated pigskin through a mob? Freudians might say that in playing with balls we men are simply toying with the prize portion of our anatomies. Darwinians might claim that we are competing for the attention of females, like so many preening peacocks or head-butting rams. Physicians might attribute the sporting frenzy to testosterone, economists might point to our dreams of professional paychecks, feminists might appeal to our machismo, philosophers to our fear of death.

No doubt all of those explanations, like buckets put out in the rain, catch some of the truth. But none of them catches all of the truth. None of them explains, for example, what moves a boy to bang a rubber ball against a wall for hours, for entire summers, as my father did in his youth, as I did in mine, as Jesse still does. That boy, throwing and catching in the lee of garage or barn, dwells for a time wholly in his body, and that is reward enough. He aims the ball at a knothole, at a crack, then leaps to snag the rebound, mastering a skill, working himself into a trance. How different is his rapture from the dancing and drumming of a young brave? How different is his solitude from that of any boy seeking visions?

The less use we have for our bodies, the more we need reminding that the body possesses its own way of knowing. To steal a line from

Pascal: The body has its reasons that reason knows nothing of. Although we struggle lifelong to dwell in the flesh without rancor, without division between act and desire, we succeed only for moments at a time. We treasure whatever brings us those moments, whether it be playing cello or playing pool, making love or making baskets, kneading bread or nursing a baby or kicking a ball. Whoever teaches us an art or skill, whoever shows us a path to momentary wholeness, deserves our love.

I am conscious of my father's example whenever I teach a game to   43
my son. Demonstrating a stroke in tennis or golf, I amplify my gestures, like a ham actor playing to the balcony. My pleasure in the part is increased by the knowledge that others, and especially Father, have played it before me. What I know about hitting a curve or shooting a hook shot or throwing a left jab, I know less by words than by feel. When I take Jesse's hand and curl his fingers over the baseball's red stitches, explaining how to make it deviously spin, I feel my father's hands slip over mine like gloves. Move like so, like so. I feel the same ghostly guidance when I hammer nails or fix a faucet or pluck a banjo. Working on the house or garden or car, I find myself wearing more than my father's hands, find myself clad entirely in his skin.

One blistering afternoon when I was a year younger than Jesse is   44
now, a flyball arched toward me in center field. I ran under it, lifted my face and glove, and lost the ball in the sun. The ball found me, however, crashing into my eye. In the split second before blacking out I saw nothing but light. We need not go hunting pain, for pain will find us. It hurts me more to see Jesse ache than to break one of my own bones. I cry out as the ground ball bangs into his throat. I wince as he comes down crookedly with a rebound and turns his ankle. I wish to spare him injury as I wish to spare him defeat, but I could not do so even if I had never lobbed him that first fat pitch.

As Jesse nears thirteen, his estimate of my knowledge and my   45
power declines rapidly. If I were a potter, say, or a carpenter, my skills would outreach his for decades to come. But where speed and stamina are the essence, a father in his forties will be overtaken by a son in his teens. Training for soccer, Jesse carries a stopwatch as he jogs around the park. I am not training for anything, only knocking rust from my joints and beguiling my heart, but I run along with him, puffing to keep up. I know that his times will keep going down, while I will never run faster than I do now. This is as it should be, for his turn has come. Slow as I am, and doomed to be slower, I relish his company.

In the game of catch, this dialogue of throw and grab we have   46
been carrying on since he was old enough to crawl, Jesse has finally begun to put questions that I cannot answer. I know the answers; I can see how my back should twist, my legs should pump; but legs and back will no longer match my vision. This faltering is the condition of our lives, of course, a condition that will grow more acute with each passing year. I mean to live the present year before rushing off to any fu-

ture ones. I mean to keep playing games with my son, so long as flesh will permit, as my father played games with me well past his own physical prime. Now that sports have begun to give me lessons in mortality, I realize they have also been giving me, all the while, lessons in immortality. These games, these contests, these grunting conversations of body to body, father to son, are not substitutes for some other way of being alive. They are the sweet and sweaty thing itself.

BERNARD COOPER

A Clack of Tiny Sparks:
Remembrances of a Gay Boyhood

Bernard Cooper (1951–) was born in Los Angeles and educated at the California Institute of the Arts, where he received both B.F.A. and M.F.A. degrees. He has been an instructor in creative writing at the Otis School of Art and Design in Los Angeles and at the Southern California Institute of Architecture. His first book, *Maps to Anywhere* (1990), is a collection of autobiographical essays, many of which explore his relationship with his father. In 1993 he published a novel, *A Year of Rhymes*, which, while largely about the sexual awakening of a teenager in the 1960s, is also somewhat autobiographical in that Cooper draws on his experience of coming to terms with the deaths of his three brothers. Recently Cooper has published another memoir, *Truth Serum* (1996), and he continues to publish essays and poems, most notably in *Grand Street, Harper's, Yale Review,* and *Kenyon Review.*

"A Clack of Tiny Sparks" was published in *Harper's* in January 1991 and appears in *Truth Serum* under the title "Where to Begin." Although the situation described is candidly realistic and the sense of humor bittersweet, the way the essay examines irrational responses to difference compares with Lois Gould's fairy tale, "X".

Theresa Sanchez sat behind me in ninth-grade algebra. When Mr. Hubbley faced the blackboard, I'd turn around to see what she was reading; each week a new book was wedged inside her copy of *Today's Equations.* The deception worked; from Mr. Hubbley's point of view, Theresa was engrossed in the value of *x*, but I knew otherwise. One week she perused *The Wisdom of the Orient,* and I could tell from Theresa's contemplative expression that the book contained exotic thoughts, guidelines handed down from high. Another week it was a paperback novel whose title, *Let Me Live My Life,* appeared in bold print atop every page, and whose cover, a gauzy photograph of a woman biting a strand of pearls, head thrown back in an attitude of ecstasy, confirmed my suspicion that Theresa Sanchez was mature beyond her years. She was the tallest girl in school. Her bouffant hairdo, streaked with blond, was higher than the flaccid bouffants of other girls. Her smooth skin, plucked eyebrows, and painted fingernails suggested hours of pampering, a worldly and sensual vanity that placed her within the domain of adults. Smiling dimly, steeped in daydreams, Theresa moved through the crowded halls with a languid, self-satisfied indifference to those around her. "You are merely children," her posture seemed to say. "I can't be bothered." The week Theresa hid *101 Ways to Cook Hamburger* behind her algebra book, I could stand it no longer and, after the bell rang, ventured a question.

"Because I'm having a dinner party," said Theresa. "Just a couple   2
of intimate friends."

No fourteen-year-old I knew had ever given a dinner party, let   3
alone used the word "intimate" in conversation. "Don't you have a mother?" I asked.

Theresa sighed a weary sigh, suffered my strange inquiry. "Don't   4
be so naive," she said. "Everyone has a mother." She waved her hand to indicate the brick school buildings outside the window. "A higher education should have taught you that." Theresa draped an angora sweater over her shoulders, scooped her books from the graffiti-covered desk, and just as she was about to walk away, she turned and asked me, "Are you a fag?"

There wasn't the slightest hint of rancor or condescension in her   5
voice. The tone was direct, casual. Still I was stunned, giving a sidelong glance to make sure no one had heard. "No," I said. Blurted really, with too much defensiveness, too much transparent fear in my response. Octaves lower than usual, I tried a "Why?"

Theresa shrugged. "Oh, I don't know. I have lots of friends who   6
are fags. You remind me of them." Seeing me bristle, Theresa added, "It was just a guess." I watched her erect, angora back as she sauntered out the classroom door.

She had made an incisive and timely guess. Only days before, I'd   7
invited Grady Rogers to my house after school to go swimming. The instant Grady shot from the pool, shaking water from his orange hair, freckled shoulders shining, my attraction to members of my own sex became a matter I could no longer suppress or rationalize. Sturdy and boisterous and gap-toothed, Grady was an inveterate backslapper, a formidable arm wrestler, a wizard at basketball. Grady was a boy at home in his body.

My body was a marvel I hadn't gotten used to; my arms and legs   8
would sometimes act of their own accord, knocking over a glass at dinner or flinching at an oncoming pitch. I was never singled out as a sissy, but I could have been just as easily as Bobby Keagan, a gentle, intelligent, and introverted boy reviled by my classmates. And although I had always been aware of a tacit rapport with Bobby, a suspicion that

I might find with him a rich friendship, I stayed away. Instead, I emulated Grady in the belief that being seen with him, being like him, would somehow vanquish my self-doubt, would make me normal by association.

Apart from his athletic prowess, Grady had been gifted with all the   9
trappings of what I imagined to be a charmed life: a fastidious, aproned mother who radiated calm, maternal concern; a ruddy, stoic father with a knack for home repairs. Even the Rogerses' small suburban house in Hollywood, with its spindly Colonial furniture and chintz curtains, was a testament to normalcy.

Grady and his family bore little resemblance to my clan of Eastern   10
European Jews, a dark and vociferous people who ate with abandon— matzo and halvah and gefilte fish; foods the goyim[1] couldn't pronounce—who cajoled one another during endless games of canasta, making the simplest remark about the weather into a lengthy philosophical discourse on the sun and the seasons and the passage of time. My mother was a chain-smoker, a dervish in a frowsy housedress. She showed her love in the most peculiar and obsessive ways, like spending hours extracting every seed from a watermelon before she served it in perfectly bite-sized, geometric pieces. Preoccupied and perpetually frantic, my mother succumbed to bouts of absentmindedness so profound she'd forget what she was saying midsentence, smile and blush and walk away. A divorce attorney, my father wore roomy, iridescent suits, and the intricacies, the deceits inherent in his profession, had the effect of making him forever tense and vigilant. He was "all wound up," as my mother put it. But when he relaxed, his laughter was explosive, his disposition prankish: "Walk this way," a waitress would say, leading us to our table, and my father would mimic the way she walked, arms akimbo, hips liquid, while my mother and I were wracked with laughter. Buoyant or brooding, my parents' moods were unpredictable, and in a household fraught with extravagant emotion it was odd and awful to keep my longing secret.

One day I made the mistake of asking my mother what a "fag"   11
was. I knew exactly what Theresa had meant but hoped against hope it was not what I thought; maybe "fag" was some French word, a harmless term like "naive." My mother turned from the stove, flew at me, and grabbed me by the shoulders. "Did someone call you that?" she cried.

"Not me," I said. "Bobby Keagan."   12

"Oh," she said, loosening her grip. She was visibly relieved. And   13
didn't answer. The answer was unthinkable.

For weeks after, I shook with the reverberations from that after   14
noon in the kitchen with my mother, pained by the memory of her

---

1. goyim: Gentiles.

shocked expression and, most of all, her silence. My longing was wrong in the eyes of my mother, whose hazel eyes were the eyes of the world, and if that longing continued unchecked, the unwieldy shape of my fate would be cast, and I'd be subjected to a lifetime of scorn.

During the remainder of the semester, I became the scientist of my own desire, plotting ways to change my yearning for boys into a yearning for girls. I had enough evidence to believe that any habit, regardless of how compulsive, how deeply ingrained, could be broken once and for all: The plastic cigarette my mother purchased at the Thrifty pharmacy—one end was red to approximate an ember, the other tan like a filtered tip—was designed to wean her from the real thing. To change a behavior required self-analysis, cold resolve, and the substitution of one thing for another: plastic, say, for tobacco. Could I also find a substitute for Grady? What I needed to do, I figured, was kiss a girl and learn to like it.

This conclusion was affirmed one Sunday morning when my father, seeing me wrinkle my nose at the pink slabs of lox he layered on a bagel, tried to convince me of its salty appeal. "You should try some," he said. "You don't know what you're missing."

"It's loaded with protein," added my mother, slapping a platter of sliced onions onto the dinette table. She hovered above us, cinching her housedress, eyes wet from onion fumes, the mock cigarette dangling from her lips.

My father sat there chomping with gusto, emitting a couple of hearty grunts to dramatize his satisfaction. And still I was not convinced. After a loud and labored swallow, he told me I may not be fond of lox today, but sooner or later I'd learn to like it. One's tastes, he assured me, are destined to change.

"Live," shouted my mother over the rumble of the Mixmaster. "Expand your horizons. Try new things." And the room grew fragrant with the batter of a spice cake.

The opportunity to put their advice into practice, and try out my plan to adapt to girls, came the following week when Debbie Coburn, a member of Mr. Hubbley's algebra class, invited me to a party. She cornered me in the hall, furtive as a spy, telling me her parents would be gone for the evening and slipping into my palm a wrinkled sheet of notebook paper. On it were her address and telephone number, the lavender ink in a tidy cursive. "Wear cologne," she advised, wary eyes darting back and forth. "It's a make-out party. Anything can happen."

The Santa Ana wind blew relentlessly the night of Debbie's party, careening down the slopes of the Hollywood hills, shaking the road signs and stoplights in its path. As I walked down Beachwood Avenue, trees thrashed, surrendered their leaves, and carob pods bombarded the pavement. The sky was a deep but luminous blue, the air hot, abrasive, electric. I had to squint in order to check the number of the

Coburns' apartment, a three-story building with glitter embedded in its stucco walls. Above the honeycombed balconies was a sign that read BEACHWOOD TERRACE in lavender script resembling Debbie's.

From down the hall, I could hear the plaintive strains of Little An- 22 thony's[2] "I Think I'm Going Out of My Head." Debbie answered the door bedecked in an Empire dress, the bodice blue and orange polka dots, the rest a sheath of black and white stripes. "Op art,"[3] proclaimed Debbie. She turned in a circle, then proudly announced that she'd rolled her hair in orange juice cans. She patted the huge unmoving curls and dragged me inside. Reflections from the swimming pool in the courtyard, its surface ruffled by wind, shuddered over the ceiling and walls. A dozen of my classmates were seated on the sofa or huddled together in corners, their whispers full of excited imminence, their bodies barely discernible in the dim light. Drapes flanking the sliding glass doors bowed out with every gust of wind, and it seemed that the room might lurch from its foundations and sail with its cargo of silhouettes into the hot October night.

Grady was the last to arrive. He tossed a six-pack of beer into Deb- 23 bie's arms, barreled toward me, and slapped my back. His hair was slicked back with Vitalis, lacquered furrows left by the comb. The wind hadn't shifted a single hair. "Ya ready?" he asked, flashing the gap between his front teeth and leering into the darkened room. "You bet," I lied.

Once the beers had been passed around, Debbie provoked every- 24 one's attention by flicking on the overhead light. "Okay," she called. "Find a partner." This was the blunt command of a hostess determined to have her guests aroused in an orderly fashion. Everyone blinked, shuffled about, and grabbed a member of the opposite sex. Sheila Garabedian landed beside me—entirely at random, though I wanted to believe she was driven by passion—her timid smile giving way to plain fear as the light went out. Nothing for a moment but the heave of the wind and the distant banter of dogs. I caught a whiff of Sheila's perfume, tangy and sweet as Hawaiian Punch. I probed her face with my own, grazing the small scallop of an ear, a velvety temple, and though Sheila's trembling made me want to stop, I persisted with my mission until I found her lips, tightly sealed as a private letter. I held my mouth over hers and gathered her shoulders closer, resigned to the possibility that, no matter how long we stood there, Sheila would be too scared to kiss me back. Still, she exhaled through her nose, and I listened to the squeak of every breath as though it were a sigh of inordinate pleasure. Diving within myself, I monitored my heartbeat and respiration, trying to will stimulation into being, and all the while an image intruded, an

2. Little Anthony: soul singer during the 1950s and 1960s.
3. Op art: optical art, mid-20th century geometric art that deals with optical illusions.

image of Grady erupting from our pool, rivulets of water sliding down his chest. "Change," shouted Debbie, switching on the light. Sheila thanked me, pulled away, and continued her routine of gracious terror with every boy throughout the evening. It didn't matter whom I held—Margaret Sims, Betty Vernon, Elizabeth Lee—my experiment was a failure; I continued to picture Grady's wet chest, and Debbie would bellow "change" with such fervor, it could have been my own voice, my own incessant reprimand.

Our hostess commandeered the light switch for nearly half an hour. Whenever the light came on, I watched Grady pivot his head toward the newest prospect, his eyebrows arched in expectation, his neck blooming with hickeys, his hair, at last, in disarray. All that shuffling across the carpet charged everyone's arms and lips with static, and eventually, between low moans and soft osculations, I could hear the clack of tiny sparks and see them flare here and there in the dark like meager, short-lived stars.

I saw Theresa, sultry and aloof as ever, read three more books— *North American Reptiles, Bonjour Tristesse,* and *MGM: A Pictorial History—* before she vanished early in December. Rumors of her fate abounded. Debbie Coburn swore that Theresa had been "knocked up" by an older man, a traffic cop, she thought, or a grocer. Nearly quivering with relish, Debbie told me and Grady about the home for unwed mothers in the San Fernando Valley, a compound teeming with pregnant girls who had nothing to do but touch their stomachs and contemplate their mistake. Even Bobby Keagan, who took Theresa's place behind me in algebra, had a theory regarding her disappearance colored by his own wish for escape; he imagined that Theresa, disillusioned with society, booked passage to a tropical island, there to live out the rest of her days without restrictions or ridicule. "No wonder she flunked out of school," I overheard Mr. Hubbley tell a fellow teacher one afternoon. "Her head was always in a book."

Along with Theresa went my secret, or at least the dread that she might divulge it, and I felt, for a while, exempt from suspicion. I was, however, to run across Theresa one last time. It happened during a period of torrential rain that, according to reports on the six o'clock news, washed houses from the hillsides and flooded the downtown streets. The halls of Joseph Le Conte Junior High were festooned with Christmas decorations: crepe-paper garlands, wreaths studded with plastic berries, and one requisite Star of David twirling above the attendance desk. In Arts and Crafts, our teacher, Gerald (he was the only teacher who allowed us—*required* us— to call him by his first name), handed out blocks of balsa wood and instructed us to carve them into bugs. We would paint eyes and antennae with tempera and hang them on a Christmas tree he'd made the previous night. "Voilà," he crooned, unveiling his creation from a burlap sack. Before us sat a tortured scrub, a wardrobe-worth of wire hangers that were bent like branches and soldered together. Gerald credited his inspiration to a Charles Addams[4] cartoon he'd seen in which Morticia, grimly preparing for the holidays, hangs vampire bats on a withered pine. "All that red and green," said Gerald. "So predictable. So *boring.*"

As I chiseled a beetle and listened to rain pummel the earth, Gerald handed me an envelope and asked me to take it to Mr. Kendrick, the drama teacher. I would have thought nothing of his request if I hadn't seen Theresa on my way down the hall. She was cleaning out her locker, blithely dropping the sum of its contents—pens and textbooks and mimeographs—into a trash can. "Have a nice life," she sang as I passed. I mustered the courage to ask her what had happened. We stood alone in the silent hall, the reflections of wreaths and garlands submerged in brown linoleum.

"I transferred to another school. They don't have grades or bells, and you get to study whatever you want." Theresa was quick to sense my incredulity. "Honest," she said. "The school is progressive." She gazed into a glass cabinet that held the trophies of track meets and intramural spelling bees. "God," she sighed, "this place is so . . . barbaric." I was still trying to decide whether or not to believe her story when she asked me where I was headed. "Dear," she said, her exclamation pooling in the silence, "that's no ordinary note, if you catch my drift." The envelope was blank and white; I looked up at Theresa, baffled. "Don't be so naive," she muttered, tossing an empty bottle of nail polish into the trash can. It struck bottom with a resolute thud. "Well," she said, closing her locker and breathing deeply, "bon voyage." Theresa swept through the double doors and in seconds her figure was obscured by rain.

As I walked toward Mr. Kendrick's room, I could feel Theresa's insinuation burrow in. I stood for a moment and watched Mr. Kendrick through the pane in the door. He paced intently in front of the class, handsome in his shirt and tie, reading from a thick book. Chalked on the blackboard behind him was THE ODYSSEY BY HOMER. I have no recollection of how Mr. Kendrick reacted to the note, whether he accepted it with pleasure or embarrassment, slipped it into his desk drawer or the pocket of his shirt. I have scavenged that day in retrospect, trying to see Mr. Kendrick's expression, wondering if he acknowledged me in any way as his liaison. All I recall is the sight of his mime through a pane of glass, a lone man mouthing an epic, his gestures ardent in empty air.

Had I delivered a declaration of love? I was haunted by the need to know. In fantasy, a kettle shot steam, the glue released its grip, and I read the letter with impunity. But how would such a letter begin? Did

4. Charles Addams: 20th-century cartoonist whose ghoulish work inspired the television series *The Addams Family.*

the common endearments apply? This was a message between two
men, a message for which I had no precedent, and when I tried to en-
vision the contents, apart from a hasty, impassioned scrawl, my imagination faltered.

Once or twice I witnessed Gerald and Mr. Kendrick walk together   32
into the faculty lounge or say hello at the water fountain, but there
was nothing especially clandestine or flirtatious in their manner. Besides, no matter how acute my scrutiny, I wasn't sure, short of a kiss,
exactly what to look for—what semaphore of gesture, what encoded
word. I suspected there were signs, covert signs that would give them
away, just as I'd unwittingly given myself away to Theresa.

In the school library, a *Webster's* unabridged dictionary lay on a   33
wooden podium, and I padded toward it with apprehension; along
with clues to the bond between my teachers, I risked discovering information that might incriminate me as well. I had decided to consult
the dictionary during lunch period, when most of the students would
be on the playground. I clutched my notebook, moving in such a way
as to appear both studious and nonchalant, actually believing that, unless I took precautions, someone would see me and guess what I was
up to. The closer I came to the podium, the more obvious, I thought,
was my endeavor; I felt like the model of The Visible Man in our science class, my heart's undulations, my overwrought nerves legible
through transparent skin. A couple of kids riffled through the card catalogue. The librarian, a skinny woman whose perpetual whisper and
rubber-soled shoes caused her to drift through the room like a phantom, didn't seem to register my presence. Though I'd looked up dozens
of words before, the pages felt strange beneath my fingers. *Homer* was
the first word I saw. *Hominid. Homogenize.* I feigned interest and skirted
other words before I found the word I was after. Under the heading HO
· MO · SEX · U · AL was the terse definition: *adj. Pertaining to, characteristic
of, or exhibiting homosexuality.—n. A homosexual person.* I read the definition again and again, hoping the words would yield more than they
could. I shut the dictionary, swallowed hard, and, none the wiser, hurried away.

As for Gerald and Mr. Kendrick, I never discovered evidence to   34
prove or disprove Theresa's claim. By the following summer, however,
I had overheard from my peers a confounding amount about homosexuals: They wore green on Thursday, couldn't whistle, hypnotized
boys with a piercing glance. To this lore, Grady added a surefire test to
ferret them out.

"A test?" I said.   35

"You ask a guy to look at his fingernails, and if he looks at them   36
like this"—Grady closed his fingers into a fist and examined his nails
with manly detachment—"then he's okay. But if he does this"—he
held out his hands at arm's length, splayed his fingers, and coyly

cocked his head—"you'd better watch out." Once he'd completed his demonstration, Grady peeled off his shirt and plunged into our pool. I dove in after. It was early June, the sky immense, glassy, placid. My father was cooking spareribs on the barbecue, an artist with a basting brush. His apron bore the caricature of a frazzled French chef. Mother curled on a chaise longue, plumes of smoke wafting from her nostrils. In a stupor of contentment she took another drag, closed her eyes, and arched her face toward the sun.

Grady dog-paddled through the deep end, spouting a fountain of 37 chlorinated water. Despite shame and confusion, my longing for him hadn't diminished; it continued to thrive without air and light, like a luminous fish in the dregs of the sea. In the name of play, I swam up behind him, encircled his shoulders, astonished by his taut flesh. The two of us flailed, pretended to drown. Beneath the heavy press of water, Grady's orange hair wavered, a flame that couldn't be doused.

I've lived with a man for seven years. Some nights, when I'm half- 38 asleep and the room is suffused with blue light, I reach out to touch the expanse of his back, and it seems as if my fingers sink into his skin, and I feel the pleasure a diver feels the instant he enters a body of water.

I have few regrets. But one is that I hadn't said to Theresa, "Of 39 course I'm a fag." Maybe I'd have met her friends. Or become friends with her. Imagine the meals we might have concocted: hamburger Stroganoff, Swedish meatballs in a sweet translucent sauce, steaming slabs of Salisbury steak.

NOEL PERRIN

The Androgynous Man

[handwritten annotation: having the characteristics of both male and female nature ? strong lines together]

Noel Perrin (1927–) teaches English and Environmental Studies at Dartmouth College, farms, and write essays, which are collected in *A Passport Secretly Green* (1961), *First Person Rural* (1978), *Second Person Rural* (1980), *Third Person Rural* (1983), and *Last Person Rural* (1991). He also takes a lively interest in literature that lies somewhat off the beaten path. His *Dr. Bowdler's Legacy* (1970) is a history of expurgated books, and *A Reader's Delight* (1988) contains essays on meritorious works so unfamiliar that many of them are out of print. *A Child's Delight* (1997) contains similar essays on underappreciated children's books. Recently Perrin has focused his attention on the environment. In response to a student who made note of his driving to work in a "gas-guzzling pickup," Perrin bought an electric car; a book resulted,

Solo: Life with an Electric Car (1993), which has been the subject of numerous reviews in environmental, literary, and automobile magazines.

"The Androgynous Man" appeared in the "About Men" column of *The New York Times Magazine* on February 5, 1984. Like Michael Norman's "Against Androgyny" and Deborah Tannen's "Every Choice a Woman Makes," it demonstrates the success of the short personal essay in making a direct statement about gender roles.

The summer I was 16, I took a train from New York to Steamboat Springs, Colo., where I was going to be assistant horse wrangler at a camp. The trip took three days, and since I was much too shy to talk to strangers, I had quite a lot of time for reading. I read all of *Gone With the Wind.* I read all the interesting articles in a couple of magazines I had, and then I went back and read all the dull stuff. I also took all the quizzes, a thing of which magazines were even fuller then than now.

The one that held my undivided attention was called "How Masculine/Feminine Are You?" It consisted of a large number of inkblots. The reader was supposed to decide which of four objects each blot most resembled. The choices might be a cloud, a steam engine, a caterpillar and a sofa.

When I finished the test, I was shocked to find that I was barely masculine at all. On a scale of 1 to 10, I was about 1.2. Me, the horse wrangler? (And not just wrangler, either. That summer, I had to skin a couple of horses that died—the camp owner wanted the hides.)

The results of that test were so terrifying to me that for the first time in my life I did a piece of original analysis. Having unlimited time on the train, I looked at the "masculine" answers over and over, trying to find what it was that distinguished real men from people like me—and eventually I discovered two very simple patterns. It was "masculine" to think the blots looked like man-made objects, and "feminine" to think they looked like natural objects. It was masculine to think they looked like things capable of causing harm, and feminine to think of innocent things.

Even at 16, I had the sense to see that the compilers of the test were using rather limited criteria—maleness and femaleness are both more complicated than *that*—and I breathed a huge sigh of relief. I wasn't necessarily a wimp, after all.

That the test did reveal something other than the superficiality of its makers I realized only many years later. What it revealed was that there is a large class of men and women both, to which I belong, who are essentially androgynous. That doesn't mean we're gay, or low in the appropriate hormones, or uncomfortable performing the jobs traditionally assigned our sexes. (A few years after that summer, I was leading troops in combat and, unfashionable as it now is to admit this, having a very good time. War is exciting. What a pity the 20th century went and spoiled it with high-tech weapons.)

What it does mean to be spiritually androgynous is a kind of free- 7
dom. Men who are all-male, or he-man, or 100 percent red-blooded
Americans, have a little biological set that causes them to be attracted
to physical power, and probably also to dominance. Maybe even to
watching football. I don't say this to criticize them. Completely masculine men are quite often wonderful people: good husbands, good
(though sometimes overwhelming) fathers, good members of society.
Furthermore, they are often so unself-consciously at ease in the world
that other men seek to imitate them. They just aren't as free as us androgynes. They pretty nearly have to be what they are; we have a
range of choices open.

The sad part is that many of us never discover that. Men who are 8
not 100 percent red-blooded Americans—say, those who are only 75
percent red-blooded—often fail to notice their freedom. They are too
busy trying to copy the he-men ever to realize that men, like women,
come in a wide variety of acceptable types. Why this frantic imitation?
My answer is mere speculation, but not casual. I have speculated on
this for a long time.

Partly they're just envious of the he-man's unconscious ease. 9
Mostly they're terrified of finding that there may be something wrong
with them deep down, some weakness at the heart. To avoid discovering that, they spend their lives acting out the role that the he-man naturally lives. Sad.

One thing that men owe to the women's movement is that this kind 10
of failure is less common than it used to be. In releasing themselves
from the single ideal of the dependent woman, women have more or
less incidentally released a lot of men from the single ideal of the dominant male. The one mistake the feminists have made, I think, is in supposing that *all* men need this release, or that the world would be a
better place if all men achieved it. It wouldn't. It would just be duller.

So far I have been pretty vague about just what the freedom of the 11
androgynous man is. Obviously it varies with the case. In the case I
know best, my own, I can be quite specific. It has freed me most as a
parent. I am, among other things, a fairly good natural mother. I like
the nurturing role. It makes me feel good to see a child eat—and it
turns me to mush to see a 4-year-old holding a glass with both small
hands, in order to drink. I even enjoyed sewing patches on the knees
of my daughter Amy's Dr. Dentons when she was at the crawling
stage. All that pleasure I would have lost if I had made myself stick to
the notion of the paternal role that I started with.

Or take a smaller and rather ridiculous example. I feel free to kiss 12
cats. Until recently it never occurred to me that I would want to,
though my daughters have been doing it all their lives. But my elder
daughter is now 22, and in London. Of course, I get to look after her
cat while she is gone. He's a big, handsome farm cat named Petrushka,

very unsentimental, though used from kittenhood to being kissed on the top of the head by Elizabeth. I've gotten very fond of him (he's the adventurous kind of cat who likes to climb hills with you), and one night I simply felt like kissing him on the top of the head, and did. Why did no one tell me sooner how silky cat fur is?

Then there's my relation to cars. I am completely unembarrassed   13
by my inability to diagnose even minor problems in whatever object I happen to be driving, and don't have to make some insider's remark to mechanics to try to establish that I, too, am a "Man With His Machine."

The same ease extends to household maintenance, I do it, of   14
course. Service people are expensive. But for the last decade my house had functioned better than it used to because I've had the aid of a volume called "Home Repairs Any Woman Can Do," which is pitched just right for people at my technical level. As a youth, I'd as soon have touched such a book as I would have become a transvestite. Even though common sense says there is really nothing sexual whatsoever about fixing sinks.

Or take public emotion. All my life I have easily been moved by   15
certain kinds of voices. The actress Siobhan McKenna's, to take a notable case. Give her an emotional scene in a play, and within 10 words my eyes are full of tears. In boyhood, my great dread was that someone might notice. I struggled manfully, you might say, to suppress this weakness. Now, of course, I don't see it as a weakness at all, but as a kind of fulfillment. I even suspect that the true he-men feel the same way, or one kind of them does, at least, and it's only the poor imitators who have to struggle to repress themselves.

Let me come back to the inkblots, with their assumption that mas-   16
culine equates with machinery and science, and feminine with art and nature. I have no idea whether the right pronoun for God is He, She, or It. But this I'm pretty sure of. If God could somehow be induced to take that test, God would not come out macho, and not feminismo, either, but right in the middle. Fellow androgynes, it's a nice thought.

MICHAEL NORMAN

Against Androgyny

Michael Norman (1947–), an ex-Marine and a veteran of the Vietnam War, has been on the metropolitan staff of *The New York Times* and has done considerable free-lance writing, much of it published in *The New York Times Magazine*. He has also worked as a reporter-producer for public television and is the co-author (with Beth Scott) of a series of spooky tales from across the country, including *Haunted*

Heartland (1985) and *Haunted America* (1994). *These Good Men: Friendship Forged from War* (1990), his book about the comradeship of soldiers, stems directly from his experience in Vietnam.

"Against Androgyny" appeared in *The New York Times Magazine*
on December 11, 1994. The essay is a response not only to the issues
Noel Perrin raises in "The Androgynous Man," but also to more recent displays of androgyny in our society. In its decided stance on the
difference between genders, it is also a useful companion to Lois
Gould's "X."

A TALE OUT OF SCHOOL. The summer had been miserable. We had
moved and renovated. We were broke, spent and at each other's
throats. One night the master bedroom filled with storm clouds; I was
sitting on the edge of the chaise, aimlessly browsing a book, when they
broke. I don't remember what was said, but the next thing I knew, she
had knocked the book from my hand and was pummeling me. She
yelled, I yelled, we bickered, back and forth, for hours. Later we with-
drew to the far perimeters of the bed, alone and bitter and as far apart
as we've been. And then, suddenly, I understood: even in our most intimate moments, we were aliens, not for want of tenderness or ap-
petite, not for lack of understanding or a will to be one, but because
she was a woman and I was a man, and nothing—not 22 years of taking each other's measure, not even our boys, our unassailable alliance
of blood—could bridge that biological gap.

AN IDEA—NOT MINE. Men should be more like women, women
should be more like men. Androgyny is the goal, the perfect paradigm
for social equity: more freedom and opportunity for her, more insight
and humanity for him. The sexes should be desexed, the genders made
generic. And there is nothing in nature to argue otherwise: XX can be
made to mimic XY; give a female rat the right toy and she's likely to develop more of the neuronal nexuses of a male. The time has arrived to
liquidate the labels, to smash the stereotypes: pin a barrette on that
Tom Sawyer of a boy, then hand his sister Becky a broadsword.

A MOVIE. Conan is with child, the Terminator has come to term.
Arnold Schwarzenegger, in other words, is pregnant. In his new film,
"Junior," the well-ligatured protagonist plays a research scientist who
decides to carry a bit of research for nine months. Along the way, he
changes in his physiognomy, in his attitudes, in his behavior. At one
point, his research partner tries to convince him to abort his baby, in
effect arguing that the difference between the sexes is a difference to
be devoutly preserved:

"You're a guy, Alex! This is totally against the natural order! Guys
don't have babies! We leave that to the women! It's part of the beauty
of being a guy."

But the Terminator is determined to have it his way, to have it
both ways. "If you could feel for one minute the sense of absolute joy

and <u>connection that carrying your baby brings</u>," he says, so empathetically, "you would understand."

A QUESTION. Is biology really destiny? James Baldwin, echoing Virginia Woolf, echoing Coleridge, says we have within us "<u>the spiritual resources of both sexes</u>," but "the idea of <u>one's sexuality can only with great violence be</u> divorced or <u>distanced from the idea of the self</u>." In other words, I can, through the force of my imagination, draw on the woman in me, but I will always be—in my mind's eye and in my metaphysics—a man. And there's not a blessed thing wrong with that. Nothing. I don't want to be the woman who knocked the book from my hand.

A PAGE FROM MY NOTEBOOK. Writing in the journal *Society,* the associate dean of Rutgers University, David Popenoe, calls Sweden "probably the word's most androgynous society" because more than anywhere else, <u>men there involve themselves with raising their children.</u> In many cases they are as "<u>domestic</u>" as their wives. Yet this New Age domesticity has a dark side—at least in Sweden. Marriage counselors there told Professor Popenoe that in three-quarters of the couples they see, <u>it is the wife, not the husband,</u> who has <u>become disaffected in the marriage.</u> Why? In the age of androgyny, she has "<u>simply become bored with her husband and has lost sexual interest.</u>"

A FEMINIST'S CAVEAT. In "Writing a Woman's Life," Carolyn G. Heilbrun introduces us to the work of the late British writer Winifred Holtby, a sometimes-feminist essayist who makes allowances for human nature, then takes those allowances and celebrates them. "We are still greatly <u>ignorant of our own natures,</u>" she wrote. "We do not know how much of what we usually describe as 'feminine characteristics' are really 'masculine,' and how much 'masculinity' is common to both sexes. I think the real object behind our demand is not to reduce all men and women to the same dull pattern. It is rather to <u>release their richness of variety.</u>"

Richness of variety—there's a phrase sure to rankle all those culturally correct cooks stirring their sexless stews.

A BIG JOKE. The idea of Arnold Schwarzenegger's magnificent shell being reshaped from within is a biological scandal—wicked, ironic, in the end <u>good farce</u>. The film's simple conceit—a man with child—is funny because it is absurd, but, as Baldwin might have argued, not beyond the imagination of our second selves, our <u>secret sensibilities: the woman in every man, the man in every woman.</u> We laugh because the film has the good sense to spoof the sexes instead of hectoring them, <u>hectoring</u> for an age of androgynes.

AN EPILOGUE. We've pulled back from the edge now. The boxes are unpacked, the workmen gone, the memory of a hard summer fading in the late autumnal light. I won't soon forget our fight, however. I don't want to. It reminds me that I sleep with a feminist who loves being a woman, a "maternal" woman, to use her word, the word that always seems to come to her. Her maternalism—her woman's sensibility perhaps, her woman's physiology for certain—separates us and sometimes sets us at odds, but without those differences I would not want her. I love the stranger she is to me, the conundrum that makes her so inscrutable. Here in this new house we thrive on the tension our differences create, the tension that nature has given us—her estrogens sending her in one direction, my androgens in the other, often on a collision course. Sometimes we come to blows, all right, but more often than not we rush headlong into each other's arms.

DAVE BARRY

Lost in the Kitchen

Dave Barry (1947–) is a nationally syndicated columnist for the *Miami Herald* and the 1988 winner of the Pulitzer Prize for Commentary. After being honored as Class Clown at New York's Pleasantville High School, Barry went on to take his B.A. in English from Haverford College. He then worked as a small-town newspaper reporter in Pennsylvania and as a consultant on effective writing for various businesses. In 1983 humor became his full-time job. Besides writing his weekly column, he has been a guest on Garrison Keillor's "Radio Company of the Air" and has written countless books, including *Taming the Screw: Several Million Homeowners' Problems* (1983), *Stay Fit Until You're Dead* (1985), *Dave Barry Turns 40* (1990), *Dave Barry Talks Back* (1991), *Dave Barry's Guide to Guys* (1995), and *Dave Barry Is from Mars and Venus* (1997). Recently Barry's humor has landed him on a wide variety of talk shows and his life has been commemorated through a highly rated TV sitcom, *Dave's World*.

"Lost in the Kitchen" appeared in the *Miami Herald* and other newspapers in May 1986. Writers interested in using humor to get their ideas across may find imitating the essay's structure and style useful. Michael Norman's "Against Androgyny," which also highlights differences between man and woman, is a natural companion essay in showing how much difference a shift in tone can make.

Men are still basically scum when it comes to helping out in the kitchen. This is one of two insights I had last Thanksgiving, the other one being that Thanksgiving night must be the slowest night of the year in terms of human sexual activity. Nobody wants to engage in human sexual activity with somebody who smells vaguely like yams and is covered with a thin layer of turkey grease, which describes pretty much everybody in the United States on Thanksgiving except the Detroit Lions, who traditionally play football that day and would therefore be too tired.

But that, as far as I can tell, is not my point. My point is that despite all that has been said in the past 20 years or so about sexual equality, most men make themselves as useful around the kitchen as ill-trained Labrador retrievers. This is not just my opinion: It is a scientific finding based on an exhaustive study of what happened last Thanksgiving when my family had dinner at the home of friends named Arlene and Gene.

Picture a typical Thanksgiving scene: On the floor, three small children and a dog who long ago had her brain eaten by fleas are running as fast as they can directly into things, trying to injure themselves. On the television, the Detroit Lions are doing pretty much the same thing.

In the kitchen, Arlene, a prosecuting attorney responsible for a large staff, is doing something with those repulsive organs that are placed in little surprise packets inside turkeys, apparently as a joke. Surrounding Arlene are thousands of steaming cooking containers. I would no more enter that kitchen than I would attempt to park a nuclear aircraft carrier, but my wife, who runs her own business, glides in very casually and picks up EXACTLY the right kitchen implement and starts doing EXACTLY the right thing without receiving any instructions whatsoever. She quickly becomes enshrouded in steam.

So Gene and I, feeling like the scum we are, finally bumble over and ask what we can do to help, and from behind the steam comes Arlene's patient voice asking us to please keep an eye on the children. Which we try to do.

But there is a famous law of physics that goes: "You cannot watch small children and the Detroit Lions at the same time, and let's face it, the Detroit Lions are more interesting." So we would start out watching the children, and then one of us would sneak a peek at the TV and say, "Hey! Look at this tackle!" And then we'd have to watch for a while to see the replay and find out whether the tackled person was dead or just permanently disabled. By then the children would have succeeded in injuring themselves or the dog, and this voice from behind the kitchen steam would call, VERY patiently, "Gene, PLEASE watch the children."

I realize this is awful. I realize this sounds just like Ozzie and Harriet. I also realize that there are some males out there, with hyphenated last names, who have advanced much farther than Gene and I have, who are not afraid to stay home full time and get coated with baby vomit while their wives work as test pilots, and who go into the kitchen on a daily basis to prepare food for other people, as opposed to going in there to get a beer and maybe some peanut butter on a spoon.

But I think Gene and I are fairly typical. I think most males rarely prepare food for others, and when they do, they have their one specialty dish (spaghetti, in my case) that they prepare maybe twice a year in a very elaborate production, for which they expect to be praised as if they had developed, right there in the kitchen, a cure for heart disease.

In defense of men, let me say this: Women do not make it easy to learn. Let's say a woman is in the kitchen, working away after having been at her job all day, and the man, feeling guilty, finally shuffles in and offers to help. So the woman says something like: "Well, you can cut up the turnips." Now to the WOMAN, who had all this sexist Home Economics training back in the pre-feminism era, this is a very simple instruction. It is the absolute simplest thing she can think of.

I asked my wife to read this and tell me what she thought. This is what she said: She said before Women's Liberation, men took care of the cars and women took care of the kitchen, whereas now that we have Women's Liberation, men no longer feel obligated to take care of the cars. This seemed pretty accurate to me, so I thought I'd just tack it on to the end here, while she makes waffles.

ELIZABETH BARRETT BROWNING

A Musical Instrument

Elizabeth Barrett Browning (1806–1861) was probably the most popular female poet in England during the nineteenth century, far more famous than her husband, Robert Browning, during her lifetime. Subject to poor health and an overly protective father, Elizabeth Barrett lived much of her life as an invalid. At the age of forty, she eloped with Browning, and the two lived in Italy for several years. There Barrett Browning regained her health, became involved in Italian politics, produced a large volume of poetry, and raised their son. For many years, Barrett Browning was best known for her love poems, collected in *Sonnets from the Portuguese* (1850) and praised for their moral integrity. More recently, however, critics have turned their attention to poems such as *Aurora Leigh* (1857), a lengthy narrative poem that portrays an artist as a young woman, refusing marriage to pursue her own career. Barrett Browning was not an outspoken advocate for women's rights, but twentieth-century critics are finding in poems like *Aurora Leigh* and "A Musical Instrument" (1860) evidence of her concern for each woman's right to choose and shape her own identity. That power to do so is often outside a woman's control is a concern of this poem as well as of Deborah Tannen's "Every Choice a Woman Makes Sends a Message."

What was he doing, the great god Pan,[1]   1
  Down in the reeds by the river?
Spreading ruin and scattering ban,
Splashing and paddling with hoofs of a goat,
And breaking the golden lilies afloat
  With the dragon-fly on the river.

He tore out a reed, the great god Pan,   2
  From the deep cool bed of the river:
The limpid water turbidly ran,
And the broken lilies a-dying lay,
And the dragon-fly had fled away
  Ere he brought it out of the river.

High on the shore sat the great god Pan   3
  While turbidly flowed the river;
And hacked and hewed as a great god can,
With his hard bleak steel at the patient reed,
Till there was not a sign of the leaf indeed
  To prove it fresh from the river.

He cut it short, did the great god Pan,   4
  (How tall it stood in the river!)
Then drew the pith, like the heart of a man,
Steadily from the outside ring,
And notched the poor dry empty thing
  In holes, as he sat by the river.

"This is the way," laughed the great god Pan   5
  (Laughed while he sat by the river),
"The only way, since gods began
To make sweet music, they could succeed."
Then, dropping his mouth to a hole in the reed,
  He blew in power by the river.

Sweet, sweet, sweet, O Pan!   6
  Piercing sweet by the river!
Blinding sweet, O great god Pan!
The sun on the hill forgot to die,
And the lilies revived, and the dragon-fly
  Came back to dream on the river.

---

1. Pan: in Greek mythology, god of fields and flocks, who is represented as half-man, half-goat; pursued by Pan, the nymph Syrinx was changed into a reed, from which Pan made his famous musical pipe.

Yet half a beast is the great god Pan,
   To laugh as he sits by the river,
Making a poet out of a man:
The true gods sigh for the cost and pain,—
For the reed which grows nevermore again
   As a reed with the reeds in the river.

7

COMMUNITIES

We find ourselves in a place we call home.

Overview

There is no such thing as an independent ant. The caste distinctions in the colony are so strict that the specialists in reproduction—the blimplike queens and feeble males—would perish without the aid of the female workers and soldiers. But there is more to it than feeding and breeding. Take a worker out of the nest and put her in a separate jar with food and water and dirt to dig in. Sheer loneliness will make her disorganized and lazy. Her productivity (which entomologists have measured in volume of dirt moved) will drop to a fraction of what it had been. Whether kept alone or with only half a dozen others, she will pine away for the bustle of the community and will die prematurely.

Humans are not ants, of course, but we too are tribal creatures, dependent for health and happiness on the family and community even when we are most eager to assert out independence. Aristotle saw this interdependence 2,500 years ago and declared that "man is a political animal," a creature designed to live in the *polis*, the community. "The person who by nature, not by accident, does not belong to a *polis* is either a wild animal or a god." The pieces in this unit describe various neighborhoods—rural and urban, ancient and modern, vibrant and dying. They provide us a basis for thinking about our own ties, spiritual and practical, to our communities.

KARLA F. C. HOLLOWAY

The Thursday Ladies

Karla F. C. Holloway (1949–   ), daughter of a public school superintendent and an English teacher, was educated at Talladega College
in Talladega, Alabama, and at Michigan State University. She is presently a professor of English and African-American Literature at Duke
University, and is the author of *Codes of Conduct: Race, Ethics, and the
Color of Our Character* (1996). Even in her academic writings on linguistic and literary theory, her prose carries the ease and the drama of
a spoken voice. "If there are passages in my books or essays that read
with some difficulty," she reports, "I often suggest that my readers
read them aloud. It is often a cadence that's missing: something only
the spoken voice can supply. I hear this voice as I write." Listen
for the sound of Holloway's voice as you read the following essay,
written for *Double Stitch: Black Women Write About Mothers and
Daughters* (1991). The essay may provide a model for readers interested in writing their own recollections of learning, in childhood, certain lessons about community life—lessons that no one learns in
school.

for Gloria and her memory

I wasn't coaxed awake that morning. My sister didn't nudge me   1
off her side of the bed. Mama didn't call, quietly expecting no answer,
or louder, getting irritated. No summer morning breeze blew through
our window, rattling the shell chimes I'd made on the back porch.
Nothing Sunday woke me up—no vaseline-shined shoes waiting to be
worn or church waiting to be filled. Nothing but the intermittent
squeak of the back screen door, followed by muffled good mornings
". . . them sweeties still sleep?" constantly echoing through the house
woke me. I knew it was Thursday after the fourth or fifth squeak . . .
and so I punched Shirley in the back and told her, "Get up—those
ladies are back."

We called them the Thursday ladies. But they could have been the   2
summer ladies or weekday ladies or servant ladies. They were all of
those things. In our small Michigan town ours was one of the few
Black families. We lived apart from the town's center. I never knew the
reason we lived past the main highway, almost to the church we
shared with the next town's Black Baptist congregation. I wasn't sure
whether it was to be close to the church where we spent so much of
our family time or to be distant from the town that had only grudgingly admitted us into the outskirts of its community. It was the town

185

where my Papa brought Mama after they'd married and left Sedalia, and he'd made a living for all of us there. Mama, me, my sister Shirley, and my three brothers. My brothers were gone now, army, college, dead (hit by a car in the town my mama avoided) and only me and Shirley were home. Mama was obviously proud that her family had made it—even into the fringes of that community where we lived. So she accepted the town because it grounded our family. But Shirl and me thought she must have hated it some too by the way she never went to town unless it was to shop (on Wednesday) or to school to see about us.

Those ladies were the most constant event in our lives. They con-   3
nected the time before our brother Junior (we called him June Bug) died and the time after. They'd always been coming on Thursday, and they were always the same.

I don't mean that they were all softly warm brown. Some were   4
night-dark, deep black women with loving, caring eyes. Some were high-yellow. Like Mama. Some were so slender that I wondered how they took care of all those children they always talked about. They were too fragile, I thought. Some were large and big-boned, and their gentleness was marked in their smiles and the weariness in their eyes. They carried pocketbooks when they came to see us, they all wore the same shoes—"nurse's shoes" Shirl and I called them—and they never acknowledged that they knew. Shirl and I would sneak down the hall when we heard them coming, hide behind the stove closet (where Mama kept cooking stuff), and spend most of Thursday listening to the strange community that entered our kitchen.

They didn't talk like us—me, or Shirl or Mama. They sounded like   5
M'dear, our grandmama back in Sedalia. They kissed (when we came out to grab a biscuit or bacon) like those ladies in M'dear's church. Their voices were soft and their feelings were loud. And Mama smiled more on those summer Thursdays than on any other day.

Their community was well-established. They had ritualized those   6
mornings spent in Mama's kitchen, the evenings on our porch. All of the ladies worked for white families who had come to Michigan to escape the summer heat of places like Charleston or Natchez or New Orleans. They brought their "girls" with them to take care of the children (and them) while they vacationed in our Lake Michigan town. These ladies weren't on vacation—except on Thursday. That was their day off and the day when they gathered in the home of one of the only Black families in town and relieved themselves of the burdens of working for white folks. So Shirl and I knew to come to the kitchen without coaxing that morning, and to be there while they were coming, slowly filling in the spaces around our kitchen table, leaning up against the cupboard, standing duty near the ice box in case someone wanted

something, or helping Mama roll biscuits. Shirl and I knew they'd talk first about their "people" and we didn't want to miss any of the ritual. "Girl, you should'a seen . . ." or "She didn't have no better sense than to . . ." or "Well, what chu do when they . . . ?" We'd listen in on the fascinating world of Southern white women who didn't seem to want to see their children all day (except after their naps, or after they'd been fed, or after they were dressed for bed). That would intrigue us, but even more compelling was the aura of the community of these Black women who talked like M'dear and who were absolutely out of place in our sophisticated preadolescent vision of the world. I think now that we kind of resented the woman our mother became on Thursdays because on those days she was happy in ways that we never could make her and she laughed at things we didn't think were funny, and she seemed a part of them instead of us.

So most Thursdays, we'd pick on these ladies like they picked at   7
the white folks they worked for. "Girl, did you see those ankles on that lady by the window?" We'd exaggerate their dialect and ridicule the country manners that caused the younger ladies to call our Mama "Ma'am." "Yes, chile!" I'd pitch my voice real high to sound thin and reed-like like the cocoa-brown lady who'd just joined the group this summer. "Lawd knows my feet cain't take much more of runnin after these chillun." I rubbed my feet like I had seen her do. "Mah Jesus— mah ankles so swole I speck they'll bust!"

"Do Jesus!" Shirl would roll her eyes up and then we'd hit the   8
floor, laughing at our laughing at them. But we'd make sure to get down the hall before the talk about their people was done and shifted to the talk about what they were going to do on their day off.

Our house was the base for Thursday breakfast, supper, late night   9
talk and a kind of gathering of spirit that I didn't understand then, but respected (or feared, or envied) for the strength that was obviously a part of these women's meetings.

On that Thursday Mamie, the new lady, announced she was going   10
to the movie house in town. The other ladies just glanced at her, a smiling acknowledgment of her intent and went on back to their con- versations. They were talking about men . . . and that was the ritual talk (after breakfast and before the late afternoon lethargy when a lot of them napped on the porch swing or on the davenport in the living room) that Shirl and I had to be really quiet and careful listeners for, because we reviewed it in our beds Thursday nights. So we didn't pay much attention when Mamie put her bag on her left arm, pulled on her gloves (like she was going to church, Shirl said later) and straight- ened that black triangle hat she always wore. She went out the front door. We heard it bang shut, but our attention quickly went back to their conversation—certain we'd hear something new about men,

something that demanded review, or experimentation or a conference with some of our older girl friends from church. So we sat, our backs firmly pressed against the hall wall, munching peaches and collecting the seeds for planting in our backyard spot that we always forgot the location of.

We did hear Mamie come back. The door's slam punctuated a   11 point that one of the older ladies made: ". . . ain't that just like them mens." And the noise broke our concentration, because it was too early. By the time the movie let out, we should have been back in the kitchen, cutting up tomatoes for supper or heating the frying pan in the oven for the corn bread being stirred on the table. But she was too early for that evening kitchen time. And so Shirl and I looked at each other, then at her, sure we would see some indication of why Mamie had returned too early from the movie house.

But she just smiled—and said, "Scuse me, y'all," in that high   12 squeaky voice of hers and shyly (we agreed later her moves weren't sneaky, just shy) made her way through the living room, past us in the hall and down the passage to the bathroom. She closed the door and turned the water on. We could hear the tinkling into the toilet and the flush even though the water was running. Then she came back out, smiled that "scuse me, y'all" smile and the front door slammed behind her. We jumped up and ran back to the kitchen window where we could see her making her way back down the road to town—back to the movie house.

We looked at each other for just a moment until the truth hit us   13 and then we burst into hysterical, derisive laughter. "She came back just to use the bathroom!" Shirl shouted.

"Countre-e-e-e-e!" I giggled. "Maybe she thought the toilet was   14 outside the movie house and she just kept walking till she got back here!"

"Maybe the girl on the 'Ladies' sign didn't look enough like her so   15 she didn't think she could go in!" Shirl's voice was broken by the hilarity that had descended on us both.

I yelled back, "Maybe she couldn't read!"   16

We were both just about overcome with her obvious ignorance   17 and our own delightful sophistication when Mama appeared in the kitchen doorway. She spoke to us in a voice that controlled her rage but could not suppress her unhappiness. Later we both said that we thought she was going to cry instead of talk, but she did talk and it seemed to come out of a memory. Shirl said later that it felt like she hadn't even been in the kitchen with us.

"Maybe," Mama said quietly "maybe in that little country town in   18 Mississippi that's so funny and so foreign to you two, where Mamie works her life away in a home that will never be hers and for a family that will never love her back . . . maybe the bathrooms in movies houses there say something that hurts her so bad she wishes she couldn't read."

And she looked at us like she knew we didn't know what she   19
meant and went back to the room and to her community of Thursday ladies who lived the memory Mama had left in Sedalia.

N. SCOTT MOMADAY

The Way to Rainy Mountain

N(avarre) Scott Momaday (1934–   ) is the son of a Kiowa father and a mother of mixed white and Cherokee ancestry. He spent his earliest years among Kiowas on a family farm in Oklahoma. Later he moved with his parents to New Mexico, where they taught in reservation schools. Momaday took a B.A. in English from the University of New Mexico and an M.A. and Ph.D. from Stanford University, and he has been a professor of English at the University of Arizona since 1982. Like his father, he is an accomplished artist, and, like his mother, he is a skilled writer. Among his best-known works are *House Made of Dawn* (1968), a Pulitzer Prize–winning novel; *The Gourd Dancer* (1976), a book of poems he also illustrated; and *The Way to Rainy Mountain* (1969), a collection of traditional Kiowa stories. Many of the stories in *Rainy Mountain* were told to Momaday by his father (who illustrated the book), his grandmother, and several of his grandmother's friends, "who were in close touch with the oral tradition of the tribe." Its introduction, first published as a separate essay in *The Reporter* (1967), gives a sense of what Momaday values in his Kiowa heritage and what he sees threatened by the dominance of white civilization. Momaday's latest projects include *In the Presence of the Sun: Stories and Poems 1961–1991* (1992) and *Circle of Wonder: A Native American Christmas Story* (1993). He has also narrated a PBS documentary, *Winds of Change,* focusing on contemporary Native American experiences. Readers may be interested in comparing Momaday's discussion of the rituals that shaped Kiowa communal life with the Midwestern middle-class rituals of Scott Russell Sanders's "The Common Life."

A single knoll rises out of the plain in Oklahoma, north and west   1
of the Wichita Range. For my people, the Kiowas, it is an old landmark, and they gave it the name Rainy Mountain. The hardest weather in the world is there. Winter brings blizzards, hot tornadic winds arise in the spring, and in the summer the prairie is an anvil's edge. The grass turns brittle and brown, and it cracks beneath your feet. There are green belts along the rivers and creeks, linear groves of hickory and pecan, willow, and witch hazel. At a distance in July or August the

steaming foliage seems almost to writhe in fire. Great green-and-yellow grasshoppers are everywhere in the tall grass, popping up like corn to sting the flesh, and tortoises crawl about on the red earth, going nowhere in the plenty of time. Loneliness is an aspect of the land. All things in the plain are isolate; there is no confusion of objects in the eye, but *one* hill or *one* tree or *one* man. To look upon that landscape in the early morning, with the sun at your back, is to lose the sense of proportion. Your imagination comes to life, and this, you think, is where Creation was begun.

I returned to Rainy Mountain in July. My grandmother had died   2
in the spring, and I wanted to be at her grave. She had lived to be very old and at last infirm. Her only living daughter was with her when she died, and I was told that in death her face was that of a child.

I like to think of her as a child. When she was born, the Kiowas   3
were living the last great moment of their history. For more than a hundred years they had controlled the open range from the Smoky Hill River to the Red, from the headwaters of the Canadian to the fork of the Arkansas and Cimarron. In alliance with the Comanches, they had ruled the whole of the southern Plains. War was their sacred business, and they were among the finest horsemen the world has ever known. But warfare for the Kiowas was preeminently a matter of disposition rather than of survival, and they never understood the grim, unrelenting advance of the U.S. Cavalry. When at last, divided and ill-provisioned, they were driven onto the Staked Plains in the cold rains of autumn, they fell into panic. In Palo Duro Canyon they abandoned their crucial stores to pillage and had nothing then but their lives. In order to save themselves, they surrendered to the soldiers at Fort Sill and were imprisoned in the old stone corral that now stands as a military museum. My grandmother was spared the humiliation of those high gray walls by eight or ten years, but she must have known from birth the affliction of defeat, the dark brooding of old warriors.

Her name was Aho, and she belonged to the last culture to evolve   4
in North America. Her forebears came down from the high country in western Montana nearly three centuries ago. They were a mountain people, a mysterious tribe of hunters whose language has never been positively classified in any major group. In the late seventeenth century they began a long migration to the south and east. It was a long journey toward the dawn, and it led to a golden age. Along the way the Kiowas were befriended by the Crows, who gave them the culture and religion of the Plains. They acquired horses, and their ancient nomadic spirit was suddenly free of the ground. They acquired Tai-me, the sacred Sun Dance doll, from that moment the object and symbol of their worship, and so shared in the divinity of the sun. Not least, they acquired the sense of destiny, therefore courage and pride. When they entered upon the southern Plains, they had been transformed. No

longer were they slaves to the simple necessity of survival; they were a lordly and dangerous society of fighters and thieves, hunters and priests of the sun. According to their origin myth, they entered the world through a hollow log. From one point of view, their migration was the fruit of an old prophecy, for indeed they emerged from a sunless world.

Although my grandmother lived out her long life in the shadow of Rainy Mountain, the immense landscape of the continental interior lay like memory in her blood. She could tell of the Crows, whom she had never seen, and of the Black Hills, where she had never been. I wanted to see in reality what she had seen more perfectly in the mind's eye, and traveled fifteen hundred miles to begin my pilgrimage. ⁵

Yellowstone, it seemed to me, was the top of the world, a region of deep lakes and dark timber, canyons and waterfalls. But, beautiful as it is, one might have the sense of confinement there. The skyline in all directions is close at hand, the high wall of the woods and deep cleavages of shade. There is a perfect freedom in the mountains, but it belongs to the eagle and the elk, the badger and the bear. The Kiowas reckoned their stature by the distance they could see, and they were bent and blind in the wilderness. ⁶

Descending eastward, the highland meadows are a stairway to the plain. In July the inland slope of the Rockies is luxuriant with flax and buckwheat, stonecrop and larkspur. The earth unfolds and the limit of the land recedes. Clusters of trees and animals grazing far in the distance cause the vision to reach away and wonder to build upon the mind. The sun follows a longer course in the day, and the sky is immense beyond all comparison. The great billowing clouds that sail upon it are shadows that move upon the grain like water, dividing light. Farther down, in the land of the Crows and Blackfeet, the plain is yellow. Sweet clover takes hold of the hills and bends upon itself to cover and seal the soil. There the Kiowas paused on their way; they had come to the place where they must change their lives. The sun is at home on the plains. Precisely there does it have the certain character of a god. When the Kiowas came to the land of the Crows, they could see the dark lees of the hill at dawn across the Bighorn River, the profusion of light on the grain shelves, the oldest deity ranging after the solstices. Not yet would they veer southward to the caldron of the land that lay below; they must wean their blood from the northern winter and hold the mountains a while longer in their view. They bore Tai-me in procession to the east. ⁷

A dark mist lay over the Black Hills, and the land was like iron. At the top of a ridge I caught sight of Devil's Tower upthrust against the gray sky as if in the birth of time the core of the earth had broken through its crust and the motion of the world was begun. There are things in nature that engender an awful quiet in the heart of man; ⁸

Devil's Tower is one of them. Two centuries ago, because they could not do otherwise, the Kiowas made a legend at the base of the rock. My grandmother said:

> Eight children were there at play, seven sisters and their brother. Suddenly the boy was struck dumb; he trembled and began to run upon his hands and feet. His fingers became claws, and his body was covered with fur. Directly there was a bear where the boy had been. The sisters were terrified; they ran, and the bear after them. They came to the stump of a great tree, and the tree spoke to them. It bade them climb upon it and as they did so, it began to rise into the air. The bear came to kill them, but they were just beyond its reach. It reared against the tree and scored the bark all around with its claws. The seven sisters were borne into the sky, and they became the stars of the Big Dipper.

From that moment, and so long as the legend lives, the Kiowas have kinsmen in the night sky. Whatever they were in the mountains, they could be no more. However tenuous their well-being, however much they had suffered and would suffer again, they had found a way out of the wilderness.

My grandmother had a reverence for the sun, a holy regard that   9
now is all but gone out of mankind. There was a wariness in her and an ancient awe. She was a Christian in her later years, but she had come a long way about, and she never forgot her birthright. As a child she had been to the Sun Dances; she had taken part in those annual rites, and by them she had learned the restoration of her people in the presence of Tai-me. She was about seven when the last Kiowa Sun Dance was held in 1887 on the Washita River above Rainy Mountain Creek. The buffalo were gone. In order to consummate the ancient sacrifice—to impale the head of a buffalo bull upon the medicine tree—a delegation of old men journeyed into Texas, there to beg and barter for an animal from the Goodnight herd. She was ten when the Kiowas came together for the last time as a living Sun Dance culture. They could find no buffalo; they had to hang an old hide from the sacred tree. Before the dance could begin, a company of soldiers rode out from Fort Sill under orders to disperse the tribe. Forbidden without cause the essential act of their faith, having seen the wild herds slaughtered and left to rot upon the ground, the Kiowas backed away forever from the medicine tree. That was July 20, 1890, at the great bend of the Washita. My grandmother was there. Without bitterness, and for as long as she lived, she bore a vision of deicide.

Now that I can have her only in memory, I see my grandmother in   10
the several postures that were peculiar to her: standing at the wood stove on a winter morning and turning meat in a great iron skillet; sitting at the south window, bent above her beadwork, and afterwards, when her vision had failed, looking down for a long time into the fold

of her hands; going out upon a cane, very slowly as she did when the weight of age came upon her; praying. I remember her most often at prayer. She made long, rambling prayers out of suffering and hope, having seen many things. I was never sure that I had the right to hear, so exclusive were they of all mere custom and company. The last time I saw her she prayed standing by the side of her bed at night, naked to the waist, the light of a kerosene lamp moving upon her dark skin. Her long, black hair, always drawn and braided in the day, lay upon her shoulders and against her breasts like a shawl. I do not speak Kiowa, and I never understood her prayers, but there was something inherently sad in the sound, some merest hesitation upon the syllables of sorrow. She began in a high and descending pitch, exhausting her breath to silence; then again and again—and always the same intensity of effort, of something that is, and is not, like urgency in the human voice. Transported so in the dancing light among the shadows of her room, she seemed beyond the reach of time. But that was illusion; I think I knew then that I should not see her again.

Houses are like sentinels in the plain, old keepers of the weather   11 watch. There, in a very little while, wood takes on the appearance of great age. All colors wear soon away in the wind and rain, and then the wood is burned gray and the grain appears and the nails turn red with rust. The windowpanes are black and opaque; you imagine there is nothing within, and indeed there are many ghosts, bones given up to the land. They stand here and there against the sky, and you approach them for a longer time then you expect. They belong in the distance; it is their domain.

Once there was a lot of sound in my grandmother's house, a lot of   12 coming and going, feasting and talk. The summers there were full of excitement and reunion. The Kiowas were a summer people; they abide the cold and keep to themselves; but when the season turns and the land becomes warm and vital, they cannot hold still; an old love of going returns upon them. The aged visitors who came to my grandmother's house when I was a child were made of lean and leather, and they bore themselves upright. They wore great black hats and bright ample shirts that shook in the wind. They rubbed fat upon their hair and wound their braids with strips of colored cloth. Some of them painted their faces and carried the scars of old and cherished enmities. They were an old council of warlords, come to remind and be reminded of who they were. Their wives and daughters served them well. The women might indulge themselves; gossip was at once the mark and compensation of their servitude. They made loud and elaborate talk among themselves, full of jest and gesture, fright and false alarm. They went abroad in fringed and flowered shawls, bright beadwork, and German silver. They were at home in the kitchen, and they prepared meals that were banquets.

There were frequent prayer meetings, and great nocturnal feasts.   13
When I was a child, I played with my cousins outside, where the lamp-
light fell upon the ground and the singing of the old people rose up
around us and carried away into the darkness. There were a lot of
good things to eat, a lot of laughter and surprise. And afterwards,
when the quiet returned, I lay down with my grandmother and could
hear the frogs away by the river and feel the motion of the air.

Now there is a funeral silence in the rooms, the endless wake of   14
some final word. The walls have closed in upon my grandmother's
house. When I returned to it in mourning, I saw for the first time in
my life how small it was. It was late at night, and there was a white
moon, nearly full. I sat for a long time on the stone steps by the
kitchen door. From there I could see out across the land; I could see
the long row of trees by the creek, the low light upon the rolling
plains, and the stars of the Big Dipper. Once I looked at the moon and
caught sight of a strange thing. A cricket had perched upon the
handrail, only a few inches away from me. My line of vision was such
that the creature filled the moon like a fossil. It had gone there, I
thought, to live and die, for there of all places, was its small definition
made whole and eternal. A warm wind rose up and purled like the
longing within me.

The next morning I awoke at dawn and went out on the dirt road   15
to Rainy Mountain. It was already hot, and the grasshoppers began to
fill the air. Still, it was early in the morning, and the birds sang out of
the shadows. The long yellow grass on the mountain shone in the
bright light, and a scissortail hied above the land. There, where it
ought to be, at the end of a long and legendary way, was my grandmother's grave. Here and there on the dark stones were ancestral
names. Looking back once, I saw the mountain and came away.

H. D. F. KITTO

The Polis

H(enry) D(avy) F(indley) Kitto (1897–1982) was born in Gloucester-
shire, England, and received his B.A. in classics from Cambridge University. He continued his study while serving as a lecturer in ancient
Greek at the University of Glasgow from 1920 to 1944, interrupting
his scholarly life long enough to travel extensively in Greece and
record his observations of the modern culture and land in *In the
Mountains of Greece* (1933). In 1944 he became Professor at the University of Bristol, where he remained for the rest of his career. Kitto's
reputation as a leading Greek scholar was established with works

such as *Greek Tragedy* (1939) and *Form and Meaning in Drama* (1956),
in which he concentrated on recovering the cultural context surrounding works of the classical period. By far his most influential
book, however, has been *The Greeks* (1951), which offers the student
unfamiliar with classical culture an in-depth portrait of the history
and character of Greek civilization. This book, admired as much for
the wit and vigor of its prose as for its excellent scholarship, has been
reprinted over thirty times and translated into six languages. "The
Polis" is excerpted from *The Greeks*. Though most obviously connected
with Plato's *Crito*, the chapter invites a comparison between the
Greek idea of community and any of the American ideas presented in
this portion of the book.

"Polis" is the Greek word which we translate "city-state." It is a   1
bad translation, because the normal polis was not much like a city, and
was very much more than a state. But translation, like politics, is the
art of the possible; since we have not got the thing which the Greeks
called "the polis," we do not possess an equivalent word. From now
on, we will avoid the misleading term "city-state," and use the Greek
word instead. In this chapter we will first inquire how this political system arose, then we will try to reconstitute the word "polis" and recover its real meaning by watching it in action. It may be a long task,
but all the time we shall be improving our acquaintance with the
Greeks. Without a clear conception what the polis was, and what it
meant to the Greeks, it is quite impossible to understand properly
Greek history, the Greek mind, or the Greek achievement.

First then, what was the polis? In the *Iliad* we discern a political   2
structure that seems not unfamiliar—a structure that can be called an
advanced or a degenerate form of tribalism, according to taste. There
are kings, like Achilles, who rule their people, and there is the great
king, Agamemnon, King of Men, who is something like a feudal over-
lord. He is under obligation, whether of right or of custom, to consult
the other kings or chieftains in matters of common interest. They form
a regular council, and in its debates the sceptre, symbol of authority, is
held by the speaker for the time being. This is recognizably European,
not Oriental; Agamemnon is no despot, ruling with the unquestioned
authority of a god. There are also signs of a shadowy Assembly of the
People, to be consulted on important occasions: though Homer, a
courtly poet, and in any case not a constitutional historian, says little
about it.

Such, in outline, is the tradition about pre-conquest Greece. When   3
the curtain goes up again after the Dark Age we see a very different picture. No longer is there a "wide-ruling Agamemnon" lording it in Mycenae. In Crete, where Idomeneus had been ruling as sole king, we find
over fifty quite independent poleis, fifty small "states" in the place of

one. It is a small matter that the kings have disappeared; the important thing is that the kingdoms have gone too. What is true of Crete is true of Greece in general, or at least of those parts which play any considerable part in Greek history—Ionia, the islands, the Peloponnesus except Arcadia, Central Greece except the western parts, and South Italy and Sicily when they became Greek. All these were divided into an enormous number of quite independent and autonomous political units.

It is important to realize their size. The modern reader picks up a   4 translation of Plato's *Republic* or Aristotle's *Politics;* he finds Plato ordaining that his ideal city shall have 5,000 citizens, and Aristotle that each citizen should be able to know all the others by sight; and he smiles, perhaps, at such philosophic fantasies. But Plato and Aristotle are not fantasts. Plato is imagining a polis on the normal Hellenic scale; indeed he implies that many existing Greek poleis are too small—for many had less than 5,000 citizens. Aristotle says, in his amusing way— Aristotle sometimes sounds very like a don[1]—that a polis of ten citizens would be impossible, because it could not be self-sufficient, and that a polis of a hundred thousand would be absurd, because it could not govern itself properly. And we are not to think of these "citizens" as a "master-class" owning and dominating thousands of slaves. The ordinary Greek in these early centuries was a farmer, and if he owned a slave he was doing pretty well. Aristotle speaks of a hundred thousand citizens; if we allow each to have a wife and four children, and then add a liberal number of slaves and resident aliens, we shall arrive at something like a million—the population of Birmingham; and to Aristotle an independent "state" as populous as Birmingham is a lecture-room joke. Or we may turn from the philosophers to a practical man, Hippodamas, who laid out the Piraeus in the most up-to-date American style; he said that the ideal number of citizens was ten thousand, which would imply a total population of about 100,000.

In fact, only three poleis had more than 20,000 citizens—Syracuse   5 and Acragas (Girgenti) in Sicily, and Athens. At the outbreak of the Peloponnesian War the population of Attica was probably about 350,000, half Athenian (men, women and children), about a tenth resident aliens, and the rest slaves. Sparta, or Lacedaemon, had a much smaller citizen-body, though it was larger in area. The Spartans had conquered and annexed Messenia, and possessed 3,200 square miles of territory. By Greek standards this was an enormous area: it would take a good walker two days to cross it. The important commercial city of Corinth had a territory of 330 square miles—about the size of Huntingdonshire. The island of Ceos, which is about as big as Bute, was divided into four poleis. It had therefore four armies, four govern-

---

1. don: a tutor or fellow of one of the colleges at Oxford or Cambridge. That is, Aristotle sounds professorial.

ments, possibly four different calendars, and, it may be, four different currencies and systems of measures—though this is less likely. Mycenae was in historical times a shrunken relic of Agamemnon's capital, but still independent. She sent an army to help the Greek cause against Persia at the battle of Plataea; the army consisted of eighty men. Even by Greek standards this was small, but we do not hear that any jokes were made about an army sharing a cab.

To think on this scale is difficult for us, who regard a state of ten 6 million as small, and are accustomed to states which, like the U.S.A. and the U.S.S.R., are so big that they have to be referred to by their initials; but when the adjustable reader has become accustomed to the scale, he will not commit the vulgar error of confusing size with significance. The modern writer is sometimes heard to speak with splendid scorn of "those petty Greek states, with their interminable quarrels." Quite so; Plataea, Sicyon, Aegina and the rest are petty, compared with modern states. The Earth itself is petty, compared with Jupiter—but then, the atmosphere of Jupiter is mainly ammonia, and that makes a difference. We do not like breathing ammonia—and the Greeks would not much have liked breathing the atmosphere of the vast modern State. They knew of one such, the Persian Empire—and thought it very suitable, for barbarians. Difference of scale, when it is great enough, amounts to difference of kind.

But before we deal with the nature of the polis, the reader might 7 like to know how it happened that the relatively spacious pattern of pre-Dorian Greece became such a mosaic of small fragments. The Classical scholar too would like to know; there are no records, so that all we can do is to suggest plausible reasons. There are historical, geographical and economic reasons; and when these have been duly set forth, we may conclude perhaps that the most important reason of all is simply that this is the way in which the Greeks preferred to live.

The coming of the Dorians was not an attack made by one orga- 8 nized nation upon another. The invaded indeed had their organization, loose though it was; some of the invaders—the main body that conquered Lacedaemon—must have been a coherent force; but others must have been small groups of raiders, profiting from the general turmoil and seizing good land where they could find it. A sign of this is that we find members of the same clan in different states. Pindar, for example, was a citizen of Thebes and a member of the ancient family of the Aegidae. But there were Aegidae too in Aegina and Sparta, quite independent poleis, and Pindar addresses them as kinsmen. This particular clan therefore was split up in the invasions. In a country like Greece this would be very natural.

In a period so unsettled the inhabitants of any valley or island 9 might at a moment's notice be compelled to fight for their fields. Therefore a local strong-point was necessary, normally a defensible hill-top somewhere in the plain. This, the "acropolis" ("high-town"), would be fortified, and here would be the residence of the king. It would also be the natural place of assembly, and the religious centre.

This is the beginning of the town. What we have to do is to give   10
reasons why the town grew, and why such a small pocket of people re-mained an independent political unit. The former task is simple. To begin with, natural economic growth made a central market necessary. We saw that the economic system implied by Hesiod and Homer was "close household economy"; the estate, large or small, produced nearly everything that it needed, and what it could not produce it did with-out. As things became more stable a rather more specialized economy became possible: more goods were produced for sale. Hence the growth of a market.

At this point we may invoke the very sociable habits of the Greeks,   11
ancient or modern. The English farmer likes to build his house on his land, and to come into town when he has to. What little leisure he has he likes to spend on the very satisfying occupation of looking over a gate. The Greek prefers to live in the town or village, to walk out to his work, and to spend his rather ampler leisure talking in the town or vil-lage square. Therefore the market becomes a market-town, naturally beneath the Acropolis. This became the centre of the communal life of the people—and we shall see presently how important that was.

But why did not such towns form larger units? This is the impor-   12
tant question.

There is an economic point. The physical barriers which Greece has   13
so abundantly made the transport of goods difficult, except by sea, and the sea was not yet used with any confidence. Moreover, the variety of which we spoke earlier enabled quite a small area to be reasonably self-sufficient for a people who made such small material demands on life as the Greek. Both of these facts tend in the same direction; there was in Greece no great economic interdependence, no reciprocal pull be-tween the different parts of the country, strong enough to counteract the desire of the Greek to live in small communities.

There is a geographical point. It is sometimes asserted that this sys-   14
tem of independent poleis was imposed on Greece by the physical character of the country. The theory is attractive, especially to those who like to have one majestic explanation of any phenomenon, but it does not seem to be true. It is of course obvious that the physical sub-division of the country helped; the system could not have existed, for example, in Egypt, a country which depends entirely on the proper management of the Nile flood, and therefore must have a central gov-ernment. But there are countries cut up quite as much as Greece—Scotland, for instance—which have never developed the polis-system; and conversely there were in Greece many neighbouring poleis, such

as Corinth and Sicyon, which remained independent of each other although between them there was no physical barrier that would seriously incommode a modern cyclist. Moreover, it was precisely the
most mountainous parts of Greece that never developed poleis, or not
until later days—Arcadia and Aetolia, for example, which had something like a canton-system. The polis flourished in those parts where
communications were relatively easy. So that we are still looking for
our explanation.

Economics and geography helped, but the real explanation is the   15
character of the Greeks—which those determinists may explain who
have the necessary faith in their omniscience. As it will take some time
to deal with this, we may first clear out of the way an important historical point. How did it come about that so preposterous a system was
able to last for more than twenty minutes?

The ironies of history are many and bitter, but at least this must be   16
put to the credit of the gods, that they arranged for the Greeks to have
the Eastern Mediterranean almost to themselves long enough to work
out what was almost a laboratory-experiment to test how far, and in
what conditions, human nature is capable of creating and sustaining a
civilization. In Asia, the Hittite Empire had collapsed, the Lydian kingdom was not aggressive, and the Persian power, which eventually
overthrew Lydia, was still embryonic in the mountainous recesses of
the continent; Egypt was in decay; Macedon, destined to make nonsense of the polis-system, was and long remained in a state of ineffec-
tive semi-barbarism; Rome had not yet been heard of, nor any other
power in Italy. There were indeed the Phoenicians, and their western
colony, Carthage, but these were traders first and last. Therefore this
lively and intelligent Greek people was for some centuries allowed to
live under the apparently absurd system which suited and developed
its genius instead of becoming absorbed in the dull mass of a large empire, which would have smothered its spiritual growth, and made it
what it afterwards became, a race of brilliant individuals and oppor-
tunists. Obviously some day somebody would create a strong central-
ized power in the Eastern Mediterranean—a successor to the ancient
sea-power of King Minos. Would it be Greek, Oriental, or something
else? This question must be the theme of a later chapter, but no history
of Greece can be intelligible until one has understood what the polis
meant to the Greek; and when we have understood that, we shall also
understand why the Greeks developed it, and so obstinately tried to
maintain it. Let us then examine the word in action.

It meant at first that which was later called the Acropolis, the   17
stronghold of the whole community and the centre of its public life.
The town which nearly always grew up around this was designated by
another word, "asty." But "polis" very soon meant either the citadel or

the whole people which, as it were, "used" this citadel. So we read in Thucydides, "Epidamnus is a polis on the right as you sail into the Ionian gulf." This is not like saying "Bristol is a city on the right as you sail up the Bristol Channel," for Bristol is not an independent state which might be at war with Gloucester, but only an urban area with a purely local administration. Thucydides' words imply that there is a town— though possibly a very small one—called Epidamnus, which is the political centre of the Epidamnians, who live in the territory of which the town is the centre—not the "capital"—and are Epidamnians whether they live in the town or in one of the villages in this territory.

Sometimes the territory and the town have different names. Thus,   18
Attica is the territory occupied by the Athenian people; it comprised Athens—the "polis" in the narrower sense—the Piraeus, and many villages; but the people collectively were Athenians, not Attics, and a citizen was an Athenian in whatever part of Attica he might live.

In this sense "polis" is our "state." In Sophocles' *Antigone* Creon   19
comes forward to make his first proclamation as king. He begins, "Gentlemen, as for the polis, the gods have brought it safely through the storm, on even keel." It is the familiar image of the Ship of State, and we think we know where we are. But later in the play he says what we should naturally translate, "Public proclamation has been made . . ." He says in fact, "It has been proclaimed to the polis . . ."— not to the "state," but to the "people." Later in the play he quarrels violently with his son: "What?" he cries, "is anyone but me to rule in this land?" Haemon answers, "It is no polis that is ruled by one man only." The answer brings out another important part of the whole conception of a polis, namely that it is a community, and that its affairs are the affairs of all. The actual business of governing might be entrusted to a monarch, acting in the name of all according to traditional usages, or to the heads of certain noble families, or to a council of citizens owning so much property, or to all the citizens. All these, and many modifications of them, were natural forms of "polity"; all were sharply distinguished by the Greek from Oriental monarchy, in which the monarch is irresponsible, not holding his powers in trust by the grace of god, but being himself a god. If there was irresponsible government there was no polis. Haemon is accusing his father of talking like a "tyranos"[2] and thereby destroying the polis—but not "the State."

To continue our exposition of the word. The chorus in Aris-   20
tophanes' *Acharnians*, admiring the conduct of the hero, turns to the audience with an appeal which I render literally, "Dost thou see, O whole polis?" The last words are sometimes translated "thou thronging

---

2. I prefer to use the Greek form of this (apparently) Oriental word. It is the Greek equivalent of "dictator," but it does not necessarily have the colour of our word "tyrant." [author's note]

city," which sounds better, but obscures an essential point, namely that the size of the polis made it possible for a member to appeal to all his fellow-citizens in person, and this he naturally did if he thought that another member of the polis had injured him. It was the common assumption of the Greeks that the polis took its origin in the desire for Justice. Individuals are lawless, but the polis will see to it that wrongs are redressed. But not by an elaborate machinery of state-justice, for such a machine could not be operated except by individuals, who may be as unjust as the original wrongdoer. The injured party will be sure of obtaining justice only if he can declare his wrongs to the whole polis. The word therefore now means "people" in actual distinction from "state."

Iocasta, the tragic Queen in the *Oedipus,* will show us a little more 21 of the range of the word. It becomes a question if Oedipus her husband is not after all the accursed man who had killed the previous king Laius. "No, no," cries Iocasta, "it cannot be! The slave said it was 'brigands' who had attacked them, not a 'brigand.' He cannot go back on his word now. The polis heard him, not I alone." Here the word is used without any "political" association at all; it is, as it were, off duty, and signifies "the whole people." This is a shade of meaning which is not always so prominent, but is never entirely absent.

Then Demosthenes the orator talks of a man who, literally, "avoids 22 the city"—a translation which might lead the unwary to suppose that he lived in something corresponding to the Lake District, or Purley. But the phrase "avoids the polis" tells us nothing about his domicile; it means that he took no part in public life—and was therefore something of an oddity. The affairs of the community did not interest him.

We have now learned enough about the word polis to realize that 23 there is no possible English rendering of such a common phrase as, "It is everyone's duty to help the polis." We cannot say "help the state," for that arouses no enthusiasm; it is "the state" that takes half our incomes from us. Not "the community," for with us "the community" is too big and too various to be grasped except theoretically. One's village, one's trade union, one's class, are entities that mean something to us at once, but "work for the community," though an admirable sentiment, is to most of us vague and flabby. In the years before the war, what did most parts of Great Britain know about the depressed areas? How much do bankers, miners and farmworkers understand each other? But the "polis" every Greek knew; there it was, complete, before his eyes. He could see the fields which gave it its sustenance—or did not, if the crops failed; he could see how agriculture, trade and industry dove-tailed into one another; he knew the frontiers, where they were strong and where weak; if any malcontents were planning a *coup,* it was difficult for them to conceal the fact. The entire life of the polis, and the relation between its parts, were much easier to grasp, because of the small scale of things. Therefore to say "It is everyone's duty to help the polis" was not to express a fine sentiment but to speak the plainest and most urgent common sense.[3] Public affairs had an immediacy and a concreteness which they cannot possibly have for us.

One specific example will help. The Athenian democracy taxed the rich with as much disinterested enthusiasm as the British, but this could be done in a much more gracious way, simply because the State was so small and intimate. Among us, the payer of super-tax (presumably) pays much as the income-tax payer does: he writes his cheque and thinks, "There! *That's* gone down the drain!" In Athens, the man whose wealth exceeded a certain sum had, in a yearly rota, to perform certain "liturgies"—literally, "folk-works." He had to keep a warship in commission for one year (with the privilege of commanding it, if he chose), or finance the production of plays at the Festival, or equip a religious procession. It was a heavy burden, and no doubt unwelcome, but at least some fun could be got out of it and some pride taken in it. There was satisfaction and honour to be gained from producing a trilogy worthily before one's fellow-citizens. So, in countless other ways, the size of the polis made vivid and immediate, things which to us are only abstractions or wearisome duties. Naturally this cut both ways. For example, an incompetent or unlucky commander was the object not of a diffused and harmless popular indignation, but of direct accusation; he might be tried for his life before an Assembly, many of whose past members he had led to death.

Pericles' Funeral Speech, recorded or recreated by Thucydides, will illustrate this immediacy, and will also take our conception of the polis a little further. Each year, Thucydides tells us, if citizens had died in war—and they had, more often than not—a funeral oration was delivered by "a man chosen by the polis." Today, that would be someone nominated by the Prime Minister, or the British Academy, or the B.B.C. In Athens it meant that someone was chosen by the Assembly who had often spoken to that Assembly; and on this occasion Pericles spoke from a specially high platform, that his voice might reach as many as possible. Let us consider two phrases that Pericles used in that speech.

He is comparing the Athenian polis with the Spartan, and makes the point that the Spartans admit foreign visitors only grudgingly, and from time to time expel all strangers, "while we make our polis common to all." "Polis" here is not the political unit; there is no question of naturalizing foreigners—which the Greeks did rarely, simply because the polis was so intimate a union. Pericles means here: "We throw open to all our common cultural life," as is shown by the words that follow, difficult though they are to translate: "nor do we deny them any instruction or spectacle"—words that are almost meaningless until

24

25

26

3. It did not, of course, follow that the Greek obeyed common sense any oftener than we do. [author's note]

we realize that the drama, tragic and comic, the performance of choral hymns, public recitals of Homer, games, were all necessary and normal parts of "political" life. This is the sort of thing Pericles has in mind when he speaks of "instruction and spectacle," and of "making the polis open to all."

But we must go further than this. A perusal of the speech will show that in praising the Athenian polis Pericles is praising more than a state, a nation, or a people: he is praising a way of life; he means no less when, a little later, he calls Athens the "school of Hellas."—And what of that? Do not we praise "the English way of life"? The difference is this; we expect our State to be quite indifferent to "the English way of life"—indeed, the idea that the State should actively try to promote it would fill most of us with alarm. The Greeks thought of the polis as an active, formative thing, training the minds and characters of the citizens; we think of it as a piece of machinery for the production of safety and convenience. The training in virtue, which the medieval state left to the Church, and the polis made its own concern, the modern state leaves to God knows what. 27

"Polis," then, originally "citadel," may mean as much as "the whole communal life of the people, political, cultural, moral"—even "economic," for how else are we to understand another phrase in this same speech, "the produce of the whole world comes to us, because of the magnitude of our polis"? This must mean "our national wealth." 28

Religion too was bound up with the polis—though not every form of religion. The Olympian gods were indeed worshipped by Greeks everywhere, but each polis had, if not its own gods, at least its own particular cults of these gods. Thus, Athena of the Brazen House was worshipped at Sparta, but to the Spartans Athena was never what she was to the Athenians, "Athena Polias," Athena guardian of the City. So Hera, in Athens, was a goddess worshipped particularly by women, as the goddess of hearth and home, but in Argos "Argive Hera" was the supreme deity of the people. We have in these gods tribal deities, like Jehovah, who exist as it were on two levels at once, as gods of the individual polis, and gods of the whole Greek race. But beyond these Olympians, each polis had its minor local deities, "heroes" and nymphs, each worshipped with his immemorial rite, and scarcely imagined to exist outside the particular locality where the rite was performed. So that in spite of the panhellenic Olympian system, and in spite of the philosophic spirit which made merely tribal gods impossible for the Greek, there is a sense in which it is true to say that the polis is an independent religious, as well as political, unit. The tragic poets at least could make use of the old belief that the gods desert a city which is about to be captured. The gods are the unseen partners in the city's welfare. 29

How intimately religious and "political" thinking were connected we can best see from the *Oresteia* of Aeschylus. This trilogy is built 30 around the idea of Justice. It moves from chaos to order, from conflict to reconciliation; and it moves on two planes at once, the human and the divine. In the *Agamemnon* we see one of the moral Laws of the universe, that punishment must follow crime, fulfilled in the crudest possible way; one crime evokes another crime to avenge it, in apparently endless succession—but always with the sanction of Zeus. In the *Choephori* this series of crimes reaches its climax when Orestes avenges his father by killing his mother. He does this with repugnance, but he is commanded to do it by Apollo, the son and the mouthpiece of Zeus—Why? Because in murdering Agamemnon the King and her husband, Clytemnestra has committed a crime which, unpunished, would shatter the very fabric of society. It is the concern of the Olympian gods to defend Order; they are particularly the gods of the Polis. But Orestes' matricide outrages the deepest human instincts; he is therefore implacably pursued by other deities, the Furies. The Furies have no interest in social order, but they cannot permit this outrage on the sacredness of the blood-tie, which it is their office to protect. In the *Eumenides* there is a terrific conflict between the ancient Furies and the younger Olympians over the unhappy Orestes. The solution is that Athena comes with a new dispensation from Zeus. A jury of Athenian citizens is empanelled to try Orestes on the Acropolis where he has fled for protection—this being the first meeting of the Council of the Areopagus. The votes on either side are equal; therefore, as an act of mercy, Orestes is acquitted. The Furies, cheated of their legitimate prey, threaten Attica with destruction, but Athena persuades them to make their home in Athens, with their ancient office not abrogated (as at first they think) but enhanced, since henceforth they will punish violence within the polis, not only within the family.

So, to Aeschylus, the mature polis becomes the means by which 31 the Law is satisfied without producing chaos, since public justice supersedes private vengeance; and the claims of authority are reconciled with the instincts of humanity. The trilogy ends with an impressive piece of pageantry. The awful Furies exchange their black robes for red ones, no longer Furies, but "Kindly Ones" (Eumenides); no longer enemies of Zeus, but his willing and honoured agents, defenders of his now perfected social order against intestine violence. Before the eyes of the Athenian citizens assembled in the theatre just under the Acropolis—and indeed guided by citizen-marshals—they pass out of the theatre to their new home on the other side of the Acropolis. Some of the most acute of man's moral and social problems have been solved, and the means of the reconciliation is the Polis.

A few minutes later, on that early spring day of 458 B.C., the 32 citizens too would leave the theatre, and by the same exits as the Eumenides. In what mood? Surely no audience has had such an experience since. At the time, the Athenian polis was confidently riding the crest of the wave. In this trilogy there was exaltation, for they had seen their polis emerge as the pattern of Justice, of Order, of what the Greeks called Cosmos; the polis, they saw, was—or could be—the very crown and summit of things. They had seen their goddess herself acting as President of the first judicial tribunal—a steadying and sobering thought. But there was more than this. The rising democracy had recently curtailed the powers of the ancient Court of the Areopagus, and the reforming statesman had been assassinated by his political enemies. What of the Eumenides, the awful inhabitants of the land, the transformed Furies, whose function it was to avenge the shedding of a kinsman's blood? There was warning here, as well as exaltation, in the thought that the polis had its divine as well as its human members. There was Athena, one of those Olympians who had presided over the formation of ordered society, and there were the more primitive deities who had been persuaded by Athena to accept this pattern of civilized life, and were swift to punish any who, by violence from within, threatened its stability.

To such an extent was the religious thought of Aeschylus inter- 33 twined with the idea of the polis; and not of Aeschylus alone, but of many other Greek thinkers too—notably of Socrates, Plato, and Aristotle. Aristotle made a remark which we most inadequately translate "Man is a political animal." What Aristotle really said is "Man is a creature who lives in a polis"; and what he goes on to demonstrate, in his *Politics*, is that the polis is the only framework within which man can fully realize his spiritual, moral and intellectual capacities.

Such are some of the implications of this word: we shall meet 34 more later, for I have deliberately said little about its purely "political" side—to emphasize the fact that it is so much more than a form of political organization. The polis was a living community, based on kinship, real or assumed—a kind of extended family, turning as much as possible of life into family life, and of course having its family quarrels, which were the more bitter because they were family quarrels.

This it is that explains not only the polis but also much of what the 35 Greek made and thought, that he was essentially social. In the winning of his livelihood he was essentially individualist: in the filling of his life he was essentially "communist." Religion, art, games, the discussion of things—all these were needs of life that could be fully satisfied only through the polis—not, as with us, through voluntary associations of like-minded people, or through *entrepreneurs* appealing to individuals. (This partly explains the difference between Greek drama and the modern cinema.) Moreover, he wanted to play his own part in running the affairs of the community. When we realize how many of the necessary, interesting and exciting activities of life the Greek enjoyed through the polis, all of them in the open air, within sight of the same acropolis, with the same ring of mountains or of sea visibly enclosing the life of every member of the state—then it becomes possible to understand Greek history, to understand that in spite of the promptings of common sense the Greek could not bring himself to sacrifice the polis, with its vivid and comprehensive life, to a wider but less interesting unity. We may perhaps record an Imaginary Conversation between an Ancient Greek and a member of the Athenaeum. The member regrets the lack of political sense shown by the Greeks. The Greek replies, "How many clubs are there in London?" The member, at a guess, says about five hundred. The Greek then says, "Now, if all these combined, what splendid premises they could build. They could have a club-house as big as Hyde Park." "But," says the member, "that would no longer be a club." "Precisely," says the Greek, "and a polis as big as yours is no longer a polis."

After all, modern Europe, in spite of its common culture, common   36
interests, and ease of communication, finds it difficult to accept the idea of limiting national sovereignty, though this would increase the security of life without notably adding to its dullness; the Greek had possibly more to gain by watering down the polis—but how much more to lose. It was not common sense that made Achilles great, but certain other qualities.

GRETEL   EHRLICH

Wyoming: The Solace of Open Spaces

Gretel Ehrlich (1946–   ) grew up in Santa Barbara, California, so close to the beach that on quiet nights she could "hear the seals barking on the channel islands." Educated at Bennington College in Vermont and at U.C.L.A., she worked briefly in New York as a film editor. She went to Wyoming in 1976 to make a documentary film and quickly fell in love with her surroundings. Today, Ehrlich is a rancher near Shell. If she were to ride a horse north, she says, it would take her three days to reach the nearest fence, and in three directions, she has an unobstructed horizon for a hundred miles. Ehrlich has published three books of poetry and a novel, but is best known for her essays and books of nonfiction: *The Solace of Open Spaces* (1985), from which the following essay is drawn; *A Match to the Heart* (1994), which tells the story of her being struck by lightning; *Yellowstone: and of Fire and Ice* (1995); and *Questions of Heaven: The Chinese Journeys of an American Buddhist* (1997). Readers may wish to contrast Ehrlich's presentation of rural neighborliness with Robert Frost's (in "Mending Wall"), or they may want to compare the neighborliness of the city people described in Jane Jacobs's "The Uses of Sidewalks."

It's May, and I've just awakened from a nap, curled against sage-   1
brush the way my dog taught me to sleep—sheltered from wind. A

front is pulling the huge sky over me, and from the dark a hailstone has hit me on the head. I'm trailing a band of 2000 sheep across a stretch of Wyoming badland, a fifty-mile trip that takes five days because sheep shade up in hot sun and won't budge until it cools. Bunched together now, and excited into a run by the storm, they drift across dry land, tumbling into draws like water and surging out again onto the rugged, choppy plateaus that are the building blocks of this state.

The name Wyoming comes from an Indian word meaning "at the great plains," but the plains are really valleys, great arid valleys, 1600 square miles, with the horizon bending up on all sides into mountain ranges. This gives the vastness a sheltering look.

Winter lasts six months here. Prevailing winds spill snowdrifts to the east, and new storms from the northwest replenish them. This white bulk is sometimes dizzying, even nauseating, to look at. At twenty, thirty, and forty degrees below zero, not only does your car not work but neither do your mind and body. The landscape hardens into a dungeon of space. During the winter, while I was riding to find a new calf, my legs froze to the saddle, and in the silence that such cold creates I felt like the first person on earth, or the last.

Today the sun is out—only a few clouds billowing. In the east, where the sheep have started off without me, the benchland tilts up in a series of red-earthed, eroded mesas, planed flat on top by a million years of water; behind them, a bold line of muscular scarps rears up 10,000 feet to become the Big Horn Mountains. A tidal pattern is engraved into the ground, as if left by the sea that once covered this state. Canyons curve down like galaxies to meet the oncoming rush of flat land.

To live and work in this kind of open country, with its hundred-mile views, is to lose the distinction between background and foreground. When I asked an older ranch hand to describe Wyoming's openness, he said, "It's all a bunch of nothing—wind and rattlesnakes—and so much of it you can't tell where you're going or where you've been and it don't make much difference." John, a sheepman I know, is tall and handsome and has an explosive temperament. He has a perfect intuition about people and sheep. They call him "Highpockets," because he's so long-legged; his graceful stride matches the distance he has to cover. He says, "Open space hasn't affected me at all. It's all the people moving in on it." The huge ranch he was born on takes up much of one county and spreads into another state; to put 100,000 miles on his pickup in three years and never leave home is not unusual. A friend of mine has an aunt who ranched on Powder River and didn't go off her place for eleven years. When her husband died, she quickly moved to town, bought a car, and drove around the States to see what she'd been missing.

Most people tell me they've simply driven through Wyoming, as if there were nothing to stop for. Or else they've skied in Jackson Hole, a place Wyomingites acknowledge uncomfortably, because its green beauty and chic affluence are mismatched with the rest of the state. Most of Wyoming has a "lean-to" look. Instead of big, roomy barns and Victorian houses, there are dugouts, low sheds, log cabins, sheep camps, and fence lines that look like driftwood blown haphazardly into place. People here still feel pride because they live in such a harsh place, part of the glamorous cowboy past, and they are determined not to be the victims of a mining-dominated future.

Most characteristic of the state's landscape is what a developer euphemistically describes as "indigenous growth right up to your front door"—a reference to waterless stands of salt sage, snakes, jackrabbits, deerflies, red dust, a brief respite of wildflowers, dry washes, and no trees. In the Great Plains, the vistas look like music, like kyries of grass, but Wyoming seems to be the doing of a mad architect—tumbled and twisted, ribboned with faded, deathbed colors, thrust up and pulled down as if the place had been startled out of a deep sleep and thrown into a pure light. 7

I came here four years ago. I had not planned to stay, but I couldn't make myself leave. John, the sheepman, put me to work immediately. It was spring, and shearing time. For fourteen days of fourteen hours each, we moved thousands of sheep through sorting corrals to be sheared, branded, and deloused. I suspect that my original motive for coming here was to "lose myself" in new and unpopulated territory. Instead of producing the numbness I thought I wanted, life on the sheep ranch woke me up. The vitality of the people I was working with flushed out what had become a hallucinatory rawness inside me. I threw away my clothes and bought new ones; I cut my hair. The arid country was a clean slate. Its absolute indifference steadied me. 8

Sagebrush covers 58,000 square miles of Wyoming. The biggest city has a population of 50,000, and there are only five settlements that could be called cities in the whole state. The rest are towns, scattered across the expanse with as much as sixty miles between them, their populations 2000, fifty, or ten. They are fugitive-looking, perched on a barren, windblown bench, or tagged onto a river or a railroad, or laid out straight in a farming valley with implement stores and a block-long Mormon church. In the eastern part of the state, which slides down into the Great Plains, the new mining settlements are boom-towns, trailer cities, metal knots on flat land. 9

Despite the desolate look, there's a coziness to living in this state. There are so few people (only 470,000) that ranchers who buy and sell cattle know each other statewide; the kids who choose to go to college usually go to the state's one university, in Laramie; hired hands work their way around Wyoming in a lifetime of hirings and firings. And, despite the physical separation, people stay in touch, often driving two or three hours to another ranch for dinner. 10

Seventy-five years ago, when travel was by buckboard or horse-   11
back, cowboys who were temporarily out of work rode the grub line—
drifting from ranch to ranch, mending fences or milking cows, and
receiving in exchange a bed and meals. Gossip and messages traveled
this slow circuit with them, creating an intimacy between ranchers
who were three and four weeks' ride apart. One old-time couple I
know, whose turn-of-the-century homestead was used by an outlaw
gang as a relay station for stolen horses, recall that if you were traveling, desperado or not, any lighted ranch house was a welcome sign.
Even now, for someone who lives in a remote spot, arriving at a ranch
or coming to town for supplies is cause for celebration. To emerge from
isolation can be disorienting. Everything looks bright, new, vivid. After
I had been herding sheep for only three days, the sound of the camp-
tender's pickup flustered me. Longing for human company, I felt a
foolish grin take over my face, yet I had to resist an urgent temptation
to run and hide.

Things happen suddenly in Wyoming: the change of seasons and   12
weather; for people, the violent swings in and out of isolation. But
goodnaturedness is concomitant with severity. Friendliness is a tradition. Strangers passing on the road wave hello. A common sight is two
pickups stopped side by side far out on a range, on a dirt track winding
through the sage. The drivers will share a cigarette, uncap their thermos bottles, and pass a battered cup, steaming with coffee, between
windows. These meetings summon up the details of several generations, because in Wyoming, private histories are largely public knowledge.

Because ranch work is a physical and, these days, economic strain,   13
being "at home on the range" is a matter of vigor, self-reliance, and
common sense. A person's life is not a series of dramatic events for
which he or she is applauded or exiled but a slow accumulation of
days, seasons, years, fleshed out by the generational weight of one's
family and anchored by a land-bound sense of place.

In most parts of Wyoming, the human population is visibly out-   14
numbered by the animal. Not far from my town of fifty, I rode into a
narrow valley and startled a herd of 200 elk. Eagles took like small
people as they eat car-killed deer by the road. Antelope, moving in
small, graceful bands, travel at 60 miles an hour, their mouths open as
if drinking in the space.

The solitude in which westerners live makes them quiet. They   15
telegraph thoughts and feelings by the way they tilt their heads and listen; pulling their Stetsons into a steep dive over their eyes, or pigeon-
toeing one boot over the other, they lean against a fence with a fat
wedge of snoose beneath their lower lips and take the whole scene in.
These detached looks of quiet amusement are sometimes cynical, but
they can also come from a dry-eyed humility as lucid as the air is clear.

Conversation goes on in what sounds like a private code; a few   16
phrases imply a complex of meanings. Asking directions, you get a curious list of details. While trailing sheep, I was told to "ride up to that
kinda upturned rock, follow the pink wash, turn left at the dump, and
then you'll see the waterhole." One friend told his wife on roundup to
"turn at the salt lick and the dead cow," which turned out to be a scattering of bones and no salt lick at all.

Sentence structure is shortened to the skin and bones of a thought.   17
Descriptive words are dropped, even verbs; a cowboy looking over a
corral full of horses will say to a wrangler, "Which one needs rode?"
People hold back their thoughts in what seems to be a dumbfounded
silence, then erupt with an excoriating, perceptive remark. Language,
so compressed, becomes metaphorical. A rancher ended a relationship
with one remark: "You're a bad check," meaning bouncing in and out
was intolerable, and even coming back would be no good.

What's behind this laconic style is shyness. There is no vocabulary   18
for the subject of feelings. It's not a hangdog shyness, or anything
coy—always there's a robust spirit in evidence behind the restraint, as
if the earth-dredging wind that pulls across Wyoming had carried its
people's voices away but everything else in them had shouldered confidently into the breeze.

I've spent hours riding to sheep camp at dawn in a pickup when   19
nothing was said; eaten meals in the cookhouse when the only words
spoken were a mumbled "Thank you, ma'am" at the end of dinner.
The silence is profound. Instead of talking, we seem to share one eye.
Keenly observed, the world is transformed. The landscape is engorged
with detail, every movement on it chillingly sharp. The air between
people is charged. Days unfold, bathed in their own music. Nights become hallucinatory; dreams, prescient.

Spring weather is capricious and mean. It snows, then blisters with   20
heat. There have been tornadoes. They lay their elephant trunks out in
the sage until they find houses, then slurp everything up and leave.
I've noticed that melting snowbanks hiss and rot, viperous, then drip
into calm pools where ducklings hatch and livestock, being trailed to
summer range, drink. With the ice cover gone, rivers churn a milk-
shake brown, taking culverts and small bridges with them. Water in
such an arid place (the average annual rainfall where I live is less than
eight inches) is like blood. It festoons drab land with green veins: a line
of cottonwoods following a stream; a strip of alfalfa; and on ditch-
banks, wild asparagus growing.

I've moved to a small cattle ranch owned by friends. It's at the foot   21
of the Big Horn Mountains. A few weeks ago, I helped them deliver a
calf who was stuck halfway out of his mother's body. By the time he
was freed, we could see a heartbeat, but he was straining against a

swollen tongue for air. Mary and I held him upside down by his back feet, while Stan, on his hands and knees in the blood, gave the calf mouth-to-mouth resuscitation. I have a vague memory of being pneumonia-choked as a child, my mother giving me her air, which may account for my romance with this windswept state.

If anything is endemic to Wyoming, it is wind. This big room of space is swept out daily, leaving a boneyard of fossils, agates, and carcasses in every stage of decay. Though it was water that initially shaped the state, wind is the meticulous gardener, raising dust and pruning the sage. 22

I try to imagine a world of uncharted land, in which one could look over an uncompleted map and ride a horse past where all the lines have stopped. There is no wilderness left; wildness, yes, but true wilderness has been gone on this continent since the time of Lewis and Clark's overland journey. 23

Two hundred years ago, the Crow, Shoshone, Arapaho, Cheyenne, and Sioux roamed the intermountain West, orchestrating their movements according to hunger, season, and warfare. Once they acquired horses, they traversed the spines of all the big Wyoming ranges—the Absarokas, the Wind Rivers, the Tetons, the Big Horns—and wintered on the unprotected plains that fan out from them. Space was life. The world was their home. 24

What was life-giving to native Americans was often nightmarish to sodbusters who arrived encumbered with families and ethnic pasts to be transplanted in nearly uninhabitable land. The great distances, the shortage of water and trees, and the loneliness created unexpected hardships for them. In her book *O Pioneers!*, Willa Cather gives a settler's version of the bleak landscape: 25

> The little town behind them had vanished as if it had never been, had fallen behind the swell of the prairie, and the stern frozen country received them into its bosom. The homesteads were few and far apart; here and there a windmill gaunt against the sky, a sod house crouching in a hollow.

The emptiness of the West was for others a geography of possibility. Men and women who amassed great chunks of land and struggled to preserve unfenced empires were, despite their self-serving motives, unwitting geographers. They understood the lay of the land. But by the 1850s, the Oregon and Mormon trails sported bumper-to-bumper traffic. Wealthy landowners, many of them aristocratic absentee landlords, known as remittance men because they were paid to come West and get out of their families' hair, overstocked the range with more than a million head of cattle. By 1885, the feed and water were desperately short, and the winter of 1886 laid out the gaunt bodies of dead animals so closely together that when the thaw came, one 26 rancher from Kaycee claimed to have walked on cowhide all the way to Crazy Woman Creek, twenty miles away.

Territorial Wyoming was a boy's world. The land was generous   27
with everything but water. At first there was room enough, food enough, for everyone. And, as with all beginnings, an expansive mood set in. The young cowboys, drifters, shopkeepers, schoolteachers, were heroic, lawless, generous, rowdy, and tenacious. The individualism and optimism generated during those times have endured.

John Tisdale rode north with the trail herds from Texas. He was a   28
college-educated man with enough money to buy a small outfit near the Powder River. While driving home from the town of Buffalo with a buckboard full of Christmas toys for his family and a winter's supply of food, he was shot in the back by an agent of the cattle barons who resented the encroachment of small-time stockmen like him. The wealthy cattlemen tried to control all the public grazing land by re-stricting membership in the Wyoming Stock Growers Association, as if it were a country club. They ostracized from roundups and brandings cowboys and ranchers who were not members, then denounced them as rustlers. Tisdale's death, the second such cold-blooded murder, kicked off the Johnson County cattle war, which was no simple good-guy-bad-guy shootout but a complicated class struggle between landed gentry and less affluent settlers—a shocking reminder that the West was not an egalitarian sanctuary after all.

Fencing ultimately enforced boundaries, but barbed wire abro-   29
gated space. It was stretched across the beautiful valleys, into the mountains, over desert badlands, through buffalo grass. The "anything is possible" fever—the lure of any new place—was constricted. The in-tegrity of the land as a geographic body, and the freedom to ride any-where on it, was lost.

I punched cows with a young man named Martin, who is the   30
great-grandson of John Tisdale. His inheritance is not the open land that Tisdale knew and prematurely lost but a rage against restraint.

Wyoming tips down as you head northeast; the highest ground—   31
the Laramie Plains—is on the Colorado border. Up where I live, the Big Horn River leaks into difficult, arid terrain. In the basin here it's dammed, sandhill cranes gather and, with delicate legwork, slice through the stilled water. I was driving by with a rancher one morning when he commented that cranes are "old-fashioned." When I asked why, he said, "Because they mate for life." Then he looked at me with a twinkle in his eyes, as if to say he really did believe in such things but also understood why we break our own rules.

In all this open space, values crystallize quickly. People are strong on   32
scruples but tenderhearted about quirky behavior. A friend and I found one ranch hand, who's "not quite right in the head," sitting in front of

the badly decayed carcass of a cow, shaking his finger and saying, "Now, I don't want you to do this ever again!" When I asked what was wrong with him, I was told, "He's goofier than hell, just like the rest of us." Perhaps because the West is historically new, conventional morality is still felt to be less important than rock-bottom truths. Though there's always a lot of teasing and sparring around, people are blunt with each other, sometimes even cruel, believing honesty is stronger medicine than sympathy, which may console but often conceals.

The formality that goes hand in hand with the rowdiness is known as "the Western Code." It's a list of practical dos and don'ts, faithfully observed. A friend, Cliff, who runs a trapline in the winter, cut off half his foot while axing a hole in the ice. Alone, he dragged himself to his pickup and headed for town, stopping to open the ranch gate as he left, and getting out to close it again, thus losing, in his observance of rules, precious time and blood. Later, he commented, "How would it look, them having to come to the hospital to tell me their cows had gotten out?" 33

Accustomed to emergencies, my friends doctor each other from the vet's bag with relish. When one old-timer suffered a heart attack in hunting camp, his partner quickly stirred up a brew of red horse liniment and hot water and made the half-conscious victim drink it, then tied him onto a horse and led him twenty miles to town. He regained consciousness and lived. 34

The roominess of the state has affected political attitudes as well. Ranchers keep up with world politics and the convulsions of the economy but are basically isolationists. Being used to running their own small empires of land and livestock, they're suspicious of big government. It's a "don't fence me in" holdover from a century ago. They still want the elbow room their grandfathers had, so they're strongly conservative, but with a populist twist. 35

Summer is the season when we get our "cowboy tans"—on the lower parts of our faces and on three fourths of our arms. Excessive heat, in the nineties and higher, sends us outside with the mosquitoes. In winter, we're tucked inside our houses, and the white wasteland outside appears to be expanding, but in summer, all the greenery abridges space. Summer is a go-ahead season. Every living thing is off the block and in the race: battalions of bugs in flight and biting; bats swinging around my log cabin as if the bases were loaded and someone had hit a home run. Some of summer's high-speed growth is ominous: larkspur, death camas, and green greasewood can kill sheep—an ironic idea, dying in this desert from eating what is too verdant. With sixteen hours of daylight, farmers and ranchers irrigate feverishly. There are first, second, and third cuttings of hay, some crews averaging only four hours of sleep a night for weeks. And, like the cowboys who 36 in summer ride the night rodeo circuit, nighthawks make daredevil dives at dusk with an eerie whirring that sounds like a plane going down on the shimmering horizon.

In the town where I live, they've had to board up the dance-hall windows because there have been so many fights. There's so little to do except work that people wind up in a state of idle agitation that becomes fatalistic, as if there were nothing to be done about all this untapped energy. So the dark side to the grandeur of these spaces is the small-mindedness that seals people in. Men become hermits; women go mad. Cabin fever explodes into suicides, or into grudges and life-long family feuds. Two sisters in my area inherited a ranch but found they couldn't get along. They fenced the place in half. When one's cows got out and mixed with the other's, the women went at each other with shovels. They ended up in the same hospital room, but never spoke a word to each other for the rest of their lives. 37

Eccentricity ritualizes behavior. It's a shortcut through unmanageable emotions and strict social conventions. I knew a sheepherder named Fred who, at seventy-eight, still had a handsome face, which he kept smooth by plastering it each day with bag balm and Vaseline. He was curious, well-read, and had a fact-keeping mind to go along with his penchant for hoarding. His reliquary of gunnysacks, fence wire, wood, canned food, unopened Christmas presents, and magazines matched his odd collages of meals: sardines with maple syrup; vegetable soup garnished with Fig Newtons. His wagon was so overloaded that he had to sleep sitting up because there was no room on the bed. Despite his love of up-to-date information, Fred died from gangrene when an old-timer's remedy of fresh sheep manure, applied as a poultice to a bad cut, failed to save him. 38

After the brief lushness of summer, the sun moves south. The range grass is brown. Livestock has been trailed back down from the mountains. Waterholes begin to frost over at night. Last fall Martin asked me to accompany him on a pack trip. With five horses, we followed a river into the mountains behind the tiny Wyoming town of Meeteetse. Groves of aspen, red and orange, gave off a light that made us look toasted. Our hunting camp was so high that clouds skidded across our foreheads, then slowed to sail out across the warm valleys. Except for a bull moose who wandered into our camp and mistook our black gelding for a rival, we shot at nothing. 39

One of our evening entertainments was to watch the night sky. My dog, who also came on the trip, a dingo bred to herd sheep, is so used to the silence and empty skies that when an airplane flies over he always looks up and eyes the distant intruder quizzically. The sky, lately, seems to be much more crowded than it used to be. Satellites make their silent passes in the dark with great regularity. We counted eighteen in one hour's viewing. How odd to think that while they cir- 40 cumnavigated the planet, Martin and I had moved only six miles into our local wilderness, and had seen no other human for the two weeks we stayed there.

At night, by moonlight, the land is whittled to slivers—a ridge, a 41
river, a strip of grassland stretching to the mountains, then the huge sky. One morning a full moon was setting in the west just as the sun was rising. I felt precariously balanced between the two as I loped across a meadow. For a moment, I could believe that the stars, which were still visible, work like cooper's bands, holding everything above Wyoming together.

Space has a spiritual equivalent, and can heal what is divided and 42
burdensome in us. My grandchildren will probably use space shuttles for a honeymoon trip or to recover from heart attacks, but closer to home we might also learn how to carry space inside ourselves in the effortless way we carry our skins. Space represents sanity, not a life purified, dull, or "spaced out" but one that might accommodate intelligently any idea or situation.

From the clayey soil of northern Wyoming is mined bentonite, 43
which is used as a filler in candy, gum, and lipstick. We Americans are great on fillers, as if what we have, what we are, is not enough. We have a cultural tendency toward denial, but, being affluent, we strangle ourselves with what we can buy. We have only to look at the houses we build to see how we build *against* space, the way we drink against pain and loneliness. We fill up space as if it were a pie shell, with things whose opacity further obstructs our ability to see what is already there.

JAMES BALDWIN

Fifth Avenue, Uptown: A Letter from Harlem

James Arthur Baldwin (1924–1987) was born and raised in Harlem, the stepson of an evangelical preacher. Baldwin himself underwent a dramatic religious conversion when he was fourteen years old and later realized that involvement with the church had sheltered him from the despair and bitterness many of his classmates felt as they grew up in a segregated society. After graduating from high school, Baldwin worked as a handyman, dishwasher, waiter, and office boy before Richard Wright helped him win the first of a series of literary fellowships that allowed him to write his novel *Go Tell It on the Mountain* (1953). From 1948 to 1957, unable to find his individual voice and perspective in the segregated United States, he lived in Paris. When he returned, he threw himself into his writing and into the civil rights struggle, writing novels, short stories, and plays. It was Baldwin's essays, however, that established his stature as a writer. His earliest and most famous essays are collected in *Notes of a Native Son* (1955), *Nobody Knows My Name* (1961), and *The Fire Next Time* (1963). His collected essays were published in *The Price of the Ticket* (1985). "Fifth Avenue, Uptown" was first published in *Esquire,* July 1960. A valuable companion essay is N. Scott Momaday's "The Way to Rainy Mountain," which examines another community dying—perhaps for related reasons.

There is a housing project standing now where the house in which   1
we grew up once stood, and one of those stunted city trees is snarling where our doorway used to be. This is on the rehabilitated side of the avenue. The other side of the avenue—for progress takes time—has not been rehabilitated yet and it looks exactly as it looked in the days when we sat with our noses pressed against the windowpane, longing to be allowed to go "across the street." The grocery store which gave us credit is still there, and there can be no doubt that it is still giving credit. The people in the project certainly need it—far more, indeed, than they ever needed the project. The last time I passed by, the Jewish proprietor was still standing among his shelves, looking sadder and heavier but scarcely any older. Farther down the block stands the shoe-repair store in which our shoes were repaired until reparation became impossible and in which, then, we bought all our "new" ones. The Negro proprietor is still in the window, head down, working at the leather.

These two, I imagine, could tell a long tale if they would (perhaps   2
they would be glad to if they could), having watched so many, for so long, struggling in the fishhooks, the barbed wire, of this avenue.

The avenue is elsewhere the renowned and elegant Fifth. The area   3
I am describing, which, in today's gang parlance, would be called "the turf," is bound by Lenox Avenue on the west, the Harlem River on the east, 135th Street on the north, and 130th Street on the south. We never lived beyond these boundaries; this is where we grew up. Walking along 145th Street—for example—familiar as it is, and similar, does not have the same impact because I did not know any of the people on the block. But when I turn east on 131st Street and Lenox Avenue, there is first a soda-pop joint, then a shoeshine "parlor," then a grocery store, then a dry cleaners', then the houses. All along the street there are people who watched me grow up, people who grew up with me, people I watched grow up along with my brothers and sisters; and, sometimes in my arms, sometimes underfoot, sometimes at my shoulder—or on it—their children, a riot, a forest of children, who include my nieces and nephews.

When we reach the end of this long block, we find ourselves on   4
wide, filthy, hostile Fifth Avenue, facing that project which hangs over

the avenue like a monument to the folly, and the cowardice, of good intentions. All along the block, for anyone who knows it, are immense human gaps, like craters. These gaps are not created merely by those who have moved away, inevitably into some other ghetto; or by those who have risen, almost always into a greater capacity for self-loathing and self-delusion; or yet by those who, by whatever means—War II, the Korean war, a policeman's gun or billy, a gang war, a brawl, madness, an overdose of heroin, or, simply, unnatural exhaustion—are dead. I am talking about those who are left, and I am talking principally about the young. What are they doing? Well, some, a minority, are fanatical churchgoers, members of the more extreme of the Holy Roller sects. Many, many more are "moslems," by affiliation or sympathy, that is to say that they are united by nothing more—and nothing less—than a hatred of the white world and all its works. They are present, for example, at every Buy Black street corner meeting—meetings in which the speaker urges his hearers to cease trading with white men and establish a separate economy. Neither the speaker nor his hearers can possibly do this, of course, since Negroes do not own General Motors or RCA or the A & P, nor, indeed, do they own more than a wholly insufficient fraction of anything else in Harlem (those who *do* own anything are more interested in their profits than in their fellows). But these meetings nevertheless keep alive in the participators a certain pride of bitterness without which, however futile this bitterness may be, they could scarcely remain alive at all. Many have given up. They stay home and watch the TV screen, living on the earnings of their parents, cousins, brothers, or uncles, and only leave the house to go to the movies or to the nearest bar. "How're you making it?" one may ask, running into them along the block, or in the bar. "Oh, I'm TV-ing it"; with the saddest, sweetest, most shame-faced of smiles, and from a great distance. This distance one is compelled to respect; anyone who has traveled so far will not easily be dragged again into the world. There are further retreats, of course, than the TV screen or the bar. There are those who are simply sitting on their stoops, "stoned," animated for a moment only, and hideously, by the approach of someone who may lend them the money for a "fix." Or by the approach of someone from whom they can purchase it, one of the shrewd ones, on the way to prison or just coming out.

And the others, who have avoided all of these deaths, get up in the morning and go downtown to meet "the man." They work in the white man's world all day and come home in the evening to this fetid block. They struggle to instill in their children some private sense of honor or dignity which will help the child survive. This means, of course, that they must struggle, stolidly, incessantly, to keep this sense alive in themselves, in spite of the insults, the indifference, and the cruelty they are certain to encounter in their working day. They patiently browbeat the landlord into fixing the heat, the plaster, the plumbing; this demands prodigious patience; nor is patience usually enough. In trying to make their hovels habitable, they are perpetually throwing good money after bad. Such frustration, so long endured, is driving many strong, admirable men and women whose only crime is color to the very gates of paranoia.

One remembers them from another time—playing handball in the ₆ playground, going to church, wondering if they were going to be promoted at school. One remembers them going off to war—gladly, to escape this block. One remembers their return. Perhaps one remembers their wedding day. And one sees where the girl is now—vainly looking for salvation from some other embittered, trussed, and struggling boy— and sees the all-but-abandoned children in the streets.

Now I am perfectly aware that there are other slums in which ₇ white men are fighting for their lives, and mainly losing. I know that blood is also flowing through those streets and that the human damage there is incalculable. People are continually pointing out to me the wretchedness of white people in order to console me for the wretchedness of blacks. But an itemized account of the American failure does not console me and it should not console anyone else. That hundreds of thousands of white people are living, in effect, no better than the "niggers" is not a fact to be regarded with complacency. The social and moral bankruptcy suggested by this fact is of the bitterest, most terrifying kind.

The people, however, who believe that this democratic anguish has ₈ some consoling value are always pointing out that So-and-So, white, and So-and-So, black, rose from the slums into the big time. The existence—the public existence—of, say, Frank Sinatra and Sammy Davis, Jr. proves to them that America is still the land of opportunity and that inequalities vanish before the determined will. It proves nothing of the sort. The determined will is rare—at the moment, in this country, it is unspeakably rare—and the inequalities suffered by the many are in no way justified by the rise of a few. A few have always risen—in every country, every era, and in the teeth of regimes which can by no stretch of the imagination be thought of as free. Not all of these people, it is worth remembering, left the world better than they found it. The determined will is rare, but it is not invariably benevolent. Furthermore, the American equation of success with the big times reveals an awful disrespect for human life and human achievement. This equation has placed our cities among the most dangerous in the world and has placed our youth among the most empty and most bewildered. The situation of our youth is not mysterious. Children have never been very good at listening to their elders, but they have never failed to imitate them. They must, they have no other models. That is exactly what our children are doing. They are imitating our immorality, our disrespect for the pain of others.

All other slum dwellers, when the bank account permits it, can 9
move out of the slum and vanish altogether from the eye of persecution. No Negro in this country has ever made that much money and it
will be a long time before any Negro does. The Negroes in Harlem,
who have no money, spend what they have on such gimcracks as they
are sold. These include "wider" TV screens, more "faithful" hi-fi sets,
more "powerful" cars, all of which, of course, are obsolete long before
they are paid for. Anyone who has ever struggled with poverty knows
how extremely expensive it is to be poor; and if one is a member of a
captive population, economically speaking, one's feet have simply
been placed on the treadmill forever. One is victimized, economically,
in a thousand ways—rent, for example, or car insurance. Go shopping
one day in Harlem—for anything—and compare Harlem prices and
quality with those downtown.

The people who have managed to get off this block have only got 10
as far as a more respectable ghetto. This respectable ghetto does not
even have the advantages of the disreputable one—friends, neighbors,
a familiar church, and friendly tradesmen; and it is not, moreover, in
the nature of any ghetto to remain respectable long. Every Sunday,
people who have left the block take the lonely ride back, dragging
their increasingly discontented children with them. They spend the
day talking, not always with words, about the trouble they've seen
and the trouble—one must watch their eyes as they watch their children—they are only too likely to see. For children do not like ghettos.
It takes them nearly no time to discover exactly why they are there.

The projects in Harlem are hated. They are hated almost as much 11
as policemen, and this is saying a great deal. And they are hated for the
same reason: both reveal, unbearably, the real attitude of the white
world, no matter how many liberal speeches are made, no matter how
many lofty editorials are written, no matter how many civil-rights
commissions are set up.

The projects are hideous, of course, there being a law, apparently 12
respected throughout the world, that popular housing shall be as
cheerless as a prison. They are lumped all over Harlem, colorless,
bleak, high, and revolting. The wide windows look out on Harlem's in-
vincible and indescribable squalor: the Park Avenue railroad tracks,
around which, about forty years ago, the present dark community
began; the unrehabilitated houses, bowed down, it would seem, under
the great weight of frustration and bitterness they contain; the dark,
the ominous schoolhouses from which the child may emerge maimed,
blinded, hooked, or enraged for life; and the churches, churches, block
upon block of churches, niched in the walls like cannon in the walls of
a fortress. Even if the administration of the projects were not so in-
sanely humiliating (for example: one must report raises in salary to the

management, which will then eat up the profit by raising one's rent; the management has the right to know who is staying in your apartment; the management can ask you to leave, at their discretion), the projects would still be hated because they are an insult to the meanest intelligence.

Harlem got its first private project, Riverton[1]—which is now, naturally, a slum—about twelve years ago because at that time Negroes were not allowed to live in Stuyvesant Town. Harlem watched Riverton go up, therefore, in the most violent bitterness of spirit, and hated it long before the builders arrived. They began hating it at about the time people began moving out of their condemned houses to make room for this additional proof of how thoroughly the white world despised them. And they had scarcely moved in, naturally, before they began smashing windows, defacing walls, urinating in the elevators, and fornicating in the playgrounds. Liberals, both white and black, were appalled at the spectacle. I was appalled by the liberal innocence—or cynicism, which comes out in practice as much the same thing. Other people were delighted to be able to point to proof positive that nothing could be done to better the lot of the colored people. They were, and are, right in one respect: that nothing can be done as long as they are treated like colored people. The people in Harlem know they are living there because white people do not think they are good enough to live anywhere else. No amount of "improvement" can sweeten this fact. Whatever money is now being earmarked to improve this, or any other ghetto, might as well be burnt. A ghetto can be improved in one way only: out of existence.

Similarly, the only way to police a ghetto is to be oppressive. None of the Police Commissioner's men, even with the best will in the world, have any way of understanding the lives led by the people they swagger about in twos and threes controlling. Their very presence is an insult, and it would be, even if they spent their entire day feeding gumdrops to children. They represent the force of the white world, and the world's real intentions are, simply, for the world's criminal profit and ease, to keep the black man corraled up here, in his place. The badge, the gun in the holster, and the swinging club make vivid what will happen should his rebellion become overt. Rare, indeed, is

13

14

---

1. The inhabitants of Riverton were much embittered by this description; they have, apparently, forgotten how their project came into being; and have repeatedly informed me that I cannot possibly be referring to Riverton, but to another housing project which is directly across the street. It is quite clear, I think, that I have no interest in accusing any individuals or families of the depredations herein described: but neither can I deny the evidence of my own eyes. Nor do I blame anyone in Harlem for making the best of a dreadful bargain. But anyone who lives in Harlem and imagines that he has *not* struck this bargain, or that what he takes to his status (in whose eyes?) protects him against the common pain, demoralization, and danger, is simply self deluded. [author's note]

the Harlem citizen, from the most circumspect church member to the most shiftless adolescent, who does not have a long tale to tell of police incompetence, injustice, or brutality. I myself have witnessed and endured it more than once. The businessmen and racketeers also have a story. And so do the prostitutes. (And this is not, perhaps, the place to discuss Harlem's very complex attitude toward black policemen, nor the reasons, according to Harlem, that they are nearly all downtown.)

It is hard, on the other hand, to blame the policeman, blank, good-natured, thoughtless, and insuperably innocent, for being such a perfect representative of the people he serves. He, too, believes in good intentions and is astounded and offended when they are not taken for the deed. He has never, himself, done anything for which to be hated—which of us has?—and yet he is facing, daily and nightly, people who would gladly see him dead, and he knows it. There is no way for him not to know it: there are few things under heaven more unnerving than the silent, accumulating contempt and hatred of a people. He moves through Harlem, therefore, like an occupying soldier in a bitterly hostile country; which is precisely what, and where, he is, and is the reason he walks in twos and threes. And he is not the only one who knows why he is always in company; the people who are watching him know why, too. Any street meeting, sacred or secular, which he and his colleagues uneasily cover has as its explicit or implicit burden the cruelty and injustice of the white domination. And these days, of course, in terms increasingly vivid and jubilant, it speaks of the end of that domination. The white policeman standing on a Harlem street corner finds himself at the very center of the revolution now occurring in the world. He is not prepared for it—naturally, nobody is—and, what is possibly much more to the point, he is exposed, as few white people are, to the anguish of the black people around him. Even if he is gifted with the merest mustard grain of imagination, something must seep in. He cannot avoid observing that some of the children, in spite of their color, remind him of children he has known and loved, perhaps even of his own children. He knows that he certainly does not want *his* children living this way. He can retreat from his uneasiness in only one direction: into a callousness which very shortly becomes second nature. He becomes more callous, the population becomes more hostile, the situation grows more tense, and the police force is increased. One day, to everyone's astonishment, someone drops a match in the powder keg and everything blows up. Before the dust has settled or the blood congealed, editorials, speeches, and civil-rights commissions are loud in the land, demanding to know what happened. What happened is that Negroes want to be treated like men.

Negroes want to be treated like men: a perfectly straightforward statement, containing only seven words. People who have mastered Kant,

Hegel, Shakespeare, Marx, Freud, and the Bible find this statement utterly impenetrable. The idea seems to threaten profound, barely conscious assumptions. A kind of panic paralyzes their features, as though they found themselves trapped on the edge of a steep place. I once tried to describe to a very well-known American intellectual the conditions among Negroes in the South. My recital disturbed him and made him indignant; and he asked me in perfect innocence, "Why don't all the Negroes in the South move North?" I tried to explain what *has* happened, unfailingly, whenever a significant body of Negroes move North. They do not escape Jim Crow: they merely encounter another, not-less-deadly variety. They do not move to Chicago, they move to the South Side; they do not move to New York, they move to Harlem. This pressure within the ghetto causes the ghetto walls to expand, and this expansion is always violent. White people hold the line as long as they can, and in as many ways as they can, from verbal intimidation to physical violence. But inevitably the border which has divided the ghetto from the rest of the world falls into the hands of the ghetto. The white people fall back bitterly before the black horde; the landlords make a tidy profit by raising the rent, chopping up the rooms, and all but dispensing with the upkeep; and what has once been a neighborhood turns into a "turf." This is precisely what happened when the Puerto Ricans arrived in their thousands—and the bitterness thus caused is, as I write, being fought out all up and down those streets.

Northerners indulge in an extremely dangerous luxury. They seem 17 to feel that because they fought on the right side during the Civil War, and won, they have earned the right merely to deplore what is going on in the South, without taking any responsibility for it; and that they can ignore what is happening in Northern cities because what is happening in Little Rock or Birmingham is worse. Well, in the first place, it is not possible for anyone who has not endured both to know which is "worse." I know Negroes who prefer the South and white Southerners, because "At least there, you haven't got to play any guessing games!" The guessing games referred to have driven more than one Negro into the narcotics ward, the madhouse, or the river. I know another Negro, a man very dear to me, who says with conviction and with truth, "The spirit of the South is the spirit of America." He was born in the North and did his military training in the South. He did not, as far as I can gather, find the South "worse"; he found it, if anything, all too familiar. In the second place, though, even if Birmingham *is* worse, no doubt Johannesburg, South Africa, beats it by several miles, and Buchenwald was one of the worst things that ever happened in the entire history of the world. The world has never lacked for horrifying examples; but I do not believe that these examples are meant to be used as justification for our own crimes. This perpetual justification empties the heart of all human feeling. The emptier our hearts become, the greater will be our crimes. Thirdly, the South is not merely an embarrassingly backward region, but a part of this country, and what happens there concerns every one of us.

As far as the color problem is concerned, there is but one difference between the Southern white and the Northerner: the Southerner remembers, historically and in his own psyche, a kind of Eden in which he loved black people and they loved him. Historically, the flaming sword laid across this Eden is the Civil War. Personally, it is the Southerner's sexual coming of age, when, without any warning, unbreakable taboos are set up between himself and his past. Everything, thereafter, is permitted him except the love he remembers and has never ceased to need. The resulting, indescribable torment affects every Southern mind and is the basis of the Southern hysteria. [18]

None of this is true for the Northerner. Negroes represent nothing to him personally, except, perhaps, the dangers of carnality. He never sees Negroes. Southerners see them all the time. Northerners never think about them whereas Southerners are never really thinking of anything else. Negroes are, therefore, ignored in the North and are under surveillance in the South, and suffer hideously in both places. Neither the Southerner nor the Northerner is able to look on the Negro simply as a man. It seems to be indispensable to the national self-esteem that the Negro be considered either as a kind of ward (in which case we are told how many Negroes, comparatively, bought Cadillacs last year and how few, comparatively, were lynched), or as a victim (in which case we are promised that he will never vote in our assemblies or go to school with our kids). They are two sides of the same coin and the South will not change—*cannot* change—until the North changes. The country will not change until it re-examines itself and discovers what it really means by freedom. In the meantime, generations keep being born, bitterness is increased by incompetence, pride, and folly, and the world shrinks around us. [19]

It is a terrible, an inexorable, law that one cannot deny the humanity of another without diminishing one's own: in the face of one's victim, one sees oneself. Walk through the streets of Harlem and see what we, this nation, have become. [20]

JANE JACOBS

The Uses of Sidewalks

One of the most influential urban theorists of the latter half of the twentieth century, Jane Jacobs (1916–   ) was born in Scranton, Pennsylvania. Although Jacobs attended Columbia University, she never graduated. She married architect Robert Hyde Jacobs in 1944. Her best-known book, *The Death and Life of Great American Cities* (1961), helped to end the prevailing practice of destroying neighborhoods in the name of urban renewal. "A common mistake," Jacob argues, "is for people to look at a distressed part of a city and ask what's wrong with it. But they don't consider what's already there and look at those things as assets." In 1969, to protest the Vietnam War, Jacobs and her family moved to Toronto, where she remained actively involved in preserving cities. Her other works include *The Economy of Cities* (1969), *Cities and the Wealth of Nations* (1984), and more recently (1995), a memoir of her great-aunt, Hannah Breece, who spent fourteen years in the early 1900s as a schoolteacher in Alaska. A useful companion essay is James Baldwin's "Fifth Avenue, Uptown," a more personal testimonial to the damage done by midcentury ideas of community improvement.

Streets in cities serve many purposes besides carrying vehicles, and 1 city sidewalks—the pedestrian parts of the streets—serve many purposes besides carrying pedestrians. These uses are bound up with circulation but are not identical with it and in their own right they are at least as basic as circulation to the proper workings of cities.

A city sidewalk by itself is nothing. It is an abstraction. It means 2 something only in conjunction with the buildings and other uses that border it, or border other sidewalks very near it. The same might be said of streets, in the sense that they serve other purposes besides carrying wheeled traffic in their middles. Streets and their sidewalks, the main public places of a city, are its most vital organs. Think of a city and what comes to mind? Its streets. If a city's streets look interesting, the city looks interesting; if they look dull, the city looks dull.

More than that, and here we get down to the first problem, if a 3 city's streets are safe from barbarism and fear, the city is thereby tolerably safe from barbarism and fear. When people say that a city, or a part of it, is dangerous or is a jungle what they mean primarily is that they do not feel safe on the sidewalks.

But sidewalks and those who use them are not passive beneficia- 4 ries of safety or helpless victims of danger. Sidewalks, their bordering uses, and their users, are active participants in the drama of civilization versus barbarism in cities. To keep the city safe is a fundamental task of a city's streets and its sidewalks.

This task is totally unlike any service that sidewalks and streets in little towns or true suburbs are called upon to do. Great cities are not like towns, only larger. They are not like suburbs, only denser. They differ from towns and suburbs in basic ways, and one of these is that cities are, by definition, full of strangers. To any one person, strangers are far more common in big cities than acquaintances. More common not just in places of public assembly, but more common at a man's own doorstep. Even residents who live near each other are strangers, and must be, because of the sheer number of people in small geographical compass.

The bedrock attribute of a successful city district is that a person must feel personally safe and secure on the street among all these strangers. He must not feel automatically menaced by them. A city district that fails in this respect also does badly in other ways and lays up for itself, and for its city at large, mountain on mountain of trouble.

Today barbarism has taken over many city streets, or people fear it has, which comes to much the same thing in the end. "I live in a lovely, quiet residential area," says a friend of mine who is hunting another place to live. "The only disturbing sound at night is the occasional scream of someone being mugged." It does not take many incidents of violence on a city street, or in a city district, to make people fear the streets. And as they fear them, they use them less, which makes the streets still more unsafe.

To be sure, there are people with hobgoblins in their heads, and such people will never feel safe no matter what the objective circumstances are. But this is a different matter from the fear that besets normally prudent, tolerant and cheerful people who show nothing more than common sense in refusing to venture after dark—or in a few places, by day—into streets where they may well be assaulted, unseen or unrescued until too late.

The barbarism and the real, not imagined, insecurity that gives rise to such fears cannot be tagged a problem of the slums. The problem is most serious, in fact, in genteel-looking "quiet residential areas" like that my friend was leaving.

It cannot be tagged as a problem of older parts of cities. The problem reaches its most baffling dimensions in some examples of rebuilt parts of cities, including supposedly the best examples of rebuilding, such as middle-income projects. The police precinct captain of a nationally admired project of this kind (admired by planners and lenders) has recently admonished residents not only about hanging around outdoors after dark but has urged them never to answer their doors without knowing the caller. Life here has much in common with life for the three little pigs or the seven little kids of the nursery thrillers.

The problem of sidewalk and doorstep insecurity is as serious in cities which have made conscientious efforts at rebuilding as it is in those cities that have lagged. Nor is it illuminating to tag minority groups, or the poor, or the outcast with responsibility for city danger. There are immense variations in the degree of civilization and safety found among such groups and among the city areas where they live. Some of the safest sidewalks in New York City, for example, at any time of day or night, are those along which poor people or minority groups live. And some of the most dangerous are in streets occupied by the same kinds of people. All this can also be said of other cities.

Deep and complicated social ills must lie behind delinquency and crime, in suburbs and towns as well as in great cities. This book will not go into speculation on the deeper reasons. It is sufficient, at this point, to say that if we are to maintain a city society that can diagnose and keep abreast of deeper social problems, the starting point must be, in any case, to strengthen whatever workable forces for maintaining safety and civilization do exist—in the cities we do have. To build city districts that are custom made for easy crime is idiotic. Yet that is what we do. 11

The first thing to understand is that the public peace—the side-walk and street peace—of cities is not kept primarily by the police, necessary as police are. It is kept primarily by an intricate, almost un-conscious, network of voluntary controls and standards among the people themselves, and enforced by the people themselves. In some city areas—older public housing projects and streets with very high population turnover are often conspicuous examples—the keeping of public sidewalk law and order is left almost entirely to the police and special guards. Such places are jungles. No amount of police can en-force civilization where the normal, casual enforcement of it has bro-ken down. 12

The second thing to understand is that the problem of insecurity cannot be solved by spreading people out more thinly, trading the characteristics of cities for the characteristics of suburbs. If this could solve danger on the city streets, then Los Angeles should be a safe city because superficially Los Angeles is almost all suburban. It has virtu-ally no districts compact enough to qualify as dense city areas. Yet Los Angeles cannot, any more than any other great city, evade the truth that, being a city, it *is* composed of strangers not all of whom are nice. Los Angeles' crime figures are flabbergasting. Among the seventeen standard metropolitan areas with populations over a million, Los An-geles stands so pre-eminent in crime that it is in a category by itself. And this is markedly true of crimes associated with personal attack, the crimes that make people fear the streets. 13

Los Angeles, for example, has a forcible rape rate (1958 figures) of 31.9 per 100,000 population, more than twice as high as either of the next two cities, which happen to be St. Louis and Philadelphia; three 14 times as high as the rate of 10.1 for Chicago, and more than four times as high as the rate of 7.4 for New York.

In aggravated assault, Los Angeles has a rate of 185, compared with 149.5 for Baltimore and 139.2 for St. Louis (the two next highest), and with 90.9 for New York and 79 for Chicago.

The overall Los Angeles rate for major crimes is 2,507.6 per 100,000 people, far ahead of St. Louis and Houston, which come next with 1,634.5 and 1,541.1, and of New York and Chicago, which have rates of 1,145.3 and 943.5.

The reasons for Los Angeles' high crime rates are undoubtedly complex, and at least in part obscure. But of this we can be sure: thinning out a city does not insure safety from crime and fear of crime. This is one of the conclusions that can be drawn within individual cities too, where pseudosuburbs or superannuated suburbs are ideally suited to rape, muggings, beatings, hold ups and the like.

Here we come up against an all-important question about any city street: How much easy opportunity does it offer to crime? It may be that there is some absolute amount of crime in a given city, which will find an outlet somehow (I do not believe this). Whether this is so or not, different kinds of city streets garner radically different shares of barbarism and fear of barbarism.

Some city streets afford no opportunity to street barbarism. The streets of the North End of Boston are outstanding examples. They are probably as safe as any place on earth in this respect. Although most of the North End's residents are Italian or of Italian descent, the district's streets are also heavily and constantly used by people of every race and background. Some of the strangers from outside work in or close to the district; some come to shop and stroll; many, including members of minority groups who have inherited dangerous districts previously abandoned by others, make a point of cashing their paychecks in North End stores and immediately making their big weekly purchases in streets where they know they will not be parted from their money between the getting and the spending.

Frank Havey, director of the North End Union, the local settlement house, says, "I have been here in the North End twenty-eight years, and in all that time I have never heard of a single case of rape, mugging, molestation of a child or other street crime of that sort in the district. And if there had been any, I would have heard of it even if it did not reach the papers." Half a dozen times or so in the past three decades, says Havey, would-be molesters have made an attempt at luring a child or, late at night, attacking a woman. In every such case the try was thwarted by passers-by, by kibitzers from windows, or shopkeepers.

Meantime, in the Elm Hill Avenue section of Roxbury, a part of inner Boston that is suburban in superficial character, street assaults

and the ever present possibility of more street assaults with no kibitzers to protect the victims, induce prudent people to stay off the sidewalks at night. Not surprisingly, for this and other reasons that are
related (dispiritedness and dullness), most of Roxbury has run down.
It has become a place to leave.

I do not wish to single out Roxbury or its once fine Elm Hill Av-   21
enue section especially as a vulnerable area; its disabilities, and especially its Great Blight of Dullness, are all too common in other cities
too. But differences like these in public safety within the same city are
worth noting. The Elm Hill Avenue section's basic troubles are not
owing to a criminal or a discriminated against or a poverty-stricken
population. Its troubles stem from the fact that it is physically quite
unable to function safely and with related vitality as a city district.

Even within supposedly similar parts of supposedly similar places,   22
drastic differences in public safety exist. An incident at Washington
Houses, a public housing project in New York, illustrates this point. A
tenants' group at this project, struggling to establish itself, held some
outdoor ceremonies in mid-December 1958, and put up three Christmas trees. The chief tree, so cumbersome it was a problem to transport,
erect, and trim, went into the project's inner "street," a landscaped
central mall and promenade. The other two trees, each less than six
feet tall and easy to carry, went on two small fringe plots at the outer
corners of the project where it abuts a busy avenue and lively cross
streets of the old city. The first night, the large tree and all its trim-
mings were stolen. The two smaller trees remained intact, lights, ornaments and all, until they were taken down at New Year's. "The place
where the tree was stolen, which is *theoretically* the most safe and sheltered place in the project, is the same place that is unsafe for people
too, especially children," says a social worker who had been helping
the tenants' group. "People are no safer in that mall than the Christmas tree. On the other hand, the place where the other trees were
safe, where the project is just one corner out of four, happens to be
safe for people."

This is something everyone already knows: A well-used city street   23
is apt to be a safe street. A deserted city street is apt to be unsafe. But
how does this work, really? And what makes a city street well used or
shunned? Why is the sidewalk mall in Washington Houses, which is
supposed to be an attraction, shunned? Why are the sidewalks of the
old city just to its west not shunned? What about streets that are busy
part of the time and then empty abruptly?

A city street equipped to handle strangers, and to make a safety   24
asset, in itself, out of the presence of strangers, as the streets of successful city neighborhoods always do, must have three main qualities:

First, there must be a clear demarcation between what is public   25
space and what is private space. Public and private spaces cannot ooze
into each other as they do typically in suburban settings or in projects.

Second, there must be eyes upon the street, eyes belonging to   26
those we might call the natural proprietors of the street. The buildings
on a street equipped to handle strangers and to insure the safety of
both residents and strangers, must be oriented to the street. They cannot turn their backs or blank sides on it and leave it blind.

And third, the sidewalk must have users on it fairly continuously,   27
both to add to the number of effective eyes on the street and to induce
the people in buildings along the street to watch the sidewalks in sufficient numbers. Nobody enjoys sitting on a stoop or looking out a window at an empty street. Almost nobody does such a thing. Large
numbers of people entertain themselves, off and on, by watching
street activity.

In settlements that are smaller and simpler than big cities, controls   28
on acceptable public behavior, if not on crime, seem to operate with
greater or lesser success through a web of reputation, gossip, approval,
disapproval and sanctions, all of which are powerful if people know
each other and word travels. But a city's streets, which must control
not only the behavior of the people of the city but also of visitors from
suburbs and towns who want to have a big time away from the gossip
and sanctions at home, have to operate by more direct, straightforward methods. It is a wonder cities have solved such an inherently difficult problem at all. And yet in many streets they do it magnificently.

It is futile to try to evade the issue of unsafe city streets by at-   29
tempting to make some other features of a locality, say interior court-
yards, or sheltered play spaces, safe instead. By definition again, the
streets of a city must do most of the job of handling strangers for this is
where strangers come and go. The streets must not only defend the
city against predatory strangers, they must protect the many, many
peaceable and well-meaning strangers who use them, insuring their
safety too as they pass through. Moreover, no normal person can
spend his life in some artificial haven, and this includes children.
Everyone must use the streets.

On the surface, we seem to have here some simple aims: To try to   30
secure streets where the public space is unequivocally public, physically unmixed with private or with nothing-at-all space, so that the
area needing surveillance has clear and practicable limits; and to see that
these public street spaces have eyes on them as continuously as possible.

But it is not so simple to achieve these objects, especially the latter.   31
You can't make people use streets they have no reason to use. You
can't make people watch streets they do not want to watch. Safety on
the streets by surveillance and mutual policing of one another sounds

grim, but in real life it is not grim. The safety of the street works best, most casually, and with least frequent taint of hostility or suspicion precisely where people are using and most enjoying the city streets voluntarily and are least conscious, normally, that they are policing.

The basic requisite for such surveillance is a substantial quantity of stores and other public places sprinkled along the sidewalks of a district; enterprises and public places that are used by evening and night must be among them especially. Stores, bars and restaurants, as the chief examples, work in several different and complex ways to abet sidewalk safety.

First, they give people—both residents and strangers—concrete reasons for using the sidewalks on which these enterprises face.

Second, they draw people along the sidewalks past places which have no attractions to public use in themselves but which become traveled and peopled as routes to somewhere else; this influence does not carry very far geographically, so enterprises must be frequent in a city district if they are to populate with walkers those other stretches of street that lack public places along the sidewalk. Moreover, there should be many different kinds of enterprises, to give people reasons for crisscrossing paths.

Third, storekeepers and other small businessmen are typically strong proponents of peace and order themselves; they hate broken windows and holdups; they hate having customers made nervous about safety. They are great street watchers and sidewalk guardians if present in sufficient numbers.

Fourth, the activity generated by people on errands, or people aiming for food or drink, is itself an attraction to still other people.

This last point, that the sight of people attracts still other people, is something that city planners and city architectural designers seem to find incomprehensible. They operate on the premise that city people seek the sight of emptiness, obvious order and quiet. Nothing could be less true. People's love of watching activity and other people is constantly evident in cities everywhere. This trait reaches an almost ludicrous extreme on upper Broadway in New York, where the street is divided by a narrow central mall, right in the middle of traffic. At the cross-street intersections of this long north-south mall, benches have been placed behind big concrete buffers and on any day when the weather is even barely tolerable these benches are filled with people at block after block after block, watching the pedestrians who cross the mall in front of them, watching the traffic, watching the people on the busy sidewalks, watching each other. Eventually Broadway reaches Columbia University and Barnard College, one to the right, the other to the left. Here all is obvious order and quiet. No more stores, no more activity generated by the stores, almost no more pedestrians crossing— and no more watchers. The benches are there but they go empty in even the finest weather. I have tried them and can see why. No place could be more boring. Even the students of these institutions shun the solitude. They are doing their outdoor loitering, outdoor homework and general street watching on the steps overlooking the busiest campus crossing.

It is just so on city streets elsewhere. A lively street always has both its users and pure watchers. Last year I was on such a street in the Lower East Side of Manhattan, waiting for a bus. I had not been there longer than a minute, barely long enough to begin taking in the street's activity of errand goers, children playing, and loiterers on the stoops, when my attention was attracted by a woman who opened a window on the third floor of a tenement across the street and vigorously yoo-hooed at me. When I caught on that she wanted my attention and responded, she shouted down, "The bus doesn't run here on Saturdays!" Then by a combination of shouts and pantomime she directed me around the corner. This woman was one of thousands upon thousands of people in New York who casually take care of the streets. They notice strangers. They observe everything going on. If they need to take action, whether to direct a stranger waiting in the wrong place or to call the police, they do so. Action usually requires, to be sure, a certain self-assurance about the actor's proprietorship of the street and the support he will get if necessary, matters which will be gone into later in this book. But even more fundamental than the action and necessary to the action, is the watching itself.

Not everyone in cities helps to take care of the streets, and many a city resident or city worker is unaware of why his neighborhood is safe. The other day an incident occurred on the street where I live, and it interested me because of this point.

My block of the street, I must explain, is a small one, but it contains a remarkable range of buildings, varying from several vintages of tenements to three- and four-story houses that have been converted into low-rent flats with stores on the ground floor, or returned to single-family use like ours. Across the street there used to be mostly four-story brick tenements with stores below. But twelve years ago several buildings, from the corner to the middle of the block, were converted into one building with elevator apartments of small size and high rents.

The incident that attracted my attention was a suppressed struggle going on between a man and a little girl of eight or nine years old. The man seemed to be trying to get the girl to go with him. By turns he was directing a cajoling attention to her, and then assuming an air of nonchalance. The girl was making herself rigid, as children do when they resist, against the wall of one of the tenements across the street.

As I watched from our second-floor window, making up my mind how to intervene if it seemed advisable, I saw it was not going to be necessary. From the butcher shop beneath the tenement had emerged the woman who, with her husband, runs the shop; she was standing within earshot of the man, her arms folded and a look of determination on her face. Joe Cornacchia, who with his sons-in-law keeps the delicatessen, emerged about the same moment and stood solidly to the other side. Several heads poked out of the tenement windows above, one was withdrawn quickly and its owner reappeared a moment later in the doorway behind the man. Two men from the bar next to the butcher shop came to the doorway and waited. On my side of the street, I saw that the locksmith, the fruit man and the laundry proprietor had all come out of their shops and that the scene was also being surveyed from a number of windows besides ours. That man did not know it, but he was surrounded. Nobody was going to allow a little girl to be dragged off, even if nobody knew who she was.

I am sorry—sorry purely for dramatic purposes—to have to report   43
that the little girl turned out to be the man's daughter.

Throughout the duration of the little drama, perhaps five minutes   44
in all, no eyes appeared in the windows of the high-rent, small-apartment building. It was the only building of which this was true. When we first moved to our block, I used to anticipate happily that perhaps soon all the buildings would be rehabilitated like that one. I know better now, and can only anticipate with gloom and foreboding the recent news that exactly this transformation is scheduled for the rest of the block frontage adjoining the high-rent building. The high-rent tenants, most of whom are so transient we cannot even keep track of their faces,[1] have not the remotest idea of who takes care of the street, or how. A city neighborhood can absorb and protect a substantial number of these birds of passage, as our neighborhood does. But if and when the neighborhood finally *becomes* them, they will gradually find the streets less secure, they will be vaguely mystified about it, and if things get bad enough they will drift away to another neighborhood which is mysteriously safer.

In some rich city neighborhoods, where there is little do-it-   45
yourself surveillance, such as residential Park Avenue or upper Fifth Avenue in New York, street watchers are hired. The monotonous sidewalks of residential Park Avenue, for example, are surprisingly little used; their putative users are populating, instead, the interesting store-, bar- and restaurant-filled sidewalks of Lexington Avenue and Madison Avenue to east and west, and the cross streets leading to these. A network of doormen and superintendents, of delivery boys and nurse-maids, a form of hired neighborhood, keeps residential Park Avenue supplied with eyes. At night, with the security of the doormen as a bulwark, dog walkers safely venture forth and supplement the door-

1. Some, according to the storekeepers, live on beans and bread and spend their sojourn looking for a place to live where all their money will not go for rent. [author's note]

men. But this street is so blank of built-in eyes, so devoid of concrete reasons for using or watching it instead of turning the first corner off of it, that if its rents were to slip below the point where they could support a plentiful hired neighborhood of doormen and elevator men, it would undoubtedly become a woefully dangerous street.

Once a street is well equipped to handle strangers, once it has both 46 a good, effective demarcation between private and public spaces and has a basic supply of activity and eyes, the more strangers the merrier.

Strangers become an enormous asset on the street on which I live, 47 and the spurs off it, particularly at night when safety assets are most needed. We are fortunate enough, on the street, to be gifted not only with a locally supported bar and another around the corner, but also with a famous bar that draws continuous troops of strangers from adjoining neighborhoods and even from out of town. It is famous because the poet Dylan Thomas used to go there, and mentioned it in his writing. This bar, indeed, works two distinct shifts. In the morning and early afternoon it is a social gathering place for the old community of Irish longshoremen and other craftsmen in the area, as it always was. But beginning in midafternoon it takes on a different life, more like a college bull session with beer, combined with a literary cocktail party, and this continues until the early hours of the morning. On a cold winter's night, as you pass the White Horse, and the doors open, a solid wave of conversation and animation surges out and hits you; very warming. The comings and goings from this bar do much to keep our street reasonably populated until three in the morning, and it is a street always safe to come home to. The only instance I know of a beating in our street occurred in the dead hours between the closing of the bar and dawn. The beating was halted by one of our neighbors who saw it from his window and, unconsciously certain that even at night he was part of a web of strong street law and order, intervened.

A friend of mine lives on a street uptown where a church youth 48 and community center, with many night dances and other activities, performs the same service for his street that the White Horse bar does for ours. Orthodox planning is much imbued with puritanical and Utopian conceptions of how people should spend their free time, and in planning, these moralisms on people's private lives are deeply confused with concepts about the workings of cities. In maintaining city street civilization, the White Horse bar and the church-sponsored youth center, different as they undoubtedly are, perform much the same public street civilizing service. There is not only room in cities for such differences and many more in taste, purpose and interest of occupation; cities also have a need for people with all these differences in taste and proclivity. The preferences of Utopians, and of other compulsive managers of other people's leisure, for one kind of legal enterprise over others is worse than irrelevant for cities. It is harmful. The greater and more plentiful the range of all legitimate interests (in the strictly legal sense) that city streets and their enterprises can satisfy, the better for the streets and for the safety and civilization of the city.

Bars, and indeed all commerce, have a bad name in many city districts precisely because they do draw strangers, and the strangers do not work out as an asset at all. 49

This sad circumstance is especially true in the dispirited gray belts of great cities and in once fashionable or at least once solid inner residential areas gone into decline. Because these neighborhoods are so dangerous, and the streets typically so dark, it is commonly believed that their trouble may be insufficient street lighting. Good lighting is important, but darkness alone does not account for the gray areas' deep, functional sickness, the Great Blight of Dullness. 50

The value of bright street lights for dispirited gray areas rises from the reassurance they offer to some people who need to go out on the sidewalk, or would like to, but lacking the good light would not do so. Thus the lights induce these people to contribute their own eyes to the upkeep of the street. Moreover, as is obvious, good lighting augments every pair of eyes, makes the eyes count for more because their range is greater. Each additional pair of eyes, and every increase in their range, is that much to the good for dull gray areas. But unless eyes are there, and unless in the brains behind those eyes is the almost unconscious reassurance of general street support in upholding civilization, lights can do no good. Horrifying public crimes can, and do, occur in well-lighted subway stations when no effective eyes are present. They virtually never occur in darkened theaters where many people and eyes are present. Street lights can be like that famous stone that falls in the desert where there are no ears to hear. Does it make a noise? Without effective eyes to see, does a light cast light? Not for practical purposes. 51

Suppose we continue with building, and with deliberate rebuilding, of unsafe cities. How do we live with this insecurity? From the evidence thus far, there seem to be three modes of living with it; maybe in time others will be invented but I suspect these three will simply be further developed, if that is the word for it. 52

The first mode is to let danger hold sway, and let those unfortunate enough to be stuck with it take the consequences. This is the policy now followed with respect to low-income housing projects, and to many middle-income housing projects. 53

The second mode is to take refuge in vehicles. This is a technique practiced in the big wild-animal reservations of Africa, where tourists are warned to leave their cars under no circumstances until they reach a lodge. It is also the technique practiced in Los Angeles. Surprised visitors to that city are forever recounting how the police of Beverly Hills stopped them, made them prove their reasons for being afoot, and 54 warned them of the danger. This technique of public safety does not seem to work too effectively yet in Los Angeles, as the crime rate shows, but in time it may. And think what the crime figures might be if more people without metal shells were helpless upon the vast, blind-eyed reservation of Los Angeles.

People in dangerous parts of other cities often use automobiles as protection too, of course, or try to. A letter to the editor in the *New York Post,* reads, "I live on a dark street off Utica Avenue in Brooklyn and therefore decided to take a cab home even though it was not late. The cab driver asked that I get off at the corner of Utica, saying he did not want to go down the dark street. If I had wanted to walk down the dark street, who needed him?"

The third mode . . . was developed by hoodlum gangs and has been adopted widely by developers of the rebuilt city. This mode is to cultivate the institution of Turf.

Under the Turf system in its historical form, a gang appropriates as its territory certain streets or housing projects or parks—often a combination of the three. Members of other gangs cannot enter this Turf without permission from the Turf-owning gang, or if they do so it is at peril of being beaten or run off. In 1956, the New York City Youth Board, fairly desperate because of gang warfare, arranged through its gang youth workers a series of truces among fighting gangs. The truces were reported to stipulate, among other provisions, a mutual under-standing of Turf boundaries among the gangs concerned and agree-ment not to trespass.

The city's police commissioner, Stephen P. Kennedy, thereupon ex-pressed outrage at agreements respecting Turf. The police, he said, aimed to protect the right of every person to walk any part of the city in safety and with impunity as a basic right. Pacts about Turf, he indicated, were intolerably subversive both of public rights and public safety.

I think Commissioner Kennedy was profoundly right. However, we must reflect upon the problem facing the Youth Board workers. It was a real one, and they were trying as well as they could to meet it with whatever empirical means they could. The safety of the city, on which public right and freedom of movement ultimately depend, was missing from the unsuccessful streets, parks and projects dominated by these gangs. Freedom of the city, under these circumstances, was a rather academic ideal.

Now consider the redevelopment projects of cities: the middle- and upper-income housing occupying many acres of city, many former blocks, with their own grounds and their own streets to serve these "islands within the city," "cities within the city," and "new concepts in city living," as the advertisements for them say. The technique here is also to designate the Turf and fence the other gangs out. At first the fences were never visible. Patrolling guards were sufficient to enforce the line. But in the past few years the fences have become literal.

Perhaps the first was the high cyclone fence around a Radiant Gar-   61
den City project adjoining Johns Hopkins Hospital in Baltimore (great
educational institutions seem to be deplorably inventive with Turf devices). In case anyone mistakes what the fence means, the signs on the
project street also say "Keep Out. No Trespassing." It is uncanny to see
a city neighborhood, in a civilian city, walled off like this. It looks not
only ugly, in a deep sense, but surrealistic. You can imagine how it sits
with the neighbors, in spite of the antidote message on the project
church's bulletin board: "Christ's Love Is The Best Tonic Of All."

New York has been quick to copy the lesson of Baltimore, in its   62
own fashion. Indeed, at the back of Amalgamated Houses on the
Lower East Side, New York has gone further. At the northern end of
the project's parklike central promenade, an iron-bar gate has been
permanently padlocked and is crowned not with mere metal netting
but with a tangle of barbed wire. And does this defended promenade
give out on depraved old megalopolis? Not at all. Its neighbor is a public playground and beyond this more project housing for a different income class.

In the rebuilt city it takes a heap of fences to make a balanced   63
neighborhood. The "juncture" between two differently price-tagged
populations, again in the rebuilt Lower East Side, that between middle-
income cooperative Corlears Hook and low-income Vladeck Houses, is
especially elaborate. Corlears Hook buffers its Turf against its next-
door neighbors with a wide parking lot running the full width of the
super-block juncture, next a spindly hedge and a six-foot-high cyclone
fence, next a completely fenced-in no man's land some thirty feet wide
consisting mainly of dirty blowing papers and deliberately inaccessible
to anything else. Then begins the Vladeck Turf.

Similarly, on the Upper West Side, the rental agent of the Park   64
West Village, "Your Own World in the Heart of New York," on whom
I have foisted myself as a prospective tenant, tells me reassuringly,
"Madam, as soon as the shopping center is completed, the entire
grounds will be fenced in."

"Cyclone fences?"   65

"That is correct, madam. And eventually"—waving his hand at the   66
city surrounding his domain—"all that will go. Those people will go.
We are the pioneers here."

I suppose it is rather like pioneer life in a stockaded village, except   67
that the pioneers were working toward greater security for their civilization, not less.

Some members of the gangs on the new Turfs find this way of life   68
hard to take. Such was one who wrote a letter to the *New York Post* in
1959: "The other day for the first time my pride at being a resident of
Stuyvesant Town and of New York City was replaced by indignation
and shame. I noticed two boys about 12 years old sitting on a
Stuyvesant Town bench. They were deep in conversation, quiet, well-

behaved—and Puerto Rican. Suddenly two Stuyvesant Town guards were approaching—one from the north and one from the south. The one signaled the other by pointing to the two boys. One went up to the boys and after several words, quietly spoken on both sides, the boys rose and left. They tried to look unconcerned . . . How can we expect people to have dignity and self-respect if we rip it from them even before they reach adulthood? How really poor are we of Stuyvesant Town and of New York City, too, that we can't share a bench with two boys."

The Letters Editor gave this communication the headline, "Stay in Your Own Turf."   69

But on the whole, people seem to get used very quickly to living in a Turf with either a figurative or a literal fence, and to wonder how they got on without it formerly. This phenomenon was described, before the Turf fences came into the city, by the *New Yorker*, with reference not to fenced city but to fenced town. It seems that when Oak Ridge, Tennessee, was de-militarized after the war, the prospect of losing the fence that went with the militarization drew frightened and impassioned protests from many residents and occasioned town meetings of high excitement. Everyone in Oak Ridge had come, not many years before, from unfenced towns or cities, yet stockade life had become normal and they feared for their safety without the fence.   70

Just so, my ten-year-old nephew David, born and brought up in Stuyvesant Town, "A City Within a City," comments in wonder that anyone at all can walk on the street outside our door. "Doesn't anybody keep track whether they pay rent on this street?" he asks. "Who puts them out if they don't belong here?"   71

The technique of dividing the city into Turfs is not simply a New York solution. It is a Rebuilt American City solution. At the Harvard Design Conference of 1959, one of the topics pondered by city architectural designers turned out to be the puzzle of Turf, although they did not use that designation. The examples discussed happened to be the Lake Meadows middle-income project of Chicago and the Lafayette Park high-income project of Detroit. Do you keep the rest of the city out of these blind-eyed purlieus? How difficult and how unpalatable. Do you invite the rest of the city in? How difficult and how impossible.   72

Like the Youth Board workers, the developers and residents of Radiant City and Radiant Garden City and Radiant Garden City Beautiful have a genuine difficulty and they have to do the best they can with it by the empirical means at their disposal. They have little choice. Wherever the rebuilt city rises the barbaric concept of Turf must follow, because the rebuilt city has junked a basic function of the city street and with it, necessarily, the freedom of the city.   73

Under the seeming disorder of the old city, wherever the old city is working successfully, is a marvelous order for maintaining the safety of   74 the streets and the freedom of the city. It is a complex order. Its essence is intricacy of sidewalk use, bringing with it a constant succession of eyes. This order is all composed of movement and change, and although it is life, not art, we may fancifully call it the art form of the city and liken it to the dance—not to a simple-minded precision dance with everyone kicking up at the same time, twirling in unison and bowing off en masse, but to an intricate ballet in which the individual dancers and ensembles all have distinctive parts which miraculously reinforce each other and compose an orderly whole. The ballet of the good city sidewalk never repeats itself from place to place, and in any one place is always replete with new improvisations.

The stretch of Hudson Street where I live is each day the scene of 75 an intricate sidewalk ballet. I make my own first entrance into it a little after eight when I put out the garbage can, surely a prosaic occupation, but I enjoy my part, my little clang, as the droves of junior high school students walk by the center of the stage dropping candy wrappers. (How do they eat so much candy so early in the morning?)

While I sweep up the wrappers I watch the other rituals of morning: 76 Mr. Halpert unlocking the laundry's handcart from its mooring to a cellar door, Joe Cornacchia's son-in-law stacking out the empty crates from the delicatessen, the barber bringing out his sidewalk folding chair. Mr. Goldstein arranging the coils of wire which proclaim the hardware store is open, the wife of the tenement's superintendent depositing her chunky three-year-old with a toy mandolin on the stoop, the vantage point from which he is learning the English his mother cannot speak. Now the primary children, heading for St. Luke's, dribble through to the south; the children for St. Veronica's cross, heading to the west, and the children for P.S. 41, heading toward the east. Two new entrances are being made from the wings: well-dressed and even elegant women and men with briefcases emerge from doorways and side streets. Most of these are heading for the bus and subways, but some hover on the curbs, stopping taxis which have miraculously appeared at the right moment, for the taxis are part of a wider morning ritual: having dropped passengers from midtown in the downtown financial district, they are now bringing downtowners up to midtown. Simultaneously, numbers of women in housedresses have emerged and as they crisscross with one another they pause for quick conversations that sound with either laughter or joint indignation, never, it seems, anything between. It is time for me to hurry to work too, and I exchange my ritual farewell with Mr. Lofaro, the short, thick-bodied, white-aproned fruit man who stands outside his doorway a little up the street, his arms folded, his feet planted, looking solid as earth itself. We nod; we each glance quickly up and down the street, then look back to each other and smile. We have done this many a morning for more than ten years, and we both know what it means: All is well.

The heart-of-the-day ballet I seldom see, because part of the nature   77
of it is that working people who live there, like me, are mostly gone,
filling the roles of strangers on other sidewalks. But from days off, I
know enough of it to know that it becomes more and more intricate.
Longshoremen who are not working that day gather at the White
Horse or the Ideal or the International for beer and conversation. The
executives and business lunchers from the industries just to the west
throng the Dorgene restaurant and the Lion's Head coffee house; meat-
market workers and communications scientists fill the bakery lunch-
room. Character dancers come on, a strange old man with strings of old
shoes over his shoulders, motor-scooter riders with big beards and girl
friends who bounce on the back of the scooters and wear their hair
long in front of their faces as well as behind, drunks who follow the advice of the Hat Council and are always turned out in hats, but not hats
the Council would approve. Mr. Lacey, the locksmith, shuts up his
shop for a while and goes to exchange the time of day with Mr. Slube
at the cigar store. Mr. Koochagian, the tailor, waters the luxuriant jungle of plants in his window, gives them a critical look from the outside,
accepts a compliment on them from two passers-by, fingers the leaves
on the plane tree in front of our house with a thoughtful gardener's appraisal, and crosses the street for a bite at the Ideal where he can keep
an eye on customers and wigwag across the message that he is coming.
The baby carriages come out, and clusters of everyone from toddlers
with dolls to teen-agers with homework gather at the stoops.

When I get home after work, the ballet is reaching its crescendo.   78
This is the time of roller skates and stilts and tricycles, and games in the
lee of the stoop with bottletops and plastic cowboys; this is the time of
bundles and packages, zigzagging from the drug store to the fruit stand
and back over to the butcher's; this is the time when teen-agers, all
dressed up, are pausing to ask if their slips show or their collars look
right; this is the time when beautiful girls get out of MG's; this is the
time when the fire engines go through; this is the time when anybody
you know around Hudson Street will go by.

As darkness thickens and Mr. Halpert moors the laundry cart to   79
the cellar door again, the ballet goes on under lights, eddying back and
forth but intensifying at the bright spotlight pools of Joe's sidewalk
pizza dispensary, the bars, the delicatessen, the restaurant and the drug
store. The night workers stop now at the delicatessen, to pick up
salami and a container of milk. Things have settled down for the
evening but the street and its ballet have not come to a stop.

I know the deep night ballet and its seasons best from waking long   80
after midnight to tend a baby and, sitting in the dark, seeing the shadows and hearing the sounds of the sidewalk. Mostly it is a sound like
infinitely pattering snatches of party conversation and, about three in
the morning, singing, very good singing. Sometimes there is sharpness

and anger or sad, sad weeping, or a flurry of search for a string of beads broken. One night a young man came roaring along, bellowing terrible language at two girls whom he had apparently picked up and who were disappointing him. Doors opened, a wary semicircle formed around him, not too close, until the police came. Out came the heads, too, along Hudson Street, offering opinion, "Drunk . . . Crazy . . . A wild kid from the suburbs."[2]

Deep in the night, I am almost unaware how many people are on the street unless something calls them together, like the bagpipe. Who the piper was and why he favored our street I have no idea. The bagpipe just skirled out in the February night, and as if it were a signal the random, dwindled movements of the sidewalk took on direction. Swiftly, quietly, almost magically a little crowd was there, a crowd that evolved into a circle with a Highland fling inside it. The crowd could be seen on the shadowy sidewalk, the dancers could be seen, but the bagpiper himself was almost invisible because his bravura was all in his music. He was a very little man in a plain brown overcoat. When he finished and vanished, the dancers and watchers applauded, and applause came from the galleries too, half a dozen of the hundred windows on Hudson Street. Then the windows closed, and the little crowd dissolved into the random movements of the night street.

The strangers on Hudson Street, the allies whose eyes help us natives keep the peace of the street, are so many that they always seem to be different people from one day to the next. That does not matter. Whether they are so many always-different people as they seem to be, I do not know. Likely they are. When Jimmy Rogan fell through a plate-glass window (he was separating some scuffling friends) and almost lost his arm, a stranger in an old T shirt emerged from the Ideal bar, swiftly applied an expert tourniquet and, according to the hospital's emergency staff, saved Jimmy's life. Nobody remembered seeing the man before and no one has seen him since. The hospital was called in this way: a woman sitting on the steps next to the accident ran over to the bus stop, wordlessly snatched the dime from the hand of a stranger who was waiting with his fifteen-cent fare ready, and raced into the Ideal's phone booth. The stranger raced after her to offer the nickel too. Nobody remembered seeing him before, and no one has seen him since. When you see the same stranger three or four times on Hudson Street, you begin to nod. This is almost getting to be an acquaintance, a public acquaintance, of course.

I have made the daily ballet of Hudson Street sound more frenetic than it is, because writing it telescopes it. In real life, it is not that way.

81

82

83

---

2. He turned out to be a wild kid from the suburbs. Sometimes, on Hudson Street, we are tempted to believe the suburbs must be a difficult place to bring up children. [author's note]

In real life, to be sure, something is always going on, the ballet is never at a halt, but the general effect is peaceful and the general tenor even leisurely. People who know well such animated city streets will know how it is. I am afraid people who do not will always have it a little wrong in their heads—like the old prints of rhinoceroses made from travelers' descriptions of rhinoceroses.

On Hudson Street, the same as in the North End of Boston or in any other animated neighborhoods of great cities, we are not innately more competent at keeping the sidewalk safe than are the people who try to live off the hostile truce of Turf in a blind-eyed city. We are the lucky possessors of a city order that makes it relatively simple to keep the peace because there are plenty of eyes on the street. But there is nothing simple about that order itself, or the bewildering number of components that go into it. Most of those components are specialized in one way or another. They unite in their joint effect upon the sidewalk, which is not specialized in the least. That is its strength.

SCOTT RUSSELL SANDERS

The Common Life

Born in Memphis, Tennessee, Scott Russell Sanders (1945–   ) received a B.A. from Brown University (1967) and a Ph.D. from Cambridge University (1971). A recipient of an NEA fellowship (1983–1984) and several fiction awards, including the Penrod Award (1986) for *Stone Country* and the American Library Association Award (1987) for *Bad Man Ballad*, Sanders chose, in his early twenties, to write fiction rather than to pursue an interest in theoretical physics. Currently teaching at Indiana University, Sanders has said of his writing, "In all of my work, regardless of period or style, I am concerned with the practical problems of living on a small planet, in nature and in communities. I am concerned with the life people make together, in marriages and families and towns, more than with the life of isolated individuals." The following selection is from *Writing from the Center* (1995). Readers may want to compare the pressures that Sanders views as building or endangering his middle-class community with the pressures on the "deviant neighborhood" of Toni Cade Bambara's "The Hammer Man."

One delicious afternoon while my daughter Eva was home from college for spring vacation, she invited two neighbor girls to help her make bread. The girls are sisters, five-year-old Alexandra and ten-year-old Rachel, both frolicky, with eager dark eyes and shining faces.

They live just down the street from us here in Bloomington, Indiana, and whenever they see me pass by, on bicycle or on foot, they ask about Eva, whom they adore.

I was in the yard that afternoon mulching flower beds with com- 2
post, and I could hear the girls chattering as Eva led them up the sidewalk to our door. I had plenty of others chores to do in the yard, where every living thing was urgent with April. But how could I stay outside, when so much beauty and laughter and spunk were gathered in the kitchen?

I kept looking in on the cooks, until Eva finally asked, "Daddy, you 3
wouldn't like to knead some dough, would you?"

"I'd love to," I said. "You sure there's room for me?" 4

"There's room," Eva replied, "but you'll have to wash in the base- 5
ment."

Hands washed, I took my place at the counter beside Rachel and 6
Alexandra, who perched on a stool I had made for Eva when she was a toddler. Eva had still needed that stool when she learned to make bread on this counter; and my son, now six feet tall, had balanced there as well for his own first lessons in cooking. I never needed the stool, but I needed the same teacher—my wife Ruth, a woman with eloquent fingers.

Our kitchen is small; Ruth and I share that cramped space by mov- 7
ing in a kind of dance we have been practicing for years. When we bump one another, it is usually for the pleasure of bumping. But Eva and the girls and I jostled like birds too numerous for a nest. We spattered flour everywhere. We told stories. We joked. All the while I bobbed on a current of bliss, delighting in the feel of live dough beneath my fingers, the smell of yeast, the piping of child-voices so much like the birdsong cascading through our open windows, the prospect of whole-wheat loaves hot from the oven.

An artist might paint this kitchen scene in pastels for a poster, with 8
a tender motto below, as evidence that all is right with the world. All is manifestly *not* right with the world. The world, most of us would agree, is a mess: rife with murder and mayhem, abuse of land, extinction of species, lying and theft and greed. There are days when I can see nothing but a spectacle of cruelty and waste, and the weight of dismay pins me to my chair. On such days I need a boost merely to get up, uncurl my fists, and go about my work. The needed strength may come from family, from neighbors, from a friend's greeting in the mail, from the forked leaves of larkspur breaking ground, from rainstorms and music and wind, from the lines of a handmade table or the lines in a well-worn book, from the taste of an apple or the brash trill of finches in our backyard trees. Strength also comes to me from memories of times when I have felt a deep and complex joy, a sense of being exactly where I should be and doing exactly what I should do, as I felt on that breadmaking afternoon.

I wish to reflect on the sources of that joy, that sense of being ut- 9
terly in place, because I suspect they are the sources of all that I find
authentic in my life. So much in life seems to me unauthentic, I cannot afford to let the genuine passages slip by without considering what
makes them ring true. It is as though I spend my days wandering
about, chasing false scents, lost, and then occasionally, for a few ticks
of the heart, I stumble onto the path. While making bread with my
daughter and her two young friends, I was on the path. So I recall that
time now as a way of keeping company with Eva, who has gone back
to college, but also as a way of discovering in our common life a reservoir of power and hope.

What is so powerful, so encouraging, in that kitchen scene? To 10
begin with, I love my three fellow cooks; I relish every tilt of their
heads and turn of their voices. In their presence I feel more alive and
alert, as if the rust had been knocked off my nerves. The armor of self
dissolves, ego relaxes its grip, and I am simply there, on the breeze of
the moment.

Rachel and Alexandra belong to the Abed family, with whom we 11
often share food and talk and festivities. We turn to the Abeds for advice, for starts of plants, for cheer, and they likewise turn to us. Not
long ago they received troubling news that may force them to move
away, and we have been sharing in their distress. So the Abed girls
brought into our kitchen a history of neighborliness, a history all the
more valuable because it might soon come to an end.

The girls also brought a readiness to learn what Eva had to teach. 12
Eva, as I mentioned, had learned from Ruth how to make bread, and
Ruth had learned from a Canadian friend, and our friend had learned
from her grandmother. As Rachel and Alexandra shoved their hands
into the dough, I could imagine the rope of knowledge stretching back
and back through generations, to folks who ground their grain with
stones and did their baking in wood stoves or fireplaces or in pits of
glowing coals.

If you have made yeast bread, you know how at first the dough 13
clings to your fingers, and then gradually, as you knead in more flour,
it begins to pull away and take on a life of its own, becoming at last as
resilient as a plump belly. If you have not made yeast bread, no
amount of hearing or reading about it will give you that knowledge,
because you have to learn through your body, through fingers and
wrists and aching forearms, through shoulders and backs. Much of
what we know comes to us that way, passed on from person to person,
age after age, surviving in muscle and bone. I learned from my mother
how to transplant a seedling, how to sew on a button; I learned from
my father how to saw a board square, how to curry a horse, how to
change the oil in a car. The pleasure I take in sawing or currying, in
planting or sewing, even in changing oil, like my pleasure in making

bread, is bound up with the affection I feel for my teachers and the respect I feel for the long, slow accumulation of knowledge that informs
our simplest acts.

Those simple acts come down to us because they serve real needs.   14
You plant a tree or sweep a floor or rock a baby without asking the
point of your labors. You patch the roof to stop a leak, patch a sweater
to keep from having to throw it out. You pluck the banjo because it
tickles your ears and rouses Grandpa to dance. None of us can live entirely by such meaningful acts; our jobs, if nothing else, often push us
through empty motions. But unless at least some of what we do has a
transparent purpose, answering not merely to duty or fashion but to
actual needs, then the heart has gone out of our work. What art could
be more plainly valuable than cooking? The reason for baking bread is
as palpable as your tongue. After our loaves were finished, Eva and I
delivered two of them to the Abeds, who showed in their faces a perfect understanding of the good of bread.

When I compare the dough to a plump belly, I hear the sexual   15
overtones, of course. By making the comparison, I do not wish to say,
with Freud, that every sensual act is a surrogate for sex; on the contrary, I believe sex comes closer to being a stand-in, rather brazen and
obvious, like a ham actor pretending to be the whole show, when it is
only one player in the drama of our sensual life. That life flows
through us constantly, so long as we do not shut ourselves off. The
sound of birds and the smell of April dirt and the brush of wind
through the open door were all ingredients in the bread we baked.

Before baking, the yeast was alive, dozing in the refrigerator.   16
Scooped out of its jar, stirred into warm water, fed on sugar, it soon
bubbled out gas to leaven the loaves. You have to make sure the water
for the yeast, like milk for a baby, is neither too hot nor too cold, and
so, as for a baby's bottle, I test the temperature on my wrist. The flour,
too, had been alive not long before as wheat thriving in sun and rain.
Our nourishment is borrowed life. You need not be a Christian to feel,
in a bite of bread, a sense of communion with the energy that courses
through all things. The lump in your mouth is a chunk of earth; there
is nothing else to eat. In our house we say grace before meals, to remind ourselves of that gift and that dependence.

The elements of my kitchen scene—loving company, neighborli-   17
ness, inherited knowledge and good work, shared purpose, sensual delight, and union with the creation—sum up for me what is vital in
community. Here is the spring of hope I have been led to by my trail of
bread. In our common life we may find the strength not merely to
carry on in face of the world's bad news, but to resist cruelty and
waste. I speak of it as common because it is ordinary, because we make
it together, because it binds us through time to the rest of humanity
and through our bodies to the rest of nature. By honoring this common life, nurturing it, carrying it steadily in mind, we might renew our

households and neighborhoods and cities, and in doing so might redeem ourselves from the bleakness of private lives spent in frenzied
pursuit of sensation and wealth.

Ever since the eclipse of our native cultures, the dominant Ameri- 18
can view has been more nearly the opposite: that we should cultivate
the self rather than the community; that we should look to the individual as the source of hope and the center of value, while expecting
hindrance and harm from society.

What other view could have emerged from our history? The first 19
Europeans to reach America were daredevils and treasure seekers, as
were most of those who mapped the interior. Many colonists were
renegades of one stripe or another, some of them religious nonconformists, some political rebels, more than a few of them fugitives from
the law. The trappers, hunters, traders, and freebooters who pushed
the frontier westward seldom recognized any authority beyond the
reach of their own hands. Coast to coast, our land has been settled and
our cities have been filled by generations of immigrants more intent
on leaving behind old tyrannies than on seeking new social bonds.

Our government was forged in rebellion against alien control. Our 20
economy was founded on the sanctity of private property, and thus our
corporations have taken on a sacred immunity through being defined
under the law as persons. Our criminal justice system is so careful to
protect the rights of individuals that it may require years to convict a
bank robber who killed a bystander in front of a crowd, or a bank official who left a trail of embezzlement as wide as the Mississippi.

Our religion has been marked by an evangelical Protestantism that 21
emphasizes personal salvation rather than social redemption. To "Get
Right with God," as signs along the roads here in the Midwest gravely
recommend, does not mean to reconcile your fellow citizens to the divine order, but to make a separate peace, to look after the eternal future of your own singular soul. True, we have a remarkable history of
communal experiments, most of them religiously inspired—from Plymouth Colony, through the Shaker villages, Robert Owen's New Harmony, the settlements at Oneida, Amana, and countless other places,
to the communes in our own day. But these are generally known to
us, if they are known at all, as utopian failures.

For much of the present century, Americans have been fighting 22
various forms of collectivism—senile empires during World War I, then
Nazism, communism, and now fundamentalist theocracies—and these
wars, the shouting kind as well as the shooting kind, have only
strengthened our commitment to individualism. We have understood
freedom for the most part negatively rather than positively, as release
from constraints rather than as the condition for making a decent life
in common. Hands off, we say; give me elbow room; good fences make
good neighbors; my home is my castle; don't tread on me. I'm looking

out for number one, we say; I'm doing my own thing. We have a Bill of Rights, which protects each of us from a bullying society, but no Bill of Responsibilities, which would oblige us to answer the needs of others.

Even where America's founding documents clearly address the   23
public good, they <u>have</u> often been turned to private ends. Consider just one notorious example, the Second Amendment to the Constitution:

> As well regulated Militia, being necessary to the security of a free State, the right of the people to keep and bear Arms, shall not be infringed.

It would be difficult to say more plainly that arms are to be kept for the sake of a militia, and a militia is to be kept for defense of the country. In our day, a reasonable person might judge that the Pentagon deploys quite enough weapons, without requiring any supplement from household arsenals. Yet this lucid passage has been construed to justify a domestic arms race, until we now have in America more gun shops than gas stations, we have nearly as many handguns as hands, and we have concentrated enough firepower in the average city to carry on a war—which is roughly what, in some cities, is going on. Thus, by reading the Second Amendment through the lens of our obsessive individualism, we have turned a provision for public safety into a guarantee of public danger.

Observe how zealously we have carved up our cities and paved our   24
land and polluted our air and burned up most of the earth's petroleum within a single generation—all for the sake of the automobile, a symbol of personal autonomy even more potent than the gun. There is a contemptuous ring to the word "mass" in mass transportation, as if the only alternative to private cars were cattle cars. Motorcycles and snowmobiles and three-wheelers fill our public lands with the din of engines and tear up the terrain, yet any effort to restrict their use is denounced as an infringement of individual rights. Millions of motorists exercise those rights by hurling the husks of their pleasures onto the roadside, boxes and bottles and bags. Ravines and ditches in my part of the country are crammed with rusty cars and refrigerators, burst couches and stricken TVs, which their former owners would not bother to haul to the dump. Meanwhile, advertisers sell us everything from jeeps to jeans as tokens of freedom, and we are so infatuated with the sovereign self that we fall for the spiel, as if by purchasing one of a million identical products we could distinguish ourselves from the herd.

The cult of the individual shows up everywhere in American lore,   25
which celebrates drifters, rebels, and loners, while pitying or reviling the pillars of the community. The backwoods explorer like Daniel Boone, the riverboat rowdy like Mike Fink, the lumberjack, the prospector, the rambler and gambler, the daring crook like Jesse James and the resourceful killer like Billy the Kid, along with countless lonesome cowboys, all wander, unattached, through the great spaces of our imagination. When society begins to close in, making demands and

asking questions, our heroes hit the road. Like Huckleberry Finn, they are forever lighting out for the Territory, where nobody will tell them what to do. Huck Finn ran away from what he called civilization in order to leave behind the wickedness of slavery, and who can blame him, but he was also running away from church and school and neighbors, from aunts who made him wash before meals, from girls who cramped his style, from chores, from gossip, from the whole nuisance of living alongside other people.

In our literature, when community enters at all, it is likely to appear as a conspiracy against the free soul of a hero or heroine. Recall how restless Natty Bumppo becomes whenever Cooper drags him in from the woods to a settlement. Remember how strenuously Emerson preaches against conforming to society and in favor of self-reliance, how earnestly Hawthorne warns us about the tyranny of those Puritan villages. Think of Thoreau running errands in Concord, rushing in the front door of a house and out the back, then home to his cabin in the woods, never pausing, lest he be caught in the snares of the town. Think of the revulsion Edna Pontellier feels toward the Creole society of New Orleans in Kate Chopin's *The Awakening*. Think of Willa Cather's or Toni Morrison's or James Baldwin's high-spirited women and men who can only thrive by fleeing their home communities. Think of Spoon River, Winesburg, Gopher Prairie, Zenith, all those oppressive fictional places, the backward hamlets and stifling suburbs and heartless cities that are fit only for drones and drudges and mindless Babbitts. 26

In *The Invasion of the Body Snatchers*, a film from my childhood that still disturbs my dreams, an alien life form takes over one person after another in a small town, merging them into a single creature with a single will, until just one freethinking individual remains, and even he is clearly doomed. Along with dozens of other invasion tales, the film was a warning against communism, I suppose, but it was also a caution against the perils of belonging, of losing your one sweet self in the group, and thus it projected a fear as old as America. 27

Of course you can find American books and films that speak as passionately for the virtues of our life together as for the virtues of our lives apart. To mention only a few novels from the past decade, I think of Gloria Naylor's *Mama Day*, Wendell Berry's *A Place on Earth*, Ursula Le Guin's *Always Coming Home*, and Ernest Gaines's *A Gathering of Old Men*. But they represent a minority opinion. The majority opinion fills bestseller lists and cinema screens and billboards with isolated, alienated, rebellious figures who are too potent or sensitive for membership in any group. 28

I have been shaped by this history, and I, too, am uneasy about groups, especially large ones, above all those that are glued together by hatred, those that use a color of skin or a cut of clothes for admission tickets, and those that wrap themselves in scriptures or flags. I have 29 felt a chill from blundering into company where I was not wanted. I have known women and men who were scorned because they refused to fit the molds their neighbors had prepared for them. I have seen Klansmen parading in white hoods, their crosses burning on front lawns. I have seen a gang work its way through a subway car, picking on the old, the young, the weak. Through film I have watched the Nuremberg rallies, watched policemen bashing demonstrators in Chicago, missiles parading in Red Square, tanks crushing dissidents in Tiananmen Square. Like everyone born since World War II, I have grown up on television images of atrocities carried out, at home and abroad, with the blessing of governments or revolutionary armies or charismatic thugs.

In valuing community, therefore, I do not mean to approve of any 30 and every association of people. Humans are drawn together by a variety of motives, some of them worthy, some of them ugly. Anyone who has spent recess on a school playground knows the terror of mob rule. Anyone who has lived through a war knows that mobs may pretend to speak for an entire nation. I recently saw, for the first time in a long while, a bumper sticker that recalled for me the angriest days of the Vietnam War: AMERICA—LOVE IT OR LEAVE IT. What loving America seemed to mean, for those who brandished that slogan back around 1970, was the approval of everything the government said or the army did in our name. "All those who seek to destroy the liberty of a democratic nation ought to know," Alexis de Tocqueville observed in *Democracy in America*, "that war is the surest and the shortest means to accomplish it." As a conscientious objector, with a sister who studied near my home in Ohio on a campus where National Guardsmen killed several protestors, I felt the force of despotism in that slogan.

Rather than give in to despotism, some of my friends went to jail 31 and others into exile. My wife and I considered staying in England, where we had been studying for several years and where I had been offered a job. But instead we chose to come home, here to the Midwest where we had grown up, to work for change. In our idealism, we might have rephrased that bumper sticker to read: AMERICA—LOVE IT AND REDEEM IT. For us, loving America had little to do with politicians and even less with soldiers, but very much to do with what I have been calling the common life: useful work, ordinary sights, family, neighbors, ancestors, our fellow creatures, and the rivers and woods and fields that make up our mutual home.

During the more than twenty years since returning to America, I 32 have had some of the idealism knocked out of me, but I still believe that loving your country or city or neighborhood may require you to resist, to call for change, to speak on behalf of what you believe in, especially if what you believe in has been neglected.

What we have too often neglected, in our revulsion against 33 tyranny and our worship of the individual, is the common good. The

results of that neglect are visible in the decay of our cities, the despoiling of our land, the fouling of our rivers and air, the haphazard commercial sprawl along our highways, the gluttonous feeding at the
public trough, the mortgaging of our children's and grandchildren's
future through our refusal to pay for current consumption. Only a
people addicted to private pleasure would allow themselves to be
defined as consumers—rather than conservers or restorers—of the
earth's abundance.

In spite of the comforting assurances, from Adam Smith onward,   34
that the unfettered pursuit of private wealth should result in unlimited
public good, we all know that to be mostly a lie. If we needed re-
minders of how great that lie is, we could look at the savings and loan
industry, where billions of dollars were stolen from small investors by
rich managers who yearned to be richer; we could look at the Pentagon, where contracts are routinely encrusted with graft, or at Wall
Street, where millionaires finagle to become billionaires through insider trading; we could look at our national forests, where logging
companies buy timber for less than the cost to taxpayers of harvesting
it; or we could look at our suburbs, where palaces multiply, while
downtown more and more people are sleeping in cardboard boxes.
Wealth does not precipitate like dew from the air; it comes out of the
earth and from the labor of many hands. When a few hands hold onto
great wealth, using it only for personal ease and display, that is a betrayal of the common life, the sole source of riches.

Fortunately, while our tradition is heavily tilted in favor of private   35
life, we also inherit a tradition of caring for the community. Although
Tocqueville found much to fear and quite a bit to despise in this raw
democracy, he praised Americans for having "carried to the highest
perfection the art of pursuing in common the object of their common
desires." Writing of what he had seen in the 1830s, Tocqueville judged
Americans to be avaricious, self-serving, and aggressive; but he was
also amazed by our eagerness to form clubs, to raise barns or town
halls, to join together in one cause or another: "In no country in the
world, do the citizens make such exertions for the common weal. I
know of no people who have established schools so numerous and ef-
ficacious, places of public worship better suited to the wants on the inhabitants, or roads kept in better repair."

Today we might revise his estimate of our schools or roads, but we   36
can still see all around us the fruits of that concern for the common
weal—the libraries, museums, courthouses, hospitals, orphanages, universities, parks, on and on. Born as most of us are into places where
such amenities already exist, we may take them for granted; but they
would not be there for us to use had our forebears not cooperated in
building them. No matter where we live, our home places have also
benefited from the Granges and unions, the volunteer fire brigades,

the art guilds and garden clubs, the charities, food kitchens, homeless shelters, soccer and baseball teams, the Scouts and 4-H, the Girls and Boys Clubs, the Lions and Elks and Rotarians, the countless gatherings of people who saw a need and responded to it.

This history of local care hardly ever makes it into our literature, 37 for it is less glamorous than rebellion, yet it is a crucial part of our heritage. Any of us could cite examples of people who dug in and joined with others to make our home places better places. Women and men who invest themselves in their communities, fighting for good schools or green spaces, paying attention to where they are, seem to me as worthy of celebration as those adventurous loners who keep drifting on, prospecting for pleasure.

A few days after our breadmaking, Eva and I went to a concert in 38 Bloomington's newly opened arts center. The old limestone building had once been the town hall, then a fire station and jail, then for several years an abandoned shell. Volunteers bought the building from the city for a dollar, then renovated it with materials, labor, and money donated by local people. Now we have a handsome facility that is in constant use for pottery classes, theater productions, puppet shows, art exhibits, poetry readings, and every manner of musical event.

The music Eva and I heard was *Hymnody of Earth*, for hammer dul- 39 cimer, percussion, and children's choir. Composed by our next-door neighbor, Malcolm Dalglish, and featuring lyrics by our Ohio Valley neighbor, Wendell Berry, it was performed that night by Malcolm, percussionist Glen Velez, and the Bloomington Youth Chorus. As I sat there with Eva in a sellout crowd—about a third of whom I knew by name, another third by face—I listened to music that had been elaborated within earshot of my house, and I heard my friend play his instrument, and I watched those children's faces shining with the colors of the human spectrum, and I felt the restored building clasping us all like the cupped hands of our community. I knew once more that I was in the right place, a place created and filled and inspired by our lives together.

A woman who recently moved from Los Angeles to Bloomington 40 told me that she would not be able to stay here long, because she was already beginning to recognize people in the grocery stores, on the sidewalks, in the library. Being surrounded by familiar faces made her nervous, after years in a city where she could range about anonymously. Every traveler knows the sense of liberation that comes from journeying to a place where nobody expects anything of you. Everyone who has gone to college knows the exhilaration of slipping away from the watchful eyes of Mom and Dad. We all need seasons of withdrawal from responsibility. But if we make a career of being unaccountable, we have lost something essential to our humanity, and we may well become a burden or a threat to those around us. A community can support a number of people who are just passing through, or who care about no one's needs but their own; the greater the proportion of such people, however, the more vulnerable the community, until eventually it breaks down. That is true on any scale, from a household to a planet.

The words *community, communion,* and *communicate* all derive from 41 *common,* and the two syllables of *common* grow from separate roots, the first meaning "together" or "next to," the second having to do with barter or exchange. Embodied in that word is a sense of our shared life as one of giving and receiving—music, touch, ideas, recipes, stories, medicine, tools, the whole range of artifacts and talents. After twenty-five years with Ruth, that is how I have come to understand marriage, as a constant exchange of labor and love. We do not calculate who gives how much; if we had to, the marriage would be in trouble. Looking outward from this community of two, I see my life embedded in ever larger exchanges—those of family and friendship, neighborhood and city, countryside and country—and on every scale there is giving and receiving, calling and answering.

Many people shy away from community out of a fear that it may 42 become suffocating, confining, even vicious; and of course it may, if it grows rigid or exclusive. A healthy community is dynamic, stirred up by the energies of those who already belong, open to new members and fresh influences, kept in motion by the constant bartering of gifts. It is fashionable just now to speak of this open quality as "tolerance," but that word sounds too grudging to me—as though, to avoid strife, we must grit our teeth and ignore whatever is strange to us. The community I desire is not grudging; it is exuberant, joyful, grounded in affection, pleasure, and mutual aid. Such a community arises not from duty or money but from the free interchange of people who share a place, share work and food, sorrows and hope. Taking part in the common life means dwelling in a web of relationships, the many threads tugging at you while also holding you upright.

I have told elsewhere the story of a man who lived in the Ohio 43 township where I grew up, a builder who refused to join the volunteer fire department. Why should he join, when his house was brick, properly wired, fitted out with new appliances? Well, one day that house caught fire. The wife dialed the emergency number, the siren wailed, and pretty soon the volunteer firemen, my father among them, showed up with the pumper truck. But they held back on the hoses, asking the builder if he still saw no reason to join, and the builder said he could see a pretty good reason to join right there and then, and the volunteers let the water loose.

I have also told before the story of a family from that township 44 whose house burned down. The fire had been started accidentally by the father, who came home drunk and fell asleep smoking on the couch. While the place was still ablaze, the man took off, abandoning his wife and several young children. The local people sheltered the family, then built them a new house. This was a poor township. But nobody thought to call in the government or apply to a foundation. These were neighbors in a fix, and so you helped them, just as you would harvest corn for an ailing farmer or pull a flailing child from the creek or put your arm around a weeping friend.

I am not harking back to some idyllic past, like the one embalmed   45
in the *Saturday Evening Post* covers by Norman Rockwell or the prints of Currier and Ives. The past was never golden. As a people, we still need to unlearn some of the bad habits formed during the long period of settlement. One good habit we might reclaim, however, is that of looking after those who live nearby. For much of our history, neighbors have kept one another going, kept one another sane. Still today, in town and country, in apartment buildings and barrios, even in suburban estates, you are certain to lead a narrower life without the steady presence of neighbors. It is neither quaint nor sentimental to advocate neighborliness; it is far more sentimental to suggest that we can do without such mutual aid.

Even Emerson, preaching self-reliance, knew the necessity of   46
neighbors. He lived in a village, gave and received help, and delivered his essays as lectures for fellow citizens whom he hoped to sway. He could have left his ideas in his journals, where they first took shape, but he knew those ideas would only have effect when they were shared. I like to think he would have agreed with the Lakota shaman, Black Elk, that "a man who has a vision is not able to use the power of it until after he has performed the vision on earth for the people to see." If you visit Emerson's house in Concord, you will find leather buckets hanging near the door, for he belonged to the village fire brigade, and even in the seclusion of his study, in the depths of thought, he kept his ears open for the alarm bell.

We should not have to wait until our houses are burning before   47
we see the wisdom of facing our local needs by joining in common work. We should not have to wait until gunfire breaks out in our schools, rashes break out on our skin, dead fish float in our streams, or beggars sleep on our streets before we act on behalf of the community. On a crowded planet, we had better learn how to live well together, or we will live miserably apart.

In cultural politics these days there is much talk of diversity and   48
difference. This is all to the good, insofar as it encourages us to welcome the many distinctive traditions and visions that have flowed into America from around the world. But if, while respecting how we differ, we do not also recognize how much we have in common, we will

have climbed out of the melting pot into the fire. Every day's newspaper brings word of people suffering and dying in the name of one distinction or another. We have never been slow to notice differences—of accent, race, dress, habits. If we merely change how those differences are valued, celebrating what had formerly been despised or despising what had been celebrated, we continue to define ourselves and one another in the old divisive ways.

Ethnic labels are especially dangerous, for, while we pin them on   49
as badges of pride, we may have difficulty taking them off when others decide to use them as targets. The larger the group identified by a label, the less likely it is to be a genuine community. Haste or laziness may lead us to speak of blacks and whites, of Christians and Muslims and Jews, of Armenians and Mexicans, yet the common life transcends such categories. Sharing a national anthem, a religion, or a skin color may be grounds for holding rallies or waging war, but community is more intimate than nationality, more subtle than race or creed, arising not from abstract qualities but from the daily give-and-take among particular people in a particular place.

It is also dangerous to separate a concern for human diversity from   50
a concern for natural diversity. Since Europeans arrived in North America, we have been drawing recklessly on beaver and bison, trees and topsoil, petroleum, coal, iron and copper ore, clean air and water. Many of the achievements on which we pride ourselves are the result not of our supposed virtues but of this plundered bounty. We do not have another continent to use up; unless we learn to inhabit this one more conservingly, we will see our lives, as well as the land, swiftly degraded. There is no contradiction between caring for our fellow human beings and caring for the rest of nature; on the contrary, only by attending to the health of the land can we measure our true needs or secure a lasting home.

Just before Eva was to leave again for college, she and I went for a   51
hike in a nature preserve along Clear Creek, near Bloomington, to look at the hepatica and bloodroot and listen to the spring-high water. At the edge of the preserve, a wooden sign declared that the riding of horses was prohibited. The trail had been freshly gouged by horseshoes and was eroding badly. Trash snagged in the roots of sycamores along the stream. Much of the soil and its cover of wildflowers had washed from the slopes where people scrambled up to picnic on the limestone bluff. Some of the cans they had left behind glinted among white stars of trillium.

I wondered what it would take to persuade the riders to get down   52
off their horses and go on foot. What would it take to discourage people from dumping their worn-out washing machines in ditches? What would convince farmers to quit spraying poisons on their fields, suburbanites to quit spraying poisons on their lawns? What power in

heaven or earth could stop loggers from seeing every tree as lumber, stop developers from seeing every acre of land as real estate, stop oil-company executives from seeing our last few scraps of wilderness as pay dirt waiting to be drilled? What would it take to persuade all of us to eat what we need, rather than what we can hold; to buy what we need, rather than what we can afford; to draw our pleasure from inexhaustible springs?

Signs will not work that change of mind, for in a battle of signs the billboards always win. Police cannot enforce it. Tongue lashings and sermons and earnest essays will not do it, nor will laws alone bring it about. The framers of the Constitution may have assumed that we did not need a Bill of Responsibilities because religion and reason and the benign impulses of our nature would lead us to care for one another and for our home. At the end of a bloody century, on the eve of a new millennium that threatens to be still bloodier, few of us now feel much confidence in those redeeming influences. Only a powerful ethic might restrain us, retrain us, restore us. Our survival is at stake, yet worrying about our survival alone is too selfish a motive to carry us as far as we need to go. Nothing short of reimagining where we are and what we are will be radical enough to transform how we live. 53

Aldo Leopold gave us the beginnings of this new ethic nearly half a century ago, in *A Sand Country Almanac,* where he described the land itself as a community made up of rock, water, soil, plants, and animals—including Homo sapiens, the only species clever enough to ignore, for a short while, the conditions of membership. "We abuse land because we see it as a commodity belonging to us," Leopold wrote. "When we see land as a community to which we belong, we may begin to use it with love and respect." To use our places with love and respect demands from us the same generosity and restraint that we show in our dealings with a wife or husband, a child or parent, a neighbor, a stranger in trouble. 54

Once again this spring, the seventy-seventh of her life, my mother put out lint from her clothes dryer for the birds to use in building their nests. "I know how hard it is to make a home from scratch," she says, "I've done it often enough myself." That is not anthropomorphism; it is fellow feeling, the root of all kindness. 55

Doctors the world over study the same physiology, for we are one species, woven together by strands of DNA that stretch back to the beginnings of life. There is, in fact, only one life, one pulse animating the dust. Sycamores and snakes, grasshoppers and grass, hawks and humans all spring from the same source and all return to it. We need to make of this common life not merely a metaphor, although we live by metaphors, and not merely a story, although we live by stories; we need to make the common life a fact of the heart. That awareness, that 56 concern, that love needs to go as deep in us as the feeling we have when a child dashes into the street and we hear a squeal of brakes, or when a piece of our home ground goes under concrete, or when a cat purrs against our palms or rain sends shivers through our bones or a smile floats back to us from another face.

With our own population booming, with frogs singing in the April ponds, with mushrooms cracking the pavement, life may seem the most ordinary of forces, like hunger or gravity; it may seem cheap, since we see it wasted every day. But in truth life is expensive, life is extraordinary, having required five billion years of struggle and luck on one stony, watery planet to reach its present precarious state. And so far as we have been able to discover from peering out into the great black spaces, the life that is common to all creatures here on earth is exceedingly uncommon, perhaps unique, in the universe. How, grasping that, can we remain unchanged? 57

It may be that we will not change, that nothing can restrain us, that we are incapable of reimagining our relations to one another or our place in creation. So many alarm bells are ringing, we may be tempted to stuff our ears with cotton. Better that we should keep ears and eyes open, take courage as well as joy from our common life, and work for what we love. What I love is curled about a loaf of bread, a family, a musical neighbor, a building salvaged for art, a town of familiar faces, a creek and a limestone bluff and a sky full of birds. Those may seem like frail threads to hold anyone in place while history heaves us about, and yet, when they are braided together, I find them to be amazingly strong. 58

PLATO

Crito

Plato (c. 427–347 B.C.) was probably born in Athens and is regarded as the father of rationalist philosophy. His works such as the *Republic* and the *Laws* suggest that Plato had the makings of a great statesman, but he retreated from public life in 399 B.C., disillusioned by the political system of Athens and claiming that the only hope for Greek cities was for "philosophers [to] become kings or kings philosophers." When Plato returned to Athens after traveling for several years, he founded the Academy, establishing an educational community that made Athens the center of educational life in Greece. There he taught for forty years, educating several famous thinkers and statesmen, most notably the philosopher Aristotle. Scholars are hard pressed to distinguish between Plato's thought and that of his mentor, Socrates, largely because Plato's writings are dialogues that feature Socrates as a character. The dialogue, which resembles what we might call today a cross-examination, pits Socrates against an antagonist who is inexorably led to concede the point Socrates wishes to make. The question of whether Plato is faithfully recording the debate or putting words in the mouths of his "characters" cannot be answered. His works include *Gorgias, Symposium, Timaeus,* and the following dialogue, *Crito.* Readers may want to measure Socrates' level of commitment to a community against their own level, or to the level of commitment shown by the protagonist in Toni Cade Bambara's "The Hammer Man" or by N. Scott Momaday's grandmother in "The Way to Rainy Mountain."

Socrates.[1]   Why have you come at this hour, Crito? it must be quite early?   1

Crito.   Yes, certainly.

Soc.   What is the exact time?

Cr.   The dawn is breaking.

Soc.   I wonder that the keeper of the prison would let you in.   5

Cr.   He knows me, because I often come, Socrates; moreover, I have done him a kindness.

Soc.   And are you only just arrived?

Cr.   No, I came some time ago.

Soc.   Then why did you sit and say nothing, instead of at once awakening me?

Cr.   I should not have liked myself, Socrates, to be in such great trouble and unrest as you are—indeed I should not: I have been   10 watching with amazement your peaceful slumbers; and for that reason I did not awake you, because I wished to minimize the pain. I have always thought you to be of a happy disposition; but never did I see anything like the easy, tranquil manner in which you bear this calamity.

Soc.   Why, Crito, when a man has reached my age he ought not to be repining at the approach of death.

Cr.   And yet other old men find themselves in similar misfortunes, and age does not prevent them from repining.

Soc.   That is true. But you have not told me why you come at this early hour.

1. Socrates (469–399 B.C.), a Greek teacher and philosopher, is known to posterity through the writings of Plato. Accused of corrupting the youth of Athens by his questioning manner of teaching, he was brought to trial and sentenced to death; subsequently, he was given poison hemlock to drink. Crito, a friend and follower of Socrates, here tries to persuade him to escape from prison, but Socrates refuses to break the laws of Athens.

Cr. I come to bring you a message which is sad and painful; not, as I believe, to yourself, but to all of us who are your friends, and saddest of all to me.

Soc. What? Has the ship come from Delos, on the arrival of which I am to die?

Cr. No, the ship has not actually arrived, but she will probably be here to-day, as persons who have come from Sunium tell me that they left her there; and therefore tomorrow, Socrates, will be the last day of your life.

Soc. Very well, Crito; if such is the will of God, I am willing; but my belief is that there will be a delay of a day.

Cr. Why do you think so?

Soc. I will tell you. I am to die on the day after the arrival of the ship.

Cr. Yes; that is what the authorities say.

Soc. But I do not think that the ship will be here until tomorrow; this I infer from a vision which I had last night, or rather only just now, when you fortunately allowed me to sleep.

Cr. And what was the nature of the vision?

Soc. There appeared to me the likeness of a woman, fair and comely, clothed in bright raiment, who called to me and said: O Socrates,

The third day hence to fertile Phthia shalt thou go.

Cr. What a singular dream, Socrates!

Soc. There can be no doubt about the meaning, Crito, I think.

Cr. Yes; the meaning is only too clear. But, oh! my beloved Socrates, let me entreat you once more to take my advice and escape. For if you die I shall not only lose a friend who can never be replaced, but there is another evil: people who do not know you and me will believe that I might have saved you if I had been willing to give money, but that I did not care. Now, can there be a worse disgrace than this—that I should be thought to value money more than the life of a friend? For the many will not be persuaded that I wanted you to escape, and that you refused.

Soc. But why, my dear Crito, should we care about the opinion of the many? Good men, and they are the only persons who are worth considering, will think of these things truly as they occurred.

Cr. But you see, Socrates, that the opinion of the many must be regarded, for what is now happening shows that they can do the greatest evil to any one who has lost their good opinion.

Soc. I only wish it were so, Crito; and that the many could do the greatest evil; for then they would also be able to do the greatest good—and what a fine thing this would be! But in reality they can do neither;

for they cannot make a man either wise or foolish; and whatever they do is the result of chance.

Cr. Well, I will not dispute with you; but please to tell me, Socrates, whether you are not acting out of regard to me and your other friends: are you not afraid that if you escape from prison we may get into trouble with the informers for having stolen you away, and lose either the whole or a great part of our property; or that even a worse evil may happen to us? Now, if you fear on our account, be at ease; for in order to save you, we ought surely to run this, or even a greater risk; be persuaded, then, and do as I say.

Soc. Yes, Crito, that is one fear which you mention, but by no means the only one.

Cr. Fear not—there are persons who are willing to get you out of prison at no great cost; and as for the informers, they are far from being exorbitant in their demands—a little money will satisfy them. My means, which are certainly ample, are at your service, and if you have a scruple about spending all mine, here are strangers who will give you the use of theirs; and one of them, Simmias the Theban, has brought a large sum of money for this very purpose; and Cebes and many others are prepared to spend their money in helping you to escape. I say, therefore, do not hesitate on our account, and do not say, as you did in the court, that you will have a difficulty in knowing what to do with yourself anywhere else. For men will love you in other places to which you may go, and not in Athens only; there are friends of mine in Thessaly, if you like to go to them, who will value and protect you, and no Thessalian will give you any trouble. Nor can I think that you are at all justified, Socrates, in betraying your own life when you might be saved; in acting thus you are playing into the hands of your enemies, who are hurrying on your destruction. And further I should say that you are deserting your own children; for you might bring them up and educate them; instead of which you go away and leave them, and they will have to take their chance; and if they do not meet with the usual fate of orphans, there will be small thanks to you. No man should bring children into the world who is unwilling to persevere to the end of their nurture and education. But you appear to be choosing the easier part, not the better and manlier, which would have been more becoming in one who professes to care for virtue in all his actions, like yourself. And, indeed, I am ashamed not only of you, but of us who are your friends, when I reflect that the whole business will be attributed entirely to our want of courage. The trial need never have come on, or might have been managed differently; and this last act, or crowning folly, will seem to have occurred through our negligence and cowardice, who might have saved you, if we had been good for anything; and you might have saved yourself, for there was no difficulty at all. See now, Socrates, how sad and discreditable are the consequences, both to us and you. Make your mind, then, or rather have your mind already made up, for the time of deliberation is over, and there is only one thing to be done, which must be done this very night, and if we delay at all will be no longer practicable or possible; I beseech you therefore, Socrates, be persuaded by me, and do as I say.

Soc. Dear Crito, your zeal is invaluable, if a right one; but if wrong, the greater the zeal the greater the danger; and therefore we ought to consider whether I shall or shall not do as you say. For I am and always have been one of those natures who must be guided by reason, whatever the reason may be which upon reflection appears to me to be the best; and now that this chance has befallen me, I cannot repudiate my own words: the principles which I have hitherto honoured and revered I still honour, and unless we can at once find other and better principles, I am certain not to agree with you; no, not even if the power of the multitude could inflict many more imprisonments, confiscations, deaths, frightening us like children with hobgoblin terrors. What will be the fairest way of considering the question? Shall I return to our old argument about the opinions of men?—we were saying that some of them are to be regarded, and others, not. Now, were we right in maintaining this before I was condemned? And has the argument which was once good now proved to be talk for the sake of talking—mere childish nonsense? That is what I want to consider with your help, Crito:—whether, under my present circumstances, the argument appears to be in any way different or not; and is to be allowed by me or disallowed. That argument, which, as I believe, is maintained by many persons of authority, was to the effect, as I was saying, that the opinions of some men are to be regarded, and of other men not to be regarded. Now you, Crito, are not going to die tomorrow—at least, there is no human probability of this—and therefore you are disinterested and not liable to be deceived by the circumstances in which you are placed. Tell me, then, whether I am right in saying that some opinions, and the opinions of some men only, are to be valued, and that other opinions, and the opinions of other men, are not to be valued. I ask you whether I was right in maintaining this?

Cr. Certainly.

Soc. The good are to be regarded, and not the bad?   35

Cr. Yes.

Soc. And the opinions of the wise are good, and the opinions of the unwise are evil?

Cr. Certainly.

Soc. And what was said about another matter? Is the pupil who devotes himself to the practice of gymnastic supposed to attend to the praise and blame and opinion of every man, or of one man only—his physician or trainer, whoever he may be?

Cr. Of one man only.   40

Soc. And he ought to fear the censure and welcome the praise of that one only, and not of the many?

Cr. Clearly so.

Soc. And he ought to act and train, and eat and drink in the way which seems good to his single master who has understanding, rather than according to the opinion of all other men put together?

Cr. True.

Soc. And if he disobeys and disregards the opinion and approval   45
of the one, and regards the opinion of the many who have no understanding, will he not suffer evil?

Cr. Certainly he will.

Soc. And what will the evil be, whither tending and what affecting, in the disobedient person?

Cr. Clearly, affecting the body; that is what is destroyed by the evil.

Soc. Very good; and is not this true, Crito, of other things which
we need not separately enumerate? In questions of just and unjust,
fair and foul, good and evil, which are the subjects of our present con-
sultation, ought we to follow the opinion of the many and to fear
them; or the opinion of the one man who has understanding? ought
we not to fear and reverence him more than all the rest of the world:
and if we desert him shall we not destroy and injure that principle in
us which may be assumed to be improved by justice and deteriorated
by injustice;—there is such a principle?

Cr. Certainly there is, Socrates.   50

Soc. Take a parallel instance:—if, acting under the advice of those
who have no understanding, we destroy that which is improved by
health and is deteriorated by disease, would life be worth having? And
that which has been destroyed is—the body?

Cr. Yes.

Soc. Could we live, having an evil and corrupted body?

Cr. Certainly not.

Soc. And will life be worth having, if that higher part of man be   55
destroyed, which is improved by justice and depraved by injustice? Do
we suppose that principle, whatever it may be in man, which has to do
with justice and injustice, to be inferior to the body?

Cr. Certainly not.

Soc. More honourable than the body?

Cr. Far more.

Soc. Then, my friend, we must not regard what the many say of
us: but what he, the one man who has understanding of just and unjust, will say, and what the truth will say. And therefore you begin in
error when you advise that we should regard the opinion of the many
about just and unjust, good and evil, honourable and dishonourable.—"Well," some one will say, "But the many can kill us."

Cr. Yes, Socrates; that will clearly be the answer.   60

Soc.   And it is true: but still I find with surprise that the old argument is unshaken as ever. And I should like to know whether I may say the same of another proposition—that not life, but a good life, is to be chiefly valued?

Cr.   Yes, that also remains unshaken.

Soc.   And a good life is equivalent to a just and honourable one—that holds also?

Cr.   Yes, it does.

Soc.   From these premises I proceed to argue the question   65
whether I ought or ought not to try to escape without the consent of the Athenians: and if I am clearly right in escaping, then I will make the attempt; but if not, I will abstain. The other considerations which you mention, of money and loss of character and the duty of educating one's children, are, I fear, only the doctrines of the multitude, who would be as ready to restore people to life, if they were able, as they are to put them to death—and with as little reason. But now, since the argument has thus far prevailed, the only question which remains to be considered is, whether we shall do rightly either in escaping or in suffering others to aid in our escape and paying them in money and thanks, or whether in reality we shall not do rightly; and if the latter, then death or any other calamity which may ensue on my remaining here must not be allowed to enter into the calculation.

Cr.   I think that you are right, Socrates; how then shall we proceed?

Soc.   Let us consider the matter together, and do you either refute me if you can, and I will be convinced; or else cease, my dear friend, from repeating to me that I ought to escape against the wishes of the Athenians; for I highly value your attempts to persuade me to do so, but I may not be persuaded against my own better judgment. And now please to consider my first position, and try how you can best answer me.

Cr.   I will.

Soc.   Are we to say that we are never intentionally to do wrong, or that in one way we ought and in another way we ought not to do wrong, or is doing wrong always evil and dishonourable, as I was just now saying, and as has been already acknowledged by us? Are all our former admissions which were made within a few days to be thrown away? And have we, at our age, been earnestly discoursing with one another all our life long only to discover that we are no better than children? Or, in spite of the opinion of the many, and in spite of consequences whether better or worse, shall we insist on the truth of what was then said, that injustice is always an evil and dishonour to him who acts unjustly? Shall we say so or not?

Cr.   Yes.   70

Soc.   Then we must do no wrong?

Cr.   Certainly not.

Soc. Nor when injured injure in return, as the many imagine; for we must injure no one at all?

Cr. Clearly not.

Soc. Again, Crito, may we do evil? 75

Cr. Surely not, Socrates.

Soc. And what of doing evil in return for evil, which is the morality of the many—is that just or not?

Cr. Not just.

Soc. For doing evil to another is the same as injuring him?

Cr. Very true. 80

Soc. Then we ought not to retaliate or render evil for evil to any one, whatever evil we may have suffered from him. But I would have you consider, Crito, whether you really mean what you are saying. For this opinion has never been held, and never will be held, by any considerable number of persons; and those who are agreed and those who are not agreed upon this point have no common ground, and can only despise one another when they see how widely they differ. Tell me, then, whether you agree with and assent to my first principle, that neither injury nor retaliation nor warding off evil is ever right. And shall that be the premise of our argument? Or do you decline and dissent from this? For so I have ever thought, and continue to think; but, if you are of another opinion, let me hear what you have to say. If, however, you remain of the same mind as formerly, I will proceed to the next step.

Cr. You may proceed, for I have not changed my mind.

Soc. Then I will go on to the next point, which may be put in the form of a question:—Ought a man to do what he admits to be right, or ought he to betray the right?

Cr. He ought to do what he thinks right.

Soc. But if this is true, what is the application? In leaving the 85 prison against the will of the Athenians, do I wrong any? or rather do I not wrong those whom I ought least to wrong? Do I not desert the principles which were acknowledged by us to be just—what do you say?

Cr. I cannot tell, Socrates; for I do not know.

Soc. Then consider the matter in this way:—Imagine that I am about to play truant (you may call the proceeding by any name which you like), and the laws and the government come and interrogate me: "Tell us, Socrates," they say; "what are you about? are you not going by an act of yours to overturn us—the laws, and the whole state, as far as in you lies? Do you imagine that a state can subsist and not be overthrown, in which the decisions of law have no power, but are set aside and trampled upon by individuals?" What will be our answer, Crito, to these and the like words? Any one, and especially a rhetorician, will have a good deal to say on behalf of the law which requires a sentence to be carried out. He will argue that this law should not be set aside;

and shall we reply, "Yes; but the state has injured us and given an un-just sentence." Suppose I say that?

    Cr.   Very good, Socrates.

    Soc.   "And was that our agreement with you?" the laws would answer; "or were you to abide by the sentence of the state?" And if I were to express my astonishment at their words, the laws would prob-ably add: "Answer, Socrates, instead of opening your eyes—you are in the habit of asking and answering questions. Tell us,—What complaint have you to make against us which justifies you in attempting to de-stroy us and the state? In the first place did we not bring you into exis-tence? Your father married your mother by our aid and begat you. Say whether you have any objection to urge against those of us who regu-late marriage?" None, I should reply. "Or against those of us who after birth regulate the nurture and education of children, in which you also were trained? Were not the laws, which have the charge of education, right in commanding your father to train you in music and gymnas-tic?" Right, I should reply. "Well, then, since you were brought into the world and nurtured and educated by us, can you deny in the first place that you are our child and slave, as your fathers were before you? And if this is true, you are not on equal terms with us; nor can you think that you have a right to do to us what we are doing to you. Would you have any right to strike or revile or do any other evil to your father or your master, if you had one, because you have been struck or reviled by him, or received some other evil at his hands?— you would not say this? And because we think right to destroy you, do you think that you have any right to destroy us in return, and your country as far as in you lies? Will you, O professor of true virtue, pre-tend that you are justified in this? Has a philosopher like you failed to discover that our country is more to be valued and higher and holier far than mother or father or any ancestor, and more to be regarded in the eyes of the gods and men of understanding? also to be soothed, and gently and reverently entreated when angry, even more than a fa-ther, and either to be persuaded, or if not persuaded, to be obeyed? And when we are punished by her, whether with imprisonment or stripes, the punishment is to be endured in silence; and if she lead us to wounds or death in battle, thither we follow as is right; neither may any one yield or retreat or leave his rank, but whether in battle or in a court of law, or in any other place, he must do what his city and his country order him; or he must change their view of what is just: and if he may do no violence to his father or mother, much less may he do violence to his country." What answer shall we make to this, Crito? Do the laws speak truly, or do they not?

    Cr.   I think that they do.

    Soc.   Then the laws will say: "Consider, Socrates, if we are speak-ing truly that in your present attempt you are going to do us an injury.

90

For, having brought you into the world, and nurtured and educated you, and given you and every other citizen a share in every good which we had to give, we further proclaim to any Athenian by the liberty which we allow him, that if he does not like us when he has become of age and has seen the ways of the city, and made our acquaintance, he may go where he pleases and take his goods with him. None of our laws will forbid him or interfere with him. Any one who does not like us and the city, and who wants to emigrate to a colony or to any other city, may go where he likes, retaining his property. But he who has experience of the manner in which we order justice and administer the State, and still remains, has entered into an implied contract that he will do as we command him. And he who disobeys us is, as we maintain, thrice wrong; first, because in disobeying us he is disobeying his parents; secondly, because we are the authors of his education; thirdly, because he has made an agreement with us that he will duly obey our commands; and he neither obeys them nor convinces us that our commands are unjust; and we do not rudely impose them, but give him the alternative of obeying or convincing us;—that is what we offer, and he does neither.

"These are the sort of accusations to which, as we were saying, you, Socrates, will be exposed if you accomplish your intentions; you, above all other Athenians." Suppose now I ask, why I rather than anybody else? they will justly retort upon me that I above all other men have acknowledged the agreement. "There is clear proof," they will say, "Socrates, that we and the city were not displeasing to you. Of all Athenians you have been the most constant resident in the city, which, as you never leave, you may be supposed to love. For you never went out of the city either to see the games, except once when you went to the Isthmus, or to any other place unless when you were on military service; nor did you travel as other men do. Nor had you any curiosity to know other States or their laws: your affections did not go beyond us and our State; we were your special favourites, and you acquiesced in our government of you; and here in this city you begat your children, which is a proof of your satisfaction. Moreover, you might in the course of the trial, if you had liked, have fixed the penalty at banishment; the State which refuses to let you go now would have let you go then. But you pretended that you preferred death to exile, and that you were not unwilling to die. And now you have forgotten these fine sentiments, and pay no respect to us, the laws, of whom you are the destroyer; and are doing what only a miserable slave wouid do, running away and turning your back upon the compacts and agreements which you made as a citizen. And, first of all, answer this very question: Are we right in saying that you agreed to be governed according to us in deed, and not in word only? Is that true or not?" How shall we answer, Crito? Must we not assent?

Cr. We cannot help it, Socrates.

Soc.   Then will they not say: "You, Socrates, are breaking the covenants and agreements which you made with us at your leisure, not in any haste or under any compulsion or deception, but after you have had seventy years to think of them, during which time you were at liberty to leave the city, if we were not to your mind, or if our covenants appeared to you to be unfair. You had your choice, and might have gone either to Lacedaemon or Crete, both which States are often praised by you for their good government, or to some other Hellenic or foreign State. Whereas you, above all other Athenians, seemed to be so fond of the State, or, in other words, of us, her laws (and who would care about a State which has no laws?), that you never stirred out of her; the halt, the blind, the maimed were not more stationary in her than you were. And now you run away and forsake your agreements. Not so, Socrates, if you will take our advice; do not make yourself ridiculous by escaping out of the city.

"For just consider, if you transgress and err in this sort of way,   95 what good will you do either to yourself or to your friends? That your friends will be driven into exile and deprived of citizenship, or will lose their property, is tolerably certain; and you yourself, if you fly to one of the neighbouring cities, as, for example, Thebes or Megara, both of which are well governed, will come to them as an enemy, Socrates, and their government will be against you, and all patriotic citizens will cast an evil eye upon you as a subverter of the laws, and you will confirm in the minds of the judges the justice of their own condemnation of you. For he who is a corrupter of the laws is more than likely to be a corrupter of the young and foolish portion of mankind. Will you then flee from well-ordered cities and virtuous men? and is existence worth having on these terms? Or will you go to them without shame, and talk to them, Socrates? And what will you say to them? What you say here about virtue and justice and institutions and laws being the best things among men? Would that be decent of you? Surely not. But if you go away from well-governed states to Crito's friends in Thessaly, where there is great disorder and license, they will be charmed to hear the tale of your escape from prison, set off with ludicrous particulars of the manner in which you were wrapped in a goatskin or some other disguise, and metamorphosed as the manner is of runaways; but will there be no one to remind you that in your old age you were not ashamed to violate the most sacred laws for a miserable desire of a little more life? Perhaps not, if you keep them in a good temper; but if they are out of temper you will hear many degrading things; you will live, but how?—as the flatterer of all men, and the servant of all men; and doing what?—eating and drinking in Thessaly, having gone abroad in order that you may get a dinner. And where will be your fine sentiments about justice and virtue? Say that you wish to live for the sake of your children—you want to bring them up and educate them—will you take them into Thessaly and deprive them of Athenian citizenship? Is this the benefit which you will confer upon them? Or are you under the impression that they will be better cared for and educated here if you are still alive, although absent from them; for your friends will take care of them? Do you fancy that if you are an inhabitant of Thessaly they will take care of them, and if you are an inhabitant of the other world that they will not take care of them? Nay; but if they who call themselves friends are good for anything, they will—to be sure they will.

"Listen, then, Socrates, to us who have brought you up. Think not of life and children first, and of justice afterward, but of justice first, that you may be justified before the princes of the world below. For neither will you nor any that belong to you be happier or holier or juster in this life, or happier in another, if you do as Crito bids. Now you depart in innocence, a sufferer and not a doer of evil; a victim, not of the laws but of men. But if you go forth, returning evil for evil, and injury for injury, breaking the covenants and agreements which you have made with us, and wronging those whom you ought least of all to wrong, that is to say, yourself, your friends, your country, and us, we shall be angry with you while you live, and our brethren, the laws in the world below, will receive you as an enemy; for they will know that you have done your best to destroy us. Listen, then, to us and not to Crito."

This, dear Crito, is the voice which I seem to hear murmuring in my ears, like the sound of the flute in the ears of the mystic; that voice, I say, is humming in my ears, and prevents me from hearing any other. And I know that anything more which you may say will be vain. Yet speak, if you have anything to say.

Cr.   I have nothing to say, Socrates.

Soc.   Leave me then, Crito, to fulfill the will of God, and to follow whither he leads.

TONI CADE BAMBARA

The Hammer Man

Toni Cade Bambara (1939–1995) grew up in Harlem and the Bedford-Stuyvesant district of New York City. She began writing as a child, most notably influenced by the women of Harlem who surrounded her; Bambara claimed they taught her that "the laws of hospitality, kinship obligation, and caring neighborliness remain eternal, 'cause first and foremost there's us: community.'" Bambara valued writing, then, because she saw it as a "legitimate way, an important way, to participate in the empowerment of the community that names [her]." Primarily educated at Queen's College and City College, New York, Bambara studied theater, mime, dance, film, and linguistics at eight other institutions in Europe and America. Prodigiously talented and politically committed, she was a welfare investigator, a community organizer, a college professor, and a director of plays and films. At the same time, she published two books of short stories, *Gorilla, My Love* (1972) and *The Sea Birds Are Still Alive* (1977), two novels, *The Salt Eaters* (1980) and *If Blessing Comes* (1987), and numerous screenplays. In 1991 Bambara collaborated on a book about the films of Spike Lee, *Five for Five*. "The Hammer Man" was first published in *Negro Digest* in 1966. Readers may find a surprising connection between the way Bambara's young protagonist understands community and the way Socrates talks about the concept in Plato's *Crito*.

1 I was glad to hear that Manny had fallen off the roof. I had put out the tale that I was down with yellow fever, but nobody paid me no mind, least of all Dirty Red who stomped right in to announce that Manny had fallen off the roof and that I could come out of hiding now. My mother dropped what she was doing, which was the laundry, and got the whole story out of Red. "Bad enough you gots to hang around with boys," she said. "But fight with them too. And you would pick the craziest one at that."

2 Manny was supposed to be crazy. That was his story. To say you were bad put some people off. But to say you were crazy, well, you were officially not to be messed with. So that was his story. On the other hand, after I called him what I called him and said a few choice things about his mother, his face did go through some piercing changes. And I did kind of wonder if maybe he sure was nuts. I didn't wait to find out. I got in the wind. And then he waited for me on my stoop all day and all night, not hardly speaking to the people going in and out. And he was there all day Saturday, with his sister bringing him peanut-butter sandwiches and cream sodas. He must've gone to the bathroom right there cause every time I looked out the kitchen window, there he was. And Sunday, too. I got to thinking the boy was mad.

3 "You got no sense of humor, that's your trouble," I told him. He looked up, but he didn't say nothing. All at once I was real sorry about the whole thing. I should've settled for hitting off the little girls in the school yard, or waiting for Frankie to come in so we could raise some kind of hell. This way I had to play sick when my mother was around cause my father had already taken away my BB gun and hid it.

4 I don't know how they got Manny on the roof finally. Maybe the Wakefield kids, the ones who keep the pigeons, called him up. Manny was a sucker for sick animals and things like that. Or maybe Frankie got

some nasty girls to go up on the roof with him and got Manny to join him. I don't know. Anyway, the catwalk had lost all its cement and the roof always did kind of slant downward. So Manny fell off the roof. I got over my yellow fever right quick, needless to say, and ventured outside. But by this time I had already told Miss Rose that Crazy Manny was after me. And Miss Rose, being who she was, quite naturally went over to Manny's house and said a few harsh words to his mother, who, being who she was, chased Miss Rose out into the street and they commenced to get with it, snatching bottles out of the garbage cans and breaking them on the johnny pumps and stuff like that.

Dirty Red didn't have to tell us about this. Everybody could see and hear all. I never figured the garbage cans for an arsenal, but Miss Rose came up with sticks and table legs and things, and Manny's mother had her share of scissor blades and bicycle chains. They got to rolling in the streets and all you could see was pink drawers and fat legs. It was something else. Miss Rose is nutty but Manny's mother's crazier than Manny. They were at it a couple of times during my sick spell. Everyone would congregate on the window sills or the fire escape, commenting that it was still much too cold for this kind of nonsense. But they watched anyway. And then Manny fell off the roof. And that was that. Miss Rose went back to her dream books and Manny's mother went back to her tumbled-down kitchen of dirty clothes and bundles and bundles of rags and children.

My father got in on it too, cause he happened to ask Manny one night why he was sitting on the stoop like that every night. Manny told him right off that he was going to kill me first chance he got. Quite naturally this made my father a little warm, me being his only daughter and planning to become a doctor and take care of him in his old age. So he had a few words with Manny first, and then he got hold of the older brother, Bernard, who was more his size. Bernard didn't see how any of it was his business or my father's business, so my father got mad and jammed Bernard's head into the mailbox. Then my father started getting messages from Bernard's uncle about where to meet him for a showdown and all. My father didn't say a word to my mother all this time; just sat around mumbling and picking up the phone and putting it down, or grabbing my stickball bat and putting it back. He carried on like this for days till I thought I would scream if the yellow fever didn't have me so weak. And then Manny fell off the roof, and my father went back to his beer-drinking buddies.

I was in the school yard, pitching pennies with the little boys from the elementary school, when my friend Violet hits my brand-new Spaudeen over the wall. She came running back to tell me that Manny was coming down the block. I peeked beyond the fence and there he was all right. He had his head all wound up like a mummy and his arm in a sling and his leg in a cast. It looked phony to me, especially that walking cane. I figured Dirty Red had told me a tale just to get me out there so Manny could stomp me, and Manny was playing it up with costume and all till he could get me.

"What happened to him?" Violet's sister whispered. But I was too busy trying to figure out how this act was supposed to work. Then Manny passed real close to the fence and gave me a look. **8**

"You had enough, Hammer Head," I yelled. "Just bring your crummy self in this yard and I'll pick up where I left off." Violet was knocked out and the other kids went into a huddle. I didn't have to say anything else. And when they all pressed me later, I just said, "You know that hammer he always carries in his fatigues?" And they'd all nod waiting for the rest of a long story. "Well, I took it away from him." And I walked off nonchalantly. **9**

Manny stayed indoors for a long time. I almost forgot about him. New kids moved into the block and I got all caught up with that. And then Miss Rose finally hit the numbers and started ordering a whole lot of stuff through the mail and we would sit on the curb and watch these weird-looking packages being carried in, trying to figure out what simple-minded thing she had thrown her money away on when she might just as well wait for the warm weather and throw a block party for all her godchildren. **10**

After a while a center opened up and my mother said she'd increase my allowance if I went and joined because I'd have to get out of my pants and stay in skirts, on account of that's the way things were at the center. So I joined and got to thinking about everything else but old Hammer Head. It was a rough place to get along in, the center, but my mother said that I needed to be be'd with and she needed to not be with me, so I went. And that time I sneaked into the office, that's when I really got turned on. I looked into one of those not-quite-white folders and saw that I was from a deviant family in a deviant neighborhood. I showed my mother the word in the dictionary, but she didn't pay me no mind. It was my favorite word after that. I ran it in the ground till one day my father got the strap just to show how deviant he could get. So I gave up trying to improve my vocabulary. And I almost gave up my dungarees. **11**

Then one night I'm walking past the Douglas Street park cause I got thrown out of the center for playing pool when I should've been sewing, even though I had already decided that this was going to be my last fling with boy things, and starting tomorrow I was going to fix my hair right and wear skirts all the time just so my mother would stop talking about her gray hairs, and Miss Rose would stop calling me by my brother's name by mistake. So I'm walking past the park and there's ole Manny on the basketball court, perfecting his lay-ups and talking with himself. Being me, I quite naturally walk right up and ask what the hell he's doing playing in the dark, and he looks up and all **12** around like the dark had crept up on him when he wasn't looking. So I knew right away that he'd been out there for a long time with his eyes just going along with the program.

"There was two seconds to go and we were one point ahead," he said, shaking his head and staring at his sneakers like they was somebody. "And I was in the clear. I'd left the men in the backcourt and there I was, smiling, you dig, cause it was in the bag. They passed the ball and I slid the ball up nice and easy cause there was nothing to worry about. And . . ." He shook his head. "I muffed the goddamn shot. Ball bounced off the rim . . ." He stared at his hands. "The game of the season. Last game." And then he ignored me altogether, though he wasn't talking to me in the first place. He went back to the lay-ups, always from the same spot with his arms crooked in the same way, over and over. I must've gotten hypnotized cause I probably stood there for at least an hour watching like a fool till I couldn't even see the damn ball, much less the basket. But I stood there anyway for no reason I know of. He never missed. But he cursed himself away. It was torture. And then a squad car pulled up and a short cop with hair like one of the Marx Brothers came out hitching up his pants. He looked real hard at me and then at Manny. 13

"What are you two doing?" 14

"He's doing a lay-up. I'm watching," I said with my smart self. 15

Then the cop just stood there and finally turned to the other one who was just getting out of the car. 16

"Who unlocked the gate?" the big one said. 17

"It's always unlocked," I said. Then we three just stood there like a bunch of penguins watching Manny go at it. 18

"This on the level?" the big guy asked, tilting his hat back with the thumb the way big guys do in hot weather. "Hey you," he said, walking over to Manny. "I'm talking to you." He finally grabbed the ball to get Manny's attention. But that didn't work. Manny just stood there with his arms out waiting for the pass so he could save the game. He wasn't paying no mind to the cop. So, quite naturally, when the cop slapped him upside his head it was a surprise. And when the cop starting counting three to go, Manny had already recovered from the slap and was just ticking off the seconds before the buzzer sounded and all was lost. 19

"Gimme the ball, man." Manny's face was tightened up and ready to pop. 20

"Did you hear what I said, black boy?" 21

Now, when somebody says that word like that, I gets warm. And crazy or no crazy, Manny was my brother at that moment and the cop was the enemy. 22

"You better give him back his ball," I said. "Manny don't take no mess from no cops. He ain't bothering nobody. He's gonna be Mister 23

Basketball when he grows up. Just trying to get a little practice in before the softball seasons starts."

"Look here, sister, we'll run you in too," Harpo said.   24

"I damn sure can't be your sister seeing how I'm a black girl. Boy,   25
I sure will be glad when you run me in so I can tell everybody about
that. You must think you're in the South, Mister."

The big guy screwed his mouth up and let out one of them hard-   26
day sighs. "The park's closed, little girl, so why don't you and your
boyfriend go on home."

That really got me. The "little girl" was bad enough but that   27
"boyfriend" was too much. But I kept cool, mostly because Manny
looked so pitiful waiting there with his hands in a time-out and there
being no one to stop the clock. But I kept my cool mostly cause of that
hammer in Manny's pocket and no telling how frantic things can get
what with a big-mouth like me, a couple of wise cops, and a crazy boy
too.

"The gates are open," I said real quiet-like, "and this here's a free   28
country. So why don't you give him back his ball?"

The big cop did another one of those sighs, his specialty I guess,   29
and then he bounced the ball to Manny who went right into his gliding thing clear up to the backboard, damn near like he was some kind
of very beautiful bird. And then he swooshed that ball in, even if there
was no net, and you couldn't really hear the swoosh. Something happened to the bones in my chest. It was something.

"Crazy kids anyhow," the one with the wig said and turned to go.   30
But the big guy watched Manny for a while and I guess something
must've snapped in his head, cause all of a sudden he was hot for taking Manny to jail or court or somewhere and starting yelling at him
and everything, which is a bad thing to do to Manny, I can tell you.
And I'm standing there thinking that none of my teachers, from
kindergarten right on up, none of them knew what they were talking
about. I'll be damned if I ever knew one of them rosy-cheeked cops
that smiled and helped you get to school without neither you or your
little raggedy dog getting hit by a truck that had a smile on its face, too.
Not that I ever believed it. I knew Dick and Jane was full of crap from
the get-go, especially them cops. Like this dude, for example, pulling
on Manny's clothes like that when obviously he had just done about
the most beautiful thing a man can do and not be a fag. No cop could
swoosh without a net.

"Look out, man," was all Manny said, but it was the way he   31
pushed the cop that started the real yelling and threats. And I thought
to myself, Oh God here I am trying to change my ways, and not talk
back in school, and do like my mother wants, but just have this last
fling, and now this—getting shot in the stomach and bleeding to death
in Douglas Street park and poor Manny getting pistol-whipped by

those bastards and whatnot. I could see it all, practically crying too. And it just wasn't no kind of thing to happen to a small child like me with my confirmation picture in the paper next to my weeping parents and schoolmates. I could feel the blood sticking to my shirt and my eyeballs slipping away, and then that confirmation picture again; and my mother and her gray hair; and Miss Rose heading for the precinct with a shotgun; and my father getting old and feeble with no one to doctor him up and all.

And I wished Manny had fallen off the damn roof and died right   32
then and there and saved me all this aggravation of being killed with him by these cops who surely didn't come out of no fifth-grade reader. But it didn't happen. They just took the ball and Manny followed them real quiet-like right out of the park into the dark, then into the squad car with his head drooping and his arms in a crook. And I went on home cause what the hell am I going to do on a basketball court, and it getting to be nearly midnight?

I didn't see Manny no more after he got into that squad car. But   33
they didn't kill him after all cause Miss Rose heard he was in some kind of big house for people who lose their marbles. And then it was spring finally, and me and Violet was in this very boss fashion show at the center. And Miss Rose bought me my first corsage—yellow roses to match my shoes.

ROBERT FROST

Mending Wall

Robert Frost (1874–1963), son of a San Francisco newspaperman and a schoolteacher, published his first poem in 1894 and continued to publish actively until 1962. After attending classes at Dartmouth and Harvard, but graduating from neither, he farmed and taught school in New Hampshire before turning full-time to poetry. His numerous honors and awards include four Pulitzer Prizes for Poetry (1924, 1931, 1937, and 1943), the American Academy of Poets Award (1953), and induction into the American Poet's Corner at the Cathedral of St. John the Divine in 1986. Having lived most of his adult life in New England, Frost was heavily influenced by the region's characteristic speech and landscape, but it might be a mistake to think of him as having been entirely at home there: The speakers in his poems often seem to view both their Yankee neighbors and the natural landscape with an outsider's eye. "Mending Wall" was first published in *North of Boston* (1914).

Something there is that doesn't love a wall,
That sends the frozen-ground-swell under it,
And spills the upper boulders in the sun;
And makes gaps even two can pass abreast.
The work of hunters if another thing: 5
I have come after them and made repair
Where they have left not one stone on a stone,
But they would have the rabbit out of hiding,
To please the yelping dogs. The gaps I mean,
No one has seen them made or heard them made,   10
But at spring mending-time we find them there.
I let my neighbor know beyond the hill;
And on a day we meet to walk the line
And set the wall between us once again.
We keep the wall between us as we go.   15
To each the boulders that have fallen to each.
And some are loaves and some so nearly balls
We have to use a spell to make them balance:
'Stay where you are until our backs are turned!'
We wear our fingers rough with handling them.   20
Oh, just another kind of outdoor game,
One on a side. It comes to little more:
There were it is we do not need the wall:
He is all pine and I am apple orchard.
My apple trees will never get across   25
And eat the cones under his pines. I tell him.
He only says, 'Good fences make good neighbors.'
Spring is the mischief in me, and I wonder
If I could put a notion in his head:
'Why do they make good neighbors? Isn't it   30
Where there are cows? But here there are no cows.
Before I built a wall I'd ask to know
What I was walling in or walling out,
And to whom I was like to give offense.
Something there is that doesn't love a wall,   35
That wants it down.' I could say, 'Elves' to him,
But it's not elves exactly, and I'd rather
He said it for himself. I see him there
Bringing a stone grasped firmly by the top
In each hand, like an old-stone savage armed.   40
He moves in darkness as it seems to me,
Not of woods only and the shade of trees.
He will not go behind his father's saying,
And he likes having thought of it so well
He says again, 'Good fences make good neighbors.'   45

INSIDERS AND
OUTSIDERS

We find ourselves dislodged and excluded.

Overview

"To an ordinary human being," George Orwell once wrote, "love means nothing if it does not mean loving some individuals more than others." One way or another, all the selections in this unit have to do with the problems created by our inability to spread love, admiration, or even respect, evenly in society. Every circle that defines a cozy "us" leaves the rest of the world defined as less-welcome "them."

The writers in this unit sometimes focus on the ironies and even the humor of our struggles to find a place inside what C. S. Lewis calls "the Inner Ring." But we can hardly read them without feeling the ache of exclusion. Simply because of being human, most of us have stories to tell about being outsiders struggling for acceptance, or insiders trying to maintain our position. Writing about such experiences can deepen our understanding—and our readers' understanding—of a social force that can control us from the day we enter preschool until the day we die.

The unit also opens up some opportunities for research. You might want to examine the social forces that have created prejudices against entire groups of people. How can we account for attitudes toward African-Americans, Jews, and women that were overtly expressed a generation or two ago but now are almost universally condemned? You might look for answers not only in the writings of historians and sociologists, but in primary sources: Examine for yourself the books, newspapers, and magazines people used to read; see what you can learn from autobiographies and fiction. You might also examine the ways that groups of "outsiders" are treated by the media today. Is our society freer of irrational biases than it was fifty years ago, or is the level of prejudice about the same, with some change of targets or code words?

C. S. LEWIS   The Inner Ring   281

> I believe that in all men's lives at certain periods, and in many men's lives at all periods between infancy and extreme old age, one of the most dominant elements is the desire to be inside the local Ring and the terror of being left outside.

GEORGE ORWELL   Shooting an Elephant   288

> In Moulmein, in Lower Burma, I was hated by large numbers of people—the only time in my life that I have been important enough for this to happen to me. I was sub-divisional police officer of the town, and in an aimless, petty kind of way anti-European feeling was very bitter.

For the first two days, I was invisible. When I spoke, people tapped impatiently, waiting for the interruption to end. No one took either my presence or my words seriously. At meals, I sat with my colleagues' wives.

The truth was that I was ashamed of my handicap. I wanted to have something more visibly wrong with me. I wanted to be in the same league as the girl who'd lost her right leg in a car accident; her artificial leg attracted a bevy of awestruck campers.

Watching myself being watched by all the white campers, I experienced that strange combination of power and powerlessness that you feel when the actions of another black person affect your own life, simply because you both are black.

All segregation statutes are unjust because segregation distorts the soul and damages the personality. It gives the segregator a false sense of superiority and the segregated a false sense of inferiority.

You may never have met such people, but you've heard what they do: they pile up money, vote in blocs, and elect right-wing crazies; they censor books; they carry handguns; they fight fluoride in the drinking water and evolution in the schools; probably they would lynch people if they could get away with it.

The more extreme forms aside, one most important function of medical jargon is to help doctors maintain some distance from their patients. By reformulating a patient's pain and problems into a language that the patient doesn't even speak, I suppose we are in some sense taking those pains and problems under our jurisdiction . . .

"I'm going because I've been invited," she said. "And I've been invited because Luciana is my friend. So there."

"Ah yes, your friend," her mother grumbled. She paused. "Listen, Rosaura," she said at last. "That one's not your friend. You know what you are to them? The maid's daughter, that's what."

So will my page be colored that I write?
Being me, it will not be white.
But it will be a part of you, instructor.
You are white—

The Inner Ring

C. S. Lewis (1898–1963), professor of medieval and Renaissance English at Cambridge University, was also a novelist, a writer of children's books, and a popular speaker on moral and religious issues. In the early 1940s, he delivered a series of radio talks on the BBC that were later collected in *Mere Christianity* (1952), a book still very popular among Christians of all denominations. In 1942 he published his best-known book, *The Screwtape Letters*, in which he impersonated a veteran devil in hell who writes letters encouraging the efforts of a novice devil hard at work on earth. Lewis's witty, intelligent defenses of traditional morality and religion led him to challenge many of the secular orthodoxies of the twentieth century. "The Inner Ring" was the Memorial Lecture at King's College, University of London, in 1944. In it readers will find a challenge to Sigmund Freud's assumption that sex is the strongest of all human drives. This challenge is echoed, in different terms, in almost every essay, poem, or story in this section of *The Dolphin Reader.*

May I read you a few lines from Tolstoi's *War and Peace?* 1

When Boris entered the room, Prince Andrey was listening to an old general, wearing his decorations, who was reporting something to Prince Andrey, with an expression of soldierly servility on his purple face. "Alright. Please wait!" he said to the general, speaking in Russian with the French accent which he used when he spoke with contempt. The moment he noticed Boris he stopped listening to the general who trotted imploringly after him and begged to be heard, while Prince Andrey turned to Boris with a cheerful smile and a nod of the head. Boris now clearly understood—what he had already guessed—that side by side with the system of discipline and subordination which were laid down in the Army Regulations, there existed a different and a more real system—the system which compelled a tightly laced general with a purple face to wait respectfully for his turn while a mere captain like Prince Andrey chatted with a mere second lieutenant like Boris. Boris decided at once that he would be guided not by the official system but by this other unwritten system.[1]

When you invite a middle-aged moralist to address you, I suppose 2
I must conclude, however unlikely the conclusion seems, that you have a taste for middle-aged moralising. I shall do my best to gratify it. I shall in fact give you advice about the world in which you are going to live. I do not mean by this that I am going to attempt to talk on what are called current affairs. You probably know quite as much about

---

1. Part III, chapter 9. [author's note]

them as I do. I am not going to tell you—except in a form so general that you will hardly recognise it—what part you ought to play in post-war reconstruction. It is not, in fact, very likely that any of you will be able, in the next ten years, to make any direct contribution to the peace or prosperity of Europe. You will be busy finding jobs, getting married, acquiring facts. I am going to do something more old-fashioned than you perhaps expected. I am going to give advice. I am going to issue warnings. Advice and warnings about things which are so perennial that no one calls them "current affairs."

And of course everyone knows what a middle-aged moralist of my ³ type warns his juniors against. He warns them against the World, the Flesh, and the Devil. But one of this trio will be enough to deal with today. The Devil, I shall leave strictly alone. The association between him and me in the public mind has already gone quite as deep as I wish: in some quarters it has already reached the level of confusion, if not of identification. I begin to realise the truth of the old proverb that he who sups with that formidable host needs a long spoon. As for the Flesh, you must be very abnormal young people if you do not know quite as much about it as I do. But on the World I think I have something to say.

In the passage I have just read from Tolstoi, the young second lieu- ⁴ tenant Boris Dubretskoi discovers that there exist in the army two different systems or hierarchies. The one is printed in some little red book and anyone can easily read it up. It also remains constant. A general is always superior to a colonel and a colonel to a captain. The other is not printed anywhere. Nor is it even a formally organised secret society with officers and rules which you would be told after you had been admitted. You are never formally and explicitly admitted by anyone. You discover gradually, in almost indefinable ways, that it exists and that you are outside it; and then later, perhaps, that you are inside it. There are what correspond to passwords, but they too are spontaneous and informal. A particular slang, the use of particular nicknames, an allusive manner of conversation, are the marks. But it is not constant. It is not easy, even at a given moment, to say who is inside and who is outside. Some people are obviously in and some are obviously out, but there are always several on the border-line. And if you come back to the same Divisional Headquarters, or Brigade Headquarters, or the same regiment or even the same company, after six weeks' absence, you may find this second hierarchy quite altered. There are no formal admissions or expulsions. People think they are in it after they have in fact been pushed out of it, or before they have been allowed in: this provides great amusement for those who are really inside. It has no fixed name. The only certain rule is that the insiders and outsiders call it by different names. From inside it may be designated, in simple cases, by mere enumeration: it may be called "You and Tony and me." When it is very secure and comparatively stable in membership it calls itself "we." When it has to be suddenly expanded to meet a particular emergency it calls itself "All the sensible people at this place." From outside, if you have despaired of getting into it, you call it "That gang" or "They" or "So-and-so and his set" or "the Caucus" or "the Inner Ring." If you are a candidate for admission you probably don't call it anything. To discuss it with the other outsiders would make you feel outside yourself. And to mention it in talking to the man who is inside, and who may help you if this present conversation goes well, would be madness.

Badly as I may have described it, I hope you will all have recog- 5 nised the thing I am describing. Not, of course, that you have been in the Russian Army or perhaps in any army. But you have met the phenomenon of an Inner Ring. You discovered one in your house at school before the end of the first term. And when you had climbed up to somewhere near it by the end of your second year, perhaps you discovered that within the Ring there was a Ring yet more inner, which in its turn was the fringe of the great school Ring to which the house Rings were only satellites. It is even possible that the School Ring was almost in touch with a Masters' Ring. You were beginning, in fact, to pierce through the skins of the onion. And here, too, at your university—shall I be wrong in assuming that at this very moment, invisible to me, there are several rings—independent systems or concentric rings—present in this room? And I can assure you that in whatever hospital, inn of court, diocese, school, business, or college you arrive after going down, you will find the Rings—what Tolstoi calls the second or unwritten systems.

All this is rather obvious. I wonder whether you will say the same 6 of my next step, which is this. I believe that in all men's lives at certain periods, and in many men's lives at all periods between infancy and extreme old age, one of the most dominant elements is the desire to be inside the local Ring and the terror of being left outside. This desire, in one of its forms, has indeed had ample justice done to it in literature. I mean, in the form of snobbery. Victorian fiction is full of characters who are hag-ridden by the desire to get inside that particular Ring which is, or was, called Society. But it must be clearly understood that "Society," in that sense of the word, is merely one of a hundred Rings and snobbery therefore only one form of the longing to be inside. People who believe themselves to be free, and indeed are free, from snobbery, and who read satires on snobbery with tranquil superiority, may be devoured by the desire in another form. It may be the very intensity of their desire to enter some quite different Ring which renders them immune from the allurements of high life. An invitation from a duchess would be very cold comfort to a man smarting under the sense of exclusion from some artistic or communist côterie. Poor man—it is not large, lighted rooms, or champagne, or even scandals about peers and Cabinet Ministers that he wants: it is the sacred little attic or studio, the heads bent together, the fog of tobacco smoke, and the delicious knowledge that we—we four or five all huddled beside this stove—are the people who *know*. Often the desire conceals itself so well that we hardly recognise the pleasures of fruition. Men tell not only their wives but themselves that it is a hardship to stay late at the office or the school on some bit of important extra work which they have been let in for because they and So-and-so and the two others are the only people left in the place who really know how things are run. But it is not quite true. It is a terrible bore, of course, when old Fatty Smithson draws you aside and whispers "Look here, we've got to get you in on this examination somehow" or "Charles and I saw at once that you've got to be on this committee." A terrible bore . . . ah, but how much more terrible if you were left out! It is tiring and unhealthy to lose your Saturday afternoons: but to have them free because you don't matter, that is much worse.

Freud would say, no doubt, that the whole thing is a subterfuge of the sexual impulse. I wonder whether the shoe is not sometimes on the other foot. I wonder whether, in ages of promiscuity, many a virginity has not been lost less in obedience to Venus than in obedience to the lure of the caucus. For of course, when promiscuity is the fashion, the chaste are outsiders. They are ignorant of something that other people know. They are uninitiated. And as for lighter matters, the number who first smoked or first got drunk for a similar reason is probably very large.

I must now make a distinction. I am not going to say that the existence of Inner Rings is an evil. It is certainly unavoidable. There must be confidential discussions: and it is not only not a bad thing, it is (in itself) a good thing, that personal friendship should grow up between those who work together. And it is perhaps impossible that the official hierarchy of any organisation should quite coincide with its actual workings. If the wisest and most energetic people invariably held the highest posts, it might coincide; since they often do not, there must be people in high positions who are really deadweights and people in lower positions who are more important than their rank and seniority would lead you to suppose. In that way the second, unwritten system is bound to grow up. It is necessary; and perhaps it is not a necessary evil. But the desire which draws us into Inner Rings is another matter. A thing may be morally neutral and yet the desire for that thing may be dangerous. As Byron has said:

> *Sweet is a legacy, and passing sweet*
> *The unexpected death of some old lady.*

The painless death of a pious relative at an advanced age is not an evil. But an earnest desire for her death on the part of her heirs is not reck-

oned a proper feeling, and the law frowns on even the gentlest attempt
to expedite her departure. Let Inner Rings be an unavoidable and even
an innocent feature of life, though certainly not a beautiful one: but
what of our longing to enter them, our anguish when we are excluded, and the kind of pleasure we feel when we get in?

I have no right to make assumptions about the degree to which
any of you may already be compromised. I must not assume that you
have ever first neglected, and finally shaken off, friends whom you
really loved and who might have lasted you a lifetime, in order to
court the friendship of those who appeared to you more important,
more esoteric. I must not ask whether you have ever derived actual
pleasure from the loneliness and humiliation of the outsiders after you
yourself were in: whether you have talked to fellow members of the
Ring in the presence of outsiders simply in order that the outsiders
might envy; whether the means whereby, in your days of probation,
you propitiated the Inner Ring, were always wholly admirable. I will
ask only one question—and it is, of course, a rhetorical question which
expects no answer. In the whole of your life as you now remember it,
has the desire to be on the right side of that invisible line ever
prompted you to any act or word on which, in the cold small hours of
a wakeful night, you can look back with satisfaction? If so, your case is
more fortunate than most.

But I said I was going to give advice, and advice should deal with
the future, not the past. I have hinted at the past only to awake you to
what I believe to be the real nature of human life. I don't believe that
the economic motive and the erotic motive account for everything
that goes on in what we moralists call the World. Even if you add Ambition I think the picture is still incomplete. The lust for the esoteric,
the longing to be inside, take many forms which are not easily recog-
nisable as Ambition. We hope, no doubt, for tangible profits from
every Inner Ring we penetrate: power, money, liberty to break rules,
avoidance of routine duties, evasion of discipline. But all these would
not satisfy us if we did not get in addition the delicious sense of secret
intimacy. It is no doubt a great convenience to know that we need fear
no official reprimands from our official senior because he is old Percy,
a fellow-member of our Ring. But we don't value the intimacy only for
the sake of convenience; quite equally we value the convenience as a
proof of the intimacy.

My main purpose in this address is simply to convince you that
this desire is one of the great permanent mainsprings of human action.
It is one of the factors which go to make up the world as we know it—
this whole pell-mell of struggle, competition, confusion, graft, disappointment, and advertisement, and if it is one of the permanent
mainsprings then you may be quite sure of this. Unless you take measures to prevent it, this desire is going to be one of the chief motives of

unless you recognize it; it will consume you

your life, from the first day on which you enter your profession until the day when you are too old to care. That will be the natural thing— the life that will come to you of its own accord. Any other kind of life, if you lead it, will be the result of conscious and continuous effort. If you do nothing about it, if you drift with the stream, you will in fact be an "inner ringer." I don't say you'll be a successful one; that's as may be. But whether by pining and moping outside Rings that you can never enter, or by passing triumphantly further and further in—one way or the other you will be that kind of man.

I have already made it fairly clear that I think it better for you not   12
to be that kind of man. But you may have an open mind on the question. I will therefore suggest two reasons for thinking as I do.

It would be polite and charitable, and in view of your age reason-   13
able too, to suppose that none of you is yet a scoundrel. On the other hand, by the mere law of averages (I am saying nothing against free will) it is almost certain that at least two or three of you before you die will have become something very like scoundrels. There must be in this room the makings of at least that number of unscrupulous, treacherous, ruthless egotists. The choice is still before you: and I hope you will not take my hard words about your possible future characters as a token of disrespect to your present characters. And the prophecy I make is this. To nine out of ten of you the choice which could lead to scoundrelism will come, when it does come, in no very dramatic colours. Obviously bad men, obviously threatening or bribing, will almost certainly not appear. Over a drink or a cup of coffee, disguised as a triviality and sandwiched between two jokes, from the lips of a man, or woman, whom you have recently been getting to know rather better and whom you hope to know better still—just at the moment when you are most anxious not to appear crude, or naïf, or a prig—the hint will come. It will be the hint of something which is not quite in accordance with the technical rules of fair play: something which the public, the ignorant, romantic public, would never understand: something which even the outsiders, in your own profession are apt to make a fuss about: but something, says your new friend, which "we"—and at the word "we" you try not to blush for mere pleasure— something "we always do." And you will be drawn in, if you are drawn in, not by desire for gain or ease, but simply because at that moment, when the cup was so near your lips, you cannot bear to be thrust back again into the cold outer world. It would be so terrible to see the other man's face—that genial, confidential, delightfully sophisticated face—turn suddenly cold and contemptuous, to know that you had been tried for the Inner Ring and rejected. And then, if you are drawn in, next week it will be something a little further from the rules, and next year something further still, but all in the jolliest, friendliest spirit. It may end in a crash, a scandal, and penal servitude: it may end

in millions, a peerage and giving the prizes at your old school. But you will be a scoundrel.

That is my first reason. Of all the passions the passion for the Inner Ring is most skillful in making a man who is not yet a very bad man do very bad things. 14

My second reason is this. The torture allotted to the Danaids in the classical underworld, that of attempting to fill sieves with water, is the symbol not of one vice but of all vices. It is the very mark of a perverse desire that it seeks what is not to be had. The desire to be inside the invisible line illustrates this rule. As long as you are governed by that desire you will never get what you want. You are trying to peel an onion: if you succeed there will be nothing left. Until you conquer the fear of being an outsider, an outsider you will remain. 15

This is surely very clear when you come to think of it. If you want to be made free of a certain circle for some wholesome reason—if, say, you want to join a musical society because you really like music—then there is a possibility of satisfaction. You may find yourself playing in a quartet and you may enjoy it. But if all you want is to be in the know, your pleasure will be short-lived. The circle cannot have from within the charm it had from outside. By the very act of admitting you it has lost its magic. Once the first novelty is worn off the members of this circle will be no more interesting than your old friends. Why should they be? You were not looking for virtue or kindness or loyalty or humour or learning or wit or any of the things that can be really enjoyed. You merely wanted to be "in." And that is a pleasure that cannot last. As soon as your new associates have been staled to you by custom, you will be looking for another Ring. The rainbow's end will still be ahead of you. The old Ring will now be only the drab background for your endeavour to enter the new one. 16

And you will always find them hard to enter, for a reason you very well know. You yourself, once you are in, want to make it hard for the next entrant, just as those who are already in made it hard for you. Naturally. In any wholesome group of people which holds together for a good purpose, the exclusions are in a sense accidental. Three or four people who are together for the sake of some piece of work exclude others because there is work only for so many or because the others can't in fact do it. Your little musical group limits its numbers because the rooms they meet in are only so big. But your genuine Inner Ring exists for exclusion. There'd be no fun if there were no outsiders. The invisible line would have no meaning unless most people were on the wrong side of it. Exclusion is no accident: it is the essence. 17

The quest of the Inner Ring will break your hearts unless you break it. But if you break it, a surprising result will follow. If in your working hours you make the work your end, you will presently find yourself all unawares inside the only circle in your profession that 18 really matters. You will be one of the sound craftsmen, and other sound craftsmen will know it. This group of craftsmen will by no means coincide with the Inner Ring or the Important People or the People in the Know. It will not shape that professional policy or work up that professional influence which fights for the profession as a whole against the public: nor will it lead to those periodic scandals and crises which the Inner Ring produces. But it will do those things which that profession exists to do and will in the long run be responsible for all the respect which that profession in fact enjoys and which the speeches and advertisements cannot maintain. And if in your spare time you consort simply with the people you like, you will again find that you have come unawares to a real inside: that you are indeed snug and safe at the centre of something which, seen from without, would look exactly like an Inner Ring. But the difference is that its secrecy is accidental, and its exclusiveness a by-product, and no one was led thither by the lure of the esoteric: for it is only four or five people who like one another meeting to do things that they like. This is friendship. Aristotle placed it among the virtues. It causes perhaps half of all the happiness in the world, and no Inner Ring can ever have it.

We are told in Scripture that those who ask get. That is true, in senses I can't now explore. But in another sense there is much truth in the schoolboy's principle "them as asks shan't have." To a young person, just entering on adult life, the world seems full of "insides," full of delightful intimacies and confidentialities, and he desires to enter them. But if he follows that desire he will reach no "inside" that is worth reaching. The true road lies in quite another direction. It is like the house in *Alice Through the Looking Glass*.[2]

GEORGE ORWELL

Shooting an Elephant

George Orwell (1903–1950), originally named Eric Arthur Blair, was born in Bengal, India. His father was a minor British colonial officer and his mother the daughter of a French merchant. When his family moved to England in 1911, Orwell spent six unpleasant years in a snobbish preparatory school before winning a scholarship to Eton, a still more exclusive school where his relative poverty made him feel

---

2. Lewis Carroll's Alice imagines that the mirror over her mantel is actually a window through which she sees another room in another house.

like an outsider. On the advice of one of his tutors, he elected not to enter Cambridge University, but instead to join the Indian Imperial Police in Burma, a job he held until 1927, when guilt at being "part of that evil despotism" drove him out. To experience life unprotected by the privileges of the British middle class, he then lived among the poor in Paris and London, working as a dishwasher and day laborer. In 1933 he published an account of this life in *Down and Out in Paris and London* under the pseudonym by which he has been known ever since. While Orwell is perhaps best known for his novels *Animal Farm* (1945) and *1984* (1949), he is considered one of the finest essayists of this century; among his collections of nonfiction are *Dickens, Dali and Others* (1946) and *Shooting an Elephant* (1950). "Shooting an Elephant" was first published in *New Writing*, Autumn 1936. The essay is justly regarded as a model for writers who want to discuss large issues through examining personal experience.

In Moulmein, in Lower Burma, I was hated by large numbers of people—the only time in my life that I have been important enough for this to happen to me. I was sub-divisional police officer of the town, and in an aimless, petty kind of way anti-European feeling was very bitter. No one had the guts to raise a riot, but if a European woman went through the bazaars alone somebody would probably spit betel juice over her dress. As a police officer I was an obvious target and was baited whenever it seemed safe to do so. When a nimble Burman tripped me up on the football field and the referee (another Burman) looked the other way, the crowd yelled with hideous laughter. This happened more than once. In the end the sneering yellow faces of young men that met me everywhere, the insults hooted after me when I was at a safe distance, got badly on my nerves. The young Buddhist priests were the worst of all. There were several thousands of them in the town and none of them seemed to have anything to do except stand on street corners and jeer at Europeans.

All this was perplexing and upsetting. For at that time I had already made up my mind that imperialism was an evil thing and the sooner I chucked up my job and got out of it the better. Theoretically—and secretly, of course—I was all for the Burmese and all against their oppressors, the British. As for the job I was doing, I hated it more bitterly than I can perhaps make clear. In a job like that you see the dirty work of Empire at close quarters. The wretched prisoners huddling in the stinking cages of the lockups, the grey, cowed faces of the long-term convicts, the scarred buttocks of the men who had been flogged with bamboos—all these oppressed me with an intolerable sense of guilt. But I could get nothing into perspective. I was young and ill-educated and I had to think out my problems in the utter silence that is imposed on every Englishman in the East. I did not even know that the British Empire is dying, still less did I know that it is a great deal better than the younger empires that are going to supplant it. All I knew was that I was stuck between my hatred of the empire I served and my rage against the evil-spirited little beasts who tried to make my job impossible. With one part of my mind I thought of the British Raj as an unbreakable tyranny, as something clamped down, *in saecula saeculorum*,[1] upon the will of prostrate peoples; with another part I thought that the greatest joy in the world would be to drive a bayonet into a Buddhist priest's guts. Feelings like these are the normal byproducts of imperialism; ask any Anglo-Indian official, if you can catch him off duty.

One day something happened which in a roundabout way was enlightening. It was a tiny incident in itself, but it gave me a better glimpse than I had had before of the real nature of imperialism—the real motives for which despotic governments act. Early one morning the sub-inspector at a police station at the other end of the town rang me up on the 'phone and said that an elephant was ravaging the bazaar. Would I please come and do something about it? I did not know what I could do, but I wanted to see what was happening and I got on to a pony and started out. I took my rifle, an old .44 Winchester and much too small to kill an elephant, but I thought the noise might be useful *in terrorem*. Various Burmans stopped me on the way and told me about the elephant's doings. It was not, of course, a wild elephant, but a tame one which had gone "must." It had been chained up, as tame elephants always are when their attack of "must" is due, but on the previous night it had broken its chain and escaped. Its mahout, the only person who could manage it when it was in that state, had set out in pursuit but had taken the wrong direction and was now twelve hours' journey away, and in the morning the elephant had suddenly reappeared in the town. The Burmese population had no weapons and were quite helpless against it. It had already destroyed somebody's bamboo hut, killed a cow and raided some fruit-stalls and devoured the stock; also it had met the municipal rubbish van and, when the driver jumped out and took to his heels, had turned the van over and inflicted violences upon it.

The Burmese sub-inspector and some Indian constables were waiting for me in the quarter where the elephant had been seen. It was a very poor quarter, a labyrinth of squalid bamboo huts, thatched with palm-leaf, winding all over a steep hillside. I remember that it was a cloudy, stuffy morning at the beginning of the rains. We began questioning the people as to where the elephant had gone and, as usual, failed to get any definite information. That is invariably the case

---

1. *in saecula saeculorum*: "for ages of ages" (Latin); until the end of time.

in the East; a story always sounds clear enough at a distance, but the nearer you get to the scene of events the vaguer it becomes. Some of the people said that the elephant had gone in one direction, some said that he had gone in another, some professed not even to have heard of any elephant. I had almost made up my mind that the whole story was a pack of lies, when we heard yells a little distance away. There was a loud, scandalized cry of "Go away, child! Go away this instant!" and an old woman with a switch in her hand came round the corner of a hut, violently shooing away a crowd of naked children. Some more women followed, clicking their tongues and exclaiming; evidently there was something that the children ought not to have seen. I rounded the hut and saw a man's dead body sprawling in the mud. He was an Indian, a black Dravidian coolie, almost naked, and he could not have been dead many minutes. The people said that the elephant had come suddenly upon him round the corner of the hut, caught him with its trunk, put its foot on his back and ground him into the earth. This was the rainy season and the ground was soft, and his face had scored a trench a foot deep and a couple of yards long. He was lying on his belly with arms crucified and head sharply twisted to one side. His face was coated with mud, the eyes wide open, the teeth bared and grinning with an expression of unendurable agony. (Never tell me, by the way, that the dead look peaceful. Most of the corpses I have seen look devilish.) The friction of the great beast's foot had stripped the skin from his back as neatly as one skins a rabbit. As soon as I saw the dead man I sent an orderly to a friend's house nearby to borrow an elephant rifle. I had already sent back the pony, not wanting it to go mad with fright and throw me if it smelt the elephant.

The orderly came back in a few minutes with a rifle and five cartridges, and meanwhile some Burmans had arrived and told us that the elephant was in the paddy fields below, only a few hundred yards away. As I started forward practically the whole population of the quarter flocked out of the houses and followed me. They had seen the rifle and were all shouting excitedly that I was going to shoot the elephant. They had not shown much interest in the elephant when he was merely ravaging their homes, but it was different now that he was going to be shot. It was a bit of fun to them, as it would be to an English crowd; besides they wanted the meat. It made me vaguely uneasy. I had no intention of shooting the elephant—I had merely sent for the rifle to defend myself if necessary—and it is always unnerving to have a crowd following you. I marched down the hill, looking and feeling a fool, with the rifle over my shoulder and an ever-growing army of people jostling at my heels. At the bottom, when you got away from the huts, there was a metalled road and beyond that a miry waste of paddy fields a thousand yards across, not yet ploughed but soggy from the first rains and dotted with coarse grass. The elephant was standing eight yards from the road, his left side towards us. He took not the slightest notice of the crowd's approach. He was tearing up bunches of grass, beating them against his knees to clean them and stuffing them into his mouth.

I had halted on the road. As soon as I saw the elephant I knew with perfect certainty that I ought not to shoot him. It is a serious matter to shoot a working elephant—it is comparable to destroying a huge and costly piece of machinery—and obviously one ought not to do it if it can possibly be avoided. And at that distance, peacefully eating, the elephant looked no more dangerous than a cow. I thought then and I think now that his attack of "must" was already passing off; in which case he would merely wander harmlessly about until the mahout came back and caught him. Moreover, I did not in the least want to shoot him. I decided that I would watch him for a little while to make sure that he did not turn savage again, and then go home.

But at that moment I glanced round at the crowd that had followed me. It was an immense crowd, two thousand at the least and growing every minute. It blocked the road for a long distance on either side. I looked at the sea of yellow faces above the garish clothes—faces all happy and excited over this bit of fun, all certain that the elephant was going to be shot. They were watching me as they would watch a conjurer about to perform a trick. They did not like me, but with the magical rifle in my hands I was momentarily worth watching. And suddenly I realized that I should have to shoot the elephant after all. The people expected it of me and I had got to do it; I could feel their two thousand wills pressing me forward, irresistibly. And it was at this moment, as I stood there with the rifle in my hands, that I first grasped the hollowness, the futility of the white man's dominion in the East. Here was I, the white man with his gun, standing in front of the unarmed native crowd—seemingly the leading actor of the piece; but in reality I was only an absurd puppet pushed to and fro by the will of those yellow faces behind. I perceived in this moment that when the white man turns tyrant it is his own freedom that he destroys. He becomes a sort of hollow, posing dummy, the conventionalized figure of a sahib. For it is the condition of his rule that he shall spend his life in trying to impress the "natives," and so in every crisis he has got to do what the "natives" expect of him. He wears a mask, and his face grows to fit it. I had got to shoot the elephant. I had committed myself to doing it when I sent for the rifle. A sahib has got to act like a sahib; he has got to appear resolute, to know his own mind and do definite things. To come all that way, rifle in hand, with two thousand people marching at my heels, and then to trail feebly away, having done nothing—no, that was impossible. The crowd would laugh at me. And my whole life, every white man's life in the East, was one long struggle not to be laughed at.

But I did not want to shoot the elephant. I watched him beating   8
his bunch of grass against his knees, with that preoccupied grand-
motherly air that elephants have. It seemed to me that it would be
murder to shoot him. At that age I was not squeamish about killing animals, but I had never shot an elephant and never wanted to. (Somehow it always seems worse to kill a *large* animal.) Besides, there was
the beast's owner to be considered. Alive, the elephant was worth at
least a hundred pounds; dead, he would only be worth the value of his
tusks, five pounds, possibly. But I had got to act quickly. I turned to
some experienced-looking Burmans who had been there when we arrived, and asked them how the elephant had been behaving. They all
said the same thing; he took no notice of you if you left him alone, but
he might charge if you went too close to him.

It was perfectly clear to me what I ought to do. I ought to walk up   9
to within, say, twenty-five yards of the elephant and test his behavior.
If he charged, I could shoot; if he took no notice of me, it would be safe
to leave him until the mahout came back. But also I knew that I was
going to do no such thing. I was a poor shot with a rifle and the ground
was soft mud into which one would sink at every step. If the elephant
charged and I missed him, I should have about as much chance as a
toad under a steamroller. But even then I was not thinking particularly
of my own skin, only of the watchful yellow faces behind. For at that
moment, with the crowd watching me, I was not afraid in the ordinary
sense, as I would have been if I had been alone. A white man mustn't
be frightened in front of "natives"; and so, in general, he isn't frightened. The sole thought in my mind was that if anything went wrong
those two thousand Burmans would see me pursued, caught, trampled
on and reduced to a grinning corpse like that Indian up the hill. And if
that happened it was quite probable that some of them would laugh.
That would never do. There was only one alternative. I shoved the cartridges into the magazine and lay down on the road to get a better aim.

The crowd grew very still, and a deep, low, happy sigh, as of   10
people who see the theatre curtain go up at last, breathed from innumerable throats. They were going to have their bit of fun after all. The
rifle was a beautiful German thing with cross-hair sights. I did not then
know that in shooting an elephant one would shoot to cut an imaginary bar running from ear-hole to ear-hole. I ought, therefore, as the
elephant was sideways on, to have aimed straight at his ear-hole; actually I aimed several inches in front of this, thinking the brain would be
further forward.

When I pulled the trigger I did not hear the bang or feel the kick—   11
one never does when a shot goes home—but I heard the devilish roar
of glee that went up from the crowd. In that instant, in too short a
time, one would have thought, even for the bullet to get there, a mysterious, terrible change had come over the elephant. He neither stirred

nor fell, but every line of his body had altered. He looked suddenly stricken, shrunken, immensely old, as though the frightful impact of the bullet had paralysed him without knocking him down. At last, after what seemed a long time—it might have been five seconds, I dare say—he sagged flabbily to his knees. His mouth slobbered. An enormous senility seemed to have settled upon him. One could have imagined him thousands of years old. I fired again into the same spot. At the second shot he did not collapse but climbed with desperate slowness to his feet and stood weakly upright, with legs sagging and head drooping. I fired a third time. That was the shot that did for him. You could see the agony of it jolt his whole body and knock the last remnant of strength from his legs. But in falling he seemed for a moment to rise, for as his hind legs collapsed beneath him he seemed to tower upward like a huge rock toppling, his trunk reaching skywards like a tree. He trumpeted, for the first and only time. And then down he came, his belly towards me, with a crash that seemed to shake the ground even where I lay.

I got up. The Burmans were already racing past me across the   12
mud. It was obvious that the elephant would never rise again, but he was not dead. He was breathing very rhythmically with long rattling gasps, his great mound of a side painfully rising and falling. His mouth was wide open—I could see far down into caverns of pale pink throat. I waited a long time for him to die, but his breathing did not weaken. Finally I fired my two remaining shots into the spot where I thought his heart must be. The thick blood welled out of him like red velvet, but still he did not die. His body did not even jerk when the shots hit him, the tortured breathing continued without a pause. He was dying, very slowly and in great agony, but in some world remote from me where not even a bullet could damage him further. I felt that I had got to put an end to that dreadful noise. It seemed dreadful to see the great beast lying there, powerless to move and yet powerless to die, and not even to be able to finish him. I sent back for my small rifle and poured shot after shot into his heart and down his throat. They seemed to make no impression. The tortured gasps continued as steadily as the ticking of a clock.

In the end I could not stand it any longer and went away. I heard   13
later that it took him half an hour to die. Burmans were bringing dahs and baskets even before I left, and I was told they had stripped his body almost to the bones by the afternoon.

Afterwards, of course, there were endless discussions about the   14
shooting of the elephant. The owner was furious, but he was only an Indian and could do nothing. Besides, legally I had done the right thing, for a mad elephant has to be killed, like a mad dog, if its owner fails to control it. Among the Europeans opinion was divided. The older men said I was right, the younger men said it was a damn shame to shoot an elephant for killing a coolie, because an elephant was

worth more than any damn Coringhee coolie. And afterwards I was very glad that the coolie had been killed; it put me legally in the right and it gave me a sufficient pretext for shooting the elephant. I often wondered whether any of the others grasped that I had done it solely to avoid looking a fool.

CYNTHIA OZICK

We Are the Crazy Lady and Other Feisty Feminist Fables

*Avoid looking a
fool → fool has
a different
connotation*

Cynthia Ozick (1928–   ) was born in New York City into a family of storytellers. She remembers her grandmother's tales of growing up in a Russian village and her parents' accounts of the lives of their neighbors, who sounded—she later realized—like characters from a novel by Jane Austen or Anthony Trollope. Ozick took her B.A. in English from New York University in 1949 and her M.A. from Ohio State University the next year; she is also a student of Hebrew language and Jewish literature. Among her works of fiction are *Trust* (1966), *The Pagan Rabbi and Other Stories* (1971), *Bloodshed and Three Novellas* (1976), *The Messiah of Stockholm* (1987), *and The Puttermesser Papers* (1997). Her essays have been collected in *Art and Ardor* (1983), *Metaphor and Memory* (1988), and *Fame and Folly* (1996). Ozick describes herself as a "classical feminist"—one who objects to the segregation of men's and women's intellectual, social, and political lives. Lately, she has complained that those who present women's literature as a separate realm "instigate and inflame the old prejudices *in the name* of feminism." "We Are the Crazy Lady" was first published in *Ms Magazine* in the spring of 1973. Like Orwell's "Shooting an Elephant," Ozick's essay makes a point about public politics by examining personal experience. Unlike Orwell's essay, it is a model of humor with a serious intent.

I. THE CRAZY LADY DOUBLE

A long, long time ago, in another century—1951, in fact—when 1 you, dear younger readers, were most likely still in your nuclear-family playpen (where, if female, you cuddled a rag-baby to your potential titties, or, if male, let down virile drool over your plastic bulldozer), The Famous Critic[1] told me never, never to use a parenthesis in the very first sentence. This was in a graduate English seminar at

1. The Famous Critic: Lionel Trilling, influential literary critic and writer (1905–1975).

Columbia University. To get into this seminar, you had to submit to a grilling wherein you renounced all former allegiance to the then-current literary religion, New Criticism, which considered that only the text existed, not the world. I passed the interview by lying—cunningly, and against my real convictions. I said that probably the world *did* exist—and walked triumphantly into the seminar room.

There were four big tables arranged in a square, with everyone's   2 feet sticking out into the open middle of the square. You could tell who was nervous, and how much, by watching the pairs of feet twist around each other. The Great Man presided awesomely from the high bar of the square. His head was a majestic granite-gray, like a centurion in command; he *looked* famous. His clean shoes twitched only slightly, and only when he was angry.

It turned out he was angry at me a lot of the time. He was angry   3 because he thought me a disrupter, a rioter, a provocateur, and a fool; also crazy. And this was twenty years ago, before these things were *de rigueur*[2] in the universities. Everything was very quiet in those days: there were only the Cold War and Korea and Joe McCarthy and the Old Old Nixon, and the only revolutionaries around were in Henry James's *The Princess Casamassima.*

Habit governed the seminar. Where you sat the first day was   4 where you settled forever. So, to avoid the stigmatization of the ghetto, I was careful not to sit next to the other woman in the class: the Crazy Lady.

At first the Crazy Lady appeared to be remarkably intelligent. She   5 was older than the rest of us, somewhere in her thirties (which was why we thought of her as a Lady), with wild tan hair, a noticeably breathing bosom, eccentric gold-rimmed old-pensioner glasses, and a tooth-crowded wild mouth that seemed to get wilder the more she talked. She talked like a motorcycle, fast and urgent. Everything she said was almost brilliant, only not actually on point, and frenetic with hostility. She was tough and negative. She volunteered a lot and she stood up and wobbled with rage, pulling at her hair and mouth. She fought the Great Man point for point, piecemeal and wholesale, mixing up queerly-angled literary insights with all sorts of private and public fury. After the first meetings he was fed up with her. The rest of us accepted that she probably wasn't all there, but in a room where everyone was on the make for recognition—you talked to save your life and the only way to save your life was to be the smartest one that day—she was a nuisance, a distraction, a pain in the ass. The class became a bunch of Good Germans, determinedly indifferent onlookers to a vindictive match between the Critic and the Crazy Lady, until finally

2. *de rigueur*: indispensable, required (French). In this instance Ozick means "a matter of course, usual."

he subdued her by shutting his eyes, and, when that didn't always work, by cutting her dead and lecturing right across the sound of her strong, strange voice.

All this was before R. D. Laing[3] had invented the superiority of madness, of course, and, cowards all, no one liked the thought of being tarred with the Crazy Lady's brush. Ignored by the boss, in the middle of everything she would suddenly begin to mutter to herself. She mentioned certain institutions she'd been in, and said we all belonged there. The people who sat on either side of her shifted chairs. If the Great Man ostracized the Crazy Lady, we had to do it too. But one day the Crazy Lady came in late and sat down in the seat next to mine, and stayed there the rest of the semester.

Then an odd thing happened. There, right next to me, was the noisy Crazy Lady, tall, with that sticking-out sighing chest of hers, orangey curls dripping over her nose, snuffling furiously for attention. And there was I, a brownish runt, a dozen years younger and flatter and shyer than the Crazy Lady, in no way her twin, physically or psychologically. In those days I was bone-skinny, small, sallow and myopic, and so scared I could trigger diarrhea at one glance from the Great Man. All this stress on looks is important: the Crazy Lady and I had our separate bodies, our separate brains. We handed in our separate papers.

But the Great Man never turned toward me, never at all, and if ambition broke feverishly through shyness so that I dared to push an idea audibly out of me, he shut his eyes when I put up my hand. This went on for a long time. I never got to speak, and I began to have the depressing feeling that he hated me. It was no small thing to be hated by the man who had written the most impressive criticism of the century. What in hell was going on? I was in trouble; like everyone else in that demented contest, I wanted to excel. Then, one slow afternoon, wearily, the Great Man let his eyes fall on me. He called me by name, but it was not my name—it was the Crazy Lady's. The next week the papers came back—and there, right at the top of mine, in the Great Man's own handwriting, was a rebuke to the Crazy Lady for starting an essay with a parenthesis in the first sentence, a habit he took to be a continuing sign of that unruly and unfocused mentality so often exhibited in class. And then a Singular Revelation crept coldly through me: because the Crazy Lady and I sat side by side, because we were a connected blur of Woman, the Famous Critic, master of ultimate distinctions, couldn't tell us apart. The Crazy Lady and I! He couldn't tell us apart! It didn't matter that the Crazy Lady was crazy! *He couldn't tell us apart!*

---

3. R. D. Laing: Scottish psychiatrist (b. 1927) whose lifework has been devoted to the study of insanity, especially schizophrenia.

Moral 1: All cats are gray at night,
    all darkies look alike.   9

Moral 2: Even among intellectual humanists, every woman has a   10
    Doppelgänger[4]—every other woman.

II. THE LECTURE, 1

I was invited by a women's group to be guest speaker at a Book   11
Author Luncheon. The women themselves had not really chosen me:
the speaker had been selected by a male leader and imposed on them.
The plan was that I would autograph copies of my book, eat a good
meal, and then lecture. The woman in charge of the programming
telephoned to ask me what my topic would be. This was a matter of
some concern, since they had never had a woman author before, and
no one knew how the idea would be received. I offered as my subject
"The Contemporary Poem."

When the day came, everything went as scheduled—the auto-   12
graphing, the food, the welcoming addresses. Then it was time to go to
the lectern. I aimed at the microphone and began to speak of poetry. A
peculiar rustling sound flew up from the audience. All the women
were lifting their programs to the light, like hundreds of wings. Confused murmurs ran along the walls. Something was awry; I began to
feel very uncomfortable. Then I too took up the program. It read:
"Topic: The Contemporary Home."

Moral: Even our ears practice the caste system.   13

III. THE LECTURE, 2

I was in another country, the only woman at a philosophical sem-   14
inar lasting three days. On the third day, I was to read a paper. I had
accepted the invitation with a certain foreknowledge. I knew, for instance, that I could not dare to be the equal of any other speaker. To be
an equal would be to be less. I understood that mine had to be the
most original and powerful paper of all. I had no choice; I had to toil
beyond my most extreme possibilities. This was not ambition, but only
fear of disgrace.

For the first two days, I was invisible. When I spoke, people tapped   15
impatiently, waiting for the interruption to end. No one took either my
presence or my words seriously. At meals, I sat with my colleagues'
wives.

The third day arrived, and I read my paper. It was successful beyond   16
my remotest imaginings. I was interviewed, and my remarks appeared

---

4. *Doppelgänger:* "double-goer," a ghostly double (German).

in newspapers in a language I could not understand. The Foreign Minister invited me to his home. I hobnobbed with famous poets.

Now my colleagues noticed me. But they did not notice me as a colleague. They teased and kissed me. I had become their mascot. [17]

Moral: There is no route out of caste which does not instantly lead back into it. [18]

IV. PROPAGANDA

For many years I had noticed that no book of poetry by a woman was ever reviewed without reference to the poet's sex. The curious thing was that, in the two decades of my scrutiny, there were *no* exceptions whatever. It did not matter whether the reviewer was a man or woman: in every case the question of the "feminine sensibility" of the poet was at the center of the reviewer's response. The maleness of the male poets, on the other hand, hardly ever seemed to matter. [19]

Determined to ridicule this convention, I wrote a tract, a piece of purely tendentious mockery, in the form of a short story. I called it "Virility." [20]

The plot was, briefly, as follows: A very bad poet, lustful for fame, is despised for his pitiful lucubrations and remains unpublished. But luckily, he comes into possession of a cache of letters written by his elderly spinster aunt, who lives an obscure and secluded working-class life in a remote corner of England. The letters contain a large number of remarkable poems; the aunt, it turns out, is a genius. The bad poet publishes his find under his own name, and instantly attains worldwide adulation. Under the title *Virility*, the poems become immediate classics. They are translated into dozens of languages and are praised and revered for their unmistakably masculine qualities: their strength, passion, wisdom, energy, boldness, brutality, worldliness, robustness, authenticity, sensuality, compassion. A big, handsome, sweating man, the poet swaggers from country to country, courted everywhere, pursued by admirers, yet respected by the most demanding critics. [21]

Meanwhile, the old aunt dies. The supply of genius runs out. Bravely and contritely the poor poet confesses his ruse, and, in a burst of honesty, publishes the last batch under the real poet's name; the book is entitled *Flowers from Liverpool*. But the poems are at once found negligible and dismissed: "Thin feminine art," say the reviews, "a lovely girlish voice." And: "Limited one-dimensional vision." "Choked with female inwardness." "The fine womanly intuition of a competent poetess." The poems are utterly forgotten. [22]

I included this fable in a collection of short stories. In every review the salvo went unnoticed. Not one reviewer recognized that the story was a sly tract. Not one reviewer saw the smirk or the point. There was [23]

one delicious comment, though. "I have some reservations," a man in
Washington, D.C., wrote, "about the credibility of some of her male
characters when they are chosen as narrators."

Moral: In saying what is obvious, never choose cunning. Yelling   24
works better.

V. HORMONES

During a certain period of my life, I was reading all the time, and   25
fairly obsessively. Sometimes, though, sunk in a book of criticism or
philosophy, I would be brought up short. Consider: here is a paragraph
that excites the intellect; inwardly, one assents passionately to its
premises; the writer's idea is an exact diagram of one's own deepest
psychology or conviction; one feels oneself seized as for a portrait.
Then the disclaimer, the excluding shove: "It is, however, otherwise
with the female sex . . ." A rebuke from the World of Thinking: *I didn't
mean you, lady.* In the instant one is in possession of one's humanity
most intensely, it is ripped away.

These moments I discounted. What is wrong—intrinsically, psy-   26
chologically, culturally, morally—can be dismissed.

But to dismiss in this manner is to falsify one's most genuine actu-   27
ality. A Jew reading of the aesthetic glories of European civilization
without taking notice of his victimization during, say, the era of the
building of the great cathedrals, is self-forgetful in the most dangerous
way. So would be a black who read of King Cotton[5] with an economist's objectivity.

I am not offering any strict analogy between the situation of   28
women and the history of Jews or colonialized blacks, as many politically radical women do (though the analogy with blacks is much the
more frequent one). It seems to me to be abusive of language in the extreme when some women speak, in the generation after Auschwitz, of
the "oppression" of women. Language makes culture, and we make a
rotten culture when we abuse words. We raise up rotten heroines. I
use "rotten" with particular attention to its precise meaning: foul, pu-
trid, tainted, stinking. I am thinking now especially of a radical
women's publication, *Off Our Backs,* which not long ago presented Leila
Khaled, terrorist and foiled murderer, as a model for the political conduct of women.

But if I would not support the extreme analogy (and am never   29
surprised when black women, who have a more historical comprehension of actual, not figurative, oppression, refuse to support the analogy), it is anyhow curious to see what happens to the general culture

5. The reference is to the importance of cotton in the economy of the American South
in the first half of the nineteenth century—a condition heavily dependent on the labor
of black slaves.

when any enforced class in any historical or social condition is compelled to doubt its own self- understanding—when identity is externally defined, when individual humanity is called into question as being different from "standard" humanity. What happens is that the general culture, along with the object of its debasement, is also debased. If you laugh at women, you play Beethoven in vain.

If you laugh at women, your laboratory will lie.   30

We can read in Charlotte Perkins Gilman's[6] 1912 essay, "Are   31
Women Human Beings?", an account of an opinion current sixty years ago. Women, said one scientist, are not only "not the human race—they are not even half the human race, but a sub-species set apart for purposes of reproduction merely."

A physician said: "No doctor can ever lose sight of the fact that the   32
mind of woman is always threatened with danger from the reverberations of her physiological emergencies." He concluded this entirely on the basis of his invalid patients.

Though we are accustomed to the idea of "progress" in science and   33
medicine, if not in civilization generally, the fact is that more information has led to something very like regression.

I talked with an intelligent physician, the Commissioner of Health   34
of a middle-sized city in Connecticut, a man who sees medicine not discretely but as part of the social complex—was treated to a long list of all the objective differences between men and women, including particularly an account of current endocrinal studies relating to female hormones. Aren't all of these facts? he asked. How can you distrust facts? Very good, I said, I'm willing to take your medically-educated word for it. I'm not afraid of facts, I welcome facts—*but a congeries of facts is not equivalent to an idea*. This is the essential fallacy of the so-called "scientific" mind. People who mistake facts for ideas are incomplete thinkers; they are gossips.

You tell me, I said, that my sense of my own humanity as being   35
"standard" humanity—which is, after all, a subjective idea—is refuted by hormonal research. My psychology, you tell me, which in your view is the source of my ideas, is the result of my physiology: it is not I who express myself, it is my hormones which express me. A part is equal to the whole, you say. Worse yet, the whole is simply the issue of the part: my "I" is a flash of chemicals. You are willing to define all my humanity by hormonal investigation under a microscope: this you call "objective irrefutable fact," as if tissue-culture were equivalent to culture. But each scientist can assemble his own (subjective) constellation of "objective irrefutable fact," just as each social thinker can assemble his own (subjective) selection of traits to define "humanity" by. Who can prove what is "standard" humanity, and which sex, class, or race is

6. Charlotte Perkins Gilman: American feminist writer (1860–1935).

to be exempted from whole participation in it? On what basis do you regard female hormones as causing a modification from normative humanity? And what better right do you have to define normative humanity by what males have traditionally apperceived than by what females have traditionally apperceived—assuming (as I, lacking presumptuousness, do not) that their apperceptions have not been the same? Only Tiresias—that mythological character who was both man and woman[7]—is in a position to make the comparison and present the proof. And then not even Tiresias, because to be a hermaphrodite is to be a monster, and not human.

"Why are you so emotional about all this?" said the Commissioner of Health. "You see how it is? Those are your female hormones working on you right now."

Moral: Defamation is only applied research.

VI. AMBITION

After thirteen years, I at last finished a novel. The first seven years were spent in a kind of apprenticeship—the book that came out of that time was abandoned without much regret. A second one was finished in six weeks and buried. It took six years to write the third novel, and this one was finally published.

How I lived through those years is impossible to recount in a short space. I was a recluse, a priest of Art. I read seas of books. I believed in the idea of masterpieces. I was scornful of the world of journalism, jobs, everydayness. I did not live like any woman I knew, although it never occurred to me to reflect on this of my own volition. I lived like some men I had read about—Flaubert, or Proust, or James: the subjects of those literary biographies I endlessly drank in. I did not think of them as men but as writers. I read the diaries of Virginia Woolf, and biographies of George Eliot, but I did not think of them as women. I thought of them as writers. I thought of myself as a writer. I went on reading and writing.

It goes without saying that all this time my relatives regarded me as abnormal. I accepted this. It seemed to me, from what I had read, that most writers were abnormal. Yet on the surface I could easily have passed for normal. The husband goes to work, the wife stays home—that is what is normal. Well, I was married. My husband went to his job every day. His job paid the rent and bought the groceries. I stayed home, reading and writing, and felt myself to be an economic parasite. To cover guilt, I joked that I had been given a grant from a very private, very poor, foundation; I meant my husband.

7. In Greek mythology, Tiresias the seer, after being transformed for a time into a woman, was asked by the gods to settle an argument as to whether men or women enjoyed love more. Having seen it from both sides, he voted in favor of women.

But my relatives never thought of me as a parasite. The very thing 41
I was doubtful about—my economic dependence—they considered
my due as a woman. They saw me not as a failed writer without an income, but as a childless housewife, a failed woman. They did not think
me abnormal because I was a writer, but because I was not properly
living my life as a woman. In one respect we were in agreement utterly—my life was failing terribly, terribly. For me it was because, already deep into my thirties, I had not yet published a book. For them,
it was because I had not yet borne a child.

I was a pariah,[8] not only because I was a deviant, but because I 42
was not recognized as the kind of deviant I meant to be. A failed
woman is not the same as a failed writer. Even as a pariah I was the
wrong kind of pariah.

Still, relations are only relations, and what I aspired to, what I was 43
in thrall to, was Art; was Literature; not familial contentment. I knew
how to distinguish the trivial from the sublime. In Literature and in
Art, I saw, my notions were not pariah notions: *there*, I inhabited the
mainstream. So I went on reading and writing; I went on believing in
Art, and my intention was to write a masterpiece. Not a saucer of well-
polished craft (the sort of thing "women writers" are always accused of
being accomplished at), but something huge, contemplative, Tol-
stoyan. My ambition was a craw.

I called the book *Trust*. I began it in the summer of 1957 and fin- 44
ished it in November of 1963, on the day President John Kennedy was
assassinated. In manuscript it was 801 pages divided into four parts:
"America," "Europe," "Birth," "Death." The title was meant to be
ironic. In reality, it was about distrust. It seemed to me I had touched
on distrust in every order or form of civilization. It seemed to me I had
left nothing out. It was (though I did not know this then) a very hating
book. What it hated above all was the whole—the whole!—of Western
Civilization. It told how America had withered into another Europe; it
dreamed dark and murderous pagan dreams, and hated what it
dreamed.

In style, the book was what has come to be called "mandarin": a 45
difficult, aristocratic, unrelenting virtuoso prose. It was, in short, un-
readable. I think I knew this; I was sardonic enough to say, echoing
Joyce about *Finnegans Wake*,[9] "I expect you to spend your life at this."
In any case, I had spent a decade-and-a-half of my own life at it, and
though I did not imagine the world would fall asunder at its appearance, I thought—at the very least—the ambition, the all-
swallowingness, the wild insatiability of the writer would be plain to
everyone who read it. I had, after all, taken History for my subject: not

8. pariah: a social outcast.
9. *Finnegans Wake:* a notoriously difficult novel by Irish novelist James Joyce
(1882–1941).

merely History as an aggregate of events, but History as a judgment on events. No one could say my theme was flighty. Of all the novelists I read—and in those days I read them all, broiling in the envy of the un-published, which is like no envy on earth—who else had dared so vastly?

During that period, Françoise Sagan's[10] first novel was published. I   46
held the thin little thing and laughed. Women's pulp!

My own novel, I believed, contained everything—the whole world.   47

But there was one element I had consciously left out, though on   48
principle I did not like to characterize it or think about it much. The truth is I was thinking about it all the time. It was only a fiction-technicality, but I was considerably afraid of it. It was the question of the narrator's "sensibility." The narrator, as it happened, was a young woman; I had chosen her to be the eye—and the "I"—of the novel be-cause all the other characters in some way focused on her, and she was the one most useful to my scheme. Nevertheless I wanted her not to live. Everything I was reading in reviews of other people's books made me fearful: I would have to be very, very cautious, I would have to drain my narrator of emotive value of any kind. I was afraid to be pegged as having written a "women's" novel, and nothing was more certain to lead to that than a point-of-view seemingly lodged in a woman; no one takes a woman's novel seriously. I was in terror, above all, of sentiment and feeling, those telltale taints. I kept the fury and the passion for other, safer, characters.

So what I left out of my narrator entirely, sweepingly, with exquis-   49
ite consciousness of what exactly I *was* leaving out, was any shred of "sensibility." I stripped her of everything, even a name. I crafted and carpentered her; she was for me a bloodless device, fulcrum or pivot, a recording voice, a language-machine. She confronted moment or event, took it in, gave it out. And what to me was all the more won-derful about this nameless fiction-machine I had invented was that the machine itself, though never alive, was a character in the story, with-out ever influencing the story. My machine-narrator was there for ef-ficiency only, for flexibility, for craftiness, for subtlety, but never, never, as a "woman." I wiped the "woman" out of her. And I did it out of fear, out of vicarious vindictive critical imagination, out of the terror of my ambition, out of, maybe, paranoia. I meant my novel to be taken for what it really was. I meant to make it impossible for it to be mis-taken for something else.

Publication.   50

Review in *The New York Times* Sunday Book Review.   51

Review is accompanied by a picture of a naked woman seen from   52
the back. Her bottom is covered by some sort of drapery.

---

10. Françoise Sagan: French novelist (b. 1935). Her first work, *Bonjour Tristesse* ("Hello, Sadness"), is the story of an adolescent's tragic attempt to prevent her father's remarriage.

Title of review: "Daughter's Reprieve."   53

Excerpts from review: "These events, interesting in themselves,   54
exist to reveal the sensibility of the narrator." "She longs to play some
easy feminine role." "She has been unable to define herself as a
woman." "Thus the daughter, at the age of twenty-two, is eager for the
prerequisites that should have been hers as a woman, but is flounder-
ing badly in their pursuit." "Her protagonist insists on coming to terms
with the recalcitrant sexual elements in her life." "The main body of
the novel, then, is a revelation of the narrator's inner, turbulent, psychic dream."

O rabid rotten Western Civilization, where are you? O judging His-   55
tory, O foul Trust and fouler Distrust, where?

O Soap Opera, where did you come from?   56

(Meanwhile the review in *Time* was calling me a "housewife.")   57

Pause.   58

All right, let us take up the rebuttals one by one.   59

Q. Maybe you *did* write a soap opera without knowing it. Maybe   60
you only *thought* you were writing about Western Civilization when
you were really only rewriting Stella Dallas.[11]

A. A writer may be unsure of everything—trust the tale not the   61
teller is a good rule—but not of his obsessions; of these he is certain. If
I were rewriting Stella Dallas, I would turn her into the Second Crusade and demobilize her.

Q. Maybe you're like the blind Jew who wants to be a pilot, and   62
when they won't give him the job he says they're anti-Semitic. Look,
the book was lousy, you deserved a lousy review.

A. You mistake me, I never said it was a bad review. It was in fact   63
an extremely favorable review, full of gratifying adjectives.

Q. But your novel languished anyhow?   64

A. Perished, is dead and buried. I sometimes see it exhumed on   65
the shelf in the public library. It's always there. No one ever borrows it.

Q. Dummy! You should've written a soap opera. Women are good   66
at that.

A. Thank you. You almost remind me of another Moral: In con-   67
ceptual life, junk prevails. Even if you do not produce junk, it will be
taken for junk.

Q. What does that have to do with women?   68

A. The products of women are frequently taken for junk.   69

Q. And if a woman *does* produce junk . . .?   70

A. Glory—they will treat her almost like a man who produces   71
junk. They will say her name on television.

Q. Bitter, bitter!   72

---

11. *Stella Dallas* (1923) was originally a magazine serial by Olive Higgins Prouty. The
story was taken up by almost every conceivable genre (novel, film, play) and finally became a long-running soap opera, which is what its name connotes today.

A. Not at all. Again you misunderstand. You see, I have come   73
round to thinking (I learned it from television commercials, as a matter of fact) that there is a Women's Culture—a sort of tribal, separatist,
ghettoized thing. And I propose that we cultivate it.

Q. You mean *really* writing Women's Novels? On purpose?   74

A. Nothing like that. The novel was invented by men. It isn't ours,   75
you see, and to us it is to *assimilate*. I see now where I went wrong! So
I propose that we return to our pristine cultural origins, earn the respect of the male race, and regain our self-esteem.

Q. All that? Really? How?   76

A. *We will revive the Quilting Bee!*   77

Q. Oh, splendid, splendid! What a genius you are!   78

A. I always knew it.   79

TERRY GALLOWAY

I'm Listening as Hard as I Can

Terry Galloway (1950–   ) is a deaf playwright. poet, and performer who grew up in Germany and Texas. She holds a degree in
American Studies from the University of Texas at Austin and had, she
reports, a "two years combative relationship with Columbia University." In the early eighties, she began presenting one-woman shows,
one of which she opens by noting, "I'm a Texan and am proud of it.
Unfortunately, I share with most Texans a fatal flaw. I presume an intimacy—and most often where there is none." The combination of
tough humor and assumed intimacy in the monologues make Galloway, as one reviewer said, "a hoot and a provocateur from the get-
go." Galloway's shows have been produced throughout the United
States and in England, Canada. and Mexico. She has also created alternative theater groups in Austin. Texas. and Tallahassee, Florida. To
date she has published a play, a performance text, a book of poetry.
several individual poems, and many comic and dramatic monologues. She also co-wrote an award-winning children's show for PBS.
Her more personal life, she reports, "is the subject of gossipy speculation." The following essay was first published in *Texas Monthly* in April
1981. Galloway's elaborate sense of being inside some circles and outside others might be compared with that of Henry Louis Gates, Jr.
("Living Under Grace").

At the age of twelve I won the swimming award at the Lions Camp   1
for Crippled Children. When my name echoed over the PA system the
girl in the wheelchair next to me grabbed the box speaker of my hear-

ing aid and shouted, "You won!" My ear quaking, I took the cue. I stood up straight—the only physically unencumbered child in a sea of braces and canes—affixed a pained but brave grin to my face, then limped all the way to the stage.

Later, after the spotlight had dimmed, I was overcome with re- 2 morse, but not because I'd played the crippled heroine. The truth was that I was ashamed of my handicap. I wanted to have something more visibly wrong with me. I wanted to be in the same league as the girl who'd lost her right leg in a car accident; her artificial leg attracted a bevy of awestruck campers. I, on the other hand, wore an unwieldy box hearing aid huckled to my body like a dog halter. It attracted no one. Deafness wasn't, in my eyes, a blue-ribbon handicap. Mixed in with my envy, though, was an overwhelming sense of guilt; at camp I was free to splash in the swimming pool, while most of the other children were stranded at the shallow end, where lifeguards floated them in lazy circles. But seventeen years of living in the "normal" world has diminished my guilt considerably, and I've learned that every handicap has its own particular hell.

I'm something of an anomaly in the deaf world. Unlike most deaf 3 people, who were either born deaf or went deaf in infancy, I lost my hearing in chunks over a period of twelve years. Fortunately I learned to speak before my loss grew too profound, and that ability freed me from the most severe problem facing the deaf—the terrible difficulty of making themselves understood. My opinion of deafness was just as biased as that of a person who can hear. I had never met a deaf child in my life, and I didn't know how to sign. I imagined deaf people to be like creatures from beyond: animallike because their language was so physical, threatening because they were unable to express themselves with sophistication—that is, through speech. I could make myself understood, and because I had a talent for lipreading it was easy for me to pass in the wider world. And for most of my life that is exactly what I did—like a black woman playing white, I passed for something other than what I was. But in doing so I was avoiding some very painful facts. And for many years I was inhibited not only by my deafness but my own idea of what it meant to be deaf.

My problems all started when my mother, seven months pregnant 4 with me, developed a serious kidney infection. Her doctors pumped her full of antibiotics. Two months later I was born, with nothing to suggest that I was anything more or less than a normal child. For years nobody knew that the antibiotics had played havoc with my fetal nervous system. I grew up bright, happy, and energetic.

But by the time I was ten I knew, if nobody else did, that some- 5 thing somewhere had gone wrong. The people around me had gradually developed fuzzy profiles, and their speech had taken on a blurred and foreign character. But I was such a secure and happy child that it didn't enter my mind to question my new perspective or mention the changes to anyone else. Finally, my behavior became noticeably erratic—I would make nonsensical replies to ordinary questions or simply fail to reply at all. My teachers, deciding that I was neither a particularly creative child nor an especially troublesome one, looked for a physical cause. They found two: I wasn't quite as blind as a bat, but I was almost as deaf as a doornail.

My parents took me to Wilford Hall Air Force Hospital in San Antonio, where I was examined from ear to ear. My tonsils were removed and studied, ice water was injected into my inner ear, and I underwent a series of inexplicable and at times painful exploratory tests. I would forever after associate deafness with kind attention and unusual punishment. Finally a verdict was delivered: "Congenital; interference has resulted in a neural disorder for which there is no known medical or surgical treatment." My hearing loss was severe and would grow progressively worse. 6

I was fitted with my first hearing aid and sent back home to resume my childhood. I never did. I had just turned twelve, and my body was undergoing enormous changes. I had baby fat, baby breasts, hairy legs, and thick pink cat-eye glasses. My hearing aid was about the size of a small transistor radio and rode in a white linen pouch that hit exactly at breast level. It was not a welcome addition to my pubescent woe. 7

As a vain child trapped in a monster's body, I was frantic for a way to survive the next few years. Glimpsing my reflection in mirrors became such agony that I acquired a habit of brushing my teeth and hair with my eyes closed. Everything I did was geared to making my body more inhabitable, but I only succeeded in making it less so. I kept my glasses in my pocket and developed an unbecoming squint; I devised a smile that hid two broken front teeth, but it looked disturbingly like the grin of a piranha; I kept my arms folded over my would-be breasts. But the hearing aid was a different story. There was no way to disguise it. I could tuck it under my blouse, but then all I could hear was the static of cotton. Besides, whenever I took a step the box bounced around like a third breast. So I resigned myself: a monster I was, a monster I would be. 8

I became more withdrawn, more suspicious of other people's intentions. I imagined that I was being deliberately excluded from schoolyard talk because the other children didn't make much of an effort to involve me—they simply didn't have the time or patience to repeat snatches of gossip ten times and slowly. Conversation always reached the point of ridiculousness before I could understand something as simple as "The movie starts at five." (The groovy shark's alive? The moving stars that thrive?) I didn't make it to many movies. I culti- 9 vated a lofty sense of superiority, and I was often brutal with people who offered the "wrong" kind of help at the "wrong" time. Right after my thirteenth birthday some well-meaning neighbors took me to a revivalist faith healing. I already had doubts about exuberant religions, and the knee-deep hysteria of the preacher simply confirmed them. He bounded to my side and put his hands on my head. "O Lord," he cried, "heal this poor little lamb!"

I leaped up as if transported and shouted, "I can walk!" 10

For the first few years my parents were as bewildered as I was. 11
Nothing had prepared them for a handicapped child on the brink of adolescence. They sensed a whole other world of problems, but in those early stages I still seemed so normal that they just couldn't see me in a school for the deaf. They felt that although such schools were there to help, they also served to isolate. I have always been grateful for their decision. Because of it, I had to contend with public schools, and in doing so I developed two methods of survival: I learned to read not just lips but the whole person, and I learned the habit of clear speech by taking every speech and drama course I could.

That is not to say my adolescent years were easy going—they were 12
misery. The lack of sound cast a pall on everything. Life seemed less fun than it had been before. I didn't associate that lack of fun with the lack of sound. I didn't begin to make the connection between the failings of my body and the failings of the world until I was well out of college. I simply did not admit to myself that deafness caused certain problems—or even that I was deaf.

From the time I was twelve until I was twenty-four, the loss of my 13
hearing was erratic. I would lose a decibel or two of sound and then my hearing would stabilize. A week or a year later there would be another slip and then I'd have to adjust all over again. I never knew when I would hit bottom. I remember going to bed one night still being able to make out the reassuring purr of the refrigerator and the late-night conversation of my parents, then waking the next morning to nothing—even my own voice was gone. These fits and starts continued until my hearing finally dropped to the last rung of amplifiable sound. I was a college student at the time, and whenever anyone asked about my hearing aid, I admitted to being only slightly hard of hearing.

My professors were frequently alarmed by my almost maniacal in- 14
tensity in class. I was petrified that I'd have to ask for special privileges just to achieve marginal understanding. My pride was in flames. I became increasingly bitter and isolated. I was terrified of being marked a deaf woman, a label that made me sound dumb and cowlike, enveloped in a protective silence that denied me my complexity. I did everything I could to hide my handicap. I wore my hair long and never

wore earrings, thus keeping attention away from my ears and their riders. I monopolized conversations so that I wouldn't slip up and reveal what I was or wasn't hearing; I took on a disdainful air at large parties, hoping that no one would ask me something I couldn't instantly reply to. I lied about the extent of my deafness so l could avoid the stigma of being thought "different" in a pathetic way.

It was not surprising that in my senior year I suffered a nervous collapse and spent three days in the hospital crying like a baby. When I stopped crying I knew it was time to face a few things—I had to start asking for help when I needed it because I couldn't handle my deafness alone, and I had to quit being ashamed of my handicap so I could begin to live with its consequences and discover what (if any) were its rewards.   15

When I began telling people that I was *really* deaf I did so with grim determination. Some were afraid to talk to me at any length, fearing perhaps that they were talking into a void; others assumed that I was somehow an unsullied innocent and always inquired in carefully enunciated sentences: "Doooooooo youuuuuuuu driiinnk liquor?" But most people were surprisingly sympathetic—they wanted to know the best way to be understood, they took great pains to talk directly to my face, and they didn't insult me by using only words of one syllable.   16

It was, in part, that gentle acceptance that made me more curious about my own deafness. Always before it had been an affliction to wrestle with as one would with angels, but when I finally accepted it as an inevitable part of my life, I relaxed enough to do some exploring. I would take off my hearing aid and go through a day, a night, an hour or two— as long as I could take it—in absolute silence. I felt as if I were indulging in a secret vice because I was perceiving the world in a new way—stripped of sound.   17

Of course I had always known that sound is vibration, but I didn't know, until I stopped straining to hear, how truly sound is a refinement of feeling. Conversations at parties might elude me, but I seldom fail to pick up on moods. I enjoy watching people talk. When I am too far away to read lips I try reading postures and imagining conversations. Sometimes, to everyone's horror, I respond to things better left unsaid when I'm trying to find out what's going on around me. I want to see, touch, taste, and smell everything within reach; I especially have to curb a tendency to judge things by their smell—not just potato salad but people as well—a habit that seems to some people entirely too barbaric for comfort. I am not claiming that my other senses stepped up their work to compensate for the loss, but the absence of one does allow me to concentrate on the others. Deafness has left me acutely aware of both the duplicity that language is capable of and the many expressions the body cannot hide.   18

Over the last twenty years I've worked exclusively in speaking   19 theatre. I've performed both male and female roles in a variety of Shakespearean productions; co-wrote and starred in a PBS children's show; toured my performance art pieces, nationally and internationally; helped found, then wrote and performed for two major musical/satirical cabarets; and still I make my living performing and conducting workshops in performance. Some people think it's odd that, as deaf as I am, I've spent so much of my life working in the theater, but I find it to be a natural consequence of my particular circumstance. The loss of sound has enhanced my fascination with language and the way meaning is conveyed. I love to perform. Exactly the same processes occur onstage as off—except that onstage, once I've memorized the script, I know what everybody is saying as they say it. I am delighted to be so immediately in the know. It has provided a direct way to keep in touch with the rest of-the world despite the imposed isolation.

Silence is not empty; it is simply more sobering than sound. At times I prefer the sobriety. I can still "hear" with a hearing aid—that is. I can discern noise, but I can't tell you where it's coming from or if it is laughter or a faulty drain. When there are many people talking together I hear a strange music, a distant rumbling in my consciousness. But when I take off my hearing aid at night and lie in bed surrounded by my fate, I wonder, "What is this—a foul subtraction or a blessing in disguise?" For despite my fears there is a kind of peace in the silence— albeit an uneasy one. There is, after all, less to distract me from my thoughts. 20

But I know what I've lost. The process of becoming deaf has at times been frightening, akin perhaps to dying, and early in life it took away my happy confidence in the image of a world where things always work right. When I first came back from the Lions Camp that summer I cursed heaven and earth for doing such terrible wrong to me and to my friends. My grandmother tried to comfort me by promising, "Honey, God's got something special planned for you." 21

But I thought, "Yes. He plans to make me deaf." 22

HENRY LOUIS GATES, JR.

Living Under Grace

Henry Louis Gates, Jr. (1950–   ), grew up in the small town of Piedmont, West Virginia, and is now Director of the Afro-American Studies Department and W.E.B. Du Bois Professor of Humanities at Harvard. As a student at Yale in the late 1960s, Gates received fellowships that allowed him to spend a year in East Africa, working as a general anesthetist for the Anglican Mission Hospital in Tanzania. After graduating from Yale in 1973, Gates entered Cambridge University, where, in 1979, he became the first African-American to receive a Ph.D. Although he had gone to Cambridge to study medicine, after studying literature there under Nobel laureate Wole Soyinka, Gates decided to pursue degrees in English. He held teaching positions at Yale, Cornell, and Duke before accepting the position at Harvard in 1991. Gates has edited several works on African-American writers, including the thirty-volume *Schomburg Library of Nineteenth-Century Black Women Writers* and collections of essays on Wole Soyinka and Frederick Douglass. His studies in literary criticism include *Black Literature and Literary Theory* (1984) and *The Signifying Monkey: Towards a Theory of Afro-American Literary Criticism* (1988). In 1997, Gates published both *Thirteen Ways of Looking at a Black Man* and *The Norton Anthology of Afro-American Literature*. In sharp contrast to his scholarly writing is Gates's *Colored People* (1994), the story of his coming-of-age during the 1950s and 1960s. In writing this memoir, Gates worked deliberately to simplify his writing, wishing to regain the child's perspective on small-town life. "Living Under Grace" is excerpted from this work.

It was at Peterkin, an Episcopal church camp in West Virginia that   1
I attended that summer—the summer of 1965—and the two summers following, that I was given an opportunity to explore the contours of my new faith, and the world beyond Piedmont.

Spending two weeks at Peterkin, made possible by a scholarship,   2
was like stepping into a dream world. It was populated by well over a hundred seemingly self-confident, generous-spirited teenagers, their ages ranging from fifteen to eighteen; they were rebellious, worldly, questioning, cosmopolitan, articulate, bold, and smart. I learned so much at that camp, I don't even know where to begin.

Following a regular regime of breakfast, morning prayers in the   3
chapel, cleanup, seminars, then lunch, we'd sit for long hours in the afternoon, playing hands of bridge, which I was learning as I went along. We'd play on the front porch of the main house, which used to be an elegant hunting lodge, complete with a huge stone fireplace. I had beginner's luck: a couple of small slams, a grand slam, hands with lots of points. We'd play, the four of us—Tandy Tully and her boyfriend, Peter Roberts, Andrea Strader and I—all afternoon sometimes, watching the other campers come and go, and we'd talk about this and that and everything, books and ideas, people and concepts. The war in Vietnam. Smoking. The existence of God.

Andrea was smart and well-read, intuitive and analytical. She was   4
also beautiful, cocoa-colored, with a wide plum-purple mouth that tasted delicious. It was Andrea who told me early on that I should go

to prep school, and then to the Ivy League. (What's a prep school? I asked her.) That I should travel and read this and that. She was petite and elegant, and she sang like an angel. Every night we'd have a campfire, and every night I'd sit next to her, trying to learn the words of the traditional gospel songs and the camp songs, listening to my past and future through Andrea's lovely voice. She had large black eyes and long, straightened hair that was soft to the touch. I couldn't believe that she even existed or that she would want to be with me.

The third black camper at Peterkin was Eddie James— Edward Lawrence James, The Third, thank you very much. Eddie was rich. His grandfather had founded a produce business in Charleston at the turn of the century, and it had prospered. Everybody in Charleston knew and respected the Jameses, he let us know. All the Democratic politicians kissed Mr. James II's black behind. Money can't erase color, Andrea would explain to me, but sometimes it can help you blend a bit better. The Jameses were proof of that. Eddie was dating a white girl at camp, which was giving the director, Mary Jo Fitts, fits. She chain-smoked so much that her teeth looked like yellow fangs, and her personality matched her teeth.

Sex was everywhere at Peterkin—everywhere but in my bed. Maybe it could have been there, but I didn't know it, and I didn't know how to put it there. I was fond of making all sorts of lofty pronouncements, like: I'm naturally high, or I'll wait to do it until I get married. I was the walking, talking equivalent of those wall plaques that you can buy in Woolworth's that attest to such sentiments as "M Is for the Many Things She Gave Me" or "Lord, Help Us to Accept the Things We Cannot Change." I wonder how people could stand me. But I was being honest, in the same way that people who collect paintings on black velvet are being honest. I thought I was thinking the right things, remaining pure of heart. I was terribly earnest: the Pentheus[1] of Peterkin. Meantime, everybody else was getting down with somebody or other. You could feel the sexual energy flowing. There was a charge in the air.

A month shy of my fifteenth birthday, I felt I had died and gone to Heaven. I was living in a kingdom, one of the princes. We drank ideas and ate controversy. Is God dead? we asked. Can you love two people at the same time? I feasted on the idea of learning about the world and being a citizen of it.

And yet my sense of this citizenship would be jeopardized not long after I arrived. After a solid week of complete isolation, a deliveryman bringing milk and bread to the camp told the head counselor that "all hell has broken loose in Los Angeles" and the "colored people have

---

1. In Euripides' play *The Bacchae*, Pentheus attempts to suppress the followers of Dionysus, god of wine, drunkenness, and fertility, to his own demise—he is torn apart by the Bacchae, a group of frenzied women.

gone crazy." He handed him a Sunday paper, which screamed the news about Negroes rioting in some place called Watts. Andrea had overheard and was the one to tell me. Your soul brothers have gone totally crazy, she said. Rioting and shit. I stared at the headline: NE-GROES RIOT IN WATTS.[2] We were all trying to understand what was really happening, to judge from one screaming headline.

I was bewildered. I didn't understand what a riot was. Were col-   9
ored people being killed by white people, or were they killing white people? Watching myself being watched by all the white campers, I experienced that strange combination of power and powerlessness that you feel when the actions of another black person affect your own life, simply because you both are black. I realized that the actions of people I did not know had become my responsibility as surely as if the black folk in Watts had been my relatives in Piedmont, just twenty or so miles away.

Sensing my mixture of pride and discomfiture, a priest handed me   10
a book later that day. From the cover, the wide-spaced eyes of a black man transfixed me. *Notes of a Native Son*, the book was called, by James Baldwin.[3] Was this man the *author*, I wondered, this man with a closely cropped "natural," with brown skin, splayed nostrils, and wide lips, so very Negro, so seemingly comfortable to be so?

From the book's first few sentences, I was caught up thoroughly in   11
the sensibility of another person—a black person. It was the first time I had heard a voice capturing the terrible exhilaration and anxiety of being a person of African descent in this country. The book performed for me the Adamic function of naming the complex racial dynamic of the American cultural imagination. I could not put it down.

It became all the more urgent to deal with the upheaval I had felt   12
when I read that headline.

We were pioneers, people my age, in cross-race relations, able to   13
get to know each other across cultures and classes in a way that was unthinkable in our parents' generation. Honest hatreds, genuine friendships, rivalries bred from contiguity rather than from the imagination. Love and competition. In school, I had been raised with white kids, from first grade. To speak to white people was just to speak. Period. No artificial tones, no hypercorrectness. And yet I have known so many Negroes who were separated from white people by an abyss of fear. Whenever one of my uncles would speak to a white person, his head would bow, his eyes would widen, and the smile he would force on his

2. Watts: a southwestern district of Los Angeles. There, August 11–16, 1965, in the face of insurmountable racial problems, thousands of African-Americas rioted, resulting in thirty-four deaths and more than a thousand injuries.
3. One of the most distinguished essayists and novelists of the twentieth century, James Baldwin (1924–1987) published his earliest essays in *Notes of a Native Son* in 1955.

lips said: I won't hurt you, boss, an' I'm your faithful friend. Just come here and let ole me help you. Laughing much too loud and too long at their jokes, he assumed the same position with his head and his body as when he was telling a lie.

But there, at Peterkin, on that day especially, we were all trying to understand what had just happened and what it might mean for our lives, and to do so with a measure of honesty. 14

What the news of the riots did for us was to remind everybody in one fell swoop that there was a racial context outside Peterkin that affected relations between white and black Americans; we had suddenly to remember that our roles were scripted by that larger context. We had for a blissful week been functioning outside these stereotypes of each other—functioning as best we could, that is—when all of a sudden the context had come crashing down upon us once again. I hated that newspaper. But we overcame it: with difficulty, with perseverance, we pushed away the racial context and could interact not as allegories but as people. It felt like something of an achievement. 15

I didn't want to leave. I cried when I had to go . . . but then everybody cried. When I got home, my wonderful room full of books and records looked like Cinderella's hovel must have, when she returned from the ball at half-past midnight. My beautiful mountain valley on the banks of the mighty Potomac looked like a dirty, smelly mill town, full of people who cared more about basketball and baseball and eating than anything else. Somehow, between the six weeks of the hospital[4] and the two weeks of Peterkin, some evil blight had stricken my magical kingdom. It made me heartsick, especially the once or twice I was foolhardy enough to try to explain all this to Linda Hoffman or to Johnny DiPilato.[5] There are *lots* of nice church camps, was all that Hoffman said. 16

MARTIN LUTHER KING, JR.

Letter from Birmingham Jail

Martin Luther King, Jr. (1929–1968), was the dominant leader of the American civil rights movement from 1955 until his assassination. A gifted student and the son and grandson of eloquent Baptist ministers, he received his B.A. from Morehouse College when he was

4. Earlier in *Colored People*, Gates describes a prolonged hospital stay after intensive surgery to correct a slipped epithesis, which had resulted from a touch-football knee injury.
5. Linda Hoffman, Johnny DiPilato: two of Gates's white friends.

nineteen years old. At Crozer Theological Seminary, where he studied until 1951, he became acquainted with the ideas of Mohandas Gandhi, the great Indian advocate of nonviolent protest. After taking his Ph.D. from Boston University in 1955, he became pastor of a church in Montgomery, Alabama, where he led the famous bus boycott that initiated more than a decade of civil rights protests. Soon King organized the Southern Christian Leadership Conference, a network of civil rights leaders extending throughout the South. Arrested in 1963 during desegregation demonstrations in Birmingham, Alabama, King wrote his "Letter from Birmingham Jail" in response to a public letter from a group of eight clergymen who opposed the demonstrations. His letter received national attention when it was republished in *The Christian Century* and *The Atlantic Monthly*. The following version is from King's *Why We Can't Wait* (1964). Readers may want to note ways that King, even while articulating the impatience of an excluded minority, stresses values shared with his largely white audience.

April 16, 1963[1]

My Dear Fellow Clergymen:

While confined here in the Birmingham city jail, I came across   1
your recent statement calling my present activities "unwise and untimely." Seldom do I pause to answer criticism of my work and ideas. If I sought to answer all the criticisms that cross my desk, my secretaries would have little time for anything other than such correspondence in the course of the day, and I would have no time for constructive work. But since I feel that you are men of genuine good will and that your criticisms are sincerely set forth, I want to try to answer your statement in what I hope will be patient and reasonable terms.

I think I should indicate why I am here in Birmingham, since you   2
have been influenced by the view which argues against "outsiders coming in." I have the honor of serving as president of the Southern Christian Leadership Conference, an organization operating in every southern state, with headquarters in Atlanta, Georgia. We have some eighty-five affiliated organizations across the South, and one of them is the Alabama Christian Movement for Human Rights. Frequently we

1. This response to a published statement by eight fellow clergymen from Alabama (Bishop C. C. J. Carpenter. Bishop Joseph A. Durick, Rabbi Hilton L. Grafman, Bishop Paul Hardin, Bishop Holan B. Harmon, the Reverend George M. Murray, the Reverend Edward V. Ramage and the Reverend Earl Stallings) was composed under somewhat constricting circumstances. Begun on the margins of the newspaper in which the statement appeared while I was in jail, the letter was continued on scraps of writing paper supplied by a friendly Negro trusty, and concluded on a pad my attorneys were eventually permitted to leave me. Although the text remains in substance unaltered. I have indulged in the author's prerogative of polishing it for publication. [author's note]

share staff, educational, and financial resources with our affiliates. Several months ago the affiliate here in Birmingham asked us to be on call to engage in a nonviolent direct-action program if such were deemed necessary. We readily consented, and when the hour came we lived up to our promise. So I, along with several members of my staff, am here because I was invited here. I am here because I have organizational ties here.

But more basically, I am in Birmingham because injustice is here. 3 Just as the prophets of the eighth century B.C. left their villages and carried their "thus saith the Lord" far beyond the boundaries of their home towns, and just as the Apostle Paul left his village of Tarsus and carried the gospel of Jesus Christ to the far corners of the Greco-Roman world, so am I compelled to carry the gospel of freedom beyond my own home town. Like Paul, I must constantly respond to the Macedonian call for aid.

Moreover, I am cognizant of the interrelatedness of all communities and states. I cannot sit idly by in Atlanta and not be concerned about what happens in Birmingham. Injustice anywhere is a threat to justice everywhere. We are caught in an inescapable network of mutuality, tied in a single garment of destiny. Whatever affects one directly, affects all indirectly. Never again can we afford to live with the narrow, provincial "outside agitator" idea. Anyone who lives inside the United States can never be considered an outsider anywhere within its bounds.

You deplore the demonstrations taking place in Birmingham. But 5 your statement, I am sorry to say, fails to express a similar concern for the conditions that brought about the demonstrations. I am sure that none of you would want to rest content with the superficial kind of social analysis that deals merely with effects and does not grapple with underlying causes. It is unfortunate that demonstrations are taking place in Birmingham, but it is even more unfortunate that the city's white power structure left the Negro community with no alternative.

In any nonviolent campaign there are four basic steps: collection 6 of the facts to determine whether injustices exist; negotiation; self-purification; and direct action. We have gone through all these steps in Birmingham. There can be no gainsaying the fact that racial injustice engulfs this community. Birmingham is probably the most thoroughly segregated city in the United States. Its ugly record of brutality is widely known. Negroes have experienced grossly unjust treatment in the courts. There have been more unsolved bombings of Negro homes and churches in Birmingham than in any other city in the nation. These are the hard, brutal facts of the case. On the basis of these conditions, Negro leaders sought to negotiate with the city fathers. But the latter consistently refused to engage in good-faith negotiation.

Then, last September, came the opportunity to talk with leaders of 7 Birmingham's economic community. In the course of the negotiations, certain promises were made by the merchants—for example, to remove the stores' humiliating racial signs. On the basis of these promises, the Reverend Fred Shuttlesworth and the leaders of the Alabama Christian Movement for Human Rights agreed to a moratorium on all demonstrations. As the weeks and months went by, we realized that we were the victims of a broken promise. A few signs, briefly removed, returned; the others remained.

As in so many past experiences, our hopes had been blasted, and the shadow of deep disappointment settled upon us. We had no alternative except to prepare for direct action, whereby we would present our very bodies as a means of laying our case before the conscience of the local and the national community. Mindful of the difficulties involved, we decided to undertake a process of self-purification. We began a series of workshops on nonviolence, and we repeatedly asked ourselves: "Are you able to accept blows without retaliating?" "Are you able to endure the ordeal of jail?" We decided to schedule our direct-action program for the Easter season, realizing that except for Christmas, this is the main shopping period of the year. Knowing that a strong economic withdrawal program would be the by-product of direct action, we felt that this would be the best time to bring pressure to bear on the merchants for the needed change.

Then it occurred to us that Birmingham's mayoral election was coming up in March, and we speedily decided to postpone action until after election day. When we discovered that the Commissioner of Public Safety, Eugene "Bull" Connor, had piled up enough votes to be in the runoff, we decided again to postpone action until the day after the run-off so that the demonstrations could not be used to cloud the issues. Like many others, we waited to see Mr. Connor defeated, and to this end we endured postponement after postponement. Having aided in this community need, we felt that our direct-action program could be delayed no longer.

You may well ask: "Why direct action? Why sit-ins, marches, and so forth? Isn't negotiation a better path?" You are quite right in calling for negotiation. Indeed, this is the very purpose of direct action. Nonviolent direct action seeks to create such a crisis and foster such a tension that a community which has constantly refused to negotiate is forced to confront the issue. It seeks so to dramatize the issue that it can no longer be ignored. My citing the creation of tension as part of the work of the nonviolent-resister may sound rather shocking. But I must confess that I am not afraid of the word "tension." I have earnestly opposed violent tension, but there is a type of constructive, nonviolent tension which is necessary for growth. Just as Socrates felt that it was necessary to create a tension in the mind so that individuals could rise from the bondage of myths and half-truths to the unfettered realm of creative analysis and objective appraisal, so must we see the need for nonviolent gadflies to create the kind of tension in society that will help men rise from the dark depths of prejudice and racism to the majestic heights of understanding and brotherhood.

The purpose of our direct-action program is to create a situation so 11 crisis-packed that it will inevitably open the door to negotiation. I therefore concur with you in your call for negotiation. Too long has our beloved Southland been bogged down in a tragic effort to live in monologue rather than dialogue.

One of the basic points in your statement is that the action that I 12 and my associates have taken in Birmingham is untimely. Some have asked: "Why didn't you give the new city administration time to act?" The only answer that I can give to this query is that the new Birmingham administration must be prodded about as much as the outgoing one, before it will act. We are sadly mistaken if we feel that the election of Albert Boutwell as mayor will bring the millennium to Birmingham. While Mr. Boutwell is a much more gentle person than Mr. Connor, they are both segregationists, dedicated to maintenance of the status quo. I have hope that Mr. Boutwell will be reasonable enough to see the futility of massive resistance to desegregation. But he will not see this without pressure from devotees of civil rights. My friends, I must say to you that we have not made a single gain in civil rights without determined legal and nonviolent pressure. Lamentably, it is an historical fact that privileged groups seldom give up their privileges voluntarily. Individuals may see the moral light and voluntarily give up their unjust posture; but, as Reinhold Niebuhr has reminded us, groups tend to be more immoral than individuals.

We know through painful experience that freedom is never volun- 13 tarily given by the oppressor; it must be demanded by the oppressed. Frankly, I have yet to engage in a direct action campaign that was "well timed" in the view of those who have not suffered unduly from the disease of segregation. For years now I have heard the word "Wait!" It rings in the ear of every Negro with piercing familiarity. This "Wait" has almost always meant "Never." We must come to see, with one of our distinguished jurists, that "justice too long delayed is justice denied."

We have waited for more than 340 years for our constitutional and 14 God-given rights. The nations of Asia and Africa are moving with jet-like speed toward gaining political independence, but we still creep at horse-and-buggy pace toward gaining a cup of coffee at a lunch counter. Perhaps it is easy for those who have never felt the stinging darts of segregation to say, "Wait." But when you have seen vicious mobs lynch your mothers and fathers at will and drown your sisters and brothers at whim; when you have seen hate-filled policemen curse, kick, and even kill your black brothers and sisters; when you see the vast majority of your twenty million Negro brothers smothering in an airtight cage of poverty in the midst of an affluent society; when you suddenly find your tongue twisted and your speech stammering as you seek to explain to your six-year-old daughter why she can't go to the public amusement park that has just been advertised on television, and see tears welling up in her eyes when she is told that Funtown is closed to colored children, and see ominous clouds of inferiority beginning to form in her little mental sky, and see her beginning to distort her personality by developing an unconscious bitterness toward white people; when you have to concoct an answer for a five-year-old son who is asking: "Daddy, why do white people treat colored people so mean?"; when you take a cross-country drive and find it necessary to sleep night after night in the uncomfortable corners of your automobile because no motel will accept you; when you are humiliated day in and day out by nagging signs reading "white" and "colored"; when your first name becomes "nigger," your middle name becomes "boy" (however old you are) and your last name becomes "John," and your wife and mother are never given the respected title "Mrs."; when you are harried by day and haunted by night by the fact that you are a Negro, living constantly at tiptoe stance, never quite knowing what to expect next, and are plagued with inner fears and outer resentments; when you are forever fighting a degenerating sense of "nobodiness"— then you will understand why we find it difficult to wait. There comes a time when the cup of endurance runs over, and men are no longer willing to be plunged into the abyss of despair. I hope, sirs, you can understand our legitimate and unavoidable impatience.

You express a great deal of anxiety over our willingness to break laws. This is certainly a legitimate concern. Since we so diligently urge people to obey the Supreme Court's decision of 1954 outlawing segregation in the public schools, at first glance it may seem rather paradoxical for us consciously to break laws. One may well ask: "How can you advocate breaking some laws and obeying others?" The answer lies in the fact that there are two types of laws: just and unjust. I would be the first to advocate obeying just laws. One has not only a legal but a moral responsibility to obey just laws. Conversely, one has a moral responsibility to disobey unjust laws. I would agree with St. Augustine that "an unjust law is no law at all." 15

Now, what is the difference between the two? How does one determine whether a law is just or unjust? A just law is a man-made code that squares with the moral law or the law of God. An unjust law is a code that is out of harmony with the moral law. To put it in the terms of St. Thomas Aquinas: An unjust law is a human law that is not rooted in eternal law and natural law. Any law that uplifts human personality is just. Any law that degrades human personality is unjust. All segregation statutes are unjust because segregation distorts the soul and damages the personality. It gives the segregator a false sense of superiority and the segregated a false sense of inferiority. Segregation, to use the terminology of the Jewish philosopher Martin Buber, substitutes an "I—it" relationship for an "I–thou" relationship and ends up 16 relegating persons to the status of things. Hence segregation is not only politically, economically, and sociologically unsound, it is morally wrong and sinful. Paul Tillich has said that sin is separation. Is not segregation an existential expression of man's tragic separation, his awful estrangement, his terrible sinfulness? Thus it is that I can urge men to obey the 1954 decision of the Supreme Court, for it is morally right; and I can urge them to disobey segregation ordinances, for they are morally wrong.

Let us consider a more concrete example of just and unjust laws. An unjust law is a code that a numerical or power majority group compels a minority group to obey but does not make binding on itself. This is *difference* made legal. By the same token, a just law is a code that a majority compels a minority to follow and that it is willing to follow itself. This is *sameness* made legal.   17

Let me give another explanation. A law is unjust if it is inflicted on a minority that, as a result of being denied the right to vote, had no part in enacting or devising the law. Who can say that the legislature of Alabama which set up that state's segregation laws was democratically elected? Throughout Alabama all sorts of devious methods are used to prevent Negroes from becoming registered voters, and there are some counties in which, even though Negroes constitute a majority of the population, not a single Negro is registered. Can any law enacted under such circumstances be considered democratically structured?   18

Sometimes a law is just on its face and unjust in its application. For instance, I have been arrested on a charge of parading without a permit. Now, there is nothing wrong in having an ordinance which requires a permit for a parade. But such an ordinance becomes unjust when it is used to maintain segregation and to deny citizens the First-Amendment privilege of peaceful assembly and protest.   19

I hope you are able to see the distinction I am trying to point out. In no sense do I advocate evading or defying the law, as would the rabid segregationist. That would lead to anarchy. One who breaks an unjust law must do so openly, lovingly, and with a willingness to accept the penalty. I submit that an individual who breaks a law that conscience tells him is unjust, and who willingly accepts the penalty of imprisonment in order to arouse the conscience of the community over its injustice, is in reality expressing the highest respect for law.   20

Of course, there is nothing new about this kind of civil disobedience. It was evidenced sublimely in the refusal of Shadrach, Meshach, and Abednego to obey the laws of Nebuchadnezzar,[2] on the ground that a higher moral law was at stake. It was practiced superbly by the early Christians, who were willing to face hungry lions and the excruciating pain of chopping blocks rather than submit to certain unjust laws of the Roman Empire. To a degree, academic freedom is a reality   21

2. King refers to the biblical story recorded in Dan. 3.

today because Socrates practiced civil disobedience. In our own nation, the Boston Tea Party represented a massive act of civil disobedience.

We should never forget that everything Adolf Hitler did in Germany was "legal" and everything the Hungarian freedom fighters did in Hungary was "illegal." It was "illegal" to aid and comfort a Jew in Hitler's Germany. Even so, I am sure that, had I lived in Germany at the time, I would have aided and comforted my Jewish brothers. If today I lived in a Communist country where certain principles dear to the Christian faith are suppressed, I would openly advocate disobeying that country's antireligious laws.   22

I must make two honest confessions to you, my Christian and Jewish brothers. First, I must confess that over the past few years I have been gravely disappointed with the white moderate. I have almost reached the regrettable conclusion that the Negro's great stumbling block in his stride toward freedom is not the White Citizen's Counciler or the Ku Klux Klanner, but the white moderate, who is more devoted to "order" than to justice; who prefers a negative peace which is the absence of tension to a positive peace which is the presence of justice; who constantly says: "I agree with you in the goal you seek, but I cannot agree with your methods of direct action"; who paternalistically believes he can set the timetable for another man's freedom; who lives by a mythical concept of time and who constantly advises the Negro to wait for a "more convenient season." Shallow understanding from people of good will is more frustrating than absolute misunderstanding from people of ill will. Lukewarm acceptance is much more bewildering than outright rejection.   23

I had hoped that the white moderate would understand that law and order exist for the purpose of establishing justice and that when they fail in this purpose they become the dangerously structured dams that block the flow of social progress. I had hoped that the white moderate would understand that the present tension in the South is a necessary phase of the transition from an obnoxious negative peace, in which the Negro passively accepted his unjust plight, to a substantive and positive peace, in which all men will respect the dignity and worth of human personality. Actually, we who engage in nonviolent direct action are not the creators of tension. We merely bring to the surface the hidden tension that is already alive. We bring it out in the open, where it can be seen and dealt with. Like a boil that can never be cured so long as it is covered up but must be opened with all its ugliness to the natural medicines of air and light, injustice must be exposed, with all the tension its exposure creates, to the light of human conscience and the air of national opinion before it can be cured.   24

In your statement you assert that our actions, even though peaceful, must be condemned because they precipitate violence. But is this a logical assertion? Isn't this like condemning a robbed man because his possession of money precipitated the evil act of robbery? Isn't this like   25 condemning Socrates because his unswerving commitment to truth and his philosophical inquiries precipitated the act by the misguided populace in which they made him drink hemlock? Isn't this like condemning Jesus because his unique God-consciousness and never-ceasing devotion to God's will precipitated the evil act of crucifixion? We must come to see that, as the federal courts have consistently affirmed, it is wrong to urge an individual to cease his efforts to gain his basic constitutional rights because the quest may precipitate violence. Society must protect the robbed and punish the robber.

26   I had also hoped that the white moderate would reject the myth concerning time in relation to the struggle for freedom. I have just received a letter from a white brother in Texas. He writes: "All Christians know that the colored people will receive equal rights eventually, but it is possible that you are in too great a religious hurry It has taken Christianity almost two thousand years to accomplish what it has. The teachings of Christ take time to come to earth." Such an attitude stems from a tragic misconception of time, from the strangely irrational notion that there is something in the very flow of time that will inevitably cure all ills. Actually, time itself is neutral; it can be used either destructively or constructively. More and more I feel that the people of ill will have used time much more effectively than have the people of good will. We will have to repent in this generation not merely for the hateful words and actions of the bad people but for the appalling silence of the good people. Human progress never rolls in on wheels of inevitability; it comes through the tireless efforts of men willing to be co-workers with God, and without this hard work, time itself becomes an ally of the forces of social stagnation. We must use time creatively, in the knowledge that the time is always ripe to do right. Now is the time to make real the promise of democracy and transform our pending national elegy into a creative psalm of brotherhood. Now is the time to lift our national policy from the quicksand of racial injustice to the solid rock of human dignity.

27   You speak of our activity in Birmingham as extreme. At first I was rather disappointed that fellow clergymen would see my nonviolent efforts as those of an extremist. I began thinking about the fact that I stand in the middle of two opposing forces in the Negro community. One is a force of complacency, made up in part of Negroes who, as a result of long years of oppression, are so drained of self-respect and a sense of "somebodiness" that they have adjusted to segregation; and in part of a few middle-class Negroes who, because of a degree of academic and economic security and because in some ways they profit by segregation, have become insensitive to the problems of the masses. The other force is one of bitterness and hatred, and it comes perilously close to advocating violence. It is expressed in the various black nationalist groups that are springing up across the nation, the largest and best-known being Elijah Muhammad's Muslim movement. Nourished

by the Negro's frustration over the continued existence of racial discrimination, this movement is made up of people who have lost faith in America, who have absolutely repudiated Christianity, and who have concluded that the white man is an incorrigible "devil."

I have tried to stand between these two forces, saying that we need emulate neither the "do-nothingism" of the complacent nor the hatred and despair of the black nationalist. For there is the more excellent way of love and nonviolent protest. I am grateful to God that, through the influence of the Negro church, the way of nonviolence became an integral part of our struggle.   28

If this philosophy had not emerged, by now many streets of the South would, I am convinced, be flowing with blood. And I am further convinced that if our white brothers dismiss as "rabble-rousers" and "outside agitators" those of us who employ nonviolent direct action, and if they refuse to support our nonviolent efforts, millions of Negroes will, out of frustration and despair, seek solace and security in black-nationalist ideologies—a development that would inevitably lead to a frightening racial nightmare.   29

Oppressed people cannot remain oppressed forever. The yearning for freedom eventually manifests itself, and that is what has happened to the American Negro. Something within has reminded him of his birthright of freedom, and something without has reminded him that it can be gained. Consciously or unconsciously, he has been caught up by the *Zeitgeist*,[3] and with his black brothers of Africa and his brown and yellow brothers of Asia, South America and the Caribbean, the United States Negro is moving with a sense of great urgency toward the promised land of racial justice. If one recognizes this vital urge that has engulfed the Negro community, one should readily understand why public demonstrations are taking place. The Negro has many pent-up resentments and latent frustrations, and he must release them. So let him march; let him make prayer pilgrimages to the city hall; let him go on freedom rides—and try to understand why he must do so. If his repressed emotions are not released in nonviolent ways, they will seek expression through violence; this is not a threat but a fact of history. So I have not said to my people: "Get rid of your discontent." Rather, I have tried to say that this normal and healthy discontent can be channeled into the creative outlet of nonviolent direct action. And now this approach is being termed extremist.   30

But though I was initially disappointed at being categorized as an extremist, as I continued to think about the matter I gradually gained a measure of satisfaction from the label. Was not Jesus an extremist for love: "Love your enemies, bless them that curse you, do good to them that hate you, and pray for them which despitefully use you, and persecute you." Was not Amos an extremist for justice: "Let justice roll   31

---

3. *Zeitgeist*: spirit of the age (German).

down like waters and righteousness like an ever-flowing stream." Was not Paul an extremist for the Christian gospel: "I bear in my body the marks of the Lord Jesus." Was not Martin Luther an extremist: "Here I stand; I cannot do otherwise, so help me God." And John Bunyan: "I will stay in jail to the end of my days before I make a butchery of my conscience." And Abraham Lincoln: "This nation cannot survive half slave and half free." And Thomas Jefferson: We hold these truths to be self-evident, that all men are created equal . . ." So the question is not whether we will be extremists, but what kind of extremists we will be. Will we be extremists for hate or for love? Will we be extremists for the preservation of injustice or for the extension of justice? In that dramatic scene on Calvary's hill three men were crucified. We must never forget that all three were crucified for the same crime— the crime of extremism. Two were extremists for immorality, and thus fell below their environment. The other, Jesus Christ, was an extremist for love, truth, and goodness, and thereby rose above his environment. Perhaps the South, the nation, and the world are in dire need of creative extremists.

I had hoped that the white moderate would see this need. Perhaps I was too optimistic; perhaps I expected too much. I suppose I should have realized that few members of the oppressor race can understand the deep groans and passionate yearnings of the oppressed race, and still fewer have the vision to see that injustice must be rooted out by strong, persistent, and determined action. I am thankful, however, that some of our white brothers in the South have grasped the meaning of this social revolution and committed themselves to it. They are still all too few in quantity, but they are big in quality. Some—such as Ralph McGill, Lillian Smith, Harry Golden, James McBride Dabbs, Ann Braden, and Sarah Patton Boyle—have written about our struggle in eloquent and prophetic terms. Others have marched with us down nameless streets to the South. They have languished in filthy, roach-infested jails, suffering the abuse and brutality of policemen who view them as "dirty nigger-lovers." Unlike so many of their moderate brothers and sisters, they have recognized the urgency of the moment and sensed the need for powerful "action" antidotes to combat the disease of segregation.

Let me take note of my other major disappointment. I have been so greatly disappointed with the white church and its leadership. Of course, there are some notable exceptions. I am not unmindful of the fact that each of you has taken some significant stands on this issue. I commend you, Reverend Stallings, for your Christian stand on this past Sunday, in welcoming Negroes to your worship service on a non-segregated basis. I commend the Catholic leaders of this state for integrating Spring Hill College several years ago.

But despite these notable exceptions, I must honestly reiterate that I have been disappointed with the church. I do not say this as one of those negative critics who can always find something wrong with the church. I say this as a minister of the gospel, who loves the church; who was nurtured in its bosom; who has been sustained by its spiritual blessings and who will remain true to it as long as the cord of life shall lengthen.

When I was suddenly catapulted into the leadership of the bus protest in Montgomery, Alabama, a few years ago, I felt we would be supported by the white church. I felt that the white ministers, priests, and rabbis of the South would be among our strongest allies. Instead, some have been outright opponents, refusing to understand the freedom movement and misrepresenting its leaders; all too many others have been more cautious than courageous and have remained silent behind the anesthetizing security of stained-glass windows.

In spite of my shattered dreams, I came to Birmingham with the hope that the white religious leadership of this community would see the justice of our cause and, with deep moral concern, would serve as the channel through which our just grievances could reach the power structure. I had hoped that each of you would understand. But again I have been disappointed.

I have heard numerous southern religious leaders admonish their worshipers to comply with a desegregation decision because it is the law, but I have longed to hear white ministers declare: "Follow this decree because integration is morally right and because the Negro is your brother." In the midst of blatant injustices inflicted upon the Negro, I have watched white churchmen stand on the sideline and mouth pious irrelevancies and sanctimonious trivialities. In the midst of a mighty struggle to rid our nation of racial and economic injustice, I have heard many ministers say: "Those are social issues, with which the gospel has no real concern." And I have watched many churches commit themselves to a completely otherworldly religion which makes a strange, un-Biblical distinction between body and soul, between the sacred and the secular.

I have traveled the length and breadth of Alabama, Mississippi, and all the other southern states. On sweltering summer days and crisp autumn mornings I have looked at the South's beautiful churches with their lofty spires pointing heavenward. I have beheld the impressive outlines of her massive religious-education buildings. Over and over I have found myself asking: "What kind of people worship here? Who is their God? Where were their voices when the lips of Governor Barnett[4] dripped with words of interposition and nullification? Where were they when Governor Wallace[5] gave a clarion call for defiance and

35

36

37

38

---

4. Ross Barnett, governor of Mississippi, in 1962 ordered resistance to the registration of a black student, James Meredith, at the University of Mississippi.
5. George Wallace, governor of Alabama, stood in a doorway of the University of Alabama in a symbolic effort to block the registration of two black students in 1963.

hatred? Where were their voices of support when bruised and weary Negro men and women decided to rise from the dark dungeons of complacency to the bright hills of creative protest?"

Yes, these questions are still in my mind. In deep disappointment I have wept over the laxity of the church. But be assured that my tears have been tears of love. There can be no deep disappointment where there is not deep love. Yes, I love the church. How could I do otherwise? I am in the rather unique position of being the son, the grandson and the great-grandson of preachers. Yes, I see the church as the body of Christ. But, oh! How we have blemished and scarred that body through social neglect and through fear of being nonconformists.

There was a time when the church was very powerful—in the time when the early Christians rejoiced at being deemed worthy to suffer for what they believed. In those days the church was not merely a thermometer that recorded the ideas and principles of popular opinion; it was a thermostat that transformed the mores of society. Whenever the early Christians entered a town, the people in power became disturbed and immediately sought to convict the Christians for being "disturbers of the peace" and "outside agitators." But the Christians pressed on, in the conviction that they were "a colony of heaven," called to obey God rather than man. Small in number, they were big in commitment. They were too God-intoxicated to be "astronomically intimidated." By their effort and example they brought an end to such ancient evils as infanticide and gladiatorial contests.

Things are different now. So often the contemporary church is a weak, ineffectual voice with an uncertain sound. So often it is an archdefender of the status quo. Far from being disturbed by the presence of the church, the power structure of the average community is consoled by the church's silent—and often even vocal—sanction of things as they are.

But the judgment of God is upon the church as never before. If today's church does not recapture the sacrificial spirit of the early church, it will lose its authenticity, forfeit the loyalty of millions, and be dismissed as an irrelevant social club with no meaning for the twentieth century. Every day I meet young people whose disappointment with the church has turned into outright disgust.

Perhaps I have once again been too optimistic. Is organized religion too inextricably bound to the status quo to save our nation and the world? Perhaps I must turn my faith to the inner spiritual church, the church within the church, as the true *ekklesia*[6] and the hope of the world. But again I am thankful to God that some noble souls from the ranks of organized religion have broken loose from the paralyzing chains of conformity and joined us as active partners in the struggle for

6. *ekklesia*: literally, "assembly of the people" (Greek).

freedom. They have left their secure congregations and walked the streets of Albany, Georgia, with us. They have gone down the highways of the South on tortuous rides for freedom. Yes, they have gone to jail with us. Some have been dismissed from their churches, have lost the support of their bishops and fellow ministers. But they have acted in the faith that right defeated is stronger than evil triumphant. Their witness has been the spiritual salt that has preserved the true meaning of the gospel in these troubled times. They have carved a tunnel of hope through the dark mountain of disappointment.

I hope the church as a whole will meet the challenge of this decisive hour. But even if the church does not come to the aid of justice, I have no despair about the future. I have no fear about the outcome of our struggle in Birmingham, even if our motives are at present misunderstood. We will reach the goal of freedom in Birmingham and all over the nation, because the goal of America is freedom. Abused and scorned though we may be, our destiny is tied up with America's destiny. Before the pilgrims landed at Plymouth, we were here. Before the pen of Jefferson etched the majestic words of the Declaration of Independence across the pages of history, we were here. For more than two centuries our forebears labored in this country without wages; they made cotton king; they built the homes of their masters while suffering gross injustice and shameful humiliation—and yet out of a bottomless vitality they continued to thrive and develop. If the inexpressible cruelties of slavery could not stop us, the opposition we now face will surely fail. We will win our freedom because the sacred heritage of our nation and the eternal will of God are embodied in our echoing demands. 44

Before closing I feel impelled to mention one other point in your statement that has troubled me profoundly. You warmly commended the Birmingham police force for keeping "order" and "preventing violence." I doubt that you would have so warmly commended the police force if you had seen its dogs sinking their teeth into unarmed, nonviolent Negroes. I doubt that you would so quickly commend the policemen if you were to observe their ugly and inhumane treatment of Negroes here in the city jail; if you were to watch them push and curse old Negro women and young Negro girls; if you were to see them slap and kick old Negro men and young boys; if you were to observe them, as they did on two occasions, refuse to give us food because we wanted to sing our grace together. I cannot join you in your praise of the Birmingham police department. 45

It is true that the police have exercised a degree of discipline in handling the demonstrators. In this sense they have conducted themselves rather "nonviolently" in public. But for what purpose? To preserve the evil system of segregation. Over the past few years I have consistently preached that nonviolence demands that the means we 46 use must be as pure as the ends we seek. I have tried to make clear that it is wrong to use immoral means to attain moral ends. But now I must affirm that it is just as wrong, or perhaps even more so, to use moral means to preserve immoral ends. Perhaps Mr. Connor and his policemen have been rather nonviolent in public, as was Chief Pritchett in Albany, Georgia, but they have used the moral means of nonviolence to maintain the immoral end of racial injustice. As T. S. Eliot has said: "The last temptation is the greatest treason: To do the right deed for the wrong reason."

I wish you had commended the Negro sit-inners and demonstrators of Birmingham for their sublime courage, their willingness to suffer, and their amazing discipline in the midst of great provocation. One day the South will recognize its real heroes. They will be the James Merediths, with the noble sense of purpose that enables them to face jeering and hostile mobs, and with the agonizing loneliness that characterizes the life of the pioneer. They will be old, oppressed, battered Negro women, symbolized in a seventy-two-year-old woman in Montgomery, Alabama, who rose up with a sense of dignity and with her people decided not to ride segregated buses, and who responded with ungrammatical profundity to one who inquired about her weariness: "My feets is tired, but my soul is at rest." They will be the young high school and college students, the young ministers of the gospel and a host of their elders, courageously and nonviolently sitting in at lunch counters and willingly going to jail for conscience' sake. One day the South will know that when these disinherited children of God sat down at lunch counters, they were in reality standing up for what is best in the American dream and for the most sacred values in our Judaeo-Christian heritage, thereby bringing our nation back to those great wells of democracy which were dug deep by the founding fathers in their formulation of the Constitution and the Declaration of Independence. 47

Never before have I written so long a letter. I'm afraid it is much too long to take your precious time. I can assure you that it would have been much shorter if I had been writing from a comfortable desk, but what else can one do when he is alone in a narrow jail cell, other than write long letters, think long thoughts, and pray long prayers? 48

If I have said anything in this letter that overstates the truth and indicates an unreasonable impatience, I beg you to forgive me. If I have said anything that understates the truth and indicates my having a patience that allows me to settle for anything less than brotherhood, I beg God to forgive me. 49

I hope this letter finds you strong in the faith. I also hope that circumstances will soon make it possible for me to meet each of you, not as an integrationist or a civil-rights leader but as a fellow clergyman and a Christian brother. Let us all hope that the dark clouds of racial prejudice will soon pass away and the deep fog of misunderstanding 50 will be lifted from our fear-drenched communities, and in some not too distant tomorrow the radiant stars of love and brotherhood will shine over our great nation with all their scintillating beauty.

Yours for the cause of Peace and Brotherhood,

MARTIN LUTHER KING. JR.

ANNIE DILLARD

Singing with the Fundamentalists

Annie Dillard was born in 1945, in Pittsburgh. She is the author of nine books including *An American Childhood, The Writing Life,* and *Holy the Firm. The Living,* a novel, is the story of four men on the coast of Puget Sound in the second half of the nineteenth century. In 1975, *Pilgrim at Tinker Creek* was awarded the Pulitzer Prize in nonfiction. Her writing appears in the *Atlantic, Harper's,* the *New York Times Magazine,* the *Yale Review, American Heritage,* and in many anthologies. She has received fellowship grants from the Guggenheim Foundation and the National Endowment for the Arts; her writing has received the Washington Governor's Award, the Connecticut Governor's Award, the New York Press Club Award, and the Ambassador Book Award in Arts and Letters from the English-Speaking Union.

She lives in Middletown, Connecticut, with her husband, Robert D. Richardson, Jr., biographer of Thoreau and Emerson, and young daughter Rosie.

"Singing with the Fundamentalists" (from *Yale Review,* January 1985), describing her experiences with a group often ostracized on college campuses, is one of these. Like many of her best essays, it combines minute observation with contemplation of large questions about the value and meaning of human life. Some fundamentalist readers of the essay have thought it profoundly offensive. Readers may want to decide whether or not this reaction is justified.

It is early spring. I have a temporary office at a state university on 1
the West Coast. The office is on the third floor. It looks down on the Square, the enormous open courtyard at the center of campus. From my desk I see hundreds of people moving between classes. There is a large circular fountain in the Square's center.

Early one morning, on the first day of spring quarter, I hear sing- 2
ing. A pack of students has gathered at the fountain. They are singing something which, at this distance, and through the heavy window, sounds good.

I know who these singing students are: they are the Fundamental- 3
ists. This campus has a lot of them. Mornings they sing on the Square; it is their only perceptible activity. What are they singing? Whatever it

is, I want to join them, for I like to sing; whatever it is, I want to take my stand with them, for I am drawn to their very absurdity, their innocent indifference to what people think. My colleagues and students here, and my friends everywhere, dislike and fear Christian fundamentalists. You may never have met such people, but you've heard what they do: they pile up money, vote in blocs, and elect right-wing crazies; they censor books; they carry handguns; they fight fluoride in the drinking water and evolution in the schools; probably they would lynch people if they could get away with it. I'm not sure my friends are correct. I close my pen and join the singers on the Square.

There is a clapping song in progress. I have to concentrate to follow it:

> Come on, rejoice,
> And let your heart sing.
> Come on, rejoice,
> Give praise to the king.
> Singing alleluia—
> He is the king of kings;
> Singing alleluia—
> He is the king of kings.

Two song leaders are standing on the broad rim of the fountain; the water is splashing just behind them. The boy is short, hard-faced, with a moustache. He bangs his guitar with the backs of his fingers. The blonde girl, who leads the clapping, is bouncy; she wears a bit of makeup. Both are wearing blue jeans.

The students beside me are wearing blue jeans too—and athletic jerseys, parkas, football jackets, turtlenecks, and hiking shoes or jogging shoes. They all have canvas or nylon book bags. They look like any random batch of seventy or eighty students at this university. They are grubby or scrubbed, mostly scrubbed; they are tall, fair, or redheaded in large proportions. Their parents are white-collar workers, blue-collar workers, farmers, loggers, orchardists, merchants, fishermen; their names are, I'll bet. Olsen, Jensen, Seversen, Hansen, Klokker. Sigurdsen.

Despite the vigor of the clapping song, no one seems to be giving it much effort. And no one looks at anyone else; there are no sentimental glances and smiles, no glances even of recognition. These kids don't seem to know each other. We stand at the fountain's side, out on the broad, bricked Square in front of the science building, and sing the clapping song through three times.

It is quarter to nine in the morning. Hundreds of people are crossing the Square. These passersby—faculty, staff, students—pay very little attention to us; this morning singing has gone on for years. Most of them look at us directly, then ignore us, for there is nothing to see: no animal sacrifices, no lynchings, no collection plate for Jesse Helms,[1] no seizures, snake handling, healing, or glossolalia. There is barely anything to hear. I suspect the people glance at us to learn if we are really singing: how could so many people make so little sound? My fellow singers, who ignore each other, certainly ignore passersby as well. Within a week, most of them will have their eyes closed anyway.

We move directly to another song, a slower one.   8

> *He is my peace*
> *Who has broken down every wall;*
> *He is my peace,*
> *He is my peace.*

> *Cast all your cares on him,*
> *For he careth for you—oo—oo*
> *He is my peace,*
> *He is my peace.*

I am paying strict attention to the song leaders, for I am singing at   9
the top of my lungs and I've never heard any of these songs before. They are not the old American low-church Protestant hymns; they are not the old European high-church Protestant hymns. These hymns seem to have been written just yesterday, apparently by the same people who put out lyrical Christian greeting cards and bookmarks.

"Where do these songs come from?" I ask a girl standing next to   10
me. She seems appalled to be addressed at all, and startled by the question. "They're from the praise albums!" she explains, and moves away.

The songs' melodies run dominant, subdominant, dominant, tonic,   11
dominant. The pace is slow, about the pace of "Tell Laura I Love Her," and with that song's quavering, long notes. The lyrics are simple and repetitive; there are very few of them to which a devout Jew or Mohammedan could not give whole-hearted assent. These songs are similar to the things Catholics sing in church these days. I don't know if any studies have been done to correlate the introduction of contemporary songs into Catholic churches with those churches' decline in membership, or with the phenomenon of Catholic converts' applying to enter cloistered monasteries directly, without passing through parish churches.

> *I'm set free to worship,*
> *I'm set free to praise him,*
> *I'm set free to dance before the Lord . . .*

---

1. Jesse Helms: an ultraconservative U.S. Senator from North Carolina.

At nine o'clock sharp we quit and scatter. I hear a few quiet "see 12
you"s. Mostly the students leave quickly, as if they didn't want to be
seen. The Square empties.

The next day we show up again, at twenty to nine. The same two 13
leaders stand on the fountain's rim; the fountain is pouring down behind them.

After the first song, the boy with the moustache hollers, "Move on 14
up! Some of you guys aren't paying attention back there! You're talking to each other. I want you to concentrate!" The students laugh, embarrassed for him. He sounds like a teacher. No one moves. The girl
breaks into the next song, which we join at once:

> *In my life, Lord,*
> *Be glorified, be glorified, be glorified;*
> *In my life, Lord,*
> *Be glorified, be glorified, today.*

At the end of this singularly monotonous verse, which is straining my
tolerance for singing virtually anything, the boy with the moustache
startles me by shouting, "Classes!"

At once, without skipping a beat, we sing, "In my classes, Lord, be 15
glorified, be glorified . . ." I give fleet thought to the class I'm teaching
this afternoon. We're reading a little "Talk of the Town"[2] piece called
"Eggbag," about a cat in a magic store on Eighth Avenue. "Relationships!" the boy calls. The students seem to sing "In my relationships,
Lord," more easily than they sang "classes." They seemed embarrassed
by "classes." In fact, to my fascination, they seem embarrassed by almost everything. Why are they here? I will sing with the Fundamentalists every weekday morning all spring; I will decide, tentatively, that
they come pretty much for the same reasons I do: each has a private
relationship with "the Lord" and will put up with a lot of junk for it.

I have taught some Fundamentalist students here, and know a bit 16
of what they think. They are college students above all, worried about
their love lives, their grades, and finding jobs. Some support moderate
Democrats; some support moderate Republicans. Like their classmates,
most support nuclear freeze, ERA, and an end to the draft. I believe
they are divided on abortion and busing. They are not particularly political. They read *Christianity Today* and *Campus Life* and *Eternity*—moderate, sensible magazines, I think; they read a lot of C. S. Lewis. (One
such student, who seemed perfectly tolerant of me and my shoddy

2. "The Talk of the Town" is a regular feature of *The New Yorker*, consisting of short, informal essays.

Christianity, introduced me to C. S. Lewis's critical book on Charles Williams.) They read the Bible. I think they all "believe in" organic evolution. The main thing about them is this: there isn't any "them." Their views vary. They don't know each other.

Their common Christianity puts them, if anywhere, to the left of their classmates. I believe they also tend to be more able than their classmates to think well in the abstract, and also to recognize the complexity of moral issues. But I may be wrong. 17

In 1980, the media were certainly wrong about television evangelists. Printed estimates of Jerry Falwell's television audience ranged from 18 million to 30 million people. In fact, according to Arbitron's actual counts, fewer than 1.5 million people were watching Falwell. And, according to an Emory University study, those who did watch television evangelists didn't necessarily vote with them. Emory University sociologist G. Melton Mobley reports, "When that message turns political, they cut it off." Analysis of the 1982 off-year election turned up no Fundamentalist bloc voting. The media were wrong, but no one printed retractions. 18

The media were wrong, too, in a tendency to identify all fundamentalist Christians with Falwell and his ilk, and to attribute to them, across the board, conservative views. 19

Someone has sent me two recent issues of *Eternity: The Evangelical Monthly*. One lead article criticizes a television preacher for saying that the United States had never used military might to take land from another nation. The same article censures Newspeak, saying that government rhetoric would have us believe in a "clean bomb," would have us believe that we "defend" America by invading foreign soil, and would have us believe that the dictatorships we support are "democracies." "When the President of the United States says that one reason to support defense spending is because it creates jobs," this lead article says, "a little bit of *1984* begins to surface." Another article criticizes a "heavy-handed" opinion of Jerry Falwell Ministries—in this case a broadside attack on artificial insemination, surrogate motherhood, and lesbian motherhood. Browsing through *Eternity*, I find a double crostic.[3] I find an intelligent, analytical, and enthusiastic review of the new London Philharmonic recording of Mahler's second symphony—a review which stresses the "glorious truth" of the Jewish composer's magnificent work, and cites its recent performance in Jerusalem to celebrate the recapture of the Western Wall following the Six Day War. Surely, the evangelical Christians who read this magazine are not book-burners. If by chance they vote with the magazine's editors, then 20

---

3. double-crostic: a difficult word puzzle that requires the solver to re-create a long quotation.

it looks to me as if they vote with the American Civil Liberties Union and Americans for Democratic Action.

Every few years some bold and sincere Christian student at this 21 university disagrees with a professor in class—usually about the professor's out-of-hand dismissal of Christianity. Members of the faculty, outraged, repeat the stories of these rare and uneven encounters for years on end, as if to prove that the crazies are everywhere, and gaining ground. The notion is, apparently, that these kids can't think for themselves. Or they wouldn't disagree.

Now again the moustached leader asks us to move up. There is no 22 harangue, so we move up. (This will be a theme all spring. The leaders want us closer together. Our instinct is to stand alone.) From behind the tall fountain comes a wind; on several gusts we get sprayed. No one seems to notice.

We have time for one more song. The leader, perhaps sensing that 23 no one likes him, blunders on. "I want you to pray this one through," he says. "We have a lot of people here from a lot of different fellowships, but we're all one body. Amen?" They don't like it. He gets a few polite Amens. We sing:

> *Bind us together, Lord,*
> *With a bond that can't be broken;*
> *Bind us together, Lord,*
> *With love.*

Everyone seems to be in a remarkably foul mood today. We don't like this song. There is no one here under seventeen, and, I think, no one here who believes that love is a bond that can't be broken. We sing the song through three times; then it is time to go.

The leader calls after our retreating backs, "Hey, have a good day! 24 Praise Him all day!" The kids around me roll up their eyes privately. Some groan; all flee.

The next morning is very cold. I am here early. Two girls are talk- 25 ing on the fountain's rim; one is part Indian. She says, "I've got all the Old Testament, but I can't get the New. I screw up the New." She takes a breath and rattles off a long list, ending with "Jonah, Micah, Nahum, Habakkuk, Zephaniah, Haggai, Zechariah, Malachi." The other girl produces a slow, sarcastic applause. I ask one of the girls to help me with the words to a song. She is agreeable, but says, "I'm sorry, I can't. I just became a Christian this year, so I don't know all the words yet."

The others are coming; we stand and separate. The boy with the 26 moustache is gone, replaced by a big, serious fellow in a green down jacket. The bouncy girl is back with her guitar; she's wearing a skirt and wool knee socks. We begin, without any preamble, by singing a song that has so few words that we actually stretch one syllable over eleven separate notes. Then we sing a song in which the men sing one phrase and the women echo it. Everyone seems to know just what to do. In the context of our vapid songs, the lyrics of this one are extraordinary:

> *I was nothing before you found me.*
> *Heartache! Broken people! Ruined lives*
> *Is why you died on Calvary.*

The last line rises in a regular series of half-notes. Now at last some people are actually singing; they throw some breath into the business. There is a seriousness and urgency to it: "Heartache! Broken people! Ruined lives . . . I was nothing."

We don't look like nothing. We look like a bunch of students of every stripe, ill-shaven or well-shaven, dressed up or down, but dressed warmly against the cold: jeans and parkas, jeans and heavy sweaters, jeans and scarves and blow-dried hair. We look ordinary. But I think, quite on my own, that we are here because we know this business of nothingness, brokenness, and ruination. We sing this song over and over. 27

Something catches my eye. Behind us, up in the science building, professors are standing alone at opened windows. 28

The long brick science building has three upper floors of faculty offices, thirty-two windows. At one window stands a bearded man, about forty; his opening his window is what caught my eye. He stands full in the open window, his hands on his hips, his head cocked down toward the fountain. He is drawn to look, as I was drawn to come. Up on the building's top floor, at the far right window, there is another: an Asian-American professor, wearing a white shirt, is sitting with one hip on his desk, looking out and down. In the middle of the row of windows, another one, an old professor in a checked shirt, stands sideways to the opened window, stands stock-still, his long, old ear to the air. Now another window cranks open, another professor—or maybe a graduate student—leans out, his hands on the sill. 29

We are all singing, and I am watching these five still men, my colleagues, whose office doors are surely shut—for that is the custom here: five of them alone in their offices in the science building who have opened their windows on this very cold morning, who motionless hear the Fundamentalists sing, utterly unknown to each other. 30

We sing another four songs, including the clapping song, and one which repeats, "This is the day which the Lord hath made; rejoice and be glad in it." All the professors but one stay by their opened windows, figures in a frieze. When after ten minutes we break off and scatter, each cranks his window shut. Maybe they have nine o'clock classes too. 31

* * *

I miss a few sessions. One morning of the following week, I rejoin 32 the Fundamentalists on the Square. The wind is blowing from the north; it is sunny and cold. There are several new developments.

Someone has blown up rubber gloves and floated them in the 33 fountain. I saw them yesterday afternoon from my high office window, and couldn't quite make them out: I seemed to see hands in the fountain waving from side to side, like those hands wagging on springs which people stick in the back windows of their cars. I saw these many years ago in Quito and Guayaquil, where they were a great fad long before they showed up here. The cardboard hands said, on their palms, HOLA GENTE, hello people. Some of them just said HOLA, hello, with a little wave to the universe at large, in case anybody happened to be looking. It is like our sending radio signals to planets in other galaxies: HOLA, if anyone is listening. Jolly folk, these Ecuadorians, I thought.

Now, waiting by the fountain for the singing, I see that these particular 34 hands are long surgical gloves, yellow and white, ten of them, tied off at the cuff. They float upright and they wave, *hola, hola, hola;* they mill around like a crowd, bobbing under the fountain's spray and back again to the pool's rim, *hola.* It is a good prank. It is far too cold for the university's maintenance crew to retrieve them without turning off the fountain and putting on rubber boots.

From all around the Square, people are gathering for the singing. 35 There is no way I can guess which kids, from among the masses crossing the Square, will veer off to the fountain. When they get here, I never recognize anybody except the leaders.

The singing begins without ado as usual, but there is something 36 different about it. The students are growing prayerful, and they show it this morning with a peculiar gesture. I'm glad they weren't like this when I first joined them, or I never would have stayed.

Last night there was an educational television special, part of 37 "Middletown."[4] It was a segment called "Community of Praise," and I watched it because it was about Fundamentalists. It showed a Jesus-loving family in the Midwest; the treatment was good and complex. This family attended the prayer meetings, healing sessions, and church services of an unnamed sect—a very low-church sect, whose doctrine and culture were much more low-church than those of the kids I sing with. When the members of this sect prayed, they held their arms over their heads and raised their palms, as if to feel or receive a blessing or energy from above.

Now today on the Square there is a new serious mood. The leaders 38 are singing with their eyes shut. I am impressed that they can bang their guitars, keep their balance, and not fall into the pool. It is the

4. "Middletown": a 1983 PBS series that updated a book published in 1929, *Middletown: A Study in Contemporary American Culture,* by Robert and Helen Merrell Lynd.

same bouncy girl and earnest boy. Their eyeballs are rolled back a bit. I look around and see that almost everyone in this crowd of eighty or so has his eyes shut and is apparently praying the words of this song or praying some other prayer.

Now as the chorus rises, as it gets louder and higher and simpler in   39
melody—

> *I exalt thee,*
> *I exalt thee,*
> *I exalt thee,*
> *Thou art the Lord—*

then, at this moment, hands start rising. All around me, hands are going up—that tall girl, that blond boy with his head back, the red-headed boy up front, the girl with the McDonald's jacket. Their arms rise as if pulled on strings. Some few of them have raised their arms very high over their heads and are tilting back their palms. Many, many more of them, as inconspicuously as possible, have raised their hands to the level of their chins.

What is going on? Why are these students today raising their   40
palms in this gesture, when nobody did it last week? Is it because the leaders have set a prayerful tone this morning? Is it because this gesture always accompanies this song, just as clapping accompanies other songs? Or is it, as I suspect, that these kids watched the widely publicized documentary last night just as I did; and are adopting, or trying out, the gesture?

It is a sunny morning, and the sun is rising behind the leaders and   41
the fountain, so those students have their heads tilted, eyes closed, and palms upraised toward the sun. I glance up at the science building and think my own prayer: thank God no one is watching this.

The leaders cannot move around much on the fountain's rim. The   42
girl has her eyes shut; the boy opens his eyes from time to time, glances at the neck of his guitar, and closes his eyes again.

When the song is over, the hands go down, and there is some   43
desultory chatting in the crowd, as usual: can I borrow your library card? And, as usual, nobody looks at anybody.

All our songs today are serious. There is a feudal theme to them, or   44
a feudal analogue:

> *I will eat from abundance of your household.*
> *I will dream beside your streams of righteousness.*
>
> *You are my king.*
>
> *Enter his gates*
> *with thanksgiving in your heart;*
> *come before his courts with praise.*

He is the king of kings

Thou art the Lord.

All around me, eyes are closed and hands are raised. There is no   45
social pressure to do this, or anything else. I've never known any
group to be less cohesive, imposing fewer controls. Since no one looks
at anyone, and since passersby no longer look, everyone out here is in-
conspicuous and free. Perhaps the palm-raising has begun because the
kids realize by now that they are not on display; they're praying in
their closets, right out here on the Square. Over the course of the next
weeks, I will learn that the palm-raising is here to stay.

The sun is rising higher. We are singing our last song. We are pray-   46
ing. We are alone together.

> *He is my peace*
> *Who has broken down every wall . . .*

When the song is over, the hands go down. The heads lower, the   47
eyes open and blink. We stay still a second before we break up. We
have been standing in a broad current; now we have stepped aside. We
have dismantled the radar cups; we have closed the telescope's vault.
Students gather their book bags and go. The two leaders step down
from the fountain's rim and pack away their guitars. Everyone scatters.
I am in no hurry, so I stay after everyone is gone. It is after nine
o'clock, and the Square is deserted. The fountain is playing to an
empty house. In the pool the cheerful hands are waving over the
water, bobbing under the fountain's veil and out again in the current,
hola.

PERRI KLASS

Learning the Language

Perri Klass (1958–   ) graduated from Harvard Medical School in
1986. During her years as a medical student, she not only published a
novel (*Recombinations,*1985) and gave birth to a son but also contributed essays to *Mademoiselle, Discover, Massachusetts Medicine,* and *The
New York Times.* These essays gave a fresh and sometimes discomfort-
ing picture of medical school education; several were later collected
in *A Not Entirely Benign Procedure: Four Years as a Medical Student*
(1987). In 1990 she published a second novel, *Other Women's Children,*
and in 1992 continued the story of her medical training with *Baby
Doctor,* an account of her years as a pediatric resident. Now a practicing pediatrician, Klass is also a regular contributor of articles and sto-

ries to several magazines. Klass says that writing about medical
school while going through it changed the nature of the experience:
"I have found that in order to write about my training so that people
outside the medical profession can understand what I am talking
about I have had to preserve a certain level of naiveté for myself." In
"Learning the Language," first published in the "Hers" column of *The
New York Times* in 1984, Klass's naiveté allows her to see some hidden
functions of medical jargon. Like Orwell's "Shooting an Elephant,"
this essay looks at the problem of exclusion from the perspective of
someone in a privileged position.

"Mrs. Tolstoy is your basic LOL in NAD, admitted for a soft rule-   1
out MI," the intern announces. I scribble that on my patient list. In
other words, Mrs. Tolstoy is a Little Old Lady in No Apparent Distress
who is in the hospital to make sure she hasn't had a heart attack (rule
out a Myocardial Infarction). And we think it's unlikely that she has
had a heart attack (a *soft* rule-out).

If I learned nothing else during my first three months of working   2
in the hospital as a medical student, I learned endless jargon and ab-
breviations. I started out in a state of primeval innocence, in which I
didn't even know that "s̄ CP, SOB, N/V" meant "without chest pain,
shortness of breath, or nausea and vomiting." By the end I took the ab-
breviations so much for granted that I would complain to my mother
the English professor, "And can you believe I had to put down *three* NG
tubes last night?"

"You'll have to tell me what an NG tube is if you want me to sym-   3
pathize properly," my mother said. NG, nasogastric—isn't it obvious?

I picked up not only the specific expressions but also the patterns   4
of speech and the grammatical conventions; for example, you never
say that a patient's blood pressure fell or that his cardiac enzymes rose.
Instead, the patient is always the subject of the verb: "He dropped his
pressure." "He bumped his enzymes." This sort of construction probably reflects the profound irritation of the intern when the nurses come
in the middle of the night to say that Mr. Dickinson has disturbingly
low blood pressure. "Oh, he's gonna hurt me bad tonight," the intern
might say, inevitably angry at Mr. Dickinson for dropping his pressure
and creating a problem.

When chemotherapy fails to cure Mrs. Bacon's cancer, what we   5
say is, "Mrs. Bacon failed chemotherapy."

"Well, we've already had one hit today, and we're up next, but at   6
least we've got mostly stable players on our team." This means that
our team (group of doctors and medical students) has already gotten
one new admission today, and it is our turn again, so we'll get who-

ever is admitted next in emergency, but at least most of the patients we already have are fairly stable, that is, unlikely to drop their pressures or in any other way get suddenly sicker and hurt us bad. Baseball metaphor is pervasive. A no-hitter is a night without any new admissions. A player is always a patient—a nitrate player is a patient on nitrates, a unit player is a patient in the intensive care unit, and so on, until you reach the terminal player.

It is interesting to consider what it means to be winning, or doing 7 well, in this perennial baseball game. When the intern hangs up the phone and announces, "I got a hit," that is not cause for congratulations. The team is not scoring points; rather, it is getting hit, being bombarded with new patients. The object of the game from the point of view of the doctors, considering the players for whom they are already responsible, is to get as few new hits as possible.

This special language contributes to a sense of closeness and pro- 8 fessional spirit among people who are under a great deal of stress. As a medical student, I found it exciting to discover that I'd finally cracked the code, that I could understand what doctors said and wrote, and could use the same formulations myself. Some people seem to become enamored of the jargon for its own sake, perhaps because they are so deeply thrilled with the idea of medicine, with the idea of themselves as doctors.

I knew a medical student who was referred to by the interns on 9 the team as Mr. Eponym because he was so infatuated with eponymous terminology, the more obscure the better. He never said "capillary pulsations" if he could say "Quincke's pulses." He would lovingly tell over the multinamed syndromes—Wolff-Parkinson-White, Lown-Ganong-Levine, Schönlein- Henoch—until the temptation to suggest Schleswig-Holstein or Stevenson-Kefauver or Baskin-Robbins became irresistible to his less reverent colleagues.

And there is the jargon that you don't ever want to hear yourself 10 using. You know that your training is changing you, but there are certain changes you think would be going a little too far.

The resident was describing a man with devastating terminal pan- 11 creatic cancer. "Basically he's CTD," the resident concluded. I reminded myself that I had resolved not to be shy about asking when I didn't understand things. "CTD?" I asked timidly.

The resident smirked at me. "Circling The Drain."   12

The images are vivid and terrible. "What happened to Mrs. 13 Melville?"

"Oh, she boxed last night." To box is to die, of course.   14

Then there are the more pompous locutions that can make the be- 15 ginning medical student nervous about the effects of medical training. A friend of mine was told by his resident, "A pregnant woman with sickle-cell represents a failure of genetic counseling."

Mr. Eponym, who tried hard to talk like the doctors, once ex-   16
plained to me, "An infant is basically a brainstem preparation." The
term "brainstem preparation," as used in neurological research, refers
to an animal whose higher brain functions have been destroyed so
that only the most primitive reflexes remain, like the sucking reflex,
the startle reflex, and the rooting reflex.

And yet at other times the harshness dissipates into a strangely elu-   17
sive euphemism. "As you know, this is a not entirely benign procedure," some doctor will say, and that will be understood to imply agony,
risk of complications, and maybe even a significant mortality rate.

The more extreme forms aside, one most important function of   18
medical jargon is to help doctors maintain some distance from their
patients. By reformulating a patient's pain and problems into a language that the patient doesn't even speak, I suppose we are in some
sense taking those pains and problems under our jurisdiction and also
reducing their emotional impact. This linguistic separation between
doctors and patients allows conversations to go on at the bedside that
are unintelligible to the patient. "Naturally, we're worried about
adeno-CA," the intern can say to the medical student, and lung cancer
need never be mentioned.

I learned a new language this past summer. At times it thrills me to   19
hear myself using it. It enables me to understand my colleagues, to
communicate effectively in the hospital. Yet I am uncomfortably aware
that I will never again notice the peculiarities and even atrocities of
medical language as keenly as I did this summer. There may be specific
expressions I manage to avoid, but even as I remark them, promising
myself I will never use them, I find that this language is becoming my
professional speech. It no longer sounds strange in my ears—or coming from my mouth. And I am afraid that as with any new language, to
use it properly you must absorb not only the vocabulary but also the
structure, the logic, the attitudes. At first you may notice these new
and alien assumptions every time you put together a sentence, but
with time and increased fluency you stop being aware of them at all.
And as you lose that awareness, for better or for worse, you move
closer and closer to being a doctor instead of just talking like one.

LILIANA HEKER

The Stolen Party

Liliana Heker (1943–   ), born in Buenos Aires, began writing as a teenager. Her first book of short stories, *Los que vieron la zarza* (*Those Who Beheld the Burning Bush*), was published in 1966, and she has been writing ever since. Most of Heker's career has been devoted to serving as editor in chief for *El ornitorrinco* (*The Platypus*), a literary magazine that survived years of chaos in Argentina's civil life. In addition to short stories, Heker writes novels; her second, *Zona de clivaje* (*Zone of Cleavage*, 1987), won the Buenos Aires Municipal Prize. In her journalism and fiction, Heker encourages loyalty to Argentina, believing that writers should stay in the country and work to improve it rather than writing about its problems in exile. "The Stolen Party" was translated into English by Alberto Manguel for his *Other Fires. Short Fiction by Latin American Women* (1986). Readers may be painfully reminded of episodes from their own childhood as they read this story, and those very episodes could become germs of strong personal essays.

As soon as she arrived she went straight to the kitchen to see if the   1
monkey was there. It was: what a relief! She wouldn't have liked to admit that her mother had been right. *Monkeys at a birthday?* her mother had sneered. *Get away with you, believing any nonsense you're told!* She was cross, but not because of the monkey, the girl thought; it's just because of the party.

"I don't like you going," she told her. "It's a rich people's party."   2

"Rich people go to Heaven too," said the girl, who studied religion   3
at school.

"Get away with Heaven," said the mother. "The problem with you,   4
young lady, is that you like to fart higher than your ass."

The girl didn't approve of the way her mother spoke. She was   5
barely nine, and one of the best in her class.

"I'm going because I've been invited," she said. "And I've been in-   6
vited because Luciana is my friend. So there."

"Ah yes, your friend," her mother grumbled. She paused. "Listen,   7
Rosaura," she said at last. "That one's not your friend. You know what you are to them? The maid's daughter, that's what."

Rosaura blinked hard: she wasn't going to cry. Then she yelled: 8
"Shut up! You know nothing about being friends!"

Every afternoon she used to go to Luciana's house and they would   9
both finish their homework while Rosaura's mother did the cleaning.

They had their tea in the kitchen and they told each other secrets. Rosaura loved everything in the big house, and she also loved the people who lived there.

"I'm going because it will be the most lovely party in the whole 10 world, Luciana told me it would. There will be a magician, and he will bring a monkey and everything."

The mother swung around to take a good look at her child, and 11 pompously put her hands on her hips.

"Monkeys at a birthday?" she said. "Get away with you, believing 12 any nonsense you're told!"

Rosaura was deeply offended. She thought it unfair of her mother 13 to accuse other people of being liars simply because they were rich. Rosaura too wanted to be rich, of course. If one day she managed to live in a beautiful palace, would her mother stop loving her? She felt very sad. She wanted to go to that party more than anything else in the world.

"I'll die if I don't go," she whispered, almost without moving her 14 lips.

And she wasn't sure whether she had been heard, but on the 15 morning of the party she discovered that her mother had starched her Christmas dress. And in the afternoon, after washing her hair, her mother rinsed it in apple vinegar so that it would be all nice and shiny. Before going out, Rosaura admired herself in the mirror, with her white dress and glossy hair, and thought she looked terribly pretty

Señora Ines also seemed to notice. As soon as she saw her, she said: 16
"How lovely you look today, Rosaura." 17

Rosaura gave her starched skirt a slight toss with her hands and 18 walked into the party with a firm step. She said hello to Luciana and asked about the monkey. Luciana put on a secretive look and whispered into Rosaura's ear: "He's in the kitchen. But don't tell anyone, because it's a surprise."

Rosaura wanted to make sure. Carefully she entered the kitchen 19 and there she saw it: deep in thought, inside its cage. It looked so funny that the girl stood there for a while, watching it, and later, every so often, she would slip out of the party unseen and go and admire it. Rosaura was the only one allowed into the kitchen. Señora Ines had said: "You yes, but not the others, they're much too boisterous, they might break something." Rosaura had never broken anything. She even managed the jug of orange juice, carrying it from the kitchen into the dining room. She held it carefully and didn't spill a single drop. And Señora Ines had said: "Are you sure you can manage a jug as big as that?" Of course she could manage. She wasn't a butterfingers, like the others. Like that blonde girl with the bow in her hair. As soon as she saw Rosaura, the girl with the bow had said:

"And you? Who are you?" 20

"I'm a friend of Luciana," said Rosaura.   21

"No," said the girl with the bow, "you are not a friend of Luciana be-   22
cause I'm her cousin and I know all her friends. And I don't know you."

"So what," said Rosaura. "I come here every afternoon with my   23
mother and we do our homework together."

"You and your mother do your homework together?" asked the   24
girl, laughing.

"I and Luciana do our homework together," said Rosaura, very se-   25
riously.

The girl with the bow shrugged her shoulders.   26

"That's not being friends," she said. "Do you go to school together?"   27
"No."   28

"So where do you know her from?" said the girl, getting impatient.   29

Rosaura remembered her mother's words perfectly. She took a   30
deep breath.

"I'm the daughter of the employee," she said.   31

Her mother had said very clearly: "If someone asks, you say you're   32
the daughter of the employee, that's all." She also told her to add:
"And proud of it." But Rosaura thought that never in her life would
she dare to say something of the sort.

"What employee?" said the girl with the bow. "Employee in a   33
shop?"

"No," said Rosaura angrily. "My mother doesn't sell anything in   34
any shop, so there."

So how come she's an employee?" said the girl with the bow.   35

Just then Señora Ines arrived saying *shh shh*, and asked Rosaura if   36
she wouldn't mind helping serve out the hot-dogs, as she knew the
house so much better than the others.

"See?" said Rosaura to the girl with the bow, and when no one   37
was looking she kicked her in the shin.

Apart from the girl with the bow, all the others were delightful.   38
The one she liked best was Luciana, with her golden birthday crown;
and then the boys. Rosaura won the sack race, and nobody managed
to catch her when they played tag. When they split into two teams to
play charades, all the boys wanted her for their side. Rosaura felt she
had never been so happy in all her life.

But the best was still to come. The best came after Luciana blew   39
out the candles. First the cake. Señora Ines had asked her to help pass
the cake around, and Rosaura had enjoyed the task immensely, because everyone called out to her, shouting "Me, me!" Rosaura remembered a story in which there was a queen who had the power of life or
death over her subjects. She had always loved that, having the power
of life or death. To Luciana and the boys she gave the largest pieces,
and to the girl with the bow she gave a slice so thin one could see
through it.

After the cake came the magician, tall and bony, with a fine red 40
cape. A true magician: he could untie handkerchiefs by blowing on
them and make a chain with links that had no openings. He could
guess what cards were pulled out from a pack, and the monkey was his
assistant. He called the monkey "partner." "Let's see here, partner," he
would say, "Turn over a card." And, "Don't run away, partner; time to
work now."

The final trick was wonderful. One of the children had to hold the 41
monkey in his arms and the magician said he would make him disappear.

"What, the boy?" they all shouted. 42

"No, the monkey!" shouted back the magician. 43

Rosaura thought that this was truly the most amusing party in the 44
whole world.

The magician asked a small fat boy to come and help, but the small 45
fat boy got frightened almost at once and dropped the monkey on the
floor. The magician picked him up carefully, whispered something in
his ear, and the monkey nodded almost as if he understood.

"You mustn't be so unmanly, my friend," the magician said to the 46
fat boy.

"What's unmanly?" said the fat boy. 47

The magician turned around as if to look for spies. 48

"A sissy," said the magician. "Go sit down." 49

Then he stared at all the faces, one by one. Rosaura felt her heart 50
tremble.

"You, with the Spanish eyes," said the magician. And everyone 51
saw that he was pointing at her.

She wasn't afraid. Neither holding the monkey, nor when the ma- 52
gician made him vanish; not even when, at the end, the magician flung
his red cape over Rosaura's head and uttered a few magic words . . .
and the monkey reappeared, chattering happily, in her arms. The children clapped furiously. And before Rosaura returned to her seat, the
magician said:

"Thank you very much, my little countess." 53

She was so pleased with the compliment that a while later, when 54
her mother came to fetch her, that was the first thing she told her.

"I helped the magician and he said to me, 'Thank you very much, 55
my little countess.'"

It was strange because up to then Rosaura had thought that she was 56
angry with her mother. All along Rosaura had imagined that she would
say to her: "See that the monkey wasn't a lie?" But instead she was so
thrilled that she told her mother all about the wonderful magician.

Her mother tapped her on the head and said: "So now we're a 57
countess!"

But one could see that she was beaming.   58

And now they both stood in the entrance, because a moment ago   59
Señora Ines, smiling, had said: "Please wait here a second."

Her mother suddenly seemed worried.   60

"What is it?" she asked Rosaura.   61

"What is what?" said Rosaura. "It's nothing; she just wants to get   62
the presents for those who are leaving, see?"

She pointed at the fat boy and at a girl with pigtails who were also   63
waiting there, next to their mothers. And she explained about the presents. She knew, because she had been watching those who left before
her. When one of the girls was about to leave, Señora Ines would give
her a bracelet. When a boy left, Señora Ines gave him a yo-yo. Rosaura
preferred the yo-yo because it sparkled, but she didn't mention that to
her mother. Her mother might have said: "So why don't you ask for
one, you blockhead?" That's what her mother was like. Rosaura didn't
feel like explaining that she'd be horribly ashamed to be the odd one
out. Instead she said:

"I was the best-behaved at the party."   64

And she said no more because Señora Ines came out into the hall   65
with two bags, one pink and one blue.

First she went up to the fat boy, gave him a yo-yo out of the blue   66
bag, and the fat boy left with his mother. Then she went up to the girl
and gave her a bracelet out of the pink bag, and the girl with the pigtails left as well.

Finally she came up to Rosaura and her mother. She had a big   67
smile on her face and Rosaura liked that. Señora Ines looked down at
her, then looked up at her mother, and then said something that made
Rosaura proud:

"What a marvellous daughter you have, Herminia."   68

For an instant, Rosaura thought that she'd give her two presents: 69
the bracelet and the yo-yo. Señora Ines bent down as if about to look
for something. Rosaura also leaned forward, stretching out her arm.
But she never completed the movement.

Señora Ines didn't look in the pink bag. Nor did she look in the   70
blue bag. Instead she rummaged in her purse. In her hand appeared
two bills.

"You really and truly earned this," she said handing them over.   71
"Thank you for all your help, my pet."

Rosaura felt her arms stiffen, stick close to her body, and then she   72
noticed her mother's hand on her shoulder. Instinctively she pressed
herself against her mother's body. That was all. Except her eyes.
Rosaura's eyes had a cold, clear look that fixed itself on Señora Ines's
face.

Señora Ines, motionless, stood there with her hand outstretched.   73

As if she didn't dare draw it back. As if the slightest change might shatter an infinitely delicate balance.

Translated by Alberto Manguel

LANGSTON HUGHES

Theme for English B

Poet, playwright, novelist, translator, and lecturer, Langston Hughes (1902–1967) was born in Joplin, Missouri. An influential literary figure of the Harlem Renaissance, Hughes attended Columbia University (1921–1922) and received an A.B. from Lincoln University (1929). His best-known works include *The Weary Blues* (1926), *Not without Laughter* (1930), and *Montage of a Dream Deferred* (1951). In "The Negro Artist and the Racial Mountain" (1926) Hughes wrote, "to my mind, it is the duty of the younger Negro artist, if he accepts any duties at all from outsiders, to change through the force of his art that old whispering 'I want to be white,' hidden in the aspirations of his people, to 'why should I want to be white?'" The same strong sense of a connection between racial and personal identity shows in "Theme for English B," a poem published in 1949, more than a decade before the civil rights movement changed American assumptions about relations between races.

The instructor said,

Go home and write
a page tonight.
And let that page come out of you—
Then, it will be true. 5

I wonder if it's that simple?
I am twenty-two, colored, born in Winston-Salem.
I went to school there, then Durham, then here
to this college[1] on the hill above Harlem.
I am the only colored student in my class. 10
The steps from the hill lead down into Harlem,
through a park, then I cross St. Nicholas,
Eighth Avenue, Seventh, and I come to the Y,
the Harlem Branch Y, where I take the elevator
up to my room, sit down, and write this page:

---

1. college: Columbia University

It's not easy to know what is true for you or me   15
at twenty-two, my age. But I guess I'm what
I feel and see and hear, Harlem, I hear you:
hear you, hear me—we two—you, me, talk on this page:

(I hear New York, too.) Me—who?   20
Well, I like to eat, sleep, drink, and be in love.
I like to work, read, learn, and understand life.
I like a pipe for a Christmas present,
or records—Bessie,[2] bop, or Bach.
I guess being colored doesn't make me *not* like   25
the same things other folks like who are other races.
So will my page be colored that I write?
Being me, it will not be white.
But it will be
A part of you, instructor.   30
You are white—
yet a part of me, as I am a part of you.
That's American.
Sometimes perhaps you don't want to be a part of me.
Nor do I often want to be a part of you.   35
But we are, that's true!
As I learn from you,
I guess you learn from me—
although you're older—and white—
and somewhat more free.   40

This is my page for English B.

2. Bessie: Bessie Smith (1894–1937), the great blues singer.

NATURE AND CIVILIZATION

We find ourselves among the beasts.

Overview

Asking whether humans live in nature or in civilization is in some ways like asking whether they walk on their left feet or on their right. Since Darwin's time, we have come to know ourselves as well-dressed apes, bundles of animal instincts barely covered by the veneer of civilization. On the other hand, what we *know* is not always what we *feel*, and these days more and more of us feel that our "natural" environment is indoors, in rooms without weather or insects or decay. Close encounters with even little fragments of the natural world can feel uncomfortable, yet most of us cannot shake off a deep, perhaps even spiritual, connection to nature—even if we prefer to experience it outside the cage bars at the zoo or behind glass in a moving car. From a variety of perspectives, the essays in this unit offer us intense observation of creatures, both human and nonhuman, and insight into their interactions with one another.

And then, occasionally, when he came up for apples, or I took apples to him, he looked at me. It was a look so piercing, so full of grief, a look so *human*, I almost laughed (I felt too sad to cry) to think there are people who do not know that animals suffer.

My grandmother in Bacon County, Georgia, raised biddies: tiny cheeping bits of fluff that city folk allow their children to squeeze to death at Easter. But city children are not the only ones who love biddies; hawks love them, too.

"We evolved over millions of years in the wild, where survival depended on our awareness of the landscape, the weather, and the animals. We haven't been domesticated long enough to have lost those senses. . . . We can design a zoo that will make the hair stand up on the back of your neck."

The notion that "nature" and "nature study" are somehow "nice" for children, regardless of the children's own temperament, is a sentimental piety—and often a hypocritical one, like the piety which thinks Sunday School nice for *them* though we don't go to church ourselves.

I will begin to feel better about us, and about our future, when we finally start learning about some of the things that are still mystifications. Start with the events in the mind of a cricket, I'd say, and then go on from there. Comprehend my cat Jeoffry and we'll be on our way.

The questions asked by animal-rights activists are flawed, because they are built on the concept that the origin of rights is in the avoidance of suffering rather than in the pursuit of happiness.

"Turtle, I believe I got you and you got me," Homer said. He slipped a turn of rope around his left foot with his free arm. He kept pulling back as hard as he could to free his sleeve but the turtle had it. "I understand you, Turtle," he said, "you don't like to let go."

RANDALL JARRELL   Field and Forest   423

The boy stands looking at the fox
As if, if he looked long enough—

                                        he looks at it
Or is it the fox that's looking at the boy?
The trees can't tell the two of them apart.

E. B. WHITE

Twins

E(lwyn) B(rooks) White (1899–1985), after failing as a newspaper reporter, became the principal writer of short comments for *The New
Yorker.* Harold Ross, the magazine's founder and editor, insisted that
these comments be unsigned and employ the editorial *we*, a practice
that, White complained, could make the writer sound like "a composite personality." White, however, retained his singularity and his
sanity: "Once in a while we think of ourself as 'we,' but not often." In
1938 White and his wife, Katharine Angell, moved to a farm in
Maine, now famous as the setting of *Charlotte's Web* (1952), and
White temporarily left *The New Yorker* to write monthly essays for
Harper's, which are collected in *One Man's Meat* (1942). Other important collections include *The Second Tree from the Corner* (1954) and *Essays of E. B. White* (1977).

   "Twins," originally published as an unsigned comment in *The
New Yorker* on June 12, 1948, shows White at the top of his form. By
using contrasting images to illuminate the tension between nature
and civilization, he provides a model of descriptive writing. A useful
companion essay is Annie Dillard's "The Fixed," in which contact
with nature is less idyllic than what White describes.

On a warm, miserable morning last week we went up to the Bronx   1
Zoo to see the moose calf and to break in a new pair of black shoes. We
encountered better luck than we had bargained for. The cow moose
and her young one were standing near the wall of the deer park below
the monkey house, and in order to get a better view we strolled down
to the lower end of the park, by the brook. The path there is not much
travelled. As we approached the corner where the brook trickles under
the wire fence, we noticed a red deer getting to her feet. Beside her, on
legs that were just learning their business, was a spotted fawn, as small
and perfect as a trinket seen though a reducing glass. They stood there,
mother and child, under a gray beech whose trunk was engraved with
dozens of hearts and initials. Stretched on the ground was another
fawn, and we realized that the doe had just finished twinning. The second fawn was still wet, still unrisen. Here was a scene of rare sylvan
splendor, in one of our five favorite boroughs, and we couldn't have
asked for more. Even our new shoes seemed to be working out all
right and weren't hurting much.

   The doe was only a couple of feet from the wire, and we sat down   2
on a rock at the edge of the footpath to see what sort of start young
fawns get in the deep fastnesses of Mittel Bronx. The mother, mildly
resentful of our presence and dazed from her labor, raised one forefoot

and stamped primly. Then she lowered her head, picked up the after-birth, and began dutifully to eat it, allowing it to swing crazily from her mouth, as though it were a bunch of withered beet greens. From the monkey house came the loud, insane hooting of some captious primate, filling the whole woodland with a wild hooroar. As we watched, the sun broke weakly through, brightened the rich red of the fawns, and kindled their white spots. Occasionally a sightseer would appear and wander aimlessly by, but of all who passed none was aware that anything extraordinary had occurred. "Looka the kangaroos!" a child cried. And he and his mother stared sullenly at the deer and then walked on.

In a few moments the second twin gathered all his legs and all his   3
ingenuity and arose, to stand for the first time sniffing the mysteries of a park for captive deer. The doe, in recognition of his achievement, quit her other work and began to dry him, running her tongue against the grain and paying particular attention to the key points. Meanwhile the first fawn tiptoed toward the shallow brook, in little stops and goes, and started across. He paused midstream to make a slight contribution, as a child does in bathing. Then, while his mother watched, he continued across, gained the other side, selected a hiding place, and lay down under a skunk-cabbage leaf next to the fence, in perfect concealment, his legs folded neatly under him. Without actually going out of sight, he had managed to disappear completely in the shifting light and shade. From somewhere a long way off a twelve-o'clock whistle sounded. We hung around awhile, but he never budged. Before we left, we crossed the brook ourself, just outside the fence, knelt, reached through the wire, and tested the truth of what we had once heard: that you can scratch a new fawn between the ears without starting him. You can indeed.

ANNIE DILLARD

The Fixed

Annie Dillard was born in 1945, in Pittsburgh. She is the author of nine books including *An American Childhood, The Writing Life,* and *Holy the Firm. The Living,* a novel, is the story of four men on the coast of Puget Sound in the second half of the nineteenth century. In 1975, *Pilgrim at Tinker Creek* was awarded the Pulitzer Prize in nonfiction. Her writing appears in the *Atlantic, Harper's,* the *New York Times Magazine,* the *Yale Review, American Heritage,* and in many anthologies. She has received fellowship grants from the Guggenheim Foundation and the National Endowment for the Arts; her writing has received the Washington Governor's Award, the Connecticut Governor's Award, the New York Press Club Award, and the Ambassador Book Award in Arts and Letters from the English-Speaking Union.

She lives in Middletown, Connecticut, with her husband, Robert
D. Richardson, Jr., biographer of Thoreau and Emerson, and young
daughter Rosie.

Pilgrim at Tinker Creek, from which "The Fixed" is excerpted, is a
guidebook to the author's neighborhood: Its most common gesture is
a pointing finger and a plea for us to look at what we commonly
overlook. If we follow her instructions, we discover again that our
neighborhood is the earth and that our relationship with our neighbors is often troubling. Because Harry Crews's "Pages from the Life of
a Georgia Innocent" also peers undauntedly into brutal aspects of our
connection to nature, it makes a useful companion essay.

I have just learned to see praying mantis egg cases. Suddenly I see   1
them everywhere; a tan oval of light catches my eye, or I notice a blob
of thickness in a patch of slender weeds. As I write I can see the one I
tied to the mock orange hedge outside my study window. It is over an
inch long and shaped like a bell, or like the northern hemisphere of an
egg cut through its equator. The full length of one of its long sides is affixed to a twig; the side that catches the light is perfectly flat. It has a
dead straw, deadweed color, and a curious brittle texture, hard as varnish, but pitted minutely, like frozen foam. I carried it home this afternoon, holding it carefully by the twig, along with several others—they
were light as air. I dropped one without missing it until I got home and
made a count.

Within the week I've seen thirty or so of these egg cases in a rose-   2
grown field on Tinker Mountain, and another thirty in weeds along
Carvin's Creek. One was on a twig of tiny dogwood on the mud lawn
of a newly built house. I think the mail-order houses sell them to gar-
deners at a dollar apiece. It beats spraying, because each case contains
between one hundred twenty-five to three hundred fifty eggs. If the
eggs survive ants, woodpeckers, and mice—and most do—then you
get the fun of seeing the new mantises hatch, and the smug feeling of
knowing, all summer long, that they're out there in your garden de-
vouring gruesome numbers of fellow insects all nice and organically.
When a mantis has crunched up the last shred of its victim, it cleans its
smooth green face like a cat.

In late summer I often see a winged adult stalking the insects that   3
swarm about my porch light. Its body is a clear, warm green; its naked,
triangular head can revolve uncannily, so that I often see one twist its
head to gaze at me as it were over its shoulder. When it strikes, it jerks
so suddenly and with such a fearful clatter of raised wings, that even a
hardened entomologist like J. Henri Fabre[1] confessed to being startled
witless every time.

1. Fabre: a noted French observer of the behavior of insects (1823–1915).

Adult mantises eat more or less everything that breathes and is   4
small enough to capture. They eat honeybees and butterflies, including monarch butterflies. People have actually seen them seize and devour garter snakes, mice, and even *hummingbirds*. Newly hatched
mantises, on the other hand, eat small creatures like aphids and each
other. When I was in elementary school, one of the teachers brought
in a mantis egg case in a Mason jar. I watched the newly hatched mantises emerge and shed their skins; they were spidery and translucent,
all over joints. They trailed from the egg case to the base of the Mason
jar in a living bridge that looked like Arabic calligraphy, some baffling
text from the Koran inscribed down the air by a fine hand. Over a period of several hours, during which time the teacher never summoned
the nerve or the sense to release them, they ate each other until only
two were left. Tiny legs were still kicking from the mouths of both. The
two survivors grappled and sawed in the Mason jar; finally both died
of injuries. I felt as though I myself should swallow the corpses, shutting my eyes and washing them down like jagged pills, so all that life
wouldn't be lost.

When mantises hatch in the wild, however, they straggle about   5
prettily, dodging ants, till all are lost in the grass. So it was in hopes of
seeing an eventual hatch that I pocketed my jackknife this afternoon
before I set out to walk. Now that I can see the egg cases, I'm embarrassed to realize how many I must have missed all along. I walked east
through the Adams' woods to the cornfield, cutting three undamaged
egg cases I found at the edge of the field. It was a clear, picturesque
day, a February day without clouds, without emotion or spirit, like a
beautiful woman with an empty face. In my fingers I carried the
thorny stems from which the egg cases hung like roses; I switched the
bouquet from hand to hand, warming the free hand in a pocket. Passing the house again, deciding not to fetch gloves, I walked north to the
hill by the place where the steers come to drink from Tinker Creek.
There in the weeds on the hill I found another eight egg cases. I was
stunned—I cross this hill several times a week, and I always look for
egg cases here, because it was here that I had once seen a mantis laying her eggs.

It was several years ago that I witnessed this extraordinary proce-   6
dure, but I remember, and confess, an inescapable feeling that I was
watching something not real and present, but a horrible nature movie,
a "secrets-of-nature" short, beautifully photographed in full color, that
I had to sit through unable to look anywhere else but at the dimly
lighted EXIT signs along the walls, and that behind the scenes some amateur moviemaker was congratulating himself on having stumbled
across this little wonder, or even on having contrived so natural a setting, as though the whole scene had been shot very carefully in a ter-
rarium in someone's greenhouse.

* * *

I was ambling across this hill that day when I noticed a speck of 7
pure white. The hill is eroded; the slope is a rutted wreck of red clay
broken by grassy hillocks and low wild roses whose roots clasp a pittance of topsoil. I leaned to examine the white thing and saw a mass of
bubbles like spittle. Then I saw something dark like an engorged leech
rummaging over the spittle, and then I saw the praying mantis.

She was upside-down, clinging to a horizontal stem of wild rose by 8
her feet which pointed to heaven. Her head was deep in dried grass.
Her abdomen was swollen like a smashed finger; it tapered to a fleshy
tip out of which bubbled a wet, whipped froth. I couldn't believe my
eyes. I lay on the hill this way and that, my knees in thorns and my
cheeks in clay, trying to see as well as I could. I poked near the female's
head with a grass; she was clearly undisturbed, so I settled my nose
an inch from that pulsing abdomen. It pulled like a concertina, it
throbbed like a bellows; it roved, pumping, over the glistening, clab-
bered surface of the egg case testing and patting, thrusting and
smoothing. It seemed to act so independently that I forgot the panting
brown stick at the other end. The bubble creature seemed to have two
eyes, a frantic little brain, and two busy, soft hands. It looked like a
hideous, harried mother slicking up a fat daughter for a beauty pageant, touching her up, slobbering over her, patting and hemming and
brushing and stroking.

The male was nowhere in sight. The female had probably eaten 9
him. Fabre says that, at least in captivity, the female will mate with and
devour up to seven males, whether she has laid her egg cases or not.
The mating rites of mantises are well known: a chemical produced in
the head of the male insect says, in effect, "No, don't go near her, you
fool, she'll eat you alive." At the same time a chemical in his abdomen
says, "Yes, by all means, now and forever yes."

While the male is making up what passes for his mind, the female 10
tips the balance in her favor by eating his head. He mounts her. Fabre
describes the mating, which sometimes lasts six hours, as follows: "The
male, absorbed in the performance of his vital functions, holds the female in a tight embrace. But the wretch has no head; he has no neck;
he has hardly a body. The other, with her muzzle turned over her
shoulder continues very placidly to gnaw what remains of the gentle
swain. And, all the time, that masculine stump, holding on firmly, goes
on with the business! . . . I have seen it done with my own eyes and
have not yet recovered from my astonishment."

I watched the egg-laying for over an hour. When I returned the 11
next day, the mantis was gone. The white foam had hardened and
browned to a dirty suds; then, and on subsequent days, I had trouble
pinpointing the case, which was only an inch or so off the ground. I
checked on it every week all winter long. In the spring the ants discov-

ered it; every week I saw dozens of ants scrambling over the sides, unable to chew a way in. Later in the spring I climbed the hill every day, hoping to catch the hatch. The leaves of the trees had long since unfolded, the butterflies were out, and the robins' first broods were fledged; still the egg case hung silent and full on the stem. I read that I should wait for June, but still I visited the case every day. One morning at the beginning of June everything was gone. I couldn't find the lower thorn in the clump of three to which the egg case was fixed. I couldn't find the clump of three. Tracks ridged the clay, and I saw the lopped stems: somehow my neighbor had contrived to run a tractor-mower over that steep clay hill on which there grew nothing to mow but a few stubby thorns.

So. Today from this same hill I cut another three undamaged cases   12
and carried them home with the others by their twigs. I also collected a suspiciously light cynthia moth cocoon. My fingers were stiff and red with cold, and my nose ran. I had forgotten the Law of the Wild, which is, "Carry Kleenex." At home I tied the twigs with their egg cases to various sunny bushes and trees in the yard. They're easy to find because I used white string; at any rate, I'm unlikely to mow my own trees. I hope the woodpeckers that come to the feeder don't find them, but I don't see how they'd get a purchase on them if they did.

Night is rising in the valley; the creek has been extinguished for an   13
hour, and now only the naked tips of trees fire tapers into the sky like trails of sparks. The scene that was in the back of my brain all afternoon, obscurely, is beginning to rise from night's lagoon. It really has nothing to do with praying mantises. But this afternoon I threw tiny string lashings and hitches with frozen hands, gingerly, fearing to touch the egg cases even for a minute because I remembered the Polyphemus moth.[2]

I have no intention of inflicting all my childhood memories on   14
anyone. Far less do I want to excoriate my old teachers who, in their bungling, unforgettable way, exposed me to the natural world, a world covered in chitin, where implacable realities hold sway. The Polyphemus moth never made it to the past; it crawls in that crowded, pellucid pool at the lip of the great waterfall. It is as present as this blue desk and brazen lamp, as this blackened window before me in which I can no longer see even the white string that binds the egg case to the hedge, but only my own pale, astonished face.

Once, when I was ten or eleven years old, my friend Judy brought   15
in a Polyphemus moth cocoon. It was January; there were doily snowflakes taped to the schoolroom panes. The teacher kept the co-

2. Polyphemus: in classical mythology, a one-eyed giant (a Cyclops) whom the hero Odysseus blinded (*Odyssey,* Book 9).

coon in her desk all morning and brought it out when we were getting
restless before recess. In a book we found what the adult moth would
look like; it would be beautiful. With a wingspread of up to six inches,
the Polyphemus is one of the few huge American silk moths, much
larger than, say, a giant or tiger swallowtail butterfly. The moth's enormous wings are velveted in a rich, warm brown, and edged in bands of
blue and pink delicate as a watercolor wash. A startling "eyespot," immense, and deep blue melding to an almost translucent yellow, luxuri-
ates in the center of each hind wing. The effect is one of a masculine
splendor foreign to the butterflies, a fragility unfurled to strength. The
Polyphemus moth in the picture looked like a mighty wraith, a beating
essence of the hardwood forest, alien-skinned and brown, with spread,
blind eyes. This was the giant moth packed in the faded cocoon. We
closed the book and turned to the cocoon. It was an oak leaf sewn into
a plump oval bundle; Judy had found it loose in a pile of frozen leaves.

We passed the cocoon around; it was heavy. As we held it in our 16
hands, the creature within warmed and squirmed. We were delighted,
and wrapped it tighter in our fists. The pupa began to jerk violently, in
heart-stopping knocks. Who's there? I can still feel those thumps, urgent through a muffling of spun silk and leaf, urgent through the
swaddling of many years, against the curve of my palm. We kept passing it around. When it came to me again it was hot as a bun; it jumped
half out of my hand. The teacher intervened. She put it, still heaving
and banging, in the ubiquitous Mason jar.

It was coming. There was no stopping it now, January or not. One 17
end of the cocoon dampened and gradually frayed in a furious battle.
The whole cocoon twisted and slapped around in the bottom of the jar.
The teacher fades, the classmates fade, I fade: I don't remember anything but that thing's struggle to be a moth or die trying. It emerged at
last, a sodden crumple. It was a male; his long antennae were thickly
plumed, as wide as his fat abdomen. His body was very thick, over an
inch long, and deeply furred. A gray, furlike plush covered his head; a
long, tan furlike hair hung from his wide thorax over his brown-
furred, segmented abdomen. His multijointed legs, pale and powerful,
were shaggy as a bear's. He stood still, but he breathed.

He couldn't spread his wings. There was no room. The chemical 18
that coated his wings like varnish, stiffening them permanently, dried,
and hardened his wings as they were. He was a monster in a Mason
jar. Those huge wings stuck on his back in a torture of random pleats
and folds, wrinkled as a dirty tissue, rigid as leather. They made a single nightmare clump still wracked with useless, frantic convulsions.

The next thing I remember, it was recess. The school was in 19
Shadyside, a busy residential part of Pittsburgh. Everyone was playing
dodgeball in the fenced playground or racing around the concrete
schoolyard by the swings. Next to the playground a long delivery drive
sloped downhill to the sidewalk and street. Someone—it must have

been the teacher—had let the moth out. I was standing in the drive-way, alone, stock-still, but shivering. Someone had given the Polyphe-mus moth his freedom, and he was walking away.

He heaved himself down the asphalt driveway by infinite degrees, 20 unwavering. His hideous crumpled wings lay glued and rucked on his back, perfectly still now, like a collapsed tent. The bell rang twice; I had to go. The moth was receding down the driveway, dragging on. I went; I ran inside. The Polyphemus moth is still crawling down the driveway, crawling down the driveway hunched, crawling down the driveway on six furred feet, forever.

DIANE ACKERMAN

The Moon by Whale Light

Diane Ackerman (1948–   ) received her M.F.A., M.A., and Ph.D. from Cornell University. She taught English at the University of Pitts-burgh and then was the director of the writers' program at Washing-ton University in St. Louis (1984–1986). Since then she has been a staff writer for *The New Yorker* and has served as a visiting writer at several universities. Ackerman's many interests include skin diving, horseback riding, flying an airplane, and counseling for a crisis hot-line. Although an accomplished poet, Ackerman is best known for many collections of her nonfiction, including *A Natural History of the Senses* (1990), *The Moon by Whale Light* (1991), *The Rarest of the Rare: Vanishing Animals, Timeless Worlds* (1995), and *Bats* (1996). These works have established Ackerman as a science and nature writer of the sta-ture of Stephen Jay Gould, John McPhee, and Annie Dillard. A recent book brings her diverse experiences together: *A Slender Thread: A Year of Changing Seasons in the Life of a Poet, Naturalist, and Crisis Counselor* (1996).

The following excerpt from *A Moon by Whale Light* offers us a glimpse into Ackerman's life as a naturalist and a taste of her poetic writing style; her description of swimming with whales demonstrates the power of metaphorical language to make experience come alive for the reader. Readers may want to compare Alice Walker's "Am I Blue?"; both essays explore similarities between animals and hu-mans, but at the same time they remind us of the alienness of an-other species.

. . . We cut the motor about two hundred yards from the whales. 1 Juan[1] and I slipped over the side of the boat and began to swim toward them, approaching as quietly as possible, so that they wouldn't con-

1. Juan: a student from the University of Buenos Aires spending the summer in Patago-nia conducting research on whales.

strue any of our movements as aggressive. In a few minutes, we were only yards from the mother's head. Looking down, I saw the three-month-old baby beside her underwater, its callosities bright in the murky green water. Slowly, Juan and I swam all the way around them, getting closer and closer. The long wound on Fang's[2] flank looked red and angry. When her large tail lifted out of the water, its beauty stunned me for a moment, and then I yanked Juan's hand, to draw his attention, and we pulled back. At fifty feet long, weighing about fifty tons, all she would have needed to do was hit us with a flipper to crush us, or swat us with her tail to kill us instantly. But she was moving her tail gently, slowly, without malice. It would be as if a human being, walking across a meadow, had come upon a strange new animal. Our instinct wouldn't be to kill it but to get closer and have a look, perhaps touch it. Right whales are grazers, which have balleen plates, not teeth. We did not look like lunch. She swung her head around so that her mouth was within two feet of me, then turned her head on edge to reveal a large white patch and, under that, an eye shaped much like a human eye. I looked directly into her eye, and she looked directly back at me, as we hung in the water, studying each other.

I wish you well, I thought, applying all the weight of my concentration, in case it was possible for her to sense my mood. I did not imagine she could decipher the words, but many animals can sense fear in humans. Perhaps they can also sense other emotions.

Her dark, plumlike eye fixed me and we stared deeply at one another for some time. The curve of her mouth gave her a Mona Lisa smile, but that was just a felicity of her anatomy. The only emotion I sensed was her curiosity. That shone through her watchfulness, her repeated turning toward us, her extreme passivity, her caution with flippers and tail. Apparently, she was doing what we were—swimming close to a strange, fascinating life-form, taking care not to frighten or hurt it. Perhaps, seeing us slip over the side of the Zodiac,[3] she thought it had given birth and we were its young. In that case, she might have been thinking how little we resembled our parent. Or perhaps she understood only too well that we were intelligent beasts who lived in the strange, dangerous world of the land, where whales can get stranded, lose their bearings and equilibrium, and die. Perhaps she knew somehow that we live in that desert beyond the waves from which whales rarely return, a kingdom we rule, where we thrive. A whale's glimpse of us is almost as rare as our glimpse of a whale. They have never seen us mating, they have rarely if at all seen us feeding, they have never seen us give birth, suckle our young, die of old age. They have never

2. Fang: the mother whale who had been so frequently observed she had earned herself a name.
3. Zodiac: the small boat Ackerman used during her whaling explorations.

observed our society, our normal habits. They would not know how to tell our sex, since we hide our reproductive organs. Perhaps they know that human males tend to have more facial hair than females, just as we know that male right whales tend to have more callosities on their faces than females. But they would still find it hard to distinguish between a clothed, short-haired, clean-shaven man and a clothed, short-haired woman.

When Fang had first seen us in the Zodiac, we were wearing large smoked plastic eyes. Now we had small eyes shaped like hers—but two on the front of the head, like a flounder or a seal, not an eye on either side, like a fish or a whale. In the water, our eyes were encased in a glass jar, our mouths stretched around a rubber tube, and our feet were flippers. Instead of diving like marine mammals, we floated on the surface. To Fang, I must have looked spastic and octopuslike, with my thin limbs dangling. Human beings possess such immense powers that few animals cause us to feel truly humble. A whale does, swimming beside you, as big as a reclining building, its eye carefully observing you. It could easily devastate you with a twitch, and yet it doesn't. Still, although it lives in a gliding, quiet, investigate-it-first realm, it is not as benign as a Zen monk.[4] Aggression plays a big role in its life, especially during courtship. Whales have weapons that are equal in their effects to our pointing a gun at somebody, squeezing a finger, and blowing him away. When they strike each other with their flukes in battles, they hit flat, but they sometimes slash the water with the edge. That fluke edge could break a person in two instantly. But such an attack has never happened in the times people have been known to swim with whales. On rare occasions, unprovoked whales have struck boats with their flukes, perhaps by accident, on at least one occasion killing a man. And there are three reported instances of a whale breaching onto a boat, again resulting in deaths. But they don't attack swimmers. In many of our science-fiction stories, aliens appear on earth and terrible fights ensue, with everyone shooting weapons that burn, sting, or blow others up. To us, what is alien is treacherous and evil. Whales do not visualize aliens in that way. So although it was frightening to float beside an animal as immense and powerful as a whale, I knew that if I showed her where I was and what I was and that I meant her no harm, she would return the courtesy.

Suddenly, Juan pulled me back a few feet and, turning, I saw the calf swimming around to our side, though staying close to its mother. Big as an elephant, it still looked like a baby. Only a few months old, it was a frisky pup and rampantly curious. It swam right up, turned one

4. Zen monk: A member of a secluded community of men leading a stoic lifestyle dedicated to the principles of Zen Buddhism, a sect of Buddhism that stresses the practice of meditation as the means of enlightenment.

eye at us, took a good look, then wheeled its head around to look at us with the other eye. When it turned, it swung its mouth right up to my chest, and I reached out to touch it, but Juan pulled my hand back. I looked at him and nodded. A touch could have startled the baby, which might not have known its own strength yet. In a reflex, its flipper or tail could have swatted us. It might not have known that if humans are held underwater—by a playful flipper, say—they can drown. Its flippers hung in the water by its sides, and its small callosities looked like a crop of fieldstones. When it rolled, it revealed a patch of white on its belly and an anal slit. Swimming forward, it fanned its tail, and the water suddenly felt chillier as it stirred up cold from the bottom. The mother was swimming forward to keep up with it, and we followed, hanging quietly in the water, trying to breathe slowly and kick our flippers as little as possible. Curving back around, Fang turned on her side so that she could see us, and waited as we swam up close again. Below me, her flipper hovered large as a freight elevator. Tilting it very gently in place, she appeared to be sculling; her tail, too, was barely moving. Each time she and the baby blew, a fine mist sprayed into the air, accompanied by a *whumping* sound, as of a pedal organ. Both mother and calf made no sudden moves around us, no acts of aggression.

We did not have their insulation of blubber to warm us in such frigid waters and, growing cold at last after an hour of traveling slowly along the bay with them, we began to swim back toward the beach. To save energy, we rolled onto our backs and kicked with our fins. When we were a few hundred yards away from her, Fang put her head up in a spy hop. Then she dove, rolled, lifted a flipper high into the air like a black rubber sail, and waved it back and forth. The calf did the same. Juan and I laughed. They were not waving at us, only rolling and playing now that we were out of the way. But it was so human a gesture that we automatically waved our arms overhead in reply. Then we turned back onto our faces again. Spears of sunlight cut through the thick green water and disappeared into the depths, a bottom soon revealed itself as tawny brown about thirty feet below us, and then the sand grew visible, along with occasional shells, and then the riot of shells near shore, and finally the pebbles of the shallows. Taking off our fins, we stepped from one liquid realm to another, from the whale road, as the Anglo-Saxons called the ocean, back onto the land of humans.

DALE PETERSON

To Snare the Nimble Marmoset

Dale Peterson (1944–   ) has written about anthropology, art, chimpanzees, computers, literature, psychiatry, travel, and tropical forests. His recent works include *Chimpanzee Travels* (1995), a humorous narrative about looking for apes in tropical forests, and the scholarly *Demonic Males: Apes and the Origins of Human Violence* (1996), co-authored with Harvard University anthropologist Richard Wrangham. In addition to teaching freshman English at Tufts University in Massachusetts, Peterson is currently finishing the story of his 20,000-mile journey by car to oddly named small towns in the United States and working on the first full biography of chimpanzee expert Jane Goodall. Goodall was the co-author of Peterson's seventh book, *Visions of Caliban: On Chimpanzees and People* (1993), which was named a *New York Times* Notable Book.

This excerpt from *Visions of Caliban* demonstrates the beauty of serendipity; by immersing himself in the experience, Peterson makes remarkable and surprising discoveries. Like E. B. White ("Twins") and Randall Jarrell ("Field and Forest"), he discovers both real and imagined barriers separating nature and civilization.

Chimpanzees in West Africa, west of the Sassandra River in Ivory Coast, use pieces of flat stone and wood as anvils. They hammer on these anvils with specially selected, large, often rounded stone hammers and also stick hammers. This stone-tool culture persists among chimpanzee communities from the Sassandra through Liberia and Guinea as far west as the Moa River in Sierra Leone. Yet this tradition varies in detail from one locality to the next. Altogether, the nut-cracking chimps of West Africa use their hammers and anvils to crack hard nuts of six varieties—but in every area where this practice has been studied, the chimps seem to prefer a different menu.[1] Why? The differences could very well result solely from ecological factors—availability of trees, quality of nuts, and so on. We don't know yet. Nonetheless, the differing nut choices of chimps in different parts of West Africa could be at least partially cultural, artifacts of tradition.

---

1. My comments on chimpanzee stone-tool culture are based on recent work by Paul Marchesi and Christophe Boesch (in press). Chimps in the Tai Forest of Ivory Coast crack and eat *Coula edolis* (African walnut), *Panda oleosa,* and *Parinari* (gray plum) nuts. *Panda* nuts are very hard, harder than any nut currently harvested by human hunter-gatherers; to break them, Tai chimps use only stone hammers, never wood, and the hammers weigh as much as forty-five pounds. [author's note]

Africans at the edge of the great Tai Forest, near Ivory Coast's bor-   2
der with Liberia, used to claim that a tribe of forest-dwelling pygmies
lived there. The pygmies specialized in cracking nuts, they said, and if
you went deep into the forest, you might find them. The French colonial government, wishing to leave no rumor uninvestigated and no
tribe unsubjugated, sent a military detachment into the forest to "civi-
lize" the nut-cracking pygmies. They found no one.

I went into the Tai Forest, and I lay down one night in the camp of   3
Swiss scientists Christophe and Hedwige Boesch, listening to noises
that were mostly rhythmic—ten thousand insects in three dimensions—and fell asleep imagining myself in the midst of some great living, breathing body. Every few minutes I was startled awake by a
random and mysterious motion in the leaves, or by a call or a series of
hoots or shrieks or agonized and strangulated cries.

It was still dark when Christophe Boesch and I left camp in the   4
morning. We walked into a pitch-black forest, blinking our flashlights
once in a while to find our way, stumbling along dark trails for perhaps
half an hour before we stopped walking and sat down on a log.
Chimps were in the trees above us, in their sleeping nests, and we listened to them wake up. They made a few brief, sleepy, half-hearted
hoots—uh-hooo, uh-hooo, uh-hooo—and a few low cries and inhale-
exhalations. We listened to rainfall noises of these chimps urinating
from high in the trees, and then we heard brief splashing in the leaves,
as some of them jumped from one tree to another. After a while we
heard some real hooting, then a crackling of leaves and branches
above us. We sat there on the log as dawn moved into the forest, and
we looked up into the trees towering high above us and watched the
apes, dark shapes moving, trees and tree branches waving with their
weight, while detritus dropped into our faces and hair. We listened to
more splashes in the leaves, a coughing, then a mild and brief screaming off to one side: wraaaa wraaaaa wraaaaa! I saw one chimp perhaps
eighty feet above us, behind a screen of leaves, squatting on a branch
and eating leaves, plucking them with his hands. But mostly I just saw
moving leaves high up and once in a while a dark, humanlike shape
behind pale green leaves before speckles of a pale white sky.

They began leaving their nests and descending. The dark shape of   5
a female leapt into a tree and climbed down it. A young male climbed
into the top of a thin, polelike tree that sank, bent down with his
weight—and he rode it down calmly, as if it were his private elevator. I
heard some screams, a brief chorusing of calls, some grunts and
rustling and falling of debris. High above, I saw a chase: a chimp leapt
from one tree to another at sixty feet above the forest floor and clam-
bered down the second tree, and a second chimp chased the first. We
heard the thumping of feet and hands on branches as the chase pro-

gressed and moved out of our vision. We saw, a few minutes later, two big males sitting side by side on the ground. "It's the alpha male,"[2] Boesch said, referring to the larger of the two, and soon this one began swaying, rising slowly, then inhale-exhaling until his voice was rising into hoots. He stood up, smashed through some low vegetation, and dove into a rotten tree that disintegrated and crashed into a hundred flying pieces—but not before this displaying male, without losing balance or pace, had already burst into a green cluster of leaves and vines and then jumped into a tree right above us.

There were other chases, screams and squabbles and noisy displays, even some brief grooming, as the dozen or so chimps I was able to see in our part of the forest gradually began their day. Boesch said that nearly fifty chimps belong to this community, though he has never seen them together at one time. Chimpanzees live in what has been called a *fusion-fission* social structure. With remarkable fluidity, the chimps of any community will gather into large groups or splinter into very small units, one or two or three individuals. In fact, sometimes during this day we followed (so far as I could see) only a couple of apes; other times we followed, indeed became part of, a moving band of perhaps twenty or more.

The disorganized start to this day became even more so when one of the chimps, walking along the ground with several others, suddenly stopped, leapt directly backward, and began crying out strangely. The rest of the group stopped too and began screaming. The chimps seemed to be looking at one particular spot in the underbrush. Some of them climbed trees to get a better look. Eventually they stopped screaming and looking at the spot and began moving again, so Boesch and I, walking a few yards behind the chimps, were able to move up to that spot and see for ourselves. I saw nothing but the olive and tan chaos of dry sticks and grass and dead leaves. For at least thirty seconds that was all I saw, until suddenly the chaos reorganized itself in my vision as pattern: a flattened, dully gleaming weave; a reptilian tesselation within leaves and grass. "Rhinoceros viper," Boesch said. Deadly.

As the morning developed, as the forest became warmer and brighter, we progressed from food to food with regular resting and some male displaying and juvenile playing in between. The rests were a pleasure, actually, as we all sat or lay down together, two people and roughly a half-dozen or a dozen chimps. The chimps would sometimes turn to each other and start grooming, one scratching away at the other's back, plucking into the fur, holding up discovered particles to

2. alpha male: in any group of animals, the male that has, through brute strength, achieved the respect and submission of the others, both female and male.

examine them, smacking lips or clacking teeth as if to emphasize the intensity of this procedure. Meanwhile, from other parts of the forest, we would regularly hear the hooting or buttress thumping of other chimps from the same community, moving with different companions.

When our chimps rested, they did so with abandon: I remember 9 watching one lie flat down on the forest floor, both arms thrown behind him, curled back so that his hands met just above the top of his head—it was a dancer's pose. A female near us lay on her back, yawned a huge yawn, flung her arms behind her, and lifted both legs straight up to prop her feet against a branch just above. Farther away, a lying-down male suddenly sat up and looked at us, at Boesch and me, with some intensity. What are *these* apes doing here? he may have been asking himself. Then, having decided not to worry about it further, perhaps, he lay down again. Once one of the males in our group was lying back, arms spread out, as still as sleep—but a single hoot in the distance seemed to startle this guy awake and send him screaming and running on all fours into the bushes. He leapt across a fallen tree, then sat down and scratched himself, slowly, as if in thought.

There were mercurial shifts in mood. It seemed as if some chimp 10 would look at the wrong male with the wrong expression, and then there would be swaying, hair raising, inhale-exhalations, working up to a frenzy, explosions of noise and tearing through the bush, screaming, charging around—but soon enough peace would return.

Sometimes the chimps would take to the trees, very abruptly. A 11 big chimp might ascend a hundred-foot tree in ten or fifteen seconds; another might climb right up a hanging liana for forty feet before leaping over into a tree; we would be left looking up, leaves spinning down and falling into our faces, sometimes big branches crashing down.

Late in the morning I heard a noise, a thumping, a light hammer- 12 ing. I looked down a brief slope to see an adult female squatting at the base of a big tree, hammering with a reddish piece of log, both hands lifting up and dropping down one end of this log. I watched her stop hammering and pick up some white fragments and place them in her mouth and eat them. She was cracking nuts. She put another nut in place, on top of a root, and began hammering again. She was squatting before the root anvil, both hands lifting up one end of a three-foot log, and hammering away. The log worked like a lever, one end resting on the ground, the other moving up and down as the chimp hammered. The sound had a distinct pattern—a series of thunking taps that continued until the nut cracked: thunk thunk thunk thunk thunk thunk crack! Then she would stop, put down the log hammer, pick through the pieces, place the nutmeat in her mouth, put another nut on the anvil, and begin again: thunk thunk thunk thunk thunk thunk crack!

Soon I heard more hammering, and I looked over to see on the 13
other side of the tree another female, this one with an infant clinging
to her breast. In a third area, I heard more labor—thunk thunk thunk
thunk thunk thunk crack! I heard hammering at a fourth site and
saw a big chimp facing away from me, squatting at a root anvil like the
others, lifting and dropping one end of a log, bent intently over the
work, pausing to pick through and chew nut fragments before resum-
ing work with the same tempo and pattern as the others: thunk thunk
thunk thunk thunk thunk crack! Sometimes the chimps would get up
from their work, walk around under the tree, gather more nuts, and
take the new supply back to the anvil. But eventually they ran out of
nuts, and finally Boesch and I were left at the top of the slope by ourselves.

These were *Coula* nuts, Boesch informed me; about 85 percent of 14
the time chimps use wood hammers to break *Coula*. He pulled three
green, golfball-sized nuts out of his pocket and handed them to me.
"Now it's your turn," he said. We walked down the slope to where the
chimps had been, and I squatted beneath a tree and picked up the log
hammer. It was an irregular piece of hard wood, perhaps three feet
long and quite heavy. I found a root with a worn dent in it, placed a nut
in the dent, and with both hands lifted the heavy log on one end, hammering down just as I had seen the chimp do: I went thunk, thunk, and
after about the sixth blow, the nut went crack! The nut was broken. I
reached down and pulled out a piece of the white meat and ate it. It
tasted rather like dry coconut, slightly sweet, tasty and satisfying.

I tried the second nut, but it wouldn't crack. Finally, after several 15
frustrating attempts, I threw it away and placed the third nut down.
"Typical infant behavior," Boesch said coolly. "That's just what the
chimp infants do when they're first learning. If it doesn't crack, you
blame it on the nut and try another. The nut is not the problem. It's
your technique. Aiming is very important."

But the chimps were on the move again, so we left the log ham- 16
mers and anvils and caught up with them; they walked at a steady
pace for some time, pausing to climb this tree, eat those leaves, drink
that water. When they were tired of moving, they rested. At one of our
resting spots, I watched a shaking bush with laughter coming out. The
laughter emerged irregular and breathy, infectious; it continued for
perhaps twenty minutes. There was a whistling bird here, lots of motion and splashing in the leaves—and two chimps, juveniles I imagined, laughing and laughing and laughing. The laughter was becoming
more and more frantic. It sounded like a fast sawing of wood: whuuu,
whuuu, whuuu. A whole area of branches and leaves, an entire bush,
shook as the laughter coming from inside became frantic. An arm, a
head, an ear, a body would appear and disappear into the bush.

We traveled again, juveniles riding piggyback on their mothers. 17
We entered a small swamp where the chimps drank and then ate the
pith from the leaf stem of a knee-high plant with oblong green leaves.
A male stood upright and gobbled leaves; he was perhaps three and a
half feet tall. We watched a brief mating, the female on the ground on
all fours, the male behind her, quiet. A bird went valvoline valvoline
valvoline. Somewhere a hornbill played a buzzy kazoo, then flew
away with noisy feathers.

A male chimpanzee, walking upright on two legs and revealing an 18
urgent erection, chased a female—who fled.

We stopped at a place in the forest where a massive tree had fallen, 19
breaking open the canopy. Sunlight poured through and the fallen
trunk provided a pleasant place for several of the chimps to sit, sprawl,
loll, nap, groom, and be groomed. Around the fallen tree several more
chimps lolled about, some on the forest floor, some in trees. Once I
counted ten chimps on the log, and perhaps another ten in the forest
around the log. The adults seemed mostly to be napping. Two juveniles
were wrestling and tumbling and laughing in an open area near the
log; later I watched one big male with a gray splotch on his back play
and wrestle and tickle a toddler—a one year old. The big male chased
him around and around a tree, then tickled and tickled and tickled the
toddler, who laughed desperately. Up on the fallen log, one young
male was blissfully sacked out, knees up, eyes closed, arms flung back
into a remarkable concave fit around the big trunk. The light fell across
his body, and he seemed to keep his face pointed toward the sun, as if
working on that tan. There was also grooming going on, on the log—
one male bent over in a salaam[3] position, head in hands, rump high,
being groomed by a neighbor.

After perhaps an hour, the siesta was over—abruptly, it seemed to 20
me—and the group started moving with some unanimity and cohe-
sion. We walked fast, and when we entered parts of the forest where it
was relatively open, I was surprised to see how many chimpanzees
were in our group. We crossed an invisible border. "They've entered
the territory of the neighbors," Boesch commented. Soon we came to
a gargantuan tree, towering, with a giant crown high above us and
perhaps twenty or thirty great lianas hanging down like cables. The
chimps, hooting and screaming, climbed straight up the lianas, which
swayed softly, and about eighty feet up entered the crown of the tree
and disappeared from sight. All I could see then were old leaves falling
down and dust passing through beams of late-afternoon sunlight.

*   *   *

3. salaam: an Eastern salutation that involves bowing very low and placing the right
palm on the forehead.

Time passed. We continued moving. It seemed as if at some point   21
we were joined by more members of the group, and finally I felt in the
midst of a mass migration—all around us chimpanzees, male and female adults, youngsters, infants, were on the move. We came at last to
a big area of several nut trees, and presently half the apes started
cracking nuts with wood hammers on wood anvils. Soon there was
hammering all around us, a thunk thunk thunking from many directions at once. To the right, thirty-five feet away, one laborer with a
short log hammer lifted it wholly into the air before crashing it down
on a nut and anvil: both hands in the center of the log hammer, lift
and slam, lift and slam. Under the tree right in front of us, three different apes worked at three anvils, hammering away. And to the left, as
well. Behind us another used a log hammer, lever style.

A young chimp tried to crack open nuts using a fallen tree as the   22
anvil. He kept knocking the nut off—couldn't quite get the hang of it.
A second juvenile came over, pushing the first one away. He couldn't
get the hang of it either.

The whole forest was filled with the industrious sound of hammer-   23
ing. By then it was late afternoon and the light was fading. I turned to
watch a mother play with her baby, nibbling on his toes, wrestling with
him, looking into his little face with a goofy bliss. In another spot three
young adult females surrounded and played with an infant, all four of
them hanging in a low cluster of vines and branches. One of the adults
was below the baby, the other two above it, and all three seemed to be
sharing it, tickling and kissing the infant. I saw familiar expressions on
their faces, absolutely familiar: human expressions, Madonna-like expressions of pure adoration.[4] It was astonishing!

All my chimpanzee experiences before this moment had been   24
fragmented, I from my world peering briefly into theirs. Now for the
briefest time I had been blessed to pass through a door into another
universe. Christophe Boesch and I were accepted, tolerated, as a
strange and perhaps mildly parasitic species of ape—yet fundamentally
harmless, neither predator nor prey—and so we were able momentarily to merge with the coming and going, the fusion and fission, the
motion and rest and play and occasional squabbles and struggles that
make up the chimpanzee world. It was a richer and more satisfying
world than I had imagined.

My co-author could have told me this. I should have understood it   25
from my reading. But perhaps it was necessary to discover it for myself. I suddenly recognized why I or anyone should care about what
happens to the African great apes. Not, ultimately, because chimpanzees so resemble us, anatomically, behaviorally. Not because they

---

4. The writer is alluding to countless works of art depicting the mother of Christ admiring her newborn child.

can solve problems, learn language, recognize themselves as individuals in mirrors. Not because they have their own forest medicines and cultures, nor because they use tools and know how to snare the nimble marmoset.[5] And not because they are intellectual beings. But because they are emotional beings, as we are, and because their emotions are so obviously similar to ours. In the course of the day I had witnessed anger, fear, and irritation—but also, I thought, real comradeship, affection, and love.

Surely some of my reaction had to do with the beauty of the forest itself, but mostly I was moved by the play, the incredible laughter in the bushes, the adult male chasing a toddler round and round a tree, the mother nibbling her baby's toes and looking blissful, the three females playing with and adoring a single infant. These remarkable beings have our emotions. They feel! That was my discovery. 26

ALICE WALKER

Am I Blue?

Alice Walker (1944–   ) was born in Eatonton, Georgia, the youngest of eight children. Her father, who she says was "wonderful at math" but "a terrible farmer," earned only about three hundred dollars a year as a sharecropper. The example of her mother, a determined woman who helped in the fields and worked as a maid, helped make Walker a "womanist," a term she invented to mean "a black feminist or woman of color." Both her parents were storytellers: Walker's career began when she was eight and started to write their stories down. After graduating at the top of her high school class, Walker attended Spelman College in Atlanta, then graduated from Sarah Lawrence College in Bronxville, New York, in 1965. Best known for her third novel, *The Color Purple* (1982), which won the American Book Award and the Pulitzer Prize, Walker is also an accomplished essayist and poet. Her essays have been collected in *In Search of Our Mothers' Gardens: Womanist Prose* (1983), *Living by the Word* (1988), and *Anything We Love Can be Saved: A Writer's Activism* (1997).

"Am I Blue?" was first published in *Living by the Word*. In that it addresses, among other things, the humane treatment of animals, the essay connects logically to Vicki Hearne's "What's Wrong with Animal Rights."

5. Peterson is referring to a line in Shakespeare's *The Tempest* (Act 2, Scene 2), spoken by Caliban, the beastlike man or manlike beast whose true nature is the subject of considerable critical debate.

"Ain't these tears in these eyes tellin' you?"[1]

For about three years my companion and I rented a small house in the country that stood on the edge of a large meadow that appeared to run from the end of our deck straight into the mountains. The mountains, however, were quite far away, and between us and them there was, in fact, a town. It was one of the many pleasant aspects of the house that you never really were aware of this.

It was a house of many windows, low, wide, nearly floor to ceiling in the living room, which faced the meadow, and it was from one of these that I first saw our closest neighbor, a large white horse, cropping grass, flipping its mane, and ambling about—not over the entire meadow, which stretched well out of sight of the house, but over the five or so fenced-in acres that were next to the twenty-odd that we had rented. I soon learned that the horse, whose name was Blue, belonged to a man who lived in another town, but was boarded by our neighbors next door. Occasionally, one of the children, usually a stocky teen-ager, but sometimes a much younger girl or boy, could be seen riding Blue. They would appear in the meadow, climb up on his back, ride furiously for ten or fifteen minutes, then get off, slap Blue on the flanks, and not be seen again for a month or more.

There were many apple trees in our yard, and one by the fence that Blue could almost reach. We were soon in the habit of feeding him apples, which he relished, especially because by the middle of summer the meadow grasses—so green and succulent since January—had dried out from lack of rain, and Blue stumbled about munching the dried stalks half-heartedly. Sometimes he would stand very still just by the apple tree, and when one of us came out he would whinny, snort loudly, or stamp the ground. This meant, of course: I want an apple.

It was quite wonderful to pick a few apples, or collect those that had fallen to the ground overnight, and patiently hold them, one by one, up to his large, toothy mouth. I remained as thrilled as a child by his flexible dark lips, huge, cubelike teeth that crunched the apples, core and all, with such finality, and his high broad-breasted *enormity;* beside which, I felt small indeed. When I was a child, I used to ride horses, and was especially friendly with one named Nan until the day I was riding and my brother deliberately spooked her and I was thrown, head first, against the trunk of a tree. When I came to, I was in bed and my mother was bending worriedly over me; we silently agreed that perhaps horseback riding was not the safest sport for me. Since then I have walked, and prefer walking to horseback riding—but I had forgotten the depth of feeling one could see in horses' eyes.

---

1. The quoted line is from "Am I Blue?", a song popularized by the great jazz singer Billie Holiday.

I was therefore unprepared for the expression in Blue's. Blue was lonely. Blue was horribly lonely and bored. I was not shocked that this should be the case; five acres to tramp by yourself, endlessly, even in the most beautiful of meadows—and his was—cannot provide many interesting events, and once rainy season turned to dry that was about it. No, I was shocked that I had forgotten that human animals and nonhuman animals can communicate quite well; if we are brought up around animals as children we take this for granted. By the time we are adults we no longer remember. However, the animals have not changed. They are in fact *completed* creations (at least they seem to be, so much more than we) who are not likely *to* change; it is their nature to express themselves. What else are they going to express? And they do. And, generally speaking, they are ignored.

After giving Blue the apples, I would wander back to the house, aware that he was observing me. Were more apples not forthcoming then? Was that to be his sole entertainment for the day? My partner's small son had decided he wanted to learn how to piece a quilt; we worked in silence on our respective squares as I thought . . .

Well, about slavery: about white children, who were raised by black people, who knew their first all-accepting love from black women, and then, when they were twelve or so, were told they must "forget" the deep levels of communication between themselves and "mammy" that they knew. Later they would be able to relate quite calmly, "My old mammy was sold to another good family." "My old mammy was ————." Fill in the blank. Many more years later a white woman would say: "I can't understand these Negroes, these blacks. What do they want? They're so different from us."

And about the Indians, considered to be "like animals" by the "settlers" (a very benign euphemism for what they actually were), who did not understand their description as a compliment.

And about the thousands of American men who marry Japanese, Korean, Filipina, and other non-English-speaking women and of how happy they report they are, *"blissfully,"* until their brides learn to speak English, at which point the marriages tend to fall apart. What then did the men see, when they looked into the eyes of the women they married, before they could speak English? Apparently only their own reflections.

I thought of society's impatience with the young. "Why are they playing the music so loud?" Perhaps the children have listened to much of the music of oppressed people their parents danced to before they were born, with its passionate but soft cries for acceptance and love, and they have wondered why their parents failed to hear.

I do not know how long Blue had inhabited his five beautiful, boring acres before we moved into our house; a year after we had arrived—

and had also traveled to other valleys, other cities, other worlds—he was still there.

But then, in our second year at the house, something happened in   12
Blue's life. One morning, looking out the window at the fog that lay like a ribbon over the meadow, I saw another horse, a brown one, at the other end of Blue's field. Blue appeared to be afraid of it, and for several days made no attempt to go near. We went away for a week. When we returned, Blue had decided to make friends and the two horses ambled or galloped along together, and Blue did not come nearly as often to the fence underneath the apple tree.

When he did, bringing his new friend with him, there was a differ-   13
ent look in his eyes. A look of independence, of self-possession, of in- alienable *horse*ness. His friend eventually became pregnant. For months and months there was, it seemed to me, a mutual feeling be- tween me and the horses of justice, of peace. I fed apples to them both. The look in Blue's eyes was one of unabashed, "this is *it*ness."

It did not, however, last forever. One day, after a visit to the city, I   14
went out to give Blue some apples. He stood waiting, or so I thought, though not beneath the tree. When I shook the tree and jumped back from the shower of apples, he made no move. I carried some over to him. He managed to half-crunch one. The rest he let fall to the ground. I dreaded looking into his eyes—because I had of course noticed that Brown, his partner, had gone—but I did look. If I had been born into slavery, and my partner had been sold or killed, my eyes would have looked like that. The children next door explained that Blue's partner had been "put with him" (the same expression that old people used, I had noticed, when speaking of an ancestor during slavery who had been impregnated by her owner) so that they could mate and she con- ceive. Since that was accomplished, she had been taken back by her owner, who lived somewhere else.

Will she be back? I asked.   15

They didn't know.   16

Blue was like a crazed person. Blue *was,* to me, a crazed person. He   17
galloped furiously, as if he were being ridden, around and around his five beautiful acres. He whinnied until he couldn't. He tore at the ground with his hooves. He butted himself against his single shade tree. He looked always and always toward the road down which his partner had gone. And then, occasionally, when he came up for ap- ples, or I took apples to him, he looked at me. It was a look so piercing, so full of grief, a look so *human,* I almost laughed (I felt too sad to cry) to think there are people who do not know that animals suffer. People like me who have forgotten, and daily forget, all that animals try to tell us. "Everything you do to us will happen to you; we are your teachers, as you are ours. We are one lesson" is essentially it, I think. There are those who never once have even considered animals' rights: those who have been taught that animals actually want to be used and

abused by us, as small children "love" to be frightened, or women "love" to be mutilated and raped. . . . They are the great-grandchildren of those who honestly thought, because someone taught them this: "Women can't think," and "niggers can't faint." But most disturbing of all, in Blue's large brown eyes was a new look, more painful than the look of despair: the look of disgust with human beings, with life, the look of hatred. And it was odd what the look of hatred did. It gave him, for the first time, the look of a beast. And what that meant was that he had put up a barrier within to protect himself from further violence; all the apples in the world wouldn't change that fact.

And so Blue remained, a beautiful part of our landscape, very 18 peaceful to look at from the window, white against the grass. Once a friend came to visit and said, looking out on the soothing view: "And it *would* have to be a *white* horse; the very image of freedom." And I thought, yes, the animals are forced to become for us merely "images" of what they once so beautifully expressed. And we are used to drinking milk from containers showing "contented" cows, whose real lives we want to hear nothing about, eating eggs and drumsticks from "happy" hens, and munching hamburgers advertised by bulls of integrity who seem to command their fate.

As we talked of freedom and justice one day for all, we sat down to 19 steaks. I am eating misery, I thought, as I took the first bite. And spit it out.

HARRY CREWS

Pages from the Life of a Georgia Innocent

Harry Crews (1935–   ) grew up in Bacon County, Georgia, part of a poor family living in one of the most impoverished regions of the rural South. He now teaches English at the University of Florida at Gainesville and is the author of many novels, including *The Knockout Artist* (1988), and *Body* (1990), both of which depict confrontations between the urban and the rural. Recent novels include *Scar Lover* (1992) and *The Mulching of America* (1995). Crews is known for mixing pain, humor, and deliberate roughness of style. One critic has said that reading his work is like undergoing major surgery while under the influence of laughing gas. You can read more about Crews's difficult early years in Bacon County in his autobiography, *A Childhood: A Biography of a Place* (1978).

"Pages from the Life of a Georgia Innocent" appeared in Crews's monthly column in *Esquire* in July 1976. That Crews chose to call the column "Grits" (a slang term for rough-edged Southerners) tells a great deal about where he is, quite literally, coming from, and the essay is a model for anyone writing about the effect of "place" on one's character. Crews's earthy skepticism about nature in this essay contrasts well with Brigid Brophy's more cerebral skepticism in "The Menace of Nature."

Not very long ago I went with my twelve-year-old boy to a Disney 1 movie, one of those things that show a farm family, poor but God knows honest, out there on the land building character through hunger and hard work. The hunger and hard work seemed to be a hell of a lot of fun. The deprivation was finally so rewarding you could hardly stand it. The farm was full of warm, fuzzy, furry, damp-nosed creatures: bawling calves and braying mules and dogs that were treated like people. There was a little pain here and there but just so much as would teach important lessons to all of us. It sometimes even brought a tear to the eye, but not a real tear because the tear only served to prove that a family out in the middle of nowhere scratching in the earth for survival didn't have it so bad after all. Somebody was forever petting and stroking the plump little animals, crooning to them, as they were raised for strange, unstated reasons, but surely not to be castrated and slaughtered and skinned and eaten. They were, after all, friends.

If somebody got sick, he'd just pop into an old, rattling but trust- 2 worthy pickup truck and go off to town, where a kindly doctor would receive him immediately into his office and effect an instant cure by looking down his throat and asking him to say Ah. No mention was made of payment.

As my boy and I came out of the movie, blinking in the sunlight, it 3 occurred to me that Disney and others—the folks who bring you *The Waltons,* say, or *The Little House on the Prairie*—had managed to sell this strange vision of poverty and country life not only to suburbanites, while the suburbanites stuffed themselves with malt balls and popcorn, but also to people in little towns throughout the South who had proof in their daily lives to the contrary.

All fantasy. Now there is nothing wrong with fantasy. I love it, 4 even live off it at times. But driving home, the reality behind the fantasy began to go bad on me. It seemed immoral and dangerous to show so many smiles without an occasional glimpse of the skull underneath.

As we were going down the driveway, my boy, Byron, said: "That 5 was a great movie, huh, Dad?"

"Yeah," I said. "Great." 6

"I wish I could've lived in a place like that," he said. 7

"No, you don't," I said. "You just think you do." 8

My grandmother in Bacon County, Georgia, raised biddies: tiny 9 cheeping bits of fluff that city folk allow their children to squeeze to death at Easter. But city children are not the only ones who love biddies; hawks love them, too. Hawks like to swoop into the yard and carry off one impaled on their curved talons. Perhaps my grandmother, in her secret heart, knew that hawks even then were approaching the time when they would be on the endangered-species list. Whether she did or not, I'm sure she often felt she and her kind were already on the list. It would not do.

I'll never forget the first time I saw her get rid of a hawk. Chickens, [10] as everybody knows, are cannibals. Let a biddy get a spot of blood on it from a scrape or a raw place and the other biddies will simply eat it alive. My grandmother penned up all the biddies except the puniest one, already half pecked to death by the other cute little bits of fluff, and she set it out in the open yard by itself. First, though, she put arsenic on its head. I—about five years old and sucking on a sugar-tit— saw the hawk come in low over the fence, its red tail fanned, talons stretched, and nail the poisoned biddy where it squatted in the dust. The biddy never made a sound as it was carried away. My gentle grandmother watched it all with satisfaction before she let her other biddies out of the pen.

Another moment from my childhood that comes instantly to mind [11] was about a chicken, too; a rooster. He was boss cock of the whole farm, a magnificent bird nearly two feet tall. At the base of a chicken's throat is its craw, a kind of pouch into which the bird swallows food, as well as such things as grit, bits of rock and shell. For reasons I don't understand they sometimes become craw-bound. The stuff in the craw does not move; it remains in the craw and swells and will ultimately cause death. That's what would have happened to the rooster if the uncle who practically raised me hadn't said one day: "Son, we got to fix him."

He tied the rooster's feet so we wouldn't be spurred and took out [12] his castrating knife, honed to a razor's edge, and sterilized it over a little fire. He soaked a piece of fine fishing line and a needle in alcohol. I held the rooster on its back, a wing in each hand. With the knife my uncle split open the craw, cleaned it out, then sewed it up with the fishing line. The rooster screamed and screamed. But it lived to be cock of the walk again.

Country people never did anything worse to their stock than they [13] sometimes were forced to do to themselves. We had a man who farmed with us, a man from up north somewhere who had drifted down into Georgia with no money and a mouth full of bad teeth. Felix was his name and he was good with a plow and an ax, a hard worker. Most of the time you hardly knew he was on the place, he was so quiet and well-mannered. Except when his teeth began to bother him. And they bothered him more than a little. He lived in a shedlike little room off the side of the house. The room didn't have much in it: a ladder-back chair, a kerosene lamp, a piece of broken glass hanging on the wall over a pan of water where he shaved as often as once a week, a slatboard bed, and in one corner a chamber pot—which we called a slop jar—for use in the middle of the night when nature called. I slept in a room on the other side of the wall from him. I don't remember how old I was the night of his terrible toothache, but I do remember I was still young enough to wear a red cotton gown with five little pearl buttons down the front my grandmother had made for me.

When I heard him kick the slop jar, I knew it was his teeth. I just 14 didn't know how bad it was. When the ladder-back chair splintered, I knew it was a bad hurt, even for Felix. A few times that night I managed to slip off to sleep only to be jarred awake when he would run blindly into the thin wall separating us. He groaned and cursed, not loudly but steadily, sometimes for as long as half an hour. Ordinarily, my mother would have fixed a hot poultice for his jaw or at least tried to do *something*, but he was a proud man and when he was really dying from his teeth, he preferred to suffer, if not in silence, at least by himself. The whole house was kept awake most of the night by his thrashing and groaning, by the wash pan being knocked off the shelf, by his broken shaving mirror being broken again, and by his blind charges into the wall.

See, our kindly country dentist would not have gotten out of his 15 warm bed for anything less than money. And Felix didn't have any money. Besides, the dentist was in town ten miles away and we didn't have a rattling, trustworthy old truck. The only way we had to travel was two mules. And so there was nothing for Felix to do but what he was doing and it built practically no character at all. Looking back on it now, I can see that it wasn't even human. The sounds coming through the wall sure as hell weren't human anyway. On a Georgia dirt farm, pain reduced everything—man and beast alike—to the lowest common denominator. And it was pretty low and pretty common. Not something you'd want to watch while you ate malt balls and popcorn.

I was huddled under the quilts shaking with dread—my nerves 16 were shot by the age of four and so they have remained—when I heard Felix kick open the door to his room and thump down the wooden steps in his heavy brogan work shoes, which he'd not taken off all night. I couldn't imagine where he was going but I knew I wanted to watch whatever was about to happen. The only thing worse than my nerves is my curiosity, which has always been untempered by pity or compassion, a serious character failing in most societies but a sanity-saving virtue in Georgia when I was a child.

It was February and I went out the front door barefoot onto the 17 frozen ground. I met Felix coming around the corner of the house. In the dim light I could see the craziness in his eyes, the same craziness you see in the eyes of a trapped fox when it has not quite been able to chew through its own leg. Felix headed straight for the well, with me behind him, shaking in my thin cotton gown. He took the bucket from the nail on the rack built over the open well and sent it shooting down hard as he could to break the inch of ice that was over the water. As he was drawing the bucket up on the pulley, he seemed to see me for the first time.

"What the hell, boy! What the hell!" His voice was as mad as his [18] eyes and he either would not or could not say anything else. He held the bucket and took a mouthful of the freezing water. He held it a long time, spat it out, and filled his mouth again.

He turned the bucket loose and let it fall again into the well instead [19] of hanging it back on the nail where it belonged. With his cheeks swelling with water he took something out of the back pocket of his overalls. As soon as I saw what he had I knew beyond all belief and good sense what he meant to do, and suddenly I was no longer cold but stood on the frozen ground in a hot passion waiting to see him do it, to see if he *could* do it.

He had a piece of croker sack about the size of a half-dollar in his [20] left hand and a pair of wire pliers in his right. He spat the water out and reached way back in his rotten mouth and put the piece of sack over the tooth. He braced his feet against the well and stuck the pliers in over the sackcloth. He took the pliers in both hands and immediately a forked vein leapt in his forehead. The vein in his neck popped big as a pencil. He pulled and twisted and pulled and never made a sound.

It took him a long time and finally as he fought with the pliers and [21] with himself his braced feet slipped so that he was flat on his back when the blood broke from his mouth, followed by the pliers holding a tooth with roots half an inch long. He got slowly to his feet, sweat running off his face, and held the bloody tooth up between us.

He looked at the tooth and said in his old, recognizable voice: [22] *"Hurt now, you sumbitch!"*

MELISSA GREENE

No Rms, Jungle Vu

Melissa Greene (1952–) is a freelance writer in Atlanta. After graduating from Oberlin College in 1975, she joined VISTA as a volunteer in McIntosh County, Georgia. The knowledge she gained through personal contacts there resulted in her first book, *Praying for Sheetrock* (1991), a portrait of a community belatedly struggling with the issue of civil rights. In her recent work *The Temple Bombing* (1996), Greene returns to this issue by reconstructing the story of an Atlanta synagogue bombed in 1958 as a warning to its outspoken rabbi.

Greene once said that her motive in writing was to preserve the memory of things that might otherwise vanish unnoticed. This motive has led not only to books about civil rights, but also to an interest in zoologist Jon Coe, who impressed Greene because he, too, was a preservationist, working to save or re-create fragments of natural habitats. Greene was eager to meet the man who said he could design a zoo that would make the zoo-goer's hair stand on end. Her account of this meeting, "No Rms, Jungle Vu" appeared in a slightly longer form in *The Atlantic Monthly* in December 1987. For reasons obvious and not-so-obvious, it makes a useful companion to E. B. White's "Twins."

"The Egyptians have been civilized for four thousand years . . . my own ancestors probably a lot less," Jon Charles Coe says. "We evolved over millions of years in the wild, where survival depended on our awareness of the landscape, the weather, and the animals. We haven't been domesticated long enough to have lost those senses. In my opinion, it is the business of the zoo to slice right through that sophisticated veneer, to recall us to our origins. I judge the effectiveness of a zoo exhibit in the pulse rate of the zoo-goer. We can design a zoo that will make the hair stand up on the back of your neck." [1]

A revolution is under way in zoo design, which was estimated to be a $20 million business last year. Jon Coe and Grant Jones are the vanguard. Coe, forty-six, is a stocky man with a long, curly beard. He is an associate professor of landscape architecture at the University of Pennsylvania and a senior partner in the zoo-design firm of Coe Lee Robinson Roesch, in Philadelphia. Grant Jones, a senior partner in the architectural firm Jones & Jones, in Seattle, is at forty-eight a trendsetter in the design of riverfront areas, botanical gardens, and historical parks, as well as zoos. Coe and Jones were classmates at the Harvard School of Design, and Coe worked for Jones & Jones until 1981. [2]

Ten years ago in Seattle they created the Woodland Park gorilla exhibit in collaboration with Dennis Paulson, a biologist, and with David Hancocks, an architect and the director of the Woodland Park Zoo. The exhibit is still praised by experts as the best ever done. It has become an international standard for the replication of wilderness in a zoo exhibit and for the art of including and engaging the zoo-goer. Dian Fossey, the field scientist who lived for fifteen years near the wild mountain gorillas of Rwanda before her murder there, in December of 1985, flew to Seattle as a consultant to the designers of Woodland Park. When the exhibit was completed, Johnpaul Jones, Grant Jones's partner (the two are not related), sent photographs to her. She wrote back that she had shown the photos to her colleagues at the field station and they had believed them to be photos of wild gorillas in Rwanda. "Your firm, under the guidance of [Mr.] Hancocks, has made a tremendously im- [3]

portant advancement toward the captivity conditions of gorillas," Fossey wrote. "Had such existed in the past, there would undoubtedly be more gorillas living in captivity."

"Woodland Park has remained a model for the zoo world," says 4
Terry Maple, the new director of Zoo Atlanta, a professor of comparative psychology (a field that examines the common origins of animal and human behavior) at the Georgia Institute of Technology, and the author of numerous texts and articles on primate behavior. "Woodland Park changed the way we looked at the zoo environment. Before Woodland Park, if the gorillas weren't in cages, they were on beautiful mown lawns, surrounded by moats. In good zoos they had playground equipment. In Woodland Park the staff had to teach the public not to complain that the gorilla exhibit looked unkempt."

"As far as gorilla habitats go," Maple says, "Cincinnati's is pretty 5
good; San Diego's is pretty good; Columbus's has a huge cage, so aesthetically it loses a great deal, but socially it's terrific; San Francisco's is a more technical solution, naturalistic but surrounded by walls. Woodland Park's is the best in the world."

In Woodland Park the zoo-goer must step off the broad paved cen- 6
tral boulevard onto a narrow path engulfed by vegetation to get to the gorillas. Coe planted a big-leaf magnolia horizontally, into the bank of a man-made hill, so that it would grow over the path. ("People forget that a landscape architect not only can do this," he said on a recent tour of the exhibit, indicating a pretty circle of peonies, "but can also do *this*" —he pointed to a shaggy, weed-covered little hill. "I *designed* that hill.")

The path leads to a wooden lean-to with a glass wall on one side 7
that looks into a rich, weedy, humid clearing. Half a dozen heavy-set, agile gorillas part the tall grasses, stroll leaning on their knuckles, and sit nonchalantly among clumps of comfrey, gnawing celery stalks. The blue-black sheen of their faces and fur on a field of green is electrifying. The social organization of the gorillas is expressed by their interaction around a couple of boulders in the foreground of the exhibit. All the gorillas enjoy climbing on the boulders, but the young ones yield to their elders and the adult females yield to the adult males, two silverback gorillas. The silverbacks drum their chests with their fists rapidly and perfunctorily while briefly rising on two feet—not at all like Tarzan. The fists make a rapid thudding noise, which seems to mean, "Here I come." Each silverback climbs to his rostrum, folds his arms, and glares at the other. As in nature, their relationship is by turns civil but not friendly, and contentious but not bullying.

The zoo-goers in the lean-to, observing all this, feel fortunate that 8
the troop of gorillas chooses to stay in view, when it apparently has acres and acres in which to romp. Moss-covered boulders overlap other boulders in the distance, a stream fringed with ferns wanders among them, birds roost in the forty-foot-high treetops, and caves and

nests beyond the bend in the stream are available to the gorillas as a place of retreat. "Flight distance" is the zoological term for the distance an animal needs to retreat from an approaching creature in order to feel safe—the size of the cushion of empty space it wishes to maintain around itself. (Several years ago Jon Coe accepted an assignment to design a nursing home, a conventional job that was unusual for him. He designed the home with flight distance. Sitting rooms and visiting areas were spacious near the front door but grew smaller as one progressed down the hall toward the residents' rooms. A resident overwhelmed by too much bustle in the outer areas could retreat down the hall to quieter and quieter environments.)

In fact the gorillas in Woodland Park do not have so much space to 9 explore. The exhibit is 13,570 square feet (about a third of an acre), which is generous but not limitless. The arrangement of overlapping boulders and trees in the distance is meant to trick the eye. There are no fences or walls against which to calculate depth, and the visitor's peripheral vision is deliberately limited by the dimensions of the lean-to. Wider vision might allow a visitor to calculate his position within Woodland Park, or might give him an inappropriate glimpse—as happens in almost every other zoo in the world—of a snowshoe rabbit or an Amazon porcupine or a North American zoo-goer, over the heads of the West African gorillas. Coe measured and calculated the sight lines to ensure that the view was an uncorrupted one into the heart of the rain forest.

The boulders themselves contain a trick. Coe designed them to 10 contain heating coils, so that in the miserable, misty Seattle winter they give off a warm aura, like an electric blanket. The boulders serve two purposes: they help the tropical gorillas put up with the Seattle winter, and they attract the gorillas to within several feet of the lean-to and the zoo-goers. It is no coincidence that much of the drama of the gorillas' everyday life is enacted three feet away from the lean-to. The patch of land in front of the lean-to is shady and cool in summer. The gorillas freely choose where to spend their day, but the odds have been weighted heavily in favor of their spending it in front of the lean-to.

"Their old exhibit was a six-hundred-square-foot tile bathroom," 11 says Grant Jones, a tall, handsome, blue-eyed man. "The gorillas displayed a lot of very neurotic behavior. They were aggressive, sad, angry, lethargic. They had no flight distance. The people were behind the glass day and night, the people pounded on the glass, the gorillas were stressed out, totally, all the time. Their only way to deal with it was to sleep or to show intense anger. They'd pick up their own feces and smear it across the glass. They were not interacting with one another.

"My assumption was that when they left their cage to enter their 12 new outdoor park, that behavior would persist. On the first day, although they were frightened when they came into the new park, they were tranquil. They'd never felt the wind; they'd never seen a bird fly over; they'd never seen water flowing except for the drain in the bottom of their cubicle. Instantly they became quiet and curious. The male was afraid to enter into the environment and stood at the door for hours. His mate came and took him by the hand and led him. They only went about halfway. They stopped at a small stream. They sat and picked up some leaves and dipped them in the water and took a bite of the leaves. They leaned back and saw clouds moving over. It was spellbinding. I assumed they would never recover from the trauma of how they'd been kept. It turned out to be a matter of two or three days."

"Picture the typical zoo exhibit," Jon Coe says. "You stroll along a sidewalk under evenly spaced spreading maples, beside colorful bedding plants. On your right is a polar-bear exhibit. There is a well-pruned hedge of boxwood with a graphic panel in it. The panel describes interesting features of the species, including the fact that polar bears often are seen swimming far out to sea. In the exhibit a bear is splashing in a bathtub. Very little is required of the viewers and very little is gained by them. The visitor is bored for two reasons: first because the setting is too obvious, and second because of a feeling of security despite the close presence of a wild animal.

"When planning this exhibit, we learned that in the wild, gorillas like to forage at the edge of a forest, in clearings created by tribal people who fell the trees, burn off the undergrowth, farm for a couple of years, then move on. After they move on, the forest moves back in and the gorillas forage there. We set about to re-create that scene. We got lots of charred stumps, and we took a huge dead tree from a power-line clearing a few miles from here. The story is plant succession, and how the gorillas exploit the early plants growing back over the abandoned farmland."

Coe relies on stagecraft and drama to break down the zoo-goer's sense of security. When walking through a client zoo for the first time, long before he has prepared a master plan, he offers a few suggestions: Get rid of the tire swings in the chimp exhibit. Get rid of the signs saying NIMBA THE ELEPHANT and JOJO THE CHEETAH. Stop the publicized feeding of the animals, the baby elephant's birthday party, and any other element contributing to either an anthropomorphized view ("Do the elephants call each *other* Nimba and Bomba?") or a view of wild beasts as tame pets.

"How can we improve our ability to get and hold the attention of the zoo-goer?" he asks. "We must create a situation that transcends the range of stimulation people are used to and enhances the visitor's perception of the animal. A zoo animal that *appears* to be unrestrained and dangerous should receive our full attention, possibly accompanied by an adrenal rush, until its potential for doing us harm is determined."

For ten years Coe and others have been experimenting with the relative positions of zoo-goers and zoo animals. Coe now designs exhibits in which the animal terrain surrounds and is actually higher than the zoo paths, so that zoo-goers must look up to see the animals. The barriers between animals and people are camouflaged so effectively that zoo-goers may be uncertain whether an animal has access to them or not. In JungleWorld, the Bronx Zoo's recently opened $9.5 million indoor tropical forest nearly an acre in size, conceived by William Conway, the director of the zoo, a python lives inside a tree trunk that apparently has fallen across the zoo-goers' walkway. "We made the interior of the log brighter and tilted the glass away from the outside light to avoid all reflections," says Charles Beier, an associate curator. "It's an old jeweler's trick. When people glance overhead, there appears to be no barrier between them and the snake." The screams of horror provoked by the python are quite a different matter from the casual conversations that people engage in while strolling past rows of terrariums with snakes inside.

"We are trying to get people to be prepared to look for animals in the 18 forest, not have everything brightly lighted and on a platform in front of them," says John Gwynne, the deputy director for design of the New York Zoological Society, which operates the Bronx Zoo. "We have lots of dead trees and dead grass in here. It's actually very hard to train a gardener not to cut off the dead branches. We're trying to create a wilderness, not a garden—something that can catch people by surprise."

.   .   .

The profession of zoo design is a relatively new one. In the past, 19 when a zoo director said that a new lion house was required, the city council solicited bids and hired a popular local architect—the one who did the suburban hospital and the new high school—and paid him to fly around the country and get acquainted with lion houses. He visited four or five and learned design tips from each: how wide to space the bars, for example, and how thick to pour the cement. Then he flew home and drew a lion house.

"As recently as fifteen years ago there was no Jones & Jones or Jon 20 Coe," says William Conway, of the Bronx Zoo. "There were very few architects around then who had any concept of what animals were all about or who would go—as Jon Coe has gone—to Africa to see and sketch and try to understand, so that he knew what the biologist was talking about. The problem of the zoologist in the zoo was that, in the past, he was very often dealing with an architect who wanted to make a monument."

"The downfall of most zoos has been that they've hired architects," 21 says Ace Torre, a designer in New Orleans, who holds degrees in architecture and landscape architecture. "Some of the more unfortunate zoos hired six different architects. Each one made his own statement. As a result, the zoo is a patchwork of architectural tributes."

In 1975 the City of Seattle asked Grant Jones, whose firm had re-   22
stored the splendid Victorian copper-roofed pergolas and the elegant
walkways and the granite statuary of the city's Pioneer Square Historic
District, to design the Woodland Park Zoo gorilla house. The City of
Seattle—specifically, David Hancocks, the zoo director—had made a
novel choice. Jones was an anomaly in the world of architecture in
that he prided himself on having never designed anything taller than
three stories. Most of his buildings were made of wood, and they
tended to be situated in national parks. Instead of making a grand tour
of gorilla houses, Jones consulted field scientists and gorilla experts
who had seen how gorillas lived in the wild.

"When they asked me to design a gorilla exhibit," Jones says, "I   23
naturally rephrased the problem in my own mind as designing a landscape with gorillas in it. In what sort of landscape would I want to be-
hold gorillas? I would want to include mystery and discovery. I'd like
to see the gorillas from a distance first, and then up close. I'd like to be
able to intrude on them and see what's going on without their knowing I'm there. I'd want to give them flight distance, a place to back off
and feel secure. And I would want an experience that would take me
back to a primordial depth myself. How did I spend my day some millions of years ago, living in proximity to this animal?"

"We asked Dian Fossey to visit Seattle," David Hancocks says, "and   24
she became the most crucial member of the design team. We had so
many people telling us we were being very foolish. A zoo director on
the East Coast called to say he'd put a potted palm in a cage where a
gorilla had lived for fifteen years. The gorilla pulled it out by the roots,
ate it, and got sick."

"Driving in from the airport, we asked Fossey what the rain forest   25
looked like," Jon Coe says. "She kept turning this way and that way in
her seat, saying, 'It looks like that! It looks just like that!' Of course,
Seattle is in a belt of temperate rain forest Fossey was in an alpine
tropical rain forest. The plants are not identical, but they are very similar. We realized that we could stand back and let the native plants take
over the exhibit and the overall effect would be very much the same.

"And there were trees, forty-foot-tall trees, in the area slated for   26
the gorillas. What to do about the trees? No zoo in the world had let
gorillas have unlimited access to trees. We thought of the gorilla as a
terrestrial animal. The wisdom at the time said that the trees had to
come down. We brought George Schaller, probably the world's preem-
inent field scientist, to Seattle, and asked him about the trees. His response was, 'I don't know if they're going to fall out of them or not,
but somebody has to do this.'"

"They didn't fall out of the trees," Jones says, "but Kiki [one of the   27
silverbacks] escaped. We'd brought in some rock-climbers to try to get
out of the exhibit when it was finished, and we'd made a few modifi-

cations based on their suggestions. Jon figured out an elaborate jumping matrix: if a gorilla can jump this far on the horizontal, how far can
he go on a downward slope, et cetera. The problem is, you can't program in motivation. At some point the motivation may be so great that
you'll find yourself saying, 'Whoops, the tiger can jump thirteen feet,
not twelve. Guess we should have made it wider.'

"We had planted some hawthorn trees about four to five inches in   28
diameter, ten feet high, and had hoped they were large enough that
the gorillas would accept them. They accepted everything else, but
these trees were standing too much alone, too conspicuous. Kiki
pulled all the branches off of one, then ripped it out of the ground. It
stood by itself; the roots were like a tripod. He played with that thing
for a number of days.

"The keepers were aware of how we must never let them have a   29
big long stick because they might put it across the moat, walk across it,
and get out. They saw that tree but it was clearly not long enough to
bridge the moat. We all discussed it, and decided it wasn't a problem.
During that same period Kiki began disappearing for three hours at a
time, and we didn't know where he was. It's a large environment, and
he could have been off behind some shrubbery. One of the keepers
told us later that he'd seen Kiki sitting on the edge of the big dry moat
at the back of the habitat. One day Kiki climbed down into the moat.

"I imagine he took his tree with him to the far corner, leaned it up   30
against the wall, and considered it. At some point he must have made
a firm decision. He got a toehold on the roots, pressed his body to the
wall, lifted himself up in one lunge, and hung from the top of the
moat. Then he pulled himself up and landed in the rhododendrons. He
was out, he was in the park."

"He was sitting in the bushes and some visitors saw him," Coe   31
says. "They raced to the director's office and reported it to Hancocks."
His response was calm, according to Coe. Anxious visitors often reported that there were gorillas loose in the trees. "The gorilla's not
out," said Hancocks. "The exhibit, you see, is called landscape immer-
sion. It's intended to give you the *impression* that the gorillas are free."

The visitors thanked Hancocks and left. He overheard one remark   32
to the other, "Still, it just doesn't seem right having him sit there on
the sidewalk like that."

"Sidewalk?" Hancocks said.   33

"We called the police," says Hancocks, "not to control the gorilla   34
but to stop people from coming into the zoo. Jim Foster, the vet, fed
fruit to Kiki and calmed him down while we tried to figure out what to
do. We put a ladder across the moat and Jim climbed on it to show Kiki
how to cross. Kiki actually tried it, but the ladder wobbled and fell, and
he retreated. It was getting dark. We finally had to tranquilize him and
carry him back."

"It's been seven years since," Jones says, "and Kiki never has tried 35 again, although he clearly knows how to do it. He doesn't want to leave. In fact I am frequently called in by zoos that are having problems with escape. They always want to know, Should we make the moats wider? The bars closer together? Should we chain the animal? Yet escape is almost never a design problem. It is a question of motivation. It is a social problem."

"One of the roles a silverback has in life," Coe says, "is to patrol his 36 territory. Kiki wasn't escaping *from* something. He was exploring outward from the center of his territory to define its edges."

"If Kiki had escaped from a conventional ape house, the city 37 would have panicked," Hancocks says. "But in the year or two the exhibit has been open, Seattle had lost the hairy-monster-of-the-apehouse image, and saw gorillas as quiet and gentle."

Shortly after, one of the local papers carried a cartoon of Kiki 38 roller-skating arm-in-arm with two buxom beauties through the adjacent Greenlake Park, and another had a cartoon of him pole-vaulting over the moat.

.   .   .

The current revolution in zoo design—the landscape revolution— 39 is driven by three kinds of change that have occurred during this century. First are great leaps in animal ecology, veterinary medicine, landscape design, and exhibit technology, making possible unprecedented realism in zoo exhibits. Second, and perhaps most important, is the progressive disappearance of wilderness—the very subject of zoos—from the earth. Third is knowledge derived from market research and from environmental psychology, making possible a sophisticated focus on the zoo-goer.

Zoo-related sciences like animal ecology and veterinary medicine 40 for exotic animals barely existed fifty years ago and tremendous advances have been made in the last fifteen years. Zoo veterinarians now inoculate animals against diseases they once died of. Until recently, keeping the animals alive required most of a zoo's resources. A cage modeled after a scientific laboratory or an operating room—tile-lined and antiseptic, with a drain in the floor—was the best guarantee of continued physical health. In the late 1960s and early 1970s zoo veterinarians and comparative psychologists began to realize that stress was as great a danger as disease to the captive wild animals. Directors thus sought less stressful forms of confinement than the frequently-hosed-down sterile cell.

Field scientists also published findings about the complex social relations among wild animals. Zoos began to understand that captive animals who refused to mate often were reacting to the improper social 41

configurations in which they were confined. Gorillas, for example, live
in large groups in the wild. Zoos had put them in pairs, and then only
at breeding time—"believing them monogamous, as we'd like to think
we are," Coe says. Interaction between the male and the female gorilla
was stilted, hostile, abnormal. Successful breeding among captive gorillas didn't begin until they were housed in large family groups. Golden
lion tamarins, in contrast, refused to mate when they were caged in
groups. Only very recently did researchers affiliated with the National
Zoo discover that these beautiful little monkeys *are* monogamous.

Science first affected the design of zoos in 1735, when Linnaeus   42
published his *Systema Naturae* and people fell in love with classification.
The resultant primate house, carnivore house, and reptile house allowed the public to grasp the contemporary scientific understanding of
the animal world. "At the turn of the century a zoo was a place where
you went to learn what kinds of animals there were," Conway says.
"The fact that they were in little cages didn't matter. You could see this
was an Arabian oryx, a scimitar-horned oryx, a beisa oryx, and so on.
It wasn't at that time so important to have an idea of what they do, or
the way they live, or how they evolved." The taxonomic approach informed the design of science museums, aquariums, botanical gardens,
and arboretums.

Today zoo directors and designers can draw on whole libraries of   43
information about animal behavior and habitat. Exhibit designers can
create entire forests of epoxy and fiber-glass trees, reinforced concrete
boulders, waterfalls, and artificial vines, with mist provided by cloud
machines. A zoo director can oversee the creation of astoundingly realistic habitats for the animals.

But zoo directors and designers cannot simply create magnificent   44
animal habitats and call them a zoo. That would be something else—a
wildlife preserve, a national park. A zoo director has to think about
bathrooms: zoos are for people, not animals. A zoo director has to
think about bond issues and the fact that the city council, which also
finances garbage collection, trims a little more from his budget each
year. He has to be aware that the zoo is competing with a vast entertainment industry for the leisure hours and dollars of the public.

"If you're not smiling at Disney World, you're fired the next   45
day," says Robert Yokel, the director of the Miami Metrozoo. He is a
laid-back, blue-jeaned, suntanned man with wild, scant hair. "Happy,
happy, happy, that's the whole concept. They are the premier opera-
tors. They taught the rest of the industry how a park should be run:
keep it clean, make it convenient, make the ability to spend dollars
very easy. They do everything top drawer. They drew over thirteen
million people last year. It's an escape. It's a fantasy." Obviously, the director of the Miami zoo, more than most, has to worry about Disney

World. He is surrounded, as well, by Monkey Jungle, the Miami Sea-quarium, Busch Gardens, Parrot Jungle, Orchid Jungle, Flamingo Gardens, Lion Country Safari, and the beach. If Florida legalizes gambling, he may never see anyone again. But Yokel is not alone in the zoo world in appreciating what commercial entertainment parks offer the public.

The public today has more leisure time and disposable income 46 than ever before, more children than at any time since the 1950s, and more sophistication about animals—thanks to television, movies, and libraries—than at any time in history. Although a Greek in the age of Homer might not have been able to identify an anteater or a koala, many two-year-olds today can. However, there are other claims on people's time. Although, according to statistics, zoo-going is an entrenched habit with Americans, it is no longer likely that a station wagon packed with kids and heading down the highway on Sunday afternoon will turn in at the zoo. The family has been to Disney World, to Six Flags; they've been to theme parks where the hot-dog vendors wear period costumes and the concession stands look like log cabins; they've visited amusement parks where the whole environment, from the colorful banners to the trash cans, all sparkling clean and brightly painted, shrieks of fun. The local zoo, with its broad tree-lined avenues, pacing leopards, and sleeping bears, seems oddly antiquated and sobering by comparison. So zoo directors must ask, Are our visitors having a good time? Will they come back soon? Would they rather be at Disney World? What will really excite them?

Zoos used to be simpler. Once upon a time—in pharaonic Egypt, in 47 Imperial Rome, in the Austro-Hungarian Empire, in the traveling menageries and bear shows of Western Europe and Russia in the 1800s, even in the United States at the turn of the century—it was sufficient for the zoo to pluck an animal from the teeming wild populations in Asia and Africa and display it, as an exotic specimen, to an amazed populace. (And if the animal sickened in captivity, there was nothing to do but wait for it to die and send for another one. Not only had veterinary medicine not evolved adequately but there was no pressure by concerned wildlife groups for zoos to maintain and reproduce their own stock. The animals were out there.)

Already occupied with the welfare of their animals and the amuse- 48 ment of their zoo-goers, zoo directors today must be responsible to the larger reality that the wilderness is disappearing and the animals with it. Today the cement-block enclosure or quarter-acre plot allotted by a zoo may be the last protected ground on earth for an animal whose habitat is disappearing under farmland, villages, or cities. The word *ark* is used with increasing frequency by zoo professionals. In this country, zoos house members of half a dozen species already extinct in the wild, and of hundreds more on the verge of extinction. Zoo-goers are confronted by skull logos denoting vanishing animals. The new designers like Coe and Jones, and directors like Conway, Maple, Graham, Dolan, George Rabb, at Chicago Brookfield, and Michael Robinson, at the National Zoo, belong as no designers or directors ever before belonged to the international community of zoologists and conservationists who have as their goal the preservation of the wild.

"This is a desperate time," William Conway says. The New York   49
Zoological Society, under his leadership, also operates one of the largest and oldest wildlife-conservation organizations in the world, Wildlife Conservation International, which sponsors sixty-two programs in thirty-two countries. Conway is a slender, distinguished, avuncular gentleman with a pencil-line moustache. For him it seems quite a personal matter, a subject of intense private distress, that the earth is losing its wildlife and he doesn't know how many species are going, or what they are, or where they are, or how to save them.

"We are certainly at the rate of losing a species a day now, proba-   50
bly more," he says. "Who knows how many species there are on earth? Suppose, for the sake of argument, there are ten million species of animals out there. If we have one million in the year 2087 we will be doing very well. The human population is increasing at the rate of a hundred and fifty a minute. The tropical moist forest is decreasing at the rate of fifty acres a minute. And there is not a hope in the world of slowing this destruction and this population increase for quite some time. Most of the animals we hold dear, the big, charismatic megavertebrates, almost all of them will be endangered within the next twenty years. The people who are going to do that have already been born.

"And the destruction is being effected by some poor guy and his   51
wife and their five children who are hacking out a few acres of ground to try to eat. That's where most of the fifty acres a minute are going: forty-eight that way and two to the bulldozers. In Rwanda there is a mountain-gorilla preserve that supports two hundred and forty gorillas. It recently was calculated that the park could sustain two thousand human families, people with no other place to live, no land. Now, how can you justify saving the land for two hundred and forty gorillas when you could have two thousand human families? That's one side of the story. Here's the other: if you were to do that, to put those two thousand families in there, the mountain gorilla would disappear completely, and that would take care of Rwanda's population-expansion needs for slightly less than three months. It's a very discouraging picture."

Michael Robinson, the director of the National Zoo, is a rotund   52
and rosy-cheeked Englishman. "I have spent twenty years in the tropics, and it is difficult to talk about them in a detached, scientific manner," he says. "They are the richest ecosystem on earth. They have

been here for millions of years. Perhaps eighty percent of all the animals in the world live there and have evolved relationships of breathtaking complexity. The northern hardwood forests have perhaps forty species of trees per hectare. The rain forest has closer to a hundred and fifty to two hundred species per hectare. Once the rain forest is cut down, it takes about a hundred years for the trees to grow back. We estimate that it would take at least six hundred years before the forest has returned to its original state, with all the plants and animals there."

"The American Association of Zoological Parks and Aquariums Species Survival Plan has only thirty-seven endangered species," Conway says. "We should have at least a thousand. How are we going to do it? My God, there are only one thousand seven hundred and eighty-five spaces for big cats in the United States. One thousand seven hundred and eighty-five. How many races of tigers are out there? Five or six. Several races of lions. Several races of leopards, to say nothing of snow leopards, jaguars, fishing cats, cheetahs, and so on. And you have to maintain a minimum population of two to three hundred animals each to have a population that is genetically and demographically sound. What in bloody hell are we going to do?"

Zoos in America are doing two things to try to save the wild animals. The front-line strategy is conservation biology and captive propagation, employing all the recent discoveries in human fertility, such as *in vitro* fertilization, embryo transplantation, and surrogate motherhood. Zoos around the world have hooked into a computerized database called ISIS, so that if a rare Indian rhino goes into heat in Los Angeles—or, for that matter, in the wilds of India—a healthy male rhino to donate sperm can be located.

The second-line strategy is to attempt to save the wilderness itself through educating the public. Zoo directors and designers point out that there are 115 million American zoo-goers each year, and that if even 10 percent of them were to join conservation organizations, to boycott goods produced from the bones, horns, organs, and hides of endangered species, to vote to assist poor nations that are attempting to preserve their forests (perhaps by allowing debt payments to be eased in proportion to the numbers of wild acres preserved), their strength would be felt. The point of the landscape-immersion exhibits is to give the public a taste of what is out there, what is being lost.

It is dawning on zoo professionals that they are, in part, responsible for the American public's unfamiliarity with ecology and lack of awareness that half a dozen species a week are being driven into extinction, and that the precious tropical rain forest may vanish within our lifetime. "By itself, the sight of caged animals does not engender respect for animals," the environmental psychologist Robert Sommer wrote in 1972 in a pioneering essay titled "What Did We Learn at the Zoo?" "Despite excellent intentions, even the best zoos may be creating animal stereotypes that are not only incorrect but that actually work against the interests of wildlife preservation." Terry Maple says, "Zoos used to teach that animals are weird and they live alone."

In the past the only zoo people who paid much attention to zoo-goers were the volunteers assigned to drum up new members. The question they usually asked about zoo-goers was, Can we attract ten thousand of them in August? rather than, How have we influenced their attitudes about wildlife? With the decline of the wild and the dedication of zoos to educating the public, zoo professionals have grown curious about zoo-goers. What do they think? What are they saying as they nudge each other and point? Why do they shoot gum balls at the hippos? What exactly *are* they learning at the zoo? In search of answers to such questions, behavioral scientists are strolling through zoos around the country. They clock the number of seconds zoo-goers look at an exhibit. They count how many zoo-goers read the educational placards. They record the casual utterances of passers-by. And they note the age and gender of the zoo-goers who carve their initials on the railings. (They excite the envy of their co-equals in the science-museum world. "Researchers [at zoos] can linger for inordinate amounts of time at exhibits under the guise of waiting for an animal to do something," Beverly Serrell wrote in *Museum News* in 1980. "Standing next to a skeleton doesn't afford such a convenient cover.")

A fairly sharply focused portrait of the average North American zoo-goer has emerged. For example, data collected by the Smithsonian Institution at the National Zoo in 1979 revealed that zoo-goers arrive at the gates in any one of eighty-four "visitor constellations." One of the most common constellations is one parent accompanied by one or more children. On weekdays mothers predominate. On weekends fathers are sighted. In another study Professor Edward G. Ludwig, of State University College at Fredonia, New York, observed that the adult unaccompanied by children seemed to have "an aura of embarrassment." A survey published in 1976 found that zoo-goers tend to have more education and larger annual incomes than the population at large, and a 1979 survey found that zoo-goers are ignorant of basic ecological principles much more than are backpackers, birdwatchers, and members of wildlife organizations.

In a group of four zoo-goers, it's likely that only one or two will read an informational sign. Nearly all conversation will be confined to the friends and family members with whom the zoo-goer arrives. The most common form of conversation at the zoo is a declarative sentence following "Watch!" or "Look!" The second most common form is a question. Robert Yokel, in Miami, believes that the two questions asked most frequently by zoo-goers are "Where is the bathroom?" and

57

58

59

"Where is the snack bar?" Zoo-goers typically look at exhibits for about ninety seconds. Some never stop walking. Ludwig found that most people will stop for animals that beg, animals that are feeding, baby animals, animals that make sounds, or animals that are mimicking human behavior. People express irritation or annoyance with animals that sleep, eliminate, or regurgitate.

Zoo visitors do not like to lose their way within a zoo, and they get   60 disgruntled when they find themselves backtracking. "We do not enjoy walking in circles and we invariably do," said one of the 300 respondents to the Smithsonian study. "Then we get irritated with ourselves."

Jim Peterson, a senior partner in the natural-history exhibit design   61 firm of Bios, in Seattle, has identified the "first-fish syndrome." Within twenty feet of the entrance to an aquarium, visitors need to see a fish or they become unhappy. They will rush past the finest backlighted high-tech hands-on exhibitry to find that first fish. Similarly, Peterson has noted that visitors in zoos can tolerate only fifty feet between animals. Any greater distance inspires them to plow through foliage and create their own viewing blind.

Most "noncompliant behavior," such as unauthorized feeding of   62 animals or attempting to climb over barriers, comes from juveniles and teens in mixed-gender groupings and children accompanied by both parents. A 1984 study by Valerie D. Thompson suggested that two parents tend to be involved with each other, freeing the children to perform antisocial acts; and that among teenagers there is "a close tie between noncompliant behavior and attempting to impress a member of the opposite sex."

Ted Finlay, a graduate student working with Terry Maple at Zoo   63 Atlanta, wrote a mater's thesis titled "The Influence of Zoo Environments on Perceptions of Animals," one of the first studies to focus on zoo design. Finlay majored in psychology and animal behavior with a minor in architecture, with the intention of becoming a zoo psychologist. For the research for his dissertation he prepared a slide show of animals in three environments: free, caged, and in various types of naturalistic zoo exhibits. Two hundred and sixty-seven volunteers viewed the slides and rated their feelings about the animals. The free animals were characterized as "free," "wild," and "active." Caged animals were seen as "restricted," "tame," and "passive." Animals in naturalistic settings were rated like the free animals if no barrier was visible. If the barrier *was* visible, they were rated like caged animals— that is to say, less favorably.

The zoo-goer who emerges from the research literature—be-   64 nighted and happy-go-lucky, chomping his hot dog, holding his nose in the elephant house and scratching under his arms in the monkey house to make his children laugh—is a walking anachronism. He is the creation of an outmoded institution—the conventional zoo—in which the primate house, carnivore house, and reptile house, all lined with tile, glow with an unreal greenish light as if the halls were subterranean, and in which giraffes, zebras, and llamas stand politely, and as if on tiptoe, on the neatly mown lawns of the moated exhibits.

Once it was education enough for the public to file past the captive [65] gorilla in its cage and simply absorb the details of its peculiar or frightening countenance. "One ape in a cage, shaking its steel bars," Terry Maple says, "was a freak show, a horror show, King Kong! You'd go there to be scared, to scream, to squeeze your girlfriend." Despite gilded, or dingy, surroundings, a tusked creature in eighteenth-century Versailles, or downtown Pittsburgh, had the aura of a savage, strange, flowered wilderness.

"Pee-you!" is the primal, universal response of schoolchildren [66] herded into an elephant house. Adults more discreetly crinkle their noses, turn their heads, and laugh. The unspoken impressions are that elephants are filthy, tread in their own feces, attract flies, require hosing down, eat mush, and no wonder they are housed in cinder-block garages. These are not the sort of impressions that might inspire a zoo-goer to resist—much less protest—the marketing of souvenirs made of ivory.

Moated exhibits display animals in garden-like settings, with bed- [67] ding plants along cement walkways. A koala seated alone in the branch of a single artificial tree above a bright-green lawn looks as if he'd be at home in a Southern California back yard, next to the patio. The visitors looking at such exhibits appreciate the animals in them more and pronounce them "beautiful" or "interesting," but the subliminal message here is that animals are like gentle pets and thrive nicely in captivity. The visitors are hard pressed to explain what the big deal is about the rain forest or why zoologists talk about it, their voices cracking, the way twelfth-century Crusaders must have discussed the Holy Land.

BRIGID BROPHY

The Menace of Nature

Brigid Brophy (1929–1995), after completing an undergraduate degree in classics at Oxford University, found work as a secretary first for a London camera firm and later for a distributor of pornographic books. By 1954, however, she had established herself as a prize-winning novelist. She later produced several novels, scores of essays, a psychoanalytic study of civilization (*Black Ship to Hell*, 1962), a book on Mozart, and another on the "decadent" artist Aubrey Beardsley. Perhaps the most characteristic of her titles, however, is *Fifty Works of English Literature We Could Do Without* (1968). Brophy is an iconoclast by nature: She challenges every complacent assumption she finds. "The Menace of Nature" (first published in London's *New Statesman* in 1965) attacks several beliefs most of us accept without a second thought: that the city is stressful and the country relaxing, that a rural landscape is more beautiful than a block of buildings, that when we get "back to the land" we are making contact with something basic to human nature. Not only does Brophy challenge beliefs some of us cherish, but she addresses us with more familiarity than we are accustomed to: She seems to pluck at our sleeves rather than address us from behind a lectern. Both the voice and the stance of the essay make it an excellent companion to Harry Crews's "Pages from the Life of a Georgia Innocent."

So? Are you just back? Or are you, perhaps, staying on there for the extra week? By "there" I mean, of course, one of the few spots left where the machine has not yet gained the upper hand; some place as yet unstrangled by motorways and unfouled by concrete mixers; a place where the human spirit can still—but for how much longer?—steep itself in natural beauty and recuperate after the nervous tension, the sheer stress, of modern living.

Well (I assume you're *enough* recuperated to stand this information?): I think you've been piously subscribing to a heresy. It's a heresy I incline offhand to trace, with an almost personally piqued sense of vendetta, to the old heresiarch himself, the sometimes great, often bathetic but never cogently thoughtful poet, William Wordsworth. Since the day he let the seeds of heresy fall (on, no doubt, the Braes of the Yarrow or the Banks of Nith), the thing has spread and enlarged itself into one of the great parroted, meaningless (but slightly paranoid) untruths of our age.

I am not trying to abolish the countryside. (I *state* this because it is true; I emphasise it because I don't want the lynch mob outside my window.) I'm not such a pig as to want the country built on or littered up with bottles and plastic bags merely because it doesn't appeal to *me*. As it happens, my own taste for countryside, though small, is existent. I've found the country very pleasant to be driven through in a tolerably fast car by someone whose driving I trust and whose company I like. But I admit that landscape as such bores me—to the extent that I have noticed myself in picture galleries automatically pausing to look at "Landscape with Ruins" or "Bandits in a Landscape" but walking straight past the pure landscapes at a speed which is obviously trying to simulate the effect of being driven past in a car.

I'm not, however, out to dissuade *you* from spending your holiday as a sort of legalised bandit in the landscape. Neither am I anti-holiday. Holidays have been sniped at lately as things everyone feels an obligation to enjoy but no one really does. Yet I suspect there would be fewer dissatisfied holiday-makers if social pressure didn't try to limit our choice to "Landscape" or "Landscape with Seascape." You can be made to feel quite guiltily antisocial in the summer months if you are, like me, constitutionally unable either to relax or to take a suntan. Indeed, relaxation is becoming this decade's social *sine qua non,* like Bridge in the 'thirties. They'll scarcely let you have a baby these days if you can't satisfy them beforehand you're adept at relaxing. But on the in some ways more private question of having a holiday, constitutional urbanites are still free, if only they can resist being shamed onto the beaches, to opt out of a rest and settle for the change which even the proverb allows to be as good as it. By simply exchanging their own for a foreign city, they are released from the routine of earning their daily bread and washing up after it, but don't suffer the disorientation, the uncorseted discomfort, which overtakes an urbanite cast up on a beach with no timetable to live by except the tides.

Still, it isn't in the holidays but during the rest of the year that the   5
great rural heresy does its damage. How many, for example, of the middle-class parents who bring up their children in London do so with unease or even apology, with a feeling that they are selfishly depriving the children of some "natural heritage" and sullying their childhood with urban impurities? Some parents even let this guilt drive them out to the suburbs or further, where they believe they cancel the egocentricity of their own need or desire for the town by undergoing the martyrdom of commuting. This parental masochism may secure the child a rural heritage (though parents should enquire, before moving, whether their child has the rural temperament and *wants* the rural heritage) but it deprives him of the cultural one; he gains the tennis club but is condemned to the tennis club light-opera society's amateur production of *No, No, Nanette* because the trains don't run late enough to bring him home after Sadler's Wells.[1]

The notion that "nature" and "nature study" are somehow "nice"   6
for children, regardless of the children's own temperament, is a sentimental piety—and often a hypocritical one, like the piety which thinks Sunday School nice for *them* though we don't go to church ourselves. (In fact, it is we middle-aged who may need fresh air and exercise; the young are cat-like enough to remain lithe without.) Historically, it is not inept to trace the supposed affinity between children and "nature" to Wordsworth's time. It was about that time that there settled on England, like a drizzle, the belief that sex is *not* "nice" for children. Children's sexual curiosity was diverted to "the birds and the bees" and gooseberry bushes; and birds, bees and bushes—in other words, "nature"—have remained "suitable" for children ever since.

If the romantic belief in children's innocence is now exploded, its   7
numinous energy has only gone to strengthen the even more absurd romantic belief in the innocence of landscape's, as opposed to man-

---

1. Sadler's Wells: a theater in London, primarily used by visiting theatrical companies.

created beauty. But I reject utterly the imputation that a brook is purer than Bach or a breeze more innocent than *As You Like It*. I warn you I shall be suspicious of this aesthetic faculty of yours that renders you so susceptible to the beauty of Snowdon if it leaves you unable to see anything in All Souls', Langham Place; and I shall be downright sceptical of it if (I am making allowance for your sensibility to run exclusively in that landscape groove which mine leaves out) you dote on the Constable country but feel it vaguely impure to take a 74 to the V.&A. to see a Constable.[2]

You'll protest you feel no such impurity. Yet didn't you read the   8 first paragraph of this article without taking so much as a raised eyebrow's worth of exception? Didn't you let the assumption pass that the city is corrupt? Weren't you prepared to accept from me, as you have from a hundred august authorities—sociologists, physicians, psychologists—that *idée reçue*[3] about the nervous tension and stress of modern urban life? But what in heaven's name is this stressful modern urban life being compared with? Life in a medieval hamlet? Will no one take into account the symptoms into which the stress of *that* erupted—the epidemics of dancing madness and flagellation frenzy? Or life in a neolithic cave—whose stress one can only imagine and flinch at?

The truth is that the city is a device for *reducing* stress—by giving   9 humans a freer choice of escapes from the pressure (along with the weather) of their environment. The device doesn't always work perfectly: traffic jams *are* annoying; the motor car does maim and must be prevented from doing so: but the ambulance which arrives so mercifully quick is also powered by a motor. The city is one of the great indispensable devices of civilisation (itself only a device for centralising beauty and transmitting it as a heritage). It is one of the cardinal simple brilliant inventions, like currency. Like currency, it is a medium of exchange and thereby of choice—whereas the country is a place where one is under the thumb of chance, constrained to love one's neighbour not out of philanthropy but because there's no other company.

What's more, in the eighteenth century the city was suddenly up- 10 graded from a device of civilisation to a manifestation of it. The city became an art form. (The form had been discovered, but not very consciously remarked, earlier. It was discovered, like many art forms, by accident—often, as at Venice and Bruges, an accident of water.) We are in dire danger now of clogging up our cities as devices and at the same time despoiling them as works of art; and one of the biggest villains in this process is our rural heresy.

2. The references in the last sentence in the paragraph are *Snowdon*, highest mountain in Wales, in a district noted for scenic beauty; *All Souls', Langham Place*, church in London built from 1822 to 1825 by John Nash; *Constable country*, rural areas in southern Great Britain painted by the famous landscape painter John Constable (1776–1837); *a 74*, a bus; *the V.&A.*, the Victoria & Albert Museum in London, where a number of Constables are hung.
3. *idée reçue:* an idea generally accepted by everyone.

Most western European beings have to live in cities, and all but   11
the tiny portion of them who are temperamental rustics would do so
contentedly, without wasting energy in guilt, and with an appreciative
eye for the architecturescapes round them, had they not been told that
liking the country is purer and more spiritual. Our cities run to squalor
and our machines run amok because our citizens' minds are not on
the job of mastering the machines and using them to make the cities
efficient and beautiful. Their eyes are blind to the Chirico-esque hand-
someness of the M1,[4] because their hearts are set on a rustic Never-
Never Land. Rustic sentimentality makes us build our suburban villas
to mimic cottages, and then pebble-dash their outside walls in pious
memory of the holiday we spent sitting agonised on the shingle. The
lovely terraced façades of London are being undermined, as by subsi-
dence, by our yearning, our sickly nostalgia, for a communal country
childhood that never existed. We neglect our towns for a fantasy of
going "back" to the land, back to our "natural" state. But there isn't
and never was a natural man. We are a species that doesn't occur wild.
No pattern in his genes instructs man on what pattern to build his nest.
Instead, if he's fortunate, the Muses whisper to him the ground-plan of
an architectural folly. Even in his cave, he frescoed the walls. All that is
infallibly natural to our species is to make things that are artificial. We
are *homo artifex, homo faber, homo Fabergé.*[5] Yet we are so ignorant of our
own human nature that our cities are falling into disrepair and all we
worry about is their encroachment on "nature."

For, as I said at the start, the rural fantasy is paranoid. A glance at   12
history shows that it is human life which is frail, and civilisation which
flickers in constant danger of being blown out. But the rural fantasy
insists that every plant is a delicate plant. The true paranoid situation is
on the other foot. I wouldn't wish to do (and if we live at sensibly high
densities there's no need to do) either, but were I forced either to pull
down a Nash terrace or to build over a meadow, I'd choose the latter. If
you don't like what you've put up on the meadow, you can take it
away again and the meadow will re-seed itself in a year or two; but
human semen is lucky if it engenders an architectural genius a century. The whole Wordsworthian fallacy consists in gravely underesti-
mating the toughness of plants. In fact, no sooner does civilisation
admit a crack—no sooner does a temple of Apollo lapse into disuse—
than a weed forces its wiry stem through the crack and urges the blocks
of stone further apart. During the last war, the bomber engines were

4. The allusion is to Giorgio de Chirico, an early-twentieth-century Italian painter
whose mysterious, symbolic work influenced surrealist painters. The M1 is a major
northbound highway out of London.
5. The Latin phrase is very freely translatable either as "man the craftsman, man the
builder, man the perfumed" or as "man the tool-user, man the engineer, man the jeweler." Fabergé is the name of both an international manufacturer of fragrances and a
brilliant Russian goldsmith, known especially for his Imperial Easter eggs.

hardly out of earshot before the loosestrife[6] leapt up on the bombed site. Whether we demolish our cities in a third world war or just let them tumble into decay, the seeds of the vegetable kingdom are no doubt waiting to seize on the rubble or sprout through the cracks. *Aux armes, citoyens.*[7] To your trowels and mortar. Man the concrete mixers. The deep mindless silence of the countryside is massing in the Green Belt, ready to move in.

LEWIS THOMAS

Crickets, Bats, Cats, & Chaos

Lewis Thomas (1913–1993) was a physician by vocation and a naturalist by avocation. He became a writer almost by accident: in 1970 he was asked to deliver the keynote address at a medical symposium on inflammation. "This kind of conference," he later observed, "tends to be rather heavy going and my talk was designed to lighten the proceedings at the outset by presenting a rather skewed view of inflammation." The address was such a success that Thomas was soon asked to become a regular columnist for the *New England Journal of Medicine.* The terms were simple: no pay for Thomas but an absolutely free hand to write what he wished. Thomas's essays attracted a wide audience and were eventually collected in a series of popular books: *The Lives of a Cell* (1974), *The Medusa and the Snail* (1979), *Late Night Thoughts on Listening to Mahler's Ninth Symphony* (1983), *Et Cetera, et Cetera* (1990), and *The Fragile Species* (1992). In 1983 he published *The Youngest Science,* a mixture of memoir and history that reminds us how closely his own career paralleled the development of truly modern medicine. Thomas was president emeritus at the Memorial Sloan-Kettering Cancer Center in New York City until his death in 1993.

"Crickets, Bats, Cats, & Chaos" originally appeared in *Audubon* in 1992 and was collected in *The Best American Essays, 1993.* In linking seemingly disparate things together under one roof, the structure of Thomas's essay suggests one of its central themes: order in chaos. This approach to the essay form invites comparison with Alice Walker's "Am I Blue?"

I am not sure where to classify the mind of my cat Jeoffry. He is a   1
small Abyssinian cat, a creature of elegance, grace, and poise, a piece
of moving sculpture, and a total mystery. We named him Jeoffry after

---

6. loosestrife: a wild flowering plant.
7. *Aux armes, citoyens:* "To arms, citizens" (French)—a call to battle (the third line of *La Marseillaise,* the French national anthem).

the eighteenth-century cat celebrated by the unpredictable poet Christopher Smart in a poem titled "Jubilate Agno," one section of which begins, "For I will consider my cat Jeoffry." The following lines are selected more or less at random:

For he counteracts the powers of darkness by his electrical skin and glaring eyes.
For he counteracts the Devil, who is death, by brisking about the life . . .
For he is of the tribe of Tiger . . .
For he purrs in thankfulness, when God tells him he's a good Cat . . .
For he is an instrument for the children to learn benevolence upon . . .
For he is a mixture of gravity and waggery . . .
For there is nothing sweeter than his peace when at rest.
For there is nothing brisker than his life when in motion.

I have not the slightest notion what goes on in the mind of my cat Jeoffry, beyond the conviction that it is a genuine mind, with genuine thoughts and a strong tendency to chaos, but in all other respects a mind totally unlike mine. I have a hunch, based on long moments of observing him stretched on the rug in sunlight, that his mind has more periods of geometric order, and a better facility for switching itself almost, but not quite, entirely off, and accordingly an easier access to pure pleasure. Just as he is able to hear sounds that I cannot hear, and smell important things of which I am unaware, and suddenly leap like a crazed gymnast from chair to chair, upstairs and downstairs through the house, flawless in every movement and searching for something he never finds, he has periods of meditation on matters I know nothing about.

While thinking about what nonhumans think is, in most biological   2
quarters, an outlandish question, even an impermissible one, to which the quick and easy answer is nothing, or almost nothing, or certainly nothing like *thought* as we use the word, I still think about it. For while none of them may have real thoughts, foresee the future, regret the past, or be self-aware, most of us up here at the peak of evolution cannot manage the awareness of our own awareness, a state of mind only achieved when the mind succeeds in emptying itself of all other information and switches off all messages, interior and exterior. This is the state of mind for which the Chinese Taoists long ago used a term meaning, literally, no-knowledge. With no-knowledge, it is said, you get a different look at the world, an illumination.

Falling short of this, as I do, and dispossessed of anything I could   3
call illumination, it has become my lesser satisfaction to learn secondhand whatever I can, and then to think, firsthand, about the behavior of other kinds of animals.

I think of crickets, for instance, and the thought of their unique,   4
very small thoughts—principally about mating and bats—but also

about the state of cricket society. The cricket seems to me an eminently suitable animal for sorting out some of the emotional issues bound to arise in any consideration of animal awareness. Nobody, so far as I know, not even an eighteenth-century minor poet, could imagine any connection between events in the mind of a cricket and those in the mind of a human. If there was ever a creature in nature meriting the dismissive description of a living machine, mindless and thoughtless, the cricket qualifies. So in talking about what crickets are up to when they communicate with each other, as they unmistakably do, by species-unique runs and rhythms of chirps and trills, there can be no question of *anthropomorphization,* that most awful of all terms for the deepest error a modern biologist can fall into.

If you reduce the temperature of a male cricket, the rate of his   5
emission of chirping signals is correspondingly reduced. Indeed, some of the earlier naturalists used the technical term "thermometer crickets" because of the observation that you can make a close guess at the air temperature in a field by counting the rate of chirps of familiar crickets.

This is curious, but there is a much more curious thing going on   6
when the weather changes. The female crickets in the same field, genetically coded to respond specifically to the chirp rhythm of their species, adjust their recognition mechanism to the same temperature change and the same new, slower rate of chirps. That is, as John Doherty and Ronald Hoy wrote on observing the phenomenon, "warm females responded best to the songs of warm males, and cold females responded best to the songs of cold males." The same phenomenon, known as temperature coupling, has been encountered in grasshoppers and tree frogs, and also in fireflies, with their flash communication system. The receiving mind of the female cricket, if you are willing to call it that, adjusts itself immediately to match the sending mind of the male. This has always struck me as one of the neatest examples of animals adjusting to a change in their environment.

But I started thinking about crickets with something quite differ-   7
ent in mind, namely bats. It has long been known that bats feed voraciously on the nocturnal flights of crickets and moths, which they detect on the wing by their fantastically accurate ultrasound mechanism. What should have been guessed at, considering the ingenuity of nature, is that certain cricket species, green lacewings, and certain moths have ears that can detect the ultrasound emissions of a bat, and can analyze the distance and direction from which the ultrasound is coming. These insects can employ two separate and quite distinct defensive maneuvers for evading the bat's keen sonar.

The first is simply swerving away. This is useful behavior when the   8
bat signal is coming from a safe distance, twenty to thirty meters away. At this range the insect can detect the bat, but the bat is too far off to

receive the bounced ultrasound back to its own ears. So the cricket or moth needs to do nothing more, at least for the moment, than swing out of earshot.

But when the bat is nearby, three meters or less, the insect is in   9 immediate and mortal danger, for now the bat's sonar provides an accurate localization. It is too late for swerving or veering; because of its superior speed the bat can easily track such simple evasions. What to do? The answer has been provided by Kenneth Roeder, who designed a marvelous laboratory model for field studies, including instruments to imitate the intensity and direction of bat signals.

The answer, for a cricket or moth or lacewing who hears a bat hom-   10 ing in close by, is *chaos*. Instead of swerving away, the insect launches into wild, totally erratic, random flight patterns, as unpredictable as possible. This kind of response tends to confuse the bat and results in escape for the insect frequently enough to have been selected by evolution as the final, stereotyped, "last-chance" response to the threat. It has the look of a very smart move, whether thought out or not.

So chaos is part of the useful, everyday mental equipment of a   11 cricket or a moth, and that, I submit, is something new to think about. I don't wish to push the matter beyond its possible significance, but it seems to me to justify a modest nudge. The long debate over the problem of animal awareness is not touched by the observation, but it does bring up the opposite side of that argument, the opposite of anthropomorphization. It is this: Leaving aside the deep question as to whether the lower animals have anything going on in their mind that we might accept as conscious thought, are there important events occurring in our human minds that are matched by habits of the animal mind?

Surely chaos is a capacious area of common ground. I am con-   12 vinced that my own mind spends much of its waking hours, not to mention its sleeping time, in a state of chaos directly analogous to that of the cricket hearing the sound of the nearby bat. But there is a big difference. My chaos is not induced by a bat; it is not suddenly switched on in order to facilitate escape; it is not an evasive tactic set off by any new danger. It is, I think, the normal state of affairs, and not just for my brain in particular but for human brains in general. The chaos that is my natural state of being is rather like the concept of chaos that has emerged in higher mathematical circles in recent years.

As I understand it, and I am quick to say that I understand it only   13 quite superficially, chaos occurs when any complex, dynamic system is perturbed by a small uncertainty in one or another of its subunits. The inevitable result is an amplification of the disturbance and then the spread of unpredictable, random behavior throughout the whole system. It is the total unpredictability and randomness that makes the word "chaos" applicable as a technical term, but it is not true that the behavior of the system becomes disorderly. Indeed, as James P. Crutchfield and his associates have written, "There is order in chaos: underlying chaotic behavior there are elegant geometric forms that create randomness in the same way as a card dealer shuffles a deck of cards or a blender mixes cake batter." The random behavior of a turbulent stream of water, or of the weather, or of Brownian movement, or of the central nervous system of a cricket in flight from a bat, are all determined by the same mathematical rules. Behavior of this sort has been encountered in computer models of large cities: When a small change was made in one small part of the city model, the amplification of the change resulted in enormous upheavals, none of them predictable, in the municipal behavior at remote sites in the models.

A moth or a cricket has a small enough nervous system to *seem* 14 predictable and orderly most of the time. There are not all that many neurons, and the circuitry contains what seem to be mostly simple reflex pathways. Laboratory experiments suggest that in a normal day, one thing—the sound of a bat at a safe distance, say—leads to another, predictable thing—a swerving off to one side in flight. It is only when something immensely new and important happens—the bat sound at three meters away—that the system is thrown into chaos.

I suggest that the difference with us is that chaos is the norm. Pre- 15 dictable, small-scale, orderly, cause-and-effect sequences are hard to come by and don't last long when they do turn up. Something else almost always turns up at the same time, and then another sequential thought intervenes alongside, and there come turbulence and chaos again. When we are lucky, and the system operates at its random best, something astonishing may suddenly turn up, beyond predicting or imagining. Events like these we recognize as good ideas.

My cat Jeoffry's brain is vastly larger and more commodious than 16 that of a cricket, but I wonder if it is qualitatively all that different. The cricket lives with his two great ideas in mind, mating and predators, and his world is a world of particular, specified sounds. He is a tiny machine, I suppose, depending on what you mean by "machine," but it is his occasional moments of randomness and unpredictability that entitle him to be called aware. In order to achieve that feat of wild chaotic flight, and thus escape, he has to make use, literally, of his brain. When Int 1, an auditory interneuron, is activated by the sound of a bat closing in, the message is transmitted by an axon connected straight to the insect's brain, and it is here, and only here, that the swerving is generated. This I consider to be a thought, a very small thought, but still a thought. Without knowing what to count as a thought, I figure that Jeoffry, with his kind of brain, has a trillion thoughts of about the same size in any waking moment. As for me, and my sort of brain, I can't think where to begin.

We like to think of our minds as containing trains of thought, or 17
streams of consciousness, as though they were orderly arrangements
of linear events, one notion leading in a cause-and-effect way to the
next notion. Logic is the way to go; we set a high price on logic, unlike
E. M. Forster's elderly lady in *Aspects of the Novel,* who, when accused of
being illogical, replied, "Logic? Good gracious! What rubbish! How can
I tell what I think till I see what I say?"

But with regard to our own awareness of nature, I believe we've 18
lost sight of, lost track of, lost touch with, and to some measurable degree lost respect for, the chaotic and natural in recent years—and during the very period of history when we humans have been learning
more about the detailed workings of nature than in all our previous
millennia. The more we learn, the more we seem to distance ourselves
from the rest of life, as though we were separate creatures, so different
from other occupants of the biosphere as to have arrived from another
galaxy. We seek too much to explain, we assert a duty to run the place,
to dominate the planet, to govern its life, but at the same time we ourselves seem to be less a part of it than ever before.

We leave it whenever we can, we crowd ourselves from open 19
green countrysides onto the concrete surfaces of massive cities, as far
removed from the earth as we can get, staring at it from behind insulated glass, or by way of half-hour television clips.

At the same time, we talk a great game of concern. We shout at 20
each other in high virtue, now more than ever before, about the be-
foulment of our nest and about whom to blame. We have mechanized
our lives so extensively that most of us live with the illusion that our
only connection with nature is the nagging fear that it may one day
turn on us and do us in. Polluting our farmlands and streams, even the
seas, worries us because of what it may be doing to the food and water
supplies necessary for human beings. Raising the level of CO_2, methane,
and hydrofluorocarbons in the atmosphere troubles us because of the
projected effects of climate upheaval on human habitats. These anxi-
eties do not extend, really, to nature at large. They are not the result of
any new awareness.

Nature itself, that vast incomprehensible meditative being, has 21
come to mean for most of us nothing much more than odd walks in
the nearby woods, or flowers in the rooftop garden, or the soap opera
stories of the last giant panda or whooping crane, or curiosities like the
northward approach, from Florida, of the Asiatic flying cockroach.

I will begin to feel better about us, and about our future, when we 22
finally start learning about some of the things that are still mystifications. Start with the events in the mind of a cricket, I'd say, and then
go on from there. Comprehend my cat Jeoffry and we'll be on our
way. Nowhere near home, but off and dancing, getting within a few

millennia of understanding why the music of Bach is what it is, ready at last for open outer space. Give us time, I'd say, the kind of endless time we mean when we talk about the real world.

VICKI HEARNE

What's Wrong with Animal Rights

Vicki Hearne (1946–   ), known equally for her creative writing and animal training, is a professor of English at Yale and consultant for the Yale Institution for Social and Policy Studies. Born in Austin, Texas, Hearne received her B.A. from the University of California at Riverside, where she served as a lecturer in the early eighties. Her books of poetry include *Nervous Horses* (1980) and *The Parts of Light: Poems* (1994), and she has also written a novel, *The White German Shepherd* (1988). Hearne is also a weekly columnist on animal issues for the *Los Angeles Times* and has published several works of nonfiction about animals, including *Adam's Task: Calling Animals by Name* (1986), *Bandit: Dossier of a Dangerous Dog* (1991), and *Animal Happiness* (1994).

In *Adam's Task*, a well-received but controversial book, Hearne spells out her philosophy of domesticated animals and their relationship to humans; this book lays the foundation for her essay "What's Wrong with Animal Rights," first published in *Harper's* (September 1991) and collected in *Best American Essays, 1992*. Like Lewis Thomas's "Crickets, Bats, Cats, & Chaos," Hearne's essay is overtly analytical and persuasive; together the essays demonstrate ways of developing a thesis through examples, illustrations, and analysis.

Not all happy animals are alike. A Doberman going over a hurdle after a small wooden dumbbell is sleek, all arcs of harmonious power. A basset hound cheerfully performing the same exercise exhibits harmonies of a more lugubrious nature. There are chimpanzees who love precision the way musicians or fanatical housekeepers or accomplished hypochondriacs do; others for whom happiness is a matter of invention and variation—chimp vaudevillians. There is a rhinoceros whose happiness, as near as I can make out, is in needing to be trained every morning, all over again, or else he "forgets" his circus routine, and in this you find a clue to the slow, deep, quiet chuckle of his happiness and to the glory of the beast. Happiness for Secretariat[1] is in his ebullient bound, that joyful length of stride. For the draft horse or the weight-pull dog, happiness is of a different shape, more awesome and

1

---

1. Secretariat: U.S. racehorse who won the Kentucky Derby in 1973.

less obviously intelligent. When the pulling horse is at its most intense, the animal goes into himself, allocating all of the educated power that organizes his desire to dwell in fierce and delicate intimacy with that power, leans into the harness, and MAKES THAT SUCKER MOVE.

If we are speaking of human beings and use the phrase "animal happiness," we tend to mean something like "creature comforts." The emblems of this are the golden retriever rolling in the grass, the horse with his nose deep in the oats, the kitty by the fire. Creature comforts are important to animals—"Grub first, then ethics" is a motto that would describe many a wise Labrador retriever, and I have a pit bull named Annie whose continual quest for the perfect pillow inspires her to awesome feats. But there is something more to animals, a capacity for satisfactions that come from work in the fullest sense—what is known in philosophy and in this country's Declaration of Independence as "happiness." This is a sense of personal achievement, like the satisfaction felt by a good wood-carver or a dancer or a poet or an accomplished dressage horse. It is a happiness that, like the artist's, must come from something within the animal, something trainers call "talent." Hence, it cannot be imposed on the animal. But it is also something that does not come *ex nihilo*.[2] If it had not been a fairly ordinary thing, in one part of the world, to teach young children to play the pianoforte, it is doubtful that Mozart's music would exist.

Happiness is often misunderstood as a synonym for pleasure or as an antonym for suffering. But Aristotle associated happiness with ethics—codes of behavior that urge us toward the sensation of getting it right, a kind of work that yields the "click" of satisfaction upon solving a problem or surmounting an obstacle. In his *Ethics*, Aristotle wrote, "If happiness is activity in accordance with excellence, it is reasonable that it should be in accordance with the highest excellence." Thomas Jefferson identified the capacity for happiness as one of the three fundamental rights on which all others are based: "life, liberty, and the pursuit of happiness."

I bring up this idea of happiness as a form of work because I am an animal trainer, and work is the foundation of the happiness a trainer and an animal discover together. I bring up these words also because they cannot be found in the lexicon of the animal-rights movement. This absence accounts for the uneasiness toward the movement of most people, who sense that rights advocates have a point but take it too far when they liberate snails or charge that goldfish at the county fair are suffering. But the problem with the animal-rights advocates is not that they take it too far; it's that they've got it all wrong.

Animal rights are built upon a misconceived premise that rights were created to prevent us from unnecessary suffering. You can't find an animal-rights book, video, pamphlet, or rock concert in which some-

2. *ex nihilo:* Latin phrase meaning "from or out of nothing."

one doesn't mention the Great Sentence, written by Jeremy Bentham in 1789. Arguing in favor of such rights, Bentham wrote: "The question is not, Can they *reason?* nor, can they *talk?* but, can they suffer?"

The logic of the animal-rights movement places suffering at the iconographic center of a skewed value system. The thinking of its proponents—given eerie expression in a virtually sadopornographic sculpture of a tortured monkey that won a prize for its compassionate vision—has collapsed into a perverse conundrum. Today the loudest voices calling for—demanding—the destruction of animals are the humane organizations. This is an inevitable consequence of the apotheosis of the drive to relieve suffering: death is the ultimate release. To compensate for their contradictions, the humane movement has demonized, in this century and the last, those who made animal happiness their business: veterinarians, trainers, and the like. We think of Louis Pasteur as the man whose work saved you and me and your dog and cat from rabies, but antivivisectionists of the time claimed that rabies increased in areas where there were Pasteur[3] Institutes.

An anti-rabies public relations campaign mounted in England in the 1880s by the Royal Society for the Prevention of Cruelty to Animals and other organizations led to orders being issued to club any dog found not wearing a muzzle. England still has her cruel and unnecessary law that requires an animal to spend six months in quarantine before being allowed loose in the country. Most of the recent propaganda about pit bulls—the crazy claim that they "take hold with their front teeth while they chew away with their rear teeth" (which would imply, incorrectly, that they have double jaws)—can be traced to literature published by the Humane Society of the United States during the fall of 1987 and earlier. If your neighbors want your dog or horse impounded and destroyed because he is a nuisance— say the dog barks, or the horse attracts flies—it will be the local Humane Society to whom your neighbors turn for action.

In a way, everyone has the opportunity to know that the history of the humane movement is largely a history of miseries, arrests, prosecutions, and death. The Humane Society is the pound, the place with the decompression chamber or the lethal injections. You occasionally find worried letters about this in Ann Landers's column.

Animal-rights publications are illustrated largely with photographs of two kinds of animals—"Helpless Fluff" and "Agonized Fluff," the two conditions in which some people seem to prefer their animals, because any other version of an animal is too complicated for propaganda. In the introduction to his book *Animal Liberation,* Peter Singer says somewhat smugly that he and his wife have no animals and, in

---

3. Pasteur (1822–1895): French chemist and microbiologist whose experiments with rabbits allowed him to develop a vaccine that protected humans from rabies and bankrolled further research at his Institute.

fact, don't much care for them. This is offered as evidence of his objectivity and ethical probity. But it strikes me as an odd, perhaps obscene underpinning for an ethical project that encourages university and high school students to cherish their ignorance of, say, great bird dogs as proof of their devotion to animals.

I would like to leave these philosophers behind, for they are inept   10
connoisseurs of suffering who might revere my Airedale for his capacity to scream when subjected to a blowtorch but not for his wit and courage, not for his natural good manners that are a gentle rebuke to ours. I want to celebrate the moment not long ago when, at his first dog show, my Airedale, Drummer, learned that there can be a public place where his work is respected. I want to celebrate his meticulousness, his happiness upon realizing at the dog show that no one would swoop down upon him and swamp him with the goo-goo excesses known as the "teddy-bear complex" but that people actually got out of his way, gave him room to work. I want to say, "There can be a six-and-a-half-month-old puppy who can care about accuracy, who can be fastidious, and whose fastidiousness will be a foundation for courage later." I want to say, "Leave my puppy alone!"

I want to leave the philosophers behind, but I cannot, in part be-   11
cause the philosophical problems that plague academicians of the animal-rights movement are illuminating. They wonder, do animals have rights or do they have interests? Or, if these rightists lead particularly unexamined lives, they dismiss that question as obvious (yes, of course animals have rights, prima facie[4]) and proceed to enumerate them, James Madison style. This leads to the issuance of bills of rights—the right to an environment, the right not to be used in medical experiments—and other forms of trivialization.

The calculus of suffering can be turned against the philosophers of   12
festering flesh, even in the case of food animals, or exotic animals who perform in movies and circuses. It is true that it hurts to be slaughtered by man, but it doesn't hurt nearly as much as some of the cunningly cruel arrangements meted out by "Mother Nature." In Africa, 75 percent of the lions cubbed do not survive to the age of two. For those who make it to two, the average age of death is ten years. Asali, the movie and TV lioness, was still working at age twenty-one. There are fates worse than death, but twenty-one years of a close working relationship with Hubert Wells, Asali's trainer, is not one of them. Dorset sheep and polled Herefords would not exist at all were they not in a symbiotic relationship with human beings.

A human being living in the "wild"—somewhere, say, without the   13
benefits of medicine and advanced social organization—would proba-

---

4. prima facie: Latin phrase meaning "at first sight" or "before close inspection."

bly have a life expectancy of from thirty to thirty-five years. A human being living in "captivity"—in, say, a middle-class neighborhood of what the Centers for Disease Control call a Metropolitan Statistical Area—has a life expectancy of seventy or more years. For orangutans in the wild in Borneo and Malaysia, the life expectancy is thirty-five years; in captivity, fifty years. The wild is not a suffering-free zone or all that frolicsome a location.

The questions asked by animal-rights activists are flawed, because   14
they are built on the concept that the origin of rights is in the avoidance of suffering rather than in the pursuit of happiness. The question that needs to be asked—and that will put us in closer proximity to the truth—is not, do they have rights? or, what are those rights? but rather, what is a right?

Rights originate in committed relationships and can be found, both   15
intact and violated, wherever one finds such relationships—in social compacts, within families, between animals, and between people and nonhuman animals. This is as true when the nonhuman animals in question are lions or parakeets as when they are dogs. It is my Airedale whose excellencies have my attention at the moment, so it is with reference to him that I will consider the question, what is a right?

When I imagine situations in which it naturally arises that A de-   16
fends or honors or respects B's rights, I imagine situations in which the relationship between A and B can be indicated with a possessive pronoun. I might say, "Leave her alone, she's my daughter" or "That's what she wants, and she is my daughter. I think I am bound to honor her wants." Similarly, "Leave her alone, she's my mother." I am more tender of the happiness of my mother, my father, my child, than I am of other people's family members: more tender of my friends' happinesses than your friends' happinesses, unless you and I have a mutual friend.

Possession of a being by another has come into more and more dis-   17
repute, so that the common understanding of one person possessing another is slavery. But the important detail about the kind of possessive pronoun that I have in mind is reciprocity: if I have a friend, she has a friend. If I have a daughter, she has a mother. The possessive does not bind one of us while freeing the other; it cannot do that. Moreover, should the mother reject the daughter, the word that applies is "disown." The form of disowning that most often appears in the news is domestic violence. Parents abuse children; husbands batter wives.

Some cases of reciprocal possessives have built-in limitations, such   18
as "my patient/my doctor" or "my student/my teacher" or "my agent/my client." Other possessive relations are extremely limited but still remarkably binding: "my neighbor" and "my country" and "my president."

The responsibilities and the ties signaled by reciprocal possession   19
typically are hard to dissolve. It can be as difficult to give up an enemy

as to give up a friend, and often the one becomes the other, as though the logic of the possessive pronoun outlasts the forms it chanced to take at a given moment, as though we were stuck with one another. In these bindings, nearly inextricable, are found the origin of our rights. They imply a possessiveness but also recognize an acknowledgment by each side of the other's existence.

The idea of democracy is dependent on the citizens' having knowledge of the government; that is, realizing that the government exists and knowing how to claim rights against it. I know this much because I get mail from the government and see its "representatives" running about in uniforms. Whether I actually have any rights in relationship to the government is less clear, but the idea that I do is symbolized by the right to vote. I obey the government, and, in theory, it obeys me, by counting my ballot, reading the *Miranda* warning[5] to me, agreeing to be bound by the Constitution. My friend obeys me as I obey her; the government "obeys" me to some extent, and, to a different extent, I obey it. 20

What kind of thing can my Airedale, Drummer, have knowledge of? He can know that I exist and through that knowledge can claim his happiness, with varying degrees of success, both with me and against me. Drummer can also know about larger human or dog communities than the one that consists only of him and me. There is my household—the other dogs, the cats, my husband. I have had enough dogs on campuses to know that he can learn that Yale exists as a neighborhood or village. My older dog, Annie, not only knows that Yale exists but can tell Yalies from townies, as I learned while teaching there during labor troubles. 21

Dogs can have elaborate conceptions of human social structures, and even of something like their rights and responsibilities within them, but these conceptions are never elaborate enough to construct a rights relationship between a dog and the state, or a dog and the Humane Society. Both of these are concepts that depend on writing and memoranda, officers in uniform, plaques and seals of authority. All of these are literary constructs, and all of them are beyond a dog's ken, which is why the mail carrier who doesn't also happen to be a dog's friend is forever an intruder—this is why dogs bark at mailmen. 22

It is clear enough that natural rights relations can arise between people and animals. Drummer, for example, can insist, "Hey, let's go outside and do something!" if I have been at my computer several days on end. He can both refuse to accept various of my suggestions and tell me when he fears for his life—such as the time when the huge, white flapping flag appeared out of nowhere, as it seemed to him, on the 23

---

5. *Miranda* warning: "You have the right to remain silent," etc. The formulaic warning police officers deliver to suspects to inform them of their right to avoid self-incrimination.

town green one evening when we were working. I can (and do) say to him, either, "Oh, you don't have to worry about that" or, "Uh, oh, you're right, Drum, that guy looks dangerous." Just as the government and I—two different species of organism—have developed improvised ways of communicating, such as the vote, so Drummer and I have worked out a number of ways to make our expressions known. Largely through obedience, I have taught him a fair amount about how to get responses from me. Obedience is reciprocal; you cannot get responses from a dog to whom you do not respond accurately. I have enfranchised him in a relationship to me by educating him, creating the conditions by which he can achieve a certain happiness specific to a dog, maybe even specific to an Airedale, inasmuch as this same relationship has allowed me to plumb the happiness of being a trainer and writing this article.

Instructions in this happiness are given terms that are alien to a 24 culture in which liver treats, fluffy windup toys, and miniature sweaters are confused with respect and work. Jack Knox, a sheepdog trainer originally from Scotland, will shake his crook at a novice handler who makes a promiscuous move to praise a dog, and will call out in his Scottish accent, "Eh! Eh! Get back, get BACK! Ye'll no be abusin' the dogs like that in my clinic." America is a nation of abused animals, Knox says, because we are always swooping at them with praise, "no gi'ing them their freedom." I am reminded of Rainer Maria Rilke's account in which the Prodigal Son leaves—has to leave—because everyone loves him, even the dogs love him, and he has no path to the delicate and fierce truth of himself. Unconditional praise and love, in Rilke's story, disenfranchise us, distract us from what truly excites our interest.

In the minds of some trainers and handlers, praise is dishonesty. 25 Paradoxically, it is a kind of contempt for animals that masquerades as a reverence for helplessness and suffering. The idea of freedom means that you do not, at least not while Jack Knox is nearby, helpfully guide your dog through the motions of, say, herding over and over—what one trainer calls "explainy-wainy." This is rote learning. It works tolerably well on some handlers, because people have vast unconscious minds and can store complex preprogrammed behaviors. Dogs, on the other hand, have almost no unconscious minds, so they can learn only by thinking. Many children are like this until educated out of it.

If I tell my Airedale to sit and stay on the town green, and some- 26 one comes up and burbles, "What a pretty thing you are," he may break his stay to go for a caress. I pull him back and correct him for breaking. Now he holds his stay because I have blocked his way to movement but not because I have punished him. (A correction blocks one path as it opens another for desire to work; punishment blocks desire and opens nothing.) He holds his stay now, and—because the stay opens this possibility of work, new to a heedless young dog—he

Vicki Hearne

watches. If the person goes on talking, and isn't going to gush with praise, I may heel Drummer out of his stay and give him an "Okay" to make friends. Sometimes something about the person makes Drummer feel that reserve is in order. He responds to an insincere approach by sitting still, going down into himself, and thinking, "This person has no business pawing me. I'll sit very still, and he will go away." If the person doesn't take the hint from Drummer, I'll give the pup a little backup by saying, "Please don't pet him, he's working," even though he was not under any command.

The pup reads this, and there is a flicker of a working trust now 27 stirring in the dog. Is the pup grateful? When the stranger leaves, does he lick my hand, full of submissive blandishments? This one doesn't. This one says nothing at all, and I say nothing much to him. This is a working trust we are developing, not a mutual congratulation society. My backup is praise enough for him; the use he makes of my support is praise enough for me.

Listening to a dog is often praise enough. Suppose it is just after 28 dark and we are outside. Suddenly there is a shout from the house. The pup and I both look toward the shout and then toward each other: "What do you think?" I don't so much as cock my head, because Drummer is growing up, and I want to know what he thinks. He takes a few steps toward the house, and I follow. He listens again and comprehends that it's just Holly, who at fourteen is much given to alarming cries and shouts. He shrugs at me and goes about his business. I say nothing. To praise him for this performance would make about as much sense as praising a human being for the same thing. Thus:

A. What's that?
B. I don't know. [Listens] Oh, it's just Holly.
A. What a goooooood human being!
B. Huh?

This is one small moment in a series of like moments that will cul- 29 minate in an Airedale who on a Friday will have the discrimination and confidence required to take down a man who is attacking me with a knife and on Saturday clown and play with the children at the annual Orange Empire Dog Club Christmas party.

People who claim to speak for animal rights are increasingly de- 30 voted to the idea that the very keeping of a dog or a horse or a gerbil or a lion is in and of itself an offense. The more loudly they speak, the less likely they are to be in a rights relation to any given animal, because they are spending so much time in airplanes or transmitting fax announcements of the latest Sylvester Stallone anti-fur rally. In a 1988 *Harper's* forum, for example, Ingrid Newkirk, the national director of People for the Ethical Treatment of Animals, urged that domestic pets be spayed and neutered and ultimately phased out. She prefers, it appears, wolves—and wolves someplace else—to Airedales and, by a logic whose interior structure is both emotionally and intellectually forever closed to Drummer, claims thereby to be speaking for "animal rights."

She is wrong. I am the only one who can own up to my Airedale's inalienable rights. Whether or not I do it perfectly at any given moment is no more refutation of this point than whether I am perfectly my husband's mate at any given moment refutes the fact of marriage. Only people who know Drummer, and whom he can know, are capable of this relationship. PETA and the Humane Society and the ASPCA and the Congress and NOW[6]—as institutions—do have the power to affect my ability to grant rights to Drummer but are otherwise incapable of creating conditions or laws or rights that would increase his happiness. Only Drummer's owner has the power to obey him—to obey who he is and what he is capable of—deeply enough to grant him his rights and open up the possibility of happiness.

JOSEPH BRUCHAC III

Turtle Meat

Joseph Bruchac III (1942–   ), a descendant of Abnaki Indians and Slovakian immigrants to the United States, has lived most of his life in upper New York state. Born in Saratoga Springs, he took his bachelor's degree at Cornell University, served three years as a high school teacher in Ghana, West Africa, and returned to his native state to do graduate work at Syracuse University, SUNY-Albany, and Union Graduate School (Ph.D., 1975). A prolific writer and translator of West African and Iroquois literature, he has contributed poems to over four hundred periodicals and published several collections, including *Entering Onondaga* (1978), *Translator's Son* (1981), and *Remembering the Dawn* (1983). He is also the author of several novels and collections of short stories, including *The Dreams of Jesse Brown* (1977), *Fox Song* (1993), and *The Earth Under Sky Bear's Feet* (1995), and a collector of Native American tales and legends, found in such works as *The Native American Sweat Lodge: History and Legends* (1993) and *The First Strawberries: A Cherokee Story* (1993). Recently Bruchac has devoted himself to promoting the works of fellow Native Americans, West Africans, and American prison inmates, and has edited numerous anthologies of their work. He has also written children's books,

---

6. PETA: People for the Ethical Treatment of Animals; ASPCA: American Society for the Prevention of Cruelty to Animals; NOW: National Organization for Women.

including *A Boy Called Slow* (1995) and *Eagle Song* (1997). Not a cloistered scholar, Bruchac says he likes "to work outside, in the earth-mother's soil, with my hands." Bruchac's religion is animism—belief in an indwelling soul in both animate beings and inanimate objects.

"Turtle Meat" appeared in *Earth Power Coming: Short Fiction in Native American Literature* (1983). It questions how the consciousness of those who live close to nature differs from that of those who live farther away; thus, it invites comparison with Melissa Green's "No Rms, Jungle Vu."

"Old Man, come in. I need you!"   1

The old woman's cracked voice carried out to the woodshed near   2
the overgrown field. Once it had been planted with corn and beans, the whole two acres. But now mustard rolled heads in the wind and wild carrot bobbed among nettles and the blue flowers of thistles. *A goat would like to eat those thistles,* Homer LaWare thought. *Too bad I'm too old to keep a goat.* He put down the ax handle he had been carving, cast one quick look at the old bamboo fishing pole hanging over the door and then stood up.

"Coming over," he called out. With slow careful steps he crossed   3
the fifty yards between his shed and the single-story house with the picture window and the gold-painted steps. He swung open the screen door and stepped over the dishes full of dog food. *Always in front of the door,* he thought.

"Where?" he called from the front room.   4

"Back here, I'm in the bathroom. I can't get up."   5

He walked as quickly as he could through the cluttered kitchen.   6
The breakfast dishes were still on the table. He pushed open the bathroom door. Mollie was sitting on the toilet.

"Amalia Wind, what's wrong?" he said.   7

"My legs seem to of locked, Homer. Please just help me to get up.   8
I've been hearing the dogs yapping for me outside the door and the poor dears couldn't even get to me. Just help me up."

He slipped his hand under her elbow and lifted her gently. He   9
could see that the pressure of his fingers on the white wrinkled flesh of her arm was going to leave marks. She's always been like that. She always bruised easy. But it hadn't stopped her from coming for him . . . and getting him, all those years ago. It hadn't stopped her from throwing Jake Wind out of her house and bringing Homer LaWare to her farm to be the hired man.

Her legs were unsteady for a few seconds but then she seemed to   10
be all right. He removed his arms from her.

"Just don't know how it happened, Homer. I ain't so old as that,   11
am I, Old Man?"

"No, Amalia. That must of was just a cramp. Nothing more than   12
that."

They were still standing in the bathroom. Her long grey dress had   13
fallen down to cover her legs but her underpants were still around her
ankles. He felt awkward. Even after all these years, he felt awkward.

"Old Man, you just get out and do what you were doing. A woman   14
has to have her privacy. Get now."

"You sure?"   15

"Sure? My Lord! If I wasn't sure you think I'd have any truck with   16
men like you?" She poked him in the ribs. "You know what you
should do, Old Man? You should go down to the pond and do that
fishing you said you were going to."

He didn't want to leave her alone, but he didn't want to tell her   17
that. And there was something in him that urged him towards that
pond, the pond where the yellow perch had been biting for the last
few days according to Jack Crandall. Jack had told him that when he
brought his ax by to have Homer fit a new handle.

"I still got Jack's ax to fix, Amalia."   18

"And when did it ever take you more than a minute to fit a handle   19
into anything, *Old Man?*" There was a wicked gleam in her eye. For a
few seconds she looked forty years younger in the old man's eyes.

He shook his head.   20

"Miss Wind, I swear those ladies were right when they said you   21
was going to hell." She made a playful threatening motion with her
hand and he backed out the door. "But I'm going."

It took him another hour to finish carving the handle to the right   22
size. It slid into the head like a hand going into a velvet glove. His
hands shook when he started the steel wedge that would hold it tight,
but it took only three strokes with the maul to put the wedge in. He
looked at his hands, remembering the things they'd done. Holding the
reins of the last horse they'd had on the farm—twenty years ago. Or
was it thirty? Lifting the sheets back from Mollie's white body that first
night. Swinging in tight fists at the face of Jake Wind the night he
came back, drunk and with a loaded .45 in his hand. He'd gone down
hard and Homer had emptied the shells out of the gun and broken its
barrel with his maul on his anvil. Though Jake had babbled of the law
that night, neither the law nor Jake ever came back to the Wind farm.
It had been Amalia's all along. Her father'd owned it and Jake had
married her for it. She'd never put the property in any man's name,
never would. That was what she always said.

"I'm not asking, Amalia," that was what Homer had said to her   23
after the first night they'd spent in the brass bed, just before he'd
dressed and gone back to sleep the night away in his cot in the shed.
He always slept there. All the years. "I'm not asking for any property,
Amalia. It's the Indian in me that don't want to own no land."

That was Homer's favorite saying. Whenever there was something   24
about him that seemed maybe different from what others expected he

would say simply, "It's the Indian in me." Sometimes he thought of it not just as a part of him but as another man, a man with a name he didn't know but would recognize if he heard it.

His father had said that same phrase often. His father had come down from Quebec and spoke French and, sometimes, to his first wife who had died when Homer was six, another language that Homer never heard again after her death. His father had been a quiet man who made baskets from the ash trees that grew on their farm. "But he never carried them into town," Homer said with pride. "He just stayed on the farm and let people come to him if they wanted to buy them." 25

The farm had gone to a younger brother who sold out and moved West. There had been two other children. None of them got a thing, except Homer who got his father's best horse. In those years Homer was working for Seneca Smith at his mill. Woods work, two-man saws and sledding the logs out in the snow. He had done it until his thirtieth year when Amalia had asked him to come and work her farm. Though people had talked, he had done it. When anyone asked why he let himself be run by a woman that way he said, in the same quiet voice his father had used, "It's the Indian in me." 26

The pond was looking glass smooth. Homer stood beside the boat. Jack Crandall had given him the key to it. He looked in the water. He saw his face, the skin lined and brown as an old map. Wattles of flesh hung below his chin like the comb of a rooster. 27

"Shit, you're a good-looking man, Homer LaWare," he said to his reflection. "Easy to see what a woman sees in you." He thought again of Mollie sitting in the rocker and looking out the picture window. As he left he heard her old voice calling the names of the small dogs she loved so much. *Those dogs were the only ones ever give back her love,* he thought, *not that no-good daughter. Last time she come was Christmas in '68 to give her that pissy green shawl and try to run me off again.* 28

Homer stepped into the boat. Ripples wiped his face from the surface of the pond. He put his pole and the can of worms in front of him and slipped the oars into the oarlocks, one at a time, breathing hard as he did so. He pulled the anchor rope into the boat and looked out across the water. A brown stick projected above the water in the middle of the pond. *Least it looks like a stick, but if it moves it . . .* The stick moved . . . slid across the surface of the water for a few feet and then disappeared. He watched with narrowed eyes until it reappeared a hundred feet further out. It was a turtle, a snapping turtle. Probably a big one. 29

"I see you out there, Turtle," Homer said. "Maybe you and me are going to see more of each other." 30

He felt in his pocket for the familiar feel of his bone-handled knife. He pushed the red handkerchief that held it deep in his pocket more firmly into place. Then he began to row. He stopped in the middle of the pond and began to fish. Within a few minutes he began to pull in 31 the fish, yellow-stomached perch with bulging dark eyes. Most of them were a foot long. He stopped when he had a dozen and began to clean them, leaving the baited line in the water. He pulled out the bone-handled knife and opened it. The blade was thin as the handle of a spoon from thirty years of sharpening. It was like a razor. Homer always carried a sharp knife. He made a careful slit from the ventral opening of the fish up to its gills and spilled out the guts into the water, leaning over the side of the boat as he did so. He talked as he cleaned the fish.

"Old Knife, you cut good," he said. He had cleaned nearly every fish, hardly wasting a moment. Almost as fast as when he was a boy. *Some things didn't go from you so . . .*

The jerking of his pole brought him back from his thoughts. It was being dragged overboard. He dropped the knife on the seat and grabbed the pole as it went over. He pulled up on it and it bent almost double. *No fish pulls like that.* It was the turtle. He began reeling the line in, slow and steady so it wouldn't break. Soon he saw it, wagging its head back and forth, coming up from the green depths of the pond where it had been gorging on the perch guts and grabbed his worm.

"Come up and talk, Turtle," Homer said.

The turtle opened its mouth as if to say something and the hook slipped out, the pole jerking back in Homer's hands. Its jaws were too tough for the hook to stick in. But the turtle stayed there, just under the water. It was big, thirty pounds at least. It was looking for more food. Homer put another worm on the hook with trembling hands and dropped it in front of the turtle's mouth.

"Turtle, take this one too."

He could see the wrinkled skin under its throat as it turned its head. A leech of some kind was on the back of its head, another hanging onto its right leg. It was an old turtle. Its skin was rough, its shell green with algae. It grabbed the hook with a sideways turn of its head. As Homer pulled up to snag the hook it reached forward with its paws and grabbed the line like a man grabbing a rope. Its front claws were as long as the teeth of a bear.

Homer pulled. The turtle kept the hook in its mouth and rose to the surface. It was strong and the old man wondered if he could hold it up. Did he want turtle meat that much? But he didn't cut the line. The mouth was big enough to take off a finger, but he kept pulling in line. It was next to the boat and the hook was only holding because of the pressure on the line. A little slack and it would be gone. Homer slipped the pole under his leg and grabbed with his other hand for the anchor rope, began to fasten a noose in it as the turtle shook its head, moving the twelve-foot boat as it struggled. He could smell it now. The heavy musk of the turtle was everywhere. It wasn't a good smell or a bad smell. It was only the smell of the turtle.

Now the noose was done. He hung it over the side. It was time for   39
the hard part now, the part that was easy for him when his arms were
young and his chest wasn't caved in like a broken box. He reached
down fast and grabbed the tail, pulling it so that the turtle came half out
of the water. The boat almost tipped but Homer kept his balance. The
turtle swung its head, mouth open and wide enough to swallow a softball. It hissed like a snake, ready to grab at anything within reach. With
his other hand, gasping as he did it, feeling the turtle's rough tail tear
the skin of his palm as it slipped from his other hand, Homer swung the
noose around the turtle's head. Its own weight pulled the slip knot
tight. The turtle's jaws clamped tight with a snap on Homer's sleeve.

"Turtle, I believe I got you and you got me," Homer said. He slipped   40
a turn of rope around his left foot with his free arm. He kept pulling
back as hard as he could to free his sleeve but the turtle had it. "I understand you, Turtle," he said, "you don't like to let go." He breathed hard,
closed his eyes for a moment. Then he took the knife in his left hand. He
leaned over and slid it across the turtle's neck. Dark fluid blossomed out
into the water. A hissing noise came from between the clenched jaws,
but the turtle held onto the old man's sleeve. For a long time the blood
came out but the turtle still held on. Finally Homer took the knife and
cut the end of his sleeve off, leaving it in the turtle's mouth.

He sat up straight for the first time since he had hooked the turtle   41
and looked around. It was dark. He could hardly see the shore. He had
been fighting the turtle for longer than he thought.

By the time he had reached the shore and docked the boat the   42
sounds of the turtle banging itself against the side of the boat had
stopped. He couldn't tell if blood was still flowing from its cut throat
because night had turned all of the water that same color. He couldn't
find the fish in the bottom of the boat. It didn't matter. The raccoons
could have them. He had his knife and his pole and the turtle. He
dragged it back up to the old Ford truck. It was too heavy to carry.

There were cars parked in the driveway when he pulled in. He had   43
to park near the small mounds beside his shed that were marked with
wooden plaques and neatly lettered names. He could hear voices as he
walked through the darkness.

"Old fool's finally come back," he heard a voice saying. The voice   44
was rough as a rusted hinge. It was the voice of Amalia's daughter.

He pushed through the door. "Where's Amalia?" he said. Someone   45
screamed. The room was full of faces and they were all looking at him.

"Old bastard looks like he scalped someone," a pock-faced man   46
with grey crew-cut hair muttered.

Homer looked at himself. His arms and hands were covered with   47
blood of the turtle. His tattered right sleeve barely reached his elbow.
His trousers were muddy. His fly was half-way open. "Where's
Amalia?" he demanded again.

"What the hell have you been up to, you old fart?" said the raspy ⁴⁸ voice of the daughter. He turned to stare into her loose-featured face. She was sitting in Amalia's rocker.

"I been fishin'." ⁴⁹

The daughter stood up and walked toward him. She looked like her ⁵⁰ father. Jake Wind was written all over her face, carved into her bones.

"You want to know where Moms is, huh? Wanta know where ⁵¹ your old sweetheart's gone to? Well, I'll tell you. She's been sent off to a home that'll take care of her, even if she is cracked. Come in and find her sittin' talking to dogs been dead for years. Dishes full of dog food for ghosts. Maybe you better eat some of it because your meal ticket's been cancelled, you old bastard. This man is a doctor and he's decided my dear mother was mentally incompetent. The ambulance took her outta here half an hour ago."

She kept talking, saying things she had longed to say for years. ⁵² Homer LaWare wasn't listening. His eyes took in the details of the room he had walked through every day for the last forty years, the furniture he had mended when it was broken, the picture window he had installed, the steps he had painted, the neatly stacked dishes he had eaten his food from three times each day for almost half a century. The daughter was still talking, talking as if this were a scene she had rehearsed for many years. But he wasn't listening. Her voice was getting louder. She was screaming. Homer hardly heard her. He closed his eyes, remembering how the turtle held onto his sleeve even after its throat was cut and its life was leaking out into the pond.

The screaming stopped. He opened his eyes and saw that the man ⁵³ with the grey crew-cut hair was holding the daughter's arms. She was holding a plate in her hands. Maybe she had been about to hit him with it. It didn't matter. He looked at her. He looked at the other people in the room. They seemed to be waiting for him to say something.

"I got a turtle to clean out," he said, knowing what it was in him ⁵⁴ that spoke. Then he turned and walked into the darkness.

RANDALL JARRELL

Field and Forest

Randall Jarrell (1914–1965), literary critic, poet, and translator, grew up in the South and in California and graduated from Vanderbilt University. He began teaching as an instructor at Kenyon College in the late 1930s and was a professor of English at several universities during his life, including the University of North Carolina, Princeton, and the University of Cincinnati. Author of several books of criticism, numerous translations, and even a few children's books, Jarrell was well respected for his poetry. His collections include *Selected Poems* (1955) and *The Woman at the Washington Zoo* (1960), which won a National Book Award. Jarrell's poetry often includes images of nature, but he generally uses these images to study the complexity, and the sadness or tragedy, he found in human nature. Jarrell was killed in an automobile accident in 1965. "Field and Forest" is from his last book of poetry, *The Lost World,* which was published that same year. The poem stresses close identification between a human and nonhuman similar to that explored in Joseph Bruchac's "Turtle Meat."

> When you look down from the airplane you see lines,
> Roads, ruts, braided into a net or web—
> Where people go, what people do: the ways of life.

1

> Heaven says to the farmer: 'What's your field?'
> And he answers: 'Farming,' with a field,
> Or: 'Dairy-farming,' with a herd of cows.
> They seem a boys' toy cows, seen from this high.

2

> Seen from this high,
> The fields have a terrible monotony.

3

> But between the lighter patches there are dark ones.
> A farmer is separated from a farmer
> By what farmers have in common: forests,
> Those dark things—what the fields were to begin with.
> At night a fox comes out of the forest, eats his chickens.
> At night the deer come out of the forest, eat his crops.

4

> If he could he'd make farm out of all the forest,
> But it isn't worth it: some of it's marsh, some rocks,
> There are things there you couldn't get rid of
> With a bulldozer, even—not with dynamite.
> Besides, he likes it. He had a cave there, as a boy;
> He hunts there now. It's a waste of land,
> But it would be a waste of time, a waste of money,
> To make it into anything but what it is.

5

> At night, from the airplane, all you see is lights,
> A few lights, the lights of houses, headlights,
> And darkness. Somewhere below, beside a light,
> The farmer, naked, takes out his false teeth:
> He doesn't eat now. Takes off his spectacles:
> He doesn't see now. Shuts his eyes:
> If he were able to he'd shut his ears,

6

And as it is, he doesn't hear with them.
Plainly, he's taken out his tongue: he doesn't talk.
His arms and legs: at least, he doesn't move them.

They are knotted together, curled up, like a child's.   7
And after he has taken off the thoughts
It has taken him his life to learn,
He takes off, last of all, the world.

When you take off everything what's left? A wish,   8
A blind wish; and yet the wish isn't blind,
What the wish wants to see, it sees.

There in the middle of the forest is the cave   9
And there, curled up inside it, is the fox.
He stands looking at it.
Around him the fields are sleeping: the fields dream.
At night there are no more farmers, no more farms.
At night the fields dream, the fields are the forest.
The boy stands looking at the fox
As if, if he looked long enough—

                              he looks at it.   10
Or is it the fox that's looking at the boy?
The trees can't tell the two of them apart.

WORK AND THE
ECONOMY

We find ourselves in our work and works.

Overview

Most people in "developed" nations have a habitual way of talking about work and income. Here in the United States, for instance, "work" is something done at the plant or, increasingly, at the office. It eats up the week and crowds our pleasures into the weekend. Its purpose is to produce income, which we can use to buy things made by other workers at other factories and in other offices. Work is not fun, and it is separate from our home lives and our spiritual lives. It is democratic in the sense that it provides roughly comparable, mildly unpleasant experiences for executives and day laborers, men and women. The income it provides is proportionate to the effort, skill, and intelligence of the worker, so there is a rough justice in the discrepancies in pay among us. The aim of this section of the book is to encourage some rethinking of this consensus view and to provide a chance to write and think about the assumptions that underlie it. We will read writers who see work primarily in spiritual rather than economic terms, writers who find the economic system unjust or irrational, writers who focus on work in the home or on volunteer work, writers who would dissolve the boundary between work and play. The writers do not themselves agree about what work is, of course, but they provide perspectives on the vast subject that may help us hone our own thinking.

There is always something to talk about with the other hands, because farming is genuinely absorbing. It has the best quality of work: nothing else seems real. And everyone doing it, even the cheapest helpers like me, can see the layout of the whole—from spring work, to cultivating, to small grain harvest, to cornpicking, to fall plowing.

Bill Dickinson is what he seems to be. Only in meeting a person whose internal life is so visible can we see how rare that quality is—the transparency that comes to each of us only when we are doing exactly what we want to do, and think we should be doing, with our lives.

Housewifery remained a full-time job irrespective of the appliances or the technological systems at the housewife's disposal. The 1950s and 1960s were particularly labor-intensive. Middle-class women were trapped in a stultifying domesticity, following "Hints from Heloise" on how to prepare homemade dog food or turn Clorox bottles into birdfeeders.

The decisive economic contribution of women in the developed industrial society is rather simple—or at least it so becomes once the disguising myth is dissolved. It is, overwhelmingly, to make possible a continuing and more or less unlimited increase in the sale and use of consumer goods.

Perhaps the most potent instance of the politics of honor plays itself out in debates about work. One reason many working-class voters despise welfare is not that they begrudge the money it costs but that they resent the message it conveys about what is worthy of honor and reward. . . . For many who "work hard and play by the rules," rewarding those who stay at home mocks the effort they expend and the pride they take in the work they do.

A little farther down the line comes the president. In calculating his height, we take account only of his direct salary. . . . He is about twenty yards high. His security guards, being only about three yards tall, have passed by many minutes ago. Obviously, at that height they would have been of little use in protecting the president. . . . After all, they come up only halfway to his shin bone.

Sometimes, you'd be surprised, some doctor has given the parents a ride before they bring the child to the clinic. You wouldn't believe it. They clean 'em out, maybe for twenty-five dollars—they maybe had to borrow—and then tell 'em to move on. It happens. Men we all know too. Pretty bad. But what can you do?

They were poor then but everyone had been poor.
He hadn't minded the sweeping,
just the thought of it—like now
when people ask him what he's thinking
and he says *I'm listening.*

DOROTHY L. SAYERS

Living to Work

Born in Oxford, England, Dorothy Leigh Sayers (1893–1957) is best known for crime novels featuring the aristocratic amateur detective Lord Peter Wimsey. She attended Oxford University before women were allowed to take degrees from that institution, passed her examinations with first-class honors in 1915, and was finally awarded two degrees in 1920, when Oxford changed its policy. Sayers and Agatha Christie inaugurated a Golden Age in British crime fiction. Her novels *Clouds of Witness* (1926), *Unnatural Death* (1927), *Murder Must Advertise* (1933), and *The Nine Tailors* (1934) continue to be widely read both in the United States and Britain. In the 1940s, having freed herself from the "mystery formula," Sayers turned her attention to essays, religious drama, and verse translations of *Tristan, The Song of Roland,* and *The Divine Comedy.* "Living to Work," written for broadcasting on British radio during World War II, was suppressed by the B.B.C. because it seemed too political and because "our public do not want to be admonished by a woman." It first appeared along with her similarly censored essays on "Christian Morality" and "Forgiveness," in *Unpopular Opinions* (1946). The essay frames in the broadest terms questions that dominate this unit: Why do we work? Is "Money" an adequate answer? Can we imagine a world where work is not a burden?

When I look at the world—not particularly at the world at war, but at our Western civilisation generally—I find myself dividing people into two main groups according to the way they think about work. And I feel sure that the new world after the war will be satisfactory or not according to the view we are all prepared to take about the work of the world. So let us look for a moment at these two groups of people.

One group—probably the larger and certainly the more discontented—look upon work as a hateful necessity, whose only use is to make money for them, so that they can escape from work and do something else. They feel that only when the day's labour is over can they really begin to live and be themselves. The other group—smaller nowadays, but on the whole far happier—look on their work as an opportunity for enjoyment and self-fulfilment. They only want to make money so that they may be free to devote themselves more single-mindedly to their work. Their work and their life are one thing; if they were to be cut off from their work, they would feel that they were cut off from life. You will realise that we have here a really fundamental difference of outlook, which is bound to influence all schemes about work, leisure and wages.

Now the first group—that of the work-haters—is not made up   3
solely of people doing very hard, uninteresting and ill-paid work. It includes a great many well-off people who do practically no work at all.
The rich man who lives idly on his income, the man who gambles or
speculates in the hope of getting money without working for it, the
woman who marries for the mere sake of being comfortably established for life—all these people look on money in the same way: as
something that saves them from the curse of work. Except that they
have had better luck, their outlook is exactly the same as that of the
sweated factory hand whose daily work is one long round of soul-and-
body-destroying toil. For all of them, work is something hateful, only
to be endured because it makes money; and money is desirable because it represents a way of escape from work. The only difference is
that the rich have already made their escape, and the poor have not.

The second group is equally mixed. It includes the artists, scholars   4
and scientists—the people really devoured with the passion for making
and discovering things. It includes also the rapidly-diminishing band of
old-fashioned craftsmen, taking a real pride and pleasure in turning
out a good job of work. It includes also—and this is very important—
those skilled mechanics and engineers who are genuinely in love with
the complicated beauty of the machines they use and look after. Then
there are those professional people in whom we recognize a clear, spiritual vocation—a call to what is sometimes very hard and exacting
work—those doctors, nurses, priests, actors, teachers, whose work is
something more to them than a mere means of livelihood; seamen
who, for all they may grumble at the hardships of the sea, return to it
again and again and are restless and unhappy on dry land; farmers and
farm-workers who devotedly serve the land and the beasts they tend;
airmen; explorers; and those comparatively rare women to whom the
nurture of children is not merely a natural function but also a full-time
and absorbing intellectual and emotional interest. A very mixed bag,
you will notice, and not exclusively confined to the "possessing classics,"[1] or even to those who, individually or collectively, "own the
means of production."

But we must also admit that, of late, the second group of workers   5
has become more and more infected with the outlook of the first
group. Agriculuture—especially in those countries where farming is
prosperous—has been directed, not to serving the land, but to bleeding
it white in the interests of moneymaking. Certain members of the
medical profession—as you may read in Dr. Cronin's book, *The
Citadel*—are less interested in preserving their patients' health than in
exploiting their weaknesses for profit. Some writers openly admit that

---

1. "possessing classics": almost certainly a misprint for "possessing classes," a term imported from Marxist thought.

their sole aim is the manufacture of best-sellers. And if we are inclined
to exclaim indignantly that this kind of conduct is bad for the work,
bad for the individual, and bad for the community, we must also confess that we ourselves—the ordinary public—have been only too ready
to acquiesce in these commercial standards, not only in trade and
manufacture, but in the professions and public services as well.

For us, a "successful" author is one whose sales run into millions;   6
any other standard of criticism is dismissed as "highbrow." We judge
the skill of a physician or surgeon, not by his hospital record, but by
whether or not he has many wealthy patients and an address in Harley
Street.[2] The announcement that a new film has cost many thousands
of pounds to make convinces us that it must be a good film; though
very often these excessive production costs are evidence of nothing
more than graft, incompetence and bad organisation in the studios.
Also, it is useless to pretend that we do not admire and encourage the
vices of the idle rich so long as our cinemas are crowded with young
men and women gaping at film-stars in plutocratic surroundings and
imbecile situations and wishing with all their hearts that they too could
live like the heroes and heroines of these witless million-dollar screen
stories. Just as it is idle to demand selfless devotion to duty in public
servants, so long as we respect roguery in business, or so long as we
say, with an admiring chuckle, about some fellow citizen who has
pulled off some shady deal with our local borough authorities, that
"Old So-and-so is hot stuff, and anybody would have to get up early to
find any flies on *him*."

We have *all* become accustomed to rate the value of work by a   7
purely money standard. The people who still cling to the old idea that
work should be served and enjoyed for its own sake are diminishing
and—what is worse—are being steadily pushed out of the control of
public affairs and out of contact with the public. We find them odd and
alien—and a subservient journalism (which we encourage by buying
and reading it) persuades us to consider them absurd and contemptible.
It is only in times of emergency and national disaster that we realise
how much we depend upon the man who puts the integrity of his job
before money, before success, before self—before all those standards
by which we have come to assess the value of work.

Consequently, in planning out our post-war economic paradise,   8
we are apt to concentrate exclusively on questions of hours, wages and
conditions, and to neglect the really fundamental question whether, in
fact, we want work to be something in which a man can enjoy the exercise of his full natural powers; or merely a disagreeable task, with its
hours as short as possible and its returns as high as possible, so that the
worker may be released as quickly as possible to enjoy his life in his

2. Harley Street: the traditional address of London's most prosperous physicians.

leisure. Mind, I do not say for a moment that hours, wages and conditions ought not to be dealt with; but we shall deal with them along different lines, according as we believe it right and natural that men should work to live or live to work.

At this point, many of you will be thinking: "Before we can do 9 anything about this, we must get rid of the capitalist system." But the much-abused "system" is precisely the system that arises when we think of work in terms of money-returns. The capitalist is faithfully carrying to its logical conclusion the opinion that work is an evil, that individual liberty means liberty to emancipate one's self from work, and that whatever pays best is right. And I see no chance of getting rid of "the system," or of the people who thrive on it, so long as in our hearts we accept the standards of that system, envy the very vices we condemn, build up with one hand what we pull down with the other, and treat with ridicule and neglect the people who acknowledge a less commercial—if you like, a more religious—conception of what work ought to be.

But now we are faced with a big difficulty. Suppose we decide that 10 we want work to provide our natural fulfilment and satisfaction, how are we to manage this in an age of industrial machinery? You will have noticed that all the workers in my second group possess three privileges. (1) Their work provides opportunity for individual initiative. (2) It is of a kind that, however laborious it may be in detail, allows them to view with satisfaction the final results of their labour. (3) It is of a kind that fits in with the natural rhythm of the human mind and body, since it involves periods of swift, exacting energy, followed by periods of repose and recuperation, and does not bind the worker to the monotonous, relentless, deadly pace of an inhuman machine.

The factory hand has none of these advantages. He is not required 11 to show initiative, but only to perform one unimaginative operation over and over again. He usually sees no step in the process of manufacture except that one operation, and so can take no interest in watching the thing he is making grow to its final perfection; often, indeed, it is some useless thing that only exists to create profits and wages, and which no worker could admire or desire for its own sake. Thirdly, it is the pace that kills—the subjection of the human frame to the unresting, unchanging, automatic movement of the machine. The other day, a journalist was talking to some miners. He says: "With one voice they told me that they think the machines are becoming monsters, draining their life-blood, and how they longed for the old days when they worked longer shifts, but with their hands, and the process of procuring the coal was less exhausting."

This last statement is very interesting, since it shows that the regu- 12 lation of hours and wages cannot by itself do away with the difficulty about certain kinds of work. The economic solution will not solve this problem, because it is not really an economic problem at all, but a problem about human nature and the nature of work.

Some people are so greatly depressed by these considerations that they can see no way out of the difficulty except to do away with machines altogether, as things evil in themselves and destructive of all good living. But this is a counsel of despair. For one thing, it is not a practical proposition in the present state of things. Also, this suggestion takes no account of the real delight and satisfaction that the machines are capable of giving. It throws on the scrap-heap the skill and creative enthusiasm of the designer, the engineer's pride in his craft, the flying man's ecstasy in being air-borne, all the positive achievements of mechanical invention, and all those products—and they are many—which are actually *better* made by machinery than by hand. To renounce the machines means, at this time of day, to renounce the world and to retire to a kind of hermitage of the spirit. But society cannot be exclusively made of saints and solitaries; the average good citizen, like the average Christian, has to live *in* the world; his task is not to run away from the machines but to learn to use them so that they work in harmony with human nature instead of injuring or oppressing it.   13

Now, I will not attempt, in the last few minutes of a short broadcast, to produce a cut-and-dried scheme for taming machinery to the service of man. I will only say that I believe it can be done, and (since my opinion would not carry very much weight) that there are many people, with personal experience of factory conditions, who have already worked out practical proposals for doing it. But it can only be done if we ourselves—all of us—know what we want and are united in wanting the same thing; if we are all prepared to revise our ideas about what work ought to be, and about what we mean by "having a good time."   14

For there is one fact we must face. Victory is the only possible condition upon which we can look forward to a "good time" of any kind; but victory will not leave us in a position where we can just relax all effort and enjoy ourselves in leisure and prosperity. We shall be living in a confused, exhausted and impoverished world, and there will be a great deal of work to do. Our best chance of having a good time will be to arrange our ideas, and our society, in such a way that everybody will have an opportunity to work hard and find happiness in doing *well* the work that will so desperately need to be done.   15

JANE SMILEY

The Case Against Chores

Born in Los Angeles, Jane Graves Smiley (1949–   ) received her
B.A. from Vassar College (1971) and her M.A. (1975), M.F.A. (1976),
and Ph.D. (1978) from the University of Iowa. Despite—or perhaps
because of—the attitudes toward work she describes in the following
essay, she has contributed to many of American's leading magazines
and has been represented in *Best American Short Stories, The Pushcart
Anthology,* and *Best of the Eighties.* She has produced eleven books, including six novels. The most recent of these, *Moo* (1995), presents life
on a Midwestern university campus in terms that might be equally
amusing to both professors and students. Her earlier novel *A Thousand Acres* (1991), a reworking of Shakespeare's *King Lear* in the contemporary Midwest, won the Pulitzer Prize, National Book Critics
Circle Award, and Heartland Award, and has been made into a popular film (1997). Smiley's light autobiographical touch as she discusses
the serious matter of how children should be encouraged to understand work may encourage some readers to respond with memoirs of
their own. Readers who want to challenge Smiley might turn to
Juliet B. Shor's "Housewives' Hours," which takes a different view of
housework, and to Michael J. Sandel's "Honor and Resentment,"
which suggests that people should learn to take pride in even the
"dirty work."

I've lived in the upper Midwest for twenty-one years now, and I'm   1
here to tell you that the pressure to put your children to work is unrelenting. So far I've squirmed out from under it, and my daughters have
led a life of almost tropical idleness, much to their benefit. My son,
however, may not be so lucky. His father was himself raised in Iowa
and put to work at an early age, and you never know when, in spite of
all my husband's best intentions, that early training might kick in.

Although "chores" are so sacred in my neck of the woods that al-   2
most no one ever discusses their purpose, I have over the years gleaned
some of the reasons parents give for assigning them. I'm not impressed.
Mostly the reasons have to do with developing good work habits or, in
the absence of good work habits, at least habits of working. No such
thing as a free lunch, any job worth doing is worth doing right, work
before play, all of that. According to this reasoning, the world is full of
jobs that no one wants to do. If we divide them up and get them over
with, then we can go on to pastimes we like. If we do them "right,"
then we won't have to do them again. Lots of times, though, in a family, that *we* doesn't operate. The operative word is *you.* The practical result of almost every child-labor scheme that I've witnessed is the child
doing the dirty work and the parent getting the fun: Mom cooks and

Sis does the dishes; the parents plan and plant the garden, the kids weed it. To me, what this teaches the child is the lesson of alienated labor: not to love the work but to get it over with; not to feel pride in one's contribution but to feel resentment at the waste of one's time.

Another goal of chores: the child contributes to the work of main-   3
taining the family. According to this rationale, the child comes to un-
derstand what it takes to have a family, and to feel that he or she is an important, even indispensable member of it. But come on. Would you really want to feel loved primarily because you're the one who gets the floors mopped? Wouldn't you rather feel that your family's love simply exists all around you, no matter what your contribution? And don't the parents love their children anyway, whether the children vacuum or not? Why lie about it just to get the housework done? Let's be frank about the other half of the equation too. In this day and age, it doesn't take much work at all to manage a household, at least in the middle class—maybe four hours a week to clean the house and another four to throw the laundry into the washing machine, move it to the dryer, and fold it. Is it really a good idea to set the sort of example my former neighbors used to set, of mopping the floor every two days, cleaning the toilets every week, vacuuming every day, dusting, dusting, dust-ing? Didn't they have anything better to do than serve their house?

Let me confess that I wasn't expected to lift a finger when I was   4
growing up. Even when my mother had a full-time job, she cleaned up after me, as did my grandmother. Later there was a housekeeper. I would leave my room in a mess when I headed off for school and find it miraculously neat when I returned. Once in a while I vacuumed, just because I liked the pattern the Hoover made on the carpet. I did learn to run water in my cereal bowl before setting it in the sink.

Where I discovered work was at the stable, and, in fact, there is no   5
housework like horsework. You've got to clean the horses' stalls, feed them, groom them, tack them up, wrap their legs, exercise them, turn them out, and catch them. You've got to clip them and shave them. You have to sweep the aisle, clean your tack and your boots, carry bales of hay and buckets of water. Minimal horsekeeping, rising just to the level of humaneness, requires many more hours than making a few beds, and horsework turned out to be a good preparation for the real work of adulthood, which is rearing children. It was a good prepa-ration not only because it was similar in many ways but also because my desire to do it, and to do a good job of it, grew out of my love of and interest in my horse. I can't say that cleaning out her bucket when she manured in it was an actual joy, but I knew she wasn't going to do it herself. I saw the purpose of my labor, and I wasn't alienated from it.

Probably to the surprise of some of those who knew me as a child,   6
I have turned out to be gainfully employed. I remember when I was in seventh grade, one of my teachers said to me, strongly disapproving,

"The trouble with you is you only do what you want to do!" That continues to be the trouble with me, except that over the years I have wanted to do more and more.

My husband worked hard as a child, out-Iowa-ing the Iowans, if 7 such a thing is possible. His dad had him mixing cement with a stick when he was five, pushing wheelbarrows not long after. It's a long sad tale on the order of two miles to school and both ways uphill. The result is, he's a great worker, much better than I am, but all the while he's doing it he wishes he weren't. He thinks of it as work; he's torn between doing a good job and longing not to be doing it at all. Later, when he's out on the golf course, where he really wants to be, he feels a little guilty, knowing there's work that should have been done before he gave in and took advantage of the beautiful day.

Good work is not the work we assign children but the work they 8 want to do, whether it's reading in bed (where would I be today if my parents had rousted me out and put me to scrubbing floors?) or cleaning their rooms or practicing the flute or making roasted potatoes with rosemary and Parmesan for the family dinner. It's good for a teenager to suddenly decide that the bathtub is so disgusting she'd better clean it herself. I admit that for the parent, this can involve years of waiting. But if she doesn't want to wait, she can always spend her time dusting.

GLORIA STEINEM

I Was a Playboy Bunny

Gloria Steinem (1934–   ) was born in Toledo, Ohio, and graduated *magna cum laude* from Smith College in 1956. Pursuing a career in journalism as a writer, lecturer, and editor, Steinem helped found both *New York Magazine* (1968) and *Ms.* (1971); she served as *Ms.* Editor for twenty years. Involved in civil rights organizations and women's groups, she helped to organize the National Women's Political Caucus and the Women's Action Alliance. In 1972, she was selected *McCall's* Woman of the Year; *World Almanac* has cited her nine times as one of the twenty-five most influential women in America. Her writings include *Marilyn: Norma Jean* (1986); *Revolution from Within* (1992), and *Moving Beyond Words* (1993). "I Was a Playboy Bunny," here presented in excerpted form, first appeared as a two-part article in *Show* magazine in 1963 and was adapted as an ABC television movie, *A Bunny's Tale*, in 1985. Those who want to read the entire essay can find it in *Outrageous Acts and Everyday Rebellions* (1983). The essay is unusual because it depicts one of America's leading feminists in one of America's least feminist environments, but it fits into a genre that some student writers handle very well: the workplace memoir. Readers may also want to compare the essay with Carol Bly's "Getting Tired" and William Carlos Williams's "Jean Beicke," both of which report on the daily reality of a job from the worker's point of view.

I undertook a reporting assignment armed with a large diary and this ad: 1

GIRLS:
Do Playboy Club Bunnies Really
Have Glamorous Jobs,
Meet Celebrities, And
Make Top Money?

Yes, it's true! Attractive young girls can now earn $200–$300 a week at the fabulous New York Playboy Club, enjoy the glamorous and exciting aura of show business, and have the opportunity to travel to other Playboy Clubs throughout the world. Whether serving drinks, snapping pictures, or greeting guests at the door, the Playboy Club is the stage—the Bunnies are the stars.

The charm and beauty of our Bunnies has been extolled in *Time, Newsweek,* and *Pageant,* and Ed Sullivan has called The Playboy Club ". . . the greatest new show biz gimmick," And the Playboy Club is now the busiest spot in New York.

If you are pretty and personable, between 21 and 24, married or single, you probably qualify. No experience necessary.

Apply in person at SPECIAL INTERVIEWS being held Saturday and Sunday, January 26–27, 10 A.M.–3 P.M. Please bring a swimsuit or leotards.

THE PLAYBOY CLUB

5 East 59th Street   PL 2-3100

THURSDAY, JANUARY 24TH, 1963

I've decided to call myself Marie Catherine Ochs. It is, may my ancestors forgive me, a family name. I have some claim to it, and I'm well versed in its European origins. Besides, it sounds much too square to be phony.   2

SATURDAY 26TH

Today I put on the most theatrical clothes I could find, packed my leotard in a hatbox, and walked to the Playboy Club. It is impossible to miss. The discreet six-story office building and art gallery that once stood there has been completely gutted and transformed into a shiny   3 rectangle of plate glass. The orange-carpeted interior is clearly visible, with a modern floating stairway spiraling upward at dead center. The total effect is cheerful and startling.

I crossed over to the club, where a middle-aged man in a private   4 guard's uniform grinned and beckoned. "Here bunny, bunny, bunny!" He jerked his thumb toward the glass door on the left. "Interviews downstairs in the Playmate Bar."

The inside of the club was so dramatically lit that it took a few sec-   5 onds to realize it was closed and empty. I walked down a short flight of stairs and was greeted by Miss Shay, a thin, thirtyish woman who sat at a desk in the darkened bar. "Bunny?" she asked briskly. "Sit over there, fill out this form, and take off your coat." I could see that two of the tables were already occupied by girls hunched over pencils, and I looked at them curiously. I had come in the middle of the interviews, hoping to see as many applicants as I could, but there were only three. *"Take off your coat,"* said Miss Shay again, and she looked at me appraisingly while I did so. One of the girls got up and crossed to the desk, her high-heeled plastic sandals slapping smartly against her heels. "Look," she said, "you want these measurements with or without a bra?"

"With," said Miss Shay.   6

"But I'm bigger without," said the girl.   7

"All right," said Miss Shay wearily, "without." Two more girls came   8 down the steps looking fresh and innocent of cosmetics. "Bunny?" said Miss Shay.

"Not really," said one, but the other took a card. Their long hair   9 and loafers looked collegiate.

The application form was short: address, phone, measurements,   10 age, and last three employers. I finished it and began to stall for time by looking at an accompanying brochure entitled *BE A PLAYBOY CLUB BUNNY!* Most of it was devoted to photographs: a group picture showed Bunnies "chosen from all over the United States" surrounding "Playboy Club President and *Playboy* Editor-Publisher Hugh M. Hefner"; there was a close-up of a Bunny serving Tony Curtis, "a Playboy Club devotee [who] will soon star in Hugh M. Hefner's film titled, appropriately enough, *Playboy*"; in another, two Bunnies smiled with Hugh M. Hefner on "Playboy's nationally syndicated television show"; Bunnies handed out copies of *Playboy* in a veterans' hospital as "just one of the many worthwhile community projects in which Bunnies participate"; a blond Bunny stood before a matronly woman, the "Bunny Mother," who offered "friendly personal counseling"; and, on the last page, a bikini-clad girl crouched on a yacht flying a Bunny flag. "When you become a Bunny," said the text, "your world will be fun-filled, pleasant, and always exciting. . . ." It cited an average salary of two hundred dollars a week.

Another girl came down the steps. She wore glasses with blue rims   11 and a coat that looked as if she had outgrown it. I watched her as she nervously asked Miss Shay if the club hired eighteen-year-olds. "Sure," said Miss Shay, "but they can't work the midnight shift." She gave the girl an application card, glanced down at her plump legs, and did not ask her to take off her coat. Two more girls came in, one in bright pink stretch pants and the other in purple. "Man, this place is a gas," said Pink.

"You think this is wild, you should see Hefner's house in Chicago," 12 said Purple. Miss Shay looked at them with approval.

"I don't have a phone," said Blue Glasses sadly. "Is it all right if I 13 give you my uncle's phone? He lives in Brooklyn, too."

"You do that," said Miss Shay, and she called me over. She pointed 14 to a spot three feet in front of her desk and told me to stand up straight. I stood.

"I want to be a Bunny so much," said Blue Glasses. "I read about it 15 in a magazine at school."

Miss Shay asked me if I were really twenty-four. "That's awfully 16 old," she warned. I said I thought I might just get in under the wire. She nodded.

"My uncle isn't home all day," the girl said, "but I'll go to his house 17 and stay by the phone."

"You do that, dear," said Miss Shay and, turning to me, she added, 18 "I've taking the liberty of making an appointment for you on Wednesday at six-thirty. You will come to the service entrance, go to the sixth floor, and ask for Miss Burgess, the Bunny Mother." I agreed, but then she added, "Are you sure you haven't applied before? Someone named Marie Ochs came in yesterday." I was startled; could Marie have escaped from my notebook? I had a thirty-second fantasy based on *Pygmalion*. Or was there another Marie Ochs? Possible, but not likely. I decided to brave it out. "How strange," I murmured, "there must be some mistake." Miss Shay shrugged and suggested I bring "bathing suit or leotard" on Wednesday.

"Could I call you?" said Blue Glasses. 19

"Don't do that, dear," said Miss Shay. "*We'll* call *you*." 20

I left the club worrying about the life expectancy of Marie Ochs. 21 Would they find out? Or did they know already? When I got halfway up the block I saw the two college girls. They were leaning against a building, their arms wrapped around themselves in a spasm of giggles, and suddenly I felt better about everything.

Everything, perhaps, except the thought of Blue Glasses sitting by 22 her uncle's phone in Brooklyn.

WEDNESDAY 30TH

I arrived at the club promptly at 6:30, and business appeared to 23 be booming. Customers were lined up in the snow to get in, and several passersby were standing outside with their faces pressed to the

glass. The elevator boy, a Valentino-handsome Puerto Rican, cheerfully jammed me in his car with two uniformed black porters, five
middle-aged male customers, two costumed Bunnies, and a stout matron in a mink coat. We stopped at the sixth floor. "Is this where I get
out?" said the matron.

"Sure, darling," drawled the elevator boy, "if you want to be a   24
Bunny." Laughter.

I looked around me. Dim lights and soft carpets had given way to   25
unpainted cement block and hanging light bulbs. There was a door
marked UNNIES; I could see the outlines where the B had been. A sign,
handwritten on a piece of torn cardboard, was taped underneath:
KNOCK!! Come on, guys. Please cooperate?!! I walked through the door and
into a bright, crowded hallway.

Two girls brushed past me. One was wearing nothing but bikini-   26
style panties; the other had on long black tights of fine mesh, and
lavender satin heels. They both rushed to a small wardrobe room on
my right, yelled out their names, collected costumes, and rushed back.
I asked the wardrobe mistress for Miss Burgess. "Honey, we just gave
her a going-away present." Four more girls bounced up to ask for costumes, collars, cuffs, and tails. They had on tights and high heels but
nothing from the waist up. One stopped to study a bulletin-board list
titled "Bunny of the Week."

I retreated to the other end of the tiny hall. It opened into a large   27
dressing room filled with metal lockers and long rows of dressing tables. Personal notes were taped to the mirrors ("Anybody want to
work B Level Saturday night?" and "I'm having a swingin' party
Wednesday at Washington Square Village, all Bunnies welcome . . . ")
Cosmetics were strewn along the counters, and three girls sat in a row
applying false eyelashes with the concentration of yogis. It looked like
a cartoon of a chorus girls' dressing room.

A girl with very red hair, very white skin, and a black satin Bunny   28
costume turned her back to me and waited. I understood that I was
supposed to zip her up, a task that took several minutes of pulling and
tugging. She was a big girl and looked a little tough, but her voice
when she thanked me was tiny and babylike. Judy Holliday could not
have done better. I asked her about Miss Burgess. "Yeah, she's in that
office," said Baby Voice, gesturing toward a wooden door with a glass
peephole in it, "but Sheralee's the new Bunny Mother." Through the
glass, I could see two girls, a blond and a brunette. Both appeared to be
in their early twenties and nothing like the matronly woman pictured
in the brochure. Baby Voice tugged and pulled some more. "This isn't
my costume," she explained, "that's why it's hard to get the crotch
up." She walked away, snapping her fingers and humming softly.

The brunette came out of the office and introduced herself to me as   29
Bunny Mother Sheralee. I told her I had mistaken her for a Bunny. "I

worked as a Bunny when the club opened last month," she said, "but now I've replaced Miss Burgess." She nodded toward the blond who was trying on a three-piece beige suit that I took to be her going-away present. "You'll have to wait a while, honey," said Sheralee. I sat down.

By 7:00 I had watched three girls tease their hair into cotton-candy shapes and four more stuff their bosoms with Kleenex. By 7:15 I had talked to two other prospective Bunnies, one a dancer, the other a part-time model from Texas. At 7:30, I witnessed the major crisis of a Bunny who had sent her costume to the cleaners with her engagement ring pinned inside. At 7:40, Miss Shay came up to the office and said, "There's no one left but Marie." By 8:00, I was sure that she was waiting for the manager of the club to come tell me that my real identity had been discovered. By 8:15, when I was finally called in, I was nervous beyond all proportion.

I waited while Sheralee looked over my application. "You don't look twenty-four," she said. *Well, that's that,* I thought. "You look much younger." I smiled in disbelief. She took several Polaroid pictures of me. "For the record," she explained. I offered her the personal history I had so painstakingly fabricated and typed, but she gave it back with hardly a glance. "We don't like our girls to have any background," she said firmly. "We just want you to fit the Bunny image." She directed me to the costume room.

I asked if I should put on my leotard.

"Don't bother with that," said Sheralee. "We just want to see that Bunny image."

The wardrobe mistress told me to take off my clothes and began to search for an old Bunny costume in my size. A girl rushed in with her costume in her hand, calling for the wardrobe mistress as a wounded solider might yell, "Medic!" "I've broken my zipper," she wailed, "I sneezed!"

"That's the third time this week," said the wardrobe mistress sternly. "It's a regular epidemic." The girl apologized, found another costume, and left.

I asked if a sneeze could really break a costume.

"Sure," she said. "Girls with colds usually have to be replaced."

She gave me a bright blue satin. It was so tight that the zipper caught my skin as she fastened the back. She told me to inhale as she zipped again, this time without mishap, and stood back to look at me critically. The bottom was cut up so high that it left my hip bones exposed as well as a good five inches of untanned derrière. The boning in the waist would have made Scarlett O'Hara blanch, and the entire construction tended to push all available flesh up to the bosom. I was sure it would be perilous to bend over. "Not too bad," said the wardrobe mistress, and began to stuff an entire plastic dry-cleaning bag into the top of my costume. A blue satin band with matching

Bunny ears attached was fitted around my head like an enlarged bicycle clip, and a grapefruit-sized hemisphere of white fluff was attached to hooks at the costume's rear-most point. "Okay, baby," she said, "put on your high heels and go show Sheralee." I looked in the mirror. The Bunny image looked back.

"Oh, you look *sweet*," said Sheralee. "Stand against the wall and smile pretty for the birdie." She took several more Polaroid shots.   39

The baby-voiced redhead came in to say she still hadn't found a costume to fit. A tiny blond in lavender satin took off her tail and perched on the desk. "Look," she said, "I don't mind the demerits— okay, I got five demerits—but don't I get points for working overtime?"   40

Sheralee looked harassed and turned to Miss Burgess. "The new kids think the girls from Chicago get special treatment, and the old kids won't train the new ones."   41

"I'll train the little buggers," said Baby Voice. "Just get me a costume."   42

I got dressed and waited. And listened: 43

". . . he gave me thirty bucks, and I only got him cigarettes."   44

"Bend over, honey, and get yourself into it."   45

"I don't know, he makes Milk of Magnesia or something."   46

"You know people commit *suicide* with those plastic bags?"   47

"Then this schmuck orders a Lace Curtain. Who ever heard of a Lace Curtain?"   48

"I told him our tails were asbestos, so he tried to burn it to find out."   49

"Last week I netted thirty bucks in tips. Big deal."   50

Sheralee called me back into the office. "So you want to be a Bunny," she said.   51

"Oh yes, very much," I said.   52

"Well . . ."—she paused significantly—"we want you to be!" I was startled. No more interviews? No investigation? "Come in tomorrow at three. We'll fit your costume and have you sign everything." I smiled and felt foolishly elated.   53

Down the stairs and up Fifth Avenue. Hippety-hop, I'm a Bunny!   54

FRIDAY, FEBRUARY 1ST

I was fitted for false eyelashes today at Larry Mathews's, a twenty-four-hour-a-day beauty salon in a West Side hotel. As a makeup expert feathered the eyelashes with a manicure scissors, she pointed out a girl who had just been fired from the club "because she wouldn't go out with a Number One keyholder." I said I thought we were forbidden to go out with customers. "You can go out with them if they've got Number One keys," the makeup girl explained. "They're for club management and reporters and big shots like that." I explained that being fired for *not* going seemed like a very different thing. "Well," she said   55 thoughtfully. "I guess it was the way she said it. She told him to go screw himself."

I paid the bill. $8.14 for the eyelashes and a cake of rouge, even 56 after the 25-percent Bunny discount. I had refused to invest in darker lipstick even though "girls get fired for looking pale." I wondered how much the Bunny beauty concession was worth to Mr. Mathews. Had beauty salons sent in sealed bids for this lucrative business?

I am home now, and I have measured the lashes. Maybe I don't 57 have to worry so much about being recognized in the club. They are three quarters of an inch long at their shortest point.

SUNDAY 3RD

I've spent an informative Sunday with the Bunny bible, or the 58 *Playboy Club Bunny Manual,* as it is officially called. From introduction ("You are holding the top job in the country for a young girl") to appendix ("Sidecar: Rim glass with lime and frost with sugar"), it is a model of clarity.

Some dozen supplements accompany the bible. Altogether, they 59 give a vivid picture of a Bunny's function. For instance:

> . . . You . . . are the only direct contact most of the readers will ever have with *Playboy* personnel. . . . We depend on our Bunnies to express the personality of the magazine.

> . . . Bunnies will be expected to contribute a fair share of personal appearances as part of their regular duties for the Club.

> . . . Bunnies are reminded that there are many pleasing means they can employ to stimulate the club's liquor volume, thereby increasing their earnings significantly. . . . The key to selling more drinks is *Customer Contact* . . . they will respond particularly to your efforts to be friendly. . . . You should make it seem that [the customer's] opinions are very important. . . .

> The Incentive System is a method devised to reward those table Bunnies who put forth an extra effort. . . . The Bunny whose [drink] average per person is highest will be the winner. . . . Prize money . . . will likewise be determined by over-all drink income.

There is a problem in being "friendly" and "pampering" the cus- 60 tomer while refusing to go out with him or even give him your last name. The manual makes it abundantly clear that Bunnies must never go out with anyone met in the club—customer or employee—and adds that a detective agency called Willmark Service Systems, Inc., has been employed to make sure that they don't. ("Of course, you can never tell when you are being checked out by a Willmark Service representative.") The explanation written for the Bunnies is simple: "Men are very excited about being in the company of Elizabeth Taylor, but they know they can't paw or proposition her. The moment they felt they could become familiar with her, she would not have the aura of glamour that now surrounds her. The same must be true of our Bunnies." In an accompanying letter from Hugh Hefner to Willmark, the explanation is still simpler: "Our licenses are laid on the line any time any of our employees in any way engages, aids, or abets traffic in prostitution. . . ." Willmark is therefore instructed to "Use your most attractive and personable male representatives to proposition the Bunnies, and even offer . . . as high as $200 on this, 'right now,' for a promise of meeting you outside the Club later." Willmark representatives are told to ask a barman or other male employee "if any of the girls are available on a cash basis for a 'friendly evening.' . . . Tell him you will pay the girls well or will pay him for the girls." If the employee does act "as a procurer," Willmark is to notify the club immediately. "We naturally do not tolerate any merchandising of the Bunnies," writes Mr. Hefner, "and are most anxious to know if any such thing is occurring."

If the idea of being merchandised isn't enough to unnerve a   61
prospective Bunny, there are other directives that may. Willmark representatives are to check girls for heels that are too low, runs in their hose, jewelry, underwear that shows, crooked or unmatched ears, dirty costumes, absence of name tags, and "tails in good order." Further: "When a show is on, check to see if the Bunnies are reacting to the performers. When a comic is on, they are supposed to laugh." Big Brother Willmark is watching you.

In fact, Bunnies must *always* appear gay and cheerful. (". . . Think   62
about something happy or funny . . . your most important commodity is personality") in spite of all worries, including the demerit system. Messy hair, bad nails, and bad makeup cost five demerits each. So does calling the room director by his first name, failing to keep a makeup appointment, or eating food in the Bunny Room. Chewing gum or eating while on duty is ten demerits for the first offense, twenty for the second, and dismissal for the third. A three-time loser for "failure to report for work without replacement" is not only dismissed but blacklisted from all other Playboy Clubs. Showing up late for work or after a break costs a demerit a minute, failure to follow a room director's instructions costs fifteen. "The dollar value of demerits," notes the Bunny bible, "shall be determined by the general manager of each club."

Once the system is mastered, there are still instructions for specific   63
jobs. Door Bunnies greet customers and check their keys. Camera Bunnies must operate Polaroids. Cigarette Bunnies explain why a pack of cigarettes can't be bought without a Playboy lighter; hat-check Bunnies learn the checking system; gift-shop Bunnies sell Playboy products; mobile-gift-shop Bunnies carry Playboy products around in baskets, and table Bunnies memorize thirteen pages of drinks.

There's more to Bunnyhood than stuffing bosoms.   64

Note: Section 523 says: "Employees may enter and enjoy the facili-   65
ties of the club as bona fide guests of 1 [Number One] keyholders." Are
these the big shots my makeup expert had in mind?

MORNING, MONDAY 4TH

At 11:00 A.M. I went to see the Playboy doctor ("Failure to keep   66
doctor's appointment, twenty demerits") at his office in a nearby hotel.
The nurse gave me a medical-history form to fill out. "Do you know
this includes an internal physical? I've been trying to get Miss Shay to
warn the girls." I said I knew, but that I didn't understand why it was
required. "It's for your own good," she said, and led me into a narrow
examining room containing a medicine chest, a scale, and a gyneco-
logical table. I put on a hospital robe and waited. It seemed I had spent
a good deal of time lately either taking off clothes, waiting, or both.

The nurse came back with the doctor, a stout, sixtyish man with   67
the pink and white skin of a baby. "So you're going to be a Bunny," he
said heartily. "Just came back from Miami myself. Beautiful club down
there. Beautiful Bunnies." I started to ask him if he had the coast-to-
coast franchise, but he interrupted to ask how I liked Bunnyhood.

"Well, it's livelier than being a secretary," I said, and he told me to 68
sit on the edge of the table. As he pounded my back and listened to me
breathe, the thought crossed my mind that every Bunny in the New
York club had rested on the same spot. "This is the part all the girls
hate," said the doctor, and took blood from my arm for a Wassermann
test. I told him that testing for venereal disease seemed a little ominous. "Don't be silly," he said, "all the employees have to do it. You'll
know everyone in the club is clean." I said that their being clean didn't
really affect me and that I objected to being put through these tests. Silence. He asked me to stand to "see if your legs are straight." "Okay," I
said, "I have to have a Wassermann. But what about an internal examination? Is that required of waitresses in New York State?"

"What do you care?" he said. "It's free, and it's for everybody's   69
good."

"How?" I asked.   70

"Look," he said impatiently, "we usually find that girls who object   71
to it strenuously have some reason . . ." He paused significantly. I
paused, too. I could either go through with it or I could march out in
protest. But in protest of what?

Back in the reception room, the nurse gave me a note to show   72
Miss Shay that I had, according to preliminary tests at least, passed. As
I put on my coat, she phoned a laboratory to pick up "a blood sample
and a smear." I asked why those tests and no urine sample? Wasn't
that the most common laboratory test of all? "It's for your own protection," she said firmly, "and anyway, the club pays."

Down in the lobby, I stopped in a telephone booth to call the board   73
of health. I asked if a Wassermann test was required of waitresses in
New York City? "No." Then what kind of physical examination *was* required? "None at all," they said.

EVENING, TUESDAY 5TH

The Bunny Room was chaotic. I was pushed and tugged and   74
zipped into my electric-blue costume by the wardrobe mistress, but
this time she allowed me to stuff my own bosom, and I was able to get
away with only half a dry cleaner's bag. I added the tiny collar with
clip-on bow tie and the starched cuffs with Playboy cuff links. My
nameplate was centered in a ribbon rosette like those won in horse
shows, and pinned just above my bare right hipbone. A major policy
change, I was told, had just shifted name tags from left hip to right.
The wardrobe mistress also gave me a Bunny jacket: it was a below-
zero night, and I was to stand by the front door. The jacket turned out
to be a brief shrug of imitation white fur that covered the shoulders
but left the bosom carefully bare.

I went in to be inspected by Bunny Mother Sheralee. "You look   75
sweet," she said, and advised that I keep any money I had with me in
my costume. "Two more girls have had things stolen from their lockers," she said, and added that I should be sure to tell the lobby director
the exact amount of money I had with me. "Otherwise they may think
you stole tips." Table Bunnies, she explained, were allowed to keep
any tips they might receive in cash (though the club did take up to 50
percent of all their charge tips), but hat-check Bunnies could keep no
tips at all. Instead, they were paid a flat twelve dollars for eight hours.
I told her that twelve dollars a day seemed a good deal less than the
salary of two to three hundred dollars mentioned in the advertisement. "Well, you won't work hat check all the time, sweetie," she said.
"When you start working as a table Bunny, you'll see how it all averages out."

I took a last look at myself in the mirror. A creature with three-   76
quarter-inch eyelashes, blue satin ears, and an overflowing bosom
looked back. I asked Sheralee if we had to stuff ourselves so much. "Of
course you do," she said. "Practically all the girls just stuff and stuff.
That's the way the Bunnies are supposed to look."

The elevator opened on the mezzanine, and I made my profes-   77
sional debut in the Playboy Club. It was crowded, noisy, and very dark.
A group of men with organizational name tags on their lapels stood
nearby. "Here's my Bunny honey now," said one, and flung his arm
around my shoulders as if we were fellow halfbacks leaving the field.

"Please, sir," I said, and uttered the ritual sentence we had learned   78
from the Bunny Father lecture: "You are not allowed to touch the

Bunnies." His companions laughed and laughed. "Boy oh boy, guess she told *you!*" said one, and tweaked my tail as I walked away.

The programmed phrases of the Bunny bible echoing in my mind, I climbed down the carpeted spiral stairs between the mezzanine ("Living Room, Piano Bar, buffet dinner now being served") and the lobby ("Check your coats; immediate seating in the Playmate Bar"), separated from the street by only a two-story sheet of glass. The alternative was a broad staircase in the back of the lobby, but that, too, could be seen from the street. All of us, customers and Bunnies alike, were a living window display. I reported to the lobby director. "Hello, Bunny Marie," he said. "How's things?" I told him that I had fifteen dollars in my costume. "I'll remember," he said. I had a quick and humiliating vision of all the hat-check Bunnies lined up for bosom inspection.

There was a four-deep crowd of impatient men surrounding the Hat Check Room. The head hat-check Bunny, a little blond who had been imported from Chicago to straighten out the system, told me to take their tickets and call the numbers out to two "hang boys" behind the counter. "I'll give you my number if you give me yours," said a balding man, and turned to the crowd for appreciation.

After an hour of helping men on with coats, scarves, and hats, the cocktail rush had subsided enough for the Chicago Bunny to show me how to pin numbers on coat lapels with straight pins or tuck them in hatbands. She gave me more ritual sentences. "Thank you, sir, here is your ticket." "The information Bunny is downstairs to your right." "Sorry, we're unable to take ladies' coats." (Only if the club was uncrowded, and the coats were not fur, was the Hat Check Room available to women.) She emphasized that I was to put all tips in a slotted box attached to the wall, smile gratefully, and not tell the customers that the tips went to the club. She moved to the other half of the check room ("The blue tickets are next door, sir") and sent a tall, heavy-set Swiss Bunny to take her place.

The two of us took care of a small stream of customers and talked a little. I settled down to my ever-present worry that someone I knew was going to come in, recognize me, and say, "Gloria!" If the rumor were true that one newspaper reporter and one news-magazine reporter had tried to become Bunnies and failed, the management must be alert to the possibility, and I had seen more than enough Sydney Greenstreet movies to worry about the club's reaction. If someone I knew did come in, I would just keep repeating "There must be some mistake" and hope for the best.

Dinner traffic began, and soon there was a crowd of twenty men waiting. We worked quickly, but coats going in and out at the same time made for confusion. One customer was blundering about behind the counter in search of a lost hat, and two more were complaining loudly that they had been waiting ten minutes. "The reason there's a line outside the Playboy Club," said one, "is because they're waiting for their coats." A man in a blue silk suit reached out to pull my tail. I dodged and held a coat for a balding man with a row of ballpoint pens in his suit pocket. He put it on, but backward, so that his arms were around me. The hang boy yelled at him in a thick Spanish accent to "Leave her alone," and he told the hang boy to shut up. Three women in mink stoles stood waiting for their husbands. I could see them staring, not with envy, but coldly, as if measuring themselves against the Swiss Bunny and me. High up on the opposite wall, a camera stared down at all of us and transmitted the scene to screens imbedded in walls all over the club, including one screen over the sidewalk: " . . . the closed-circuit television camera that flashes your arrival throughout the Club . . ." explained publicity folders. I was overcome by a nightmare sensation of walking naked through crowds but the only way back to my own clothes was the glass-encased stairway. As men pressed forward with coats outstretched, I turned to the hang boy for more tickets. "Don't worry," he said kindly, "you get used to it."

Business let up again. I asked the Swiss Bunny if she liked the work. "Not really," she shrugged. "I was an airline hostess for a while, but once you've seen Hong Kong, you've seen it." A man asked for his coat. I turned around and found myself face-to-face with two people whom I knew well, a television executive and his wife. I looked down as I took his ticket and kept my back turned while the boy found the coat, but I had to face him again to deliver it. My television friend looked directly at me, gave me fifty cents, and walked away. Neither he nor his wife had recognized me. It was depressing to be a nonperson in a Bunny suit, but it was also a victory. To celebrate, I helped a slight, shy-looking man put on his long blue-and-white scarf, asked him if he and the scarf were from Yale. He looked startled, as if he had been recognized at a masquerade. 84

There were no clocks anywhere in the club. I asked the hang boy what time it was. "One o'clock," he said. I had been working for more than five hours with no break. My fingers were perforated and sore from pushing pins through cardboard, my arms ached from holding heavy coats, I was thoroughly chilled from the icy wind that blew each time a customer opened the door, and, atop my three-inch black satin heels, my feet were killing me. I walked over to ask the Chicago Bunny if I could take a break. 85

"Yes," she said, "a half-hour to eat, but no more." 86

Down the hall from the Bunny Room was the employees' lounge, where our meal tickets entitled us to one free meal a day. I pulled a metal folding chair up to a long bare table, took my shoes off gingerly, and sat down next to two black men in gray work uniforms. They looked sympathetic as I massaged my swollen feet. One was young and quite handsome, the other middle-aged and graying at the temples: like all employees at the club, they seemed chosen, at least partly, 87 for their appearance. The older one advised me about rolling bottles under my feet to relax them and getting arch supports for my shoes. I asked what they did. "We're garbage men," said the younger. "It don't sound so good, but it's easier than your job."

They told me I should eat something and gestured to the beef stew 88 on their paper plates. "Friday we get fish," one said, "but every other day is the same stew."

"The same, except it gets worse," said the other, and laughed. The 89 older one told me he felt sorry for the Bunnies even though some of them enjoyed "showing off their looks." He advised me to be careful of my feet and not to try to work double shifts.

Back downstairs, I tried to categorize the customers as I checked 90 their coats. With the exception of a few teenage couples, the majority seemed to be middle-aged businessmen. Less than half had women with them, and the rest came in large all-male bunches that seemed entirely subsidized by expense accounts. I saw only four of the type pictured in club advertisements—the young, lean, nattily dressed Urban Man—and they were with slender, fashionable girls who looked rather appalled by our stuffed costumes and bright makeup. The least-confident wives of the businessmen didn't measure themselves against us, but seemed to assume that their husbands would be attracted to us and stood aside, looking timid and embarrassed. There were a few customers, a very few, either men or women (I counted ten), who looked at us not as objects but smiled and nodded as if we might be human beings.

The Swiss Bunny took a break, and a hang boy began to give me a 91 gentle lecture. I was foolish, he said, to put all that money in the box. The tips were cash. If we didn't take some, the man who counted it might. I told him I was afraid they would look in my costume and I didn't want to get fired. "They only check you girls once in a while," he said. "Anyway, I'll make you a deal. You give me money. I meet you outside. We split it." My feet ached, my fingers were sticky from dozens of sweaty hatbands, and my skin was gouged and sore from the bones of the costume. Even the half-hour dinner break had been on my own time, so the club was getting a full eight hours of work. I felt resentful enough to take him up on it. Still, it would hardly do to get fired for stealing. I told him that I was a new Bunny and too nervous to try it. "You'll get over that," he said. "One Saturday night last week, this check room took in a thousand dollars in tips. And you know how much we get paid. You think about that."

It was almost 4:00 A.M. Quitting time. 92

The lobby director came over to tell us that the customer count for 93 the night was about two thousand. I said that sounded good. "No," he said. "Good is four thousand."

I went back to the Bunny Room, turned in my costume, and sat 94 motionless, too tired to move. The stays had made vertical indentations around my rib cage and the zipper had left a welt over my spine.

I complained about the costume's tightness to the Bunny who was sitting next to me, also motionless. "Yeah," she said, "a lot of girls say their legs get numb from the knee up. I think it presses on a nerve or something."

The street was deserted, but a taxi waited outside by the employees' exit. The driver held a dollar bill out the window. "I got four more of these," he said. "Is that enough?" I kept on walking. "What'sa matter?" he said, irritated. "You work in there, don't you?" 95

The streets were brightly lit and sparkling with frost. As I walked the last block to my apartment, I passed a gray English car with the motor running. A woman was sitting in the driver's seat, smoking a cigarette and watching the street. Her hair was bright blond and her coat bright red. She looked at me and smiled. I smiled back. She looked available—and she was. Of the two of us, she seemed the more honest. 96

CAROL BLY

Getting Tired

Carol Bly (1930–   ) was born in Duluth, Minnesota, and graduated from Wellesley College in 1951. Between 1958 and 1971, with her husband, poet Robert Bly, she managed a literary magazine series: *Fifties, Sixties,* and finally, *Seventies.* In the 1970s she began writing essays—which she called "letters"—for *Preview* and *Minnesota Monthly,* published by Minnesota Public Radio. These essays focus on rural life in Minnesota, depicting the dullness as well as the romance, and they often encourage rural people to put aside societal expectations in order to cultivate their internal lives and learn to live passionately. Her short stories, published in *The New Yorker, Ploughshares,* and *American Review* and collected in *Backbone* (1985), echo this interest. She has recently edited an anthology of poems, essays, and stories, *Changing the Bully Who Rules the World: Reading and Thinking about Ethics* (1996). "Getting Tired" comes from Bly's collection of essays, *Letters from the Country* (1981). The essay shows Bly's remarkable ability to connect the physical sensation of "being there" with abstract philosophical and political thought. In addition to connecting with the other work memoirs in this unit, it could be read as an embodiment in concrete terms of some of the ideas presented by Dorothy L. Sayers's "Living to Work."

The men have left a gigantic 6600 combine a few yards from our grove, at the edge of the stubble. For days it was working around the farm; we heard it on the east, later on the west, and finally we could see it grinding back and forth over the windrows on the south. But 1 now it has been simply squatting at the field's edge, huge, tremendously still, very professional, slightly dangerous.

We all have the correct feelings about this new combine: this isn't the good old farming where man and soil are dusted together all day; this isn't farming a poor man can afford, either, and therefore it further threatens his hold on the American "family farm" operation. We have been sneering at this machine for days, as its transistor radio, amplified well over the engine roar, has been grinding up our silence, spreading a kind of shrill ghetto evening all over the farm.

But now it is parked, and after a while I walk over to it and climb up its neat little John-Deere-green ladder on the left. Entering the big cab up there is like coming up into a large ship's bridge on visitors' day—heady stuff to see the inside workings of a huge operation like the Queen Elizabeth II. On the other hand I feel left out, being only a dumbfounded passenger. The combine cab has huge windows flaring wider at the top; they lean forward over the ground, and the driver sits so high behind the glass in its rubber moldings it is like a movie-set spaceship. He has obviously come to dominate the field, whether he farms it or not.

The value of the 66 is that it can do anything, and to change it from a combine into a cornpicker takes one man about half an hour, whereas most machine conversions on farms take several men a half day. It frees its owner from a lot of monkeying.

Monkeying, in city life, is what little boys do to clocks so they never run again. In farming it has two quite different meanings. The first is small side projects. You monkey with poultry, unless you're a major egg handler. Or you monkey with ducks or geese. If you have a very small milk herd, and finally decide that prices plus state regulations don't make your few Holsteins worthwhile, you "quit monkeying with them." There is a hidden dignity in this word: it precludes mention of money. It lets the wife of a very marginal farmer have a conversation with a women who may be helping her husband run fifteen hundred acres. "How you coming with those geese?" "Oh, we've been real disgusted. We're thinking of quitting monkeying with them." It saves her having to say, "We lost our shirts on those darn geese."

The other meaning of monkeying is wrestling with and maintaining machinery, such as changing heads from combining to cornpicking. Farmers who cornpick the old way, in which the corn isn't shelled automatically during picking in the field but must be elevated to the top of a pile by belt and then shelled, put up with some monkeying.

Still, cornpicking and plowing is a marvelous time of the year on farms; one of the best autumns I've had recently had a few days of fieldwork in it. We were outside all day, from six in the morning to eight at night—coming in only for noon dinner. We ate our lunches on a messy truck flatbed. (For city people who don't know it: *lunch* isn't a noon meal; it is what you eat out of a black lunch pail at 9 A.M. and 3

P.M. If you offer a farmer a cup of coffee at 3:30 P.M. he or she is likely to say, "No thanks, I've already had lunch.") There were four of us hired to help—a couple to plow, Celia (a skilled farmhand who worked steady for our boss), and me. Lunch was always two sandwiches of white commercial bread with luncheon meat, and one very generous piece of cake-mix cake carefully wrapped in Saran Wrap. (I never found anyone around here self-conscious about using Saran Wrap when the Dow Chemical Company was also making napalm.)

It was very pleasant on the flatbed, squinting out over the yellow   8 picked cornstalks—each time we stopped for lunch, a larger part of the field had been plowed black. We fell into the easy psychic habit of farmworkers: admiration of the boss. "Ja, I see he's buying one of those big 4010s," someone would say. We always perked up at inside information like that. Or "Ja," as the woman hired steady told us, "he's going to plow the home fields first this time, instead of the other way round." We temporary help were impressed by that, too. Then, with real flair, she brushed a crumb of luncheon meat off her jeans, the way you would make sure to flick a gnat off spotless tennis whites. It is the true feminine touch to brush a crumb off pants that are encrusted with Minnesota Profile A heavy loam, many swipes of SAE 40 oil, and grain dust.

All those days, we never tired of exchanging information on how   9 *he* was making out, what *he* was buying, whom *he* was going to let drive the new tractor, and so on. There is always something to talk about with the other hands, because farming is genuinely absorbing. It has the best quality of work: nothing else seems real. And everyone doing it, even the cheapest helpers like me, can see the layout of the whole—from spring work, to cultivating, to small grain harvest, to cornpicking, to fall plowing.

The second day I was promoted from elevating corncobs at the   10 corn pile to actual plowing. Hour after hour I sat up there on the old Alice, as she was called (an Allis-Chalmers WC that looked rusted from the Flood). You have to sit twisted part way around, checking that the plowshares are scouring clean, turning over and dropping the dead crop and soil, not clogging. For the first two hours I was very political. I thought about what would be good for American farming—stronger marketing organizations, or maybe a law like the Norwegian Odal law, preventing the breaking up of small farms or selling them to business interests. Then the sun got high, and each time I reached the headlands area at the field's end I dumped off something else, now my cap, next my jacket, finally my sweater.

Since the headlands are the last to be plowed, they serve as a field   11 road until the very end. There are usually things parked there—a pickup or a corn trailer—and things dumped—my warmer clothing, our afternoon lunch pails, a broken furrow wheel someone picked up.

By noon I'd dropped all political interest, and was thinking only: how unlike this all is to Keats's picture of autumn, a "season of mists and mellow fruitfulness." This gigantic expanse of horizon, with everywhere the easy growl of tractors, was simply teeming with extrovert energy. It wouldn't calm down for another week, when whoever was lowest on the totem pole would be sent out to check a field for dropped parts or to drive away the last machines left around.

The worst hours for all common labor are the hours after noon dinner. Nothing is inspiring then. That is when people wonder how they ever got stuck in the line of work they've chosen for life. Or they wonder where the cool Indian smoke of secrets and messages began to vanish from their marriage. Instead of plugging along like a cheerful beast working for me, the Allis now smelled particularly gassy. To stay awake I froze my eyes onto an indented circle in the hood around the gas cap. Someone had apparently knocked the screw cap fitting down into the hood, so there was a moat around it. In this moat some overflow gas leapt in tiny waves. Sometimes the gas cap was a castle, this was the moat; sometimes it was a nuclear-fission plant, this was the horrible hot-water waste. Sometimes it was just the gas cap on the old Alice with the spilt gas bouncing on the hot metal.

Row after row. I was stupefied. But then around 2:30 the shadows appeared again, and the light, which had been dazing and white, grew fragile. The whole prairie began to gather itself for the cool evening. All of a sudden it was wonderful to be plowing again, and when I came to the field end, the filthy jackets and the busted furrow wheel were just benign mistakes: that is, if it chose to, the jacket could be a church robe, and the old wheel could be something with some pride to it, like a helm. And I felt the same about myself: instead of being someone with a half interest in literature and a half interest in farming doing a half-decent job plowing, I could have been someone desperately needed in Washington or Zurich. I drank my three o'clock coffee joyously, and traded the other plowman a Super-Valu cake-mix lemon cake slice for a Holsum baloney sandwich because it had garlic in it.

By seven at night we had been plowing with headlights for an hour. I tried to make up games to keep going, on my second wind, on my third wind, but labor is labor after the whole day of it; the mind refuses to think of ancestors. It refuses to pretend the stalks marching up to the right wheel in the spooky light are men-at-arms, or to imagine a new generation coming along. It doesn't care. Now the Republicans could have announced a local meeting in which they would propose a new farm program whereby every farmer owning less than five hundred acres must take half price for his crop, and every farmer owning more than a thousand acres shall receive triple price for his crop, and I was so tired I wouldn't have shown up to protest.

A million hours later we sit around in a daze at the dining-room table, and nobody says anything. In low, courteous mutters we ask for the macaroni hotdish down this way, please. Then we get up in ones and twos and go home. Now the farm help are all so tired we *are* a little like the various things left out on the headlands—some tools, a jacket, someone's thermos top—used up for that day. Thoughts won't even stick to us anymore.

Such tiredness must be part of farmers' wanting huge machinery   17 like the Deere 6600. That tiredness that feels so good to the occasional laborer and the athlete is disturbing to a man destined to it eight months of every year. But there is a more hidden psychology in the issue of enclosed combines versus open tractors. It is this: one gets too many impressions on the open tractor. A thousand impressions enter as you work up and down the rows: nature's beauty or nature's stubbornness, politics, exhaustion, but mainly the feeling that all this repetition—last year's cornpicking, this year's cornpicking, next year's cornpicking—is taking up your lifetime. The mere repetition reveals your eventual death.

When you sit inside a modern combine, on the other hand, you   18 are so isolated from field, sky, all the real world, that the brain is dulled. You are not sensitized to your own mortality. You aren't sensitive to anything at all.

This must be a common choice of our mechanical era: to hide from   19 life inside our machinery. If we can hide from life in there, some idiotic part of the psyche reasons, we can hide from death in there as well.

SALLIE TISDALE

Good Soldiers

Born in Yreka, California, in 1957, Sallie Tisdale received a B.S. in nursing from the University of Portland in 1983. She worked as a registered nurse for the next seven years, and her writing often draws from these experiences. Her books *The Sorcerer's Apprentice: Tales of the Modern Hospital* (1986) and *Lot's Wife: Salt and the Human Condition* (1988) both won Book of the Year Awards from *American Health*. In 1987, *Harvest Moon: Portrait of a Nursing Home* won the same honor from *American Journal of Nursing*. She received a grant from the Oregon Arts Commission in 1988 and an NEA fellowship in 1989. Her contributions have appeared in such periodicals as *The New York Times, Vogue, Esquire,* and *The New Yorker*. Tisdale's *Talk Dirty to Me: An Intimate Philosophy of Sex* was published in 1994. In her writing, Tisdale declares, she works at the "illumination of the personal, the striking for a chord of experience."

"Good Soldiers" is a particularly challenging essay in which Tisdale, a Buddhist and a leftist, encounters workers who have devoted their lives to a Christian ideal with very conservative overtones. The essay might inspire readers to investigate the world of volunteers, of people who choose their life work for reasons that are neither economic nor aesthetic. It also links workplace essays like Gloria Steinem's "I Was a Playboy Bunny" with essays like Herbert Inhaber and Sidney Carroll's "A Grand Parade" that raise questions of economic justice.

The red shield with a white letter "S," red kettles at Christmas, 1 fresh-faced young women in bonnets, street-corner brass bands. Each image means only one thing, and each is likely to evoke more amusement than respect. The Salvation Army is so conspicuous as to be invisible to most people, almost as invisible as the average person served in its kitchens and shelters. I've seen the red shield on the big white building down the street from my house, on the stately stonework of the New York headquarters on Fourteenth Street, on the architectural gloss of a new building in Santa Monica, and until recently I never paid attention. I thought of the Salvation Army as little more than a chain of thrift stores—a quaint and rather austere organization of indeterminate size.

I am not a Christian and never have been, but I think of Jesus 2 every time I pass a storefront mission and see men curled up in doorways, families lined up outside. "The least among you," He said. I am glad, when I pass the soup kitchens, that someone is doing something. I am guilty because I do too little. I am puzzled because I'm not always sure what I could and should do. But to tackle homelessness and end-stage alcoholism with cornets and a Bible reading, as I believed the Salvation Army to do, seemed rather naive. What I mostly didn't do with the Salvation Army—and do now—is take it seriously.

The Army is far larger than most people realize, claiming more 3 than 5 million members in ninety-nine countries. Last year, it raised $726 million from private donations in the United States, more than any other nonprofit organization. (The Christmas kettles alone brought in $61 million.) All money raised locally is used locally. One of the principles of charity outlined in Army literature is that any social plan "must be on a scale commensurate with the situation with which it proposes to deal." In the United States last year the Army served at least 69 million free meals and provided shelter for 9.5 million homeless people.

These are, and should be, dazzling numbers, easily outstripping 4 the income and services provided by other charities struggling directly with poverty. Certainly the Army is one of the most efficient, spending eighty-seven cents of every donated dollar on its service programs. In the name of bringing the poor and hungry up from the gutter to independence, the Salvation Army offers food and shelter, employment services, drug and alcohol recovery programs, a nationwide missing persons service, homes for pregnant women, shelter for battered women and their children, nursing care for people with AIDS, day-care centers, toy giveaways at Christmas, clothing, prison programs, hospitals, legal aid, various forms of counseling and, always, as much religion as anyone wants.

The Salvation Army is an evangelical church. Its charity is not simply service for service's sake, but service to people so much in need they cannot hear the word of the Salvationists' God. In 1992 the Army counted 133,833 "Decisions for Christ" by people attending worship or receiving charity. The Army's target has always been the most disadvantaged and the most reviled. In a way, the Salvation Army has tried to *be* the poor.

Though the Army can invoke in the thoughtful outsider an uncomfortable ambivalence, a careful reading of its policies reveals surprising layers of intelligence, tolerance and joy. My own cultural politics are far to the left of the Army's. My growing respect for it comes from the fact that the daily behavior of Salvationists is often more political and far to the left of my own. They preach and pray about the suffering of the world, but most of all, what Salvationists do in the face of suffering is act.

Captain Bill Dickinson runs the Seattle Temple Corps of the Salvation Army, a congregation of more than 400 members. He is 53 years old, mild, plainspoken, compact, graying. His voice is usually diffident, but now and then it will rise into the cantatory inflections of testimony. Bill and his wife, Mary, were childhood sweethearts in Walla Walla, Washington, where they both occasionally attended Salvation Army services. They married in 1960, a year after Bill finished his Navy Service. Bill eventually became a successful restaurant owner. He also became an alcoholic.

"I found early on that I'm the kind of person who can't take just one drink. I was always trying to find satisfaction in *something*. I thought, if I work hard enough and make enough money, that way we'll find happiness. And we were very successful, and I felt no satisfaction. We had the financial means to do all kinds of stuff, and yet it was just an *empty* life." In Spokane, Washington, the Dickinsons began attending Army services for the first time since childhood.

Bill Dickinson told me of his resistance to the whispering call. "I got to the point where I hated to go to church. The Holy Spirit had really been convicting me of my sin—my sins—and I had such a need to repent and come back to Him. But I wouldn't yield to the Holy Spirit because of my pride." He smiled, a little sheepish at the memory. "So finally it's Sunday morning and I'm sitting in the pew at church, and I couldn't wait for them to give the altar call. I thought, 'This is it, now or never.' August 29, 1982, at about 12:15, I went forward and accepted Christ as my Savior in the Lord. And I was delivered from the taste of alcohol."

Like Dickinson, many Army officers have had wide experience in the secular world. Yet there is no typical Salvationist; prejudgment fails in this real world on which so many false stereotypes are based. Bill Dickinson is what he seems to be. Only in meeting a person whose internal life is so visible can we see how rare that quality is—the transparency that comes to each of us only when we are doing exactly what we want to do, and think we should be doing, with our lives.

On a Christmas visit I made to Dickinson's temple last year, he introduced me to another kind of Salvationist, a tall, broad, laughing 35-year-old man named Ken Solts. Solts was then a second-year seminary student sent from California to help with the holiday kettle drive. Over cocoa in the Temple kitchen, Solts interrupted our conversation to ask me if I had accepted Jesus as my personal savior, accepted my refusal to discuss the matter with another laugh and went on. He eagerly told me of his own history of drug dealing and jail time. "Everything kind of caught up all at once, when I was 29." He shook his head. "There's something about what that drug—crank—does to you, something that makes you such an airhead, and it takes a long time for it to wear off. God has changed my life in such a short time, and if He can do it for me, He can do it for anyone.

"I'd made a lot of promises to God, and now I was really in a bad place. So I made another promise—that if He got me out of prison time, I would change my life. And somehow the courts ended up combining all my felonies into one, which was a miracle in itself, and then the judge suspended my sentence. I had three years probation, and all kinds of fines to pay, and there I was, with a big promise to keep.

"My parents are auxiliary captains in Sacramento. I knew if I moved there I'd have to go to church," he continued. "So, I went, but I wasn't ready to give in. One day I was just sitting there and I really felt the need to change my life. I prayed and asked Christ into my heart.

"When I was saved, I said, 'O.K., this is cool, but I'm *not* wearing that uniform.' So five months later I'm wearing a uniform, being sworn in as a senior soldier. Then my dad started talking to me about officership, and I said, 'I don't want to be an officer.' Besides, it's real strict. You can't be a cadet if you're on probation. Then the captain wrote to the probation officer, and the Army made a special grant to pay off my fines. They sent them a check. And the judge let me off."

People who join the Salvation Army church sign a covenant called the "Articles of War," and are then called soldiers. (Many people who attend Army services prefer not to sign the Articles, often because of the smoking restriction. These people are called "adherents.") Soldiers are enjoined against the use of alcohol, tobacco and other recreational drugs, and told to avoid gambling, debt and the use of profanity. They are encouraged to join trade unions and generally will side with labor during strikes. Soldiers are also urged to examine themselves for dishonesty, racism, sexism and arrogance. The Salvationist is admonished to see himself as a "stranger" on earth, and to see the church itself as "a band of pilgrims who are called to separate themselves from the oppressive patterns of the present." The death of a Salvationist is routinely referred to as a "promotion to Glory," and mourning is discouraged.

The Salvation Army's mix of social action and religion leads to a   16
number of policies unexpected in fundamentalist Christianity. The Army *is* quaint, and austere; Salvationists are also unflinchingly clear-headed about the state of the world. Naïveté, like the blush on the bonneted girl's cheek, is only an image. The Army combines radicalism and conservatism in a mix that should not work: since its inception it has been accused of being too conservative by some observers and too liberal by others—too religious in its charitable work, too secular in its religion.

Salvationists traditionally volunteer in war zones, and Army offi-   17
cers are qualified as military chaplains. But any Salvationist who declares himself to be a conscientious objector will receive the church's backing. Contraception among Salvationists is not only a private matter between husband and wife, but, to a church intimate with the problems of overpopulation and poverty, also a matter of "informed responsibility."

Two issues stand out as the traditional thorns of fundamentalism—   18
abortion and homosexuality. Abortion is strongly discouraged, but there are certain exceptions in which it is an acceptable choice. Homosexuality is considered one of several examples of "sexual misconduct," but the Doctrines of the Army are careful to distinguish between homosexual behavior and homosexual "tendencies." This doctrine is, in fact, the only example of real naïveté I've come across in Army literature. ("Some homosexuals achieve a happy heterosexual marriage," reads the position paper.) Absent from the Army's attitude toward homosexuality, however, is any trace of hate-mongering. In the words of the church, homosexuality is not "blameworthy and should not be allowed to create guilt."

Salvation Army officers receive no salary; the commitment to the   19
poor includes the experience of poverty. (William Booth, the Army's founder, told one class of newly trained officers, "I sentence you all to hard labor for the rest of your natural lives.") These days, Army officers

are provided with modest housing, a car, a portion of the cost of their uniforms, 80 percent of their medical expenses and a living allowance. At the beginning of her career, a single officer will receive $138 per week; the amount gradually increases. A married couple receives between them a beginning allowance of $229 per week. A child under the age of 5 increases the couple's allowance by $23 per week. The most any officer or officer couple can make is $282 a week. (This is, approximately, all the compensation given to the Army's general, its worldwide leader.) Most officers tithe their allowance to the church. And the tithe is not all; from its inception, the Army has occasionally called on its members and officers for Self-Denial Funds for specific projects; in 1992 the Army raised more than $20 million from its own staff.

A Salvation Army officer is expected to be in uniform whenever he or she is on duty, and officers are almost always on duty. According to church literature, the navy blue uniform is "an invitation to the people to avail themselves" of officers for any kind of help. "I tell you, if I put my uniform on and go down the street and approach somebody," Dickinson told me one afternoon, "I'll have a very easy time striking up a conversation with them and even talking to them about the Lord. If I take my uniform off and just dress up in a suit or casual clothes, and do the same thing, chances are I'll be ignored. With the uniform they know they're safe. They're probably going to hear the Gospel story, but they'll accept that. They don't have to be afraid.

"People wave and smile at me. People will even stop and tell me, 'Thank you for how you helped me out fifteen or twenty years ago, forty or fifty years ago,' or, 'Thank you for how you helped my parents. They always told me that if I was ever in trouble, I could go to the Salvation Army and they would help me."

Army founder William Booth was born in Nottingham, England, in 1829 to severe poverty. He was a teetotaler, a vegetarian, the father of eight, often ill and depressed. He was called "General" wherever he went, and once was described as being "desperately in earnest all the time." He certainly looks earnest in his photographs, earnest and infinitely weary, with a long white beard, a frosting of snow-white hair, a prominent nose and uncommonly sad eyes.

Booth began preaching as a Wesleyan Methodist, but was kicked out of the church because of his volatile outdoor sermons and his insistence on universal salvation—that God's saving grace was available to all people. (In Booth's time, the poor were either not allowed into church services or were required to stay hidden behind screens.) His sermons drew big crowds, and eventually mobs, riots and the police, especially after his young wife, Catherine Mumford, began to preach beside him. They converted hundreds of people at a time. In 1878 he changed the name of his Christian Mission to the Salvation Army, adopting as his motto "Blood and Fire."

Booth wanted the poor of London, he said, to have only what cab   24
horses could depend upon: adequate food, decent shelter, gainful employment. He believed economic conditions held people in thrall. In fact, reading his proposals today is a lesson in how very different roads can lead to the same goal, because William Booth steered close to a kind of Marxism in his love of Christ. The Army, instead, arrived at a policy of strict nonpartisanship. Only once, and not without internal dissension, has the Army taken a public political position; in 1928 it briefly endorsed Herbert Hoover for president because he supported prohibition.

George Bernard Shaw, in his introduction to *Major Barbara*, wrote   25
that Booth "would take money from the Devil himself and be only too glad to get it out of his hands and into God's." The philosophy is akin to Booth's feeling about the joy of music, which in the Army's hands is both irrepressible and reverent. "I rather enjoy robbing the Devil of his choicest tunes," said Booth.

Once the Army was established, clients were expected to pay for   26
their meals. If the bowl of soup cost a penny to make, a man should pay a penny, and if he didn't have a penny, the Army gave him a penny's worth of work to do before he ate. This policy continued well into the 1950s, but today, sheer numbers make it impossible to let every hungry person work for his or her meal. Instead, one officer told me simply, "If unemployment is the problem, we get them jobs." Eighty-two thousand jobs last year, in fact.

In the United States, the Salvation Army has seen its biggest suc-   27
cesses. The Army's first overseas missionaries, seven women and a man, were sent to America in 1880. Only one of the women was over the age of 20. A few days after docking in New York (the first Salvation sermon being delivered on the dock), the missionaries preached at Harry Hill's Variety, a saloon on the corner of Crosby and Houston Streets. The *New York World* duly reported the event as "A PECULIAR PEOPLE AMID QUEER SURROUNDINGS." Within six months there were twelve American Salvation Army Corps; within ten years, the Army was in forty-three states. And it grew, adding new Corps almost monthly, and never failing to find new forms of spectacle and display for its message—"Soup, Soap and Salvation!" The first Salvation Army Christmas kettle was a crab pot put out on a street in San Francisco, appropriated on an impulse by an officer in 1891 and labeled "Keep the Pot Boiling!"

The first Army home for alcoholics, called the Church of the   28
Homeless Outcast, was started in Detroit in 1939. Now there are 147, known as Adult Rehabilitation Centers (ARCS). The clients in such programs, who must be considered unemployable when they are admit-

ted, receive free shelter, food, detoxification, counseling and "work therapy"—training, advice, experience and placement. Clients sort used clothes, pick up donations, help with maintenance. In return, they receive a stipend of up to $15 a week.

The $726 million raised from individual donors in the United States last year represents about two-thirds of the United States Salvation Army's income. The rest comes from foundations, income-producing programs (hospitals, day-care centers), corporations and federal and state governments. In recent years, the amount of federal money accepted by the Army has dropped to less than 1 percent of its annual budget. The Army considers it "unnatural" to separate its secular work—charity—from its religious purpose. When the government pushes on the church-state separation issue, the Army shoves back—it returns the money and refuses any more with such a hitch attached. The Army now requires its other donors to sign an agreement giving it the right to keep its iconography visible.

A few months after his altar call, Bill Dickinson felt the call to become an Army officer. "I'm sitting there saying, 'Lord, I'm 43, and I know I'm too old to go into the training school, and so there's no possible way to fulfill what you're telling me to do.'" There was another complication, too: officers may only be married to another officer, or lose their rank altogether. Married couples always work together, in parallel roles or sharing the duties of a single position. Bill could never become an officer without Mary at his side.

Shortly after that Bill learned about something called an auxiliary commission that would enable him and Mary to become officers without attending seminary. He approached Mary with the idea. "She said, 'Absolutely not. There's no way that I'll ever become a Salvation Army officer,' I knew it was either both of us or neither of us."

Mary Dickinson, a shy woman who admits she "lacks confidence," is an uncommon officer because she would have been happy not to have become an officer at all. "I was very comfortable being at home, being a housewife. We had a good business, and three beautiful children, and grandchildren. Then he came to me and told me he wanted to be an officer. And I said, 'I can't. There's just no way.' Well, you never tell God never. It wasn't long after that, about a year, that God did speak in my heart." She laughs. "I said, 'Lord, you really don't mean that!' I struggled for some time, and I still struggle a lot."

When I asked Mary about the role of women in the Army she eyed me for a long moment before speaking. She had already told me she preferred to be addressed as "Mrs. Captain Bill Dickinson," rather than by her own name. "I have the feeling the women here . . . ," she trailed off, laughing. "You're not going to like this and most people don't like it when I say it, so I don't say it very often. I think women aren't equal to men. I feel the last word should be the husband's; it's a man's place behind the pulpit. People here, they get really angry with me sometimes. Because the women here *like* to be leaders."

Women have always been allowed to hold any position and have always outnumbered men in the Army both as soldiers and officers. For the past seven years (two years longer than the usual term) the general of the Salvation Army was a woman, an Australian named Eva Burrows. Until her retirement last July, she held the highest religious office of any woman in the world.   34

Catherine Mumford Booth openly advocated women's rights at a time of embryonic suffragism, and her influence on her husband was strong. William Booth wrote, "Women must be treated as equal with men in all intellectual and social relationships of life." Catherine Booth was openly condemned for preaching; in her day, women weren't allowed to hold religious office and were forbidden to take the pulpit. When a man at one of her open-air Bible meetings quoted Paul's advice to the Corinthians—"Let your women keep silence in the Churches"—she replied, "In the first place this is not a church, and in the second place I am not a Corinthian."   35

After physical and psychological testing and some education—a process lasting about a year—the Dickinsons were commissioned as auxiliary captains in November of 1985. They worked as assistants in Spokane, and then were transferred to a small congregation in Idaho, then to a larger one in Kelso, Washington. When they became full captains in 1990, they moved to Seattle.   36

The salvation Army is divided into Corps, which are evangelical units serving specific regions. As head of the Seattle Temple Corps, Bill functions largely as the pastor of any good-sized Protestant congregation does: writing and delivering sermons, ministering to the sick, conducting weddings and funerals, teaching and counseling. Mary cooks the Temple's weekly lunch for the elderly, helps clean the buildings, runs the Home League—a women's group—makes hospital visits, counsels women, designs the Sunday worship service around Bill's choice of topics, handles scheduling and, in the Christmas season, helps manage the kettle drive.   37

The Dickinsons work sixty to eighty hours a week. In its early days the Salvation Army had to force its officers to take vacations ("furloughs") because otherwise the officers worked themselves to exhaustion. "It's so difficult to find the time," says Dickinson, who, like every other Salvation Army officer I've met, seems to be in an organized hurry much of the time. "That's kind of a lame excuse, I guess, but I think we're in the last days, myself. There's so many things that need to be done, and so little time to do it in."   38

On a winter day in a cold, unceasing drizzle, Dickinson took me to Seattle's Harbor Light—the name typically given to the Army's shelters   39 for the homeless. (A new social services building, the William Booth Center, has since replaced it.) Dickinson ran this program when he first came to Seattle, before being transferred to the Temple. We walked past the line of people waiting to enter, heads down in the rain, and were greeted all the way to the door. "Hey, Captain." "How are you, Captain?"

Inside, I watched a quiet crowd of 106 men and four women file into the dim chapel. Almost everyone was black or Hispanic. The so-called ethnic ministries of the Army, aimed at blacks, Asians and Hispanics, are its fastest-growing segments in the United States. Elsewhere in Seattle an entire Salvation Army Corps is devoted to the Laotian population. Many clients are from minority groups, many are immigrants, legal and otherwise, and many don't speak English.

I had heard clients in other programs refer to the church as the "Starvation Army," in spite of the fact that this meal, like all meals for the homeless, is free. I stood in the back talking to Major Eddie Reed, a retired officer who volunteered as chaplain. Officers have to retire at 65, and in fact the Army maintains retirement homes for them if desired, but almost all volunteer back into service.

Reed said that times had changed, that unlike the "hoboes" of a few decades back, many of the homeless men he meets today don't want to work for their meals. "Maybe they think the sermon is too high a price," he added. Earlier, a Harbor Light counselor had told me that her clients were getting younger, and frequently had multiple addictions. "We're seeing people who had everything—car, job, apartment—and lost everything."

"Take off your hats!" yelled Vern, the doorman, an ex-ARC client, and at his words several dozen baseball caps and cowboy hats disappeared. Reed then delivered a five-minute sermon, taking as his theme the universal nature of God's love, and offering an invitation to anyone wanting to accept the altar call. No one did. "Let us pray. God, we ask that you bless the men in this room. Bless the women in this room. We pray that you will touch their hearts and their lives. These things we ask in the name of Our Lord Jesus Christ. Amen." The room filled with a low murmur of amens, and then Vern's loud, demanding voice: "Everybody, stay where you are! Sit down, please! Back row first!"

When Bill Dickinson was sent to the Temple Corps, Captain Sherry McWhorter was transferred from Alaska to replace him in the social services program, of which this Harbor Light is a part. A divorced mother of four adopted children with a master's degree, McWhorter had spent thirteen years running social welfare programs for the Army. She is a solid woman with steel-gray, brush-cut hair and a brusque manner ruined by her silky Texas accent: when I asked her about the need for social services in Seattle and Alaska, she didn't hesitate.

"There's a whole generation of people now in their 20s and 30s who are a wasted generation. I've felt very frustrated ever since the Reagan years, when they made so many cutbacks, especially in maternal and child health. People are so much worse off now. I'm not picketing or anything, but in every community the Salvation Army tries to help wherever we can to correct societal problems, and the helping process is often hindered by the government." The sight of Sherry McWhorter picketing in her navy blue uniform has tremendous appeal. The Army's policy of nonpartisanship is not always an equal match for the religiously inspired activism of its members.

When the health department ordered Dickinson to throw away donated food, he threatened to have T.V. cameras film the event. The department backed off. Dickinson also publicly embarrassed the city of Seattle into allowing the homeless to sleep in the foyers of public buildings during a vicious cold snap. Such occasions of, as Dickinson puts it, "throwing our weight around when we have to," are in Booth's tradition. After all, Booth wanted brass bands because brass gets attention.

After Reed's brief sermon, the crowd hurried through the basement lunch-line, taking bowls of soup, hunks of bread and apples back to long, bare tables. They ate hurriedly, coming back for seconds until the food was gone. Several men filled their pockets with apples and partial loaves of bread.

Last week I stood by a kettle in a big, crowded mall. (The kettle on the street corner has become the kettle in the mall, although many malls forbid the kettles altogether. Those that allow them often won't permit a bell.) A four-person band, three men in jaunty caps and pressed slacks and one woman in a knee-length navy skirt, adjusted their music stands, lifted their polished golden instruments and burst into the familiar strains of "Joy to the World."

A small crowd gathered. A tall man with a cap pulled down over his face strode by, dropping a handful of change into the kettle without looking up; two children sidled up and slipped in a bill; a cheerful young woman approached with both hands in front of her and emptied a pile of clanking coins. "See, I'm emptying my pockets!" she cheerfully called out. One traditional carol followed another. "Silent Night" giving way to "Here Comes Santa Claus" with extra, glittering trills. People stood nearby, smiling; the old man in a soldier's uniform, sitting by the kettle because he was too tired by then to stand, nodded in time to the trombone's beat.

And now it's me turning my pockets out. I don't have to agree with its theology to know that in Salvationism, unlike most religions, actions do speak louder than any number of words. If I want to help the poor and homeless with my money, this red kettle is a safe place to start.

JULIET B. SCHOR

Housewives' Hours

Juliet B. Schor (1955–   ), who took her Ph.D. in economics from
the University of Massachusetts in 1982, has had the sort of solid academic career that rarely produces best-sellers. After teaching briefly
at Williams College and Columbia University, she settled in at Harvard, published three books, and was promoted to associate professor
in 1989. Three years later she published *The Overworked American: The
Unexpected Decline of Leisure.* Schor found herself suddenly in the lime-
light, frequently interviewed and asked to make public appearances.
The cause of this stir was her portrait of American workers lured by
the desire for a higher and higher material standard of living into a
work-and-spend lifestyle that leaves them unhappy and unfulfilled.
The following excerpt, which surveys the effect of technology on
housework, combines Schor's interest in economics with her increasing interest in women's studies. Readers may be particularly interested in connecting the essay with others expressing different concerns
about women and their work: Carol Bly's "Getting Tired," Gloria
Steinem's "I Was a Playboy Bunny," and John Kenneth Galbraith's
"The Higher Economic Purpose of Women." Schor's footnotes citing
Scientific American, Ladies' Home Journal, Ms. magazine, and several
academic books and articles have been omitted.

The twentieth century radically transformed America. We went   1
from the horse and buggy to the Concorde, from farm to city and then
to suburb, from silent movies to VCRs. Throughout all these changes,
one thing stayed constant: the amount of work done by the American
housewife. In the 1910s, she was doing about fifty-two hours a week.
Fifty or sixty years later, the figure wasn't much different.

This conclusion comes from a set of studies recording the daily ac-   2
tivities of full-time housewives. The first was carried out in 1912–14 by
a Ph.D. candidate at Columbia University named John Leeds. Leeds
surveyed a group of sixty middle-class families, with employed husbands, full-time homemakers, and an average of 2.75 children. After
watching the routine of the housewives in his group, Leeds found that
they spent an average of fifty-six hours each week at their work. This
number is actually slightly higher than most subsequent findings, but
the difference appears not to be meaningful and is attributable to some
peculiarities of Leeds's families.

Over the next few decades, many more housewives were surveyed   3
under the auspices of the U.S. Bureau of Home Economics. Another
Ph.D. candidate, Joann Vanek from the University of Michigan, compiled the results of these surveys, all of which followed a common set

of guidelines. Vanek found that in 1926–27, and again in 1929, housewives were putting in about fifty-two hours. The strange thing is that in 1936, 1943, and 1953, years of additional studies, the findings were unchanged. The housewife was still logging in fifty-two hours. In the 1960s and 1970s, more surveys were undertaken. A large one in Syracuse, New York, in 1967 and 1968 found that housewives averaged fifty-six hours per week. And according to my own estimates, from 1973, a married, middle-class housewife with three children did an average of fifty-three hours of domestic work each week (see figure 4.1).

The odd thing about the constancy of hours is that it coincided 4
with a technological revolution in the household. When the early studies were done, American homes had little sophisticated equipment. Many were not yet wired for gas and electricity. They did not have automatic washers and dryers or refrigerators. Some homes even lacked indoor plumbing, so that every drop of water that entered the house had to be carried in by hand and then carried out again.

By 1950, the amount of capital equipment in the home had risen 5
dramatically. Major technological systems, such as indoor plumbing, electricity, and gas, had been installed virtually everywhere. At the

Figure 4.1   The Constancy of Housewives' Weekly Hours

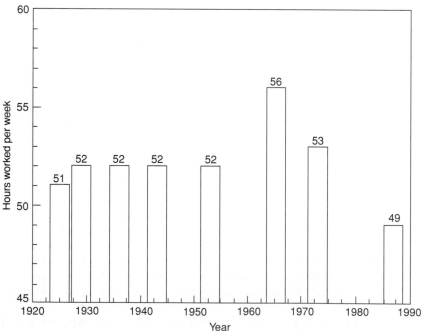

SOURCE: Estimates from 1926–27 through 1965–66 are from Joann Vanek, "Time Spent in Housework," *Scientific American,* 231 (5 November 1974): 116–20. 1973 and 1987 are author's calculations.
All data are for full-time housewives.

same time, many labor-saving appliances also came into vogue—automatic washing machines and dryers, electric irons, vacuum cleaners, refrigerators and freezers, garbage disposals. By the 1990s, we had added dishwashers, microwaves, and trash compacters. Each of these innovations had the potential to save countless hours of labor. Yet none of them did. In terms of reducing time spent on domestic work, all this expensive labor-saving technology was an abject failure.

Researchers have documented this failure. After conducting a 6 large, twelve-country study, in which conditions ranged from the most modern to rather primitive (lack of indoor plumbing, appliances, and so forth), the authors tentatively suggested the opposite: technical sophistication may *increase* the amount of time given over to household work. Studies of U.S. women also found that those with more durable equipment in their homes work no fewer hours than those with less. Only one major appliance has been shown to save significant amounts of time (the microwave oven). Some actually increase housework (freezers and washing machines).

Of course, technology was not without its effects. Some activities 7 became less time consuming and others more. Between the 1920s and the 1960s, food preparation fell almost ten hours a week, but was offset by the rise in shopping, managerial tasks, and child care. Certain innovations were labor saving on their own, but led to new tasks. The refrigerator eliminated the need for daily shopping and storing ice at home, but helped drive the door-to-door vendor out of business, thereby contributing to the rise of the supermarket, with its self-service and greater travel time.

Laundry provides the best example of how technology failed to re- 8 duce labor time. During the period from 1925 to 1965, automatic washers and dryers were introduced. The new machines did cut the time needed to wash and dry a load of clothes. Yet laundry time rose. The reason was that housewives were doing more loads—in part, because investment in household-level capital undermined commercial establishments. Laundry that had previously been sent out began to stay home. At the same time, standards of cleanliness went up.

The escalation of standards for laundering has been a long process, 9 stretching back to colonial times. In those days, washing would be done once a month at most and, in many families, much less—perhaps four times per year. Nearly everyone wore dirty clothes nearly all the time. Slowly the frequency of washing rose. When the electric washer was introduced (1925), many Americans enjoyed a clean set of clothes (or at least a fresh shirt or blouse) every Saturday night. By the 1950s and 1960s, we washed after one wearing.

Standards have crept up for nearly everything housewives do— 10 laundry, cooking, care of children, shopping, care of the sick, cleaning. Estimates from a mid-1970s survey show that the housewife spent an average of 10.3 hours a week getting the floors "spic and span," cleaning toilets, dusting, and waxing. In recent decades, homes have received "deep cleaning," with concerted attacks on "germs" and an "eat-off-the-floor" standard. Americans have taken seriously the dictim that "cleanliness is next to godliness." One 1920s housewife realized:

> Because we housewives of today have the tools to reach it, we dig every day after dust that grandmother left to a spring cataclysm. If few of us have nine children for a weekly bath, we have two or three for a daily immersion. If our consciences don't prick over vacant pie shelves or empty cookie jars, they do over meals in which a vitamin may be omitted or a calorie lacking.

But we were not always like this. Contemporary standards of housecleaning are a modern invention, like the vacuum cleaners and furniture polishes that make them possible. Europeans (and Americans) joined the cleanliness bandwagon quite recently. It was not until the late eighteenth century that people in England even began to wash themselves systematically. And it was only the rich who did so. Body odors and excretions offended no one. For example, menstrual blood just dripped onto the floor. In terms of personal hygiene, a crust of dirt was thought to foster a good complexion underneath. Noses would be blown onto clothing; feces were often left lying around the house, even among the genteel classes.

In other parts of the world, higher standards of hygiene prevailed. 11 Medieval and early modern European travelers to Asia, for example, were considered to be extremely uncouth. In matters of housekeeping, filth and neglect were the order of the day. Anything more was considered "a waste of time." These habits were transported to America with the first European settlers, whose bodies and homes reproduced European-style filth. The culture of cleanliness was at least a century away.

It was delayed because it was expensive. The labor of colonial 12 women was far too valuable to be spent creating spic-and-span. For most colonists, survival entailed the labor of both adults (and their children and perhaps someone else's children as well). Women were busy making yarn, cloth, candles, and soap. They were butchering animals, baking bread, churning butter, and brewing beer. They tended gardens and animals, concocted medicines, and cared for the sick. They sewed and mended garments, and typically had time to clean their houses only once a year. According to historian Mary Beth Norton, "it seems clear either that cleanliness was not highly valued or that farm wives, fully occupied with other tasks, simply had no time to worry about sweeping floors, airing bedding, or putting things away." Undoubtedly, some colonial women did take great pains with their homes, but sanitation could be infeasible. Rural dwellings were rudimentary, with dirt floors and few pieces of furniture or other possessions. Open-hearth fires spewed out soot. Hauling and heating water was arduous and expensive; it was used sparingly for luxuries such as washing dishes.

The less well-off segments of U.S. society, who were by no means 13 a minority, faced similar living conditions throughout the nineteenth century. Slaves, and then sharecroppers, lived in primitive cabins, which were "extremely difficult to keep clean and tidy." In urban tenements, housekeeping was hard even to recognize:

> There was no furniture to speak of, few clothes to wash, little food to prepare. . . . Washing and cleaning were difficult since all water had to be carried up the stairs. People tracked in dirt from the muddy streets; plaster crumbled; chimneys clogged and stoves smoked. . . . Cleaning was only a small part of complicated and arduous family economies. The major effort went into acquiring necessities—food, fuel and water.

As the nation grew richer, it got cleaner. Prosperity freed many married women from the burdens of earning money and producing necessities and gave them time to devote to housekeeping. As they did, higher standards emerged. The shift began among the middle classes and eventually filtered down to the less well-to-do. By the last quarter of the nineteenth century, America was well into its longstanding affair with the immaculate. Victorian-era homes were subjected to strenuous cleaning exercises, which were further complicated by the clutter and bric-a-brac that was the fashion of the day. In households with servants, requirements would be even more exacting. By the turn of the century, the once-yearly cleaning had given way to a daily routine. Each and every morning, women would be sweeping, dusting, cleaning, washing, and straightening up. And those were just the daily tasks. Bigger jobs (washing clothes, ironing clothes, baking, canning, washing walls, and so on) were done on a weekly, monthly, and seasonal basis. The rituals had become endless.

The trend to more and better was not confined to housecleaning 14 and laundry but included activities such as cooking and baking. To some extent, what occurred was a shift from the production of the food itself (gardening, raising animals, making butter or beer) to more elaborate preparation. In earlier days, "the simplest and least exerting forms of cooking had to be utilized most frequently; hence the ubiquity and centrality of those classic 'one-pot' dishes, soup and stew." Now women learned the art and craft of cooking, as soup and stew gave way to fried chicken and angel food cake. Nutrition and esthetics became preoccupations. All these changes in the standards of housekeeping helped keep the housewife's hours long even as progress made it possible to save her labor. But the area where the upgrading was most dramatic was in the care of children.

Being a mother—and increasingly, being a father as well—is a 15 highly labor-intensive and demanding job. It is an article of faith that infants and small children need constant attention, supervision, and love. As they grow older, they also require education and moral training. All these needs translate into countless hours. One might have thought that mothering was always like this. Newborn babies in the fifteenth century were just as helpless as those in the twentieth. But three hundred years ago, parents acted very differently. Children were hardly "raised" in today's sense of the term. Historians of the family and "private life" have discovered that we cannot project contemporary child-rearing practices backward in time. Like housecleaning, laundering, cooking, and many other domestic labors, the standards and norms of mothering have been dramatically upgraded.

Part of the transformation has been psychological. In the past (before about the sixteenth century in England and later in other parts of Europe), parent-child relationships appear to have been much less emotional. What is seen today as a deep biological bond between parent and child, particularly mother and child, is very much a social construction. For the most part, children were not "cared for" by their parents. The rich had little to do with their offspring until they were grown. Infants were given to wet-nurses, despite widespread evidence of neglect and markedly lower chances of survival. Older children were sent off to school. Those in less economically fortunate families fared no better. They would be sent as servants or into apprenticeships, often in the homes of strangers. In all social classes, infants and children were routinely left unattended for long periods of time. To make them less of a nuisance, babies were wrapped in swaddling clothes, their limbs completely immobilized, for the first months of their lives. Another custom was the violent rocking of infants "which puts the babe into a dazed condition, in order that he may not trouble those that have the care of him." However harmful these practices may have been for children, they were convenient for their elders.

Among the poor and laboring classes, economic stress made proper care virtually impossible. In the worst cases, there was not sufficient income to feed children, and infanticide and abandonment were not unusual. When families did keep (and feed) their offspring, they could rarely spare even the ill-paid labor of women. Time for mothering was an unaffordable luxury. Women had to work for pay, and the children were frequently left alone:

> The children are then in many cases left without any person in charge of them, a sufficient quantity [of opium] being given by the parents to keep them in a state of stupor until they return home. . . . When under the influence of this mixture, the children lie in a perfectly torpid state for hours together. "The young 'uns all lay about on the floor," said one woman to me who was in the habit of dosing her children with it, "like dead 'uns, and there's no bother with 'em. When they cry we gives 'em a little of it—p'raps half a spoonful, and that quiets 'em."

The relative lack of parental love and attention can partly be explained by the high probability that children might not survive. The ephemerality of life until at least the mid-eighteenth century is revealed by the practice of giving two children the same name, in the expectation that only one would live. Under these circumstances, the absence of deep emotional ties to children is understandable. But the picture is actually more complicated. Parental indifference was not merely a result of infant mortality. It was also a cause. Historians now realize that one reason many children died is that their parents did not, or could not, take sufficient pains to keep them alive. Neglect and abuse were dangerous, in both rich and poor families.

More caring attitudes began to emerge in the eighteenth century, in both Europe and the United States. Eventually some of the more odious child-rearing practices started to fade away, such as swaddling; and by the end of the century, wetnursing was in decline. Parental affection became more common, and the individuality of the child was recognized. Middle-class families, often religious reformers, began to devote considerable attention to the education of their children. The biggest changes came in the nineteenth century. The idealization of mother love, vigilant attention to the needs of children, and recognition of the unique potential of each individual came to dominate child-rearing ideology. These beliefs may appear natural; but, as a leading historian of the family has noted, "motherhood as we know it today is a surprisingly new institution." [18]

By the last quarter of the nineteenth century, what historians have called "conscious motherhood" and a bona-fide mothers' movement emerged. As the "century of the child" opened, mothers were providing their children with all manner of new services. They breast-fed. They began to toilet-train, schedule, and educate. They learned to worry about germs, nutrition, and the quality of the air. They practiced "scientific nursing" on sick children. The long legacy of child neglect gave way, particularly in America, to the most labor-intensive mothering process in human history. [19]

Children benefited from all this attention. "But the burden that it placed upon the new American housewife was immense. Children had to be kept in bed for weeks at a time; bedpans had to be provided and warmed . . . utensils had to be boiled, alcohol baths administered, hands scrupulously washed, mouths carefully masked." And all these practical duties were embedded in a new cultural icon: the selfless mother. She was a romantic ideal, but eventually became a reality. Mothers actually did become altruistic—and unsparing with their time. [20]

In all these ways, then, was the American household and the labor of its mistress transformed. The old tasks of animal husbandry, sewing, and candlemaking disappeared, and women took on new ones. They made their family's beds and breast-fed their own babies. The motto was more and better. Looking back on this history, some observers [21] have noted the operation of a Parkinson's Law of housework, in which "work expands to fill the time available for its completion." And there is a certain amount of truth in this characterization: the housewife's work *did* expand to fill her customary schedule. As the market economy produced low-cost versions of what women had made at home, they transferred their labor to other tasks. Housewifery remained a full-time job irrespective of the appliances or the technological systems at the housewife's disposal. The 1950s and 1960s were particularly labor-intensive. Middle-class women were trapped in a stultifying domesticity, following "Hints from Heloise" on how to prepare homemade dog food or turn Clorox bottles into birdfeeders.

JOHN KENNETH GALBRAITH

The Higher Economic Purpose of Women

Born in Iona Station, Ontario, in 1908, John Kenneth Galbraith became a naturalized U.S. citizen in 1937. He received his B.S. in agriculture from the University of Toronto (1931), and his M.S. (1933) and Ph.D. (1934) in economics from the University of California at Berkeley. During the 1930s and early 1940s Galbraith taught at Harvard and Princeton. Currently a professor emeritus at Harvard, he has also served as director of the U.S. Strategic Bombing Survey during World War II, as U.S. ambassador to India and as a presidential advisor to John F. Kennedy and Lyndon B. Johnson. "Life," Galbraith has said, "is too short to confine yourself to one career." A prolific writer, his more recent publications include *The Culture of Contentment* (1993), *Macroeconomics* (1993), *A Short History of Financial Euphoria* (1994), and *The Good Society: The Humane Agenda* (1996). The following essay is from *Annals of an Abiding Liberal* (1979). With Galbraith's typical combination of dry humor and serious analysis, it encourages us not only to reconsider the position of women, but to reconsider the commonsense assumption that working is one thing and consuming another. Obviously the essay is a valuable companion piece to Juliet B. Schor's "Housewives' Hours." It might also, like Herbert Inhaber and Sidney Carroll's "A Grand Parade" encourage us to see the remarkable social effects of America's unevenly distributed income.

In the nineteen-fifties, for reasons that were never revealed to me, 1 for my relations with academic administrators have often been somewhat painful, I was made a trustee of Radcliffe College. It was not a highly demanding position. Then, as now, the college had no faculty of its own, no curriculum of its own and, apart from the dormitories, a gymnasium and a library, no academic plant of its own. We were a committee for raising money for scholarships and a new graduate center. The meetings or nonmeetings of the trustees did, however, encourage a certain amount of reflection on the higher education of women, there being no appreciable distraction. This reflection was encouraged by the mood of the time at Harvard. As conversation and numerous formal and informal surveys reliably revealed, all but a small minority of the women students felt that they were a failure unless they were firmly set for marriage by the time they got their degree. I soon learned that my fellow trustees of both sexes thought this highly meritorious. Often at our meetings there was impressively solemn mention of our responsibility, which was to help women prepare themselves for their life's work. Their life's work, it was held, was care of home, husband and children. In inspired moments one or another of my colleagues would ask, "Is there anything else so important?"

Once, and rather mildly, for it was more to relieve tedium than to express conviction, I asked if the education we provided wasn't rather expensive and possibly also ill-adapted for these tasks, even assuming that they were combined with ultimate service to the New Rochelle Library and the League of Women Voters. The response was so chilly that I subsided. I've never minded being in a minority, but I dislike being thought eccentric.   2

It was, indeed, mentioned that a woman should be prepared for what was called a *second* career. After her children were raised and educated, she should be able to essay a re-entry into intellectual life—become a teacher, writer, researcher or some such. All agreed that this was a worthy, even imaginative design which did not conflict with *basic* responsibilities. I remember contemplating but censoring the suggestion that this fitted in well with the common desire of husbands at about this stage in life to take on new, younger and sexually more inspiring wives.   3

In those years I was working on the book that eventually became *The Affluent Society*. The task was a constant reminder that much information solemnly advanced as social wisdom is, in fact, in the service of economic convenience—the convenience of some influential economic interest. I concluded that this was so of the education of women and resolved that I would one day explore the matter more fully. This I have been doing in these last few years, and I've decided that while the rhetorical commitment of women to home and husband as a career has been weakened in the interim, the economic ideas by which they are kept persuaded to serve economic interests are still almost completely intact. Indeed, these ideas are so generally assumed that they are very little discussed.   4

Women are kept in the service of economic interests by ideas that they do not examine and that even women who are professionally involved as economists continue to propagate, often with some professional pride. The husband, home and family that were celebrated in   5 those ghastly Radcliffe meetings are no longer part of the litany. But the effect of our economic education is still the same.

Understanding of this begins with a look at the decisive but little-perceived role of women in modern economic development and at the economic instruction by which this perception is further dulled.   6

The decisive economic contribution of women in the developed industrial society is rather simple—or at least it so becomes once the disguising myth is dissolved. It is, overwhelmingly, to make possible a continuing and more or less unlimited increase in the sale and use of consumer goods.   7

The test of success in modern economic society, as all know, is the annual rate of increase in Gross National Product. At least until recent times this test was unquestioned; a successful society was one with a large annual increase in output, and the most successful society was the one with the largest increase. Even when the social validity of this measure is challenged, as on occasion it now is, those who do so are only thought to be raising an interesting question. They are not imagined to be practical.   8

Increasing production, in turn, strongly reflects the needs of the dominant economic interest, which in modern economic society, as few will doubt, is the large corporation. The large corporation seeks relentlessly to get larger. The power, prestige, pay, promotions and perquisites of those who command or who participate in the leadership of the great corporation are all strongly served by its expansion. That expansion, if it is to be general, requires an expanding or growing economy. As the corporation became a polar influence in modern economic life, economic growth became the accepted test of social performance. This was not an accident. It was the predictable acceptance of the dominant economic value system.   9

Economic growth requires manpower, capital and materials for increased production. It also, no less obviously, requires increased consumption, and if population is relatively stable, as in our case, this must be increased per-capita consumption. But there is a further and equally unimpeachable truth which, in economics at least, has been celebrated scarcely at all: just as the production of goods and services requires management or administration, so does their consumption. The one is no less essential than the other. Management is required for providing automobiles, houses, clothing, food, alcohol and recreation. And management is no less required for their possession and use.   10

The higher the standard of living, that is to say the greater the consumption, the more demanding is this management. The larger the house, the more numerous the automobiles, the more elaborate the attire, the more competitive and costly the social rites involving food and intoxicants, the more complex the resulting administration.   11

In earlier times this administration was the function of a menial 12 servant class. To its great credit, industrialization everywhere liquidates this class. People never remain in appreciable numbers in personal service if they have alternative employment. Industry supplies this employment, so the servant class, the erstwhile managers of consumption, disappears. If consumption is to continue and expand, it is an absolute imperative that a substitute administrative force be found. This, in modern industrial societies, is the function that wives perform. The higher the family income and the greater the complexity of the consumption, the more nearly indispensable this role. Within broad limits the richer the family, the more indispensably menial must be the role of the wife.

It is, to repeat, a vital function for economic success as it is now 13 measured. Were women not available for managing consumption, an upper limit would be set thereon by the administrative task involved. At some point it would become too time-consuming, too burdensome. We accept, without thought, that a bachelor of either sex will lead a comparatively simple existence. (We refer to it as the bachelor life.) This is because the administrative burden of a higher level of consumption, since it must be assumed by the individual who consumes, is a limiting factor. When a husband's income passes a certain level, it is expected that his wife will be needed "to look after the house" or simply "to manage things." So, if she has been employed, she quits her job. The consumption of the couple has reached the point where it requires full-time attention.

Although without women appropriately conditioned to the task 14 there would be an effective ceiling on consumption and thus on production and economic expansion, this would not apply uniformly. The ceiling would be especially serious for high-value products for the most affluent consumers. The latter, reflecting their larger share of total income—the upper 20 percent of income recipients received just under 42 percent of all income in 1977—account for a disproportionate share of total purchases of goods. So women are particularly important for lifting the ceiling on this kind of consumption. And, by a curious quirk, their doing so opens the way for a whole new range of consumer products—washing machines, dryers, dishwashers, vacuum cleaners, automatic furnaces, sophisticated detergents, cleaning compounds, tranquilizers, pain-relievers—designed to ease the previously created task of managing a high level of consumption.

Popular sociology and much associated fiction depict the extent 15 and complexity of the administrative tasks of the modern diversely responsible, high-bracket, suburban woman. But it seems likely that her managerial effectiveness, derived from her superior education, her accumulating experience as well as her expanding array of facilitating gadgetry and services, keeps her more or less abreast of her increasingly large and complex task. Thus the danger of a ceiling on consumption, and therefore on economic expansion, caused by the exhaustion of her administrative capacities does not seem imminent. One sees here, more than incidentally, the economic rationale, even if it was unsuspected for a long time by those involved, of the need for a superior education for the upper-bracket housewife. Radcliffe prepared wives for the higher-income family. The instinct that this required superior intelligence and training was economically sound.

The family of higher income, in turn, sets the consumption patterns to which others aspire. That such families be supplied with intelligent, well-educated women of exceptional managerial competence is thus of further importance. It allows not only for the continued high-level consumption of these families, but it is important for its demonstration effect for families of lesser income.   16

That many women are coming to sense that they are instruments of the economic system is not in doubt. But their feeling finds no support in economic writing and teaching. On the contrary, it is concealed, and on the whole with great success, by modern neoclassical economics—the everyday economics of the textbook and classroom. This concealment is neither conspiratorial nor deliberate. It reflects the natural and very strong instinct of economics for what is convenient to influential economic interest—for what I have called the convenient social virtue. It is sufficiently successful that it allows many hundreds of thousands of women to study economics each year without their developing any serious suspicion as to how they will be used.   17

The general design for concealment has four major elements: 18

First, there is the orthodox identification of an increasing consumption of goods and services with increasing happiness. The greater the consumption, the greater the happiness. This proposition is not defended; it is again assumed that only the philosophically minded will cavil. They are allowed their dissent, but, it is held, no one should take it seriously.   19

Second, the tasks associated with the consumption of goods are, for all practical purposes, ignored. Consumption being a source of happiness, one cannot get involved with the problems in managing happiness. The consumer must exercise choice; happiness is maximized when the enjoyment from an increment of expenditure for one object of consumption equals that from the same expenditure for any other object or service. As all who have ever been exposed, however inadequately, to economic instruction must remember, satisfactions are maximized when they are equalized at the margin.   20

Such calculation does require some knowledge of the quality and technical performance of goods as well as thought in general. From it   21 comes the subdivision of economics called consumer economics; this is a moderately reputable field that, not surprisingly, is thought especially appropriate for women. But this decision-making is not a burdensome matter. And once the decision between objects of expenditure is made, the interest of economics is at an end. No attention whatever is given to the effort involved in the care and management of the resulting goods.[1]

The third requisite for the concealment of women's economic role is the avoidance of any accounting for the value of household work. This greatly helps it to avoid notice. To include in the Gross National Product the labor of housewives in managing consumption, where it would be a very large item which would increase as consumption increases, would be to invite thought on the nature of the service so measured. And some women would wonder if the service was one they wished to render. To keep these matters out of the realm of statistics is also to help keep them innocuously within the sacred domain of the family and the soul. It helps sustain the pretense that, since they are associated with consumption, the toil involved is one of its joys.

The fourth and final element in the concealment is more complex and concerns the concept of the household. The intellectual obscurantism that is here involved is accepted by all economists, mostly without thought. It would, however, be defended by very few.

The avowed focus of economics is the individual. It is the individual who distributes her or his expenditures so as to maximize satisfactions. From this distribution comes the instruction to the market and ultimately to the producing firm that makes the individual the paramount power in economic society. (There are grave difficulties with this design, including the way in which it reduces General Motors to the role of a mere puppet of market forces, but these anomalies are not part of the present story.)

Were this preoccupation with the individual pursued to the limit, namely to the individual, there would be grave danger that the role of women would attract attention. There would have to be inquiry as to

1. There is a branch of learning—home economics or home science—that does concern itself with such matters. This field is a nearly exclusive preserve of women. It has never been accorded any serious recognition by economists or scholars generally; like physical education or poultry science, it is part of an academic underworld. And home economists or home scientists, in their natural professional enthusiasm for their subject matter and their natural resentment of their poor academic status, have sought to elevate their subject, homemaking, into a thing of unique dignity, profound spiritual reward, infinite social value as well as great nutritional significance. Rarely have they asked whether it cons women into a role that is exceedingly important for economic interest and also highly convenient for the men and institutions they are trained to serve. Some of the best home economists were once students of mine. I thought them superbly competent in their commitment to furthering a housewifely role for women. [author's note]

whether, within the family, it is the husband's enjoyments that are equalized and thus maximized at the margin. Or, in his gallant way, does he defer to the preference system of his wife? Or does marriage unite only men and women whose preference schedules are identical? Or does marriage make them identical?

Investigation would turn up a yet more troublesome thing. It [26] would be seen that, in the usual case, the place and style of living accord with the preferences and needs of the member of the family who makes the money—in short, the husband. Thus, at least partly, his titles: "head of the household," "head of the family." And he would be seen to have a substantial role in decisions on the individual objects of expenditure. But the management of the resulting house, automobile, yard, shopping and social life would be by the wife. It would be seen that this arrangement gives the major decisions concerning consumption extensively to one person and the toil associated with that consumption to another. There would be further question as to whether consumption decisions reflect with any precision or fairness the preferences of the person who has the resulting toil. Would the style of life and consumption be the same if the administration involved were equally shared?

None of these questions gets asked, for at precisely the point they [27] obtrude, the accepted economics abruptly sheds its preoccupation with the individual. The separate identities of men and women are merged into the concept of the household. The inner conflicts and compromises of the household are not explored; by nearly universal consent, they are not the province of economics. The household, by a distinctly heroic simplification, is assumed to be the same as an individual. It thinks, acts and arranges its expenditures as would an individual; it is so treated for all purposes of economic analysis.

That, within the household, the administration of consumption [28] requires major and often tedious effort, that decisions on consumption are heavily influenced by the member of the household least committed to such tasks, that these arrangements are extremely important if consumption is to expand, are all things that are thus kept out of academic view. Those who study and those who teach are insulated from such adverse thoughts. The concept of the household is an outrageous assault on personality. People are not people; they are parts of a composite or collective that is deemed somehow to reflect the different or conflicting preferences of those who make it up. This is both analytically and ethically indefensible. But for concealing the economic function of women even from women it works.

One notices, at this point, an interesting convergence of economics with politics. It has long been recognized that women are kept on [29] political leash primarily by urging their higher commitment to the family. Their economic role is also concealed and protected by submerging them in the family or household. There is much, no doubt, to be said for the institution of the family. And it is not surprising that conservatives say so much.

In modern society power rests extensively on persuasion. Such re-   30
verse incentives as flogging, though there are law-and-order circles that seek their revival, are in limbo. So, with increasing affluence, is the threat of starvation. And even affirmative pecuniary reward is impaired. For some, at least, enough is enough—the hope for more ceases to drive. In consequence, those who have need for a particular behavior in others resort to persuasion—to instilling the belief that the action they need is reputable, moral, virtuous, socially beneficent or otherwise good. It follows that what women are persuaded to believe about their social role and, more important, what they are taught to overlook are of prime importance in winning the requisite behavior. They must believe that consumption is happiness and that, however onerous its associated toil, it all adds up to greater happiness for themselves and their families.

If women were to see and understand how they are used, the con-   31
sequence might be a considerable change in the pattern of their lives, especially in those income brackets where the volume of consumption is large. Thus, suburban life sustains an especially large consumption of goods, and, in consequence, is especially demanding in the administration required. The claims of roofs, furniture, plumbing, crabgrass, vehicles, recreational equipment and juvenile management are all very great. This explains why unmarried people, regardless of income, favor urban living over the suburbs. If women understood that they are the facilitating instrument of this consumption and were led to reject its administration as a career, there would, one judges, be a general return to a less demanding urban life.

More certainly there would be a marked change in the character   32
of social life. Since they are being used to administer consumption, women are naturally encouraged to do it well. In consequence, much social activity is, in primary substance, a competitive display of managerial excellence. The cocktail party or dinner party is, essentially, a fair, more refined and complex than those at which embroidery or livestock are entered in competition but for the same ultimate purpose of displaying and improving the craftsmanship or breed. The cleanliness of the house, the excellence of the garden, the taste, quality and condition of the furnishings and the taste, quality and imagination of the food and intoxicants and the deftness of their service are put on display before the critical eye of those invited to appraise them. Comparisons are made with other exhibitors. Ribbons are not awarded, but the competent administrator is duly proclaimed a good housekeeper, a gracious hostess, a clever manager or, more simply, a really good wife. These competitive social rites and the accompanying titles encourage and confirm women in their role as administrators and thus facilitators

of the high levels of consumption on which the high-production economy rests. It would add measurably to economic understanding were they so recognized. But perhaps for some it would detract from their appeal.

However, the more immediate reward to women from an understanding of their economic role is in liberalizing the opportunity for choice. What is now seen as a moral compulsion—the diligent and informed administration of the family consumption—emerges as a service to economic interests. When so seen, the moral compulsion disappears. Once women see that they serve purposes which are *not* their own, they will see that they can serve purposes which *are* their own.   33

MICHAEL J. SANDEL

Honor and Resentment

.Michael J. Sandel (1953–   ), an American political theorist, has concentrated much of his attention on the conflicting demands of the individual and the community. His best-known book to date, *Liberalism and the Limits of Justice* (1982), played an important role in the debate between civil libertarians and communitarians that continues today. He was also the editor of *Liberalism and Its Critics* (1984). In his recent work *Democracy's Discontent: America in Search of a Public Philosophy* (1996), Sandel points out that the procedures which liberals have erected to ensure individuals' freedom to live as they choose hardly solve the problem of *how* we should live and what we should value. Currently, Sandel teaches government at Harvard University. "Honor and Resentment" originally appeared in *The New Republic* (December, 1996). Readers may be surprised by the way the essay approaches the controversy over "welfare rights" indirectly, asking us to connect our attitudes toward welfare to our attitudes toward all forms of work and accomplishment. Like Dorothy Sayers ("Living to Work"), Rita Dove ("The Satisfaction Coal Company"), and Carol Bly ("Getting Tired"), Sandel seems in the end more interested in the spiritual meaning of work than in its economic consequences.

The politics of the ancients was about virtue and honor, but we   1
moderns are concerned with fairness and rights. There is some truth in this familiar adage, but only to a point. On the surface, our political debates make little mention of honor, a seemingly quaint concern best suited to a status-ridden world of chivalry and duels. Not far beneath

the surface, however, some of our fiercest debates about fairness and rights reflect deep disagreement about the proper basis of social esteem.

Consider the fuss over Callie Smartt, a 15-year-old cheerleader at a high school in West Texas. Last year she was a popular freshman cheerleader, despite the fact that she has cerebral palsy and moves about in a wheelchair. As Sue Anne Pressley reported recently in *The Washington Post,* "She had plenty of school spirit to go around. . . . The fans seemed to delight in her. The football players said they loved to see her dazzling smile." But at the end of the season, Callie was kicked off the squad.

Earlier this fall, she was relegated to the status of honorary cheerleader; now, even that position is being abolished. At the urging of some other cheerleaders and their parents, school officials have told Callie that, to make the squad next year, she will have to try out like anyone else, in a rigorous routine involving splits and tumbles.

The head cheerleader's father opposes Callie's participation. He claims he is only concerned for Callie's safety. If a player comes flying off the field, he worries, "the cheerleader girls who aren't handicapped could move out of the way a little faster." But Callie has never been hurt cheerleading. Her mother suspects the opposition may be motivated by resentment of the acclaim Callie has received.

But what kind of resentment might motivate the head cheerleader's father? It cannot be fear that Callie's inclusion deprives his daughter of a place; she is already on the team. Nor is it the simple envy he might feel toward a girl who outshines his daughter at tumbles and splits, which Callie, of course, does not. The resentment more likely reflects the conviction that Callie is being accorded an honor she does not deserve, in a way that mocks the pride he takes in his daughter's cheerleading prowess. If great cheerleading is something that can be done from a wheelchair, then what becomes of the honor accorded those who excel at tumbles and splits? Indignation at misplaced honor is a moral sentiment that figures prominently in our politics, complicating and sometimes inflaming arguments about fairness and rights.

Should Callie be allowed to continue on the team? Some would answer by invoking the right of nondiscrimination: provided she can perform well in the role, Callie should not be excluded from cheerleading simply because, through no fault of her own, she lacks the physical ability to perform gymnastic routines. But the nondiscrimination argument begs the question at the heart of the controversy: What does it mean to perform well in the role of cheerleader? This question, in turn, is about the virtues and excellences that the practice of cheerleading honors and rewards. The case for Callie is that, by roaring up and down the sidelines in her wheelchair, waving her pom-poms and motivating the team, she does well what cheerleaders are supposed to do: inspire school spirit.

But if Callie should be a cheerleader because she displays, despite   7
her disability, the virtues appropriate to her role, her claim does pose a
certain threat to the honor accorded the other cheerleaders. The gymnastic skills they display no longer appear essential to excellence in
cheerleading, only one way among others of rousing the crowd. Un-
generous though he was, the father of the head cheerleader correctly
grasped what was at stake. A social practice once taken as fixed in its
purpose and in the honors it bestowed was now, thanks to Callie, re-
defined.

Disputes about the allocation of honor underlie other controver-   8
sies about fairness and rights. Consider, for example, the debate over
affirmative action in university admissions. Here too, some try to resolve the question by invoking a general argument against discrimination. Advocates of affirmative action argue it is necessary to remedy
the effects of discrimination, while opponents maintain that taking
race into account amounts to reverse discrimination. Again the
nondiscrimination argument begs a crucial question. All admissions
policies discriminate on some ground or other. The real issue is, what
kind of discrimination is appropriate to the purposes universities serve?
This question is contested, not only because it decides how educational
opportunities are distributed but also because it determines what
virtues universities define as worthy of honor.

If the sole purpose of a university were to promote scholarly excel-   9
lence and intellectual virtues, then it should admit the students most
likely to contribute to these ends. But if another mission of a university is to cultivate leadership for a pluralistic society, then it should
seek students likely to advance civic purposes as well as intellectual
ones. In a recent court case challenging its affirmative action program,
the University of Texas Law School invoked its civic purpose, arguing
that its minority admissions program had helped equip black and
Mexican-American graduates to serve in the Texas legislature, on the
federal bench and even in the president's Cabinet.

Some critics of affirmative action resent the idea that universities   10
should honor qualities other than intellectual ones, for to do so implies
that standard meritocratic virtues lack a privileged moral place. If race
and ethnicity can be relevant to university admissions, then what becomes of the proud parent's conviction that his daughter is worthy of
admission by virtue of her grades and test scores alone? Like the father's pride in his cheerleader daughter's tumbles and splits, it would
have to be qualified by the recognition that honor is relative to social
institutions, whose purposes are open to argument and revision.

Perhaps the most potent instance of the politics of honor plays it-   11
self out in debates about work. One reason many working-class voters
despise welfare is not that they begrudge the money it costs but that

they resent the message it conveys about what is worthy of honor and reward. Liberals who defend welfare in terms of fairness and rights often miss this point. More than an incentive to elicit effort and skills in socially useful ways, income is a measure of the things we prize. For many who "work hard and play by the rules," rewarding those who stay at home mocks the effort they expend and the pride they take in the work they do. Their resentment against welfare is not a reason to abandon the needy. But it does suggest that liberals need to articulate more convincingly the notions of virtue and honor that underlie their arguments for fairness and rights.

HERBERT INHABER AND SIDNEY L. CARROLL

A Grand Parade

Herbert Inhaber (1941–   ) was born in Montreal and came to the United States in 1962. He received his M.S. from the University of Illinois, Urbana, in 1964 and a Ph.D. from the University of Oklahoma in 1971. His books include *Environmental Indices* (1976), *Physics of the Environment* (1978), and *Energy Risk Assessment* (1982). Inhaber, a risk analyst, has contributed numerous articles to *American Enterprise* and has served on the editorial boards of both *Scientometrics* and *Risk Analysis*. Sidney L. Carroll, after receiving both his B.S. and his M.S. at Louisiana State University, acquired his Ph.D. in economics at Harvard University. He has contributed various articles to *Media Economics Reader, Challenge,* and the *Journal of Post-Keynesian Economics.* Carroll teaches industrial organization, government, business, and economics at the University of Tennessee in Knoxville. The following selection is an excerpt from Inhaber and Carroll's 1992 book *How Rich Is Too Rich? Income and Wealth in America.* The book is primarily about the "division between the superwealthy and the rest of us" and suggests the breaking up of enormous fortunes by severe taxation. Along the way, though, it raises larger questions about the connection (or lack of connection) between the work people do and the income they receive. Like Gloria Steinem's "I Was a Playboy Bunny" and Sallie Tisdale's "Good Soldiers," "A Grand Parade" reminds us that despite its ideals, America is not a classless society.

On hearing the words "income distribution," you may have visions of bloodless tables of numbers, your eyes blurring as you try to bring the masses of digits into focus. Income distribution can be thought of in this way, but Jan Pen, the Dutch economist, has brought the admittedly dull figures to life. While the columns themselves may be sleep-inducing, they represent millions of real Americans trying to make a living, doing the best they can for their families. We should not forget this when we are confronted by the inevitable numbers. The following is a condensed adaptation of Pen's work. . . .

Professor Pen proposes a grand parade, at least in our minds, in   2
which everyone with an income marches by. We could, in our imagination, give everyone a big sign to hold up, stating his or her earnings. It is far more interesting if we did the opposite of Procrustes. That early specialist in alterations shrank or stretched his victims to make them all the same size. What we will do is shrink or stretch everyone, to make their size *proportional* to their income. Since there is a wide array of incomes in a given year, there will be a correspondingly wide array of heights.

Pen's parade is previewed in Figure 1.1. The average income of   3
each group is measured by the height of the curve. As the horizontal axis shows, the parade lasts one hour, by our self-imposed rule.

Figure 1.1

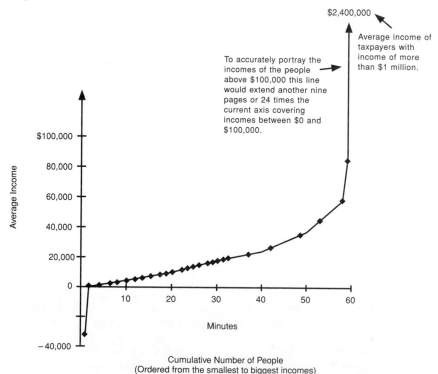

Cumulative Number of People
(Ordered from the smallest to biggest incomes)

The parade is organized by income, so that those with the smallest incomes are on the left. The height of the curve at each point represents the average income of the individuals at that level. This works quite well until the last minute of the parade. The incomes at this level are so large that it would require an additional *nine pages* to represent accurately their incomes. This is a major element of the argument that will be made in this book.

So in this grand and fanciful parade, stretching for miles, the tallest people will have the highest incomes. The midgets will have the lowest. And to avoid complicating matters further, we will not bring in questions of wealth as opposed to income. As we will see later, if we had a parade of *wealth*, the results would be even stranger than the ones we are about to see.

A few more words as we hear the band in the distance. To keep the show from getting tedious, everyone will march by in exactly one hour. We know that it is impossible to get 250 million people to move past the reviewing stand in that short a time, but it is no more impossible than getting the group to assemble in the first place. So we pretend that we are latter-day versions of Cecil B. DeMille, with superhuman powers, and can get everyone across the line within the appointed time.

We are going to ignore people in the parade with no direct income, but who share in it. Mrs. Getty may not have gotten any oil royalty checks addressed to her, but she was certainly not destitute as a result of that omission. You can live well without any income by being married or related to the right people. This applies to men as well as women. The husband of Chris Evert, one of the highest-paid women in sports, shares in her enormous income. However, our parade cannot take account of situations like this.

THE PARADE BEGINS

Now the parade begins, with the smallest in front. But even before we see the tiniest of people, we notice something even more unusual: people with negative height. These are the people who lost money in the course of the year. In the United States in recent times, there were between 800,000 to 900,000 of them.

If it is difficult to visualize the extremely small and gigantic people we will see later in the parade, it is even harder to imagine negative height. But if we can organize a march by of everyone in the country in less than half the time of a football game, anything can be accomplished.

For people of negative height, we see their feet on the ground, and their heads somehow burrowing under the earth, like human moles. Through unknown means, they move forward. The greater their losses, the deeper their heads are in the ground.

Who are these strange creatures? They are mostly businessmen   11
who have suffered capital losses during the year. Our tax laws encourage people to take tax losses every few years, so there are far more
people in this group than we would expect in prosperous times. The
tax reform law of 1986 reduced this incentive somewhat, so we may
see a smaller negative height group in the parade in coming years.

Those who suffer losses in one year generally do not in the next. If   12
incomes were averaged over five or ten years, there would probably be
very few with negative incomes over that period. Yet in any one year
we will find hundreds of thousands.

Most of the people with negative incomes do not seem miserable   13
in spite of their large losses. These losses averaged $32,000 for the en-
tire group in the year 1987, more than the average national *positive* income. And isn't the man who leads the parade, with his head perhaps
sixty yards beneath the surface, the same one whose picture was featured a few years ago in the *Forbes* list of the wealthiest people in the
country? How can he be heading the march, when he should by all
rights be at the end?

Have no fear. The gentleman in question is not likely to be found   14
in the nearest breadline. If we held the parade again next year, he
would likely be in his rightful place in the back, towering over most of
the other marchers.

After the big losers, we find smaller ones, whose negative income   15
is probably not a result of the tax lawyers' manipulations. They are a
varied group, but they may include people whose homes have burned
down without insurance, and business people whose enterprises
folded. About a third of all new firms fail within a year or two.

By way of proof of these results, consider the 1987 tax returns. Of   16
those with negative or zero income, about 3% had tax-exempt interest. These generally derive from municipal and state bonds. Rather
than the pittance you might expect from this negative income group,
their average income from these bonds was about $21,000. If the aver-
age return on a tax-free bond that year was about 6% (lower than cor-
porate or federal bond rates because of the tax-free aspect), this
implies an average wealth from this source alone of about $350,000
for this group. Not bad for people with negative incomes.

We can investigate this subterranean group further. About half of   17
them received taxable interest from banks and the like. Their average
income from these sources was about $4,700. If we assume an average
interest rate of about 8%, this in turn implies about $58,000 in the
bank. This is less than the $350,000 in municipal and state bonds we
mentioned above, but still more than most Americans have in a savings account.

The marchers with heads in the ground are numerous, but they go   18
by in about half a minute. The rest of the parade is above ground,
which makes it a little easier to see.

THE TINIEST PEOPLE

Before we see the miniature people heading up the above-ground 19 parade, we should mention the rule we are using to proportion income to height. We are assuming that the average real height of all people, male and female, is about 5ft. 7in., or 67 inches, give or take an inch. In 1987, the average reportable taxable income in the United States was about $26,000. We obtained this value by dividing all adjusted gross income (less deficits) by the 107 million taxpayers in that year.

We will take this income as corresponding to the average height. 20 Thus if someone has an income of $52,000, or twice the average, he or she would be assigned an imaginary height, for purposes of the parade, of twice 67 inches, or 134 inches. This in turn is slightly more than 11 feet tall. Similarly, someone with an income of $13,000, or half the average, would be assigned a height of half 67 inches, or 34 inches. This is less than a yard.

Now back to the reviewing stand. We have been promised that the 21 real parade would begin after the first half-minute of the economic moles buried in the earth, but where are the people? As time goes by, almost no activity is seen except some dust rising from the ground. In exasperation we seize a handy telescope, and there they are—tiny people, marching side by side, the size of a match stick or key. No wonder they were not visible from a distance. As we squint at them, and try to make out their minuscule bodies, we realize that this is truly when the faint go marching in.

Who are these people? They are truly a mixed group. Some are 22 people who may have worked for just a short time, because of illness, lack of employment skills, or other reasons. Because they have held a job for such short times, they are not eligible for unemployment insurance benefits, which help out people in more prosperous classes.

We may personally recognize some of these economic midgets. 23 Some are the teenagers bagging or checking groceries at your local grocery store for spending money. The cash earned would be the only income attributed to the teens in the parade. Allowances from parents or money from neighbors or family for mowing lawns or baby-sitting would not be represented, since they generally do not show up on tax returns. The appearance of the teenagers at this stage then does not necessarily mean they are poor.

But there are also many people in this group that we do not recog- 24 nize, unless we have seen some television documentaries on poverty. There are a goodly number of dirt farmers, some from Appalachia. These people are not as badly off as their puny size might indicate, because of the food crops they raise for themselves. Remember this is a parade of money, not goods or food. The height of the group of stunted gnomes varies, but all of them are ten inches or shorter. It is no wonder we had some difficulty in seeing them from the reviewing stand.

The procession of the smallest midgets has taken longer than we   25
would have guessed—about four minutes in all. Recall that the parade
is an hour in length, and that about four and half minutes have gone
by. There are clearly more low-income people around than we had
imagined.

UP TO THE WAIST

Now the marchers are getting bigger—10, 12, 20 inches and on up   26
to knee height. There are also a lot more of them. This array is composed of some old-age pensioners with small Social Security checks,
some divorced women without alimony, people on welfare, and yet
others who have been jobless a substantial part of the year. A few of
these unemployed, such as artists and actors, may be in that condition
voluntarily. They may describe themselves as being "between engage-
ments" or "between sales" of a canvas. Next year, they may hit it
lucky, with a choice part or a big sale. In next year's parade, we may
find them grown dramatically, and near the rear of the marchers. But
this year, they are close to the front, and reach just above our kneecaps.

This group, between 10 inches and 2 feet in height, has taken   27
about ten minutes to go by. You will note that this group is much
larger in number than the two previous ones. About a quarter hour
has gone by. Yet we are still seeing people no taller than preschool children. When will the normal people get here?

Not quite yet. For first must come those who have regular or al-   28
most regular employment, but who are the lowest paid of steady
workers. If you go into an office building late at night, some of them—
the cleaning crews and the guards—will be there. A few of this group
are at your local fast food restaurant, and you may recognize familiar
faces. Not the managers, of course—they will be seen later in the parade—but the order takers and hamburger flippers. Now clerks, un-
skilled manual laborers, and grocery workers, slightly above the
minimum wage, file by. And since this parade is American, we see
hundreds of thousands of minorities—blacks, Hispanics and others—
coming by now. In fact, the proportion of minorities seems quite high.
We would try to make a quick estimate of the proportion, but the people are moving by so fast that we can not.

How tall are these people? They go up to about three to four-and-   29
a-half feet high. But we can make a somewhat more exact estimate for
those who are paid exactly the minimum wage. In 1987, the federal
minimum was $3.35 an hour, although some states had higher values.
If someone worked forty hours a week at that rate, their equivalent
height would be a foot and a half. Because of this, many in the latest
group now filing by who are paid the minimum wage work considerably longer than forty hours a week.

HALF THE PARADE HAS GONE BY

By this time, we may have stolen a nervous glance at our watch. About twenty-five minutes of the parade have passed, and yet the marchers hardly reach to our chests. Where are the regular people, those who are supposedly the backbones of our communities and nation? 30

They still have not arrived. As Professor Pen puts it, we still keep seeing dwarfs. The marchers are gradually getting bigger, but painfully slowly. Now we begin to see the masses of so-called ordinary workers, who start to reach up to our armpits. Then on to skilled industrial workers, generally those who are not employed at the very largest corporations like General Motors. We also see office and computer employees. This latest group reach up to our shoulders. This height is referred to in the women's department of clothing stores as "petite," but the marchers in this group are mostly men. 31

Time goes on. Another seven minutes have flown by, bringing the elapsed time to about thirty-two minutes. We might expect that at the half-way point people would be at the exact average, but this is not so. Looking straight ahead brings no eye contact yet. Only after about thirty-six minutes, with twenty-four minutes left in the parade, do people with average income march by. 32

Who are these average types? They are middle management civil servants, for example. However, these civil servants are federal, not state or local. The latter two groups have already passed us by, on the whole. 33

Others at this point in the parade are experienced teachers and some principals, some junior officers and senior noncommissioned officers in the military, junior industrial managers, and some low-ranking executives just a few years out of college. A few retired couples with substantial Social Security checks and perhaps from a company pension are also represented. 34

Now only about twenty minutes remain. Heights are starting to rise more rapidly now, much faster than in the first half hour. During that first period, the rate of change seemed excruciatingly slow. By the forty-five-minute mark, with only fifteen minutes left to go, people are about as big as the tall man in the circus or the biggest player in the National Basketball Association, at about seven-and-a-half feet tall. We see a few university professors, mostly at the associate professor rank and at medium to smaller colleges. Full professors at Harvard, Cal Tech, and Yale will come by later. We also see a few people just a year or two out of college who have chosen a lucrative profession, such as chemical or petroleum engineering. 35

Now the smaller ranks of giants wheel onto the field. After apparently endless minutes of almost imperceptible height changes, we see visible alterations with each new glance. Over the next ten minutes, 36

up to the fifty-five-minute mark, successful businessmen and women, advertising agency managers, and some prosperous midwestern farmers march by. They are accompanied by the top scientists. A few Harvard and Yale professors are found in this group, but the top ones are yet to come. The height of this group is ever-increasing. They grow past the ten-foot barrier up to around twelve feet, much taller than any real human being has ever grown. It is around this point we decide to measure these giants in yards, not feet.

THE LAST FIVE MINUTES OF THE PARADE

The last five minutes of the parade are the most startling and memorable of all, even more astounding than the armies of matchstick people we saw almost an hour ago. By this point, the swarms of midgets have almost faded from our memory. 37

In the next minute or two, a few doctors loom into view. They are not the most successful surgeons, who appear just before the end of the march, but younger physicians, some of whom may work for the government in such agencies as the National Institutes of Health: five yards high. Successful engineers, top federal civil servants, and other high executives are all about the same height. The top professors, whose books appear in the *New York Review of Books* and who have consulting and royalty income in addition to their professional salary, are also here. Three- and four-star generals and admirals, with swagger sticks about six feet long, start to appear. 38

Now there is only one minute to go. While we have seen many of the major groups in our society, there are still a large number of movers and shakers of the money tree to go. Here come members of Congress, at about seven and a half yards. However, some of the more affluent Senators, with private income in addition to their salaries, will appear later at a height of ten to fifteen yards. 39

A little farther down the line comes the president. In calculating his height, we take account only of his direct salary. His fleet of aircraft, ability to live for free in one of the largest and most historic mansions in the nation, and an army of servants, do not play any part in our estimate of his height. In fact, we have done the same underestimation for many of the top executives that appear in this section of the parade. Their perks do not appear in their paycheck or capital gains. However, we will see that these executives are already so tall that it does not make all that much difference if their perks would have boosted their height by half. 40

Finally the president strides by. He is about twenty yards high. His security guards, being only about three yards tall, have passed by many minutes ago. Obviously, at that height they would have been of little use in protecting the president, even if they could accompany the 41

Chief Executive in this part of the parade. Even standing on each other's shoulders, they could not keep the president out of harm's way. After all, they come up only halfway to his shin bone.

Now the top surgeons, for heart, lung, eye, and all the other inter- 42 esting organs, file by. Their height is sometimes greater than the president's: ten, twenty, up to thirty yards high. It is a good thing that the parade will end quickly, because we would get a stiff neck from peering up at these gigantic figures. In fact, since the heads of the marchers are becoming difficult to see without binoculars, we tend to focus on their feet, which are much easier to see. The feet of the last surgeon we saw were about five yards long, about the size of a compact car.

In the last few seconds of the parade are many of the people we 43 read about in the news. Their names often appear in newspapers like the *Wall Street Journal* and magazines like *Fortune, Forbes,* and *Business Week,* although entire articles in these publications are not yet devoted to them. They tend to be the subject only of paragraphs in these national stories. However, these executives are often the theme of lengthy articles in their hometown newspaper business pages. Here we see the businessmen who run large—but not the largest—firms: twenty or thirty yards tall. No, we are not being discriminatory here. Almost all the Brobdingnagians on the field are male.

Here come the basketball, baseball, and football stars, representa- 44 tives of a different kind of business. Their heights vary tremendously, just as there was a grand variation in the heights of business executives. We saw the heights of these executives range from that of the manager of a McDonald's fast-food establishment, many minutes ago, to that of the gargantuan executives we are seeing—rather, partly seeing because of their size—now.

The smallest of the basketball players came by a few minutes ago, 45 at around twelve yards tall. These are players who were drafted in late rounds by their teams, or who are just starting their careers. Most of those with some experience are about five or six times as high. One towering and well-muscled figure from the sports world strides by at around 100 to 150 yards high. His thighs are so large that we can not make out his face, so we can not tell which sport he plays. Since we have almost given up on estimating heights, we concentrate on the length of his feet. They are fifteen to twenty yards long, about the size of a railway car.

By now, we are almost overwhelmed. The president was about the 46 size of a ten-story building. This athlete is about thirty-five to forty-five stories high, bigger than the tallest buildings in all except a handful of American cities.

The parade continues. The mix changes rapidly, with fewer enter- 47 tainers and sports figures. More people appear who seem to have thatches of white hair, and who occasionally carry canes. True, Johnny

Carson is there, about a quarter mile high. Bob Hope might also be that height. By now, people are approaching the height of the Sears Tower.

Who are the last group in the parade? They are people with accumulated wealth, mostly. Their income from that wealth can be, in some cases, astronomical. 48

In general, we do not recognize most of the faces. Some of them have appeared in annual compilations in magazines like *Forbes* or *Fortune*. However, even the excellent journalists attached to those publications have missed a large number in this last section. The journalists would say, in defense, that theirs is a compilation of wealth. The parade is one of income. They would be right. 49

Some of the giants striding by, such as Daniel Ludwig and John Kluge, make a point of staying out of the press, occasionally paying well for the privilege. In any case, almost everyone who appears in this last section is not known by face or voice to the average reporter. They have long passed the point where they got a thrill out of seeing their name in the newspaper or on television. 50

With only a second or two to go in the parade, we could not tell whose heads those enormous legs belong to, even if we could recognize the faces. The shoulders are literally in the clouds. If we had enough time, we might estimate the heights from the size of the gigantic shoes pounding by, but it all happens too fast. 51

One of the people in the reviewing stand says that he has made a rough calculation. Using surveyor's instruments, he has estimated that the length of the shoes of one of the last men in the parade—for they are almost exclusively men now—was about sixty football fields. From that, he invites us to calculate the height. But we are so astounded by what we have seen that we decline the invitation. 52

There is some dispute over the identity of the last man who strides by, the earth quaking under his footsteps. Is it a Getty heir, or one of the owners of the DuPont billions? Or is it Michael Milken, the junk-bond king, who in a court case was reported to have earned about $550 million in 1987? Nobody knows for sure. Even if we questioned one of these gentlemen, we might not get an accurate answer, assuming the respondent was perfectly honest. The fortunes and complicated stock and land transactions are too great and abstruse for all except the most ingenious accountants to decipher. 53

Still, the impression made by the last marcher is overwhelming. The average sole of a man's shoe is about one-quarter inch thick. If that was indeed Mr. Milken at the end of the parade, the soles of his 54 shoes are about *620 feet* tall. His shoes alone are higher than all the marchers who appeared in the first fifty-nine minutes of the parade.

THE PROCESSION ENDS

Suddenly, it is all over. The procession of millions has finished, and the field now rings with an unbearable silence. The ground gradually stops shaking.   55

What have we learned? At least two major facts: First, we reach the average height much after half the time has elapsed. Most of the parade consisted of small men and women, as well as the dwarfs, midgets, and matchstick figures. The reason? The average is boosted considerably by the large figures in the last ten or so minutes. Each of the towering figures bringing up the rear changes the average by himself only slightly, however.   56

Second, the end of the hour is stunning. Rather than seeing an increase of an inch or two every few minutes, as we did at the beginning, the heights rise by leaps and bounds. By the end, the increase is a yard per second or more. The size of the very last behemoths is so immense that we have difficulty in measuring it. We abandon the binoculars we used before and bring out a telescope. The last minute starts with marchers seventy yards high and then extends up into the stratosphere.   57

WILLIAM CARLOS WILLIAMS

Jean Beicke

Born in Rutherford, New Jersey, William Carlos Williams (1883–1963), is perhaps best known as a poet, particularly for his five-book collection *Paterson*, published between 1946 and 1958. In addition to poetry, Williams also wrote novels, autobiographical prose, and translations from several languages. However, he did not make his living by writing. Between 1902 and 1906 Williams attended medical school at the University of Pennsylvania, and after internships in New York hospitals, he returned to Rutherford as a general practitioner. His heavy patient load included many poor immigrant families. In his autobiography he declares, "As a writer, I have been a physician, and as a physician a writer. "Jean Beike" was one of William's own favorite stories and originally appeared in a 1933 fall edition of *Blast*. Like Carol Bly's "Getting Tired" and Gloria Steinem's "I Was A Playboy Bunny," the story reveals the ethical and political dimensions of a job, even while it gives us a ground-level view of what the work is like.

During a time like this, they kid a lot among the doctors and nurses on the obstetrical floor because of the rushing business in new babies that's pretty nearly always going on up there. It's the Depression, they say, nobody has any money so they stay home nights. But one bad result of this is that in the children's ward, another floor up, you see a lot of unwanted children. 1

The parents get them into the place under all sorts of pretexts. For instance, we have two premature brats, Navarro and Cryschka, one a boy and one a girl; the mother died when Cryschka was born, I think. We got them within a few days of each other, one weighing four pounds and one a few ounces more. They dropped down below four pounds before we got them going but there they are; we had a lot of fun betting on their daily gains in weight but we still have them. They're in pretty good shape though now. Most of the kids that are left that way get along swell. The nurses grow attached to them and get a real thrill when they begin to pick up. It's great to see. And the parents sometimes don't even come to visit them, afraid we'll grab them and make them take the kids out, I suppose. 2

A funny one is a little Hungarian Gypsy girl that's been up there for the past month. She was about eight weeks old maybe when they brought her in with something on her lower lip that looked like a chancre. Everyone was interested but the Wassermann was negative. It turned out finally to be nothing but a peculiarly situated birthmark. But that kid is still there too. Nobody can find the parents. Maybe they'll turn up some day. 3

Even when we do get rid of them, they often come back in a week or so—sometimes in terrible condition, full of impetigo, down in weight—everything we'd done for them to do over again. I think it's deliberate neglect in most cases. That's what happened to this little Gypsy. The nurse was funny after the mother had left the second time. I couldn't speak to her, she said. I just couldn't say a word I was so mad. I wanted to slap her. 4

We had a couple of Irish girls a while back named Cowley. One was a red head with beautiful wavy hair and the other a straight haired blonde. They really were good looking and not infants at all. I should say they must have been two and three years old approximately. I can't imagine how the parents could have abandoned them. But they did. I think they were habitual drunkards and may have had to beat it besides on short notice. No fault of theirs maybe. 5

But all these are, after all, not the kind of kids I have in mind. The ones I mean are those they bring in stinking dirty, and I mean stinking. 6

The poor brats are almost dead sometimes, just living skeletons, almost, wrapped in rags, their heads caked with dirt, their eyes stuck together with pus and their legs all excoriated from the dirty diapers no one has had the interest to take off them regularly. One poor little tot we have now with a thin purplish skin and big veins standing out all over its head had a big sore place in the fold of its neck under the chin. The nurse told me that when she started to undress it it had on a shirt with a neckband that rubbed right into that place. Just dirt. The mother gave a story of having had it in some sort of home in Paterson. We couldn't get it straight. We never try. What the hell? We take 'em and try to make something out of them.

Sometimes, you'd be surprised, some doctor has given the parents 7
a ride before they bring the child to the clinic. You wouldn't believe it. They clean 'em out, maybe for twenty-five dollars—they maybe had to borrow—and then tell 'em to move on. It happens. Men we all know too. Pretty bad. But what can you do?

And sometimes the kids are not only dirty and neglected but sick, 8
ready to die. You ought to see those nurses work. You'd think it was the brat of their best friend. They handle those kids as if they were worth a million dollars. Not that some nurses aren't better than others but in general they break their hearts over those kids, many times, when I, for one, wish they'd never get well.

I often kid the girls. Why not? I look at some miserable specimens 9
they've dolled up for me when I make the rounds in the morning and I tell them: Give it an enema, maybe it will get well and grow up into a cheap prostitute or something. The country needs you, brat. I once proposed that we have a mock wedding between a born garbage hustler we'd saved and a little female with a fresh mug on her that would make anybody smile.

Poor kids! You really wonder sometimes if medicine isn't all wrong 10
to try to do anything for them at all. You actually want to see them pass out, especially when they're deformed or—they're awful sometimes. Every one has rickets in an advanced form, scurvy too, flat chests, spindly arms and legs. They come in with pneumonia, a temperature of a hundred and six, maybe, and before you can do a thing, they're dead.

This little Jean Beicke was like that. She was about the worst 11
you'd expect to find anywhere. Eleven months old. Lying on the examining table with a blanket half way up her body, stripped, lying there, you'd think it a five months baby, just about that long. But when the nurse took the blanket away, her legs kept on going for a good eight inches longer. I couldn't get used to it. I covered her up and asked two of the men to guess how long she was. Both guessed at least half a foot too short. One thing that helped the illusion besides her

small face was her arms. They came about to her hips. I don't know what made that. They should come down to her thighs, you know.

She was just skin and bones but her eyes were good and she looked straight at you. Only if you touched her anywhere, she started to whine and then cry with a shrieking, distressing sort of cry that no one wanted to hear. We handled her as gently as we knew how but she had to cry just the same. 12

She was one of the damnedest looking kids I've ever seen. Her head was all up in front and flat behind, I suppose from lying on the back of her head so long the weight of it and the softness of the bones from the rickets had just flattened it out and pushed it up forward. And her legs and arms seemed loose on her like the arms and legs of some cheap dolls. You could bend her feet up on her shins absolutely flat—but there was no real deformity, just all loosened up. Nobody was with her when I saw her though her mother had brought her in. 13

It was about ten in the evening, the interne had asked me to see her because she had a stiff neck, and how! and there was some thought of meningitis—perhaps infantile paralysis. Anyhow, they didn't want her to go through the night without at least a lumbar puncture if she needed it. She had a fierce cough and a fairly high fever. I made it out to be a case of broncho-pneumonia with meningismus but no true involvement of the central nervous system. Besides she had inflamed ear drums. 14

I wanted to incise the drums, especially the left, and would have done it only the night superintendent came along just then and made me call the ear man on service. You know. She also looked to see if we had an operative release from the parents. There was. So I went home, the ear man came in a while later and opened the ears—a little bloody serum from both sides and that was that. 15

Next day we did a lumbar puncture, tapped the spine that is, and found clear fluid with a few lymphocytes in it, nothing diagnostic. The X-ray of the chest clinched the diagnosis of broncho-pneumonia, there was an extensive involvement. She was pretty sick. We all expected her to die from exhaustion before she'd gone very far. 16

I had to laugh every time I looked at the brat after that, she was such a funny looking one but one thing that kept her from being a total loss was that she did eat. Boy! how that kid could eat! As sick as she was she took her grub right on time every three hours, a big eight ounce bottle of whole milk and digested it perfectly. In this depression you got to be such a hungry baby, I heard the nurse say to her once. It's a sign of intelligence, I told her. But anyway, we all got to be crazy about Jean. She'd just lie there and eat and sleep. Or she'd lie and look straight in front of her by the hour. Her eyes were blue, a pale sort of blue. But if you went to touch her, she'd begin to scream. We just didn't, that's all, unless we absolutely had to. And she began to gain in weight. Can you imagine that? I suppose she had been so terribly run 17 down that food, real food, was an entirely new experience to her. Anyway she took her food and gained on it though her temperature continued to run steadily around between a hundred and three and a hundred and four for the first eight or ten days. We were surprised.

When we were expecting her to begin to show improvement, however, she didn't. We did another lumbar puncture and found fewer cells. That was fine and the second X-ray of the chest showed it somewhat improved also. That wasn't so good though, because the temperature still kept up and we had no way to account for it. I looked at the ears again and thought they ought to be opened once more. The ear man disagreed but I kept after him and next day he did it to please me. He didn't get anything but a drop of serum on either side.

Well, Jean didn't get well. We did everything we knew how to do except the right thing. She carried on for another two—no I think it was three—weeks longer. A couple of times her temperature shot up to a hundred and eight. Of course we knew then it was the end. We went over her six or eight times, three or four of us, one after the other, and nobody thought to take an X-ray of the mastoid regions. It was dumb, if you want to say it, but there wasn't a sign of anything but the history of the case to point to it. The ears had been opened early, they had been watched carefully, there was no discharge to speak of at any time and from the external examination, the mastoid processes showed no change from the normal. But that's what she died of, acute purulent mastoiditis of the left side, going on to involvement of the left lateral sinus and finally the meninges. We might, however, have taken a culture of the pus when the ear was first opened and I shall always, after this, in suspicious cases. I have been told since that if you get a virulent bug like the streptococcus mucosus capsulatus it's wise at least to go in behind the ear for drainage if the temperature keeps up. Anyhow she died.

I went in when she was just lying there gasping. Somehow or other, I hated to see that kid go. Everybody felt rotten. She was such a scrawny, misshapen, worthless piece of humanity that I had said many times that somebody ought to chuck her in the garbage chute—but after a month watching her suck up her milk and thrive on it—and to see those alert blue eyes in that face—well, it wasn't pleasant. Her mother was sitting by the bed crying quietly when I came in, the morning of the last day. She was a young woman, didn't look more than a girl, she just sat there looking at the child and crying without a sound.

I expected her to begin to ask me questions with that look on her face all doctors hate—but she didn't. I put my hand on her shoulder and told her we had done everything we knew how to do for Jean but that we really didn't know what, finally, was killing her. The woman didn't make any sign of hearing me. Just sat there looking in between the bars of the crib. So after a moment watching the poor kid beside her, I turned to the infant in the next crib to go on with my rounds.

There was an older woman there looking in at that baby also—no better off than Jean, surely. I spoke to her, thinking she was the mother of this one, but she wasn't.

Before I could say anything, she told me she was the older sister of Jean's mother and that she knew that Jean was dying and that it was a good thing. That gave me an idea—I hated to talk to Jean's mother herself—so I beckoned the woman to come out into the hall with me.   22

I'm glad she's going to die, she said. She's got two others home, older, and her husband has run off with another woman. It's better off dead—never was any good anyway. You know her husband came down from Canada about a year and a half ago. She seen him and asked him to come back and live with her and the children. He come back just long enough to get her pregnant with this one then he left her again and went back to the other woman. And I suppose knowing she was pregnant, and suffering, and having no money and nowhere to get it, she was worrying and this one never was formed right. I seen it as soon as it was born. I guess the condition she was in was the cause. She's got enough to worry about now without this one. The husband's gone to Canada again and we can't get a thing out of him. I been keeping them, but we can't do much more. She'd work if she could find anything but what can you do with three kids in times like this? She's got a boy nine years old but her mother-in-law sneaked it away from her and now he's with his father in Canada. She worries about him too, but that don't do no good.   23

Listen, I said, I want to ask you something. Do you think she'd let us do an autopsy on Jean if she dies? I hate to speak to her of such a thing now but to tell you the truth, we've worked hard on that poor child and we don't exactly know what is the trouble. We know that she's had pneumonia but that's been getting well. Would you take it up with her for me, if—of course—she dies.   24

Oh, she's gonna die all right, said the woman. Sure, I will. If you can learn anything, it's only right. I'll see that you get the chance. She won't make any kick, I'll tell her.   25

Thanks, I said.   26

The infant died about five in the afternoon. The pathologist was dog-tired from a lot of extra work he'd had to do due to the absence of his assistant on her vacation so he put off the autopsy till next morning. They packed the body in ice in one of the service hoppers. It worked perfectly.   27

Next morning they did the postmortem. I couldn't get the nurse to go down to it. I may be a sap, she said, but I can't do it, that's all. I can't. Not when I've taken care of them. I feel as if they're my own.   28

I was amazed to see how completely the lungs had cleared up. They were almost normal except for a very small patch of residual pneumonia here and there which really amounted to nothing. Chest   29 and abdomen were in excellent shape, otherwise, throughout—not a thing aside from the negligible pneumonia. Then he opened the head.

It seemed to me the poor kid's convolutions were unusually well developed. I kept thinking it's incredible that that complicated mechanism of the brain has come into being just for this. I never can quite get used to an autopsy.   30

The first evidence of the real trouble—for there had been no gross evidence of meningitis—was when the pathologist took the brain in his hand and made the long steady cut which opened up the left lateral ventricle. There was just a faint color of pus on the bulb of the choroid plexus there. Then the diagnosis all cleared up quickly. The left lateral sinus was completely thrombosed and on going into the left temporal bone from the inside the mastoid process was all broken down.   31

I called up the ear man and he came down at once. A clear miss, he said. I think if we'd gone in there earlier, we'd have saved her.   32

For what? said I. Vote the straight Communist ticket.   33

Would it make us any dumber? said the ear man.   34

RITA DOVE

The Satisfaction Coal Company

Born in Akron Ohio in 1952, Rita Dove received her B.A. *summa cum laude* from Miami University (1973) and her M.F.A. from the University of Iowa in 1977. She has taught at Arizona State University and Tuskegee Institute, and currently teaches (since 1989) at the University of Virginia in Charlottesville. Dove received the Pulitzer Prize in poetry in 1987 for *Thomas and Beulah* and in 1993 became the first black Poet Laureate. Her poetry publications include *The Yellow House on the Corner* (1980), *Mandolin* (1982), *Museum* (1983), *Grace Notes* (1989), and most recently, *Mother Love* (1995) and *The Poet's World* (1995). Dove has published a collection of short stories, *Fifth Sunday* (1985); *Through the Ivory Gate*, a novel, in 1992; and *The Darker Side of the Earth*, a play (1994). She is also the associate editor of *Callaloo*. One piece of advice that Dove has given to writers is to "TRUST in whatever interests you, confuses you, or compels you. Trust that those things are worth writing about." "The Satisfaction Coal Company" is one of a series of poems from *Thomas and Beulah* that consider the life of Dove's maternal grandfather. Its depiction of Thomas in retirement may remind readers of themes raised by Michael J. Sandel ("Honor and Resentment") and Dorothy Sayers ("Living to Work").

1.

What to do with a day.
Leaf through Jet. *Watch T.V.*
Freezing on the porch
but he goes anyhow, snow too high
for a walk, the ice treacherous.   5
Inside, the gas heater takes care of itself;
he doesn't even notice being warm.

Everyone says he looks great.
Across the street a drunk stands smiling
at something carved in a tree.   10
The new neighbor with the floating hips
scoots out to get the mail
and waves once, brightly,
storm door clipping her heel on the way in.

2.

Twice a week he had taken the bus down Glendale hill   15
to the corner of Market. Slipped through
the alley by the canal and let himself in.
Started to sweep
with terrible care, like a woman
brushing shine into her hair,   20
same motion, same lullaby.
No curtains—the cop on the beat
stopped outside once in the hour
to swing his billy club and glare.

It was better on Saturdays   25
when the children came along:
he mopped while they emptied
ashtrays, clang of glass on metal
then a dry scutter. Next they counted
nailheads studding the leather cushions.   30
Thirty-four! *they shouted,*
that was the year and
they found it mighty amusing.

But during the week he noticed more—
lights when they gushed or dimmed   35
at the Portage Hotel, the 10:32
picking up speed past the B & O switchyard,
floorboards trembling and the explosive
kachook kachook kachook kachook
and the oiled rails ticking underneath.   40

3.

They were poor then but everyone had been poor.
He hadn't minded the sweeping,
just the thought of it—like now
when people ask him what he's thinking
and he says I'm listening.   45

Those nights walking home alone,
the bucket of coal scraps banging his knee,
he'd hear a roaring furnace
with its dry, familiar heat. Now the nights
take care of themselves—as for the days,   50
there is the canary's sweet curdled song,
the wino smiling through his dribble.
Past the hill, past the gorge
choked with wild sumac in summer,
the corner has been upgraded.   55
Still, he'd like to go down there someday

MEDIA

We find ourselves in a hall of mirrors.

Overview

Five centuries ago, it must have seemed obvious to most people that reality was one thing and art quite another. Nature was real in a way that art was not, solid objects more real than words or music or painting. Most people spent most of their hours in the presence of unmediated natural realities: the landscape, the weather, physical labor. Exposure to experiences designed or scripted by others was limited: a few hours per week of liturgy in a mosque or church perhaps, an occasional evening at the theater, and (for the few who could read) some time spent with books. Today our exposure to art—high and low—is so extensive that it becomes part of reality. Every minute of a typical television program or movie is scripted, of course. The newspapers and magazines are professionally written, edited, and formatted, including carefully posed or drawn figures in the advertisements. Only an occasional news photo seems to have come directly from reality, and even it may be "enhanced" in the darkroom or the computer. When we go to a shopping mall, the buildings and the displays of merchandise inside are artfully prepared by architects and designers, and the background music is programmed by Muzak, Inc., or one of its competitors. Our lives have become so entangled with media that we live half-immersed in a virtual reality—and technology is beginning to offer us "real" virtual reality. The essays in this unit consider the meaning and the effect of the centuries-long shift from "natural" reality to the reality of the media.

RANDALL JARRELL   A Sad Heart at the Supermarket   513

> Let us name *our* trade journal *The Medium*. For all these media—television, radio, movies, newspapers, magazines, and the rest—are a single medium, in whose depths we are all being cultivated. This Medium . . . is the substance through which the forces of our society act upon us, and makes us into what our society needs.

KATHA POLLITT   The Smurfette Principle   527

> Do kids pick up on the sexism in children's culture? You bet. Preschoolers are like medieval philosophers: the text—a book, a movie, a TV show—is more authoritative than the evidence of their own eyes.

GLORIA STEINEM   Sex, Lies, and Advertising   530

> Food advertisers have always demanded that women's magazines publish recipes and articles on entertaining (preferably ones that name their products) in return for their ads; clothing advertisers expect to be surrounded by fashion spreads. . . . That's why women's magazines look the way they do.

In this ad, the couple (good-looking, young, affluent, happy, heterosexual) have a problem: they are stuck in a traffic jam on a hot day. Perhaps this is a symbol of a difficult or colourless life "the heat is on . . . the pace is slow." They drink Sprite and enter its magic world. Within that world the problems of heat and inertia do not exist. . . .

We have become so accustomed to [television's] discontinuities that we are no longer struck dumb, as any sane person would be, by a newscaster who having just reported that a nuclear war is inevitable goes on to say that he will be right back after this word from Burger King. . . .

But modern people, i.e., couch potatoes, do nothing that is ever shown on television (because it is either dangerous or would involve getting up from the couch). And what they do do—watch television—is far too boring to be televised for more than a fraction of a second, not even by Andy Warhol, bless his boredom-proof little heart.

As those images come to me I realize that, for nearly 20 years, I have been thinking that TV affected me more than it really did. For though what I saw on TV was important, I always saw it with people who had senses both of history and their own dignity; people who made certain that any televised message was subjected to interference. . . .

But the only movie I remember seeing for certain, some fifty-four years later, is *The Last Train From Madrid.* After we took the bus home to Ardmore Street, I burned my collection of war cards and put away my toy soldiers forever.

Irene shifted the control and invaded the privacy of several breakfast tables. She overheard demonstrations of indigestion, carnal love, abysmal vanity, faith, and despair. Irene's life was nearly as simple and sheltered as it appeared to be, and the forthright and sometimes brutal language that came from the loudspeaker that morning astonished and troubled her.

CHRISTINA ROSSETTI   In an Artist's Studio   595

A queen in opal or in ruby dress,
    A nameless girl in freshest summer-greens
    A saint, an angel—every canvass means
The same one meaning, neither more nor less.

RANDALL JARRELL

A Sad Heart at the Supermarket

Randall Jarrell (1914–1965) was one of America's best-known poets and literary critics. His best early poems, collected in such books as *Little Friend, Little Friend* (1945) and *Losses* (1948), were reactions to the horrors of World War II. By the time he published his National Book Award–winning *The Woman at the Washington Zoo* (1960), Jarrell had become alarmed by the rise of a consumer- and media-oriented culture in the United States, a culture that seemed at odds with older, weightier understandings of human nature. He became interested in psychoanalysis, dreams, myths, and folktales—ways of viewing human beings as something other than consumers of television programs and appliances. Although Jarrell was in some ways a scholarly man—he translated Chekhov from Russian, and Goethe from German—his words are plain, direct, and sharply opinionated. "A Sad Heart at the Supermarket" was published in *Daedalus* in 1960. A useful companion essay in this unit is Gloria Steinem's "Sex, Lies, and Advertising", a pertinent essay from another unit is John Kenneth Galbraith's "The Higher Economic Purpose of Women." Jarrell, Steinem, and Galbraith share a keen sense of the role that marketing plays in our society. Readers may respond with essays discussing their own experience of a society that "needs us to be buyers."

The Emperor Augustus[1] would sometimes say to his Senate: "Words fail me, my Lords; nothing I can say could possibly indicate the depth of my feelings in this matter." But in this matter of mass culture, the mass media, I am speaking not as an emperor but as a fool, a suffering, complaining, helplessly non-conforming poet-or-artist-of-a-sort, far off at the obsolescent rear of things; what I say will indicate the depth of my feelings and the shallowness and one-sidedness of my thoughts. If those English lyric poets who went mad during the eighteenth century had told you why the Age of Enlightenment was driving them crazy, it would have had a kind of documentary interest: what I say may have a kind of documentary interest. *The toad beneath the harrow knows/Exactly where each tooth-point goes:*[2] if you tell me that the field is being harrowed to grow grain for bread, and to create a world in which there will be no more famines, or toads either, I will say: "I know"; but let me tell you where the tooth-points go, and what the harrow looks like from below.

1. Augustus was the first Roman emperor (63 B.C.–A.D. 14).
2. The quotation is from English writer Rudyard Kipling's (1865–1936) *Departmental Ditties*.

513

Advertising men, businessmen speak continually of *media* or *the* 2
media or *the mass media*. One of their trade journals is named, simply,
Media. It is an impressive world: one imagines Mephistopheles offering
Faust[3] *media that no man has ever known;* one feels, while the word is in
one's ear, that abstract, overmastering powers, of a scale and intensity
unimagined yesterday, are being offered one by the technicians who
discovered and control them—offered, and at a price. The word has
the clear fatal ring of that new world whose space we occupy so luxu-
riously and precariously; the world that produces mink stoles, rocka-
billy records, and tactical nuclear weapons by the million; the world
that Attila, Galileo, Hansel and Gretel never knew.

And yet, it's only the plural of *medium*. "*Medium*," says the dic- 3
tionary, "that which lies in the middle; hence, middle condition or
degree . . . A substance through which a force acts or an effect is transmitted . . . That through or by which anything is accomplished; as, an
advertising *medium* . . . *Biol.* A nutritive mixture or substance, as broth,
gelatin, agar, for cultivating bacteria, fungi, etc."

Let us name *our* trade journal *The Medium*. For all these media— 4
television, radio, movies, newspapers, magazines, and the rest—are a
single medium, in whose depths we are all being cultivated. This Medium is of middle condition or degree, mediocre; it lies in the middle of
everything, between a man and his neighbor, his wife, his child, his
self; it, more than anything else, is the substance through which the
forces of our society act upon us, and make us into what our society
needs.

And what does it need? For us to need. 5

Oh, it needs for us to do or be many things: workers, technicians, 6
executives, soldiers, housewives. But first of all, last of all, it needs for
us to be buyers; consumers; beings who want much and will want
more—who want consistently and insatiably. Find some spell to make
us turn away from the stoles, the records, and the weapons, and our
world will change into something to us unimaginable. Find some spell
to make us see that the product or service that yesterday was an unthinkable luxury today is an inexorable necessity, and our world will
go on. It is the Medium which casts this spell—which is this spell. As
we look at the television set, listen to the radio, read the magazines,
the frontier of necessity is always being pushed forward. The Medium
shows us what our new needs are—how often, without it, we should
not have known!—and it shows us how they can be satisfied by buying something. The act of buying something is at the root of our world;

3. According to legend, Mephistopheles (the personification of the devil) offered the
learned doctor Faust youth, knowledge, and magic—in exchange for his soul. In the
German dramatist Goethe's (1749–1832) *Faust,* Mephistopheles tells Faust, "I am giving
you things that no man has ever known."

if anyone wishes to paint the genesis of things in our society, he will paint a picture of God holding out to Adam a check-book or credit card or Charge-A-Plate.

But how quickly our poor naked Adam is turned into a consumer, is linked to others by the great chain of buying!   7

> *No outcast he, bewildered and depressed:*
> *Along his infant veins are interfused*
> *The gravitation and the filial bond*
> *Of nature that connect him with the world.*[4]

Children of three or four can ask for a brand of cereal, sing some soap's commercial; by the time that they are twelve or thirteen they are not children but teen-age consumers, interviewed, graphed, analyzed. They are well on their way to becoming that ideal figure of our culture, the knowledgeable consumer. Let me define him: the knowledgeable consumer is someone who, when he comes to Weimar, knows how to buy a Weimaraner.[5]

Daisy's voice sounded like money;[6] everything about the knowledgeable consumer looks like or sounds like or feels like money, and informed money at that. To live is to consume, to understand life is to know what to consume: he has learned to understand this, so that his life is a series of choices—correct ones—among the products and services of the world. He is able to choose to consume something, of course, only because sometime, somewhere, he or someone else produced something—but just when or where or what no longer seems to us of as much interest. We may still go to Methodist or Baptist or Presbyterian churches on Sunday, but the Protestant ethic of frugal industry, of production for its own sake, is gone.   8

Production has come to seem to our society not much more than a condition prior to consumption. "The challenge of today," an advertising agency writes, "is to make the consumer raise his level of demand." This challenge has been met: the Medium has found it easy to make its people feel the continually increasing lacks, the many specialized dissatisfactions (merging into one great dissatisfaction, temporarily assuaged by new purchases) that it needs for them to feel. When in some magazine we see the Medium at its most nearly perfect, we hardly know which half is entertaining and distracting us, which half making us buy: some advertisement may be more ingeniously entertaining than the text beside it, but it is the text which has made us long for a product more passionately. When one finishes *Holiday* or *Harper's Bazaar* or *House and Garden* or *The New Yorker* or *High Fidelity* or *Road*   9

---

4. The quotation is from Wordsworth, *The Prelude*, 2: 241–44.
5. Weimaraner: breed of dog developed in Germany.
6. The author is referring to Daisy Buchanan, in F. Scott Fitzgerald's *The Great Gatsby*.

and Track or—but make your own list—buying something, going somewhere seems a necessary completion to the act of reading the magazine.

Reader, isn't buying or fantasy-buying an important part of your   10
and my emotional life? (If you reply, *No*, I'll think of you with bitter
envy as more than merely human; as deeply un-American.) It is a
standard joke that when a woman is bored or sad she buys something,
to cheer herself up; but in this respect we are all women together, and
can hear complacently the reminder of how feminine this consumer-
world of ours has become. One imagines as a characteristic dialogue of
our time an interview in which someone is asking of a vague gracious
figure, a kind of Mrs. America: "But while you waited for the inter-
continental ballistic missiles what did you *do?*" She answers: "I bought
things."

She reminds one of the sentinel at Pompeii[7]—a space among ashes,   11
now, but at his post: she too did what she was supposed to do. Our society has delivered us—most of us—from the bonds of necessity, so
that we no longer struggle to find food to keep from starving, clothing
and shelter to keep from freezing; yet if the ends for which we work
and of which we dream are only clothes and restaurants and houses,
possessions, consumption, how have we escaped?—we have ex-
changed man's old bondage for a new voluntary one. It is more than a
figure of speech to say that the consumer is trained for his job of consuming as the factory-worker is trained for his job of producing; and
the first can be a longer, more complicated training, since it is easier to
teach a man to handle a tool, to read a dial, than it is to teach him to
ask, always, for a name-brand aspirin—to want, someday, a stand-by
generator.

What is that? You don't know? I used not to know, but the readers   12
of *House Beautiful* all know, so that now I know. It is the electrical generator that stands in the basement of the suburban houseowner, shining, silent, till at last one night the lights go out, the furnace stops, the
freezer's food begins to—

Ah, but it's frozen for good, the lights are on forever; the owner   13
has switched on the stand-by generator.

But you don't see that he really needs the generator, you'd rather   14
have seen him buy a second car? He has two. A second bathroom? He
has four. When the People of the Medium doubled everything, he
doubled everything; and now that he's gone twice round he will have
to wait three years, or four, till both are obsolescent—but while he
waits there are so many new needs that he can satisfy, so many things

7. The ancient Italian city of Pompeii was buried by an eruption of Mt. Vesuvius in A.D.
79: the cinders and ashes remarkably preserved the city's ruins, including human beings
who died on the spot.

a man can buy. "Man wants but little here below/Nor wants that little long," said the poet;[8] what a lie! Man wants almost unlimited quantities of almost everything, and he wants it till the day he dies.

Sometimes in *Life* or *Look* we see a double-page photograph of 15 some family standing on the lawn among its possessions: station-wagon, swimming-pool, power-cruiser, sports-car, tape-recorder, television sets, radios, cameras, power lawn-mower, garden tractor, lathe, barbecue-set, sporting equipment, domestic appliances—all the gleaming, grotesquely imaginative paraphernalia of its existence. It was hard to get everything on two pages, soon it will need four. It is like a dream, a child's dream before Christmas; yet if the members of the family doubt that they are awake, they have only to reach out and pinch something. The family seems pale and small, a negligible appendage, beside its possessions; only a human being would need to ask: "Which owns which?" We are fond of saying that something is not just something but "a way of life"; this too is a way of life—our way, the way.

Emerson, in his spare stony New England, a few miles from 16 Walden, could write: "Things are in the saddle/And ride mankind."[9] He could say more now: that they are in the theater and studio, and entertain mankind; are in the pulpit and preach to mankind. The values of business, in a business society like our own, are reflected in every sphere: values which agree with them are reinforced, values which disagree are canceled out or have lip service paid to them. In business what sells is good, and that's the end of it—that is what *good* means; if the world doesn't beat a path to your door, your mouse-trap wasn't better. The values of the Medium—which is both a popular business itself and the cause of popularity in other businesses—are business values: money, success, celebrity. If we are representative members of our society, the Medium's values are ours; and even if we are unrepresentative, non-conforming, our hands are—too often—subdued to the element they work in, and our unconscious expectations are all that we consciously reject. Darwin said that he always immediately wrote down evidence against a theory because otherwise, he'd noticed, he would forget it; in the same way, we keep forgetting the existence of those poor and unknown failures whom we might rebelliously love and admire.

If you're so smart why aren't you rich? is the ground-bass of our soci- 17 ety, a grumbling and quite unanswerable criticism, since the society's non-monetary values *are* directly convertible into money. Celebrity

8. The author is referring to English poet Oliver Goldsmith (1728–1744).
9. American poet and philosopher Ralph Waldo Emerson (1803–1882) was a friend of Henry David Thoreau, author of *Walden*.

turns into testimonials, lectures, directorships, presidencies, the capital gains of an autobiography *Told To* some professional ghost who photographs the man's life as Bachrach[10] photographs his body. I read in the newspapers a lyric and perhaps exaggerated instance of this direct conversion of celebrity into money: his son accompanied Adlai Stevenson[11] on a trip to Russia, took snapshots of his father; and sold them (to accompany his father's account of the trip) to *Look* for $20,000. When Liberace[12] said that his critics' unfavorable reviews hurt him so much that he cried all the way to the bank, one had to admire the correctness and penetration of his press-agent's wit—in another age, what might not such a man have become!

Our culture is essentially periodical: we believe that all that is deserves to perish and to have something else put in its place. We speak of planned obsolescence, but it is more than planned, it is felt; is an assumption about the nature of the world. We feel that the present is better and more interesting, more real, than the past, and that the future will be better and more interesting, more real, than the present; but, consciously, we do not hold against the present its prospective obsolescence. Our standards have become to an astonishing degree the standards of what is called the world of fashion, where mere timeliness—being orange in orange's year, violet in violet's—is the value to which all other values are reducible. In our society the word *old-fashioned* is so final a condemnation that someone like Norman Vincent Peale[13] can say about atheism or agnosticism simply that it is old-fashioned; the homely recommendation of the phrase *Give me that good old-time religion* has become, after a few decades, the conclusive rejection of the phrase *old-fashioned atheism*.

All this is, at bottom, the opposite of the world of the arts, where commercial and scientific progress do not exist; where the bone of Homer and Mozart and Donatello is there, always, under the mere blush of fashion; where the past—the remote past, even—is responsible for the way that we understand, value, and act in, the present. (When one reads an abstract expressionist's remark that Washington studios are "eighteen months behind" those of his colleagues in New York, one realizes something of the terrible power of business and fashion over those most overtly hostile to them.) An artist's work and life presuppose continuing standards, values extended over centuries or millennia, a future that is the continuation and modification of the

18

19

10. Bachrach: well-known photography studios.
11. Adlai Stevenson: American statesman (1900–1965).
12. Liberace: American popular pianist, famous—and rich—because of his so-called tastelessness.
13. Norman Vincent Peale: American clergyman/writer (1898–1993) whose primary message was that one can help oneself through positive thinking and prayer.

past, not its contradiction of irrelevant replacement. He is working for the time that wants the best that he can do: the present, he hopes—but if not that, the future. If he sees that fewer and fewer people are any real audience for the serious artists of the past, he will feel that still fewer are going to be an audience for the serious artists of the present: for those who, willingly or unwillingly, sacrifice extrinsic values to intrinsic ones, immediate effectiveness to that steady attraction which, the artist hopes, true excellence will always exert.

The past's relation to the artist or man of culture is almost the opposite of its relation to the rest of our society. To him the present is no more than the last ring on the trunk, understandable and valuable only in terms of all the earlier rings. The rest of our society sees only that great last ring, the enveloping surface of the trunk; what's underneath is a disregarded, almost mythical foundation. When Northrop Frye[14] writes that "the preoccupation of the humanities with the past is sometimes made a reproach against them by those who forget that we face the past: it may be shadowy, but it is all that is there," he is saying what for the artist or man of culture is self-evidently true. Yet for the Medium and the People of the Medium it is as self-evidently false: for them the present—or a past so recent, so quick-changing, so soon-disappearing, that it might be called the specious present—is all that is there.

In the past our culture's body of common knowledge—its frame of reference, its possibility of comprehensible allusion—changed slowly and superficially; the amount added to it or taken away from it, in any ten years, was surprisingly small. Now in any ten years a surprisingly large proportion of the whole is replaced. Most of the information people have in common is something that four or five years from now they will not even remember having known. A newspaper story remarks in astonishment that television quiz-programs "have proved that ordinary citizens can be conversant with such esoterica as jazz, opera, the Bible, Shakespeare, poetry, and fisticuffs." You may exclaim: "Esoterica! If the Bible and Shakespeare are esoterica, what is there that's common knowledge?" The answer, I suppose, is that Elfrida von Nordroff and Teddy Nadler—the ordinary citizens on the quiz-programs—are common knowledge; though not for long. Songs disappear in two or three months, celebrities in two or three years; most of the Medium is little felt and soon forgotten. Nothing is as dead as day-before-yesterday's newspaper, the next-to-the-last number on the roulette wheel; but most of the knowledge people have in common and lose in common is knowledge of such newspapers, such numbers. Yet the novelist or poet or dramatist, when he moves a great

14. Northrop Frye: Canadian literary critic (b. 1912).

audience, depends upon the deep feelings, the living knowledge, that the people of that audience share; if so much has become contingent, superficial, ephemeral, it is disastrous for him.

New products and fashions replace the old, and the fact that they replace them is proof enough of their superiority. Similarly, the Medium does not need to show that the subjects which fill it are interesting or timely or important; the fact that they are its subjects makes them so. If *Time, Life,* and the television shows are full of Tom Fool this month, he's no fool. And when he has been gone from them a while, we do not think him a fool—we do not think of him at all. He no longer exists, in the fullest sense of the word *exist:* to be is to be perceived, to be a part of the Medium of our perception. Our celebrities are not kings, romantic in exile, but Representatives who, defeated, are forgotten; they had, always, only the qualities that we delegated to them. 22

After driving for four or five minutes along the road outside my door, I come to a row of one-room shacks about the size of kitchens, made out of used boards, metal signs, old tin roofs. To the people who live in them an electric dishwasher of one's own is as much a fantasy as an ocean liner of one's own. But since the Medium (and those whose thought is molded by it) does not perceive them, these people are themselves a fantasy. No matter how many millions of such exceptions to the general rule there are, they do not really exist, but have a kind of anomalous, statistical subsistence; our moral and imaginative view of the world is no more affected by them than by the occupants of some home for the mentally deficient a little farther along the road. If some night one of these out-moded, economically deficient ghosts should scratch at my window, I could say only: "Come back twenty or thirty years ago." And if I myself, as an old-fashioned, one-room poet, a friend of "quiet culture," a "meek lover of the good," should go out some night to scratch at another window, shouldn't I hear someone's indifferent or regretful: "Come back a century or two ago"? 23

When those whose existence the Medium recognizes ring the chimes of the writer's doorbell, fall through his letter-slot, float out onto his television-screen, what is he to say to them? A man's unsuccessful struggle to get his family food is material for a work of art—for tragedy, almost; his unsuccessful struggle to get his family a stand-by generator is material for what? Comedy? Farce? Comedy on such a scale, at such a level, that our society and its standards seem, almost, farce? And yet it is the People of the Medium—those who struggle for and get, or struggle for and don't get, the generator—whom our society finds representative: they are there, there primarily, there to be treated first of all. How shall the artist treat them? And the Medium itself—an end of life and a means of life, something essential to people's understanding and valuing of their existence, something many of their waking hours are spent listening to or looking at—how is *it* to be 24 treated as subject-matter for art? The artist cannot merely reproduce it; should he satirize or parody it? But by the time the artist's work reaches its audience, the portion of the Medium which is satirized will already have been forgotten; and parody is impossible, often, when so much of the Medium is already an unintentional parody. (Our age might be defined as the age in which real parody became impossible, since any parody had already been duplicated, or parodied, in earnest.) Yet the Medium, by now, is an essential part of its watchers. How can you explain those whom Mohammedans call the People of the Book[15] in any terms that omit the Book? We are people of the television-set, the magazine, the radio, and are inexplicable in any terms that omit them.

Oscar Wilde said that Nature imitates Art, that before Whistler 25 painted them there were no fogs along the Thames.[16] If his statement were not false, it would not be witty. But to say that Nature imitates Art, when the Nature is human nature and the Art that of television, radio, motion-pictures, magazines, is literally true. The Medium shows its People what life is, what people are, and its People believe it: expect people to be that, try themselves to be that. Seeing is believing; and if what you see in *Life* is different from what you see in life, which of the two are you to believe? For many people it is what you see in *Life* (and in the movies, over television, on the radio) that is real life; and every-day existence, mere local or personal variation, is not real in the same sense.

The Medium mediates between us and raw reality, and the media- 26 tion more and more replaces reality for us. Many radio-stations have a news-broadcast every hour, and many people like and need to hear it. In many houses either the television set or the radio is turned on during most of the hours the family is awake. It is as if they longed to be established in reality, to be reminded continually of the "real," "objective" world—the created world of the Medium—rather than to be left at the mercy of actuality, of the helpless contingency of the world in which the radio-receiver or television set is sitting. And surely we can sympathize: which of us hasn't found a similar refuge in the "real," created world of Cézanne or Goethe or Verdi? Yet Dostoievsky's world is too different from Wordsworth's, Piero della Francesca's from Goya's, Bach's from Wolf's, for us to be able to substitute one homogeneous mediated reality for everyday reality in the belief that it *is* everyday

15. People of the Book: the terms that Islam gives to Jews, Christians, and Zoroastrians because all possess divine books: the Torah, the Gospel, the Avesta. This term is to distinguish them from "heathens," whose religions are not founded on divine revelation.
16. Wilde, an Irish writer and wit (1854–1900), was turning the conventional wisdom—that Art imitates Nature—on its head. James A. M. Whistler (1834–1903) was an American painter noted for his sense of color and design (evident in many of his paintings of London scenes)—and, on occasion, for trading barbed retorts with Oscar Wilde.

reality. For many watchers, listeners, readers, the world of events and celebrities and performers—the Great World—has become the world of primary reality: how many times they have sighed at the colorless unreality of their own lives and families, and sighed for the bright reality of, say, Elizabeth Taylor's. The watchers call the celebrities by their first names, approve or disapprove of "who they're dating," handle them with a mixture of love, identification, envy, and contempt. But however they handle them, they *handle* them: the Medium has given everyone so terrible a familiarity with everyone that it takes great magnanimity of spirit not to be affected by it. These celebrities are not heroes to us, their valets.

Better to have these real ones play themselves, and not sacrifice   27 too much of their reality to art; better to have the watcher play himself, and not lose too much of himself in art. Usually the watcher is halfway between two worlds, paying full attention to neither: half distracted from, half distracted by, this distraction; and able for the moment not to be too greatly affected, have too great demands made upon him, by either world. For in the Medium, which we escape to from work, nothing is ever *work*, makes intellectual or emotional or imaginative demands which we might find it difficult to satisfy. Here in the half-world everything is homogeneous—is, as much as possible, the same as everything else: each familiar novelty, novel familiarity has the same treatment on top and the same attitude and conclusion at bottom; only the middle, the particular subject of the particular program or article, is different. If it *is* different: everyone is given the same automatic "human interest" treatment, so that it is hard for us to remember, unnecessary for us to remember, which particular celebrity we're reading about this time—often it's the same one, we've just moved on to a different magazine.

Francesco Caraccioli[17] said that the English have a hundred reli-   28 gions and one sauce; so do we; and we are so accustomed to this sauce or dye or style of presentation, the aesthetic equivalent of Standard Brands, that a very simple thing can seem obscure or perverse without it. And, too, we find it hard to have to shift from one genre to another, to vary our attitudes and expectations, to use our unexercised imaginations. Poetry disappeared long ago, even for most intellectuals; each year fiction is a little less important. Our age is the age of articles: we buy articles in stores, read articles in magazines, exist among the interstices of articles: of columns, interviews, photographic essays, documentaries; of facts condensed into headlines or expanded into non-fiction best-sellers; of real facts about real people.

Art lie to us to tell us the (sometimes disquieting) truth. The   29 Medium tells us truths, facts, in order to make us believe some reas-

---

17. Caraccioli was a Neapolitan naval commander (1752–1799), executed by British admiral Horatio Nelson for desertion to the French during the Napoleonic wars.

suring or entertaining lie or half-truth. These actually existing celebrities, of universally admitted importance, about whom we are told directly authoritative facts—how can fictional characters compete with these? These *are* our fictional characters, our Lears and Clytemnestras. (This is ironically appropriate, since many of their doings and sayings are fictional, made up by public relations officers, columnists, agents, or other affable familiar ghosts.) And the Medium gives us such facts, such tape-recordings, such clinical reports not only about the great but also about (representative samples of) the small. When we have been shown so much about so many—*can* be shown, we feel, anything about anybody—does fiction seem so essential as it once seemed? Shakespeare or Tolstoy can show us all about someone, but so can *Life;* and when *Life* does, it's someone real.

The Medium is half life and half art, and competes with both life 30
and art. It spoils its audience for both; spoils both for its audience. For the People of the Medium life isn't sufficiently a matter of success and glamor and celebrity, isn't entertaining enough, distracting enough, *mediated* enough; and art is too difficult or individual or novel, too much a matter of tradition and the past, too much a matter of special attitudes and aptitudes—its mediation sometimes is queer or excessive, and sometimes is not even recognizable as mediation. The Medium's mixture of rhetoric and reality, in which people are given what they know they want to be given in the form in which they know they want to be given it, is something more efficient and irresistible than any real art. If a man has all his life been fed a combination of marzipan and ethyl alcohol—if eating, to him, is a matter of being knocked unconscious by an ice cream soda—can he, by taking thought, come to prefer a diet of bread and wine, apples and well-water? Will a man who has spent his life watching gladiatorial games come to prefer listening to chamber music? And those who produce the bread and the wine and the quartets for him—won't they be tempted either to give up producing them, or else to produce a bread that's half sugar and half alcohol, a quartet that ends with the cellist at the violist's bleeding throat?

Any outsider who has worked for the Medium will have observed 31
that the one thing which seems to its managers most unnatural is for someone to do something naturally, to speak or write as an individual speaking or writing to other individuals, and not as a sub-contractor supplying a standardized product to the Medium. It is as if producers and editors and supervisors—middle men—were particles forming a screen between maker and public, one which will let through only particles of their own size and weight (or as they say, the public's). As you look into their strained puréed faces, their big horn-rimmed eyes, you despair of Creation itself, which seems for the instant made in their own owl-eyed image. There are so many extrinsic considerations involved in the presentation of his work, the maker finds, that by the

time it is presented almost any intrinsic consideration has come to seem secondary. No wonder that the professional who writes the ordinary commercial success—the ordinary script, scenario, or best seller—resembles imaginative writers less than he resembles editors, producers, executives. The supplier has come to resemble those he supplies, and what he supplies them resembles both. With an artist you never know what you will get; with him you know what you will get. He is a reliable source for a standard product. He is almost exactly the opposite of the imaginative artist: instead of stubbornly or helplessly sticking to what he sees and feels—to what is right for him, true to his reality, regardless of what the others think and want—he gives the others what they think and want, regardless of what he himself sees and feels.

The Medium represents, to the artist, all that he has learned not to do: its sure-fire stereotypes seem to him what any true art, true spirit, has had to struggle past on its way to the truth. The artist sees the values and textures of this art-substitute replacing those of his art, so far as most of society is concerned; conditioning the expectations of what audience his art has kept. Mass culture either corrupts or isolates the writer. His old feeling of oneness—of speaking naturally to an audience with essentially similar standards—is gone; and writers no longer have much of the consolatory feeling that took its place, the feeling of writing for the happy few, the kindred spirits whose standards are those of the future. (Today they feel: the future, should there be one, will be worse.) True works of art are more and more produced away from or in opposition to society. And yet the artist needs society as much as society needs him: as our cultural enclaves get smaller and drier, more hysterical or academic, one mourns for the artists inside and the public outside. An incomparable historian of mass culture, Ernest van den Haag, has expressed this with laconic force: "The artist who, by refusing to work for the mass market, becomes marginal, cannot create what he might have created had there been no mass market. One may prefer a monologue to addressing a mass meeting. But it is still not a conversation."

Even if the rebellious artist's rebellion is whole-hearted, it can never be whole-stomach'd, whole-unconscious'd. Part of him wants to be like his kind, is like his kind; longs to be loved and admired and successful. Our society—and the artist, in so far as he is truly a part of it—has no place set aside for the different and poor and obscure, the fools for Christ's sake: they all go willy-nilly into Limbo. The artist is tempted, consciously, to give his society what it wants—or if he won't or can't, to give it nothing at all; is tempted, unconsciously, to give it superficially independent or contradictory works which are at heart works of the Medium. But it is hard for him to go on serving both God and Mammon when God is so really ill-, Mammon so really well-organized.

"Shakespeare wrote for the Medium of his day; if Shakespeare [34] were alive now he'd be writing *My Fair Lady;* isn't *My Fair Lady,* then, our *Hamlet?* shouldn't you be writing *Hamlet* instead of sitting there worrying about your superego? I need my *Hamlet!*" So society speaks to the artist, reasons with the artist; and after he has written it its *Hamlet* it is satisfied, and tries to make sure that he will never do it again. There are many more urgent needs that it wants him to satisfy: to lecture to it; to be interviewed; to appear on television programs; to give testimonials; to attend book luncheons; to make trips abroad for the State Department; to judge books for Book Clubs; to read for publishers, judge for publishers, to be a publisher for publishers; to edit magazines; to teach writing at colleges or conferences; to write scenarios or scripts or articles—articles about his home town for *Holiday,* about cats or clothes or Christmas for *Vogue,* about "How I Wrote *Hamlet*" for anything; to—

But why go on? I once heard a composer, lecturing, say to a poet, [35] lecturing: "They'll pay us to do *anything,* so long as it isn't writing music or writing poems." I knew the reply that as a member of my society I should have made. "As long as they pay you, what do you care?" But I didn't make it: it was plain that they cared . . . But how many more learn not to care, to love what they once endured! It is a whole so comprehensive that any alternative seems impossible, any opposition irrelevant; in the end a man says in a small voice: "I accept the Medium." The Enemy of the People winds up as the People—but where there is no enemy, the people perish.

The climate of our culture is changing. Under these new rains, [36] new suns, small things grow great, and what was great grows small; whole species disappear and are replaced. The American present is very different from the American past: so different that our awareness of the extent of the changes has been repressed, and we regard as ordinary what is extraordinary—ominous perhaps—both for us and for the rest of the world. The American present is many other peoples' future: our cultural and economic sample is to much of the world mesmeric, and it is only its weakness and poverty that prevent it from hurrying with us into the Roman future. But at this moment of our power and success, our thought and art are full of a troubled sadness, of the conviction of our own decline. When the President of Yale University writes that "the ideal of the good life has faded from the educational process, leaving only miscellaneous prospects of jobs and joyless hedonism," are we likely to find it unfaded among our entertainers and executives? Is the influence of what I have called the Medium likely to lead us to any good life? to make us love and try to attain any real excellence, beauty, magnanimity? or to make us understand these as obligatory but transparent rationalizations behind which the realities of money and power are waiting?

The tourist Matthew Arnold[18] once spoke about our green culture in terms that have an altered relevance—but are not yet irrelevant—to our ripe one. He said: "What really dissatisfies in American civilization is the want of the *interesting,* a want due chiefly to the want of those two great elements of the interesting, which are elevation and beauty." This use of *interesting*—and, perhaps, this tone of a curator pointing out what is plain and culpable—shows how far along in the decline of the West Arnold came: it is only in the latter days that we ask to be interested. He had found the word, he tells us, in Carlyle.[19] Carlyle is writing to a friend to persuade him not to emigrate to the United States; he asks: "Could you banish yourself from all that is interesting to your mind, forget the history, the glorious institutions, the noble principles of old Scotland—that you might eat a better dinner, perhaps?" We smile, and feel like reminding Carlyle of the history, the glorious institutions, the noble principles of new America—of that New World which is, after all, the heir of the Old.

And yet . . . Can we smile as comfortably, today, as we could have smiled yesterday? Nor could we listen as unconcernedly, if on taking leave of us some other tourist should conclude, with the penetration and obtuseness of his kind:

"I remember reading somewhere: that which you inherit from your fathers you must earn in order to possess. I have been so much impressed with your power and your possessions that I have neglected, perhaps, your principles. The elevation or beauty of your spirit did not equal, always, that of your mountains and skyscrapers: it seems to me that your society provides you with 'all that is interesting to the mind' only exceptionally, at odd hours, in little reservations like those of your Indians. But as for your dinners, I've never seen anything like them: your daily bread comes *flambé.*[20] And yet—wouldn't you say—the more dinners a man eats, the more comforts he possesses, the hungrier and more uncomfortable some part of him becomes: inside every fat man there is a man who is starving. Part of you is being starved to death, and the rest of you is being stuffed to death. But this will change: no one goes on being stuffed to death or starved to death forever.

"This is a gloomy, an equivocal conclusion? Oh yes, I come from an older culture, where things are accustomed to coming to such conclusions; where there is no last-paragraph fairy to bring one, always, a happy ending—or that happiest of all endings, no ending at all. And

37

38

39

40

18. English poet and critic Matthew Arnold (1822–1888) traveled in the United States in the 1880s.
19. Thomas Carlyle (1795–1881) was an English writer and social critic who had considerable influence on Arnold.
20. *flambé:* served with flaming rum or brandy (generally considered very fancy).

have I no advice to give you as I go? None. You are too successful to need advice, or to be able to take it if it were offered; but if ever you should fail, it is there waiting for you, the advice or consolation of all the other failures."

KATHA POLLITT

The Smurfette Principle

Katha Pollitt (1949–   ) was born in Brooklyn and now lives and works in Manhattan as a freelance writer. After receiving her B.A. in philosophy from Radcliffe in 1972, she earned an M.F.A. in poetry and spent several years as poet-in-residence at Barnard College. Her 1982 collection, *Antarctic Traveller,* won the National Book Critics Circle Award. A committed political liberal, she often writes essays and articles for such magazines as *The Atlantic Monthly, Mother Jones, The New Yorker,* and *The Nation* (where she is an associate editor). "The Smurfette Principle" was published in *The New York Times Magazine* on April 7, 1991. In 1993 Pollitt published *The Morning After: Sex, Fear and Femininity on Campus* and in 1994 followed with *Reasonable Creatures: Essays on Women and Feminism.* Her interest in the media's presentation of women was sharpened when she began to hear her daughter talking about men and women in terms clearly not learned at home: "Suddenly it's like this little person is a radio station through which the culture is beaming itself." A useful companion essay is David Bradley's "How TV Drew Our Family Together—In Spite of Its Messages," which deals with television's presentation of race.

This Christmas, I finally caved in: I gave my 3-year-old daughter,   1
Sophie, her very own cassette of "The Little Mermaid." Now, she, too, can sit transfixed by Ariel, the perky teen-ager with the curvy tail who trades her voice for a pair of shapely legs and a shot at marriage to a prince. ("On land it's much preferred for ladies not to say a word," sings the cynical sea witch, "and she who holds her tongue will get her man." Since she's the villain, we're not meant to notice that events prove her correct.)

Usually when parents give a child some item they find repellent,   2
they plead helplessness before a juvenile filibuster. But "The Little Mermaid" was my idea. Ariel may look a lot like Barbie, and her adventure may be limited to romance and over with the wedding bells, but unlike, say, Cinderella or Sleeping Beauty, she's active, brave and determined, the heroine of her own life. She even rescues the prince.

And that makes her a rare fish, indeed, in the world of preschool culture.

Take a look at the kids' section of your local video store. You'll find that features starring boys, and usually aimed at them, account for 9 out of 10 offerings. Clicking the television dial one recent week—admittedly not an encyclopedic study—I came across not a single network cartoon or puppet show starring a female. (Nickelodeon, the children's cable channel, has one of each.) Except for the crudity of the animation and the general air of witlessness and hype, I might as well have been back in my own 1950's childhood, nibbling Frosted Flakes in front of Daffy Duck, Bugs Bunny, Porky Pig and the rest of the all-male Warner Brothers lineup.

Contemporary shows are either essentially all-male, like "Garfield," or are organized on what I call the Smurfette principle: a group of male buddies will be accented by a lone female, stereotypically defined. In the worst cartoons—the ones that blend seamlessly into the animated cereal commercials—the female is usually a little-sister type, a bunny in a pink dress and hair ribbons who tags along with the adventurous bears and badgers. But the Smurfette principle rules the more carefully made shows, too. Thus, Kanga, the only female in "Winnie-the-Pooh," is a mother. Piggy, of "Muppet Babies," is a pint-size version of Miss Piggy, the camp glamour queen of the Muppet movies. April, of the wildly popular "Teen-Age Mutant Ninja Turtles," functions as a girl Friday to a quartet of male superheroes. The message is clear. Boys are the norm, girls the variation; boys are central, girls peripheral; boys are individuals, girls types. Boys define the group, its story and its code of values. Girls exist only in relation to boys.

Well, commercial television—what did I expect? The surprise is that public television, for all its superior intelligence, charm and commitment to worthy values, shortchanges preschool girls, too. Mister Rogers lives in a neighborhood populated mostly by middle-aged men like himself. "Shining Time Station" features a cartoon in which the male characters are train engines and the female characters are passenger cars. And then there's "Sesame Street." True, the human characters are neatly divided between the genders (and among the races, too, which is another rarity). The film clips, moreover, are just about the only place on television in which you regularly see girls having fun together: practicing double Dutch, having a sleep-over. But the Muppets are the real stars of "Sesame Street," and the important ones—the ones with real personalities, who sing on the musical videos, whom kids identify with and cherish in dozens of licensed products—are *all* male. I know one little girl who was so outraged and heartbroken when she realized that even Big Bird—her last hope—was a boy that she hasn't watched the show since.

Well, there's always the library. Some of the best children's books 6
ever written have been about girls—Madeline, Frances the badger. It's
even possible to find stories with funny, feminist messages, like "The
Paper-bag Princess." (She rescues the prince from a dragon, but he's so
ungrateful that she decides not to marry him, after all.) But books
about girls are a subset in a field that includes a much larger subset of
books about boys (12 of the 14 storybooks singled out for praise in last
year's Christmas roundup in *Newsweek,* for instance) and books in
which the sex of the child is theoretically unimportant—in which case
it usually "happens to be" male. Dr. Seuss's books are less about individual characters than about language and imaginative freedom—but,
somehow or other, only boys get to go on beyond Zebra or see marvels
on Mulberry Street. Frog and Toad, Lowly Worm, Lyle the Crocodile,
all *could* have been female. But they're not.

Do kids pick up on the sexism in children's culture? You bet. 7
Preschoolers are like medieval philosophers: the text—a book, a movie,
a TV show—is more authoritative than the evidence of their own eyes.
"Let's play weddings," says my little niece. We grownups roll our eyes,
but face it: it's still the one scenario in which the girl is the central figure. "Women are *nurses,*" my friend Anna, a doctor, was informed by
her then 4-year-old, Molly. Even my Sophie is beginning to notice the
back-seat role played by girls in some of her favorite books. "Who's
that?" she asks every time we reread "The Cat in the Hat." It's Sally,
the timid little sister of the resourceful boy narrator. She wants Sally to
matter, I think, and since Sally is really just a name and a hair ribbon,
we have to say her name again and again.

The sexism in preschool culture deforms both boys and girls. Little 8
girls learn to split their consciousness, filtering their dreams and ambitions through boy characters while admiring the clothes of the
princess. The more privileged and daring can dream of becoming exceptional women in a man's world—Smurfettes. The others are being
taught to accept the more usual fate, which is to be a passenger car
drawn through life by a masculine train engine. Boys, who are rarely
confronted with stories in which males play only minor roles, learn a
simpler lesson: girls just don't matter much.

How can it be that 25 years of feminist social changes have made 9
so little impression on preschool culture? Molly, now 6 and well aware
that women can be doctors, has one theory: children's entertainment
is mostly made by men. That's true, as it happens, and I'm sure it explains a lot. It's also true that, as a society, we don't seem to care much
what goes on with kids, as long as they are reasonably quiet. Marsh-
mallow cereal, junky toys, endless hours in front of the tube—a society
that accepts all that is not going to get in a lather about a little gender
stereotyping. It's easier to focus on the bright side. I had "Cinderella,"
Sophie has "The Little Mermaid"—that's progress, isn't it?

"We're working on it," Dulcy Singer, the executive producer of 10 "Sesame Street," told me when I raised the sensitive question of those all-male Muppets. After all, the show has only been on the air for a quarter of a century; these things take time. The trouble is, our preschoolers don't have time. My funny, clever, bold, adventurous daughter is forming her gender ideas right now. I do what I can to counteract the messages she gets from her entertainment, and so does her father—Sophie watches very little television. But I can see we have our work cut out for us. It sure would help if the bunnies took off their hair ribbons, and if half of the monsters were fuzzy, blue—and female.

GLORIA STEINEM

Sex, Lies, and Advertising

Gloria Steinem (1934–   ) grew up in relative poverty, living in a trailer while her father traveled around Ohio looking for work. After his death, she moved to a basement apartment in Toledo, where she cared for her invalid mother and compiled a mediocre high school record. High entrance-test scores allowed her to attend Smith College, where she excelled academically. After traveling on a fellowship to India, she returned to the United States determined to be a journalist. The appearance of a 1962 article on the sexual revolution ("The Moral Disarmament of Betty Coed") launched her career, and she was soon writing feature stories for a number of magazines. Her feminism dates from 1968, when she attended a meeting called to protest hearings on New York's abortion laws: "Suddenly, I was no longer learning intellectually what was wrong: I knew." In 1971 Steinem became editor of *Ms.* magazine, a post she held until 1987, when financial difficulties forced the sale of the magazine to a large Australian communications conglomerate. In addition to promoting the work of feminist writers while editing *Ms.*, Steinem has produced a significant body of her own work, including *Outrageous Acts and Everyday Rebellions* (1983), *Revolution from Within* (1992), and *Moving Beyond Words* (1994).

The following article was published in the July/August 1990 issue of *Ms.* Readers may want to connect it with Guy Cook's "The Discourse of Advertising" and produce essays in which they examine the way a particular magazine article, television program, or film comes to the audience packaged with encouragements to consume.

About three years ago, as *glasnost* was beginning and *Ms.* seemed to 1 be ending. I was invited to a press lunch for a Soviet official. He entertained us with anecdotes about new problems of democracy in his country. Local Communist leaders were being criticized in their media for the first time, he explained, and they were angry.

"So I'll have to ask my American friends," he finished pointedly, "how more *subtly* to control the press." In the silence that followed, I said, "Advertising."

The reporters laughed, but later, one of them took me aside: How *dare* I suggest that freedom of the press was limited? How dare I imply that his newsweekly could be influenced by ads?

I explained that I was thinking of advertising's media-wide influence on most of what we read. Even newsmagazines use "soft" cover stories to sell ads, confuse readers with "advertorials," and occasionally self-censor on subjects known to be a problem with big advertisers.

But, I also explained, I was thinking especially of women's magazines. There, it isn't just a little content that's devoted to attracting ads, it's almost all of it. That's why advertisers—not readers—have always been the problem for *Ms.* As the only women's magazine that didn't supply what the ad world euphemistically describes as "supportive editorial atmosphere" or "complementary copy" (for instance, articles that praise food/fashion/beauty subjects to "support" and "complement" food/fashion/beauty ads), *Ms.* could never attract enough advertising to break even.

"Oh, *women's* magazines," the journalist said with contempt. "Everybody knows they're catalogs—but who cares? They have nothing to do with journalism."

I can't tell you how many times I've had this argument in 25 years of working for many kinds of publications. Except as moneymaking machines—"cash cows" as they are so elegantly called in the trade—women's magazines are rarely taken seriously. Though changes being made by women have been called more far-reaching than the industrial revolution—and though many editors try hard to reflect some of them in the few pages left to them after all the ad-related subjects have been covered—the magazines serving the female half of this country are still far below the journalistic and ethical standards of news and general interest publications. Most depressing of all, this doesn't even rate an exposé.

If *Time* and *Newsweek* had to lavish praise on cars in general and credit General Motors in particular to get GM ads, there would be a scandal—maybe a criminal investigation. When women's magazines from *Seventeen* to *Lear's* praise beauty products in general and credit Revlon in particular to get ads, it's just business as usual.

I.

When *Ms.* began, we didn't consider *not* taking ads. The most im-   9
portant reason was keeping the price of a feminist magazine low
enough for most women to afford. But the second and almost equal
reason was providing a forum where women and advertisers could
talk to each other and improve advertising itself. After all, it was (and
still is) as potent a source of information in this country as news or TV
and movie dramas.

We decided to proceed in two stages. First, we would convince   10
makers of "people products" used by both men and women but advertised mostly to men—cars, credit cards, insurance, sound equipment,
financial services, and the like—that their ads should be placed in a
women's magazine. Since they were accustomed to the division between editorial and advertising in news and general interest magazines, this would allow our editorial content to be free and diverse.
Second, we would add the best ads for whatever traditional "women's
products" (clothes, shampoo, fragrance, food, and so on) that surveys
showed *Ms.* readers used. But we would ask them to come in *without*
the usual quid pro quo of "complementary copy."

We knew the second step might be harder. Food advertisers have   11
always demanded that women's magazines publish recipes and articles
on entertaining (preferably ones that name their products) in return
for their ads; clothing advertisers expect to be surrounded by fashion
spreads (especially ones that credit their designers); and shampoo, fragrance, and beauty products in general usually insist on positive editorial coverage of beauty subjects, plus photo credits besides. That's why
women's magazines look the way they do. But if we could break this
link between ads and editorial content, then we wanted good ads for
"women's products," too.

By playing their part in this unprecedented mix of *all* the things   12
our readers need and use, advertisers also would be rewarded: ads for
products like cars and mutual funds would find a new growth market;
the best ads for women's products would no longer be lost in oceans of
ads for the same category; and both would have access to a laboratory
of smart and caring readers whose response would help create effective ads for other media as well.

I thought then that our main problem would be the imagery in ads   13
themselves. Carmakers were still draping blondes in evening gowns
over the hoods like ornaments. Authority figures were almost always
male, even in ads for products that only women used. Sadistic, he-man
campaigns even won industry praise. (For instance, *Advertising Age*
had hailed the infamous Silva Thin cigarette theme, "How to Get a
Woman's Attention: Ignore Her," as "brilliant.") Even in medical journals, tranquilizer ads showed depressed housewives standing beside
piles of dirty dishes and promised to get them back to work.

Obviously, *Ms.* would have to avoid such ads and seek out the best   14
ones—but this didn't seem impossible. *The New Yorker* had been selecting ads for aesthetic reasons for years, a practice that only seemed to
make advertisers more eager to be in its pages. *Ebony* and *Essence* were
asking for ads with positive black images, and though their struggle
was hard, they weren't being called unreasonable.

Clearly, what *Ms.* needed was a very special publisher and ad sales   15
staff. I could think of only one woman with experience on the business
side of magazines—Patricia Carbine, who recently had become a vice
president of *McCall's* as well as its editor in chief—and the reason I
knew her name was a good omen. She had been managing editor at
Look (really *the* editor, but its owner refused to put a female name at
the top of his masthead) when I was writing a column there. After I
did an early interview with Cesar Chavez, then just emerging as a
leader of migrant labor, and the publisher turned it down because he
was worried about ads from Sunkist, Pat was the one who intervened.
As I learned later, she had told the publisher she would resign if the interview wasn't published. Mainly because *Look* couldn't afford to lose
Pat, it *was* published (and the ads from Sunkist never arrived).

Though I barely knew this woman, she had done two things I al-   16
ways remembered: put her job on the line in a way that editors often
talk about but rarely do, and been so loyal to her colleagues that she
never told me or anyone outside *Look* that she had done so.

Fortunately, Pat did agree to leave *McCall's* and take a huge cut in   17
salary to become publisher of *Ms.* She became responsible for training
and inspiring generations of young women who joined the *Ms.* ad sales
force, many of whom went on to become "firsts" at the top of publishing. When *Ms.* first started, however, there were so few women with
experience selling space that Pat and I made the rounds of ad agencies
ourselves. Later, the fact that *Ms.* was asking companies to do business
in a different way meant our saleswomen had to make many times the
usual number of calls—first to convince agencies and then client companies besides—and to present endless amounts of research. I was
often asked to do a final ad presentation, or see some higher decision-
maker, or speak to women employees so executives could see the interest of women they worked with. That's why I spent more time
persuading advertisers than editing or writing for *Ms.* and why I ended
up with an unsentimental education in the seamy underside of publishing that few writers see (and even fewer magazines can publish).

Let me take you with us through some experiences, just as they   18
happened:

• Cheered on by early support from Volkswagen and one or two other   19
car companies, we scrape together time and money to put on a major
reception in Detroit. We know U.S. carmakers firmly believe that
women choose the upholstery, not the car, but we are armed with sta-

tistics and reader mail to prove the contrary: a car is an important purchase for women, one that symbolizes mobility and freedom.

But almost nobody comes. We are left with many pounds of shrimp on the table, and quite a lot of egg on our face. We blame ourselves for not guessing that there would be a baseball pennant play-off on the same day, but executives go out of their way to explain they wouldn't have come anyway. Thus begins ten years of knocking on hostile doors, presenting endless documentation, and hiring a full-time saleswoman in Detroit; all necessary before *Ms.* gets any real results. 20

This long saga has a semihappy ending: foreign and, later, domestic carmakers eventually provided *Ms.* with enough advertising to make cars one of our top sources of ad revenue. Slowly, Detroit began to take the women's market seriously enough to put car ads in other women's magazines, too, thus freeing a few pages from the hothouse of fashion-beauty-food ads. 21

But long after figures showed a third, even a half, of many car models being bought by women, U.S. makers continued to be uncomfortable addressing women. Unlike foreign carmakers, Detroit never quite learned the secret of creating intelligent ads that exclude no one, and then placing them in women's magazines to overcome past exclusion. (*Ms.* readers were so grateful for a routine Honda ad featuring rack and pinion steering, for instance, that they sent fan mail.) Even now, Detroit continues to ask, "Should we make special ads for women?" Perhaps that's why some foreign cars still have a disproportionate share of the U.S. women's market. 22

• In the *Ms.* Gazette, we do a brief report on a congressional hearing into chemicals used in hair dyes that are absorbed through the skin and may be carcinogenic. Newspapers report this too, but Clairol, a Bristol-Myers subsidiary that makes dozens of products—a few of which have just begun to advertise in *Ms.*—is outraged. Not at newspapers or newsmagazines, just at us. It's bad enough that *Ms.* is the only women's magazine refusing to provide the usual "complementary" articles and beauty photos, but to criticize one of their categories—*that* is going too far. 23

We offer to publish a letter from Clairol telling its side of the story. In an excess of solicitousness, we even put this letter in the Gazette, not in Letters to the Editors where it belongs. Nonetheless—and in spite of surveys that show *Ms.* readers are active women who use more of almost everything Clairol makes than do the readers of any other women's magazine—*Ms.* gets almost none of these ads for the rest of its natural life. 24

Meanwhile, Clairol changes its hair coloring formula, apparently in response to the hearings we reported. 25

• Our saleswomen set out early to attract ads for consumer electronics: sound equipment, calculators, computers, VCRs, and the like. We 26 know that our readers are determined to be included in the technological revolution. We know from reader surveys that *Ms.* readers are buying this stuff in numbers as high as those of magazines like *Playboy,* or "men 18 to 34," the prime targets of the consumer electronics industry. Moreover, unlike traditional women's products that our readers buy but don't need to read articles about, these are subjects they want covered in our pages. There actually *is* a supportive editorial atmosphere.

"But women don't understand technology," say executives at the end of ad presentations. "Maybe not," we respond, "but neither do men—and we all buy it." 27

"If women *do* buy it," say the decision-makers, "they're asking their husbands and boyfriends what to buy first." We produce letters from *Ms.* readers saying how turned off they are when salesmen say things like "Let me know when your husband can come in." 28

After several years of this, we get a few ads for compact sound systems. Some of them come from JVC, whose vice president, Harry Elias, is trying to convince his Japanese bosses that there is something called a women's market. At his invitation, I find myself speaking at huge trade shows in Chicago and Las Vegas, trying to persuade JVC dealers that showrooms don't have to be locker rooms where women are made to feel unwelcome. But as it turns out, the shows themselves are part of the problem. In Las Vegas, the only women around the technology displays are seminude models serving champagne. In Chicago, the big attraction is Marilyn Chambers, who followed Linda Lovelace of *Deep Throat* fame as Chuck Traynor's captive and/or employee. VCRs are being demonstrated with her porn videos. 29

In the end, we get ads for a car stereo now and then, but no VCRs; some IBM personal computers, but no Apple or Japanese ones. We notice that office magazines like *Working Woman* and *Savvy* don't benefit as much as they should from office equipment ads either. In the electronics world, women and technology seem mutually exclusive. It remains a decade behind even Detroit. 30

• Because we get letters from little girls who love toy trains, and who ask our help in changing ads and box-top photos that feature little boys only, we try to get toy-train ads from Lionel. It turns out that Lionel executives *have* been concerned about little girls. They made a pink train, and were surprised when it didn't sell. 31

Lionel bows to consumer pressure with a photograph of a boy *and* a girl—but only on some of their boxes. They fear that, if trains are associated with girls, they will be devalued in the minds of boys. Needless to say, *Ms.* gets no train ads, and little girls remain a mostly unexplored market. By 1986, Lionel is put up for sale. 32

But for different reasons, we haven't had much luck with other kinds of toys either. In spite of many articles in child-rearing; an annual listing of nonsexist, multi-racial toys by Letty Cottin Pogrebin; 33

Stories for Free Children, a regular feature also edited by Letty; and other prizewinning features for or about children, we get virtually no toy ads. Generations of *Ms.* saleswomen explain to toy manufacturers that a larger proportion of *Ms.* readers have preschool children than do the readers of other women's magazines, but this industry can't believe feminists have or care about children.

• When *Ms.* begins, the staff decides not to accept ads for feminine hygiene sprays or cigarettes: they are damaging and carry no appropriate health warnings. Though we don't think we should tell our readers what to do, we do think we should provide facts so they can decide for themselves. Since the antismoking lobby has been pressing for health warnings on cigarette adds, we decide to take them only as they comply. 34

Philip Morris is among the first to do so. One of its brands, Virginia Slims, is also sponsoring women's tennis and the first national polls of women's opinions. On the other hand, the Virginia Slims theme, "You've come a long way, baby," has more than a "baby" problem. It makes smoking a symbol of progress for women. 35

We explain to Philip Morris that this slogan won't do well in our pages, but they are convinced its success with some women means it will work with *all* women. Finally, we agree to publish an ad for a Virginia Slims calendar as a test. The letters from readers are critical—and smart. For instance: Would you show a black man picking cotton, the same man in a Cardin suit, and symbolize the antislavery and civil rights movements by smoking? Of course not. But instead of honoring the test results, the Philip Morris people seem angry to be proven wrong. They take away ads for *all* their many brands. 36

This costs *Ms.* about $250,000 the first year. After five years, we can no longer keep track. Occasionally, a new set of executives listens to *Ms.* saleswomen, but because we won't take Virginia Slims, not one Philip Morris product returns to our pages for the next 16 years. 37

Gradually, we also realize our naiveté in thinking we *could* decide against taking cigarette ads. They became a disproportionate support of magazines the moment they were banned on television, and few magazines could compete and survive without them; certainly not *Ms.*, which lacks so many other categories. By the time statistics in the 1980s showed that women's rate of lung cancer was approaching men's, the necessity of taking cigarette ads has become a kind of prison. 38

• General Mills, Pillsbury, Carnation, DelMonte, Dole, Kraft, Stouffer, Hormel, Nabisco: you name the food giant, we try it. But no matter how desirable the *Ms.* readership, our lack of recipes is lethal. 39

We explain to them that placing food ads *only* next to recipes associates food with work. For many women, it is a negative that works *against* the ads. Why not place food ads in diverse media without 40 recipes (thus reaching more men, who are now a third of the shoppers in supermarkets anyway), and leave the recipes to specialty magazines like *Gourmet* (a third of whose readers are also men)?

These arguments elicit interest, but except for an occasional ad for 41 a convenience food, instant coffee, diet drinks, yogurt, or such extras as avocados and almonds, this mainstay of the publishing industry stays closed to us. Period.

• Traditionally, wines and liquors didn't advertise to women: men 42 were thought to make the brand decisions, even if women did the buying. But after endless presentations, we begin to make a dent in this category. Thanks to the unconventional Michel Roux of Carillon Importers (distributors of Grand Marnier, Absolut Vodka, and others), who assumes that food and drink have no gender, some ads are leaving their men's club.

Beermakers are still selling masculinity. It takes *Ms.* fully eight 43 years to get its first beer ad (Michelob). In general, however, liquor ads are less stereotyped in their imagery—and far less controlling of the editorial content around them—than are women's products. But given the underrepresentation of other categories, these very facts tend to create a disproportionate number of alcohol ads in the pages of *Ms.* This in turn dismays readers worried about women and alcoholism.

▪ We hear in 1980 that women in the Soviet Union have been pro- 44 ducing feminist *samizdat* (underground, self-published books) and circulating them throughout the country. As punishment, four of the leaders have been exiled. Though we are operating on our usual shoestring, we solicit individual contributions to send Robin Morgan to interview these women in Vienna.

The result is an exclusive cover story that includes the first news of 45 a populist peace movement against the Afghanistan occupation, a prediction of *glasnost* to come, and a grass-roots, intimate view of Soviet women's lives. From the popular press to women's studies courses, the response is great. The story wins a Front Page award.

Nonetheless, this journalistic coup undoes years of efforts to get an 46 ad schedule from Revlon. Why? Because the Soviet women on our cover *are not wearing makeup.*

• Four years of research and presentations go into convincing airlines 47 that women now make travel choices and business trips. United, the first airline to advertise in *Ms.,* is so impressed with the response from our readers that one of its executives appears in a film for our ad presentations. As usual, good ads get great results.

But we have problems unrelated to such results. For instance: be- 48 cause American Airlines flight attendants include among their labor demands the stipulation that they could choose to have their last names preceded by "Ms." on their name tags—in a long-delayed revolt against the standard, "I am your pilot, Captain Rothgart, and this is your flight attendant, Cindy Sue"—American officials seem to hold the magazine responsible. We get no ads.

There is still a different problem at Eastern. A vice president cancels subscriptions for thousands of copies on Eastern flights. Why? Because he is offended by ads for lesbian poetry journals in the *Ms.* Classified. A "family airline," as he explains to me coldly on the phone, has to "draw the line somewhere."

It's obvious that *Ms.* can't exclude lesbians and serve women. We've been trying to make that point ever since our first issue included an article by and about lesbians, and both Suzanne Levine, our managing editor, and I were lectured by such heavy hitters as Ed Kosner, then editor of *Newsweek* (and now of *New York Magazine*), who insisted that *Ms.* should "position" itself *against* lesbians. But our advertisers have paid to reach a guaranteed number of readers, and soliciting new subscriptions to compensate for Eastern would cost $150,000 plus rebating money in the meantime.

Like almost everything ad-related, this presents an elaborate organizing problem. After days of searching for sympathetic members of the Eastern board, Frank Thomas, president of the Ford Foundation, kindly offers to call Roswell Gilpatrick, a director of Eastern. I talk with Mr. Gilpatrick, who calls Frank Borman, then the president of Eastern. Frank Borman calls me to say that his airline is not in the business of censoring magazines: *Ms.* will be returned to Eastern flights.

• Women's access to insurance and credit is vital, but with the exception of Equitable and a few other ad pioneers, such financial services address men. For almost a decade after the Equal Credit Opportunity Act passes in 1974, we try to convince American Express that women are a growth market—but nothing works.

Finally, a former professor of Russian named Jerry Welsh becomes head of marketing. He assumes that women should be cardholders, and persuades his colleagues to feature women in a campaign. Thanks to this 1980s series, the growth rate for female cardholders surpasses that for men.

For this article, I asked Jerry Welsh if he would explain why American Express waited so long. "Sure," he said, "they were afraid of having a 'pink' card."

• Women of color read *Ms.* in disproportionate numbers. This is a source of pride to *Ms.* staffers, who are also more racially representative than the editors of other women's magazines. But this reality is obscured by ads filled with enough white women to make a reader snowblind.

Pat Carbine remembers mostly "astonishment" when she requested African American, Hispanic, Asian, and other diverse images. Marcia Ann Gillespie, a *Ms.* editor who was previously the editor in chief of *Essence,* witnesses ad bias a second time: having tried for *Essence* to get white advertisers to use black imagés (Revlon did so eventually, but L'Oréal, Lauder, Chanel, and other companies never did), she sees similar problems getting integrated ads for an integrated magazine. Indeed, the ad world often creates black and Hispanic ads only for black and Hispanic media. In an exact parallel of the fear that marketing a product to women will endanger its appeal to men, the response is usually, "But your [white] readers won't identify."

In fact, those we are able to get—for instance, a Max Factor ad 57 made for *Essence* that Linda Wachner gives us after she becomes president—are praised by white readers, too. But there are pathetically few such images.

• By the end of 1986, production and mailing costs have risen astro- 58 nomically, ad income is flat, and competition for ads is stiffer than ever. The 60/40 preponderance of edit over ads that we promised to readers becomes 50/50; children's stories, most poetry, and some fiction are casualties of less space; in order to get variety into limited pages, the length (and sometimes the depth) of articles suffers; and, though we do refuse most of the ads that would look like a parody in our pages, we get so worn down that some slip through. (See this issue's No Comment.) Still, readers perform miracles. Though we haven't been able to afford a subscription mailing in two years, they maintain our guaranteed circulation of 450,000.

Nonetheless, media reports on *Ms.* often insist that our unprof- 59 itability must be due to reader disinterest. The myth that advertisers simply follow readers is very strong. Not one reporter notes that other comparable magazines our size (say, *Vanity Fair* or *The Atlantic*) have been losing more money in one year than *Ms.* has lost in 16 years. No matter how much never-to-be-recovered cash is poured into starting a magazine or keeping one going, appearances seem to be all that matter. (Which is why we haven't been able to explain our fragile state in public. Nothing causes ad-flight like the smell of nonsuccess.)

My healthy response is anger. My not-so-healthy response is con- 60 stant worry. Also an obsession with finding one more rescue. There is hardly a night when I don't wake up with sweaty palms and pounding heart, scared that we won't be able to pay the printer or the post office; scared most of all that closing our doors will hurt the women's movement.

Out of chutzpah and desperation, I arrange a lunch with Leonard 61 Lauder, president of Estée Lauder. With the exception of Clinique (the brainchild of Carol Phillips), none of the Lauder's hundreds of products has been advertised in *Ms.* A year's schedule of ads for just three or four of them could save us. Indeed, as the scion of a family-owned company whose ad practices are followed by the beauty industry, he is one of the few men who could liberate many pages in all women's magazines just by changing his mind about "complementary copy."

Over a lunch that costs more than we can pay for some articles, I   62
explain the need for his leadership. I also lay out the record of *Ms.*:
more literary and journalistic prizes won, more new issues introduced
into the mainstream, new writers discovered, and impact on society
than any other magazine; more articles that became books, stories that
became movies, ideas that became television series, and newly advertised products that became profitable; and, most important for him, a
place for his ads to reach women who aren't reachable through any
other women's magazine. Indeed, if there is one constant characteristic of the ever-changing *Ms.* readership, it is their impact as leaders.
Whether it's waiting until later to have first babies, or pioneering
PABA as sun protection in cosmetics, *whatever* they are doing today, a
third to a half of American women will be doing three to five years
from now. It's never failed.

But, he says, *Ms.* readers are not *our* women. They're not inter-   63
ested in things like fragrance and blush-on. If they were, *Ms.* would
write articles about them.

On the contrary, I explain, surveys show they are more likely to   64
buy such things than the readers of, say, *Cosmopolitan* or *Vogue*. They're
good customers because they're out in world enough to need several
sets of everything: home, work, purse, travel, gym, and so on. They
just don't need to read articles about these things. Would he ask a
men's magazine to publish monthly columns on how to shave before
he advertised Aramis products (his line for men)?

He concedes that beauty features are often concocted more for ad-   65
vertisers than readers. But *Ms.* isn't appropriate for his ads anyway, he
explains. Why? Because Estée Lauder is selling "a kept-woman mentality."

I can't quite believe this. Sixty percent of the users of his products   66
are salaried, and generally resemble *Ms.* readers. Besides, his company
has the appeal of having been started by a creative and hardworking
woman, his mother, Estée Lauder.

That doesn't matter, he says. He knows his customers, and they   67
would *like* to be kept women. That's why he will never advertise in *Ms.*

In November 1987, by vote of the Ms. Foundation for Education   68
and Communication (*Ms.*'s owner and publisher, the media subsidiary
of the Ms. Foundation for Women), *Ms.* was sold to a company whose
officers, Australian feminists Sandra Yates and Anne Summers, raised
the investment money in their country that *Ms.* couldn't find in its
own. They also started *Sassy* for teenage women.

In their two-year tenure, circulation was raised to 550,000 by in-   69
vestment in circulation mailings, and, to the dismay of some readers,
editorial features on clothes and new products made a more traditional
bid for ads. Nonetheless, ad pages fell below previous levels. In addition, *Sassy*, whose fresh voice and sexual frankness were an unprecedented success with young readers, was targeted by two mothers from

Indiana who began, as one of them put it, "calling every Christian organization I could think of." In response to this controversy, several crucial advertisers pulled out.

Such links between ads and editorial content were a problem in Australia, too, but to a lesser degree. "Our readers pay two times more for their magazines," Anne explained, "so advertisers have less power to threaten a magazine's viability." 70

"I was shocked," said Sandra Yates with characteristic directness. "In Australia, we think you have freedom of the press—but you don't." 71

Since Anne and Sandra had not met their budget's projections for ad revenue, their investors forced a sale. In October 1989, *Ms.* and *Sassy* were bought by Dale Lang, owner of *Working Mother, Working Woman,* and one of the few independent publishing companies left among the conglomerates. In response to a request from the original *Ms.* staff—as well as to reader letters urging that *Ms.* continue, plus his own belief that *Ms.* would benefit his other magazines by blazing a trail—he agreed to try the ad-free, reader-supported *Ms.* you hold now and to give us complete editorial control. 72

II.

Do you think, as I once did, that advertisers make decisions based on solid research? Well, think again. "Broadly speaking," says Joseph Smith of Oxtoby-Smith, Inc., a consumer research firm, "there is no persuasive evidence that the editorial context of an ad matters." 73

Advertisers who demand such "complementary copy," even in the absence of respectable studies, clearly are operating under a double standard. The same food companies place ads in *People* with no recipes. Cosmetics companies support *The New Yorker* with no regular beauty columns. So where does this habit of controlling the content of women's magazines come from? 74

Tradition. Ever since *Ladies Magazine* debuted in Boston in 1828, editorial copy directed to women has been informed by something other than its readers' wishes. There were no ads then, but in an age when married women were legal minors with no right to their own money, there was another revenue source to be kept in mind: husbands. "Husbands may rest assured," wrote editor Sarah Josepha Hale, "that nothing found in these pages shall cause her [his wife] to be less assiduous in preparing for his reception or encourage her to 'usurp station' or encroach upon prerogatives of men." 75

Hale went on to become the editor of *Godey's Lady's Book,* a magazine featuring "fashion plates": engravings of dresses for readers to take to their seamstresses or copy themselves. Hale added "how to" articles, which set the tone for women's service magazines for years to come: how to write politely, avoid sunburn, and—in no fewer than 76

1,200 words—how to maintain a goose quill pen. She advocated education for women but avoided controversy. Just as most women's magazines now avoid politics, poll their readers on issues like abortion but rarely take a stand, and praise socially approved lifestyles, Hale saw to it that *Godey's* avoided the hot topics of its day: slavery, abolition, and women's suffrage.

What definitively turned women's magazines into catalogs, however, were two events: Ellen Butterick's invention of the clothing pattern in 1863 and the mass manufacture of patent medicines containing everything from colored water to cocaine. For the first time, readers could purchase what magazines encouraged them to want. As such magazines became more profitable, they also began to attract men as editors. (Most women's magazines continued to have men as top editors until the feminist 1970s.) Edward Bok, who became editor of *The Ladies' Home Journal* in 1889, discovered the power of advertisers when he rejected ads for patent medicines and found that other advertisers canceled in retribution. In the early 20th century, *Good Housekeeping* started its Institute to "test and approve" products. Its Seal of Approval became the grandfather of current "value added" programs that offer advertisers such bonuses as product sampling and department store promotions. 77

By the time suffragists finally won the vote in 1920, women's magazines had become too entrenched as catalogs to help women learn how to use it. The main function was to create a desire for products, teach how to use products, and make products a crucial part of gaining social approval, pleasing a husband, and performing as a homemaker. Some related articles and short stories were included to persuade women to pay for these catalogs. But articles were neither consumerist nor rebellious. Even fiction was usually subject to formula: if a woman had any sexual life outside marriage, she was supposed to come to a bad end. 78

In 1965, Helen Gurley Brown began to change part of that formula by bringing "the sexual revolution" to women's magazines—but in an ad-oriented way. Attracting multiple men required even more consumerism, as the Cosmo Girl made clear, than finding one husband. 79

In response to the workplace revolution of the 1970s, traditional women's magazines—that is, "trade books" for women working at home—were joined by *Savvy, Working Woman,* and other trade books for women working in offices. But by keeping the fashion/beauty/entertaining articles necessary to get traditional ads and then adding career articles besides, they inadvertently produced the antifeminist stereotype of Super Woman. The male-imitative, dress-for-success woman carrying a briefcase became the media image of a woman worker, even though a blue-collar woman's salary was often higher than her glorified secretarial sister's, and though women at a real brief- 80 case level are statistically rare. Needless to say, these dress-for-success women were also thin, white, and beautiful.

In recent years, advertisers' control over the editorial content of [81] women's magazines has become so institutionalized that it is written into "insertion orders" or dictated to ad salespeople as official policy. The following are recent typical orders to women's magazines:

• Dow's Cleaning Products stipulates that ads for its Vivid and Spray 'n Wash products should be adjacent to "children or fashion editorial"; ads for Bathroom Cleaner should be next to "home furnishing/family" features; and so on for other brands. "If a magazine fails for ½ the brands or more," the Dow order warns, "it will be omitted from further consideration."

• Bristol-Myers, the parent of Clairol, Windex, Drano, Bufferin, and much more, stipulates that ads be placed next to "a full page of compatible editorial."

• S.C. Johnson & Son, makers of Johnson Wax, lawn and laundry products, insect sprays, hair sprays, and so on, orders that its ads *"should not be opposite extremely controversial features or material antithetical to the nature/copy of the advertised product."* (Italics theirs.)

• Maidenform, manufacturer of bras and other apparel, leaves a blank for the particular product and states: "The creative concept of the ___ campaign, and the very nature of the product itself appeal to the positive emotions of the reader/consumer. Therefore, it is imperative that all editorial adjacencies reflect that same positive tone. The editorial must not be negative in content or lend itself contrary to the ___ product imagery/message (e.g., *editorial relating to illness, disillusionment, large size fashion, etc.*)." (Italics mine.)

• The De Beers diamond company, a big seller of engagement rings, prohibits magazines from placing its ads with "adjacencies to hard news or anti/love-romance themed editorial."

• Procter & Gamble, one of this country's most powerful and diversified advertisers, stands out in the memory of Anne Summers and Sandra Yates (no mean feat in this context): its products were not to be placed in *any* issue that included *any* material on gun control, abortion, the occult, cults, or the disparagement of religion. Caution was also demanded in any issued covering sex or drugs, even for educational purposes.

Those are the most obvious chains around women's magazines. [82] There are also rules so clear they needn't be written down: for instance, an overall "look" compatible with beauty and fashion ads. Even "real" nonmodel women photographed for a woman's magazine are usually made up, dressed in credited clothes, and retouched out of all reality. When editors do include articles on less-than cheerful subjects (for instance, domestic violence), they tend to keep them short and unillustrated. The point is to be "upbeat." Just as women in the street are asked, "Why don't you smile, honey?" women's magazines acquire an institutional smile.

Within the text itself, praise for advertisers' products has become so ritualized that fields like "beauty writing" have been invented. One of its frequent practitioners explained seriously that "It's a difficult art. How many new adjectives can you find? How much greater can you make a lipstick sound? The FDA restricts what companies can say on labels, but we create illusion. And ad agencies are on the phone all the time pushing you to get their product in. A lot of them keep the business based on how many editorial clippings they produce every month. The worst are products," like Lauder's as the writer confirmed, "with their own name involved. It's all ego." 83

Often, editorial becomes one giant ad. Last November, for instance, *Lear's* featured an elegant woman executive on the cover. On the contents page, we learned she was wearing Guerlain makeup and Samsara, a new fragrance by Guerlain. Inside were full-page ads for Samsara and Guerlain antiwrinkle cream. In the cover profile, we learned that this executive was responsible for launching Samsara and is Guerlain's director of public relations. When the *Columbia Journalism Review* did one of the few articles to include women's magazines in coverage of the influence of ads, editor Frances Lear was quoted as defending her magazine because "this kind of thing is done all the time." 84

Often, advertisers also plunge odd-shaped ads into the text, no matter what the cost to the readers. At *Woman's Day,* a magazine originally founded by a supermarket chain, editor in chief Ellen Levine said, "The day the copy had to rag around a chicken leg was not a happy one." 85

Advertisers are also adamant about where in a magazine their ads appear. When Revlon was not placed as the first beauty ad in one Hearst magazine, for instance, Revlon pulled its ads from *all* Hearst magazines. Ruth Whitney, editor in chief of *Glamour,* attributes some of these demands to "ad agencies wanting to prove to a client that they've squeezed the last drop of blood out of a magazine." She also is, she says, "sick and tired of hearing that women's magazines are controlled by cigarette ads." Relatively speaking, she's right. To be as censoring as are many advertisers for women's products, tobacco companies would have to demand articles in praise of smoking and expect glamorous photos of beautiful women smoking their brands. 86

I don't mean to imply that the editors I quote here share my objections to ads: most assume that women's magazines have to be the way they are. But it's also true that only former editors can be completely honest. "Most of the pressure came in the form of direct product mentions," explains Sey Chassler, who was editor in chief of *Redbook* from the sixties to the eighties. "We got threats from the big 87 guys, the Revlons, blackmail threats. They wouldn't run ads unless we credited them.

"But it's not fair to single out the beauty advertisers because these 88 pressures came from everybody. Advertisers want to know two things: What are you going to charge me? What *else* are you going to do for me? It's a holdup. For instance, management felt that fiction took up too much space. They couldn't put any advertising in that. For the last ten years, the number of fiction entries into the National Magazine Awards had declined.

"And pressures are getting worse. More magazines are more 89 bottom-line oriented because they have been taken over by companies with no interest in publishing.

"I also think advertisers do this to women's magazines especially," 90 he concluded, "because of the general disrespect they have for women."

Even media experts who don't give a damn about women's maga- 91 zines are alarmed by the spread of this ad-edit linkage. In a climate *The Wall Street Journal* describes as an unacknowledged Depression for media, women's products are increasingly able to take their low standards wherever they go. For instance: newsweeklies publish uncritical stories on fashion and fitness. *The New York Times Magazine* recently ran an article on "firming creams," complete with mentions of advertisers. *Vanity Fair* published a profile of one major advertiser, Ralph Lauren, illustrated by the same photographer who does his ads, and turned the lifestyle of another, Calvin Klein, into a cover story. Even the outrageous *Spy* has toned down since it began to go after fashion ads.

And just to make us really worry, films and books, the last media 92 that go directly to the public without having to attract ads first, are in danger, too. Producers are beginning to depend on payments for displaying products in movies, and books are now being commissioned by companies like Federal Express.

But the truth is that women's products—like women's maga- 93 zines—have never been the subjects of much serious reporting anyway. News and general interest publications, including the "style" or "living" sections of newspapers, write about food and clothing as cooking and fashion, and almost never evaluate such products by brand name. Though chemical additives, pesticides, and animal fats are major health risks in the United States, and clothes, shoddy or not, absorb more consumer dollars than cars, this lack of information is serious. So is ignoring the contents of beauty products that are absorbed into our bodies through our skins, and that have profit margins so big they would make a loan shark blush.

III.

What could women's magazines be like if they were as free as   94
books? as realistic as newspapers? as creative as films? as diverse as
women's lives? We don't know.

But we'll only find out if we take women's magazines seriously. If   95
readers were to act in a concerted way to change traditional practices
of *all* women's magazines and the marketing of *all* women's products,
we could do it. After all, they are operating on our consumer dollars;
money that we now control. You and I could:

• write to editors and publishers (with copies of advertisers) that
we're willing to pay *more* for magazines with editorial independence,
but will *not* continue to pay for those that are just editorial extensions
of ads;

• write to advertisers (with copies to editors and publishers) that we
want fiction, political reporting, consumer reporting—whatever is, or
is not, supported by their ads;

• put as much energy into breaking advertising's control over content
as into changing the images in ads, or protesting ads for harmful products like cigarettes.;

• support only those women's magazines and products that take *us* seriously as readers and consumers.

Those of us in the magazine world can also use the carrot-and-   96
stick technique. For instance: pointing out that, if magazines were a
regulated medium like television, the demands of advertisers would be
against FCC rules. Payola and extortion could be punished. As it is,
there are probably illegalities. A magazine's postal rates are determined
by the ratio of ad to edit pages, and the former costs more than the latter. So much for the stick.

The carrot means appealing to enlightened self-interest. For in-   97
stance: there are many studies showing that the greatest factor in de-
termining an ad's effectiveness is the credibility of its surroundings.
The "higher the rating of editorial believability," concluded a 1987 survey by the *Journal of Advertising Research*," the higher the rating of the
advertising." Thus, an impenetrable wall between edit and ads would
also be in the best interest of advertisers.

Unfortunately, few agencies or clients hear such arguments. Edi-   98
tors often maintain the false purity of refusing to talk to them at all. Instead, they see ad salespeople who know little about editorial, are
trained in business as usual, and are usually paid by commission. Editors might also band together to take on controversy. That happened
once when all the major women's magazines did articles in the same
month on the Equal Rights Amendment. It could happen again.

It's almost three years away from life between the grindstones of   99
advertising pressures and readers' needs. I'm just beginning to realize
how edges got smoothed down—in spite of all our resistance.

I remember feeling put upon when I changed "Porsche" to "car" in 100 a piece about Nazi imagery in German pornography by Andrea Dworkin—feeling sure Andrea would understand that Volkswagen, the distributor of Porsche and one of our few supportive advertisers, asked only to be far away from Nazi subjects. It's taken me all this time to realize that Andrea was the one with a right to feel put upon.

Even as I write this, I get a call from a writer for *Elle*, who is doing 101 a whole article on where women part their hair. Why, she wants to know, do I part mine in the middle?

It's all so familiar. A writer trying to make something of a nothing 102 assignment; an editor laboring to think of new ways to attract ads; readers assuming that other women must want this ridiculous stuff; more women suffering for lack of information, insight, creativity, and laughter that could be on these same pages.

I ask you: Can't we do better than this? 103

GUY COOK

The Discourse of Advertising

Guy Cook is Senior Lecturer in Applied Linguistics at the London University Institute of Education and the author of *Discourse* (1989) and *The Discourse of Advertising* (1992), from which the selection below is excerpted. Like many applied linguists, Cook has been interested in such "subliterary" matters as jokes, graffiti, and popular songs—how they communicate, how they combine sounds, music, and images with words to create meaning. Cook's detailed and systematic analysis of two advertisements may provide a model useful to readers as they attempt their own analyses of television advertising in particular. His active but rather neutral interest in the way the electronic media work stands in sharp contrast to the alarms sounded by Randall Jarrell ("A Sad Heart at the Supermarket") and Neil Postman ("Now . . . This").

Let us take a fairly ordinary tv ad, firstly as words only, and sec- 1 ondly as words in interaction with music and pictures. The example raises two quite separate problems: how to transcribe music and pictures on the page; and how to analyze their interaction with each other and with language. The ad is a tv commercial for the soft drink Sprite (screened in Britain in 1990). The words are:

> *When the heat is on,*
> *And the pace is slow,*
> *There's a cool fresh world*

Where you can go:
Clear, crisp and light,
It tastes of Sprite.

A twist of lemon
For a taste sensation;
A squeeze of lime
Is the perfect combination:
Clear, crisp and light,
Sheer taste of Sprite;
Clear, crisp and light,
Sheer taste of Sprite.

During the course of the ad two small written texts appear very   2
briefly at the bottom of the screen. The first says

Sprite and Diet Sprite are registered trademarks of the Coca-Cola Company

and the second

Diet Sprite can help slimming or weight control only as part of a calorie controlled diet.

In addition, the words "Sprite" and "Diet Sprite" are visible on the product itself. The jingle, the small print, and the brand names are the only language. Along with these words go twenty camera shots of four separate locations; and the words are sung—rather than spoken—by a man's voice (with inevitable cheerfulness!).

The music and the singing voice pass through four phases, distin-   3
guished by marked changes in speed and beat. The first phase conveys a sense of urgency building to a climax; the second phase releases the tension of the first with a bouncy and regular rhythm; in the third phase this rhythm disappears, there is an absence of percussion, and sound effects creating an air of magic and mystery; finally the fourth phase repeats the second, confident and animated as before.

The relation of the words to accompanying pictures and to these   4
phases of the music is set out, approximately, below:

Words		Pictures

SCENE ONE: THE TRAFFIC JAM
MUSIC BUILDING TO A CLIMAX

Words		Pictures
When the heat is on	1	Couple in an open car in a traffic jam at the entrance to coastal (Mediterranean?) road tunnel. The driver of a truck behind has left his cab to try to see ahead.

And the pace is slow | Everyone is very hot and frustrated.
There's a cool fresh world 2 Close-up of hands reaching into a coolbox containing ice, Sprite and Diet Sprite.

Where you can go 3 Close-up of the couple in the car. The man (the driver) looks at the woman.
4 Both swig from their cans.
5 Camera's "eye" moves through the opening in the top of the can, into the Sprite inside!

SCENE TWO: THE TOBOGGAN RUN
MUSIC INTENSIFIES, SPEEDS UP, LOOSENS

Clear, crisp and light 6 A professional toboggan run as seen from a high-speed toboggan emerging from a tunnel.

It tastes of Sprite 7 Close-up of the yellow helmet of the tobogganer.
8 Toboggan run as seen by the tobogganer.
(9/10 Repeat 7/8)

A twist of lemon 11 The track is blocked by a giant slice of lemon.

For a taste sensation 12 We see the lemon reflected in the visor of the approaching tobogganer.
13 Close-up of the slice of lemon: drops of juice are oozing out of it.
14 We now see there are two people on the toboggan, one holding tightly to the other. The toboggan smashes through the lemon.

SCENE THREE: IN THE TUNNEL
MUSIC SLOWS, LOSES BEAT, GROWS WHIMSICAL

15 An underwater shot inside the toboggan tunnel and/or the can of Sprite. We are moving through ice cubes towards the surface.

A squeeze of lime 16 Camera comes to a slice of lime at the other end of the tunnel, and breaks through.

Is the perfect combination 17 The two tobogganers are out in the open again. Their toboggan is approaching another tunnel.

SCENE FOUR: MOVING TRAFFIC
MUSIC RETURNS TO REGULAR CONFIDENT BEAT

Clear, crisp and light	18	The toboggan enters the tunnel.
Sheer taste of Sprite	19	Close-up of the couple back in
Clear, crisp and light		the car, moving fast. The woman is
		drinking from a can of Sprite.
Sheer taste of Sprite	20	The car emerges from a tunnel on a
		coastal road. The man and woman are
		cool, happy and relaxed.

Taken together with the pictures of these four scenes, and the four corresponding phases of the music, the words of the jingle, which are so one-dimensional in isolation, take on new meanings, and contribute to a complex set of visual metaphors and parallels. A number of words, phrases and clauses become puns. Thus

When the heat is on,

no longer has only its dead-metaphorical sense of

When life is difficult

it also refers to the uncomfortable heat experienced in the waiting vehicles. By the same process

And the pace is slow,

refers specifically to the traffic jam, as well as, idiomatically, to a dull period of life. Alternatively, or additionally, the pictures reinstate the lost force of the dead metaphor from which the idiomatic sense of these phrases derives. In the line

There's a cool fresh world

"world" in the context of Scene Two refers to the fantasy world of the toboggan run which is apparently inside the can; the words

Where you can go

accompany the transition shot in which we see the can from the point of view of the drinker, and seem to enter into it. In this fantasy world, inside the Sprite, all the undesirable qualities of the world in the opening scene are reversed. There is cool snow and fast movement. In the lines of the bouncy chorus which accompany these new pictures, "it" refers both to this fantasy world, and to the Sprite itself.

Clear, crisp and light,
It tastes of Sprite.

The visually created puns continue.

A twist of lemon

is also on a twist (a bend) in the toboggan run, and a twist in the tale—
for who would expect to find either a toboggan run inside a soft-drink
can, or a slice of lemon on a toboggan run? The lemon, appearing on
the track, is both a fantasy within a fantasy (and thus at an even further remove) but also, because Sprite tastes of lemon, the beginning of
a transition back to the opening scene, for on the other side of the
lemon we are back in the can, and as we emerge from it the car
emerges from the tunnel in Scene Four. Perhaps it is far-fetched to say
that

> A squeeze of lime

refers punningly to the squeezing of the front rider by the pillion rider,
but I have no doubt that the words

> Is the perfect combination

occurring with the picture of the two tobogganers, refer to their athletic teamwork, to the relationship of the couple in the car (who are
presumably also the tobogganers), to the combination of Sprite with a
hot day, and to the combination of flavours in the Sprite itself.

These complex interrelationships between the three worlds (traffic   6
jam, toboggan run, Sprite can) are all aided by the image of the tunnel,
which occurs in each one, and whose darkness effects the transition
from one world to the next. Connections between the worlds are reinforced by the puns, but separated in mood by changes in the music, allowing the ad to make two suggestions—both frequent in ads—that

> The product is a panacea, the product is a bond of love.

In this ad, the couple (good-looking, young, affluent, happy, heterosexual) have a problem: they are stuck in a traffic jam on a hot day.
Perhaps this is a symbol of a difficult or colourless life "the heat is
on . . . the pace is slow." They drink Sprite and enter its magic world.
Within that world, the problems of heat and inertia do not exist; but
when they return from that world these problems have ceased to exist
in their everyday world too. We do not see what started the traffic
moving, but we feel it was the Sprite.

The young man and woman are, like the flavours in Sprite, "The   7
perfect combination." They are also dressed in the Sprite colours of
yellow and green—both in the car, and on the toboggan. As they drink
they look at each other. The product appears to contribute to their
compatibility.

What I have tried to show by this analysis is that the effect of the   8
ad is not to be found in any of the three major modes alone, but only
in their combination. Each mode gains from the other.

.   .   .

Pictures, however, do far more than carry a story. In what is still one of the best essays on advertising, "Keeping upset with the Joneses," Marshall McLuhan wrote

> The copy is merely a punning gag to distract the critical faculties while the picture . . . goes to work on the hypnotized viewer. Those who have spent their lives protesting about "false and misleading ad copy" are godsends to advertisers, as teetotallers are to brewers, and moral censors are to books and films. The protestors are the best acclaimers and accelerators. Since the advent of pictures, the job of the ad copy is as incidental and latent as the meaning of a poem is to a poem, or the words of a song are to a song. Highly literate people cannot cope with the nonverbal art of the pictorial, so they dance impatiently up and down to express a pointless disapproval that renders them futile and gives new power and authority to the ads. The unconscious depth-messages of ads are never attacked by the literate, because of their incapacity to notice or discuss nonverbal forms of arrangement and meaning. They have not the art to argue with pictures.

(McLuhan 1964: 246)[1]

The foresight of these remarks, published at a time when both ads and analyses of them tended to be quite rudimentary, is striking. Advertisers rely more and more upon pictures, while their critics still harp upon the "literal" meaning of copy. (Even a quick glance through the *British Code of Advertising Practice,* or the case reports of successful complaints against ads, reveals that a great deal of official criticism in the UK centres upon wording, despite its demonstrably subsidiary role in many cases; the same is true of Federal Trade Commission Reports in the USA.)

McLuhan, publishing at a time when tv advertising was still in its infancy, and ads were far more reliant upon words and literal meanings than now, might have been excused for misjudging the relative power of different modes. Thirty years later, not only have pictures gained ground, but also language, where it is used, leans further and further towards the meanings it derives from interaction with pictures. In addition, many ads create powerful and complex messages entirely—or almost entirely—through pictures and music, and are virtually language-free. In illustration of this, I shall examine one such ad in detail.

This is "Last Stick," a tv and cinema ad from 1990–1 for the internationally best-selling chewing gum Wrigley's Spearmint. It too is a narrative, using thirty-six frames in sixty seconds, but it is not for its skill in compressed story-telling that I wish to analyse it here. The tale unfolds to the music of "All Right Now" by Free, a pounding pop song of 1970 (successfully re-released at the same time as the ad). Though

---

1. *Understanding Media* (New York, 1964), p. 246.

the words of this song also concern a meeting between two strangers, I shall treat this ad, its message and its methods as fundamentally non-verbal, as I believe they are, though I also briefly refer to the mood of the song in the analysis. In order to discuss the significance of the different images used, I shall first need to give an outline of the story.

The ad begins with a broad panoramic shot of a bus—"The Westerner"—making its way in bright sunlight past high mountains through prairies full of ripe wheat. The camera shifts to the interior of the bus where a young man and a young woman sit across the aisle from each other, on the inner seats. Both are blond, white, conventionally good-looking. They are clearly attracted to each other, but shy. She glances at him, but as he looks back she looks away. Behind the couple, we glimpse the other passengers: a Hispanic couple (the woman holding a bunch of flowers), another white couple, an older "country couple" (the man wearing a cowboy hat). There are alternating close-up shots of the young man and young woman. She is reading a magazine. She looks at the young man again. He looks away, out of the window, but seems pleased. The scene shifts back to the prairie outside: telegraph wires along the road, distant mountains, a heat haze. The next shots are extreme close-ups just the eyes and nose of each main character in turn. He glances sideways; she looks back. The scene changes back to the exterior again: a combine harvester, a man on a horse riding past in the other direction. Back inside, the young woman is fanning herself with her magazine. The young man reaches into the pocket of his shirt. We see a close-up of his hand taking out a packet of Wrigley's Spearmint Gum. He takes out a stick of gum and then looks back into the packet. It was the last stick. He hesitates— then offers it to her and she accepts. From the seat in front, a small boy looks around curiously, until the hand of the invisible adult beside him descends firmly on to his head and twists him back towards the front. We return to the young woman who is reading the Wrigley's wrapping paper. The camera shows her hand in close-up as she breaks the stick in half, and offers one half back to the young man. There are alternating shots—again very close—of the two main characters looking affectionately towards each other. In a longer shot of the interior of the bus, she shifts her body closer towards him. He does the same.

The bus stops outside a building called "The Rosebud." Outside, there is a van parked and a horse tethered, a cartwheel leaning against the wall. An "old-timer" with a large white beard is sitting on the porch whittling a piece of wood. The young man is leaving the bus. He turns and raises his hands in a gesture of resignation. We see the young woman's face close up. She looks down sadly. Inside, the young man sits down, while outside the bus pulls away. As the young man sits dejected, the young woman enters behind him. She has got off the bus to be with him.

The final shots show his hand with half a stick of Wrigley's gum,   13
and her hand with the other half. The two halves join and fit perfectly;
they merge into one, then transform into a whole, full packet. Words
appear on the screen:

GREAT TO CHEW. EVEN BETTER TO SHARE.

A male voice says: "Cool, refreshing Wrigley's Spearmint Gum. Great
to chew. Even better to share." The hands disappear, and we see the
packet on its own.

In this ad, there are four distinct pictorial perspectives. There is the   14
broad sweep of the outside world of nature—sunlight, corn, mountains—a benign, fertile, agricultural world at harvest time, in which
the traditional (horses) and the new (combine harvesters) are in harmony. Moving in more closely, there is the social world of the bus and
the bus station. This too is harmonious, with a cross-section of American society: the old man and the little boy, the rural couple, different
races. Moving in even more closely, there are shots in which we see
the young man and woman, within this social context, forming a relationship. Lastly, closest in of all, we see their faces from so short a distance that the image is one of complete intimacy. Only in an embrace
would one see someone so close. The most dominant image is the middle perspective: the young man and young woman forming their relationship in a social context.

The overriding impression, then, is of a young man and woman   15
meeting in a beautiful landscape, as part of a harmonious and approv-
ing society. It is also a very American world: the prairie, the old-timer,
"The Rosebud" (the same name as the sled which symbolizes lost
childhood in *Citizen Kane*). It centres upon the monogamous heterosexual relationship of a man and a woman, which in turn centres
upon the product—chewing gum. The bus, the social world, moves
through the world of nature. A further harmony between the human
and natural world is effected by the echo of the colour of the corn in
the colour of the young woman's hair. In the shots of the interior of
the bus, the couple are at the middle, moving, but apparently still,
with the agricultural world visible outside the window. Like any couple, they have both a social identity (as they appear to, and with, the
other passengers) and a private identity, as they appear to each other
(the close-ups). At the very heart of this image is the stick of gum,
passed from hand to hand, which brings them together and forms the
bond between them. These concentric levels of detail are best represented diagrammatically (Figure 17).

I have been using the word "aisle" deliberately. The view of the   16
bus is reminiscent of a wedding viewed from the altar: a young man
and woman coyly sitting on either side of the aisle, the guests in the
pews behind them. (Only the little boy—like a choirboy—is in front of
them.) The woman immediately behind the young woman is holding

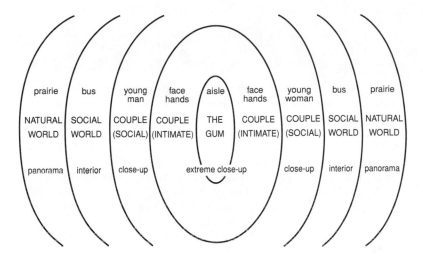

Figure 17 Concentric worlds in "Last stick" ad

a bunch of flowers like a bridesmaid. There are other parallels too. The young man reaches in his pocket for the gum as the groom reaches for the ring. He gives it to her, and it is a symbol of their union. In the final shots, we see an image of joined hands (another symbol of marriage) and also—in the only merged shot of the whole sequence—a transformation in which two become one. (The slow and significant placing of the gum in the mouth suggests both oral sex and the communion service.) There is a tension between this image of holy matrimony and the story of a casual pick-up, between a sexual union sanctified by society and one quite outside its institutionalized constraints. The casual nature of the encounter is emphasized by both the words and the period of the song. This clash of the matrimonial and the extra-marital is an image of fascination to the 1980s and 1990s; it is frequently used, for example, in the stage and video performances of Madonna.

This ad is another classic example of the product as the bond of love, presented at the centre of a sweeping view of the cosmic, social and sexual world, drawing to it the most powerful American ideological images: the Midwest wheat fields, the plural society, the marriage ceremony, and (if the wheaten-haired woman symbolizes fertility) a marriage of man and harvest, man and mother. All this in one minute! If it creates, as I have suggested, a vignette of the American ideology of marriage, then it is interesting to note that the young woman is the one who initiates every stage of the relationship but one. It is she who looks first, who returns half the stick, who shifts her body towards him, who breaks her journey to be with him, while the young man (apart from the one crucial step of offering the gum) is passive. 17

NEIL POSTMAN

"Now . . . This"

Neil Postman is a professor of media ecology and chair of the Department of Culture and Communications at New York University. He began his career as a teacher in the 1960s and published a series of influential books on the need for reforming public schools. One of his best-known books is *Teaching as a Subversive Activity* (1969). Ten years later, in *Teaching as a Conserving Activity,* Postman sounded an alarm about the effect of broadcast technology, arguing that schools must undo the damage done to children by the media's bombarding them with fragmented information. Since then, he has established himself as a leading skeptic about media technology: ". . . The question of what a technology will undo seems to me at least as important as the question of what it will do." His recent publications include *Technopoly* (1994) and *The End of Education: Redefining the Value of School* (1995). "Now . . . This" is excerpted from *Amusing Ourselves to Death* (1985). Readers may want to check the applicability of Postman's insights to today's news broadcasts by videotaping one or two and analyzing them in his terms. A useful companion essay is Barbara Ehrenreich's "Spudding Out."

The American humorist H. Allen Smith once suggested that of all the worrisome words in the English language, the scariest is "uh oh," as when a physician looks at your X-rays, and with knitted brow says, "Uh oh." I should like to suggest that the words which are the title of this chapter are as ominous as any, all the more so because they are spoken without knitted brow—indeed, with a kind of idiot's delight. The phrase, if that's what it may be called, adds to our grammar a new part of speech, a conjunction that does not connect anything to anything but does the opposite: separates everything from everything. As such, it serves as a compact metaphor for the discontinuities in so much that passes for public discourse in present-day America.

"Now . . . this" is commonly used on radio and television newscasts to indicate that what one has just heard or seen has no relevance to what one is about to hear or see, or possibly to anything one is ever likely to hear or see. The phrase is a means of acknowledging the fact that the world as mapped by the speeded-up electronic media has no order or meaning and is not to be taken seriously. There is no murder so brutal, no earthquake so devastating, no political blunder so costly—for that matter, no ball score so tantalizing or weather report so threatening—that it cannot be erased from our minds by a newscaster saying, "Now . . . this." The newscaster means that you have thought long enough on the previous matter (approximately forty-five seconds), that you must not be morbidly preoccupied with it (let us say, for ninety seconds), and that you must now give your attention to another fragment of news or a commercial.

Television did not invent the "Now . . . this" world view. As I have 3 tried to show, it is the offspring of the intercourse between telegraphy and photography. But it is through television that it has been nurtured and brought to a perverse maturity. For on television, nearly every half hour is a discrete event, separated in content, context, and emotional texture from what precedes and follows it. In part because television sells its time in seconds and minutes, in part because television must use images rather than words, in part because its audience can move freely to and from the television set, programs are structured so that almost each eight-minute segment may stand as a complete event in itself. Viewers are rarely required to carry over any thought or feeling from one parcel of time to another.

Of course, in television's presentation of the "news of the day," we 4 may see the "Now . . . this" mode of discourse in its boldest and most embarrassing form. For there, we are presented not only with fragmented news but news without context, without consequences, without value, and therefore without essential seriousness; that is to say, news as pure entertainment.

Consider for example, how you would proceed if you were given 5 the opportunity to produce a television news show for any station concerned to attract the largest possible audience. You would, first, choose a cast of players, each of whom has a face that is both "likable" and "credible." Those who apply would, in fact, submit to you their eight-by-ten glossies, from which you would eliminate those whose countenances are not suitable for nightly display. This means that you will exclude women who are not beautiful or who are over the age of fifty, men who are bald, all people who are overweight or whose noses are too long or whose eyes are too close together. You will try, in other words, to assemble a cast of talking hair-do's. At the very least, you will want those whose faces would not be unwelcome on a magazine cover.

Christine Craft has just such a face, and so she applied for a co- 6 anchor position on KMBC-TV in Kansas City. According to a lawyer who represented her in a sexism suit she later brought against the station, the management of KMBC-TV "loved Christine's look." She was accordingly hired in January 1981. She was fired in August 1981 because research indicated that her appearance "hampered viewer acceptance." What exactly does "hampered viewer acceptance" mean? And what does it have to do with the news? Hampered viewer acceptance means the same thing for television news as it does for any television show: Viewers do not like looking at the performer. It also means that viewers do not believe the performer, that she lacks credibility. In the case of a theatrical performance, we have a sense of what that implies: The actor does not persuade the audience that he or she is the character being portrayed. But what does lack of credibility imply in the case of a news show? What character is a co-anchor playing? And how do we decide that the performance lacks verisimilitude? Does the audience believe that the newscaster is lying, that what is reported did not in fact happen, that something important is being concealed?

It is frightening to think that this may be so, that the perception of the truth of a report rests heavily on the acceptability of the news-caster. In the ancient world, there was a tradition of banishing or killing the bearer of bad tidings. Does the television news show re-store, in a curious form, this tradition? Do we banish those who tell us the news when we do not care for the face of the teller? Does televi-sion countermand the warnings we once received about the fallacy of the ad hominem argument?

If the answer to any of these questions is even a qualified "Yes," then here is an issue worthy of the attention of epistemologists. Stated in its simplest form, it is that television provides a new (or, possibly, re-stores an old) definition of truth: The credibility of the teller is the ulti-mate test of the truth of a proposition. "Credibility" here does not refer to the past record of the teller for making statements that have sur-vived the rigors of reality-testing. It refers only to the impression of sincerity, authenticity, vulnerability or attractiveness (choose one or more) conveyed by the actor/reporter.

This is a mater of considerable importance, for it goes beyond the question of how truth is perceived on television news shows. If on television, credibility replaces reality as the decisive test of truth-telling, political leaders need not trouble themselves very much with reality provided that their performances consistently generate a sense of verisimilitude. I suspect, for example, that the dishonor that now shrouds Richard Nixon results not from the fact that he lied but that on television he looked like a liar. Which, if true, should bring no com-fort to anyone, not even veteran Nixon-haters. For the alternative pos-sibilities are that one may look like a liar but be telling the truth; or even worse, look like a truth-teller but in fact be lying.

As a producer of a television news show, you would be well aware of these matters and would be careful to choose your cast on the basis of criteria used by David Merrick and other successful impresarios.[1] Like them, you would then turn your attention to staging the show on principles that maximize entertainment value. You would, for exam-ple, select a musical theme for the show. All television news programs begin, end, and are somewhere in between punctuated with music. I have found very few Americans who regard this custom as peculiar,

1. Broadway producer and filmmaker David Merrick (1912–   ) has directed more than 88 shows; including Tony Award–winning *Becket, Hello Dolly,* and *42nd Street.*

which fact I have taken as evidence for the dissolution of lines of demarcation between serious public discourse and entertainment. What
has music to do with the news? Why is it there? It is there, I assume,
for the same reason music is used in the theater and films—to create a
mood and provide a leitmotif for the entertainment. If there were no
music—as is the case when any television program is interrupted for a
news flash—viewers would expect something truly alarming, possibly
life-altering. But as long as the music is there as a frame for the program, the viewer is comforted to believe that there is nothing to be
greatly alarmed about; that, in fact, the events that are reported have
as much relation to reality as do scenes in a play.

This perception of a news show as a stylized dramatic performance   11
whose content has been staged largely to entertain is reinforced by
several other features, including the fact that the average length of any
story is forty-five seconds. While brevity does not always suggest triviality, in this case it clearly does. It is simply not possible to convey a
sense of seriousness about any event if its implications are exhausted
in less than one minute's time. In fact, it is quite obvious that TV news
has no intention of suggesting that any story *has* any implications, for
that would require viewers to continue to think about it when it is
done and therefore obstruct their attending to the next story that waits
panting in the wings. In any case, viewers are not provided with much
opportunity to be distracted from the next story since in all likelihood
it will consist of some film footage. Pictures have little difficulty in
overwhelming words, and short-circuiting introspection. As a television producer, you would be certain to give both prominence and
precedence to any event for which there is some sort of visual documentation. A suspected killer being brought into a police station, the
angry face of a cheated consumer, a barrel going over Niagara Falls
(with a person alleged to be in it), the President disembarking from a
helicopter on the White House lawn—these are always fascinating or
amusing, and easily satisfy the requirements of an entertaining show.
It is, of course, not necessary that the visuals actually document the
point of a story. Neither is it necessary to explain why such images are
intruding themselves on public consciousness. Film footage justifies itself, as every television producer well knows.

It is also of considerable help in maintaining a high level of unreal-   12
ity that the newscasters do not pause to grimace or shiver when they
speak their prefaces or epilogs to the film clips. Indeed, many newscasters do not appear to grasp the meaning of what they are saying,
and some hold to a fixed and ingratiating enthusiasm as they report on
earthquakes, mass killings and other disasters. Viewers would be quite
disconcerted by any show of concern or terror on the part of newscasters. Viewers, after all, are partners with the newscasters in the
"Now . . . this" culture, and they expect the newscaster to play out his

or her role as a character who is marginally serious but who stays well clear of authentic understanding. The viewers, for their part, will not be caught contaminating their responses with a sense of reality, any more than an audience at a play would go scurrying to call home because a character on stage has said that a murderer is loose in the neighborhood.

The viewers also know that no matter how grave any fragment of news may appear (for example, on the day I write a Marine Corps general has declared that nuclear war between the United States and Russia is inevitable), it will shortly be followed by a series of commercials that will, in an instant, defuse the import of the news, in fact render it largely banal. This is a key element in the structure of a news program and all by itself refutes any claim that television news is designed as a serious form of public discourse. Imagine what you would think of me, and this book, if I were to pause here, tell you that I will return to my discussion in a moment, and then proceed to write a few words in behalf of United Airlines or the Chase Manhattan Bank. You would rightly think that I had no respect for you and, certainly, no respect for the subject. And if I did this not once but several times in each chapter, you would think the whole experience unworthy of your attention. Why, then, do we not think a news show similarly unworthy? The reason, I believe, is that whereas we expect books and even other media (such as film) to maintain a consistency of tone and a continuity of content, we have no such expectation of television, and especially television news. We have become so accustomed to its discontinuities that we are no longer struck dumb, as any sane person would be, by a newscaster who having just reported that a nuclear war is inevitable goes on to say that he will be right back after this word from Burger King; who says, in other words, "Now . . . this." One can hardly overestimate the damage that such juxtapositions do to our sense of the world as a serious place. The damage is especially massive to youthful viewers who depend so much on television for their clues as to how to respond to the world. In watching television news, they, more than any other segment of the audience, are drawn into an epistemology based on the assumption that all reports of cruelty and death are greatly exaggerated and, in any case, not to be taken seriously or responded to sanely. 13

I should go so far as to say that embedded in the surrealistic frame of a television news show is a theory of anticommunication, featuring a type of discourse that abandons logic, reason, sequence and rules of contradiction. In aesthetics, I believe the name given to this theory is Dadaism; in philosophy, nihilism; in psychiatry, schizophrenia. In the parlance of the theater, it is known as vaudeville. 14

For those who think I am here guilty of hyperbole, I offer the following description of television news by Robert MacNeil, executive editor and co-anchor of the "MacNeil-Lehrer Newshour." The idea, he 15 writes," is to keep everything brief, not to strain the attention of anyone but instead to provide constant stimulation through variety, novelty, action, and movement. You are required . . . to pay attention to no concept, no character, and no problem for more than a few seconds at a time." He goes on to say that the assumptions controlling a news show are "that bite-sized is best, that complexity must be avoided, that nuances are dispensable, that qualifications impede the simple message, that visual stimulation is a substitute for thought, and that verbal precision is an anachronism."

Robert MacNeil has more reason than most to give testimony about the television news show as vaudeville act. The "MacNeil-Lehrer Newshour" is an unusual and gracious attempt to bring to television some of the elements of typographic discourse. The program abjures visual stimulation, consists largely of extended explanations of events and in-depth interviews (which even there means only five to ten minutes), limits the number of stories covered, and emphasizes background and coherence. But television has exacted its price for MacNeil's rejection of a show business format. By television's standards, the audience is minuscule, the program is confined to public-television stations, and it is a good guess that the combined salary of MacNeil and Lehrer is one-fifth of Dan Rather's or Tom Brokaw's.

If you were a producer of a television news show for a commercial station, you would not have the option of defying television's requirements. It would be demanded of you that you strive for the largest possible audience, and, as a consequence and in spite of your best intentions, you would arrive at a production very nearly resembling MacNeil's description. Moreover, you would include some things MacNeil does not mention. You would try to make celebrities of your newscasters. You would advertise the show, both in the press and on television itself. You would do "news briefs," to serve as an inducement to viewers. You would have a weatherman as comic relief, and a sportscaster whose language is a touch uncouth (as a way of his relating to the beer-drinking common man). You would, in short, package the whole event as any producer might who is in the entertainment business.

The result of all this is that Americans are the best entertained and quite likely the least well-informed people in the Western world. I say this in the face of the popular conceit that television, as a window to the world, has made Americans exceedingly well informed. Much depends here, of course, on what is meant by being informed. I will pass over the now tiresome polls that tell us that, at any given moment, 70 percent of our citizens do not know who is the Secretary of State or the Chief Justice of the Supreme Court. Let us consider, instead, the case of Iran during the drama that was called the "Iranian Hostage Crisis." I don't suppose there has been a story in years that received more continuous attention from television. We may assume, then,

that Americans know most of what there is to know about this unhappy event. And now, I put these questions to you: Would it be an
exaggeration to say that not one American in a hundred knows what
language the Iranians speak? Or what the word "Ayatollah" means or
implies? Or knows any details of the tenets of Iranian religious beliefs?
Or the main outlines of their political history? Or knows who the Shah
was, and where he came from?

Nonetheless, everyone had an opinion about this event, for in   19
America everyone is entitled to an opinion, and it is certainly useful to
have a few when a pollster shows up. But these are opinions of a quite
different order from eighteenth- or nineteenth-century opinions. It is
probably more accurate to call them emotions rather than opinions,
which would account for the fact that they change from week to week,
as the pollsters tell us. What is happening here is that television is al-
tering the meaning of "being informed" by creating a species of information that might properly be called *disinformation*. I am using this
word almost in the precise sense in which it is used by spies in the CIA
or KGB. Disinformation does not mean false information. It means
misleading information—misplaced, irrelevant, fragmented or superficial information—information that creates the illusion of knowing
something but which in fact leads one away from knowing. In saying
this, I do not mean to imply that television news deliberately aims to
deprive Americans of a coherent, contextual understanding of their
world. I mean to say that when news is packaged as entertainment,
that is the inevitable result. And in saying that the television news
show entertains but does not inform, I am saying something far more
serious than that we are being deprived of authentic information. I am
saying we are losing our sense of what it means to be well informed.
Ignorance is always correctable. But what shall we do if we take ignorance to be knowledge?

Here is a startling example of how this process bedevils us. A *New*   20
York Times article is headlined on February 15, 1983:

REAGAN MISSTATEMENTS GETTING LESS ATTENTION

The article begins in the following way:

> President Reagan's aides used to become visibly alarmed at suggestions
> that he had given mangled and perhaps misleading accounts of his poli-
> cies or of current events in general. That doesn't seem to happen much
> anymore.
>   Indeed, the President continues to make debatable assertions of fact
> but news accounts do not deal with them as extensively as they once did.
> In the view of White House officials, the declining news coverage mirrors
> a *decline in interest by the general public.* (my italics)

This report is not so much a news story as a story about the news,   21
and our recent history suggests that it is not about Ronald Reagan's

charm. It is about how news is defined, and I believe the story would be quite astonishing to both civil libertarians and tyrants of an earlier time. Walter Lippmann, for example, wrote in 1920: "There can be no liberty for a community which lacks the means by which to detect lies." For all of his pessimism about the possibilities of restoring an eighteenth- and nineteenth-century level of public discourse, Lippmann assumed, as did Thomas Jefferson before him, that with a well-trained press functioning as a lie-detector, the public's interest in a President's mangling of the truth would be piqued, in both senses of that word. Given the means to detect lies, he believed, the public could not be indifferent to their consequences.

But this case refutes his assumption. The reporters who cover the White House are ready and able to expose lies, and thus create the grounds for informed and indignant opinion. But apparently the public declines to take an interest. To press reports of White House dissembling, the public has replied with Queen Victoria's famous line: "We are not amused." However, here the words mean something the Queen did not have in mind. They mean that what is not amusing does not compel their attention. Perhaps if the President's lies could be demonstrated by pictures and accompanied by music the public would raise a curious eyebrow. If a movie, like *All the President's Men,* could be made from his misleading accounts of government policy, if there were a break-in of some sort or sinister characters laundering money, attention would quite likely be paid. We do well to remember that President Nixon did not begin to come undone until his lies were given a theatrical setting at the Watergate hearings. But we do not have anything like that here. Apparently, all President Reagan does is *say* things that are not entirely true. And there is nothing entertaining in that.

But there is a subtler point to be made here. Many of the President's "misstatements" fall in the category of contradictions—mutually exclusive assertions that cannot possibly both, in the same context, be true. "In the same context" is the key phrase here, for it is context that defines contradiction. There is no problem in someone's remarking that he prefers oranges to apples, and also remarking that he prefers apples to oranges—not if one statement is made in the context of choosing a wallpaper design and the other in the context of selecting fruit for dessert. In such a case, we have statements that are opposites, but not contradictory. But if the statements are made in a single, continuous, and coherent context, then they are contradictions, and cannot both be true. Contradiction, in short, requires that statements and events be perceived as interrelated aspects of a continuous and coherent context. Disappear the context, or fragment it, and contradiction disappears. This point is nowhere made more clear to me than in conferences with my younger students about their writing. "Look here," I say. "In this paragraph you have said one thing. And in that you have said the opposite. Which is it to be?" They are polite, and wish to please, but they are as baffled by the question as I am by the response. "I know," they will say, "but that is *there* and this is *here*." The difference between us is that I assume "there" and "here," "now" and "then," one paragraph and the next to be connected, to be continuous, to be part of the same coherent world of thought. That is the way of typographic discourse, and typography is the universe I'm "coming from," as they say. But they are coming from a different universe of discourse altogether: the "Now . . . this" world of television. The fundamental assumption of that world is not coherence but discontinuity. And in a world of discontinuities, contradiction is useless as a test of truth or merit, because contradiction does not exist.

My point is that we are by now so thoroughly adjusted to the "Now . . . this" world of news—a world of fragments, where events stand alone, stripped of any connection to the past, or to the future, or to other events—that all assumptions of coherence have vanished. And so, perforce, has contradiction. In the context of *no context,* so to speak, it simply disappears. And in its absence, what possible interest could there be in a list of what the President says *now* and what he said *then?* It is merely a rehash of old news, and there is nothing interesting or entertaining in that. The only thing to be amused about is the bafflement of reporters at the public's indifference. There is an irony in the fact that the very group that has taken the world apart should, on trying to piece it together again, be surprised that no one notices much, or cares. 24

For all his perspicacity, George Orwell would have been stymied by this situation; there is nothing "Orwellian" about it. The President does not have the press under his thumb. *The New York Times* and *The Washington Post* are not *Pravda;* the Associated Press is not Tass. And there is no Newspeak here. Lies have not been defined as truth nor truth as lies. All that has happened is that the public has adjusted to incoherence and been amused into indifference. Which is why Aldous Huxley would not in the least be surprised by the story. Indeed, he prophesied its coming. He believed that it is far more likely that the Western democracies will dance and dream themselves into oblivion than march into it, single file and manacled. Huxley grasped, as Orwell did not, that it is not necessary to conceal anything from a public insensible to contradiction and narcoticized by technological diversions. Although Huxley did not specify that television would be our main line to the drug, he would have no difficulty accepting Robert Mac-Neil's observation that "Television is the *soma* of Aldous Huxley's *Brave New World.*" Big Brother turns out to be Howdy Doody. 25

I do not mean that the trivialization of public information is all accomplished *on* television. I mean that television is the paradigm for our conception of public information. As the printing press did in an earlier time, television has achieved the power to define the form in which news must come, and it has also defined how we shall respond 26 to it. In presenting news to us packaged as vaudeville, television induces other media to do the same, so that the total information environment begins to mirror television.

For example, America's newest and highly successful national   27
newspaper, *USA Today,* is modeled precisely on the format of television. It is sold on the street in receptacles that look like television sets. Its stories are uncommonly short, its design leans heavily on pictures, charts and other graphics, some of them printed in various colors. Its weather maps are a visual delight; its sports section includes enough pointless statistics to distract a computer. As a consequence, *USA Today,* which began publication in September 1982, has become the third largest daily in the United States (as of July 1984, according to the Audit Bureau of Circulations), moving quickly to overtake the *Daily News* and the *Wall Street Journal.* Journalists of a more traditional bent have criticized it for its superficiality and theatrics, but the paper's editors remain steadfast in their disregard of typographic standards. The paper's Editor-in-Chief, John Quinn, has said: "We are not up to undertaking projects of the dimensions needed to win prizes. They don't give awards for the best investigative paragraph." Here is an astonishing tribute to the resonance of television's epistemology: In the age of television, the paragraph is becoming the basic unit of news in print media. Moreover, Mr. Quinn need not fret too long about being deprived of awards. As other newspapers join in the transformation, the time cannot be far off when awards will be given for the best investigative sentence.

It needs also to be noted here that new and successful magazines   28
such as *People* and *Us* are not only examples of television-oriented print media but have had an extraordinary "ricochet" effect on television itself. Whereas television taught the magazines that news is nothing but entertainment, the magazines have taught television that nothing but entertainment is news. Television programs, such as "Entertainment Tonight," turn information about entertainers and celebrities into "serious" cultural content, so that the circle begins to close: Both the form and content of news become entertainment.

Radio, of course, is the least likely medium to join in the descent   29
into a Huxleyan world of technological narcotics. It is, after all, particularly well suited to the transmission of rational, complex language. Nonetheless, and even if we disregard radio's captivation by the music industry, we appear to be left with the chilling fact that such language as radio allows us to hear is increasingly primitive, fragmented, and largely aimed at invoking visceral response; which is to say, it is the linguistic analogue to the ubiquitous rock music that is radio's principal source of income. As I write, the trend in call-in shows is for the "host" to insult callers whose language does not, in itself, go much beyond humanoid grunting. Such programs have little content, as this word used to be defined, and are merely of archeological interest in

that they give us a sense of what a dialogue among Neanderthals might have been like. More to the point, the language of radio newscasts has become, under the influence of television, increasingly decontextualized and discontinuous, so that the possibility of anyone's knowing about the world, as against merely knowing *of* it, is effectively blocked. In New York City, radio station WINS entreats its listeners to "Give us twenty-two minutes and we'll give you the world." This is said without irony, and its audience, we may assume, does not regard the slogan as the conception of a disordered mind.

And so, we move rapidly into an information environment which   30 may rightly be called trivial pursuit. As the game of that name uses facts as a source of amusement, so do our sources of news. It has been demonstrated many times that a culture can survive misinformation and false opinion. It has not yet been demonstrated whether a culture can survive if it takes the measure of the world in twenty-two minutes. Or if the value of its news is determined by the number of laughs it provides.

BARBARA EHRENREICH

Spudding Out

Barbara Ehrenreich (1941–   ), who grew up in a working-class family in Butte, Montana, took her Ph.D in biology at Rockefeller University. Before she become a full-time writer, she was a staff member at the Health Policy Advisory Center and a professor of health sciences at the State University of New York in Old Westbury. Her first books, written with her husband or with Deirdre English, focus on the politics of health care; in particular, on male domination of the field of women's health: *Complaints and Disorders: The Sexual Politics of Sickness* appeared in 1973 and *For Her Own Good: One Hundred and Fifty Years of Experts' Advice to Women* in 1978. Since then she has been a columnist for *Ms., Mother Jones,* and *Time* and has published nine other books, both nonfiction and fiction. Her essays are collected in *The Snarling Citizen* (1995) and *The Worst Years of Our Lives* (1990) from which "Spudding Out" is drawn. As a radical opponent of the Vietnam War in the 1960s, Ehrenreich's impulse was, she says, "to shake my fist at people." Today her convictions remain staunchly left-wing, but her tone has changed: "I want to just say, 'calm down.'" Humor has replaced shouting in Ehrenreich's writing; some readers may find in her essay a model for lighthearted treatment of a subject about which they have serious convictions. An interesting companion essay would be Donald Hall's "Purpose, Blame, and Fire," which describes the effect of a movie in terms that might surprise Ehrenreich's couch potatoes.

Someone has to speak for them, because they have, to a person,   1
lost the power to speak for themselves. I am referring to that great
mass of Americans who were once known as the "salt of the earth,"
then as "the silent majority," more recently as "the viewing public,"
and now, alas, as "couch potatoes." What drives them—or rather,
leaves them sapped and spineless on their reclining chairs? What are
they seeking—beyond such obvious goals as a tastefully colorized version of *The Maltese Falcon?*

My husband was the first in the family to "spud out," as the ex-   2
pression now goes. Soon everyone wanted one of those zip-up "Couch
Potato Bags," to keep warm in during David Letterman. The youngest,
and most thoroughly immobilized, member of the family relies on a
remote that controls his TV, stereo, and VCR, and can also shut down
the neighbor's pacemaker at fifteen years.

But we never see the neighbors anymore, nor they us. This sad-   3
dens me, because Americans used to be a great and restless people,
fond of the outdoors in all of its manifestations, from Disney World to
miniature golf. Some experts say there are virtues in mass agorapho-
bia, that it strengthens the family and reduces highway deaths. But I
would point out that there are still a few things that cannot be done in
the den, especially by someone zipped into a body bag. These include
racquetball, voting, and meeting strange people in bars.

Most psychologists interpret the couch potato trend as a negative   4
reaction to the outside world. Indeed, the list of reasons to stay safely
tucked indoors lengthens yearly. First there was crime, then AIDS,
then side-stream smoke. To this list should be added "fear of the infra-
structure," for we all know someone who rashly stepped outside only
to be buried in a pothole, hurled from a collapsing bridge, or struck by
a falling airplane.

But it is not just the outside world that has let us down. Let's face   5
it, despite a decade-long campaign by the "profamily" movement, the
family has been a disappointment. The reason lies in an odd circular
dynamic: we watch television to escape from our families because television shows us how dull our families really are.

Compare your own family to, for example, the Huxtables, the   6
Keatons, or the peppy young people on *thirtysomething.* In those families, even the three-year-olds are stand-up comics, and the most in-
sipid remark is hailed with heartening outbursts of canned laughter.
When television families aren't gathered around the kitchen table exchanging wisecracks, they are experiencing brief but moving dilemmas, which are handily solved by the youngest child or by some cute
extraterrestrial house-guest. Emerging from *Family Ties* or *My Two Dads,*
we are forced to acknowledge that our own families are made up of
slow-witted, emotionally crippled people who would be lucky to qualify for seats in the studio audience of *Jeopardy!*

But gradually I have come to see that there is something besides   7
fear of the outside and disgust with our families that drives us to spud-
hood—some positive attraction, some deep cathexis to television itself.
For a long time it eluded me. When I watched television, mainly as a
way of getting to know my husband and children, I found that my
mind wandered to more interesting things, like whether to get up and
make ice cubes.

Only after many months of viewing did I begin to understand the   8
force that has transformed the American people into root vegetables. If
you watch TV for a very long time, day in, day out, you will begin to
notice something eerie and unnatural about the world portrayed
therein. I don't mean that it is two-dimensional or lacks a well-developed critique of the capitalist consumer culture or something superficial like that. I mean something so deeply obvious that it's almost
scary: when you watch television, you will see people doing many
things—chasing fast cars, drinking lite beer, shooting each other at
close range, etc. But you will never see people *watching television*. Well,
maybe for a second, before the phone rings or a brand-new, multira-
cial adopted child walks into the house. But never *really watching*, hour
after hour, the way *real* people do.

Way back in the beginning of the television era, this was not so   9
strange, because real people actually did many of the things people do
on TV, even if it was only bickering with their mothers-in-law about
which toilet paper to buy. But modern people, i.e., couch potatoes, do
nothing that is ever shown on television (because it is either dangerous or would involve getting up from the couch). And what they do
do—watch television—is far too boring to be televised for more than a
fraction of a second, not even by Andy Warhol, bless his boredom-
proof little heart.[1]

So why do we keep on watching? The answer, by now, should be   10
perfectly obvious: we love television because television brings us a
world in which television does not exist. In fact, deep in their hearts,
this is what the spuds crave most: a rich, new, participatory life, in
which family members look each other in the eye, in which people walk
outside and banter with the neighbors, where there is adventure, possibility, danger, feeling, all in natural color, stereophonic sound, and three
dimensions, without commercial interruptions, and starring . . . us.

"You mean some new kind of computerized interactive medium?"   11
the children asked hopefully, pert as the progeny on a Tuesday night

---

1. Artist and filmmaker Andy Warhol (1928–1987) became well-known for his use of
popular culture for high art. Warhol's intentional repetition of images and deliberately
boring recordings of mundane activities—such as *Empire,* which filmed the Empire State
Building for 24 hours from a position across the street—led one critic to announce that
"not one ounce of sentiment disturbs the numb silence of these images."

sitcom. But before I could expand on this concept—known to our ancestors as "real life"—they were back at the box, which may be, after all, the only place left to find it.

DAVID BRADLEY

How TV Drew Our Family Together— In Spite of Its Messages

David Bradley (1950–   ) grew up in Bedford County, Pennsylvania, a rural region he describes as "perilously close to the Mason-Dixon Line." Moving to Philadelphia in 1968 to attend the University of Pennsylvania, he managed to compile both a perfect academic transcript and a novel (*South Street*, 1975) based on the life stories he heard at a local bar. In 1972, he moved to London to study the United States from a British perspective, and he received an M.A. from King's College, London, in 1974. He returned to Philadelphia and worked as an editor and college teacher while he finished a ten-year struggle to complete *The Chaneyville Incident* (1981), an award-winning novel based on an incident Bradley learned about from his mother—the capture, killing, and burial of thirteen runaway slaves on a farm near Bradley's home. Currently a professor of English at Temple University in Philadelphia, Bradley is a frequent contributor to such magazines as *Esquire, Signature,* and *The New York Times Book Review.* The following essay, first published in *TV Guide* in 1987, might be called a "media autobiography," an attempt to understand and explain the writer's life as a television viewer (or moviegoer or Web surfer). It might serve as a model for readers who want to undertake a similar autobiography or memoir. Readers may also want to consider the way Bradley's detailed and personal account of television-watching confirms or contradicts the more theoretical views of Neil Postman ("Now . . . This").

Thanksgiving evening, 1986, just before 8. Home for the holiday, I   1
lie on the living-room carpet, full of pumpkin pie and pro football. My mother comes in and announces it's time for *The Cosby Show.* She says it with some trepidation; the last time she turned on *The Cosby Show,* I snorted angrily and left the room. But tonight, too stuffed to move, I only grunt as she turns on the set. I don't really mean to watch, but the announcer's voice, saying, "WJAC-TV, Johnstown, Channel 6, serving millions from atop the Alleghenies," draws my eye to the screen. As the image of Dr. Heathcliff Huxtable's Brooklyn brownstone

blossoms, it occurs to me that, while the call sign, slogan, even the announcer have been the same for as long as I can remember, a picture so sharp and free of interference is something I could only dream of when I was young.

I was born in a fringe area, a place where television signals are weakened by distance. The town was Bedford, population 5000, situated in the Allegheny Mountains of Pennsylvania, 100 miles east of Pittsburgh along the Pennsylvania Turnpike—at Exit 11, to be precise. Bedford—like most of the region—could look back on a prosperous past but forward to only a marginal future. A local TV station was an impossibility, and the mountainous terrain cut down on what could be received from a distance—some people claimed to pick up Ch. 2 from Pittsburgh, but most could receive signals from only two stations: WJAC, an NBC affiliate (although in the '50s it sometimes strayed to ABC offerings, like *Lawrence Welk* and *Ted Mack's Original Amateur Hour*) and WFGB-TV, Ch. 10, Altoona, a CBS affiliate. On neither was reception perfect. Ch. 6 always had little dots all over the screen. Ch. 10 always had multiple images. Sometimes you could hear and not see clearly; sometimes you could see and not hear. Occasionally a channel would vanish for hours. Often a broadcast would hover just beyond the threshold of intelligibility.

In such an area one quickly learned some of the jargon of TV. Before I went to school I knew that my TV watching was subject to "interference" because I lived in a "fringe area" beyond "line of sight" of cities. I even knew that the dots on Ch. 6 were called "snow" and the multiple images on Ch. 10 were called "ghosts." Of course my understanding was childishly literal-minded. I thought "line of sight" meant I could see Johnstown and Altoona if I got up on the roof with the TV antenna (I nearly broke my neck trying), and that "snow" meant it was actually snowing between Bedford and Johnstown. And I believed "ghosts" were the spirits of dead people, trapped somehow in the glowing interior of our black-and-white Motorola. For years I feared those ghosts would escape once the set was turned off, and I would sit in the darkness, staring at the screen, refusing to turn my back until the white dot that lingered there had vanished.

The set in my mother's living room now is a 20-inch General Electric, with a heart of cool germanium, not hot vacuum tubes. It does not lend itself to ghostly fantasies. Still, as the action of *The Cosby Show* commences, I find that it can at least help me to conjure the spirits of my family, to bring them into the living room as they would come 30 years ago.

My grandmother occupies an overstuffed chair in the corner beyond the fireplace. She does not have a good view of the television, but she doesn't watch TV anyway—she just listens to it. One reason she doesn't watch is she is terrifically nearsighted but refuses to wear bifocals; her glasses are propped upon her forehead so she can see. But the real reason is that she is a devotee of radio.

My grandmother was born when TV was an inventor's dream. Her 6 electronic revolution took place in 1921 or 1922, when she was invited to the home of a white neighbor to listen to one of the first commercial radio broadcasts from KDKA in Pittsburgh. It was years before she could afford a set, but by the time I was born radio was a part of her life. Every morning she would fire up her wood stove and her bulky, floor-model Zenith, and spend the day crocheting and listening to the scratchy AM broadcasts.

At dusk she would take up her cane and walk to our house to 7 spend the night with the comfort of central heating and indoor plumbing—her home had neither. After dinner she would "listen to television," which meant sitting in the corner crocheting an infinite series of antimacassars and listening to the audio portions of the programs she enjoyed (most of which were carry-overs from radio—*The Jack Benny Show, The Lone Ranger,* Groucho Marx's *You Bet Your Life*). Once I asked her why she didn't look at the characters. "I know what they look like," she said.

One thing that drew her attention to the screen was a voice that 8 seemed to belong to a black person. Eddie "Rochester" Anderson's gravelly tones would make her drop her glasses onto her nose and watch *Jack Benny* in earnest. A non-Caucasian accent from an unfamiliar source, such as a contestant on *You Bet Your Life*, would have her leaning forward and exclaiming, "Why . . . he's colored!" The only broadcast she watched from the start was one where the audio gave no clue as to the race of the participants: *The Gillette Cavalcade of Sports,* aka the Friday Night Fights.

My grandmother was not a fight fan—she could name only two 9 boxers, Joe Louis and Sugar Ray Robinson (whose bouts she had heard on radio). But on Fridays at 10 she would pull her chair out to get a better view. As the announcer, Jimmy Powers, introduced each set of combatants, she would peer through the snow of Ch. 6, examining the boxers as if she had a bet down. If both were white, she would go back to her crocheting. If both were black, she would watch, interested but passive. But if a black was pitted against a white, she would perch on the edge of her seat, the frail lace of her handwork crumpled in her fists, and mutter, "Get him, get him!" every time the black threw a punch.

At the moment, my grandmother's ghost is relishing the sight of 10 the Huxtable family—a half-dozen black faces on the screen at one time. The other ghost in the living room, however, is oblivious to the number of black faces on the screen—or anything else. My father, stretched out in his recliner, is perfectly placed for TV viewing, but, as usual, he is asleep.

* * *

If my grandmother "listened to television," my father snored to it.   11
Settled in front of the television, he would go directly to sleep, dozing
indiscriminately through laugh tracks, police sirens and war whoops.
The only sound that roused him was the theme music of the *Eleven
O'Clock News Roundup.* He would awaken to catch the national headlines, nod off through the local news, wake for the weather and then
announce it was bedtime. For years I found this behavior humorous, a
bit perverse and totally inexplicable. But later I came to understand
that putting my father to sleep was about all TV could do for him.

My father was denominational officer of the African Methodist   12
Episcopal Zion Church. Although an ordained minister, he was not assigned to a local parish but rather traveled extensively—about seven
months a year, total—on denominational business. In the mid-'50s I
began to travel with him. Our first trip was to New York, and when I
felt the thrill of actually setting foot in the city I understood why television's black-and-white images, devoid of smell and color, could only
put him to sleep. It was, I suppose, an early lesson in the difference between TV appearances and reality. But even had my father not been a
traveler, TV would have been peripheral to his existence. I discovered
that in Dinwiddie, Va., a wide place on U.S. Highway 1, south of Richmond, where the church held an annual "Institute"—a combination
Bible school, summer camp and revival meeting.

My father started taking me to the South at an odd time: the sum-   13
mer of 1956. Some Southern whites were having violent reactions to
civil-rights marches and Federal court rulings, and neither ministers
nor children were immune to their wrath: the year before, the Rev.
George Lee had been killed, and Emmett Till, a 14-year-old black boy
from Chicago, who was visiting relatives in Mississippi, had been
beaten to death, his body tied to a weight and dumped in the Talla-
hatchie River. Although I was too young to understand fully, I had
seen enough on television to be more than a little afraid. But at the Institute we were cut off from all pictures, descriptions and accounts of
the civil-rights struggle. The Institute building, a ramshackle three-
story affair built on a former plantation, didn't even have a telephone.
Television might have been a myth.

At first I was dismayed at missing *Captain Kangaroo* and *Mickey*   14
Mouse, but soon I began to enjoy Dinwiddie's brand of entertainment:
afternoon baseball games, evening firefly chases, the sweaty pomp and
pageantry of the evening worship services. My father seemed to enjoy
it too. In the afternoons he would sit beneath a shade tree, sipping iced
tea and whipping all comers at Chinese checkers. In the evenings he
would tell me a story before going to argue church politics on the
porch with the other preachers. During the years we visited the Institute it gradually dawned on me that Dinwiddie was much like Bedford

had been when my father was growing up, a place where entertainment was based on interaction between people, and I began to understand why he got annoyed at me for "sitting in front of the television," as he called it.

By then it was the mid-'60s, and a certain tension had grown between my father and me. Television did not cause it, but it became the focus of it. Whenever he saw me watching football and basketball he growled that I ought to watch things that had to do with brains, instead of brawn. He had no patience with the fantasy of *Star Trek.* We watched little together other than the *CBS Evening News,* and then Walter Cronkite's "And that's the way it is" tended to be drowned out by a frank exchange of views between my father and me, which ended when one of us—me, usually—left the room. The pattern persisted after I left home. It probably would have remained unchanged until he died if the television had not broken down.

I happened to be home visiting when the TV went dead. The repairman could only shake his head. The set was obsolete. Parts were unobtainable. The best solution was to buy a new TV. My father, then in his 70s, worried about retirement and medical bills, blanched at the price. So I went to town with my Mastercard and came back with an RCA XL-100. My father watched as I plugged it in and turned it to the channel he wanted. As I started out of the room he touched my arm. "Watch a while," he said. "OK," I said, and sat down. He smiled, looked at the screen—and fell asleep.

From that moment our relationship changed. We did not suddenly start agreeing, but, hours after one of us had made an angry exit, one of us would come back into the living room while the other was watching television, and watch, too. Sometimes my father would take his chair while I was disagreeing with the refs on *Monday Night Football.* Sometimes I would sit with him, suppressing groans, through *Little House on the Prairie.* I suppose you could call it reconciliation, but that would be a bit too grand. After all, Merlin Olsen was an ex-football player. And my father slept through every play.

My grandfather died in January of 1961, my father died in 1979. Between those dates cable came to our house. In an electronic sense the cable moved Bedford out of the fringe area, melting the snow, exorcising the ghosts. All the shows of the three major networks are available now, along with religion on the CBN Cable Network, golden oldies on the USA Network, and un-American activities like 12-man football on ESPN. In a social sense, however, the cable has made it possible for Bedford to stay on the fringe; people who believed, 30 years ago, that cities were lousy with danger and sin can find confirmation aplenty on the local news out of Pittsburgh or D.C., and can touch up their family values with the *700 Club* and reruns of *Father Knows Best.* It's a temptation too to say that, in a cultural sense, the cable has brought new opportunities for enrichment, because you can turn on PBS and watch ballet from Lincoln Center and listen to longhair music from Wolf Trap. But those aren't new opportunities for at least one person: my mother.

I am a native of the fringe area. My mother was an exile there. She was born in New Jersey in 1915, grew up there, married and lived with my father there when he was a local pastor. But, in 1948, when he became a denominational officer, they moved to Bedford. It must have been frustrating for my mother, a woman with artistic interests who was herself a pianist and a gifted soprano, after years of easy access to the culture of New York City, to be in a town where the local radio played Top 40 and country and went off the air at sundown. Although I was not born until 1950, I can recall the wistful tones in which she spoke of concerts she had attended and choirs in which she had sung. Fortunately, in the '50s, television networks had not yet learned that culture wouldn't sell and were airing programs like *Playhouse 90*, *Armstrong Circle Theater* and *The United States Steel Hour*. 19

My mother did not really watch television any more than my grandmother or my father did. She would be in the room but would almost always be doing other things—knitting, ironing, reading. The one exception came on Sunday afternoons, when she would give undivided attention to the sampler of cultural events called *Omnibus*. I watched the show with her. And so, at 4 or 5, I was exposed to Aaron Copland's "Billy the Kid" performed by the Ballet Theatre Company and Leonard Bernstein's explication of Beethoven's Fifth Symphony. I can't remember all the things we watched, but I can recall my mother's dismay when, in '56, *Omnibus* moved to ABC and was no longer broadcast in our area. But my mother did not stop watching television when *Omnibus* vanished from our airwaves. In fact, she made it a crusade to find shows of quality during the brief period between their debuts and cancellations, and was quick to recognize quality performers. She was a devotee of Richard Boone's dramatic anthology and of *East Side/West Side* with George C. Scott (both lasted only a season) and she started watching *The Garry Moore Show* when Carol Burnett joined the cast. 20

I watched those programs, too. Although most came on after my legislated bedtime, often, when my father was out of town, I would creep out into the living room, where my mother would be putting up her hair in front of the television. If my mother deemed the show "worth watching" she would pretend not to notice. When I was young what was "worth watching" tended to be what I had the least interest in seeing—I wanted *The Untouchables*, not *Alcoa Premiere*. But by the time I finished junior high school and was allowed to stay up until 11, 21 my tastes were trained. In fact, it was I who insisted, in 1965, that my mother set aside her prejudice against shoot-'em-ups to watch a witty, often moving espionage thriller call *I Spy*, co-starring somebody named Bill Cosby.

It occurs to me, now, as I watch that same Cosby registering dis-   22
may, suspicion, mollification, all at once (the bad news is another ve-
hicle crashed into the Huxtable kids' car; the good news is the other vehicle was Stevie Wonder's limo and, in addition to paying for the damage, the singer has invited the family to a recording session), that he looks different than he did back in 1965. The explanation that comes to me is that back then fringe-area interference kept Cosby's ex-pressive face a blur. But then I recall a moment when I saw Cosby's face clearly registering an even wider range of emotions. It was in one of the masterpiece episodes of *I Spy*, aired toward the end of the series, which Robert Culp directed and in which Cosby played the central role. He had been betrayed by a woman he loved, and there was noth-ing he needed to say; his face told everything. It was a powerful image then. My recollection of it now is powerful enough to challenge a line of thinking that began two decades ago.

In the fall of 1968, I left the fringe area to attend college in Phil-   23
adelphia. I couldn't afford a television, and I didn't have time to watch one anyway: I was studying or attending plays, poetry readings, con-certs or—since it was the '60s—political seminars. One of those was a panel on "Black History." The discussion was fairly tame; the panelists agreed that the white power structure had tried to brainwash blacks into accepting second-class citizenship by promoting a version of his-tory that ignored any role blacks played in the development of Amer-ica. The speakers disagreed only on the question of which medium had been the greatest brainwasher. One speaker nominated television, and suddenly I was reminded of *The Gray Ghost*.

The Gray Ghost was a syndicated dramatization of the life of John   24
Singleton Mosby, a Civil War cavalry officer who waged a guerrilla campaign that was both humorous and heroic—if you were a Confed-erate. At the time the show aired—1956 or 1957—I was too young to understand what the Civil War was about, so I cheered Mosby's es-capes from his blue-coated enemies. But one day my father saw what I was doing and gave me a brief but unequivocal lesson in American history. The panelist's argument brought back the hot chagrin I had felt at my own ignorance and at, I realized, being deceived into think-ing a "slave-holding rebel" was *my* hero.

In the weeks that followed, chagrin crystallized into a reasoned   25
hatred for the complex of finance, technology and show business that we call "television." For as I looked back to the shows I had watched in my childhood I realized that television had not only written blacks out of history, it had written them out of society. In the '50s you couldn't

see a black on TV unless the role made it absolutely necessary. Amos, Andy and Rochester were holdovers from radio—they *had* to be black. But on shows TV originated, blacks appeared nowhere. Certainly they were not heroes or heroines, and they were not even domestics in continuing roles—John Forsythe's houseboy on *Bachelor Father* was Chinese. More important from the point of view of subliminal visual messages, they were not in the background. In television America you didn't see black folks walking down the street or sitting on a bus. The image would have delighted a segregationist. Even in the '60s, when television was supposedly "making blacks more visible," the only place you were sure to see them in casual roles was on offbeat shows set in Africa, like *Cowboy in Africa,* in which Chuck Connors taught the Kikuyu to rope steers (his sidekick was a Navajo, his employer an Englishman).

The truth, I realized, was that '60s television did not make all   26
blacks more visible—only some. TV news covered riots in Northern ghettos, but it made individual leaders visible only if they were Southern and nonviolent. It was Martin Luther King on the networks—Malcolm X was on talk shows aired by independent stations in the prime time of insomniacs and night watchmen. TV entertainment made black women more visible if they were middle class and prissy, like Diahann Carroll's Julia or Peggy on *Mannix,* both of whom were widows and apparently beyond sex—both seemed dedicated to the memories of dead husbands (both of whom died in uniform). Black men were more visible only as updated domestics, like Barney on *Mission: Impossible,* whose share of the Impossible Mission was usually to crawl through a sewer pipe with a screwdriver and drive the van; or Mark Sanger on *Ironside,* whose job was to cater to a crippled white man and drive the van. The answer to, "What does a black guy have to do to be on network TV and *not* drive a van?" was given by Cosby's Alexander Scott in *I Spy:* he has to be a Rhodes scholar (not just a college graduate and an athlete), speak six languages—and carry the bags of an Ivy-League dropout who gets almost all the girls.

I saw little in the '70s to stop hating television. Black women kept   27
on losing their men while gaining about 60 pounds: Mabel King was divorced on *What's Happening,* Nell Carter was unmarried on *Gimmie a Break,* Esther Rolle, Florida on *Good Times,* started out married but was widowed midway in the series. (Isabel Sanford, Louise on *The Jeffersons,* had a husband but might have wished she didn't.) Female characters who were not nor ever had been either domestics or overweight were morally questionable good-time girls, like Willona (Ja'net DuBois) on *Good Times* . . . except for Helen Willis (Roxie Roker) on *The Jefferson,* who was married to a white man. Black men had lots of problems, too. The good news was that Florida's husband, James, finally got a job. The bad news was that it was in Mississippi. The worse news was that he died there (less violently, one hopes, than Emmett Till). George

Jefferson was short, insecure and dominated by his wife, his mother and his (black) maid. Redd Foxx was a junkman. His son Lamont was still living at home. And all the shows that focused on black people were comedies—judging from television, blacks had no emotion too deep, commitment too strong or problem too complicated to be portrayed in 30 minutes and disposed of with a laugh.

To my eye, *The Cosby Show* changed none of that. Much was made   28
of the fact that each episode was vetted by a black Harvard psychiatrist to make sure only a positive image of blacks was presented, that nothing was said to make a child feel bad that his skin was black and his hair wasn't straight, but that, to my '60s-trained eye, was the same as smearing his face with bleaching cream and cutting his hair short so you couldn't tell it was kinky. Much was made of the show's high ratings among whites, but I saw that popularity—not only in America, but in places like South Africa—as evidence that it was letting whites see exactly the blacks they wanted doing exactly what they wanted for exactly as long as they wanted—middle-class, middle-of-the-road Negroes being funny as hell, for half an hour once a week.

The recollected image of Cosby's face from *I Spy* has not made me   29
change my mind about that. It has, however, made other images come bursting into my mind, as if some interference has been removed: my grandmother's parchment-colored fists gripping her doily as she watched a black man hit a white man, the look of satisfaction on her face as she talked of how, when they put *Amos 'n' Andy* on television they had to find "real colored men"; my father's eyes flashing indignantly as he insisted that what Walter Cronkite said was not "the way it was," his mouth twisted in sarcasm as he informed me that if the Gray Ghost had been victorious my great-grandfather, a freed slave, would have been carried back to ole Virginia; my mother's uncharacterizable expression as she footnoted a televised performance by Marian Anderson with the fact that once the Daughters of the American Revolution had refused to listen to Anderson sing, or her shoulders tensing as she watched Jackie Robinson come to bat in a televised baseball game. As those images come to me I realize that, for nearly 20 years, I have been thinking that TV affected me more than it really did. For though what I saw on TV was important, I always saw it with people who had senses both of history and their own dignity; people who made certain that any televised message was subjected to interference—to make sure that, when it came to the images that could harm me, I was protected in a fringe area.

And I realize too that, while I was lucky, I was not exceptionally   30
so. Though every black child does not have a militant for a grandmother, or a world traveler for a father, or a mother who can appreciate not only the arts but the artists, there are in each child's life black people who can offer, through explanation and example, antidotes to

the poisonously . . . "negative" is too simple a word; perhaps "conventional" . . . images of blacks that television presents. There is danger in those images, of course, but those truly at risk are those who have no one to provide interference: black children whose parents do not insure that they live in a fringe area, white people who do not know the fringe is there.

Theme music rouses me. *Cosby Show* credits crawl across the screen.   31
I find I have an eerie urge to ask my mother what happened. She goes to the television, flips the dial to ESPN, where Texas is playing Texas A&M.

"Isn't there something you'd rather watch?" I ask as she resumes   32
her chair. I'm not being altruistic; I'm not interested in a game between two Southern schools.

"No," she says. "I'll just sit and put up my hair while you watch."   33

It occurs to me then that, in worrying about what television could   34
have done to me, I am forgetting what it has done for me; allowed me to keep my family. Despite the fact that we were separated by generation and politics and travel, despite the fact that I alone actually watched the thing, the television drew us, night after night, into the same room, like a fire on an ancient hearth. Like a lamp, it illuminated for me the expressions on the faces of my grandmother, my father, my mother. Like a camera, it helped me preserve their images. Now it has put them before me, clear and bright and free of interference.

And so, once again, my mother and I sit together. She puts up the   35
kinky hair *The Cosby Show* won't talk about. I doze just a bit, as we watch television together, never minding what is on the screen.

DONALD HALL

Purpose, Blame, and Fire

Donald Hall (1928–   ) was born in New Haven, Connecticut, and educated at Harvard and at Oxford University. Influenced by such undergraduate classmates as Robert Bly and Adrienne Rich, he turned his attention almost exclusively to poetry and in 1955 produced *Exiles and Marriages,* a book that won the American Academy of Poets' prestigious Lamont Award for that year. He became a professor of English at the University of Michigan in 1957 and continued to publish a steady stream of excellent poems. In 1975 he quit teaching, took up residence on a New Hampshire farm once owned by his grandparents, and devoted himself to writing full-time. Since then he has published several more volumes of award-winning poetry, as well as biographies, children's literature, textbooks, and essays. His essays are collected in *To Keep Moving: Essays 1959–1969* (1980), *Poetry and Ambition: Essays 1980–1988* (1988), and *Principal Products of Portugal: Prose Pieces* (1995). In 1994 he published *Life Work,* half of which is a discussion of his life as a working writer and half the story of his dealing with terminal cancer.

"Purpose, Blame, and Fire," written for the anthology *The Movie That Changed My Life,* was published in *Harper's* in May 1991. Like David Bradley's "How TV Kept Our Family Together . . . ," Hall's autobiographical sketch helps us see ways the media might affect us. The contrast in effect is sharp, however, and something about the media's unpredictable power might be learned by a close examination of the essays. Hall's essay might also encourage readers to write their own accounts of movies that changed their lives.

My father was too young for the Great War, not fifteen when it   1
ended, and both my grandfathers were too old. Their fathers fought in the Civil War—archaic blue figures, stiff-bearded in photographs —but in 1937, when I was eight, Gettysburg might have been Agincourt or Marathon.[1] As a second world war came closer, I understood that my father felt guilty about missing the Great War; but I understood that he wanted to miss the new one as well.

Everyone was nervous, the Depression hanging on and war   2
approaching. I was an only child, alert to my parents' anxiety. My mother was thin and attentive. She had come to Connecticut from a remote farm in New Hampshire, and as I grew up I became aware that she felt lonely in the suburbs; she paid more attention to her child, in her displacement, then she would have done if she had stayed up north with her sisters.

Sometimes she took me on excursions to New Haven—Saturdays   3
during the school year, weekdays in summer. We walked up Ardmore Street to Whitney Avenue and waited for the bus that came every ten minutes to roll us four miles down Whitney and drop us at Church and Chapel outside Liggett's across from the New Haven Green. While I tagged along, she shopped at Shartenberg's and Malley's. When we had done shopping, we ate lunch at a place where I ordered franks and beans—two grilled hot dogs and a tiny crock of pea beans dark with molasses; dessert was Jell-O with real whipped cream or dry yellow cake with white frosting. Lunch cost thirty-nine cents.

Then we went to the movies. At the theater we would see a first-   4
run film, a B-movie, one or two shorts, previews of coming attractions,

---

1. Agincourt, Marathon: Agincourt was a decisive victory of the English against the French in A.D. 1415; Marathon, a triumph of the Greeks against the Persians in 490 B.C.

and a newsreel. In the year 1937 I am almost sure that I watched Spencer Tracy in *Captains Courageous;* maybe Paul Muni in *The Life of Emile Zola*, probably *Lost Horizon* and *A Star Is Born*. But the only movie I remember seeing for certain, some fifty-four years later, is *The Last Train From Madrid*. After we took the bus home to Ardmore Street, I burned my collection of war cards and put away my toy soldiers forever.

In 1937 we boys wore long woolen stockings pulled up over the bottoms of corduroy knickers as we walked to Spring Glen Grammar School. There were no school buses. Children from my neighborhood took several different routes to school—for variety or to avoid a bully—but always passed the Glendower Drug Store, only two short blocks from the school. [5]

If we had change in our pockets, we spent it there. For a nickel, we bought big candy bars or flat pieces of gum creased into five sticks and pink as a dog's tongue. With the gum came cards that illustrated our different obsessions: Of course there were baseball cards, and I seem to recall cards for football as well; I remember G-man cards, each of which illustrated a triumph of law and order such as J. Edgar Hoover's agents flushing out Dillinger—shooting him in the lobby of a movie theater—or Pretty Boy Floyd. Although G-man cards were violent, they might have been the Society of Friends alongside another series that we bought and collected. We called them war cards, and they thrived in the bellicose air of 1937. [6]

It was a time when the war in Spain[2] shrieked from the front pages of newspapers, along with the Japanese invasion of China. In 1937 Stalin kept discovering to his astonishment that old colleagues had betrayed him; he shot seven of his best generals that year, doubtless a great advantage when Hitler invaded. In 1937 Trotsky found his way to Mexico,[3] the UAW[4] invented the sit-down strike, Neville Chamberlain[5] asked Hitler for his cooperation in the interest of peace, the *Hindenburg* exploded and burned in New Jersey, and thousands of American progressives joined the Lincoln Brigade to fight fascism in Spain. [7]

Even in the fourth grade we knew about Hitler, whose troops and planes fought alongside Franco against the Loyalists, who were aided by Stalin's troops and planes. Germany was again the enemy, less than [8]

---

2. The Spanish Civil War (1937–1939) anticipated World War II and introduced such horrors as the bombing of civilian targets. The war pitted fascist rebel General Francisco Franco against Spanish Loyalists aided by liberals and leftists from around the world.
3. Leon Trotsky (1879–1940), Russian revolutionary and political leader, was driven into exile by dictator Joseph Stalin (1879–1953).
4. UAW: United Auto Workers.
5. Neville Chamberlain: British prime minister from May 1937 through May 1940.

twenty years after the Armistice of 1918. We were good, brave, loyal, outnumbered, and victorious against all odds; they were evil, cruel, cowardly, vicious, dumb, shrewd, and doomed. We knew who was right and who was wrong. (My father's mother's family had emigrated from Germany to New Haven in the 1880s, which was confusing.) In 1937 all of us—parents, teachers, children—understood that there would be another war and that America would join this war sooner than it had the Great War. Isolationists and pacifists campaigned against the war, but everyone knew that war was inevitable—whether it was or wasn't. A phenomenon like war cards makes it now seem as if we were being prepared, as if the adults were making sure that we grew up expecting to become soldiers, accepting the guns and the bombing and the death.

At least no one—so soon after the Great War—had the temerity to   9
present war as a Cub Scout expedition. When we went to the movies, we saw a newsreel and sometimes even *The March of Time*. The late 1930s were endless parades in black and white, soldiers marching, weapons rolling past reviewing stands. I remember the bombing and strafing of refugees. I remember Hitler addressing rallies.

War cards used a lot of red ink. On the back of each card a short   10
text described a notorious incident, and on the front an artist illustrated what had happened. I remember one card that showed a Japanese bomb hitting a crowded Chinese bus, maybe in Shanghai: Bodies being torn apart hurtled through the air, intestines stretched and tangled, headless bodies littering the ground. I don't believe these cards were particularly ideological; as I recollect, the cards claimed to be educational, illustrating the Horrors of War. Blood was the whole matter.

We cherished our war cards, chewing gum as we walked home to   11
add a new one to our collections: Blood of war was the food on which we nurtured our boyish death-love. If you got a duplicate you could swap, maybe the exploded bus for a card that showed the shelling of a boat. We collected war cards as we collected ourselves for war.

Surely, at eight, my imagination was filled by war. I loved air-   12
planes and read pulp stories about dogfights over the trenches. I loved the pilot heroes of the era—Wiley Post, Amelia Earhart, later Wrong-Way Corrigan. When I imagined myself going to war it was to join the Lafayette Escadrille,[6] fly Spads, and shoot down Fokker triplanes.

Then I saw *The Last Train From Madrid*. Did it really change my life?   13
As I commit it to paper, the phrase sounds exaggerated, melodramatic. I never registered as a C.O. (Nor did I serve in the military.) Although I worked in Ann Arbor with the movement against the Vietnam War, I was never a leader. Neither did I spell the country Amerika. It was war

---

6. Lafayette Escadrille: a unit of U.S. volunteers attached to the French air force in the early years of World War I.

horror that filled my chest, not political commitment: A horror is not an idea, as a shudder is not a conviction. Certain horrors of war retain the power to burst me into tears, especially the random slaughter of civilians. And my first experience of such horrors, I now believe, must have occurred on the day in 1937 when I saw *The Last Train From Madrid.*

In September of 1990—as another war approached—I saw *The Last Train From Madrid* again. Over the years I had thought of the film often and assumed that it was antifascist, popular front. It is no such thing; the film is astonishingly without political ideology. The plot is derivative, built of romantic clichés and stereotypes, and is impossible to take seriously: a *Grand Hotel* on wheels. The writing is ghastly, from clumsy exposition to flat dialogue. Its single import is the randomness of war horror.   14

The film opens with the hurtling image of a locomotive and train. A radio newscast tells us that tonight the last train will leave Madrid, after which—we understand—the city will be overrun by the nameless army that is besieging it. The army lacks not only name but idea, and its only purpose is death. As characters speak of the train's terminus in Valencia, Valencia becomes pure symbol: The destination is Arcadian peace in a countryside antithetical to the city's panic, chaos, and violent death. Naturally, everyone wants a seat on the train. The plot of the movie turns on separate and intermingled stories of people seeking passage on the train—their stratagems, their failures and successes. At the end of the movie the train steams out of Madrid carrying some of the people we've been introduced to and leaving others behind—not only behind but dead.   15

A noble young officer (noble because he is handsome and stands straight; noble because he is Anthony Quinn) listens at the film's beginning to impassioned pleas for passes, and in his dutiful nobility refuses them. We dwell on an old lady, well played, who begs for a pass and is refused. Most of our central figures are in couples, two by two like the ark's animals: the romantic interest, which I doubtless ignored in 1937 and found myself ignoring last fall. Love between two men (Anthony Quinn and Gilbert Roland) who swore blood brotherhood as soldiers in Africa years before is standard *Beau Geste*[7] stuff, but it does provide the strongest human bond in the film—stronger for sure than the bonds each seeks to establish with Dorothy Lamour.   16

In one of the subplots a slaphappy American journalist (Lew Ayres) picks up a girl (Olympe Bradna) who wants to get to Madrid to see her father before the firing squad kills him. (Naturally, they fall in   17

---

7. *Beau Geste:* a 1939 adventure film starring Gary Cooper as a member of the French Foreign Legion.

love; later, this pair makes it onto the Valencia-bound train.) She sees her father, he is shot—and we never receive an inkling, not a *notion,* of what he did or stood for that led to his cold-blooded execution. The killing feels wholly arbitrary: No motive is supplied or suggested. In this film's eerie political emptiness, execution by firing squad is not a political act (and thus in some way purposeful) but routine, everyday—like sunrise and sunset.

One soldier on the firing squad (Robert Cummings) is tender-   18
hearted and will not fire his gun. For his sensitivity he will be sent to the front. He runs away—and runs into an unbelievable love. We see two people parting, a man and a woman whom we do not know. We understand that they have just made love, and that she is a prostitute. They seem fond of each other, happy, making plans for their next encounter. As the man walks into the street, we suddenly spy his shape down the sight of a rifle—a sniper's rifle. The sniper shoots him dead. Although we may assume that the sniper waited for this particular man, the film provides not one detail to support this assumption. We know nothing of this man or his killer or any motive; we know nothing about the shooting except the brute fact. Like the earlier execution by firing squad, this street killing—idyll destroyed by bullet—presents itself as wholly arbitrary.

It is this young prostitute (Helen Mack) with whom Cummings   19
falls in love—and she with him—immediately. After Mack and Cummings drag her dead lover's body into her flat, they talk; Cummings wants the dead man's pass for the last train. Soon enough, they scheme a double escape. During their brief courtship, the couple construct of their lovers' talk the Arcadian Valencia to which the train will deliver them. Cummings eventually makes it to the train, but alone. Mack dies on the way—again arbitrarily.

By today's standards, of course, there are actually few deaths in   20
The Last Train From Madrid. Channel-surfing the television—happening, say, upon a Chuck Norris movie—you will see more carnage before you can switch channels than you'll observe in eighty-five minutes of this old film. But the deaths I witnessed in 1937 stuck with me as those I see in movies today for the most part do not. One in particular: Near the film's end, before the train leaves the station, guards move through the cars rechecking passes. As they demand papers from everyone, our anxiety mounts because they are approaching a vulnerable protagonist. Suddenly, looking at one man's pass—a stranger to us—the guards ask him to step outside. He looks nervous; he tries to run—and they shoot him down. They kill him *on purpose,* aiming their guns, yet they kill him *for no reason* that we will ever understand.

Murderous paradox drives the film: Malignity exists everywhere,   21
yet most of the time it appears motiveless. To an eight-year-old in New Haven, the particular individuals shot and killed in the film suffered

deaths as arbitrary as if they had been killed by bombs from the sky. An air raid takes place at the center of the film, a riot of civilian panic, people running and frightened. The sound track plays fear music, camera shots are jumpy and angular, and in one quick shot nervous pigeons scurry.

In Robert Frost's "Design" he writes about the malign coincidence 22 of an invisible spider haply arranged to kill a fly; the poet asks what could have caused this coming-together except for "design of darkness to appall." Then he qualifies the question in a further line: "If design govern in a thing so small." In *The Last Train From Madrid* we are surrounded by fear of imminent death, but, horribly, we lack design. As humans, we wish or perhaps even need to understand the cause or to place blame—on an enemy, on politicians who betrayed us, on the cupidity or moral squalor of a person or a class of people—because blame implies purpose, and purpose, meaning. *The Last Train From Madrid* suggests that design may not govern in a thing so small as human life and death.

Printed words at the very start of the film scroll its neutrality: This 23 movie will not uphold or defend either side of the war. When we read of battles in old histories we study the motives of each side, although the cause may mean little to us: We want to make sense. We may not keep with us the ideas behind a conflict—what we tend to remember are stories of heroism, cowardice, and suffering; "The river ran red with blood for seven days," we remember, not "Thus Centerville retained its access to the sea." Yet we make the effort to understand the history and politics, if only to satisfy ourselves that there appeared to be reasons for the blood: a design. By eschewing history and politics, *The Last Train From Madrid* leaches war of its particular temporal context, providing an eight-year-old with his first glimpse of war as eternal anonymous suffering. The film scrolls war's utter panic and sorrow. Oh, sorrow, sorrow, sorrow—the ripe life cut by hate without purpose, by anger lacking reason, by murder without blame.

How did my mother happen to take an eight-year-old to such a 24 movie? Microfilm of the *New Haven Register* explains. The newspaper printed photographs of studio puffery that wholly misrepresented the film: "With but two pictures to her credit, both of which were outstanding successes, Dorothy Lamour, the glamorous brunette, one of the season's most sensational 'finds,' moves into the ranks of the screen's charming leading ladies. The event takes place in 'The Last Train from Madrid,' the romance laid in war-torn Spain." I find it breathtaking to read this notice of the film that horrified me. "In this story Miss Lamour appears as a beautiful patrician girl, who is the beloved of a young lieutenant in the government forces and his best friend," When I read Frank S. Nugent's *New York Times* review (6/19/37), I am almost as astonished. He notes the lack of politics in this "glib little fiction," but for Nugent also there was no horror. "True, it treats of the Spanish revolution, but merely as Hollywood has, in the past, regarded the melodramatic turmoils of Ruritania and Zenda."[8] He calls the film "a pre-tested melodrama which should suit the average palate," and in his conclusion makes a joke: "Its sympathies, neither Loyalist nor Rebel, are clearly on the side of the Ruritanians."

Frank S. Nugent was not eight years old. Was Nugent's cynicism more appropriate than my horror? At eight, I ignored the silly romance at the film's center and registered only the panic of unmotivated murder. When I returned home after the Saturday matinee, I packed my lead toy soldiers with their flattish Great War helmets into a shoebox and tucked it deep in the long closet of my bedroom. I performed the ritual with so much solemnity that I might have played taps for background music. By this time I felt not panic but a sadness that would not relent, which may have derived from another melancholy that absorbed me that weekend. The film opened in New Haven on Saturday, July 10, 1937, while Ameila Earhart was missing over the Pacific. I remember playing outside the house, keeping the window open and a radio near the window; I remember a report that the Navy had spotted her plane on an atoll; I remember the correction of the report. In my mind's eye, Amelia Earhart circled continually, high in the air, the hum of the Lockheed's engine distant and plaintive, gas almost gone, the pilot in her leather helmet peering for land as she circled . . .

A day or two later, alone in the house, I carried my war cards down to the coal furnace in the cellar. I was not allowed to open the furnace door, but I opened it anyway and threw the cards onto the red coals. At first they smoldered and turned brown, and I feared that they would not burn—would give me away when my father came home and stoked the furnace. Then one card burst into yellow flame, then another, then all together flared briefly in the shadow-and-red hellfire of the furnace on Ardmore Street.

JOHN CHEEVER

The Enormous Radio

John Cheever (1912–1982) was expelled from high school in Quincy, Massachusetts, when he was seventeen for smoking and laziness, an event that ended his formal education but gave him material for his first story, "Expelled," which was published in *The New Republic* in 1930. He left home for Boston determined to be a writer and for a

---

8. Ruritania, Zenda: fictional kingdoms in *The Prisoner of Zenda*, a swashbuckling story made into movies in 1913, 1922, and 1937.

time supported himself by writing book synopses for a film studio and other odd jobs. Meanwhile, he began to place short stories in several magazines, most significantly *The New Yorker,* where he eventually published more than one hundred. Eventually, Cheever won a dozen major literary awards, including a Pulitzer Prize in 1980 for *The Stories of John Cheever,* and was awarded an honorary doctorate from Harvard University. "The Enormous Radio," first published in *The New Yorker* on May 17, 1947, is often cited as one of his finest works.

Jim and Irene Westcott were the kind of people who seem to strike that satisfactory average of income, endeavor, and respectability that is reached by the statistical reports in college alumni bulletins. They were the parents of two young children, they had been married nine years, they lived on the twelfth floor of an apartment house near Sutton Place,.[1] they went to the theatre on an average of 10.3 times a year, and they hoped someday to live in Westchester.[2] Irene Westcott was a pleasant, rather plain girl with soft brown hair and a wide, fine fore-head upon which nothing at all had been written, and in the cold weather she wore a coat of fitch skins dyed to resemble mink. You could not say that Jim Westcott looked younger than he was, but you could at least say of him that he seemed to feel younger. He wore his graying hair cut very short, he dressed in the kind of clothes his class had worn at Andover,[3] and his manner was earnest, vehement, and intentionally naïve. The Westcotts differed from their friends, their classmates, and their neighbors only in an interest they shared in seri-ous music. They went to a great many concerts—although they sel-dom mentioned this to anyone—and they spent a good deal of time listening to music on the radio.

Their radio was an old instrument, sensitive, unpredictable, and beyond repair. Neither of them understood the mechanics of radio—or of any of the other appliances that surrounded them—and when the instrument faltered, Jim would strike the side of the cabinet with his hand. This sometimes helped. One Sunday afternoon, in the middle of a Schubert quartet, the music faded away altogether. Jim struck the cabinet repeatedly, but there was no response; the Schubert was lost to them forever. He promised to buy Irene a new radio, and on Monday when he came home from work he told her that he had got one. He refused to describe it, and said it would be a surprise for her when it came.

The radio was delivered at the kitchen door the following after-noon, and with the assistance of her maid and the handyman Irene

---

1. Sutton Place: a "gentrified" neighborhood in New York City.
2. Westchester: an upper-middle-class rustic suburb.
3. Andover: home of Phillips Academy, a prestigious preparatory school.

uncrated it and brought it into the living room. She was struck at once with the physical ugliness of the large gumwood cabinet. Irene was proud of her living room, she had chosen its furnishings and colors as carefully as she chose her clothes, and now it seemed to her that the new radio stood among her intimate possessions like an aggressive intruder. She was confounded by the number of dials and switches on the instrument panel, and she studied them thoroughly before she put the plug into a wall socket and turned the radio on. The dials flooded with a malevolent green light, and in the distance she heard the music of a piano quintet. The quintet was in the distance for only an instant; it bore down upon her with a speed greater than light and filled the apartment with the noise of music amplified so mightily that it knocked a china ornament from a table to the floor. She rushed to the instrument and reduced the volume. The violent forces that were snared in the ugly gumwood cabinet made her uneasy. Her children came home from school then, and she took them to the Park. It was not until later in the afternoon that she was able to return to the radio.

The maid had given the children their suppers and was supervising their baths when Irene turned on the radio, reduced the volume, and sat down to listen to a Mozart quintet that she knew and enjoyed. The music came through clearly. The new instrument had a much purer tone, she thought, than the old one. She decided that tone was most important and that she could conceal the cabinet behind a sofa. But as soon as she had made her peace with the radio, the interference began. A crackling sound like the noise of a burning powder fuse began to accompany the singing of the strings. Beyond the music, there was a rustling that reminded Irene unpleasantly of the sea, and as the quintet progressed, these noises were joined by many others. She tried all the dials and switches but nothing dimmed the interference, and she sat down, disappointed and bewildered, and tried to trace the flight of the melody. The elevator shaft in her building ran beside the living-room wall, and it was the noise of the elevator that gave her a clue to the character of the static. The rattling of the elevator cables and the opening and closing of the elevator doors were reproduced in her loudspeaker, and, realizing that the radio was sensitive to electrical currents of all sorts, she began to discern through the Mozart the ringing of telephone bells, the dialing of phones, and the lamentation of a vacuum cleaner. By listening more carefully, she was able to distinguish doorbells, elevator bells, electric razors, and Waring mixers, whose sounds had been picked up from the apartments that surrounded hers and transmitted through her loudspeaker. The powerful and ugly instrument, with its mistaken sensitivity to discord, was more than she could hope to master, so she turned the thing off and went into the nursery to see her children.

When Jim Westcott came home that night, he went to the radio   5
confidently and worked the controls. He had the same sort of experience Irene had had. A man was speaking on the station Jim had chosen, and his voice swung instantly from the distance into a force so
powerful that it shook the apartment. Jim turned the volume control
and reduced the voice. Then, a minute or two later, the interference
began. The ringing of telephones and doorbells set in, joined by the
rasp of the elevator doors and the whir of cooking appliances. The
character of the noise had changed since Irene had tried the radio earlier; the last of the electric razors was being unplugged, the vacuum
cleaners had all been returned to their closets, and the static reflected
that change in pace that overtakes the city after the sun goes down. He
fiddled with the knobs but couldn't get rid of the noises, so he turned
the radio off and told Irene that in the morning he'd call the people
who had sold it to him and give them hell.

The following afternoon, when Irene returned to the apartment   6
from a luncheon date, the maid told her that a man had come and
fixed the radio. Irene went into the living room before she took off her
hat or her furs and tried the instrument. From the loudspeaker came a
recording of the "Missouri Waltz." It reminded her of the thin, scratchy
music from an old-fashioned phonograph that she sometimes heard
across the lake where she spent her summers. She waited until the
waltz had finished, expecting an explanation of the recording, but
there was none. The music was followed by silence, and then the
plaintive and scratchy record was repeated. She turned the dial and
got a satisfactory burst of Caucasian music—the thump of bare feet in
the dust and the rattle of coin jewelry—but in the background she
could hear the ringing of bells and confusion of voices. Her children
came home from school then, and she turned off the radio and went to
the nursery.

When Jim came home that night, he was tired, and he took a bath   7
and changed his clothes. Then he joined Irene in the living room. He
had just turned on the radio when the maid announced dinner, so he
left it on, and he and Irene went to the table.

Jim was too tired to make even a pretense of sociability, and there   8
was nothing about the dinner to hold Irene's interest, so her attention
wandered from the food to the deposits of silver polish on the candle-
sticks and from there to the music in the other room. She listened for
a few minutes to a Chopin prelude and then was surprised to hear a
man's voice break in. "For Christ's sake, Kathy," he said, "do you always have to play the piano when I get home?" The music stopped
abruptly. "It's the only chance I have," a woman said. "I'm at the office
all day." "So am I," the man said. He added something obscene about
an upright piano, and slammed a door. The passionate and melancholy
music began again.

"Did you hear that?" Irene asked.   9

"What?" Jim was eating his dessert.   10

"The radio. A man said something while the music was still going   11
on—something dirty."

"It's probably a play."   12

"I don't think it *is* a play," Irene said.   13

They left the table and took their coffee into the living room. Irene   14
asked Jim to try another station. He turned the knob. "Have you seen
my garters?" a man asked. "Button me up," a woman said. "Have you
seen my garters?" the man said again. "Just button me up and I'll find
your garters," the woman said. Jim shifted to another station. "I wish
you wouldn't leave apple cores in the ashtrays," a man said. "I hate the
smell."

"This is strange," Jim said.   15

"Isn't it?" Irene said.   16

Jim turned the knob again. "'On the coast of Coromandel where   17
the early pumpkins blow,'" a woman with a pronounced English ac-
cent said, "'in the middle of the woods lived the Yonghy-Bonghy-Bò.
Two old chairs, and half a candle, one old jug without a handle . . .'"

"My God!" Irene cried. "That's the Sweeneys' nurse."   18

"'These were all his worldly goods,'" the British voice continued.   19

"Turn that thing off," Irene said. "Maybe they can hear *us*." Jim   20
switched the radio off. "That was Miss Armstrong, the Sweeneys'
nurse," Irene said. "She must be reading to the little girl. They live in
17-B. I've talked with Miss Armstrong in the Park. I know her voice
very well. We must be getting other people's apartments."

"That's impossible," Jim said.   21

"Well, that was the Sweeneys' nurse," Irene said hotly. "I know   22
her voice. I know it very well. I'm wondering if they can hear us."

Jim turned the switch. First from a distance and then nearer,   23
nearer, as if borne on the wind, came the pure accents of the
Sweeneys' nurse again: "'*Lady Jingly! Lady Jingly!*'" she said, "'*sitting
where the pumpkins blow, will you come and be my wife? said the Yonghy-
Bonghy-Bò . . .*'"

Jim went over to the radio and said "Hello" loudly into the   24
speaker.

"'*I am tired of living singly.*'" the nurse went on, "'*on this coast so wild   25
and shingly, I'm a-weary of my life; if you'll come and be my wife, quite serene
would be my life . . .*'"

"I guess she can't hear us," Irene said. "Try something else."   26

Jim turned to another station, and the living room was filled with   27
the uproar of a cocktail party that had overshot its mark. Someone was
playing the piano and singing the "Whiffenpoof Song,"[4] and the voices

---

4. the "Whiffenpoof Song": unofficial drinking song of Yale undergraduates.

that surrounded the piano were vehement and happy. "Eat some more sandwiches," a woman shrieked. There were screams of laughter and a dish of some sort crashed to the floor.

"Those must be the Fullers, in 11-E," Irene said. "I knew they were giving a party this afternoon. I saw her in the liquor store. Isn't this too divine? Try something else. See if you can get those people in 18-C." 28

The Westcotts overheard that evening a monologue on salmon fishing in Canada, a bridge game, running comments on home movies of what had apparently been a fortnight at Sea Island, and a bitter family quarrel about an overdraft at the bank. They turned off their radio at midnight and went to bed, weak with laughter. Sometime in the night, their son began to call for a glass of water and Irene got one and took it to his room. It was very early. All the lights in the neighborhood were extinguished, and from the boy's window she could see the empty street. She went into the living room and tried the radio. There was some faint coughing, a moan, and then a man spoke. "Are you all right, darling?" he asked. "Yes," a woman said wearily. "Yes, I'm all right, I guess," and then she added with great feeling, "But, you know, Charlie, I don't feel like myself any more. Sometimes there are about fifteen or twenty minutes in the week when I feel like myself. I don't like to go to another doctor, because the doctor's bills are so awful already, but I just don't feel like myself, Charlie. I just never feel like myself." They were not young, Irene thought. She guessed from the timbre of their voices that they were middle-aged. The restrained melancholy of the dialogue and the draft from the bedroom window made her shiver, and she went back to bed. 29

The following morning, Irene cooked breakfast for the family—the maid didn't come up from her room in the basement until ten—braided her daughter's hair, and waited at the door until her children and her husband had been carried away in the elevator. Then she went into the living room and tried the radio. "I don't want to go to school," a child screamed. "I hate school. I won't go to school. I hate school." "You will go to school," an enraged woman said. "We paid eight hundred dollars to get you into that school and you'll go if it kills you." The next number on the dial produced the worn record of the "Missouri Waltz." Irene shifted the control and invaded the privacy of several breakfast tables. She overheard demonstrations of indigestion, carnal love, abysmal vanity, faith, and despair. Irene's life was nearly as simple and sheltered as it appeared to be, and the forthright and sometimes brutal language that came from the loudspeaker that morning astonished and troubled her. She continued to listen until her maid came in. Then she turned off the radio quickly, since this insight, she realized, was a furtive one. 30

Irene had a luncheon date with a friend that day, and she left her   31
apartment at a little after twelve. There were a number of women in
the elevator when it stopped at her floor. She stared at their handsome
and impassive faces, their furs, and the cloth flowers in their hats.
Which one of them had been to Sea Island? she wondered. Which one
had overdrawn her bank account? The elevator stopped at the tenth
floor and a woman with a pair of Skye terries joined them. Her hair
was rigged high on her head and she wore a mink cape. She was humming the "Missouri Waltz."

Irene had two Martinis at lunch, and she looked searchingly at her   32
friend and wondered what her secrets were. They had intended to go
shopping after lunch, but Irene excused herself and went home. She
told the maid that she was not to be disturbed; then she went into the
living room, closed the doors, and switched on the radio. She heard, in
the course of the afternoon, the halting conversation of a woman entertaining her aunt, the hysterical conclusion of a luncheon party, and
a hostess briefing her maid about some cocktail guests. "Don't give the
best Scotch to anyone who hasn't white hair," the hostess said. "See if
you can get rid of that liver paste before you pass those hot things, and
could you lend me five dollars? I want to tip the elevator man."

As the afternoon waned, the conversations increased in intensity.   33
From where Irene sat, she could see the open sky above the East River.
There were hundreds of clouds in the sky, as though the south wind
had broken the winter into pieces and were blowing it north, and on
her radio she could hear the arrival of cocktail guests and the return of
children and businessmen from their schools and offices. "I found a
good-sized diamond on the bathroom floor this morning," a woman
said. "It must have fallen out of that bracelet Mrs. Dunston was wearing last night." "We'll sell it," a man said. "Take it down to the jeweler
on Madison Avenue and sell it. Mrs. Dunston won't know the difference, and we could use a couple of hundred bucks . . ." "'Oranges and
lemons, say the bells of St. Clement's,'" the Sweeneys' nurse sang.
"'Halfpence and farthings, say the bells of St. Martin's. When will you
pay me? say the bells at old Bailey . . .'" "It's not a hat," a woman
cried, and at her back roared a cocktail party. "It's not a hat, it's a love
affair. That's what Walter Florell said. He said it's not a hat, it's a love
affair," and then, in a lower voice, the same women added, "Talk to
somebody, for Christ's sake, honey, talk to somebody. If she catches
you standing here not talking to anybody, she'll take us off her invitation list, and I love these parties."

The Westcotts were going out for dinner that night, and when Jim   34
came home, Irene was dressing. She seemed sad and vague, and he
brought her a drink. They were dining with friends in the neighborhood, and they walked to where they were going. The sky was broad

and filled with light. It was one of those splendid spring evenings that excite memory and desire, and the air that touched their hands and faces felt very soft. A Salvation Army band was on the corner playing "Jesus Is Sweeter." Irene drew on her husband's arm and held him there for a minute, to hear the music. "They're really such nice people, aren't they?" she said. "They have such nice faces. Actually, they're so much nicer than a lot of the people we know." She took a bill from her purse and walked over and dropped it into the tambourine. There was in her face, when she returned to her husband, a look of radiant melancholy that he was not familiar with. And her conduct at the dinner party that night seemed strange to him, too. She interrupted her hostess rudely and stared at the people across the table from her with an intensity for which she would have punished her children.

It was still mild when they walked home from the party, and Irene   35
looked up at the spring stars. "'How far that little candle throws its beams,'" she exclaimed. "'So shines a good deed in a naughty world.'" She waited that night until Jim had fallen asleep, and then went into the living room and turned on the radio.

Jim came home at about six the next night. Emma, the maid, let   36
him in, and he had taken off his hat and was taking off his coat when Irene ran into the hall. Her face was shining with tears and her hair was disordered. "Go up to 16-C, Jim!" she screamed. "Don't take off your coat. Go up to 16-C. Mr. Osborn's beating his wife. They've been quarreling since four o'clock, and now he's hitting her. Go up there and stop him."

From the radio in the living room, Jim heard screams, obscenities,   37
and thuds. "You know you don't have to listen to this sort of thing," he said. He strode into the living room and turned the switch. "It's indecent," he said. "It's like looking in windows. You know you don't have to listen to this sort of thing. You can turn it off."

"Oh, it's so horrible, it's so dreadful," Irene was sobbing. "I've been   38
listening all day, and it's so depressing."

"Well, if it's so depressing, why do you listen to it? I bought this   39
damned radio to give you some pleasure," he said. "I paid a great deal of money for it. I thought it might make you happy. I wanted to make you happy."

"Don't, don't, don't, don't quarrel with me," she moaned, and laid   40
her head on his shoulder. "All the others have been quarreling all day. Everybody's been quarreling. They're all worried about money. Mrs. Hutchinson's mother is dying of cancer in Florida and they don't have enough money to send her to the Mayo Clinic. At least, Mr. Hutchinson says they don't have enough money. And some woman in this

building is having an affair with the handyman—with that hideous handyman. It's too disgusting. And Mrs. Melville has heart trouble and Mr. Hendricks is going to lose his job in April and Mrs. Hendricks is horrid about the whole thing and that girl who plays the 'Missouri Waltz' is a whore, a common whore, and the elevator man has tuber- culosis and Mr. Osborn has been beating Mrs. Osborn." She wailed, she trembled with grief and checked the stream of tears down her face with the heel of her palm.

"Well, why do you have to listen?" Jim asked again. "Why do you have to listen to this stuff if it makes you so miserable?" 41

"Oh, don't, don't don't," she cried. "Life is too terrible, too sordid and awful. But we've never been like that, have we, darling? Have we? I mean, we've always been good and decent and loving to one an- other, haven't we? And we have two children, two beautiful children. Our lives aren't sordid, are they, darling? Are they?" She flung her arms around his neck and drew his face down to hers. "We're happy, aren't we, darling? We are happy, aren't we?" 42

"Of course we're happy," he said tiredly. He began to surrender his resentment. "Of course we're happy. I'll have that damned radio fixed or taken away tomorrow." He stroked her soft hair. "My poor girl," he said. 43

"You love me, don't you?" she asked. "And we're not hypercritical or worried about money or dishonest, are we?" 44

"No, darling," he said. 45

A man came in the morning and fixed the radio. Irene turned it on cautiously and was happy to hear a California-wine commercial and a recording of Beethoven's Ninth Symphony, including Schiller's "Ode to Joy." She kept the radio on all day and nothing untoward came from the speaker. 46

A Spanish suite was being played when Jim came home. "Is every- thing all right?" he asked. His face was pale, she thought. They had some cocktails and went in to dinner to the "Anvil Chorus" from Il Trovatore. This was followed by Debussy's "La Mer." 47

"I paid the bill for the radio today," Jim said. "It cost four hundred dollars. I hope you'll get some enjoyment out of it." 48

"Oh, I'm sure I will," Irene said. 49

"Four hundred dollars is a good deal more than I can afford," he went on. "I wanted to get something that you'd enjoy. It's the last ex- travagance we'll be able to indulge in this year. I see that you haven't paid your clothing bills yet. I saw them on your dressing table." He looked directly at her. "Why did you tell me you'd paid them? Why did you lie to me?" 50

"I just didn't want you to worry, Jim," she said. She drank some 51
water. "I'll be able to pay my bills out of this month's allowance. There
were the slipcovers last month, and that party."

"You've got to learn to handle the money I give you a little more 52
intelligently, Irene," he said. "You've got to understand that we won't
have as much money this year as we had last. I had a very sobering
talk with Mitchell today. No one is buying anything. We're spending
all our time promoting new issues, and you know how long that takes.
I'm not getting any younger, you know. I'm thirty-seven. My hair will
be gray next year. I haven't done as well as I'd hoped to do. And I
don't suppose things will get any better."

"Yes, dear," she said. 53

"We've got to start cutting down," Jim said. "We've got to think of 54
the children. To be perfectly frank with you, I worry about money a
great deal. I'm not at all sure of the future. No one is. If anything
should happen to me, there's the insurance, but that wouldn't go very
far today. I've worked awfully hard to give you and the children a
comfortable life," he said bitterly. "I don't like to see all of my energies,
all of my youth, wasted in fur coats and radios and slipcovers and—"

"Please, Jim," she said. "Please. They'll hear us." 55

"*Who'll hear us?* Emma can't hear us." 56

"The radio." 57

"Oh, I'm sick!" he shouted. "I'm sick to death of your apprehen- 58
siveness. The radio can't hear us. Nobody can hear us. And what if
they can hear us? Who cares?"

Irene got up from the table and went into the living room. Jim 59
went to the door and shouted at her from there. "Why are you so
Christly all of a sudden? What's turned you overnight into a convent
girl? You stole your mother's jewelry before they probated her will.
You never gave your sister a cent of that money that was intended for
her—not even when she needed it. You made Grace Howland's life
miserable, and where was all your piety and your virtue when you
went to that abortionist? I'll never forget how cool you were. You
packed your bag and went off to have that child murdered as if you
were going to Nassau. If you'd had any reasons, if you'd had any good
reasons—"

Irene stood for a minute before the hideous cabinet, disgraced and 60
sickened, but she held her hand on the switch before she extinguished
the music and the voices, hoping that the instrument might speak to
her kindly, that she might hear the Sweeneys' nurse. Jim continued to
shout at her from the door. The voice on the radio was suave and non-
committal. "An early-morning railroad disaster in Tokyo," the loudspeaker said, "killed twenty-nine people. A fire in a Catholic hospital
near Buffalo for the care of blind children was extinguished early this

morning by nuns. The temperature is forty-seven. The humidity is eighty-nine."

CHRISTINA ROSSETTI

In an Artist's Studio

Christina Rossetti (1830–1894), daughter of an Italian politician/poet exiled in London, England, was educated at home. Like many daughters of families with more education than money she seemed destined to be a governess, but found the prospect dull. Perhaps in response, she developed during adolescence a vague illness that kept her first in her parents' house, then in the house of her brother, the famous Pre-Raphaelite poet and artist Dante Gabriel Rossetti. Surrounded by poets, and sometimes posing as a model for the painters of the Pre-Raphaelite Brotherhood, she became a social worker and a writer of essays, children's books, short stories, and much admired poetry. "In an Artist's Studio" may reflect her own experience as a model. It may also allude to Elizabeth Siddal, the favorite model of the Brotherhood, who became her brother's mistress, then his wife, and then committed suicide in 1861, the year the poem was written. The poem reminds us that the problem of representation in the media, particularly the representation of women, predates movies and television.

> One face looks out from all his canvases,
>   One selfsame figure sits or walks or leans:
>   We found her hidden just behind those screens,
> That mirror gave back all her loveliness.
> A queen in opal or in ruby dress,
>   A nameless girl in freshest summer-greens,
>   A saint, an angel—every canvas means
> The same one meaning, neither more nor less.
> He feeds upon her face by day and night,
>   And she with true kind eyes looks back on him,
> Fair as the moon and joyful as the light:
>   Not wan with waiting, not with sorrow dim;
> Not as she is, but was when hope shone bright;
>   Not as she is, but as she fills his dream.

UNDERSTANDING

We find ourselves in our findings.

Overview

In the minds of many people, understanding means the accumulation of facts. Politicians commonly complain about the number of high school students who don't know who the sixteenth president of the United States was or what year Columbus reached America. Surely factual knowledge is important: it secures our connection to history and culture, opens the door to a sophisticated understanding of the natural world, and provides educated people with a common language. But true understanding involves far more than being a Trivial Pursuit champion, for, as Samuel Scudder explains, "facts are stupid things . . . until brought into connection with some general law." In other words, facts are merely the building blocks of understanding, worth very little unless we know how to think about and interpret them, how to use them, and how *not* to use them. This unit provides opportunities, then, for exploring our means of making sense of the world—and of finding ourselves in our findings.

COUNTY ATTORNEY. I guess before we're through she may have something more serious than preserves to worry about.

HALE. Well, women are used to worrying about trifles.

I am making use
of the one thing I learned
of all the things my father tried to teach me:
the art of memory

FRANK CONROY

Think About It

Frank Conroy (1936–   ) was born in New York and received his
B.A. from Haverford College. Conroy's reputation as a writer came
with the publication of his autobiographical *Stop-Time* (1967), which
is both a picture of a family unraveling and a re-creation of the pains
and joys of early adolescence. Nineteen years later he published a collection of short prose pieces, *Midair* (1986); during the intervening
years, Conroy was teaching and, he claims, "out doing errands." In
addition, he has contributed essays and stories to several periodicals,
particularly the *New Yorker,* and he selected the stories for *The Iowa
Award: The Best Stories from Twenty Years* (1991). Conroy is a jazz pianist as well as a writer, performing with a group once a week at the
Georgetown Fish House in Washington, D.C. He also has been, since
1981, director of the literature program of the National Endowment
for the Arts.

"Think About It" was published in *Harper's* in November 1988
and collected in *Best American Essays of 1989.* Reading it can help us
write about our own flashes of understanding that illuminate what
had been mystery before. A useful companion essay is Samuel Scudder's "Learning to See," in which revelation comes to the student
through a distinct method of learning.

When I was sixteen I worked selling hot dogs at a stand in the   1
Fourteenth Street subway station in New York City, one level above
the trains and one below the street, where the crowds continually
flowed back and forth. I worked with three Puerto Rican men who
could not speak English. I had no Spanish, and although we understood each other well with regard to the tasks at hand, sensing and adjusting to each other's body movements in the extremely confined
space in which we operated, I felt isolated with no one to talk to. On
my break I came out from behind the counter and passed the time
with two old black men who ran a shoeshine stand in a dark corner of
the corridor. It was a poor location, half hidden by columns, and they
didn't have much business. I would sit with my back against the wall
while they stood or moved around their ancient elevated stand, talking to each other or to me, but always staring into the distance as they
did so.

As the weeks went by I realized that they never looked at anything   2
in their immediate vicinity—not at me or their stand or anybody who
might come within ten or fifteen feet. They did not look at approaching customers once they were inside the perimeter. Save for the instant it took to discern the color of the shoes, they did not even look at

603

what they were doing while they worked, but rubbed in polish, brushed, and buffed by feel while looking over their shoulders, into the distance, as if awaiting the arrival of an important person. Of course there wasn't all that much distance in the underground station, but their behavior was so focused and consistent they seemed somehow to transcend the physical. A powerful mood was created, and I came almost to believe that these men could see through walls, through girders, and around corners to whatever hyperspace it was where whoever it was they were waiting and watching for would finally emerge. Their scattered talk was hip, elliptical, and hinted at mysteries beyond my white boy's ken, but it was the staring off, the long, steady staring off, that had me hypnotized. I left for a better job, with handshakes from both of them, without understanding what I had seen.

Perhaps ten years later, after playing jazz with black musicians in various Harlem clubs, hanging out uptown with a few young artists and intellectuals, I began to learn from them something of the extraordinarily varied and complex riffs and rituals embraced by different people to help themselves get through life in the ghetto. Fantasy of all kinds—from playful to dangerous—was in the very air of Harlem. It was the spice of uptown life.

Only then did I understand the two shoeshine men. They were trapped in a demeaning situation in a dark corner in an underground corridor in a filthy subway system. Their continuous staring off was a kind of statement, a kind of dance. Our bodies are here, went the statement, but our souls are receiving nourishment from distant sources only we can see. They were powerful magic dancers, sorcerers almost, and thirty-five years later I can still feel the pressure of their spell.

The light bulb may appear over your head, is what I'm saying, but it may be a while before it actually goes on. Early in my attempts to learn jazz piano, I used to listen to recordings of a fine player named Red Garland, whose music I admired. I couldn't quite figure out what he was doing with his left hand, however; the chords eluded me. I went uptown to an obscure club where he was playing with his trio, caught him on his break, and simply asked him. "Sixths," he said cheerfully. And then he went away.

I didn't know what to make of it. The basic jazz chord is the seventh, which comes in various configurations, but it is what it is. I was a self-taught pianist, pretty shaky on theory and harmony, and when he said sixths I kept trying to fit the information into what I already knew, and it didn't fit. But it stuck in my mind—a tantalizing mystery.

A couple of years later, when I began playing with a bass player, I discovered more or less by accident that if the bass played the root and I played a sixth based on the fifth note of the scale, a very interesting chord involving both instruments emerged. Ordinarily, I suppose I would have skipped over the matter and not paid much attention, but I remembered Garland's remark and so I stopped and spent a week or two working out the voicings, and greatly strengthened my foundations as a player. I had remembered what I hadn't understood, you might say, until my life caught up with the information and the light bulb went on.

I remember another, more complicated example from my sopho- 8 more year at a small liberal-arts college outside Philadelphia. I seemed never to be able to get up in time for breakfast in the dining hall. I would get coffee and a doughnut in the Coop instead—a basement area with about a dozen small tables where students could get something to eat at odd hours. Several mornings in a row I noticed a strange man sitting by himself with a cup of coffee. He was in his sixties, perhaps, and sat straight in his chair with very little extraneous movement. I guessed he was some sort of distinguished visitor to the college who had decided to put in some time at a student hangout. But no one ever sat with him. One morning I approached his table and asked if I could join him.

"Certainly," he said. "Please do." He had perhaps the clearest eyes 9 I had ever seen, like blue ice, and to be held in their steady gaze was not, at first, an entirely comfortable experience. His eyes gave nothing away about himself while at the same time creating in me the eerie impression that he was looking directly into my soul. He asked a few quick questions, as if to put me at my ease, and we fell into conversation. He was William O. Douglas from the Supreme Court, and when he saw how startled I was he said, "Call me Bill. Now tell me what you're studying and why you get up so late in the morning." Thus began a series of talks that stretched over many weeks. The fact that I was an ignorant sophomore with literary pretentions who knew nothing about the law didn't seem to bother him. We talked about everything from Shakespeare to the possibility of life on other planets. One day I mentioned that I was going to have dinner with Judge Learned Hand. I explained that Hand was my girlfriend's grandfather. Douglas nodded, but I could tell he was surprised at the coincidence of my knowing the chief judge of the most important court in the country save the Supreme Court itself. After fifty years on the bench Judge Hand had become a famous man, both in and out of legal circles—a living legend, to his own dismay. "Tell him hello and give him my best regards," Douglas said.

Learned Hand, in his eighties, was a short, barrel-chested man 10 with a large, square head, huge, thick, bristling eyebrows, and soft brown eyes. He radiated energy and would sometimes bark out remarks or questions in the living room as if he were in court. His humor was sharp, but often leavened with a touch of self-mockery. When something caught his funny bone he would burst out with explosive laughter—the laughter of a man who enjoyed laughing. He had a large repertoire of dramatic expressions involving the use of his eyebrows— very useful, he told me conspiratorially, when looking down on things from behind the bench. (The court stenographer could not record the movement of his eyebrows.) When I told him I'd been talking to William O. Douglas, they first shot up in exaggerated surprise, and then lowered and moved forward in a glower.

"*Justice* William O. Douglas, young man," he admonished. "Justice 11 Douglas, if you please." About the Supreme Court in general, Hand insisted on a tone of profound respect. Little did I know that in private correspondence he had referred to the Court as "The Blessed Saints, Cherubim and Seraphim," "The Jolly Boys," "The Nine Tin Jesuses," "The Nine Blameless Ethiopians," and my particular favorite, "The Nine Blessed Chalices of the Sacred Effluvium."

Hand was badly stooped and had a lot of pain in his lower back. 12 Martinis helped, but his strict Yankee wife approved of only one before dinner. It was my job to make the second and somehow slip it to him. If the pain was particularly acute he would get out of his chair and lie flat on the rug, still talking, and finish his point without missing a beat. He flattered me by asking for my impression of Justice Douglas, instructed me to convey his warmest regards, and then began talking about the Dennis case, which he described as a particularly tricky and difficult case involving the prosecution of eleven leaders of the Communist party. He had just started in on the First Amendment and free speech when we were called into dinner.

William O. Douglas loved the outdoors with a passion, and we fell 13 into the habit of having coffee in the Coop and then strolling under the trees down toward the duck pond. About the Dennis case, he said something to this effect: "Eleven Communists arrested by the government. Up to no good, said the government; dangerous people, violent overthrow, etc., First Amendment, said the defense, freedom of speech, etc." Douglas stopped walking. "Clear and present danger."

"What?" I asked. He often talked in a telegraphic manner, and one 14 was expected to keep up with him. It was sometimes like listening to a man thinking out loud.

"Clear and present danger,"[1] he said. "That was the issue. Did they 15 constitute a clear and present danger? I don't think so. I think everybody took the language pretty far in Dennis." He began walking, striding along quickly. Again, one was expected to keep up with him. "The F.B.I. was all over them. Phones tapped, constant surveillance. How

---

1. Clear and present danger: The phrase Douglas is using was first introduced by Justice Oliver Wendell Holmes in a 1919 Supreme Court decision that allowed the suppression of an antidraft circular during World War I.

could it be clear and present danger with the F.B.I. watching every move they made? That's a ginkgo," he said suddenly, pointing at a tree. "A beauty. You don't see those every day. Ask Hand about clear and present danger."

I was in fact reluctant to do so. Douglas's argument seemed to me   16
to be crushing—the last word, really—and I didn't want to embarrass Judge Hand. But back in the living room, on the second martini, the old man asked about Douglas. I sort of scratched my nose and recapitulated the conversation by the ginkgo tree.

"What?" Hand shouted. "Speak up, sir, for heaven's sake."   17

"He said the F.B.I. was watching them all the time so there   18
couldn't be a clear and present danger," I blurted out, blushing as I said it.

A terrible silence filled the room. Hand's eyebrows writhed on his   19
face like two huge caterpillars. He leaned forward in the wing chair, his face settling, finally, into a grim expression. "I am astonished," he said softly, his eyes holding mine, "at Justice Douglas's newfound faith in the Federal Bureau of Investigation." His big, granite head moved even closer to mine, until I could smell the martini. "I had understood him to consider it a politically corrupt, incompetent organization, directed by a power-crazed lunatic." I realized I had been holding my breath throughout all of this, and as I relaxed, I saw the faintest trace of a smile cross Hand's face. Things are sometimes more complicated than they first appear, his smile seemed to say. The old man leaned back. "The proximity of the danger is something to think about. Ask him about that. See what he says."

I chewed the matter over as I returned to campus. Hand had   20
pointed out some of Douglas's language about the F.B.I. from other sources that seemed to bear out his point. I thought about the words "clear and present danger," and the fact that if you looked at them closely they might not be as simple as they had first appeared. What degree of danger? Did the word "present" allude to the proximity of the danger, or just the fact that the danger was there at all—that it wasn't an anticipated danger? Were there other hidden factors these great men were weighing of which I was unaware?

But Douglas was gone, back to Washington. (The writer in me is   21
tempted to create a scene here—to invent one for dramatic purposes— but of course I can't do that.) My brief time as a messenger boy was over, and I felt a certain frustration, as if, with a few more exchanges, the matter of *Dennis* v. *United States* might have been resolved to my satisfaction. They'd left me high and dry. But, of course, it is precisely because the matter did not resolve that has caused me to think about it, off and on, all these years. "The Constitution," Hand used to say to me flatly, "is a piece of paper. The Bill of Rights is a piece of paper." It was many years before I understood what he meant. Documents alone

do not keep democracy alive, nor maintain the state of law. There is no particular safety in them. Living men and women, generation after generation, must continually remake democracy and the law, and that involves an ongoing state of tension between the past and the present which will never completely resolve.

22

Education doesn't end until life ends, because you never know when you're going to understand something you hadn't understood before. For me, the magic dance of the shoeshine men was the kind of experience in which understanding came with a kind of click, a resolving kind of click. The same with the experience at the piano. What happened with Justice Douglas and Judge Hand was different, and makes the point that understanding does not always mean resolution. Indeed, in our intellectual lives, our creative lives, it is perhaps those problems that will never resolve that rightly claim the lion's share of our energies. The physical body exists in a constant state of tension as it maintains homeostasis, and so too does the active mind embrace the tension of never being certain, never being absolutely sure, never being done, as it engages the world. That is our special fate, our inexpressibly valuable condition.

SAMUEL SCUDDER

Learning to See

Samuel Scudder (1837–1911) was born in Boston and graduated from Williams College and Harvard University. At Harvard, Scudder studied with the celebrated zoologist and geologist Louis Agassiz. Known for laying the foundation for descriptive biology and as the leading American opponent of Darwin, Agassiz made Harvard the center for natural history instruction and research during the midnineteenth century. Adopting the scientific methods of Agassiz, Scudder became known for the incredible detail with which he worked. Considered the most productive biologist of his time, he described 630 species of insects and named 1,144 species of fossil insects. *The Butterflies of the Eastern United States and Canada* (1888–1889), his best-known work, is the result of thirty years of research on butterflies. Other works include *Catalog of Scientific Serials of All Countries 1633–1876* (1879) and *Nomenclator zoologicus* (1882–1884).

"Learning to See" was first published anonymously in *Every Saturday*, April 4, 1874. A classic description of one way that a teacher can introduce students to a topic, the essay invites readers to tell their own stories of glorious (or miserable) relationships with teachers. A useful companion essay is Malcolm X's "Learning to Read," which describes his solitary struggle to become literate.

It was more than fifteen years ago that I entered the laboratory of
Professor Agassiz, and told him I had enrolled my name in the Scientific School as a student of natural history. He asked me a few questions about my object in coming, my antecedents generally, the mode
in which I afterwards proposed to use the knowledge I might acquire,
and, finally, whether I wished to study any special branch. To the latter I replied that, while I wished to be well grounded in all depart-
ments of zoology, I purposed to devote myself specially to insects.

"When do you wish to begin?" he asked.

"Now," I replied.

This seemed to please him, and with an energetic "Very well!" he
reached from a shelf a huge jar of specimens in yellow alcohol.

"Take this fish," said he, "and look at it; we call it a haemulon; by
and by I will ask what you have seen."

With that he left me, but in a moment returned with explicit instructions as to the care of the object entrusted to me.

"No man is fit to be a naturalist," said he, "who does not know
how to take care of specimens."

I was to keep the fish before me in a tin tray, and occasionally
moisten the surface with alcohol from the jar, always taking care to replace the stopper tightly. Those were not the days of ground-glass stop-
pers and elegantly shaped exhibition jars; all the old students will
recall the huge necklace glass bottles with their leaky, wax-besmeared
corks, half eaten by insects, and begrimed with cellar dust. Entomol-
ogy was a cleaner science than ichthyology, but the example of the
Professor, who had unhesitatingly plunged to the bottom of the jar to
produce the fish, was infectious; and though this alcohol had a "very
ancient and fishlike smell,"[1] I really dared not show any aversion
within these sacred precincts, and treated the alcohol as though it
were pure water. Still I was conscious of a passing feeling of disappointment, for gazing at a fish did not commend itself to an ardent entomologist. My friends at home, too, were annoyed when they
discovered that no amount of eau-de-Cologne would drown the perfume which haunted me like a shadow.

In ten minutes I had seen all that could be seen in that fish, and
started in search of the Professor—who had, however, left the Museum; and when I returned, after lingering over some of the odd animals stored in the upper apartment, my specimen was dry all over. I
dashed the fluid over the fish as if to resuscitate the beast from a faint-
ing-fit, and looked with anxiety for a return of the normal sloppy appearance. This little excitement over, nothing was to be done but to
return to a steadfast gaze at my mute companion. Half an hour
passed—an hour—another hour; the fish began to look loathsome. I

---

1. The quotation is from Shakespeare, *The Tempest*, II, ii, 25.

turned it over and around; looked it in the face—ghastly; from behind, beneath, above, sideways, at a three-quarters' view—just as ghastly. I was in despair; at an early hour I concluded that lunch was necessary; so, with infinite relief, the fish was carefully replaced in the jar, and for an hour I was free.

On my return, I learned that Professor Agassiz had been at the Museum, but had gone, and would not return for several hours. My fellow-students were too busy to be disturbed by continued conversation. Slowly I drew forth that hideous fish, and with a feeling of desperation again looked at it. I might not use a magnifying-glass; instruments of all kinds were interdicted. My two hands, my two eyes, and the fish; it seemed a most limited field. I pushed my finger down its throat to feel how sharp the teeth were. I began to count the scales in the different rows, until I was convinced that that was nonsense. At last a happy thought struck me—I would draw the fish; and now with surprise I began to discover new features in the creature. Just then the Professor returned. 10

"That is right," he said; "a pencil is one of the best of eyes. I am glad to notice, too, that you keep your specimen wet, and your bottle corked." 11

With these encouraging words, he added: 12

"Well, what is it like?" 13

He listened attentively to my brief rehearsal of the structure of parts whose names were still unknown to me: the fringed gill-arches and movable operculum; the pores of the head, fleshy lips and lidless eyes; the lateral line, the spinous fins and forked tail; the compressed and arched body. When I had finished, he waited as if expecting more, and then, with an air of disappointment: 14

"You have not looked very carefully; why," he continued more earnestly, "you haven't even seen one of the most conspicuous features of the animal, which is as plainly before your eyes as the fish itself; look again, look again!" and he left me to my misery. 15

I was piqued; I was mortified. Still more of that wretched fish! But now I set myself to my task with a will, and discovered one new thing after another, until I saw how just the Professor's criticism had been. The afternoon passed quickly; and when, toward its close, the Professor inquired: 16

"Do you see it yet?" 17

"No," I replied, "I am certain I do not, but I see how little I saw before." 18

"That is next best," said he, earnestly, "but I won't hear you now; put away your fish and go home; perhaps you will be ready with a better answer in the morning. I will examine you before you look at the fish." 19

This was disconcerting. Not only must I think of my fish all night, studying, without the object before me, what this unknown but most 20 visible feature might be; but also, without reviewing my discoveries, I must give an exact account of them the next day. I had a bad memory; so I walked home by Charles River in a distracted state, with my two perplexities.

The cordial greeting from the Professor the next morning was re- 21 assuring; here was a man who seemed to be quite as anxious as I that I should see for myself what he saw.

"Do you perhaps mean," I asked, "that the fish has symmetrical 22 sides with paired organs?"

His thoroughly pleased "Of course! of course!" repaid the wakeful 23 hours of the previous night. After he had discoursed most happily and enthusiastically—as he always did—upon the importance of this point, I ventured to ask what I should do next.

"Oh, look at your fish!" he said, and left me again to my own de- 24 vices. In a little more than an hour he returned, and heard my new catalogue.

"That is good, that is good!" he repeated; "but that is not all; go 25 on"; and so for three long days he placed that fish before my eyes, forbidding me to look at anything else, or to use any artificial aid. "Look, look, look," was his repeated injunction.

This was the best entomological lesson I ever had— a lesson whose 26 influence has extended to the details of every subsequent study; a legacy the Professor has left to me, as he has left it to many others, of inestimable value, which we could not buy, with which we cannot part.

A year afterward, some of us were amusing ourselves with chalk- 27 ing outlandish beasts on the Museum blackboard. We drew prancing starfishes; frogs in mortal combat; hydra-headed worms; stately crawfishes, standing on their tails, bearing aloft umbrellas; and grotesque fishes with gaping mouths and staring eyes. The Professor came in shortly after, and was as amused as any at our experiments. He looked at the fishes.

"Haemulons, every one of them," he said; "Mr. —— drew them." 28

True; and to this day, if I attempt a fish, I can draw nothing but 29 haemulons.

The fourth day, a second fish of the same group was placed beside 30 the first, and I was bidden to point out the resemblances and differences between the two; another and another followed, until the entire family lay before me, and a whole legion of jars covered the table and surrounding shelves; the odor had become a pleasant perfume; and even now, the sight of an old, six-inch, worm-eaten cork brings fragrant memories.

The whole group of haemulons was thus brought in review; and, 31 whether engaged upon the dissection of the internal organs, the preparation and examination of the bony framework, or the description of the various parts, Agassiz's training in the method of observing facts and their orderly arrangement was ever accompanied by the urgent exhortation not to be content with them.

"Facts are stupid things," he would say, "until brought into con-   32
nection with some general law."

At the end of eight months, it was almost with reluctance that I   33
left these friends and turned to insects; but what I had gained by this
outside experience has been of greater value than years of later investigation in my favorite groups.

ANNIE DILLARD

Seeing

Annie Dillard was born in 1945, in Pittsburgh. She is the author of
nine books including *An American Childhood, The Writing Life,* and *Holy
the Firm. The Living,* a novel, is the story of four men on the coast of
Puget Sound in the second half of the nineteenth century. In 1975,
Pilgrim at Tinker Creek was awarded the Pulitzer Prize in nonfiction.
Her writing appears in the *Atlantic, Harper's,* the *New York Times Magazine,* the *Yale Review, American Heritage,* and in many anthologies. She
has received fellowship grants from the Guggenheim Foundation and
the national Endowment for the Arts; her writing has received the
Washington Governor's Award, the Connecticut Governor's Award,
the New York Press Club Award, and the Ambassador Book Award in
Arts and Letters from the English-speaking Union.

She lives in Middletown, Connecticut, with her husband, Robert
D. Richardson, Jr., biographer of Thoreau and Emerson, and young
daughter Rosie.

The keenness of Dillard's vision and her mystical nature are re-

flected in "Seeing," which is excerpted from *Pilgrim at Tinker Creek.*
Like Samuel Scudder in "Learning to See," Dillard dwells on the nature of observation. She concludes that despite all our clamoring for
understanding, insight often comes as "a gift and a total surprise." Because Dillard is a master of detail, her essay provides a model for descriptive writing.

I chanced on a wonderful book by Marius von Senden, called *Space* 1
and Sight. When Western surgeons discovered how to perform safe
cataract operations, they ranged across Europe and America operating
on dozens of men and women of all ages who had been blinded by
cataracts since birth. Von Senden collected accounts of such cases; the
histories are fascinating. Many doctors had tested their patients' sense
perceptions and ideas of space both before and after the operations.
The vast majority of patients, of both sexes and all ages, had, in von
Senden's opinion, no idea of space whatsoever. Form, distance, and
size were so many meaningless syllables. A patient "had no idea of
depth, confusing it with roundness." Before the operation a doctor
would give a blind patient a cube and a sphere; the patient would
tongue it or feel it with his hands, and name it correctly. After the operation the doctor would show the same objects to the patient without
letting him touch them; now he had no clue whatsoever what he was
seeing. One patient called lemonade "square" because it pricked on his
tongue as a square shape pricked on the touch of his hands. Of another
postoperative patient, the doctor writes, "I have found in her no notion of size, for example, not even within the narrow limits which she
might have encompassed with the aid of touch. Thus when I asked her
to show me how big her mother was, she did not stretch out her
hands, but set her two index-fingers a few inches apart." Other doctors
reported their patients' own statements to similar effect. "The room he
was in . . . he knew to be but part of the house, yet he could not con-
ceive that the whole house could look bigger"; "Those who are blind
from birth . . . have no real conception of height or distance. A house
that is a mile away is thought of as nearby, but requiring the taking of
a lot of steps. . . . The elevator that whizzes him up and down gives no
more sense of vertical distance than does the train of horizontal."

For the newly sighted, vision is pure sensation unencumbered 2
by meaning: "The girl went through the experience that we all go
through and forget, the moment we are born. She saw, but it did not
mean anything but a lot of different kinds of brightness." Again, "I
asked the patient what he could see; he answered that he saw an extensive field of light, in which everything appeared dull, confused, and
in motion. He could not distinguish objects." Another patient saw
"nothing but a confusion of forms and colours." When a newly sighted
girl saw photographs and paintings, she asked, "'Why do they put
those dark marks all over them?' 'Those aren't dark marks,' her

[handwritten margin note: shadows define shape]

mother explained, 'those are shadows. That is one of the ways the eye knows that things have shape. If it were not for shadows many things would look flat.' 'Well, that's how things do look,' Joan answered. 'Everything looks flat with dark patches.'"

But it is the patients' concepts of space that are most revealing. One patient, according to his doctor, "practiced his vision in a strange fashion; thus he takes off one of his boots, throws it some way off in front of him, and then attempts to gauge the distance at which it lies; he takes a few steps towards the boot and tries to grasp it; on failing to reach it, he moves on a step or two and gropes for the boot until he finally gets hold of it." "But even at this stage, after three weeks' experience of seeing," von Senden goes on, "'space,' as he conceives it, ends with visual space, i.e., with colour-patches that happen to bound his view. He does not yet have the notion that a larger object (a chair) can mask a smaller one (a dog), or that the latter can still be present even though it is not directly seen."

In general the newly sighted see the world as a dazzle of color-patches. They are pleased by the sensation of color, and learn quickly to name the colors, but the rest of seeing is tormentingly difficult. Soon after his operation a patient "generally bumps into one of these colour-patches and observes them to be substantial, since they resist him as tactual objects do. In walking about it also strikes him—or can if he pays attention—that he is continually passing in between the colours he sees, that he can go past a visual object, that a part of it then steadily disappears from view; and that in spite of this, however he twists and turns—whether entering the room from the door, for example, or returning back to it—he always has a visual space in front of him. Thus he gradually comes to realize that there is also a space behind him, which he does not see."

The mental effort involved in these reasonings proves overwhelming for many patients. It oppresses them to realize, if they ever do at all, the tremendous size of the world, which they had previously conceived of as something touchingly manageable. It oppresses them to realize that they have been visible to people all along, perhaps unattractively so, without their knowledge or consent. A disheartening number of them refuse to use their new vision, continuing to go over objects with their tongues, and lapsing into apathy and despair. "The child can see, but will not make use of his sight. Only when pressed can he with difficulty be brought to look at objects in his neighbourhood; but more than a foot away it is impossible to bestir him to the necessary effort." Of a twenty-one-year-old girl, the doctor relates, "Her unfortunate father, who had hoped for so much from this operation, wrote that his daughter carefully shuts her eyes whenever she wishes to go about the house, especially when she comes to a staircase, and that she is never happier or more at ease than when, by closing

her eyelids, she relapses into her former state of total blindness." A fifteen-year-old boy, who was also in love with a girl at the asylum for
the blind, finally blurted out, "No, really, I can't stand it any more; I
want to be sent back to the asylum again. If things aren't altered, I'll
tear my eyes out."   *love more powerful than sight*

Some do learn to see, especially the young ones. But it changes   6
their lives. One doctor comments on "the rapid and complete loss of
that striking and wonderful serenity which is characteristic only of
those who have never yet seen." A blind man who learns to see is
ashamed of his old habits. He dresses up, grooms himself, and tries to
make a good impression. While he was blind he was indifferent to objects unless they were edible; now, "a sifting of values sets in . . . his
thoughts and wishes are mightily stirred and some few of the patients
are thereby led into dissimulation, envy, theft and fraud."

On the other hand, many newly sighted people speak well of the   7
world, and teach us how dull is our own vision. To one patient, a
human hand, unrecognized, is "something bright and then holes."
Shown a bunch of grapes, a boy calls out, "It is dark, blue and
shiny. . . . It isn't smooth, it has bumps and hollows." A little girl visits
a garden. "She is greatly astonished, and can scarcely be persuaded to
answer, stands speechless in front of the tree, which she only names
on taking hold of it, and then as 'the tree with the lights on it.'" Some
delight in their sight and give themselves over to the visual world. Of a
patient just after her bandages were removed, her doctor writes, "The
first things to attract her attention were her own hands; she looked at
them very closely, moved them repeatedly to and fro, bent and
stretched the fingers, and seemed greatly astonished at the sight." One
girl was eager to tell her blind friend that "men do not really look like
trees at all," and astounded to discover that her every visitor had an
utterly different face. Finally, a twenty-two-year-old girl was dazzled
by the world's brightness and kept her eyes shut for two weeks. When
at the end of that time she opened her eyes again, she did not recognize any objects, but, "the more she now directed her gaze upon
everything about her, the more it could be seen how an expression of
gratification and astonishment overspread her features; she repeatedly
exclaimed: 'Oh God! How beautiful!'"

I saw color-patches for weeks after I read this wonderful book. It   8
was summer; the peaches were ripe in the valley orchards. When I
woke in the morning, color-patches wrapped round my eyes, intri-
cately, leaving not one unfilled spot. All day long I walked among
shifting color-patches that parted before me like the Red Sea and
closed again in silence, transfigured, wherever I looked back. Some
patched swelled and loomed, while others vanished utterly, and dark
marks flitted at random over the whole dazzling sweep. But I couldn't

sustain the illusion of flatness. I've been around for too long. Form is condemned to an eternal danse macabre[1] with meaning: I couldn't unpeach the peaches. Nor can I remember ever having seen without understanding; the color-patches of infancy are lost. My brain then must have been smooth as any balloon. I'm told I reached for the moon; many babies do. But the color-patches of infancy swelled as meaning filled them; they arrayed themselves in solemn ranks down distances which unrolled and stretched before me like a plain. The moon rocketed away. I live now in a world of shadows that shape and distance color, a world where space makes a kind of terrible sense. What gnosticism[2] is this, and what physics? The fluttering patch I saw in my nursery window—silver and green and shape-shifting blue—is gone; a row of Lombardy poplars takes its place, mute, across the distant lawn. That humming oblong creature pale as light that stole along the walls of my room at night, stretching exhilaratingly around the corners, is gone, too, gone the night I ate of the bittersweet fruit, put two and two together and puckered forever my brain. Martin Buber[3] tells this tale: "Rabbi Mendel once boasted to his teacher Rabbi Elimelekh that evenings he saw the angel who rolls away the light before the darkness, and mornings the angel who rolls away the darkness before the light. 'Yes,' said Rabbi Elimelekh, 'in my youth I saw that too. Later on you don't see these things any more.'"

Why didn't someone hand those newly sighted people paints and brushes from the start, when they still didn't know what anything was? Then maybe we all could see color-patches too, the world unraveled from reason, Eden before Adam gave names. The scales would drop from my eyes; I'd see trees like men walking; I'd run down the road against all orders, hallooing and leaping. 9

Seeing is of course very much a matter of verbalization. Unless I call my attention to what passes before my eyes, I simply won't see it. It is, as Ruskin[4] says, "not merely unnoticed, but in the full, clear sense of the word, unseen." My eyes alone can't solve analogy tests using figures, the ones which show, with increasing elaborations, a big square, then a small square in a big square, then a big triangle, and expect me to find a small triangle in a big triangle. I have to say the words, describe what I'm seeing. If Tinker Mountain erupted, I'd be likely to notice. But if I want to notice the lesser cataclysms of valley life, I have to maintain in my head a running description of the present. It's not that I'm observant; it's just that I talk too much. Other- 10

---

1. danse macabre: "dance of death" (French).
2. Gnosticism was a belief in the ability to transcend matter through faith, originating with the Gnostics of the early Christian era who believed Christ was noncorporeal.
3. Martin Buber: Austrian existential philosopher and Judaic scholar (1878–1965).
4. John Ruskin (1819–1900) was a British art critic and essayist.

wise, especially in a strange place, I'll never know what's happening. Like a blind man at the ball game, I need a radio.

When I see this way I analyze and pry. I hurl over logs and roll 11 away stones; I study the bank a square foot at a time, probing and tilting my head. Some days when a mist covers the mountains, when the muskrats won't show and the microscope's mirror shatters, I want to climb up the blank blue dome as a man would storm the inside of a circus tent, wildly, dangling, and with a steel knife claw a rent in the top, peep, and, if I must, fall.

But there is another kind of seeing that involves a letting go. 12 When I see this way I sway transfixed and emptied. The difference between the two ways of seeing is the difference between walking with and without a camera. When I walk with a camera, I walk from shot to shot, reading the light on a calibrated meter. When I walk without a camera, my own shutter opens, and the moment's light prints on my own silver gut. When I see this second way I am above all an unscrupulous observer.

It was sunny one evening last summer at Tinker Creek; the sun 13 was low in the sky, upstream. I was sitting on the sycamore log bridge with the sunset at my back, watching the shiners the size of minnows who were feeding over the muddy sand in skittery schools. Again and again, one fish, then another, turned for a split second across the current and flash! the sun shot out from its silver side. I couldn't watch for it. It was always just happening somewhere else, and it drew my vision just as it disappeared: flash, like a sudden dazzle of the thinnest blade, a sparking over a dun and olive ground at chance intervals from every direction. Then I noticed white specks, some sort of pale petals, small, floating from under my feet on the creek's surface, very slow and steady. So I blurred my eyes and gazed towards the brim of my hat and saw a new world. I saw the pale white circles roll up, roll up, like the world's turning, mute and perfect, and I saw the linear flashes, gleaming silver, like stars being born at random down a rolling scroll of time. Something broke and something opened. I filled up like a new wineskin. I breathed an air like light; I saw a light like water. I was the lip of a fountain the creek filled forever; I was ether, the leaf in the zephyr; I was flesh-flake, feather, bone.

When I see this way I see truly. As Thoreau says, I return to my 14 senses. I am the man who watches the baseball game in silence in an empty stadium. I see the game purely; I'm abstracted and dazed. When it's all over and the white-suited players lope off the green field to their shadowed dugouts, I leap to my feet; I cheer and cheer.

But I can't go out and try to see this way. I'll fail, I'll go mad. All I 15 can do is try to gag the commentator, to hush the noise of useless interior babble that keeps me from seeing just as surely as a newspaper dangled before my eyes. The effort is really a discipline requiring a lifetime of dedicated struggle; it marks the literature of saints and monks of every order East and West, under every rule and no rule, discalced[5] and shod. The world's spiritual geniuses seem to discover universally that the mind's muddy river, this ceaseless flow of trivia and trash, cannot be dammed, and that trying to dam it is a waste of effort that might lead to madness. Instead you must allow the muddy river to flow unheeded in the dim channels of consciousness; you raise your sights; you look along it, mildly, acknowledging its presence without interest and gazing beyond it into the realm of the real where subjects and objects act and rest purely, without utterance. "Launch into the deep," says Jacques Ellul,[6] "and you shall see."

16   The secret of seeing is, then, the pearl of great price. If I thought he could teach me to find it and keep it forever I would stagger barefoot across a hundred deserts after any lunatic at all. But although the pearl may be found, it may not be sought. The literature of illumination reveals this above all: although it comes to those who wait for it, it is always, even to the most practiced and adept, a gift and a total surprise. I return from one walk knowing where the killdeer nests in the field by the creek and the hour the laurel blooms. I return from the same walk a day later scarcely knowing my own name. Litanies hum in my ears; my tongue flaps in my mouth Ailinon, alleluia![7] I cannot cause light; the most I can do is try to put myself in the path of its beam. It is possible, in deep space, to sail on solar wind. Light, be it particle or wave, has force: you rig a giant sail and go. The secret of seeing is to sail on solar wind. Hone and spread your spirit till you yourself are a sail, whetted, translucent, broadside to the merest puff.

17   When her doctor took her bandages off and led her into the garden, the girl who was no longer blind saw "the tree with the lights in it." It was for this tree I searched through the peach orchards of summer, in the forests of fall and down winter and spring for years. Then one day I was walking along Tinker Creek thinking of nothing at all and I saw the tree with the lights in it. I saw the backyard cedar where the mourning doves roost charged and transfigured, each cell buzzing with flame. I stood on the grass with the lights in it, grass that was wholly fire, utterly focused and utterly dreamed. It was less like seeing than like being for the first time seen, knocked breathless by a powerful glance. The flood of fire abated, but I'm still spending the power. Gradually the lights went out in the cedar, the colors died, the cells un-

---

5. discalced: barefooted, as monks often are.
6. Jacques Ellul: French writer on law, technology, ethics, and theology (1912–   ).
7. Dillard juxtaposes words suggesting an ancient Greek dirge and an ancient Hebrew hymn of praise or thanksgiving.

flamed and disappeared. I was still ringing. I had been my whole life a bell, and never knew it until at that moment I was lifted and struck. I have since only very rarely seen the tree with the lights in it. The vision comes and goes, mostly goes, but I live for it, for the moment when the mountains open and a new light roars in spate through the crack, and the mountains slam.

MALCOLM X

Learning to Read

Malcolm X (1925–1965) was born Malcolm Little in Omaha, Nebraska, the son of a Baptist minister who was brutally murdered by a group of white supremacists who were enraged by his black separatist views. After moving from town to town, the family settled in Detroit, Michigan, where Malcolm dropped out of school and excelled at many illicit activities that eventually earned him the name "Detroit Red." In 1946 he was arrested and sent to Charleston State Prison for robbery. After being transferred to the Norfolk Prison Colony in 1948, Malcolm met a convicted burglar, Bimbi, who encouraged him to "read books with intellectual vitamins." During these years Malcolm also became a follower of the Black Muslims and began corresponding with its leader, Elijah Muhammad. After his release from prison in 1952, Malcolm became closely associated with Muhammad, but strife between the two steadily increased. After touring Mecca, the birthplace of the Muslim prophet Muhammad, Malcolm renounced his separatist views and began advocating unity among all people. His break from the Black Muslims proved deadly, however; and in 1965 he was shot and killed during a speech he was giving in a Harlem ballroom. Since his death, Malcolm X has been recognized as one of the foremost figures in the African-American movement for equality.

The following excerpt is from *The Autobiography of Malcolm X* (1964). In its focus on how the struggles and rewards of learning change us—and change the way we see ourselves and our world— the essay may lead to reevaluations of our own learning experiences. A useful companion essay is William Perry's "Examsmanship and the Liberal Arts," which describes a learning environment that contrasts sharply with Malcolm X's prison experience.

I did write to Elijah Muhammad. He lived in Chicago at that time, at 6116 South Michigan Avenue. At least twenty-five times I must have written that first one-page letter to him, over and over. I was trying to make it both legible and understandable. I practically couldn't read my handwriting myself; it shames even to remember it. My spelling and my grammar were as bad, if not worse. Anyway, as well as I could express it, I said I had been told about him by my brothers and sisters, and I apologized for my poor letter.

Mr. Muhammad sent me a typed reply. It had an all but electrical 2 effect upon me to see the signature of the "Messenger of Allah." After he welcomed me into the "true knowledge," he gave me something to think about. The black prisoner, he said, symbolized white society's crime of keeping black men oppressed and deprived and ignorant, and unable to get decent jobs, turning them into criminals.

He told me to have courage. He even enclosed some money for 3 me, a five-dollar bill. Mr. Muhammad sends money all over the country to prison inmates who write to him, probably to this day.

Regularly my family wrote to me. "Turn to Allah . . . pray to the 4 East."

The hardest test I ever faced in my life was praying. You under- 5 stand. My comprehending, my believing the teachings of Mr. Muhammad had only required my mind's saying to me, "That's right!" or "I never thought of that."

But bending my knees to pray—that *act*—well, that took me a 6 week.

You know what my life had been. Picking a lock to rob someone's 7 house was the only way my knees had ever been bent before.

I had to force myself to bend my knees. And waves of shame and 8 embarrassment would force me back up.

For evil to bend its knees, admitting its guilt, to implore the for- 9 giveness of God, is the hardest thing in the world. It's easy for me to see and to say that now. But then, when I was the personification of evil, I was going through it. Again, again, I would force myself back down into the praying-to-Allah posture. When finally I was able to make myself stay down—I didn't know what to say to Allah.

For the next years, I was the nearest thing to a hermit in the Nor- 10 folk Prison Colony. I never have been more busy in my life. I still marvel at how swiftly my previous life's thinking pattern slid away from me, like snow off a roof. It is as though someone else I knew of had lived by hustling and crime. I would be startled to catch myself thinking in a remote way of my earlier self as another person.

The things I felt, I was pitifully unable to express in the one-page 11 letter that went every day to Mr. Elijah Muhammad. And I wrote at least one more daily letter, replying to one of my brothers and sisters. Every letter I received from them added something to my knowledge of the teachings of Mr. Muhammad. I would sit for long periods and study his photographs.

I've never been one for inaction. Everything I've ever felt strongly 12 about, I've done something about. I guess that's why, unable to do anything else, I soon began writing to people I had known in the hustling world, such as Sammy the Pimp, John Hughes, the gambling house owner, the thief Jumpsteady, and several dope peddlers. I wrote them all about Allah and Islam and Mr. Elijah Muhammad. I had no idea where most of them lived. I addressed their letters in care of the Harlem or Roxbury bars and clubs where I'd known them.

I never got a single reply. The average hustler and criminal was too   13
uneducated to write a letter. I have known many slick, sharp-looking hustlers, who would have you think they had an interest in Wall Street; privately, they would get someone else to read a letter if they received one. Besides, neither would I have replied to anyone writing me something as wild as "the white man is the devil."

What certainly went on the Harlem and Roxbury wires was that   14
Detroit Red was going crazy in stir, or else he was trying some hype to shake up the warden's office.

During the years that I stayed in the Norfolk Prison Colony, never   15
did any official directly say anything to me about those letters, although, of course, they all passed through the prison censorship. I'm sure, however, they monitored what I wrote to add to the files which every state and federal prison keeps on the conversion of Negro inmates by the teachings of Mr. Elijah Muhammad.

But at that time, I felt that the real reason was that the white man   16
knew that he was the devil.

Later on, I even wrote to the Mayor of Boston, to the Governor of   17
Massachusetts, and to Harry S. Truman. They never answered; they probably never even saw my letters. I handscratched to them how the white man's society was responsible for the black man's condition in this wilderness of North America.

It was because of my letters that I happened to stumble upon start-   18
ing to acquire some kind of a homemade education.

I became increasingly frustrated at not being able to express what I   19
wanted to convey in letters that I wrote, especially those to Mr. Elijah Muhammad. In the street, I had been the most articulate hustler out there   I had commanded attention when I said something. But now, trying to write simple English, I not only wasn't articulate, I wasn't even functional. How would I sound writing in slang, the way I would *say* it, something such as, "Look, daddy, let me pull your coat about a cat, Elijah Muhammad—"

Many who today hear me somewhere in person, or on television,   20
or those who read something I've said, will think I went to school far beyond the eighth grade. This impression is due entirely to my prison studies.

It had really begun back in the Charlestown Prison, when Bimbi   21
first made me feel envy of his stock of knowledge. Bimbi had always taken charge of any conversation he was in, and I had tried to emulate him. But every book I picked up had few sentences which didn't contain anywhere from one to nearly all of the words that might as well have been in Chinese. When I just skipped those words, of course, I

really ended up with little idea of what the book said. So I had come to the Norfolk Prison Colony still going through only book-reading motions. Pretty soon, I would have quit even these motions, unless I had received the motivation that I did.

I saw that the best thing I could do was get hold of a dictionary— to study, to learn some words. I was lucky enough to reason also that I should try to improve my penmanship. It was sad. I couldn't even write in a straight line. It was both ideas together that moved me to request a dictionary along with some tablets and pencils from the Norfolk Prison Colony school.   22

I spent two days just riffling uncertainly through the dictionary's pages. I'd never realized so many words existed! I didn't know *which* words I needed to learn. Finally, just to start some kind of action, I began copying.   23

In my slow, painstaking, ragged handwriting, I copied into my tablet everything printed on that first page, down to the punctuation marks.   24

I believe it took me a day. Then, aloud, I read back, to myself, everything I'd written on the tablet. Over and over, aloud, to myself, I read my own handwriting.   25

I woke up the next morning, thinking about those words—immensely proud to realize that not only had I written so much at one time, but I'd written words that I never knew were in the world. Moreover, with a little effort, I also could remember what many of these words meant. I reviewed the words whose meanings I didn't remember. Funny thing, from the dictionary first page right now, that "aardvark" springs to my mind. The dictionary had a picture of it, a long-tailed, long-eared, burrowing African mammal, which lives off termites caught by sticking out its tongue as an anteater does for ants.   26

I was so fascinated that I went on—I copied the dictionary's next page. And the same experience came when I studied that. With every succeeding page, I also learned of people and places and events from history. Actually the dictionary is like a miniature encyclopedia. Finally the dictionary's A section had filled a whole tablet—and I went on into the B's. That was the way I started copying what eventually became the entire dictionary. It went a lot faster after so much practice helped me to pick up handwriting speed. Between what I wrote in my tablet, and writing letters, during the rest of my time in prison I would guess I wrote a million words.   27

I suppose it was inevitable that as my word-base broadened, I could for the first time pick up a book and read and now begin to understand what the book was saying. Anyone who has read a great deal can imagine the new world that opened. Let me tell you something: from then until I left that prison, in every free moment I had, if I was not reading in the library, I was reading on my bunk. You couldn't   28

have gotten me out of books with a wedge. Between Mr. Muhammad's teachings, my correspondence, my visitors—usually Ella and
Reginald[1]—and my reading of books, months passed without my even
thinking about being imprisoned. In fact, up to then, I never had been
so truly free in my life.

The Norfolk Prison Colony's library was in the school building. A
variety of classes was taught there by instructors who came from such
places as Harvard and Boston universities. The weekly debates between inmate teams were also held in the school building. You would
be astonished to know how worked up convict debaters and audiences
would get over subjects like "Should Babies Be Fed Milk?"

Available on the prison library's shelves were books on just about
every general subject. Much of the big private collection that
Parkhurst[2] had willed to the prison was still in crates and boxes in the
back of the library—thousands of old books. Some of them looked ancient: covers faded, old-time parchment-looking binding. Parkhurst,
I've mentioned, seemed to have been principally interested in history
and religion. He had the money and the special interest to have a lot of
books that you wouldn't have in general circulation. Any college library would have been lucky to get that collection.

As you can imagine, especially in a prison where there was heavy
emphasis on rehabilitation, an inmate was smiled upon if he demonstrated an unusually intense interest in books. There was a sizable
number of well-read inmates, especially the popular debaters. Some
were said by many to be practically walking encyclopedias. They were
almost celebrities. No university would ask any student to devour literature as I did when this new world opened to me, of being able to
read and *understand*.

I read more in my room than in the library itself. An inmate who
was known to read a lot could check out more than the permitted
maximum number of books. I preferred reading in the total isolation
of my own room.

When I had progressed to really serious reading, every night at
about ten P.M. I would be outraged with the "lights out." It always
seemed to catch me right in the middle of something engrossing.

Fortunately, right outside my door was a corridor light that cast a
glow into my room. The glow was enough to read by, once my eyes
adjusted to it. So when "lights out" came, I would sit on the floor
where I could continue reading in that glow.

At one-hour intervals the night guards paced past every room.
Each time I heard the approaching footsteps, I jumped into bed and

1. Ella is Malcolm's half-sister; Reginald is his brother.
2. Charles Henry Parkhurst (1842–1933) was a Presbyterian clergyman, reformer, and
author who was the president of the Society for the Prevention of Crime in the 1890s.

feigned sleep. And as soon as the guard passed, I got back out of bed onto the floor area of that light-glow, where I would read for another fifty-eight minutes—until the guard approached again. That went on until three or four every morning. Three or four hours of sleep a night was enough for me. Often in the years in the streets I had slept less than that.

PATRICIA HAMPL

Memory and Imagination

Patricia Hampl (1946–   ), poet and memoirist, was born in St. Paul, Minnesota, to parents of Czech and Irish descent. She has published two volumes of poetry, *Woman Before an Aquarium* (1978) and *Resort and Other Poems* (1983), and a much-praised autobiography, *A Romantic Education,* winner of the Houghton Mifflin Literary Fellowship in 1981. "I suppose," she has said, "I write about all the things I had intended to leave behind, to grow out of, or deny: being a Midwesterner, a Catholic, a woman." In 1987 Hampl revisited her Midwestern experience by writing a fictional account of another Czech artist's experience, *Spillville,* which is about composer Antonín Dvořák's visit to a small Iowa town in 1893. In her most recent books, *Virgin Time: In Search of the Contemplative Life* (1992) and *Burning Bright: An Anthology of Sacred Poetry* (which she edited in 1995), she returns to her Catholic upbringing to explore spirituality. Hampl now lives in St. Paul and teaches creative writing at the University of Minnesota.

Hampl wrote "Memory and Imagination" in 1986, especially for inclusion in *The Dolphin Reader.* In it we find her argument for the political importance of writing about our own pasts. The essay should make us think twice about how memory and imagination merge when we tell stories about our lives, for some of us insist that we give "just the facts," whereas others prefer to let imagination take the lead. A useful companion piece is Frank Conroy's "Think About It," which also discusses how the mind transforms past experience.

When I was seven, my father, who played the violin on Sundays 1
with a nicely tortured flair which we considered artistic, led me by the hand down a long, unlit corridor in St. Luke's School basement, a sort of tunnel that ended in a room full of pianos. There many little girls and a single sad boy were playing truly tortured scales and arpeggios in a mash of troubled sound. My father gave me over to Sister Olive Marie, who did look remarkably like an olive.

Her oily face gleamed as if it had just been rolled out of a can and laid on the white plate of her broad, spotless wimple. She was a small, plump woman; her body and the small window of her face seemed to interpret the entire alphabet of olive: her face was a sallow green olive placed upon the jumbo ripe olive of her black habit. I trusted her instantly and smiled, glad to have my hand placed in the hand of a woman who made sense, who provided the satisfaction of being what she was: an Olive who looked like an olive.

My father left me to discover the piano with Sister Olive Marie so that one day I would join him in mutually tortured piano-violin duets for the edification of my mother and brother who sat at the table meditatively spooning in the last of their pineapple sherbet until their part was called for: they put down their spoons and clapped while we bowed, while the sweet ice in their bowls melted, while the music melted, and we all melted a little into each other for a moment.

But first Sister Olive must do her work. I was shown middle C, which Sister seemed to think terribly important. I stared at middle C and then glanced away for a second. When my eye returned, middle C was gone, its slim finger lost in the complicated grasp of the keyboard. Sister Olive struck it again, finding it with laughable ease. She emphasized the importance of middle C, its central position, a sort of North Star of sound. I remember thinking, "Middle C is the belly button of the piano," an insight whose originality and accuracy stunned me with pride. For the first time in my life I was astonished by metaphor. I hesitated to tell the kindly Olive for some reason; apparently I understood a true metaphor is a risky business, revealing of the self. In fact, I have never, until this moment of writing it down, told my first metaphor to anyone.

Sunlight flooded the room; the pianos, all black, gleamed. Sister Olive, dressed in the colors of the keyboard, gleamed; middle C shimmered with meaning and I resolved never—never—to forget its location: it was the center of the world.

Then Sister Olive, who had had to show me middle C twice but who seemed to have drawn no bad conclusions about me anyway, got up and went to the windows on the opposite wall. She pulled the shades down, one after the other. The sun was too bright, she said. She sneezed as she stood at the windows with the sun shedding its glare over her. She sneezed and sneezed, crazy little convulsive sneezes, one after another, as helpless as if she had the hiccups.

"The sun makes me sneeze," she said when the fit was over and she was back at the piano. This was odd, too odd to grasp in the mind. I associated sneezing with colds, and colds with rain, fog, snow and bad weather. The sun, however, had caused Sister Olive to sneeze in this wild way, Sister Olive who gleamed benignly and who was so certain of the location of the center of the world. The universe wobbled a bit and became unreliable. Things were not, after all, necessarily what they seemed. Appearance deceived: here was the sun acting totally out of character, hurling this woman into sneezes, a woman so mild that she was named, so it seemed, for a bland object on a relish tray.

I was given a red book, the first Thompson book, and told to play 8 the first piece over and over at one of the black pianos where the other children were crashing away. This, I was told, was called practicing. It sounded alluringly adult, practicing. The piece itself consisted mainly of middle C, and I excelled, thrilled by my savvy at being able to locate that central note amidst the cunning camouflage of all the other white keys before me. Thrilled too by the shiny red book that gleamed, as the pianos did, as Sister Olive did, as my eager eyes probably did. I sat at the formidable machine of the piano and got to know middle C intimately, preparing to be as tortured as I could manage one day soon with my father's violin at my side.

But at the moment Mary Katherine Reilly was at my side, playing 9 something at least two or three lessons more sophisticated than my piece. I believe she even struck a chord. I glanced at her from the peasantry of single notes, shy, ready to pay homage. She turned toward me, stopped playing, and sized me up.

Sized me up and found a person ready to be dominated. Without 10 introduction she said, "My grandfather invented the collapsible opera hat."

I nodded, I acquiesced, I was hers. With that little stroke it was decided between us—that she should be the leader, and I the sidekick. My job was admiration. Even when she added, "But he didn't make a penny from it. He didn't have a patent"—even then, I knew and she knew that this was not an admission of powerlessness, but the easy candor of a master, of one who can afford a weakness or two.

With the clairvoyance of all fated relationships based on dominance and submission, it was decided in advance: that when the time came for us to play duets, I should always play second piano, that I should spend my allowance to buy her the Twinkies she craved but was not allowed to have, that finally, I should let her copy from my test paper, and when confronted by our teacher, confess with convincing hysteria that it was I, I who had cheated, who had reached above myself to steal what clearly belonged to the rightful heir of the inventor of the collapsible opera hat. . . .

There must be a reason I remember that little story about my first 13 piano lesson. In fact, it isn't a story, just a moment, the beginning of what could perhaps become a story. For the memoirist, more than for the fiction writer, the story seems already *there*, already accomplished and fully achieved in history ("in reality," as we naively say). For the memoirist, the writing of the story is a matter of transcription.

That, anyway, is the myth. But no memoirist writes for long without experiencing an unsettling disbelief about the reliability of memory, a hunch that memory is not, after all, *just* memory. I don't know why I remembered this fragment about my first piano lesson. I don't, for instance, have a single recollection of my first arithmetic lesson, the first time I studied Latin, the first time my grandmother tried to teach me to knit. Yet these things occurred too, and must have their stories.

It is the piano lesson that has trudged forward, clearing the haze of forgetfulness, showing itself bright with detail more than thirty years after the event. I did not choose to remember the piano lesson. It was simply there, like a book that has always been on the shelf, whether I ever read it or not, the binding and title showing as I skim across the contents of my life. On the day I wrote this fragment I happened to take that memory, not some other, from the shelf and paged through it. I found more detail, more event, perhaps a little more entertainment than I had expected, but the memory itself was there from the start. Waiting for me.

Or was it? When I reread what I had written just after I finished it, I realized that I had told a number of lies. I *think* it was my father who took me the first time for my piano lesson—but maybe he only took me to meet my teacher and there was no actual lesson that day. And did I even know then that he played the violin—didn't he take up his violin again much later, as a result of my piano playing, and not the reverse? And is it even remotely accurate to describe as "tortured" the musicianship of a man who began every day by belting out "Oh What a Beautiful Morning" as he shaved?

More: Sister Olive Marie did sneeze in the sun, but was her name Olive? As for her skin tone—I would have sworn it was olive-like; I would have been willing to spend the better part of an afternoon trying to write the exact description of imported Italian or Greek olive her face suggested: I wanted to get it right. But now, were I to write that passage over, it is her intense black eyebrows I would see, for suddenly they seem the central fact of that face, some indicative mark of her serious and patient nature. But the truth is, I don't remember the woman at all. She's a sneeze in the sun and a finger touching middle C. That, at least, is steady and clear.

Worse: I didn't have the Thompson book as my piano text. I'm sure of that because I remember envying children who did have this wonderful book with its pictures of children and animals printed on the pages of music.

As for Mary Katherine Reilly. She didn't even go to grade school with me (and her name isn't Mary Katherine Reilly—but I made that change on purpose). I met her in Girl Scouts and only went to school with her later, in high school. Our relationship was not really one of leader and follower; I played first piano most of the time in duets. She certainly never copied anything from a test paper of mine: she was a better student, and cheating just wasn't a possibility with her. Though her grandfather (or someone in her family) did invent the collapsible opera hat and I remember that she was proud of that fact, she didn't tell me this news as a deft move in a childish power play.

So, what was I doing in this brief memoir? Is it simply an example 20 of the curious relation a fiction writer has to the material of her own life? Maybe. That may have some value in itself. But to tell the truth (if anyone still believes me capable of telling the truth), I wasn't writing fiction. I was writing memoir—or was trying to. My desire was to be accurate. I wished to embody the myth of memoir: to write as an act of dutiful transcription.

Yet clearly the work of writing narrative caused me to do some- 21 thing very different from transcription. I am forced to admit that memoir is not a matter of transcription, that memory itself is not a warehouse of finished stories, not a static gallery of framed pictures. I must admit that I invented. But why?

Two whys: why did I invent, and then, if a memoirist must in- 22 evitably invent rather than transcribe, why do I—why should anybody—write memoir at all?

I must respond to these impertinent questions because they, like 23 the bumper sticker I saw the other day commanding all who read it to QUESTION AUTHORITY, challenge my authority as a memoirist and as a witness.

It still comes as a shock to realize that I don't write about what I 24 know: I write in order to find out what I know. Is it possible to convey to a reader the enormous degree of blankness, confusion, hunch and uncertainty lurking in the act of writing? When I am the reader, not the writer, I too fall into the lovely illusion that the words before me (in a story by Mavis Gallant, an essay by Carol Bly, a memoir by M.F.K. Fisher), which *read* so inevitably, must also have been *written* exactly as they appear, rhythm and cadence, language and syntax, the powerful waves of the sentences laying themselves on the smooth beach of the page one after another faultlessly.

But here I sit before a yellow legal pad, and the long page of the 25 preceding two paragraphs is a jumble of crossed-out lines, false starts, confused order. A mess. The mess of my mind trying to find out what it wants to say. This is a writer's frantic, grabby mind, not the poised mind of a reader ready to be edified or entertained.

I sometimes think of the reader as a cat, endlessly fastidious, capa- 26 ble, by turns, of mordant indifference and riveted attention, luxurious, recumbent, and ever poised. Whereas the writer is absolutely a dog, panting and moping, too eager for an affectionate scratch behind the ears, lunging frantically after any old stick thrown in the distance.

The blankness of a new page never fails to intrigue and terrify me. Sometimes, in fact, I think my habit of writing on long yellow sheets comes from an atavistic fear of the writer's stereotypic "blank white page." At least when I begin writing, my page isn't utterly blank; at least it has a wash of color on it, even if the absence of words must finally be faced on a yellow sheet as truly as on a blank white one. Well, we all have our ways of whistling in the dark.

If I approach writing from memory with the assumption that I know what I wish to say, I assume that intentionality is running the show. Things are not that simple. Or perhaps writing is even more profoundly simple, more telegraphic and immediate in its choices than the grating wheels and chugging engine of logic and rational intention. The heart, the guardian of intuition with its secret, often fearful intentions, is the boss. Its commands are what a writer obeys—often without knowing it. Or, I do.

That's why I'm a strong adherent of the first draft. And why it's worth pausing for a moment to consider what a first draft really is. By my lights, the piano lesson memoir is the first draft. That doesn't mean it exists here exactly as I first wrote it. I like to think I've cleaned it up from the first time I put it down on paper. I've cut some adjectives here, toned down the hyperbole there, smoothed a transition, cut a repetition—that sort of housekeeperly tidying-up. But the piece remains a first draft because I haven't yet gotten to know it, haven't given it a chance to tell me anything. For me, writing a first draft is a little like meeting someone for the first time. I come away with a wary acquaintanceship, but the real friendship (if any) and genuine intimacy—that's all down the road. Intimacy with a piece of writing, as with a person, comes from paying attention to the revelations it is capable of giving, not by imposing my own preconceived notions, no matter how well-intentioned they might be.

I try to let pretty much anything happen in a first draft. A careful first draft is a failed first draft. That may be why there are so many inaccuracies in the piano lesson memoir: I didn't censor, I didn't judge. I kept moving. But I would not publish this piece as a memoir on its own in its present state. It isn't the "lies" in the piece that give me pause, though a reader has the right to expect a memoir to be as accurate as the writer's memory can make it. No, it isn't the lies themselves that makes the piano lesson memoir a first draft and therefore "unpublishable."

The real trouble: the piece hasn't yet found its subject; it isn't yet about what it wants to be about. Note: what *it* wants, not what I want. The difference has to do with the relation a memoirist—any writer, in fact—has to unconscious or half-known intentions and impulses in composition.

Now that I have the fragment down on paper, I can read this little piece as a mystery which drops clues to the riddle of my feelings, like a culprit who wishes to be apprehended. My narrative self (the culprit who has invented) wishes to be discovered by my reflective self, the self who wants to understand and make sense of a half-remembered story about a nun sneezing in the sun. . . .

We only store in memory images of value. The value may be lost   33
over the passage of time (I was baffled about why I remembered that sneezing nun, for example), but that's the implacable judgment of feeling: *this,* we say somewhere deep within us, is something I'm hanging on to. And of course, often we cleave to things because they possess heavy negative changes. Pain likes to be vivid.

Over time, the value (the feeling) and the stored memory (the   34
image) may become estranged. Memoir seeks a permanent home for feeling and image, a habitation where they can live together in harmony. Naturally, I've had a lot of experiences since I packed away that one from the basement of St. Luke's School; that piano lesson has been effaced by waves of feeling for other moments and episodes. I persist in believing the event has value—after all, I remember it—but in writing the memoir I did not simply relive the experience. Rather, I explored the mysterious relationship between all the images I could round up and the even more impacted feelings that caused me to store the images safely away in memory. Stalking the relationship, seeking the congruence between stored image and hidden emotion—that's the real job of memoir.

By writing about that first piano lesson, I've come to know things   35
I could not know otherwise. But I only know these things as a result of reading this first draft. While I was writing, I was following the images, letting the details fill the room of the page and use the furniture as they wished. I was their dutiful servant—or thought I was. In fact, I was the faithful retainer of my hidden feelings which were giving the commands.

I really did feel, for instance, that Mary Katherine Reilly was far   36
superior to me. She was smarter, funnier, more wonderful in every way—that's how I saw it. Our friendship (or she herself) did not require that I become her vassal, yet perhaps in my heart that was something I wanted; I wanted a way to express my feeling of admiration. I suppose I waited until this memoir to begin to find the way.

Just as, in the memoir, I finally possess that red Thompson book   37
with the barking dogs and bleating lambs and winsome children. I couldn't (and still can't) remember what my own music book was, so I grabbed the name and image of the one book I could remember. It was only in reviewing the piece after writing it that I saw my inaccuracy. In pondering this "lie," I came to see what I was up to: I was getting what I wanted. At last.

The truth of many circumstances and episodes in the past emerges   38
for the memoirist through details (the red music book, the fascination

with a nun's name and gleaming face), but these details are not merely information, not flat facts. Such details are not allowed to lounge. They must work. Their work is the creation of symbol. But it's more accurate to call it the *recognition* of symbol. For meaning is not "attached" to the detail by the memoirist; meaning is revealed. That's why a first draft is important. Just as the first meeting (good or bad) with someone who later becomes the beloved is important and is often reviewed for signals, meanings, omens, and indications.

Now I can look at that music book and see it not only as "a detail," 39 but for what it is, how it *acts*. See it as the small red door leading straight into the dark room of my childhood longing and disappointment. That red book *becomes* the palpable evidence of that longing. In other words, it becomes symbol. There is no symbol, no life-of-the-spirit in the general or the abstract. Yet a writer wishes—indeed all of us wish—to speak about profound matters that are, like it or not, general and abstract. We wish to talk to each other about life and death, about love, despair, loss, and innocence. We sense that in order to live together we must learn to speak of peace, of history, of meaning and values. Those are a few.

We seek a means of exchange, a language which will renew these 40 ancient concerns and make them wholly and pulsingly ours. Instinctively, we go to our store of private images and associations for our authority to speak of these weighty issues. We find, in our details and broken and obscured images, the language of symbol. Here memory impulsively reaches out its arms and embraces imagination. That is the resort to invention. It isn't a lie, but an act of necessity, as the innate urge to locate personal truth always is.

All right. Invention is inevitable. But why write memoir? Why not 41 call it fiction and be done with all the hashing about, wondering where memory stops and imagination begins? And if memoir seeks to talk about "the big issues," about history and peace, death and love—why not leave these reflections to those with expert and scholarly knowledge? Why let the common or garden variety memoirist into the club? I'm thinking again of that bumper sticker: why Question Authority?

My answer, of course, is a memoirist's answer. Memoir must be 42 written because each of us must have a created version of the past. Created: that is, real, tangible, made of the stuff of a life lived in place and in history. And the down side of any created thing as well: we must live with a version that attaches us to our limitations, to the inevitable subjectivity of our points of view. We must acquiesce to our experience and our gift to transform experience into meaning and value. You tell me your story, I'll tell you my story.

If we refuse to do the work of creating this personal version of the 43 past, someone else will do it for us. That is a scary political fact. "The struggle of man against power," a character in Milan Kundera's novel

The Book of Laughter and Forgetting says, "is the struggle of memory against forgetting." He refers to willful political forgetting, the habit of nations and those in power (Question Authority!) to deny the truth of memory in order to disarm moral and ethical power. It's an efficient way of controlling masses of people. It doesn't even require much bloodshed, as long as people are entirely willing to give over their personal memories. Whole histories can be rewritten. As Czeslaw Milosz said in his 1980 Nobel Prize lecture, the number of books published that seek to deny the existence of the Nazi death camps now exceeds one hundred.

What is remembered is what *becomes* reality. If we "forget" Auschwitz,[1] if we "forget" My Lai,[2] what then do we remember? And what is the purpose of our remembering? If we think of memory naively, as a simple story, logged like a documentary in the archive of the mind, we miss its beauty but also its function. The beauty of memory rests in its talent for rendering detail, for paying homage to the senses, its capacity to love the particles of life, the richness and idiosyncrasy of our existence. The function of memory, on the other hand, is intensely personal and surprisingly political.   44

Our capacity to move forward as developing beings rests on a healthy relation with the past. Psychotherapy, that widespread method of mental health, relies heavily on memory and on the ability to retrieve and organize images and events from the personal past. We carry our wounds and perhaps even worse, our capacity to wound, forward with us. If we learn not only to tell our stories but to listen to what our stories tell us—to write the first draft and then return for the second draft—we are doing the work of memoir.   45

Memoir is the intersection of narration and reflection, of storytelling and essay-writing. It can present its story *and* reflect and consider the meaning of the story. It is a peculiarly open form, inviting broken and incomplete images, half-recollected fragments, all the mass (and mess) of detail. It offers to shape this confusion—and in shaping, of course it necessarily creates a work of art, not a legal document. But then, even legal documents are only valiant attempts to consign the truth, the whole truth and nothing but the truth to paper. Even they remain versions.   46

Locating touchstones—the red music book, the olive Olive, my father's violin playing—is deeply satisfying. Who knows why? Perhaps we all sense that we can't grasp the whole truth and nothing but the truth of our experience. Just can't be done. What can be achieved,   47

1. Auschwitz: Polish site in World War II of the concentration camp Auschwitz-Birkenau, where more than a million prisoners, most of them Jews, were exterminated.
2. My Lai: incident in 1968 in which American troops massacred unarmed Vietnamese civilians, including women and children.

however, is a version of its swirling, changing wholeness. A memoirist must acquiesce to selectivity, like any artist. The version we dare to write is the only truth, the only relationship we can have with the past. Refuse to write your life and you have no life. At least, that is the stern view of the memoirist.

Personal history, logged in memory, is a sort of slide projector flashing images on the wall of the mind. And there's precious little order to the slides in the rotating carousel. Beyond that confusion, who knows who is running the projector? A memoirist steps into this darkened room of flashing, unorganized images and stands blinking for a while. Maybe for a long while. But eventually, as with any attempt to tell a story, it is necessary to put something first, then something else. And so on, to the end. That's a first draft. Not necessarily the truth, not even *a* truth sometimes, but the first attempt to create a shape.

The first thing I usually notice at this stage of composition is the appalling inaccuracy of the piece. Witness my first piano lesson draft. Invention is screamingly evident in what I intended to be transcription. But here's the further truth: I feel no shame. In fact, it's only now that my interest in the piece truly quickens. For I can see what isn't there, what is slyly hugging the walls, hoping not to be seen. I see the filmy shape of the next draft. I see a more acute version of the episode or—this is more likely—an entirely new piece rising from the ashes of the first attempt.

The next draft of the piece would have to be a true re-vision, a new seeing of the materials of the first draft. Nothing merely cosmetic will do—no rouge buffing up the opening sentence, no glossy adjective to lift a sagging line, nothing to attempt covering a patch of gray writing. None of that. I can't say for sure, but my hunch is the revision would lead me to more writing about my father (why was I so impressed by that ancestral inventor of the collapsible opera hat? Did I feel I had nothing as remarkable in my own background? Did this make me feel inadequate?). I begin to think perhaps Sister Olive is less central to this business than she is in this draft. She is meant to be a moment, not a character.

And so I might proceed, if I were to undertake a new draft of the memoir. I begin to feel a relationship developing between a former self and me.

And, even more compelling, a relationship between an old world and me. Some people think of autobiographical writing as the precious occupation of a particularly self-absorbed person. Maybe, but I don't buy that. True memoir is written in an attempt to find not only a self but a world.

The self-absorption that seems to be the impetus and embarrassment of autobiography turns into (or perhaps always was) a hunger for the world. Actually, it begins as hunger for *a* world, one gone or lost, effaced by time or a more sudden brutality. But in the act of re-membering, the personal environment expands, resonates beyond it-self, beyond its "subject," into the endless and tragic recollection that is history.

We look at old family photographs in which we stand next to   54
black, boxy Fords and are wearing period costumes, and we do not gaze fascinated because there we are young again, or there we are standing, as we never will again in life, next to our mother. We stare and drift because there we are . . . historical. It is the dress, the black car that dazzle us now and draw us beyond our mother's bright arms which once caught us. We reach into the attractive impersonality of something more significant than ourselves. We write memoir, in other words. We accept the humble position of writing a version rather than "the whole truth."

I suppose I write memoir because of the radiance of the past—it   55
draws me back and back to it. Not that the past is beautiful. In our communal memoir, in history, the death camps *are* back there. In inti-mate life too, the record is usually pretty mixed. "I could tell you stories . . . " people say and drift off, meaning terrible things have hap-pened to them.

But the past is radiant. It has the light of lived life. A memoirist   56
wishes to touch it. No one owns the past, though typically the first act of new political regimes, whether of the left or the right, is to attempt to re-write history, to grab the past and make it over so the end comes out right. So their power looks inevitable.

No one owns the past, but it is a grave error (another age would   57
have said a grave sin) not to inhabit memory. Sometimes I think it is all we really have. But that may be a trifle melodramatic. At any rate, memory possesses authority for the fearful self in a world where it is necessary to have authority in order to Question Authority.

There may be no more pressing intellectual need in our culture   58
than for people to become sophisticated about the function of mem-ory. The political implications of the loss of memory are obvious. The authority of memory is a personal confirmation of selfhood. To write one's life is to live it twice, and the second living is both spiritual and historical, for a memoir reaches deep within the personality as it seeks its narrative form and also grasps the life-of-the-times as no political treatise can.

Our most ancient metaphor says life is a journey. Memoir is travel   59
writing, then, notes taken along the way, telling how things looked and what thoughts occurred. But I cannot think of the memoirist as a tourist. This is the traveller who goes on foot, living the journey, taking on mountains, enduring deserts, marveling at the lush green places.

Moving through it all faithfully, not so much a survivor with a harrowing tale to tell as a pilgrim, seeking, wondering.

LINDA HOGAN

Hearing Voices

A Chickasaw essayist, poet, playwright, and fiction writer, Linda Hogan (1947–   ) was born in Denver, Colorado. Hogan spent most of her childhood in Oklahoma and received her M.A. in creative writing from the University of Colorado. Her first volume of poetry, *Calling Myself Home,* appeared in 1978 and was soon followed by three others. During the 1980s she also published short fiction, including *The Big Woman* (1987). *Mean Spirit* (1990), a novel about the community of Osage Indians during the 1930s oil boom, was a finalist for the Pulitzer Prize. Hogan recently published a book of nonfiction prose, *Dwellings: A Spiritual History of the Living World* (1995), and currently teaches creative writing at the University of Colorado in Boulder. Her writing, Hogan has said, "comes from and goes back to the community, both the human and the global community. I am interested in the deepest questions, those of spirit, of shelter, of growth and movement toward peace and liberation, inner and outer."

"Hearing Voices" first appeared in Janet Sternburg's *The Writer on Her World: New Essays in New Territory* (1992). This essay is essentially about language and how we define and use it. For Hogan, language is a powerful and vital force that reveals surprising connections—science to poetry, people to corn, even politicians to armadillos. A useful companion essay is Jacob Bronowski's "The Creative Mind," which also shows how making unlikely connections can lead to understanding.

When Barbara McClintock[1] was awarded a Nobel Prize for her work on gene transposition in corn plants, the most striking thing about her was that she made her discoveries by listening to what the corn spoke to her, by respecting the life of the corn and "letting it come."

McClintock says she learned "the stories" of the plants. She "heard" them. She watched the daily green journeys of growth from

---

1. Barbara McClintock (1902–1992): a geneticist whose discovery that genes can transfer their positions on chromosomes contributed greatly to the understanding of hereditary processes. She won the Nobel Prize in 1983.

earth toward sky and sun. She knew her plants in the way a healer or mystic would have known them, from the inside, the inner voices of corn and woman speaking to one another.

As an Indian woman, I come from a long history of people who [3] have listened to the language of this continent, people who have known that corn grows with the songs and prayers of the people, that it has a story to tell, that the world is alive. Both in oral traditions and in mythology—the true language of inner life—account after account tells of the stones giving guidance, the trees singing, the corn telling of inner earth, the dragonfly offering up a tongue. This is true in the European traditions as well: Psyche received direction from the reeds and the ants, Orpheus[2] knew the languages of earth, animals, and birds.

This intuitive and common language is what I seek for my writing, [4] work in touch with the mystery and force of life, work that speaks a few of the many voices around us, and it is important to me that McClintock listened to the voices of corn. It is important to the continuance of life that she told the truth of her method and that it reminded us all of where our strength, our knowing, and our sustenance come from.

It is also poetry, this science, and I note how often scientific theo- [5] ries lead to the world of poetry and vision, theories telling us how atoms that were stars have been transformed into our living, breathing bodies. And in these theories, or maybe they should be called stories, we begin to understand how we are each many people, including the stars we once were, and how we are in essence the earth and the universe, how what we do travels clear around the earth and returns. In a single moment of our living, there is our ancestral and personal history, our future, even our deaths planted in us and already growing toward their fulfillment. The corn plants are there, and like all the rest we are forever merging our borders with theirs in the world collective.

Our very lives might depend on this listening. In the Chernobyl [6] nuclear accident,[3.] the wind told the story that was being suppressed by the people. It gave away the truth. It carried the story of danger to other countries. It was a poet, a prophet, a scientist.

Sometimes, like the wind, poetry has its own laws speaking for the [7] life of the planet. It is a language that wants to bring back together what the other words have torn apart. It is the language of life speaking through us about the sacredness of life.

---

2. In Greek mythology, Psyche lost her lover Cupid when she insisted on seeing his face; after years of hardship—during which she received assistance from nature—she was reunited with him and made immortal. Orpheus's music celebrated the sounds of nature.
3. The world's worst nuclear-reactor accident (April 26, 1986) occurred at a nuclear power plant in the Ukraine. The worldwide effects of the fallout have yet to be determined.

This life speaking life is what I find so compelling about the work   8
of poets such as Ernesto Cardenal, who is also a priest and was the
Nicaraguan Minister of Culture. He writes: "The armadillos are very
happy with this government. . . . Not only humans desired libera-
tion/the whole ecology wanted it." Cardenal has also written "The Parrots," a poem about caged birds who were being sent to the United
States as pets for the wealthy, how the cages were opened, the parrots
allowed back into the mountains and jungles, freed like the people,
"and sent back to the land we were pulled from."

How we have been pulled from the land! And how poetry has   9
worked hard to set us free, uncage us, keep us from split tongues that
mimic the voices of our captors. It returns us to our land. Poetry is a
string of words that parades without a permit. It is a lockbox of words
to put an ear to as we try to crack the safe of language, listening for the
right combination, the treasure inside. It is life resonating. It is sometimes called Prayer, Soothsaying, Complaint, Invocation, Proclamation, Testimony, Witness. Writing is and does all these things. And like
that parade, it is illegitimately insistent on going its own way, on being
part of the miracle of life, telling the story about what happened when
we were cosmic dust, what it means to be stars listening to our human
atoms.

But don't misunderstand me. I am not just a dreamer. I am also   10
the practical type. A friend's father, watching the United States stage
another revolution in another Third World country, said, "Why
doesn't the government just feed people and then let the political chips
fall where they may?" He was right. It was easy, obvious, even finan-
cially more reasonable to do that, to let democracy be chosen because
it feeds hunger. I want my writing to be that simple, that clear and direct. Likewise, I feel it is not enough for me just to write, but I need to
live it, to be informed by it. I have found over the years that my work
has more courage than I do. It has more wisdom. It teaches me, leads
me places I never knew I was heading. And it is about a new way of
living, of being in the world.

I was on a panel recently where the question was raised whether   11
we thought literature could save lives. The audience, book people,
smiled expectantly with the thought. I wanted to say, Yes, it saves
lives. But I couldn't speak those words. It saves spirits maybe, hearts. It
changes minds, but for me writing is an incredible privilege. When I sit
down at the desk, there are other women who are hungry, homeless. I
don't want to forget that, that the world of matter is still there to be
reckoned with. This writing is a form of freedom most other people do
not have. So, when I write, I feel a responsibility, a commitment to
other humans and to the animal and plant communities as well.

Still, writing has changed me. And there is the powerful need we   12
all have to tell a story, each of us with a piece of the whole pattern to

complete. As Alice Walker[4] says, we are all telling part of the same story, and as Sharon Olds[5] has said, Every writer is a cell on the body politic of America.

Another Nobel Prize laureate is Betty Williams,[6] a Northern Ireland co-winner of the 1977 Peace Prize. I heard her speak about how, after witnessing the death of children, she stepped outside in the middle of the night and began knocking on doors and yelling, behaviors that would have earned her a diagnosis of hysteria in our own medical circles. She knocked on doors that might have opened with weapons pointing in her face, and she cried out, "What kind of people have we become that we would allow children to be killed on our streets?" Within four hours the city was awake, and there were sixteen thousands names on petitions for peace. Now, that woman's work is a lesson to those of us who deal with language, and to those of us who are dealt into silence. She used language to begin the process of peace. This is the living, breathing power of the word. It is poetry. So are the names of those who signed the petitions. Maybe it is this kind of language that saves lives.   13

Writing begins for me with survival, with life and with freeing life, saving life, speaking life. It is work that speaks what can't be easily said. It originated from a compelling desire to live and be alive. For me, it is sometimes the need to speak for other forms of life, to take the side of human life, even our sometimes frivolous living, and our grief-filled living, our joyous living, our violent living, busy living, our peaceful living. It is about possibility. It is based in the world of matter. I am interested in how something small turns into an image that is large and strong with resonance, where the ordinary becomes beautiful. I believe the divine, the magic, is here in the weeds at our feet, unacknowledged. What a world this is. Where else could water rise up to the sky, turn into snow crystals, magnificently brought together, fall from the sky all around us, pile up billions deep, and catch the small sparks of sunlight as they return again to water?   14

These acts of magic happen all the time; in Chaco Canyon,[7] my sister has seen a kiva, a ceremonial room in the earth, that is in the center of the canyon. This place has been uninhabited for what seems like forever. It has been without water. In fact, there are theories that the ancient people disappeared when they journeyed after water. In the center of it a corn plant was growing. It was all alone and it had been   15

---

4. Alice Walker: (1944–   ); see headnote to "Am I Blue?".
5. Sharon Olds (1942–   ): American poet.
6. Betty Williams (1943–   ) shared the 1976 Nobel Peace Prize with Mairead Corrigan for leadership of the peace movement in Northern Ireland.
7. Chaco Canyon: in northwest New Mexico, site of ruins of the prehistoric Anasazi culture.

there since the ancient ones, the old ones who came before us all, those people who wove dog hair into belts, who witnessed the painting of flute players on the seeping canyon walls, who knew the stories of corn. And there was one corn plant growing out of the holy place. It planted itself yearly. With no water, no person to care for it, no overturning of the soil, this corn plant rises up to tell its story, and that's what this poetry is.

JACOB BRONOWSKI

The Creative Mind

Jacob Bronowski (1908–1974), born in Poland, took his Ph.D. in mathematics at Cambridge University and then published a number of books about the very unmathematical poet William Blake. Like many brilliant young people in the 1930s, Bronowski (pronounced Bron-*off*-ski) had his life shattered by Hitler's rise to power: "I suddenly realized that being happy, being human, being a scientist, being with friends was not enough." As a member of a scientific team studying the effects of the atomic bombing of Japan, Bronowski was once more jolted into a higher level of concern about the times he was living in: he "knew that we had dehumanized the enemy and ourselves at one blow." From 1945 forward, Bronowski labored to help his readers see that science and technology—so deeply implicated in the horrors of World War II—also had a human face. "The Creative Mind," originally delivered as a lecture at the Massachusetts Institute of Technology in 1953, became Chapter 1 of Bronowski's impressive short book *Science and Human Values* (1956). Wider fame came to Bronowski with the broadcast of his thirteen-part television series *The Ascent of Man*, which was published as a collection of essays in 1977. As this essay challenges beliefs about liberal education, it joins in conversation with those by Carol Bly and William Perry. In addition, Bronowski's emphasis on the "search for hidden likenesses" helps us appreciate essays like Hogan's "Hearing Voices" or poems like Lee's "This Room and Everything in It" and suggests what we can accomplish in our own thinking and writing.

1

On a fine November day in 1945, late in the afternoon, I was landed on an airstrip in southern Japan. From there a jeep was to take me over the mountains to join a ship which lay in Nagasaki Harbor. I knew nothing of the country or the distance before us. We drove off; dusk fell; the road rose and fell away, the pine woods came down to the road, straggled on and opened again. I did not know that we had left the open country until unexpectedly I heard the ship's loudspeakers broadcasting dance music. Then suddenly I was aware that we were already at the center of damage in Nagasaki. The shadows behind me were the skeletons of the Mitsubishi factory buildings, pushed backwards and sideways as if by a giant hand. What I had thought to be broken rocks was a concrete power house with its roof punched in. I could now make out the outline of two crumpled gasometers; there was a cold furnace festooned with service pipes; otherwise nothing but cockeyed telegraph poles and loops of wire in a bare waste of ashes. I had blundered into this desolate landscape as instantly as one might wake among the craters of the moon. The moment of recognition when I realized that I was already in Nagasaki is present to me as I write, as vividly as when I lived it. I see the warm night and the meaningless shapes; I can even remember the tune that was coming from the ship. It was a dance tune which had been popular in 1945, and it was called "Is You Is Or Is You Ain't Ma Baby?"

These essays, which I have called *Science and Human Values*, were   2
born at that moment. For the moment I have recalled was a universal moment; what I met was, almost as abruptly, the experience of mankind. On an evening like that evening, some time in 1945, each of us in his own way learned that his imagination had been dwarfed. We looked up and saw the power of which we had been proud loom over us like the ruins of Nagasaki.

The power of science for good and for evil has troubled other   3
minds than ours. We are not here fumbling with a new dilemma; our subject and our fears are as old as the toolmaking civilizations. Men have been killed with weapons before now: what happened at Nagasaki was only more massive (for 40,000 were killed there by a flash which lasted seconds) and more ironical (for the bomb exploded over the main Christian community in Japan). Nothing happened in 1945 except that we changed the scale of our indifference to man; and conscience, in revenge, for an instant became immediate to us. Before this immediacy fades in a sequence of televised atomic tests, let us acknowledge our subject for what it is: civilization face to face with its own implications. The implications are both the industrial slum which Nagasaki was before it was bombed, and the ashy desolation which the bomb made of the slum. And civilization asks of both ruins, "Is You Is Or Is You Ain't Ma Baby?"

2

The man whom I imagine to be asking this question, wrily with a   4
sense of shame, is not a scientist; he is civilized man. It is of course

more usual for each member of civilization to take flight from its consequences by protesting that others have failed him. Those whose education and perhaps tastes have confined them to the humanities protest that the scientists alone are to blame, for plainly no mandarin[1] ever made a bomb or an industry. The scientists say, with equal contempt, that the Greek scholars and the earnest cataloguers of cave paintings do well to wash their hands of blame; but what in fact are they doing to help direct the society whose ills grow more often from inaction than from error?

This absurd division reached its *reductio ad absurdum,* I think, when one of my teachers, G. H. Hardy, justified his great life work on the ground that it could do no one the least harm—or the least good. But Hardy was a mathematician; will humanists really let him opt out of the conspiracy of scientists? Or are scientists in their turn to forgive Hardy because, protest as he might, most of them learned their indispensable mathematics from his books?

There is no comfort in such bickering. When Shelley pictured science as a modern Prometheus[2] who would wake the world to a wonderful dream of Godwin,[3] he was alas too simple. But it is as pointless to read what has happened since as a nightmare. Dream or nightmare, we have to live our experience as it is, and we have to live it awake. We live in a world which is penetrated through and through by science, and which is both whole and real. We cannot turn it into a game simply by taking sides.

And this make-believe game might cost us what we value most: the human content of our lives. The scholar who disdains science may speak in fun, but his fun is not quite a laughing matter. To think of science as a set of special tricks, to see the scientist as the manipulator of outlandish skills—this is the root of the poison mandrake which flourishes rank in the comic strips. There is no more threatening and no more degrading doctrine than the fancy that somehow we may shelve the responsibility for making the decisions of our society by passing it to a few scientists armored with a special magic. This is another dream, the dream of H. G. Wells, in which the tall elegant engineers rule, with perfect benevolence, a humanity which has no business except to be happy. To H. G. Wells, this was a dream of heaven—a modern version of the idle, harp-resounding heaven of other childhood pieties. But in fact it is the picture of a slave society, and should make us shiver

1. *Mandarin* is sometimes used to mean a person influential in intellectual or literary circles.
2. Prometheus, one of the Titans of Greek mythology, gave humans the gift of fire.
3. William Godwin (1756–1836), a utopian socialist, dreamed of a world of perfect personal freedom in small, self-sufficient communities.

whenever we hear a man of sensibility dismiss science as someone else's concern. The world today is made, it is powered by science; and for any man to abdicate an interest in science is to walk with open eyes towards slavery.

My aim in this book is to show that the parts of civilization make a 8 whole: to display the links which give society its coherence, and, more, which give it life. In particular, I want to show the place of science in the canons of conduct which it has still to perfect.

This subject falls into three parts. The first is a study of the nature 9 of the scientific activity, and with it of all those imaginative acts of understanding which exercise "The Creative Mind." After this it is logical to ask what is the nature of the truth, as we seek it in science and in social life; and to trace the influence which this search for empirical truth has had on conduct. This influence has prompted me to call the second part "The Habit of Truth." Last I shall study the conditions for the success of science, and find in them the values of man which science would have had to invent afresh if man had not otherwise known them: the values which make up "The Sense of Human Dignity."

This, then, is a high-ranging subject which is not to be held in the 10 narrow limits of a laboratory. It disputes the prejudice of the humanist who takes his science sourly and, equally, the petty view which many scientists take of their own activity and that of others. When men misunderstand their own work, they cannot understand the work of others; so that it is natural that these scientists have been indifferent to the arts. They have been content, with the humanists, to think science mechanical and neutral; they could therefore justify themselves only by the claim that it is practical. By this lame criterion they have of course found poetry and music and painting at least unreal and often meaningless. I challenge all these judgments.

3

There is a likeness between the creative acts of the mind in art and 11 in science. Yet, when a man uses the word science in such a sentence, it may be suspected that he does not mean what the headlines mean by science. Am I about to sidle away to those riddles in the Theory of Numbers which Hardy loved, or to the heady speculations of astrophysicists, in order to make claims for abstract science which have no bearing on its daily practice?

I have no such design. My purpose is to talk about science as it is, 12 practical and theoretical. I define science as the organization of our knowledge in such a way that it commands more of the hidden potential in nature. What I have in mind therefore is both deep and matter of fact; it reaches from the kinetic theory of gases to the telephone and the suspension bridge and medicated toothpaste. It admits no sharp boundary between knowledge and use. There are of course people who like to draw a line between pure and applied science; and oddly, they are often the same people who find art unreal. To them, the word *useful* is a final arbiter, either for or against a work; and they use this word as if it can mean only what makes a man feel heavier after meals.

There is no sanction for confining the practice of science in this or another way. True, science is full of useful inventions. And its theories have often been made by men whose imagination was directed by the uses to which their age looked. Newton turned naturally to astronomy because it was the subject of his day, and it was so because finding one's way at sea had long been a practical preoccupation of the society into which he was born. It should be added, mischievously, that astronomy also had some standing because it was used very practically to cast horoscopes. (Kepler used it for this purpose; in the Thirty Years' War he cast the horoscope of Wallenstein which wonderfully told his character, and he predicted a universal disaster for 1634 which proved to be the murder of Wallenstein.)

In a setting which is more familiar, Faraday worked all his life to link electricity with magnetism because this was the glittering problem of his day; and it was so because his society, like ours, was on the lookout for new sources of power. Consider a more modest example today: the new mathematical methods of automatic control, a subject sometimes called cybernetics, have been developed now because this is a time when communication and control have in effect become forms of power. These inventions have been directed by social needs, and they are useful inventions; yet it was not their usefulness which dominated and set light to the minds of those who made them. Neither Newton nor Faraday, nor yet Norbert Wiener, spent their time in a scramble for patents.

What a scientist does is compounded of two interests: the interest of his time and his own interest. In this his behavior is no different from any other man's. The need of the age gives its shape to scientific progress as a whole. But it is not the need of the age which gives the individual scientist his sense of pleasure and of adventure, and that excitement which keeps him working late into the night when all the useful typists have gone home at five o'clock. He is personally involved in his work, as the poet is in his, and as the artist is in the painting. Paints and painting too much have been made for useful ends; and language was developed, from whatever beginnings, for practical communication. Yet you cannot have a man handle paints or language or the symbolic concepts of physics, you cannot even have him stain a microscope slide, without instantly waking in him a pleasure in the very language, a sense of exploring his own activity. This sense lies at the heart of creation.

4

The sense of personal exploration is as urgent, and as delightful, to the practical scientist as to the theoretical. Those who think otherwise are confusing what is practical with what is humdrum. Good humdrum work without originality is done every day by everyone, theoretical scientists as well as practical, and writers and painters too, as well as truck drivers and bank clerks. Of course the unoriginal work keeps the world going; but it is not therefore the monopoly of practical men. And neither need the practical man be unoriginal. If he is to break out of what has been done before, he must bring to his own tools the same sense of pride and discovery which the poet brings to words. He cannot afford to be less radical in conceiving and less creative in designing a new turbine than a new world system. 16

And this is why in turn practical discoveries are not made only by practical men. As the world's interest has shifted, since the Industrial Revolution, to the tapping of new springs of power, the theoretical scientist has shifted his interests too. His speculations about energy have been as abstract as once they were about astronomy; and they have been profound now as they were then, because the man loved to think. The Carnot cycle[4] and the dynamo grew equally from this love, and so did nuclear physics and the German V[5] weapons and Kelvin's interest in low temperatures. Man does not invent by following either use or tradition; he does not invent even a new form of communication by calling a conference of communication engineers. Who invented the television set? In any deep sense, it was Clerk Maxwell who foresaw the existence of radio waves, and Heinrich Hertz who proved it, and J. J. Thomson who discovered the electron. This is not said in order to rob any practical man of the invention, but from a sad sense of justice; for neither Maxwell nor Hertz nor J. J. Thomson would take pride in television just now. 17

Man masters nature not by force but by understanding. This is why science has succeeded when magic failed: because it has looked for no spell to cast over nature. The alchemist and the magician in the Middle Ages thought, and the addict of comic strips is still encouraged to think, that nature must be mastered by a device which outrages her laws. But in four hundred years since the Scientific Revolution we 18

4. Carnot cycle: the cycle of heat and work exchanges in an ideal steam engine, conceived by the nineteenth-century French engineer Sadi Carnot.
5. German V: the rockets with which Hitler bombarded England in World War II.

have learned that we gain our ends only *with* the laws of nature; we control her only by understanding her laws. We cannot even bully nature by any insistence that our work shall be designed to give power over her. We must be content that power is the byproduct of understanding. So the Greeks said that Orpheus played the lyre with such sympathy that wild beasts were tamed by the hand on the strings. They did not suggest that he got this gift by setting out to be a lion tamer.

5

What is the insight with which the scientist tries to see into nature? Can it indeed be called either imaginative or creative? To the literary man the question may seem merely silly. He has been taught that science is a large collection of facts; and if this is true, then the only seeing which scientists need do is, he supposes, seeing the facts. He pictures them, the colorless professionals of science, going off to work in the morning into the universe in a neutral, unexposed state. They then expose themselves like a photographic plate. And then in the darkroom or laboratory they develop the image, so that suddenly and startlingly it appears, printed in capital letters, as a new formula for atomic energy. [19]

Men who have read Balzac and Zola[6] are not deceived by the claims of these writers that they do no more than record the facts. The readers of Christopher Isherwood do not take him literally when he writes "I am a camera." Yet the same readers solemnly carry with them from their school days this foolish picture of the scientist fixing by some mechanical process the facts of nature. I have had of all people a historian tell me that science is a collection of facts, and his voice had not even the ironic rasp of one filing cabinet reproving another. [20]

It seems impossible that this historian had ever studied the beginnings of a scientific discovery. The Scientific Revolution can be held to begin in the year 1543 when there was brought to Copernicus, perhaps on his deathbed, the first printed copy of the book he had finished about a dozen years earlier. The thesis of this book is that the earth moves around the sun. When did Copernicus go out and record this fact with his camera? What appearance in nature prompted his outrageous guess? And in what odd sense is this guess to be called a neutral record of fact? [21]

Less than a hundred years after Copernicus, Kepler published (between 1609 and 1619) the three laws which described the paths of the [22]

6. Honoré de Balzac and Emile Zola were literary realists.

planets. The work of Newton and with it most of our mechanics spring from these laws. They have a solid, matter of fact sound. For example, Kepler says that if one squares the year of a planet, one gets a number which is proportional to the cube of its average distance from the sun. Does anyone think that such a law is found by taking enough readings and then squaring and cubing everything in sight? If he does, then as a scientist, he is doomed to a wasted life; he has as little prospect of making a scientific discovery as an electronic brain has.

It was not this way that Copernicus and Kepler thought, or that scientists think today. Copernicus found that the orbits of the planets would look simpler if they were looked at from the sun and not from the earth. But he did not in the first place find this by routine calculation. His first step was a leap of imagination—to lift himself from the earth, and put himself wildly, speculatively into the sun. "The earth conceives from the sun," he wrote; and "the sun rules the family of stars." We catch in his mind an image, the gesture of the virile man standing in the sun, with arms outstretched, overlooking the planets. Perhaps Copernicus took the picture from the drawings of the youth with outstretched arms which the Renaissance teachers put into their books on the proportions of the body. Perhaps he had seen Leonardo's drawings of his loved pupil Salai. I do not know. To me, the gesture of Copernicus, the shining youth looking outward from the sun, is still vivid in a drawing which William Blake in 1780 based on all these: the drawing which is usually called *Glad Day*. 23

Kepler's mind, we know, was filled with just such fanciful analogies; and we know what they were. Kepler wanted to relate the speeds of the planets to the musical intervals. He tried to fit the five regular solids into their orbits. None of these likenesses worked, and they have been forgotten; yet they have been and they remain the stepping stones of every creative mind. Kepler felt for his laws by way of metaphors, he searched mystically for likenesses with what he knew in every strange corner of nature. And when among these guesses he hit upon his laws, he did not think of their numbers as the balancing of a cosmic bank account, but as a revelation of the unity of all nature. To us, the analogies by which Kepler listened for the movement of the planets in the music of the spheres are farfetched. Yet are they more so than the wild leap by which Rutherford and Bohr in our own century found a model for the atom in, of all places, the planetary system? 24

6

No scientific theory is a collection of facts. It will not even do to call a theory true or false in the simple sense in which every fact is either so or not so. The Epicureans held that matter is made of atoms 25 two thousand years ago and we are now tempted to say that their theory was true. But if we do so we confuse their notion of matter with our own. John Dalton in 1808 first saw the structure of matter as we do today, and what he took from the ancients was not their theory but something richer, their image: the atom. Much of what was in Dalton's mind was as vague as the Greek notion, and quite as mistaken. But he suddenly gave life to the new facts of chemistry and the ancient theory together, by fusing them to give what neither had: a coherent picture of how matter is linked and built up from different kinds of atoms. The act of fusion is the creative act.

All science is the search for unity in hidden likenesses. The search 26 may be on a grand scale, as in the modern theories which try to link the fields of gravitation and electromagnetism. But we do not need to be browbeaten by the scale of science. There are discoveries to be made by snatching a small likeness from the air too, if it is bold enough. In 1935 the Japanese physicist Hideki Yukawa wrote a paper which can still give heart to a young scientist. He took as his starting point the known fact that waves of light can sometimes behave as if they were separate pellets. From this he reasoned that the forces which held the nucleus of an atom together might sometimes also be observed as if they were solid pellets. A schoolboy can see how thin Yukawa's analogy is, and his teacher would be severe with it. Yet Yukawa without a blush calculated the mass of the pellet he expected to see, and waited. He was right; his meson was found, and a range of other mesons, neither the existence nor the nature of which had been suspected before. The likeness had borne fruit.

The scientist looks for order in the appearance of nature by explor- 27 ing such likenesses. For order does not display itself of itself; if it can be said to be there at all, it is not there for the mere looking. There is no way of pointing a finger or a camera at it; order must be discovered and, in a deep sense, it must be created. What we see, as we see it, is mere disorder.

This point has been put trenchantly in a fable by Karl Popper. Sup- 28 pose that someone wished to give his whole life to science. Suppose that he therefore sat down, pencil in hand, and for the next twenty, thirty, forty years recorded in notebook after notebook everything that he could observe. He may be supposed to leave out nothing: today's humidity, the racing results, the level of cosmic radiation and the stock-market prices and the look of Mars, all would be there. He would have compiled the most careful record of nature that has ever been made; and, dying in the calm certainty of a life well spent, he would of course leave his notebooks to the Royal Society. Would the Royal Society thank him for the treasure of a lifetime of observation? It would not. The Royal Society would treat his notebooks exactly as the English bishops have treated Joanna Southcott's box.[7] It would refuse to open them at all, because it would know without looking that the notebooks contain only a jumble of disorderly and meaningless items.

7

Science finds order and meaning in our experience, and sets about this in quite a different way. It sets about it as Newton did in the story which he himself told in his old age, and of which the schoolbooks give only a caricature. In the year 1665, when Newton was twenty-two, the plague broke out in southern England, and the University of Cambridge was closed. Newton therefore spent the next eighteen months at home, removed from traditional learning, at a time when he was impatient for knowledge and, in his own phrase, "I was in the prime of my age for invention." In this eager, boyish mood, sitting one day in the garden of his widowed mother, he saw an apple fall. So far the books have the story right; we think we even know the kind of apple; tradition has it that it was a Flower of Kent. But now they miss the crux of the story. For what struck the young Newton at the sight was not the thought that the apple must be drawn to the earth by gravity; that conception was older than Newton. What struck him was the conjecture that the same force of gravity, which reaches to the top of the tree, might go on reaching out beyond the earth and its air, endlessly into space. Gravity might reach the moon: this was Newton's new thought; and it might be gravity which holds the moon in her orbit. There and then he calculated what force from the earth (falling off as the square of the distance) would hold the moon, and compared it with the known force of gravity at tree height. The forces agreed; Newton says laconically, "I found them answer pretty nearly." Yet they agreed only nearly: the likeness and the approximation go together, for no likeness is exact. In Newton's sentence modern science is full grown.

It grows from a comparison. It has seized a likeness between two unlike appearances; for the apple in the summer garden and the grave moon overhead are surely as unlike in their movements as two things can be. Newton traced in them two expressions of a single concept, gravitation: and the concept (and the unity) are in that sense his free creation. The progress of science is the discovery at each step of a new

7. Joanna Southcott (1750–1814) claimed to have transcribed divinely inspired messages concerning the Second Coming of Christ. At her death she left a locked box, instructing that it should be opened in the presence of all the bishops in a time of national emergency. It was opened, in the presence of one bishop, in 1928; nothing in it was deemed of interest, which further convinced the English religious establishment that she was merely a crank.

order which gives unity to what had long seemed unlike. Faraday did this when he closed the link between electricity and magnetism. Clerk Maxwell did it when he linked both with light. Einstein linked time with space, mass with energy, and the path of light past the sun with the flight of a bullet; and spent his dying years in trying to add to these likenesses another, which would find a single imaginative order between the equations of Clerk Maxwell and his own geometry of gravitation.

8

When Coleridge tried to define beauty, he returned always to one [31] deep thought: beauty, he said, is "unity in variety." Science is nothing else than the search to discover unity in the wild variety of nature—or more exactly, in the variety of our experience. Poetry, painting, the arts are the same search, in Coleridge's phrase, for unity in variety. Each in his own way looks for likenesses under the variety of human experience. What is a poetic image but the seizing and the exploration of a hidden likeness, in holding together two parts of a comparison which are to give depth each to the other? When Romeo finds Juliet in the tomb, and thinks her dead, he uses in his heartbreaking speech the words,

Death that hath suckt the honey of thy breath.

The critic can only haltingly take to pieces the single shock which this image carries. The young Shakespeare admired Marlowe, and Marlowe's Faustus had said of the ghostly kiss of Helen of Troy that it sucked forth his soul. But that is a pale image; what Shakespeare has done is to fire it with the single word honey. Death is a bee at the lips of Juliet, and the bee is an insect that stings; the sting of death was a commonplace phrase when Shakespeare wrote. The sting is there, under the image, Shakespeare has packed it into the word honey; but the very word rides powerfully over its own undertones. Death is a bee that stings other people, but it comes to Juliet as if she were a flower; this is the moving thought under the instant image. The creative mind speaks in such thoughts.

The poetic image here is also, and accidentally, heightened by the [32] tenderness which town dwellers now feel for country ways. But it need not be; there are likenesses to conjure with, and images as powerful, within the man-made world. The poems of Alexander Pope belong to this world. They are not countrified, and therefore readers today find them unemotional and often artificial. Let me then quote Pope: here he is in a formal satire face to face, towards the end of his life, with his own gifts. In eight lines he looks poignantly forward towards death and back to the laborious years which made him famous.

> *Years foll'wing Years, steal something ev'ry day,*
> *At last they steal us from our selves away;*
> *In one our Frolicks, one Amusements end,*
> *In one a Mistress drops, in one a Friend:*
> *This subtle Thief of Life, this paltry Time,*
> *What will it leave me, if it snatch my Rhime?*
> *If ev'ry Wheel of that unweary'd Mill*
> *That turn'd ten thousand Verses, now stands still.*

The human mind had been compared to what the eighteenth century called a mill, that is to a machine, before; Pope's own idol Bolingbroke had compared it to a clockwork. In these lines the likeness goes deeper, for Pope is thinking of the ten thousand Verses which he had translated from Homer: what he says is sad and just at the same time, because this really had been a mechanical and at times a grinding task. Yet the clockwork is present in the image too; when the wheels stand still, time for Pope will stand still for ever; we feel that we already hear, over the horizon, Faust's defiant reply to Mephistopheles, which Goethe had not yet written—"let the clock strike and stop, let the hand fall, and time be at an end."

> *Werd ich zum Augenblicke sagen:*
> *Verweile doch! du bist so schön!*
> *Dann magst du mich in Fesseln schlagen,*
> *Dann will ich gern zugrunde gehn!*
> *Dann mag die Totenglocke schallen,*
> *Dann bist du deines Dienstes frei,*
> *Die Uhr mag stehn, der Zeiger fallen*
> *Es sei die Zeit für mich vorbei!*[8]

I have quoted Pope and Goethe because their metaphor here is not poetic; it is rather a hand reaching straight into experience and arranging it with new meaning. Metaphors of this kind need not always be written in words. The most powerful of them all is simply the presence of King Lear and his Fool in the hovel of a man who is shamming madness, while lightning rages outside.[9] Or let me quote another clash of two conceptions of life, from a modern poet. In his later poems W. B. Yeats was troubled by the feeling that in shutting himself up to write, he was missing the active pleasures of life; and yet it seemed to him certain that the man who lives for these pleasures will leave no lasting work behind him. He said this at times very simply, too:

8. "If ever I say to the passing moment: Stay a while! Thou art so fair! Then may you cast me into chains. Then will I gladly perish. Then may the death-bell toll. Then are you freed from my service. Let the clock strike and stop, let the hand fall, and time be at an end." (German)
9. In Act III, scene iv of Shakespeare's *King Lear*, psychological, moral, familial, and political disorder all find a metaphor in the storm that batters these three vulnerable men.

> *The intellect of man is forced to choose*
> *Perfection of the life, or of the work.*

This problem, whether a man fulfills himself in word or in play, is of course more common than Yeats allowed; and it may be more commonplace. But it is given breadth and force by the images in which Yeats pondered it.

> *Get all the gold and silver that you can,*
> *Satisfy ambition, or animate*
> *The trivial days and ram them with the sun,*
> *And yet upon these maxims meditate:*
> *All women dote upon an idle man*
> *Although their children need a rich estate;*
> *No man has ever lived that had enough*
> *Of children's gratitude or woman's love.*

The love of women, the gratitude of children: the images fix two philosophies as nothing else can. They are tools of creative thought, as coherent and as exact as the conceptual images with which science works: as time and space, or as the proton and the neutron.

9

The discoveries of science, the works of art are explorations— 34 more, are explosions, of a hidden likeness. The discoverer or the artist presents in them two aspects of nature and fuses them into one. This is the act of creation, in which an original thought is born, and it is the same act in original science and original art. But it is not therefore the monopoly of the man who wrote the poem or who made the discovery. On the contrary, I believe this view of the creative act to be right because it alone gives a meaning to the act of appreciation. The poem or the discovery exists in two moments of vision: the moment of appreciation as much as that of creation; for the appreciator must see the movement, wake to the echo which was started in the creation of the work. In the moment of appreciation we live again the moment when the creator saw and held the hidden likeness. When a simile takes us aback and persuades us together, when we find a juxtaposition in a picture both odd and intriguing, when a theory is at once fresh and convincing, we do not merely nod over someone else's work. We reenact the creative act, and we ourselves make the discovery again. At bottom, there is no unifying likeness there until we too have seized it, we too have made it for ourselves.

How slipshod by comparison is the notion that either art or science 35 sets out to copy nature. If the task of the painter were to copy for men what they see, the critic could make only a single judgment: either that the copy is right or that it is wrong. And if science were a copy of fact, then every theory would be either right or wrong, and would be so for ever. There would be nothing left for us to say but this is so, or is not so. No one who has read a page by a good critic or a speculative scientist can ever again think that this barren choice of yes or no is all that the mind offers.

Reality is not an exhibit for man's inspection, labelled "Do not touch." There are no appearances to be photographed, no experiences to be copied, in which we do not take part. Science, like art, is not a copy of nature but a re-creation of her. We re-make nature by the act of discovery, in the poem or in the theorem. And the great poem and the deep theorem are new to every reader, and yet are his own experiences, because he himself re-creates them. They are the mark of unity in variety; and in the instant when the mind seizes this for itself, in art or in science, the heart misses a beat. 36

CAROL BLY

Growing Up Expressive

Carol Bly (1930–   ), although educated at a New England boarding school and at Wellesley College, has spent most of her life in her home state of Minnesota. She began writing in the 1970s, publishing several essays in *Preview* and *Minnesota Monthly*. At the same time, she raised four children, divorced her husband (poet Robert Bly), and gave much of her time to civil and humanitarian activities. Bly was the humanities consultant for the American Farm Project from 1978 to 1981 and since 1982 has been a consultant for the Land Stewardship Project; she has also served on the Chamber of Commerce of Madison and on the Board of Diocesan Publications for the Episcopal Church of Minnesota. In addition to collaborating on essays (with Joe Paddock and Nancy Paddock) for *Common Ground* (1981) and pamphlets such as *Soil and Survival* (1985) for the Sierra Club, Bly published several of her own essays in *Letters from the Country* (1981), from which "Growing Up Expressive" comes. Bly also writes fiction and has published two collections of short stories, *Backbone* (1985) and *The Tomcat's Wife and Other Stories* (1991), as well as a source book for creative writers, *The Passionate, Accurate Story* (1990). She recently edited *Changing the Bully who Rules the World* (1996), an anthology of poems, stories, and essays dealing with oppression and freedom. She teaches creative writing at the University of Minnesota.

In "Growing Up Expressive," Bly suggests that because public schools are too good at teaching children to be problem solvers, they blind them to the "fearless contemplation of gigantic things," like love and death and the universe, that have no easy answers. Her essay encourages us to put aside (at least temporarily) our impulse toward orderliness in our writing and generate ideas through "fear-less contemplation." A useful companion essay is William Perry's "Examsmanship and the Liberal Arts," which also sets up a di-chotomy between two approaches to understanding.

Love, death, the cruelty of power, and time's curve past the stars   1
are what children want to look at. For convenience's sake, let's say
these are the four most vitally touching things in life. Little children
ask questions about them with relish. Children, provided they are still
little enough, have no eye to doing any problem solving about love or
death or injustice or the universe; they are simply interested. I've noticed that as we read aloud literature to them, about Baba Yaga, and
Dr. Dolittle, and Ivan and the Firebird, and Rat and Mole, children are
not only interested, they are prepared to be vitally touched by the
great things of life. If you like the phrase, they are what some people
call "being as a little child." Another way of looking at it is to say that
in our minds we have two kinds of receptivity to life going on all the
time: first, being vitally touched and enthusiastic (grateful, enraged,
puzzled—but, at all events, *moved*) and, second, having a will to solve
problems.

Our gritty society wants and therefore deliberately trains problem   2
solvers, however, not mystics. We teach human beings to keep themselves conscious only of problems that *can* conceivably be solved.
There must be no hopeless causes. Now this means that some subjects,
of which death and sexual love come to mind straight off, should be
kept at as low a level of consciousness as possible. Both resist problem
solving. A single-minded problem solver focuses his consciousness, of
course, on problems to be solved, but even he realizes there is a concentric, peripheral band of other material around the problems. This
band appears to him as "issues." He is not interested in these issues for
themselves; he sees them simply as impacting on the problems. He will
allow us to talk of love, death, injustice, and eternity—he may even
encourage us to do so because his group-dynamics training advises
him to let us have our say, thus dissipating our willfulness—but his
heart is circling, circling, looking for an opening to *wrap up* these "issues" so he can return attention to discrete, solvable problems. For example, a physician who has that mentality does not wish to be near
dying patients very much. They are definitely not a solvable problem.
If he is wicked, he will regard them as a present issue with impact on a
future problem: then he will order experimentation done on them
during their last weeks with us. It means his ethic is toward the healing process only, but not toward the dying person. His ethic is toward
problem solving, not toward wonder. He will feel quite conscientious
while doing the experiments on the dying patient, because he feels he
is saving lives of future patients.

To return to little children for a second: they simply like to con- 3
template life and death. So our difficulty, in trying to educate adults so
they will be balanced but enthusiastic, is to keep both streams going—
the problem solving, which seems to be the mental genius of our
species, and the fearless contemplation of gigantic things, the spiritual
genius of our species.

The problem-solving mentality is inculcated no less in art and En- 4
glish classes than in mathematics and science. Its snake oil is hope of
success: by setting very small topics in front of people, for which it is
easy for them to see the goals, the problems, the solutions, their egos
are not threatened. They feel hopeful of being effective. Therefore, to
raise a generation of problem solvers, you encourage them to visit the
county offices (as our sixth-grade teachers do) and you lead them to
understand that this is citizenship. You carefully do not suggest that
citizenship also means comparatively complex and hopeless activities
like Amnesty International's pressure to get prisoners in far places released or at least no longer tortured. Small egos are threatened by
huge, perhaps insoluble problems. Therefore, one feeds the small ego
confidence by setting before it dozens and dozens of very simple situations. The ego is nourished by feeling it understands the relationship
between the county recorder's office and the county treasurer's office;
in later life, when young people find a couple of sticky places in county
government, they will confidently work at smoothing them. How very
different an experience such problem solving is from having put before
one the spectacle of the United States' various stances and activities
with respect to germ warfare. Educators regularly steer off all interest
in national and international government to one side, constantly feeding our rural young people on questions to which one can hope for answers on a short timeline. We do not ask them to exercise that muscle
which bears the weight of vast considerations—such as cruelty in large
governments. By the time the average rural Minnesotan is eighteen,
he or she expects to stay in cheerful places, devote some time to local
government and civic work, and "win the little ones." Rural young
people have a repertoire of pejorative language for hard causes: "opening that keg of worms," "no end to that once you get into it," "don't
worry—you can't do anything about that from where you are," "we
could go on about that forever!" They are right, of course: we could,
and our species, at its most cultivated, does go on forever about love,
death, power, time, the universe. But some of us, alas, have been conditioned by eighteen fashionably to despise those subjects because
there are no immediate answers to all the questions they ask us.

The other way we negatively reinforce any philosophical bent in 5
children is to pretend we don't see the content in their artwork. We
comment only on the technique, in somewhat the same way you can
scarcely get a comment on rural preachers' sermon content: the re-

sponse is always, He does a good (or bad) job of speaking. "Well, but what did he say?" "Oh, he talked really well. That man can preach!"

The way to devalue the content of a child's painting is to say, 6 "Wow, you sure can paint!" The average art teacher in Minnesota is at pains to find something to say to the third grader's painting of a space machine with complicated, presumably electronic equipment in it. Here is the drawing in words: A man is sitting at some controls. Outside his capsule, fire is flying from emission points on his ship toward another spaceship at right, hitting it. Explosions are coming out of its side and tail. What is an art teacher to do with this? Goodness knows. So he or she says, "My goodness, I can see there's a lot of action there!" It is said in a deliberately encouraging way but anyone can hear under the carefully supportive comment: "A lot of work going into nothing but more TV-inspired violence." One might as well have told the child, "Thank you for sharing."

I once attended a regional writers' group at which a young poet 7 wrote about his feelings of being a single parent and trying to keep his sanity as he cared for his children. In his poem, he raced up the staircase, grabbed a gun, and shot the clock. When he finished reading it aloud to us, someone told him, "I certainly am glad you shared with us. I'd like to really thank you for sharing."

If we are truly serious about life we are going to have to stop 8 thanking people for sharing. It isn't enough response to whatever has been offered. It is half ingenuous, and sometimes it is insincere, and often it is patronizing. It is the *dictum excrementi*[1] of our decade.

I would like to keep in mind for a moment the art works described 9 above: the child's painting of a spaceship assaulting another spaceship, and the harrowed father's racing up the staircase and shooting the clock. Here is a third. It is a twelve-year-old's theme for English class.

> They were their four days and nights before anyone found them. It was wet and cold down there. As little kids at the orphanage, they had been beaten every night until they could scarcely make it to bed. Now they were older. Duane and Ellen leaned together. "I love you forever," she told him. He asked her, "Even though my face is marked from getting scarlett fever and polio and small pox and newmonya and they wouldn't take decent care of me, not call the doctor or anything, so the marks will always be on me?" "You know I love you," Ellen told him. "You know that time they tortured me for information and I was there but I didn't talk and later I found out it was your uncle who did it. I didn't talk because I remembered the American flag." Just then they heard someone shout, "Anyone alive down there in this mess?" You see a bomb had gone off destroying a entire U.S.A. city where they lived. Duane had lived with his cruel uncle who took him out of the orphanage to get cheap labor and

---

1. *dictum excrementi:* The Latin translates roughly as "worthless expression."

Ellen lived at a boardinghouse where there were rats that ate pages of her diary all the time. Now they both looked up and shouted "We're here!" A head appeared at the top of the well into which they had fallen or they would of been in 6,500 pieces like all the other men and ladies even pregnant ones and little kids in that town. Now this head called down, "Oh— a boy and a girl!" then the head explained it was going for a ladder and ropes and it ducked away and where it had been they saw the beginnings of stars for that night, the stars still milky in front of the bright blue because the sky wasn't dark enough yet to show them up good.

The English teacher will typically comment on this story by observing that the spelling is uneven, and adjectives get used as adverbs. In rural Minnesota (if not elsewhere) an English teacher can spend every class hour on adjectives used as adverbs: it is meat and potatoes to a nag. But when we discuss spelling, syntax, and adverbs, we are talking method, not content. The child notices that nothing is said of the story's *plot*. No one remarks on the *feelings* in it. Now if this happens every time a child hands in fiction or a poem, the child will realize by the time he reaches twelfth grade that meaning or feelings are not worth anything, that "mechanics" (note the term) are all that matter.

It is rare for a public school English teacher to comment on a child's content unless the material is *factual*. Minnesota teachers encourage writing booklets about the state, themes on ecology and county government, on how Dad strikes the field each autumn, on how Mom avoids open-kettle canning because the USDA advises against it. In this way, our children are conditioned to regard writing as problem solving instead of contemplation, as routine thinking instead of imaginative inquiry.

How can we manage it otherwise?

I would like to suggest some questions we can ask children about their artwork which will encourage them to grow up into lovers, lobby supporters, and Amnesty International members, instead of only township officers and annual protestors against daylight saving time. Let us gather all the elements of the three artworks presented in this Letter: the little boy's spaceship-war painting, the young divorced father's narrative poem, and the twelve-year-old girl's story of love in a well. We have a set of images before us, then:

Man directing spaceship fire
Another aircraft being obliterated
Staircase, man shooting a clock; children
Cruel orphanage
Torture
Last survivors of a decimated city

Let us, instead of lending the great sneer to these images, be re-   14
spectful of them. It may help to pretend the painting is by Picasso, that
Flaubert[2] wrote the father/clock scene, and that Tolstoy[3] wrote the
well story. It helps to remember that Picasso felt the assault of historical events on us—like Guernica;[4] Flaubert, as skillfully as Dostoyevsky[5] and with less self-pity, was an observer of violent detail; and
the Tolstoy who wrote *Resurrection* or the scene of Pierre's imprisonment in *War and Peace* would turn to the well/love story without
qualm.

We know we would never say to Picasso, Flaubert, or Tolstoy,   15
"Why don't you draw something you know about from everyday life?
Why don't you write about something you know about? You say Anna
was smashed beneath a train? Thank you for sharing!"

The fact is that a child's feelings about orphanages and torture and   16
love are things that he does know about. They are psychic realities inside him, and when he draws them, he is drawing something from
everyday life. Sometimes they are from his night life of dreaming, but
in any event they are images of passion and he is drawing from his
genuine if garbled experience. A few years ago there was a stupid
movement to discourage children's reading of Grimms' fairy tales.
Later, with a more sophisticated psychology, we learned that the step-
mother who is hostile and overweening is a reality to all children; the
cutting-off of the hero's right hand and replacing of it with a hand of
silver is a reality to all children. Spaceships, witches' gingerbread
houses, orphanages, being the last two people to survive on earth—all
these are part of the inner landscape, something children know about.
Therefore, in examining their artwork, we need better sets of questions to ask them. Young people who are not repressed are going to lay
their wild stuff in front of adults (hoping for comment of some kind,
praise if possible) until the sands of life are run, so we had better try to
be good at responding to them. And unless we want to raise drones
suitable only for conveyor-belt shifts, we had better be at least half as
enthusiastic as when they tell us, Mama, I got the mowing finished.

Here are some questions to ask our young artist. How much of that   17
electronic equipment is used for firepower and how much just to run
the ship? After the other spaceship is blown up and the people in it are
dead, what will this man do? Will he go home somewhere? Were the
stars out that night? You said he'll go home to his parents. Did the
other man have parents? How soon will that man's parents find out

2. Flaubert: Gustave Flaubert (1821–1880), French author of such "realist" novels as
Madame Bovary.
3. Tolstoy: Leo Tolstoy (1828–1910), Russian novelist.
4. Guernica: a Spanish fishing village whose bombing by fascist forces in 1937 inspired
a painting by Pablo Picasso (1881–1973).
5. Dostoyevsky: Feodor Dostoyevsky (1821–1881), Russian novelist.

that his spaceship was destroyed? Could you draw in the stars? You said they were out—could you draw them into the picture some way? but don't ruin anything you've got in there now. Also, that wire you said ran to the solar plates, will you darken it so it shows better? Don't change it—just make it clearer. Yes—terrific! Can you see the planet where the other man would have returned to if he had lived till morning?

The young father's story: There is an obvious psychic complication to this story: the violence in his shooting out the clock face is gratuitous, and the plea for attention on the part of the author directed at the reader is glaring: clock faces as psychological symbols are in the public domain. Anyone who tells a friend (or a group of strangers) I am going to shoot up a clock face at 11 P.M. is asking for psychological attention. In a civil world, to ask is to receive, so if we are civilized we have to pay attention and ask the young author: Why does the father in the story blast the clock? And, when he replies, we have to ask some more. If there was ever an instance in which it was O.K. to say, "Thanks for sharing," this is not it. 18

I should like to add that this will be especially difficult for rural teachers because the traditional country way to treat any kind of mental problem is to stare it down. It didn't happen. I didn't hear that insane thing you just said, and you know you don't really hate your mother. What nice parent would shoot a clock? We uniformly do what Dr. Vaillant in *Adaptations to Life*[6] would call a denial adaptation. It takes a brave questioner when the young person brings in a crazy story. 19

The well/love story: Did you know there really are such orphanages? There are orphanages where the children have to get up at four-thirty to work in the dairy, and the girls work hours and hours in the kitchens, and the children's growth is stunted. Did you make the girl so brave on purpose? Were they a lucky couple or an unlucky couple, or is that the sort of a question you can't ask? You made a point of telling us they'd been through a lot of hardship. What would it have been like for them if they hadn't? Do you want to talk about what blew up in the city? Did you imagine yourself in the well? 20

Those are not brilliant questions; they are simply respectful, because the art works described are concerned with death by violence; cruelty by institutions; treachery by relations; bravery (or cowardice—either one is important); sexual love, either despite or encouraged by dreadful circumstances. 21

They are some of the subjects in *War and Peace,* in Dürer's[7] etchings, paintings, and woodcuts, and in *Madame Bovary.* 22

---

6. The author is referring to a book published in 1977 by Dr. George E. Vaillant, studying the ways people succeed or fail in coping with various life changes.
7. Dürer: Albrecht Dürer (1471–1528), German artist.

It is a moot question in my mind which of two disciplines will be   23
the more useful in helping people stay vitally touched by the Great
Things: psychology might do it—and English literature in high school
might do it (instruction on the college level is generally so dutiful to
methodology that it seems a lost cause to me. "How did D. H.
Lawrence foreshadow this event?" and "What metaphors does Harold
Rosenberg use in his discussion of Action Painting?" are the questions
of technocrats, not preservers of spirit. It is as if we got home from
church and the others said, "How was church?" "We had Eucharist,"
we tell them. "Well, how was it?" they ask. "Pretty good," we reply.
"Bishop Anderson was there. He held the chalice eight inches above
the rail so no one spilled, then he turned and wiped the chalice after
each use so no germs were passed along. People who had already com-
muned returned to their benches using the north aisle so there was no
bottlenecking at the chancel.")

I don't think churches will be helpful in preserving the mystical   24
outlook as long as they see life and death as a *problem*—a problem of
salvation—with a solution to be worked at. Churches have an axe to
grind. They might take the father running up the staircase to be an impact subject. they would wish to use their program to solve his problem. Churchmen often appear to be companionable counselors, but
the appearance is largely manner and habit. Under the manner, the
clergyman's mindset is nearly always to see a disturbed or grieving
person's imagery as *the issues*. From there, he swings into psychological
problem solving.

I would like to commend this responsibility to our English teach-   25
ers: that they help our children preserve pity, happiness, and grief inside themselves. They can enhance those feelings by having young
children both write and draw pictures. They can be very enthusiastic
about the children's first drawings of death in the sky. Adults, particularly mature ones who have *not* got children in school at the moment,
should make it clear that we expect this of English teachers and that
we don't give a damn if LeRoy and Merv never in their lives get the
sentence balance of past conditional and perfect subjunctive clauses
right. We need to protect some of the Things Invisible inside LeRoy
and Merv and the rest of us.

This is my last Letter from the Country. That is why it is so shrill.   26
Gadflies are always looking out a chance to be shrill anyway, so I
jumped to this one and have shouted my favorite hope: that we can
educate children not to be problem solvers but to be madly expressive
all their lives.

WILLIAM G. PERRY, JR.

Examsmanship and the Liberal Arts

William G. Perry, Jr. (1913–   ) served for many years with the Bureau of Study Counsel at Harvard University, where he advised students and studied the relation between education and the
development of personality. Perry's studies of education are used by
educators nationwide as a means of understanding and measuring
the intellectual and psychological growth of college students. *Forms of
Intellectual and Ethical Development in the College Years: A Scheme* (1970)
presents a complete account of his findings. "Examsmanship and the
Liberal Arts" grew out of a five-year study in which Perry interviewed students to learn why some thrived in Harvard's intellectual
climate but others of equal intelligence struggled unsuccessfully and
unhappily. First published in *Examining at Harvard College* (1967), the
essay suggests the general outline of Perry's answer: A university environment is essentially hostile to a simple black-and-white view of
the world, and students who are willing to see the difficulty of finding
the truth do better than their more rigid classmates. The essay, originally written for other members of the Harvard faculty, contrasts two
epistemologies, or theories of knowledge—one based on what Perry
calls "bull" and one based on what he calls "cow." Jacob Bronowski's
"The Creative Mind" is a useful companion essay for those interested
in how these epistemologies play out in the sciences.

"But sir, I don't think I really deserve it, it was mostly bull, really."   1
This disclaimer from a student whose examination we have awarded a
straight "A" is wondrously depressing. Alfred North Whitehead invented its only possible rejoinder: "Yes sir, what you wrote is nonsense, utter nonsense. But ah! Sir! It's the right *kind* of nonsense!"

Bull, in this university, is customarily a source of laughter, or a   2
problem in ethics. I shall step a little out of fashion to use the subject as
a take-off point for a study in comparative epistemology. The phenomenon of bull, in all the honor and opprobrium with which it is regarded by students and faculty, says something, I think, about our
theories of knowledge. So too, the grades which we assign on examinations communicate to students what these theories may be.

We do not have to be out-and-out logical-positivists[1] to suppose   3
that we have something to learn about "what we think knowledge is"
by having a good look at "what we do when we go about measuring

---

1. Logical positivists like Bertrand Russell insist that philosophical speculation be tightly
checked by reference to the "positive" data of experience. This position links them to the
psychological behaviorists.

it." We know the straight "A" examination when we see it, of course, and we have reason to hope that the student will understand why his work receives our recognition. He doesn't always. And those who receive lesser honor? Perhaps an understanding of certain anomalies in our customs of grading good bull will explain the students' confusion.

I must beg patience, then, both of the reader's humor and of his morals. Not that I ask him to suspend his sense of humor but that I shall ask him to go beyond it. In a great university the picture of a bright student attempting to outwit his professor while his professor takes pride in not being outwitted is certainly ridiculous. I shall report just such a scene, for its implications bear upon my point. Its comedy need not present a serious obstacle to thought.

As for the ethics of bull, I must ask for a suspension of judgment. I wish that students could suspend theirs. Unlike humor, moral commitment is hard to think beyond. Too early a moral judgment is precisely what stands between many able students and a liberal education. The stunning realization that the Harvard Faculty will often accept, as evidence of knowledge, the cerebrations of a student who has little data at his disposal, confronts every student with an ethical dilemma. For some it forms an academic focus for what used to be thought of as "adolescent disillusion." It is irrelevant that rumor inflates the phenomenon to mythical proportions. The students know that beneath the myth there remains a solid and haunting reality. The moral "bind" consequent on this awareness appears most poignantly in serious students who are reluctant to concede the competitive advantage to the bullster and who yet feel a deep personal shame when, having succumbed to "temptation," they themselves receive a high grade for work they consider "dishonest."

I have spent many hours with students caught in this unwelcome bitterness. These hours lend an urgency to my theme. I have found that students have been able to come to terms with the ethical problem, to the extent that it is real, only after a refined study of the true nature of bull and its relation to "knowledge." I shall submit grounds for my suspicion that we can be found guilty of sharing the student's confusion of moral and epistemological issues.

I

I present as my "premise," then, an amoral *fabliau*. Its hero-villain is the Abominable Mr. Metzger '47. Since I celebrate his virtuosity, I regret giving him a pseudonym, but the peculiar style of his bravado requires me to honor also his modesty. Bull in pure form is rare; there is usually some contamination by data. The community has reason to be grateful to Mr. Metzger for having created an instance of laboratory purity, free from any adulteration by matter. The more credit is due him, I think, because his act was free from premeditation, deliberation, or hope of personal gain.

Mr. Metzger stood one rainy November day in the lobby of Memorial Hall. A junior, concentrating in mathematics, he was fond of diverting himself by taking part in the drama, a penchant which may have had some influence on the events of the next hour. He was waiting to take part in a rehearsal in Sanders Theatre, but, as sometimes happens, no other players appeared. Perhaps the rehearsal had been canceled without his knowledge? He decided to wait another five minutes. 8

Students, meanwhile, were filing into the Great Hall opposite, and taking seats at the testing tables. Spying a friend crossing the lobby toward the Great Hall's door, Metzger greeted him and extended appropriate condolences. He inquired, too, what course his friend was being tested in. "Oh, Soc. Sci. something-or-other." "What's it all about?" asked Metzger, and this, as Homer remarked of Patroclus, was the beginning of evil for him. 9

"It's about Modern Perspectives on Man and Society and All That," said his friend. "Pretty interesting, really." 10

"Always wanted to take a course like that," said Metzger. "Any good reading?" 11

"Yeah, great. There's this book"—his friend did not have time to finish. 12

"Take your seats please" said a stern voice beside them. The idle conversation had somehow taken the two friends to one of the tables in the Great Hall. Both students automatically obeyed; the proctor put blue books before them; another proctor presented them with copies of the printed hour-test. 13

Mr. Metzger remembered afterwards a brief misgiving that was suddenly overwhelmed by a surge of curiosity and puckish glee. He wrote "George Smith" on the blue book, opened it, and addressed the first question. 14

I must pause to exonerate the Management. The Faculty has a rule that no student may attend an examination in a course in which he is not enrolled. To the wisdom of this rule the outcome of this deplorable story stands witness. The Registrar, charged with the enforcement of the rule, has developed an organization with procedures which are certainly the finest to be devised. In November, however, class rosters are still shaky, and on this particular day another student, named Smith, was absent. As for the culprit, we can reduce his guilt no further than to suppose that he was ignorant of the rule, or, in the face of the momentous challenge before him, forgetful. 15

We need not be distracted by Metzger's performance on the "objective" or "spot" questions on the test. His D on these sections can be explained by those versed in the theory of probability. Our interest fo- 16 cuses on the quality of his essay. It appears that when Metzger's friend picked up his own blue book a few days later, he found himself in company with a large proportion of his section in having received on the essay a C. When he quietly picked up "George Smith's" blue book to return it to Metzger, he observed that the grade for the essay was A. In the margin was a note in the section man's hand. It read "Excellent work. Could you have pinned these observations down a bit more closely? Compare . . . in . . . pp. . . . "

Such news could hardly be kept quiet. There was a leak, and the   17
whole scandal broke on the front page of Tuesday's *Crimson*. With the press Metzger was modest, as becomes a hero. He said that there had been nothing to it at all, really. The essay question had offered a choice of two books, Margaret Mead's *And Keep Your Powder Dry* or Geoffrey Gorer's *The American People*. Metzger reported that having read neither of them, he had chosen the second "because the title gave me some notion as to what the book might be about." On the test, two critical comments were offered on each book, one favorable, one unfavorable. The students were asked to "discuss." Metzger conceded that he had played safe in throwing his lot with the most laudatory of the two comments, "but I did not forget to be balanced."

I do not have Mr. Metzger's essay before me except in vivid mem-   18
ory. As I recall, he took his first cue from the name Geoffrey, and committed his strategy to the premise that Gorer was born into an "Anglo-Saxon" culture, probably English, but certainly "English speaking." Having heard that Margaret Mead was a social anthropologist, he inferred that Gorer was the same. He then entered upon his essay, centering his inquiry upon what he supposed might be the problems inherent in an anthropologist's observation of a culture which was his own, or nearly his own. Drawing in part from memories of table-talk on cultural relativity[2] and in part from creative logic, he rang changes on the relation of observer to observed, and assessed the kind and degree of objectivity which might accrue to an observer through training as an anthropologist. He concluded that the book in question did in fact contribute a considerable range of "'objective', and even 'fresh'," insights into the nature of our culture. "At the same time," he warned, "these observations must be understood within the context of their generation by a person only partly freed from his embeddedness in the culture he is observing, and limited in his capacity to transcend those particular tendencies and biases which he has himself developed as a personality in his interaction with this culture since his birth. In

2. "An important part of Harvard's education takes place during meals in the Houses." An Official Publication. [author's note] Houses are dormitories for upper-division students.

this sense the book portrays as much the character of Geoffrey Gorer as it analyzes that of the American people." It is my regrettable duty to report that at this moment of triumph Mr. Metzger was carried away by the temptations of parody and added, "We are thus much the richer."

In any case, this was the essay for which Metzger received his honor grade and his public acclaim. He was now, of course, in serious trouble with the authorities.   19

I shall leave him for the moment to the mercy of the Administrative Board of Harvard College and turn the reader's attention to the section man who ascribed the grade. He was in much worse trouble. All the consternation in his immediate area of the Faculty and all the glee in other areas fell upon his unprotected head. I shall now undertake his defense.   20

I do so not simply because I was acquainted with him and feel a respect for his intelligence; I believe in the justice of his grade! Well, perhaps "justice" is the wrong word in a situation so manifestly absurd. This is more a case in "equity." That is, the grade is equitable if we accept other aspects of the situation which are equally absurd. My proposition is this: if we accept as valid those C grades which were accorded students who, like Metzger's friend, demonstrated a thorough familiarity with the details of the book without relating their critique to the methodological problems of social anthropology, then "George Smith" deserved not only the same, but better.   21

The reader may protest that the C's given to students who showed evidence only of diligence were indeed not valid and that both these students and "George Smith" should have received E's. To give the diligent E is of course not in accord with custom. I shall take up this matter later. For now, were I to allow the protest, I could only restate my thesis: that "George Smith's" E would, in a college of liberal arts, be properly a "better" E.   22

At this point I need a short-hand. It is a curious fact that there is no academic slang for the presentation of evidence of diligence alone. "Parroting" won't do; it is possible to "parrot" bull. I must beg the reader's pardon, and, for reasons almost too obvious to bear, suggest "cow."   23

Stated as nouns, the concepts look simple enough: 24

   cow (pure): data, however relevant, without relevancies.
   bull (pure): relevancies, however relevant, without data.

The reader can see all too clearly where this simplicity would lead. I can assure him that I would not have imposed on him this way were I aiming to say that knowledge in this university is definable as some   25 neuter compromise between cow and bull, some infertile hermaphrodite. This is precisely what many diligent students seem to believe: that what they must learn to do is to "find the right mean" between "amounts" of detail and "amounts" of generalities. Of course this is not the point at all. The problem is not quantitative, nor does its solution lie on a continuum between the particular and the general. Cow and bull are not poles of a single dimension. A clear notion of what they really are is essential to my inquiry, and for heuristic purposes I wish to observe them further in the celibate state.

When the pure concepts are translated into verbs, their complexities become apparent in the assumptions and purposes of the students as they write:

> To cow (*v. intrans.*) or the act of cowing:
> To list data (or perform operations) without awareness of, or comment upon, the contexts, frames of reference, or points of observation which determine the origin, nature, and meaning of the data (or procedures). To write on the assumption that "a fact is a fact." To present evidence of hard work as a substitute for understanding, without any intent to deceive.

> To bull (*v. intrans.*) or the act of bulling:
> To discourse upon the contexts, frames of reference and points of observation which would determine the origin, nature, and meaning of data if one had any. To present evidence of an understanding of form in the hope that the reader may be deceived into supposing a familiarity with content.

At the level of conscious intent, it is evident that cowing is more moral, or less immoral, than bulling. To speculate about unconscious intent would be either an injustice or a needless elaboration of my theme. It is enough that the impression left by cow is one of earnestness, diligence, and painful naiveté. The grader may feel disappointment or even irritation, but these feelings are usually balanced by pity, compassion, and a reluctance to hit a man when he's both down and moral. He may feel some challenge to his teaching, but none whatever to his one-ups-manship. He writes in the margin: "See me."

We are now in a position to understand the anomaly of custom: As instructors, we always assign bull an E, *when we detect it;* whereas we usually give a cow a C, *even though it is always obvious.*

After all, we did not ask to be confronted with a choice between morals and understanding (or did we?). We evince a charming humanity, I think, in our decision to grade in favor of morals and pathos. "I simply *can't* give this student an E after he has *worked* so hard." At the same time we tacitly express our respect for the bullster's strength. We recognize a colleague. If he knows so well how to dish it out, we can be sure that he can also take it.

Of course it is just possible that we carry with us, perhaps from our   30
own school-days, an assumption that if a student is willing to work
hard and collect "good hard facts" he can always be taught to understand their relevance, whereas a student who has caught onto the
forms of relevance without working at all is a lost scholar.

But this is not in accord with our experience.   31

It is not in accord either, as far as I can see, with the stated values   32
of a liberal education. If a liberal education should teach students
"how to think," not only in their own fields but in fields outside their
own—that is, to understand "how the other fellow orders knowledge,"
then bulling, even in its purest form, expresses an important part of
what a pluralist university holds dear, surely a more important part
than the collecting of "facts that are facts" which schoolboys learn to
do. Here then, good bull appears not as ignorance at all but as an aspect of knowledge. It is both relevant and "true." In a university setting good bull is therefore of more value than "facts," which, without a
frame of reference, are not even "true" at all.

Perhaps this value accounts for the final anomaly: as instructors,   33
we are inclined to reward bull highly, *where we do not detect its intent*, to
the consternation of the bullster's acquaintances. And often we do not
examine the matter too closely. After a long evening of reading blue
books full of cow, the sudden meeting with a student who at least understands the problems of one's field provides a lift like a draught of refreshing wine, and a strong disposition toward trust.

This was, then, the sense of confidence that came to our unfortu-   34
nate section man as he read "George Smith's" sympathetic considerations.

II

In my own years of watching over students' shoulders as they   35
work, I have come to believe that this feeling of trust has a firmer basis
than the confidence generated by evidence of diligence alone. I believe
that the theory of a liberal education holds. Students who have dared
to understand man's real relation to his knowledge have shown themselves to be in a strong position to learn content rapidly and meaningfully, and to retain it. I have learned to be less concerned about the
education of a student who has come to understand the nature of
man's knowledge, even though he has not yet committed himself to
hard work, than I am about the education of the student who, after
one or two terms at Harvard, is working desperately hard and still believes that collected "facts" constitute knowledge. The latter, when I
try to explain to him, too often understands me to be saying that he
"doesn't *put in enough generalities*." Surely he has "put in *enough* facts."

I have come to see such quantitative statements as expressions of   36
an entire, coherent epistemology. In grammar school the student is
taught that Columbus discovered America in 1492. The *more* such
items he gets "right" on a given test the more he is credited with
"knowing." From years of this sort of thing it is not unnatural to develop the conviction that knowledge consists of the accretion of hard
facts by hard work.

The student learns that the more facts and procedures he can get   37
"right" in a given course, the better will be his grade. The more courses
he takes, the more subjects he has "had," the more credits he accumu-
lates, the more diplomas he will get, until, after graduate school, he
will emerge with his doctorate, a member of the community of scholars.

The foundation of this entire life is the proposition that a fact is a   38
fact. The necessary correlate of this proposition is that a fact is either
right or wrong. This implies that the standard against which the right-
ness or wrongness of a fact may be judged exists *someplace*—perhaps
graven upon a tablet in a Platonic world outside and above *this* cave of
tears. In grammar school it is evident that the tablets which enshrine
the spelling of a word or the answer to an arithmetic problem are visible to my teacher who need only compare my offerings to it. In high
school I observe that my English teachers disagree. This can only mean
that the tablets in such matters as the goodness of a poem are distant
and obscured by clouds. They surely exist. The pleasing of befuddled
English teachers degenerates into assessing their prejudices, a game in
which I have no protection against my competitors more glib of
tongue. I respect only my science teachers, authorities who *really know*.
Later I learn from them that "this is only what we think *now*." But
eventually, surely. . . . Into this epistemology of education, apparently
shared by teachers in such terms as "credits," "semester hours" and
"years of French," the student may invest his ideals, his drive, his com-
petitiveness, his safety, his self-esteem, and even his love.

College raises other questions: by whose calendar is it proper to   39
say that Columbus discovered America in 1492? How, when, and by
whom was the year 1 established in this calendar? What of other calendars? In view of the evidence for Leif Ericson's previous visit (and
the American Indians), what historical ethnocentrism is suggested by
the use of the word "discover" in this sentence? As for Leif Ericson, in
accord with what assumptions do you order the evidence?

These questions and their answers are not "more" knowledge.   40
They are devastation. I do not need to elaborate upon the epistemology, or rather epistemologies, they imply. A fact has become at last "an
observation or an operation performed in a frame of reference." A liberal education is founded in an awareness of frame of reference even

in the most immediate and empirical examination of data. Its acquirement involves relinquishing hope of absolutes and of the protection they afford against doubt and the glib-tongued competitor. It demands an ever widening sophistication about systems of thought and observation. It leads, not away from him, but *through* the arts of gamesmanship to a new trust.

This trust is in the value and integrity of systems, their varied character, and the way their apparently incompatible metaphors enlighten, from complementary facets, the particulars of human experience. As one student said to me: "I used to be cynical about intellectual games. Now I want to know them thoroughly. You see I came to realize that it was only when I knew the rules of the game cold that I could tell whether what I was saying was tripe."   41

We too often think of the bullster as cynical. He can be, and not always in a light-hearted way. We have failed to observe that there can lie behind cow the potential of a deeper and more dangerous despair. The moralism of sheer work and obedience can be an ethic that, unwilling to face a despair of its ends, glorifies its means. The implicit refusal to consider the relativity of both ends and means leaves the operator in an unconsidered proprietary absolutism. History bears witness that in the pinches this moral superiority has no recourse to negotiation, only to force.   42

A liberal education proposes that man's hope lies elsewhere: in the negotiability that can arise from an understanding of the integrity of systems and of their origins in man's address to his universe. The prerequisite is the courage to accept such a definition of knowledge. From then on, of course, there is nothing incompatible between such an epistemology and hard work. Rather the contrary.   43

I can now at last let bull and cow get together. The reader knows best how a productive wedding is arranged in his own field. This is the nuptial he celebrates with a straight A on examinations. The masculine context must embrace the feminine particular, though itself "born of woman." Such a union is knowledge itself, and it alone can generate new contexts and new data which can unite in their turn to form new knowledge.   44

In this happy setting we can congratulate in particular the Natural Sciences, long thought to be barren ground to the bullster. I have indeed drawn my examples of bull from the Social Sciences, and by analogy from the Humanities. Essay-writing in these fields has long been thought to nurture the art of bull to its prime. I feel, however, that the Natural Sciences have no reason to feel slighted. It is perhaps no accident that Metzger was a mathematician. As part of my researches for this paper, furthermore, a student of considerable talent has recently honored me with an impressive analysis of the art of amassing "partial credits" on examinations in advanced physics.   45

Though beyond me in some respects, his presentation confirmed my impression that instructors of Physics frequently honor on examinations operations structurally similar to those requisite in a good essay.

The very qualities that make the Natural Sciences fields of delight 46 for the eager gamesman have been essential to their marvelous fertility.

III

As priests of these mysteries, how can we make our rites more pre- 47 cisely expressive? The student who merely cows robs himself, without knowing it, of his education and his soul. The student who only bulls robs himself, as he knows full well, of the joys of inductive discovery— that is, of engagement. The introduction of frames of reference in the new curricula of Mathematics and Physics in the schools is a hopeful experiment. We do not know yet how much of these potent revelations the very young can stand, but I suspect they may rejoice in them more than we have supposed. I can't believe they have never wondered about Leif Ericson and that word "discovered," or even about 1492. They have simply been too wise to inquire.

Increasingly in recent years better students in the better high 48 schools and preparatory schools are being allowed to inquire. In fact they appear to be receiving both encouragement and training in their inquiry. I have the evidence before me.

Each year for the past five years all freshmen entering Harvard and 49 Radcliffe have been asked in freshman week to "grade" two essays answering an examination question in History. They are then asked to give their reasons for their grades. One essay, filled with dates, is 99% cow. The other, with hardly a date in it, is a good essay, easily mistaken for bull. The "official" grades of these essays are, for the first (alas!) C "because he has worked so hard," and for the second (soundly, I think) B. Each year a larger majority of freshmen evaluate these essays as would the majority of the faculty, and for the faculty's reasons, and each year a smaller minority give the higher honor to the essay offering data alone. Most interesting, a larger number of students each year, while not overrating the second essay, award the first the straight E appropriate to it in a college of liberal arts.

For us who must grade such students in a university, these devel- 50 opments imply a new urgency, did we not feel it already. Through our grades we describe for the students, in the showdown, what we believe about the nature of knowledge. The subtleties of bull are not peripheral to our academic concerns. That they penetrate to the center of our care is evident in our feelings when a student whose good work we have awarded a high grade reveals to us that he does not feel he deserves it. Whether he disqualifies himself because "there's too much bull in it," or worse because "I really don't think I've worked that hard," he presents a serious educational problem. Many students feel this sleaziness; only a few reveal it to us.

We can hardly allow a mistaken sense of fraudulence to under- 51 mine our students' achievements. We must lead students beyond their concept of bull so that they may honor relevancies that are really relevant. We can willingly acknowledge that, in lieu of the date 1492, a consideration of calendars and of the word "discovered," may well be offered with intent to deceive. We must insist that this does not make such considerations intrinsically immoral, and that, contrariwise, the date 1492 may be no substitute for them. Most of all, we must convey the impression that we grade understanding qua understanding. To be convincing, I suppose we must concede to ourselves in advance that a bright student's understanding is understanding even if he achieved it by osmosis rather than by hard work in our course.

These are delicate matters. As for cow, its complexities are not 52 what need concern us. Unlike good bull, it does not represent partial knowledge at all. It belongs to a different theory of knowledge entirely. In our theories of knowledge it represents total ignorance, or worse yet, a knowledge downright inimical to understanding. I even go so far as to propose that we award no more C's for cow. To do so is rarely, I feel, the act of mercy it seems. Mercy lies in clarity.

The reader may be afflicted by a lingering curiosity about the fate 53 of Mr. Metzger. I hasten to reassure him. The Administrative Board of Harvard College, whatever its satanic reputation, is a benign body. Its members, to be sure, were on the spot. They delighted in Metzger's exploit, but they were responsible to the Faculty's rule. The hero stood in danger of probation. The debate was painful. Suddenly one member, of a refined legalistic sensibility, observed that the rule applied specifically to "examinations" and that the occasion had been simply an hour-test. Mr. Metzger was merely "admonished."

GEORGE ORWELL

Politics and the English Language

George Orwell (1903–1950), a British writer born in India, was educated in England before serving with the Indian Imperial Police in Burma. Returning to Europe in 1927, Orwell soon plunged into a series of political and social investigations that led him to sympathize with Marxism. He lived with unemployed coal miners while he worked on *The Road to Wigan Pier* (1937) and fought with the Republican army in the Spanish Civil War before writing *Homage to Catalonia*

(1938). Shortly afterward, however, Orwell's political views changed significantly as his concern about restrictions placed on individual freedom led him to reject the totalitarianism of the left as firmly as the totalitarianism of the right. Ineligible for military service in World War II, he worked tirelessly in the British Broadcasting Corporation's propaganda war in Asia. Orwell's fame in his own time was made largely by his novels—especially the satirical *Animal Farm* (1945) and the gloomy *1984* (1949), in which he portrayed a grim future ruled by mechanized language and thought. Orwell's long-lasting influence, however, has come from his nonfiction, collected in *Inside the Whale* (1940), *Dickens, Dali and Others* (1946), *Shooting an Elephant* (1950), and *Such, Such Were the Joys* (1953). "Politics and the English Language" was first published in *Horizon,* April 1946. Like many other writers in this unit, Orwell finds powerful connections between language, understanding, and freedom. But unlike Malcolm X and Linda Hogan, who in different ways point to the liberating effect of language, Orwell worries about how language can shut down thinking and literally enslave us to a mindless political system. While Orwell's essay is clearly a response to the political situation following World War II, it ultimately offers practical advice on avoiding the pitfalls of language and adding power and clarity to writing.

Most people who bother with the matter at all would admit that 1 the English language is in a bad way, but it is generally assumed that we cannot by conscious action do anything about it. Our civilization is decadent and our language—so the argument runs—must inevitably share in the general collapse. It follows that any struggle against the abuse of language is a sentimental archaism, like preferring candles to electric light or hansom cabs to aeroplanes. Underneath this lies the half-conscious belief that language is a natural growth and not an instrument which we shape for our own purposes.

Now, it is clear that the decline of a language must ultimately have 2 political and economic causes: it is not due simply to the bad influence of this or that individual writer. But an effect can become a cause, reinforcing the original cause and producing the same effect in an intensified form, and so on indefinitely. A man may take to drink because he feels himself to be a failure, and then fail all the more completely because he drinks. It is rather the same thing that is happening to the English language. It becomes ugly and inaccurate because our thoughts are foolish, but the slovenliness of our language makes it easier for us to have foolish thoughts. The point is that the process is reversible. Modern English, especially written English, is full of bad habits which spread by imitation and which can be avoided if one is willing to take the necessary trouble. If one gets rid of these habits one can think more clearly, and to think clearly is a necessary first step towards political regeneration: so that the fight against bad English is not frivolous and is not the exclusive concern of professional writers. I will come back to this presently, and I hope that by the time the meaning of what I have said here will have become clearer. Meanwhile, here are five specimens of the English language as it is now habitually written.

These five passages have not been picked out because they are especially bad—I could have quoted far worse if I had chosen—but because they illustrate various of the mental vices from which we now suffer. They are a little below the average, but are fairly representative samples. I number them so that I can refer back to them when necessary:

3

> (1) I am not, indeed, sure whether it is not true to say that the Milton who once seemed not unlike a seventeenth-century Shelley had not become, out of an experience ever more bitter in each year, more alien [*sic*] to the founder of that Jesuit sect which nothing could induce him to tolerate.
>
> Professor Harold Laski (Essay in Freedom of Expression).

> (2) Above all, we cannot play ducks and drakes with a native battery of idioms which prescribes such egregious collocations of vocables as the Basic *put up with* for *tolerate* or *put at a loss* for *bewilder.*
>
> Professor Lancelot Hogben (Interglossa).

> (3) On the one side we have the free personality: by definition it is not neurotic, for it has neither conflict nor dream. Its desires, such as they are, are transparent, for they are just what institutional approval keeps in the forefront of consciousness; another institutional pattern would alter their number and intensity; there is little in them that is natural, irreducible, or culturally dangerous. But *on the other side*, the social bond itself is nothing but the mutual reflection of these self-secure integrities. Recall the definition of love. Is not this the very picture of a small academic? Where is there a place in this hall of mirrors for either personality or fraternity?
>
> Essay on psychology in Politics (New York).

> (4) All the "best people" from the gentlemen's clubs, and all the frantic fascist captains, united in common hatred of Socialism and bestial horror of the rising tide of the mass revolutionary movement, have turned to acts of provocation, to foul incendiarism, to medieval legends of poisoned wells, to legalize their own destruction of proletarian organizations, and rouse the agitated petty-bourgeoisie to chauvinistic fervour on behalf of the fight against the revolutionary way out of the crisis.
>
> Communist pamphlet.

> (5) If a new spirit *is* to be infused into this old country, there is one thorny and contentious reform which must be tackled, and that is the humanization and galvanization of the B.B.C. Timidity here will bespeak cancer and atrophy of the soul. The heart of Britain may be sound and of strong beat, for instance, but the British lion's roar at present is like that of Bottom in Shakespeare's *Midsummer Night's Dream*—as gentle as any

sucking dove. A virile new Britain cannot continue indefinitely to be traduced in the eyes or rather ears, of the world by the effete languors of Langham Place, brazenly masquerading as "standard English". When the Voice of Britain is heard at nine o'clock, better far and infinitely less ludicrous to hear aitches honestly dropped than the present priggish, inflated, inhibited, school-ma'amish arch braying of blameless bashful mewing maidens!

Letter in *Tribune.*

Each of these passages has faults of its own, but, quite apart from avoidable ugliness, two qualities are common to all of them. The first is staleness of imagery: the other is lack of precision. The writer either has a meaning and cannot express it, or he inadvertently says something else, or he is almost indifferent as to whether his words mean anything or not. This mixture of vagueness and sheer incompetence is the most marked characteristic of modern English prose, and especially of any kind of political writing. As soon as certain topics are raised, the concrete melts into the abstract and no one seems able to think of turns of speech that are not hackneyed: prose consists less and less of *words* chosen for the sake of their meaning, and more and more of *phrases* tacked together like the sections of a prefabricated henhouse. I list below, with notes and examples, various of the tricks by means of which the work of prose-construction is habitually dodged:

DYING METAPHORS

A newly invented metaphor assists thought by evoking a visual image, while on the other hand a metaphor which is technically "dead" (e.g. *iron resolution*) has in effect reverted to being an ordinary word and can generally be used without loss of vividness. But in between these two classes there is a huge dump of worn-out metaphors which have lost all evocative power and are merely used because they save people the trouble of inventing phrases for themselves. Examples are: *Ring the changes on, take up the cudgels for, toe the line, ride roughshod over, stand shoulder to shoulder with, play into the hands of, no axe to grind, grist to the mill, fishing in troubled waters, on the order of the day, Achilles' heel, swan song, hotbed.* Many of these are used without knowledge of their meaning (what is a "rift," for instance?), and incompatible metaphors are frequently mixed, a sure sign that the writer is not interested in what he is saying. Some metaphors now current have been twisted out of their original meaning without those who use them even being aware of the fact. For example, *toe the line* is sometimes written *tow the line.* Another example is *the hammer and the anvil,* now always used with the implication that the anvil gets the worst of it. In real life it is always the anvil that breaks the hammer, never the other way about: a writer who stopped to think what he was saying would be aware of this, and would avoid perverting the original phrase.

OPERATORS OR VERBAL FALSE LIMBS

These save the trouble of picking out appropriate verbs and nouns,   6
and at the same time pad each sentence with extra syllables which give
it an appearance of symmetry. Characteristic phrases are: *render inoper-
ative, militate against, make contact with, be subjected to, give rise to, give
grounds for, have the effect of, play a leading part (role) in, make itself felt, take
effect, exhibit a tendency to, serve the purpose of, etc., etc.* The keynote is the
elimination of simple verbs. Instead of being a single word, such as
break, stop, spoil, mend, kill, a verb becomes a *phrase,* made up of a noun
or adjective tacked on to some general-purposes verb such as *prove,
serve, form, play, render.* In addition, the passive voice is wherever possible used in preference to the active, and noun constructions are used
instead of gerunds (*by examination of* instead of *by examining*). The
range of verbs is further cut down by means of the *-ize* and *de-* formation, and the banal statements are given an appearance of profundity
by means of the *not un-* formation. Simple conjunctions and preposi-
tions are replaced by such phrases as *with respect to, having regard to, the
fact that, by dint of, in view of, in the interests of, on the hypothesis that;* and
the ends of sentences are saved from anticlimax by such resounding
commonplaces as *greatly to be desired, cannot be left out of account, a development to be expected in the near future, deserving of serious consideration,
brought to a satisfactory conclusion,* and so on and so forth.

PRETENTIOUS DICTION

7
Words like *phenomenon, element, individual* (as noun), *objective, cate-
gorical, effective, virtual, basic, primary, promote, constitute, exhibit, exploit,
utilize, eliminate, liquidate,* are used to dress up simple statements and
give an air of scientific impartiality to biased judgments. Adjectives like
*epoch-making, epic, historic, unforgettable, triumphant, age-old, inevitable, in-
exorable, veritable,* are used to dignify the sordid processes of international politics, while writing that aims at glorifying war usually takes
on an archaic colour, its characteristic words being: *realm, throne, char-
iot, mailed fist, trident, sword, shield, buckler, banner, jackboot, clarion.* Foreign words and expressions such as *cul de sac, ancien régime, deus ex
machina, mutatis mutandis, status quo, gleichschaltung, weltanschauung,* are
used to give an air of culture and elegance. Except for the useful ab-
breviations *i.e., e.g.,* and *etc.,* there is no real need for any of the hundreds of foreign phrases now current in English. Bad writers, and
especially scientific, political and sociological writers, are nearly always
haunted by the notion that Latin or Greek words are grander than
Saxon ones, and unnecessary words like *expedite, ameliorate, predict, extraneous, deracinated, clandestine, subaqueous* and hundreds of others

constantly gain ground from their Anglo-Saxon opposite numbers.[1] The jargon peculiar to Marxist writing (*hyena, hangman, cannibal, petty bourgeois, these gentry, lacquey, flunkey, mad dog, White Guard,* etc.) consists largely of words and phrases translated from Russian, German or French; but the normal way of coining a new word is to use a Latin or Greek root with the appropriate affix and, where necessary, the *-ize* formation. It is often easier to make up words of this kind (*deregionalize, impermissible, extramarital, non-fragmentatory* and so forth) than to think up the English words that will cover one's meaning. The result, in general, is an increase in slovenliness and vagueness.

MEANINGLESS WORDS

In certain kinds of writing, particularly in art criticism and literary criticism, it is normal to come across long passages which are almost completely lacking in meaning.[2] Words like *romantic, plastic, values, human, dead, sentimental, natural, vitality,* as used in art criticism, are strictly meaningless in the sense that they not only do not point to any discoverable object, but are hardly ever expected to do so by the reader. When one critic writes, "The outstanding feature of Mr. X's work is its living quality," while another writes, "The immediately striking thing about Mr. X's work is its peculiar deadness," the reader accepts this as a simple difference of opinion. If words like *black* and *white* were involved, instead of the jargon words *dead* and *living,* he would see at once that language was being used in an improper way. Many political words are similarly abused. The word *Fascism* has now no meaning except in so far as it signifies "something not desirable." The words *democracy, socialism, freedom, patriotic, realistic, justice,* have each of them several different meanings which cannot be reconciled with one another. In the case of a word like *democracy,* not only is there no agreed definition, but the attempt to make one is resisted from all sides. It is almost universally felt that when we call a country democratic we are praising it: consequently the defenders of every kind of régime claim that it is a democracy, and fear that they might have to

1. An interesting illustration of this is the way in which the English flower names which were in use till very recently are being ousted by Greek ones, *snapdragon* becoming *antirrhinum, forget-me-not* becoming *myosotis,* etc. It is hard to see any practical reason for this change of fashion: it is probably due to an instinctive turning-away from the more homely word and a vague feeling that the Greek word is scientific. [author's note]

2. Example: "Comfort's catholicity of perception and image, strangely Whitmanesque in range, almost the exact opposite in aesthetic compulsion, continues to evoke that trembling atmospheric accumulative hinting at a cruel, an inexorably serene timelessness . . . Wrey Gardiner scores by aiming at simple bull's-eyes with precision. Only they are not so simple, and through this contented sadness runs more than the surface bitter-sweet of resignation" (*Poetry Quarterly*). [author's note]

stop using the word if it were tied down to any one meaning. Words of this kind are often used in a consciously dishonest way. That is, the person who uses them has his own private definition but allows his hearer to think he means something quite different. Statements like *Marshal Pétain was a true patriot, The Soviet Press is the freest in the world, The Catholic Church is opposed to persecution,* are almost always made with intent to deceive. Other words used in variable meanings, in most cases more or less dishonestly, are: *class, totalitarian, science, progressive, reactionary, bourgeois, equality.*

Now that I have made this catalogue of swindles and perversions,   9
let me give another example of the kind of writing that they lead to. This time it must of its nature be an imaginary one. I am going to translate a passage of good English into modern English of the worst sort. Here is a well-known verse from *Ecclesiastes:*

> I returned and saw under the sun, that the race is not to the swift, nor the battle to the strong, neither yet bread to the wise, nor yet riches to men of understanding, nor yet favour to men of skill; but time and chance happeneth to them all.

Here it is in modern English: 10

> Objective consideration of contemporary phenomena compels the conclusion that success or failure in competitive activities exhibits no tendency to be commensurate with innate capacity, but that a considerable element of the unpredictable must invariably be taken into account.

This is a parody, but not a very gross one. Exhibit (3), above, for   11
instance, contains several patches of the same kind of English. It will be seen that I have not made a full translation. The beginning and ending of the sentence follow the original meaning fairly closely, but in the middle the concrete illustrations—race, battle, bread—dissolve into the vague phrase "success or failure in competitive activities." This had to be so, because no modern writer of the kind I am discussing— no one capable of using phrases like "objective consideration of contemporary phenomena"—would ever tabulate his thoughts in that precise and detailed way. The whole tendency of modern prose is away from concreteness. Now analyse the two sentences a little more closely. The first contains forty-nine words but only sixty syllables, and all its words are those of everyday life. The second contains thirty-eight words of ninety syllables: eighteen of its words are from Latin roots, and one from Greek. The first sentence contains six vivid images, and only one phrase ("time and chance") that could be called vague. The second contains not a single fresh, arresting phrase, and in spite of its ninety syllables it gives only a shortened version of the meaning contained in the first. Yet without a doubt it is the second kind of sentence that is gaining ground in modern English. I do not

want to exaggerate. This kind of writing is not yet universal, and out-crops of simplicity will occur here and there in the worst-written page. Still, if you or I were told to write a few lines on the uncertainty of human fortunes, we should probably come much nearer to my imaginary sentence than to the one from *Ecclesiastes*. 12

As I have tried to show, modern writing at its worst does not consist in picking out words for the sake of their meaning and inventing images in order to make the meaning clearer. It consists in gumming together long strips of words which have already been set in order by someone else, and making the results presentable by sheer humbug. The attraction of this way of writing is that it is easy. It is easier—even quicker, once you have the habit—to say *In my opinion it is not unjustifiable assumption that* than to say *I think*. If you use ready-made phrases, you not only don't have to hunt about for words; you also don't have to bother with the rhythms of your sentences, since these phrases are generally so arranged as to be more or less euphonious. When you are composing in a hurry—when you are dictating to a stenographer, for instance, or making a public speech—it is natural to fall into a pretentious, Latinized style. Tags like *a consideration which we should do well to bear in mind* or *a conclusion to which all of us would readily assent* will save many a sentence from coming down with a bump. By using stale metaphors, similes and idioms, you save much mental effort, at the cost of leaving your meaning vague, not only for your reader but for yourself. This is the significance of mixed metaphors. The sole aim of a metaphor is to call up a visual image. When these images clash—as in *The Fascist octopus has sung its swan song, the jackboot is thrown into the melting pot*—it can be taken as certain that the writer is not seeing a mental image of the objects he is naming; in other words he is not really thinking. Look again at the examples I gave at the beginning of this essay. Professor Laski (1) uses five negatives in fifty-three words. One of these is superfluous, making nonsense of the whole passage, and in addition there is the slip *alien* for akin, making further nonsense, and several avoidable pieces of clumsiness which increase the general vagueness. Professor Hogben (2) plays ducks and drakes with a battery which is able to write prescriptions, and, while disapproving of the everyday phrase *put up with*, is unwilling to look *egregious* up in the dictionary and see what it means. (3), if one takes an uncharitable attitude towards it, is simply meaningless: probably one could work out its intended meaning by reading the whole of the article in which it occurs. In (4), the writer knows more or less what he wants to say, but an accumulation of stale phrases chokes him like tea leaves blocking a sink. In (5), words and meaning have almost parted company. People who write in this manner usually have a general emotional meaning—they dislike one thing and want to express solidarity with another—but they are not interested in the detail of what they are saying. A scrupulous writer, in every sentence that he writes, will ask himself at least four questions, thus: What am I trying to say? What words will express it? What image or idiom will make it clearer? Is this image fresh enough to have an effect? And he will probably ask himself two more: Could I put it more shortly? Have I said anything that is avoidably ugly? But you are not obliged to go to all this trouble: You can shirk it by simply throwing your mind open and letting the ready-made phrases come crowding in. They will construct your sentences for you—even think your thoughts for you, to a certain extent—and at need they will perform the important service of partially concealing your meaning even from yourself. It is at this point that the special connection between politics and the debasement of language becomes clear.

In our time it is broadly true that political writing is bad writing. Where it is not true, it will generally be found that the writer is some kind of rebel, expressing his private opinions and not a "party line." Orthodoxy, of whatever colour, seems to demand a lifeless, imitative style. The political dialects to be found in pamphlets, leading articles, manifestos, White Papers and the speeches of under-secretaries do, of course, vary from party to party, but they are all alike in that one almost never finds in them a fresh, vivid, home-made turn of speech. When one watches some tired hack on the platform mechanically repeating the familiar phrases—*bestial atrocities, iron heel, bloodstained tyranny, free peoples of the world, stand shoulder to shoulder*—one often has a curious feeling that one is not watching a live human being but some kind of dummy: a feeling which suddenly becomes stronger at moments when the light catches the speaker's spectacles and turns them into blank discs which seem to have no eyes behind them. And this is not altogether fanciful. A speaker who uses that kind of phraseology has gone some distance towards turning himself into a machine. The appropriate noises are coming out of his larynx, but his brain is not involved as it would be if he were choosing his words for himself. If the speech he is making is one that he is accustomed to make over and over again, he may be almost unconscious of what he is saying, as one is when one utters the responses in church. And this reduced state of consciousness, if not indispensable, is at any rate favourable to political conformity.

In our time, political speech and writing are largely the defense of the indefensible. Things like the continuance of British rule in India, the Russian purges and deportations, the dropping of the atom bombs on Japan, can indeed be defended, but only by arguments which are too brutal for most people to face, and which do not square with the professed aims of political parties. Thus political language has to consist largely of euphemism, question-begging and sheer cloudy vagueness. Defenseless villages are bombarded from the air, the inhabitants driven out into the countryside, the cattle machine-gunned, the huts set on fire with incendiary bullets: this is called *pacification*. Millions of peasants are robbed of their farms and sent trudging along the roads with no more than they can carry: this is called *transfer of population* or *rectification of frontiers*. People are imprisoned for years without trial, or shot in the back of the neck or sent to die of scurvy in Arctic lumber camps: this is called *elimination of unreliable elements*. Such phraseology is needed if one wants to name things without calling up mental pictures of them. Consider for instance some comfortable English professor defending Russian totalitarianism. He cannot say outright, "I believe in killing off your opponents when you can get good results by doing so." Probably, therefore, he will say something like this:

"While freely conceding that the Soviet régime exhibits certain 15 features which the humanitarian may be inclined to deplore, we must, I think, agree that a certain curtailment of the right to political opposition is an unavoidable concomitant of transitional periods, and that the rigours which the Russian people have been called upon to undergo have been amply justified in the sphere of concrete achievement."

The inflated style is itself a kind of euphemism. A mass of Latin 16 words falls upon the facts like soft snow, blurring the outlines and covering up all the details. The great enemy of clear language is insincerity. When there is a gap between one's real and one's declared aims, one turns as it were instinctively to long words and exhausted idioms, like a cuttlefish squirting out ink. In our age there is no such thing as "keeping out of politics." All issues are political issues, and politics itself is a mass of lies, evasions, folly, hatred and schizophrenia. When the general atmosphere is bad, language must suffer. I should expect to find—this is a guess which I have not sufficient knowledge to verify— that the German, Russian and Italian languages have all deteriorated in the last ten or fifteen years, as a result of dictatorship.

But if thought corrupts language, language can also corrupt 17 thought. A bad usage can spread by tradition and imitation, even among people who should and do know better. The debased language that I have been discussing is in some ways very convenient. Phrases like *a not unjustifiable assumption, leaves much to be desired, would serve no good purpose, a consideration which we should do well to bear in mind,* are a continuous temptation, a packet of aspirins always at one's elbow. Look back through this essay, and for certain you will find that I have again and again committed the very faults I am protesting against. By this morning's post I have received a pamphlet dealing with conditions in Germany. The author tells me that he "felt impelled" to write it. I open it at random, and here is almost the first sentence that I see: "(The Allies) have an opportunity not only of achieving a radical transformation of Germany's social and political structure in such a way as to avoid a nationalistic reaction in Germany itself, but at the same time of laying the foundations of a co-operative and unified Europe." You see, he "feels impelled" to write—feels, presumably, that he has something new to say—and yet his words, like cavalry horses answering the bugle, group themselves automatically into the familiar dreary pattern. This invasion of one's mind by ready-made phrases (*lay the foundations, achieve a radical transformation*) can only be prevented if one is constantly on guard against them, and every such phrase anesthetizes a portion of one's brain.

I said earlier that the decadence of our language is probably curable. Those who deny this would argue, if they produced an argument at all, that language merely reflects existing social conditions, and that we cannot influence its development by any direct tinkering with words and constructions. So far as the general tone or spirit of a language goes, this may be true, but it is not true in detail. Silly words and expressions have often disappeared, not through any evolutionary process but owing to the conscious action of a minority. Two recent examples were *explore every avenue* and *leave no stone unturned*, which were killed by the jeers of a few journalists. There is a long list of flyblown metaphors which could similarly be got rid of if enough people would interest themselves in the job; and it should also be possible to laugh the *not un-* formation out of existence,[3] to reduce the amount of Latin and Greek in the average sentence, to drive out foreign phrases and strayed scientific words, and, in general, to make pretentiousness unfashionable. But all these are minor points. The defence of the English language implies more than this, and perhaps it is best to start by saying what it does *not* imply.

To begin with it has nothing to do with archaism, with the salvaging of obsolete words and turns of speech, or with the setting up of a "standard English" which must never be departed from. On the contrary, it is especially concerned with the scrapping of every word or idiom which has outworn its usefulness. It has nothing to do with correct grammar and syntax, which are of no importance so long as one makes one's meaning clear, or with the avoidance of Americanisms, or with having what is called a "good prose style." On the other hand it is not concerned with fake simplicity and the attempt to make written English colloquial. Nor does it even imply in every case preferring the Saxon word to the Latin one, though it does imply using the fewest and shortest words that will cover one's meaning. What is above all needed is to let the meaning choose the word, and not the other way about. In prose, the worst thing one can do with words is to surrender to them. When you think of a concrete object, you think wordlessly, and then, if you want to describe the thing you have been visualizing

---

3. One can cure oneself of the *not un-* formation by memorizing this sentence: *A not unblack dog was chasing a not unsmall rabbit across a not ungreen field.* [author's note]

you probably hunt about till you find the exact words that seem to fit. When you think of something abstract you are more inclined to use words from the start, and unless you make a conscious effort to prevent it, the existing dialect will come rushing in and do the job for you, at the expense of blurring or even changing your meaning. Probably it is better to put off using words as long as possible and get one's meaning as clear as one can through pictures or sensations. Afterwards one can choose—not simply *accept*—the phrases that will best cover the meaning, and then switch round and decide what impression one's words are likely to make on another person. This last effort of the mind cuts out all stale or mixed images, all prefabricated phrases, needless repetitions, and humbug and vagueness generally. But one can often be in doubt about the effect of a word or a phrase, and one needs rules that one can rely on when instinct fails. I think the following rules will cover most cases:

(i) Never use a metaphor, simile or other figure of speech which you are used to seeing in print.
(ii) Never use a long word where a short one will do.
(iii) If it is possible to cut a word out, always cut it out.
(iv) Never use the passive where you can use the active.
(v) Never use a foreign phrase, a scientific word or a jargon word if you can think of an everyday English equivalent.
(vi) Break any of these rules sooner than say anything outright barbarous.

These rules sound elementary, and so they are, but they demand a deep change of attitude in anyone who has grown used to writing in the style now fashionable. One could keep all of them and still write bad English, but one could not write the kind of stuff that I quoted in those five specimens at the beginning of this article.

I have not here been considering the literary use of language, but merely language as an instrument for expressing and not for concealing or preventing thought. Stuart Chase and others have come near to claiming that all abstract words are meaningless, and have used this as a pretext for advocating a kind of political quietism. Since you don't know what Fascism is, how can you struggle against Fascism? One need not swallow such absurdities as this, but one ought to recognize that the present political chaos is connected with the decay of language, and that one can probably bring about some improvement by starting at the verbal end. If you simplify your English, you are freed from the worst follies of orthodoxy. You cannot speak any of the necessary dialects, and when you make a stupid remark its stupidity will be obvious, even to yourself. Political language—and with variations this is true of all political parties, from Conservatives to Anarchists—is designed to make lies sound truthful and murder respectable, and to give an appearance of solidity to pure wind. One cannot change this all in a moment, but one can at least change one's own habits, and from time to time one can even, if one jeers loudly enough, send some worn-out and useless phrase—some *jackboot, Achilles' heel, hotbed, melting pot, acid test, veritable inferno* or other lump of verbal refuse—into the dustbin where it belongs.

SUSAN GLASPELL

Trifles

Susan Glaspell (1882–1948) was born in Davenport, Iowa, the daughter of a feed dealer and an immigrant Irish woman. She took her B.A. from Drake University in Des Moines, Iowa, in 1899 and began her professional career by writing sentimental short stories for popular magazines. In 1915 she and her husband, George Cram Cook (a Harvard graduate from her hometown), joined Eugene O'Neill in founding the Provincetown Players, one of the most influential theater groups in U.S. history. Although she was from that point on identified as part of the literary avant-garde, her work continued to show her admiration for the pioneers who had settled the Midwest and especially for strong, capable farm women. Several of Glaspell's one-act plays were collected in *Plays* (1920). Among her full-length plays are *The Inheritors* (1921), *The Comic Artist* (1927), and *Alison's House* (1930), which won a Pulitzer Prize. Her novels include *Fidelity* (1915) and *Judd Rankin's Daughter* (1945).

"Trifles," a one-act play produced by the Provincetown Players in 1916, is still a favorite of little theater groups. A careful reading will reveal Glaspell's insight into how the circumstances of our lives affect the reality we see. Useful companion essays include Annie Dillard's "Seeing," in which she describes how people very different from her—in this case blind people regaining sight—come to view the world, and Frank Conroy's "Think About It," in which an accumulation of life experiences changes the way he sees things.

Characters

GEORGE HENDERSON, *County Attorney*   MRS. PETERS
HENRY PETERS, *Sheriff*   MRS. HALE
LEWIS HALE, *A Neighboring Farmer*

SCENE
The kitchen in the now abandoned farmhouse of JOHN WRIGHT, *a gloomy kitchen , and left without having been put in order—unwashed pans under the*

sink, a loaf of bread outside the breadbox, a dish towel on the table—other
signs of incompleted work. At the rear the outer door opens and the sheriff
comes in followed by the COUNTY ATTORNEY *and* HALE. *The* SHERIFF *and* HALE
are men in middle life, the COUNTY ATTORNEY *is a young man; all are much*
bundled up and go at once to the stove. They are followed by two women—the
SHERIFF*'s wife first; she is a slightly wiry woman, a thin nervous face.* MRS.
HALE *is larger and would ordinarily be called more comfortable looking, but*
she is disturbed now and looks fearfully about as she enters. The women have
come in slowly, and stand close together near the door.

COUNTY ATTORNEY. [*Rubbing his hands.*] This feels good. Come up to the   1
   fire, ladies.

MRS. PETERS. [*after taking a step forward.*] I'm not—cold.

SHERIFF. [*Unbuttoning his overcoat and stepping away from the stove as if to*
   mark the beginning of official business.] Now, Mr. Hale, before we move
   things about, you explain to Mr. Henderson just what you saw
   when you came here yesterday morning.

COUNTY ATTORNEY. By the way, has anything been moved? Are things
   just as you left them yesterday?

SHERIFF. [*Looking about.*] It's just the same. When it dropped below zero   5
   last night I thought I'd better send Frank out this morning to make a
   fire for us—no use getting pneumonia with a big case on, but I told
   him not to touch anything except the stove—and you know Frank.

COUNTY ATTORNEY. Somebody should have been left here yesterday.

SHERIFF. Oh—yesterday. When I had to send Frank to Morris Center for
   that man who went crazy—I want you to know I had my hands full
   yesterday, I knew you could get back from Omaha by today and as
   long as I went over everything here myself—

COUNTY ATTORNEY. Well, Mr. Hale, tell just what happened when you
   came here yesterday morning.

HALE. Harry and I had started to town with a load of potatoes. We came
   along the road from my place and as I got here I said, "I'm going to
   see if I can't get John Wright to go in with me on a party telephone."
   I spoke to Wright about it once before and he put me off, saying
   folks talked too much anyway, and all he asked was peace and
   quiet—I guess you know about how much he talked himself; but I
   thought maybe if I went to the house and talked about it before his
   wife, though I said to Harry that I didn't know as what his wife
   wanted made much difference to John—

COUNTY ATTORNEY. Let's talk about that later, Mr. Hale. I do want to talk   10
   about that, but tell now just what happened when you got to the
   house.

HALE. I didn't hear or see anything; I knocked at the door, and still it
   was all quiet inside. I knew they must be up, it was past eight o'-
   clock. So I knocked again, and I thought I heard somebody say,

"Come in." I wasn't sure, I'm not sure yet, but I opened the door—
this door [*Indicating the door by which the two women are still standing*]
and there in that rocker—[*Pointing to it.*] sat Mrs. Wright. [*They all
look at the rocker.*]

COUNTY ATTORNEY. What—was she doing?

HALE. She was rockin' back and forth. She had her apron in her hand
and was kind of—pleating it.

COUNTY ATTORNEY. And how did she—look?

HALE. Well, she looked queer. 15

COUNTY ATTORNEY. How do you mean—queer?

HALE. Well, as if she didn't know what she was going to do next. And
kind of done up.

COUNTY ATTORNEY. How did she seem to feel about your coming?

HALE. Why, I don't think she minded—one way or other. She didn't
pay much attention. I said, "How do, Mrs. Wright, it's cold, ain't it?"
And she said, "Is it?"—and went on kind of pleating at her apron.
Well, I was surprised; she didn't ask me to come up to the stove, or
to set down, but just sat there, not even looking at me, so I said, "I
want to see John." And then she—laughed. I guess you would call it
a laugh. I thought of Harry and the team outside, so I said a little
sharp: "Can't I see John?" "No," she says, kind o' dull like. "Ain't he
home?" says I. "Yes," says she, "he's home." "Then why can't I see
him?" I asked her, out of patience. "'Cause he's dead," says she.
"*Dead?*" says I. She just nodded her head, not getting a bit excited,
but rockin' back and forth. "Why—where is he?" says I, not knowing what to say. She just pointed upstairs—like that [*Himself pointing
to the room above*]. I got up, with the idea of going up there. I walked
from there to here—then I says, "Why, what did he die of?" "He died
of a rope round his neck," says she, and just went on pleatin' at her
apron. Well, I went out and called Harry. I thought I might—need
help. We went upstairs and there he was lyin'—

COUNTY ATTORNEY. I think I'd rather have you go into that upstairs 20
where you can point it all out. Just go on now with the rest of the
story.

HALE. Well, my first thought was to get that rope off. It looked . . .
[*Stops, his face twitches.*] . . . but Harry, he went up to him, and he
said, "No, he's dead all right, and we'd better not touch anything."
So we went back down stairs. She was still sitting that same way.
"Has anybody been notified?" I asked. "No," says she, unconcerned.
"Who did this, Mrs. Wright?" said Harry. He said it businesslike—
and she stopped pleatin' of her apron. "I don't know," she says. "You
don't *know?*" says Harry. "No," says she. "Weren't you sleepin' in the
bed with him?" says Harry. "Yes," says she, "but I was on the inside."
"Somebody slipped a rope round his neck and strangled him and
you didn't wake up?" says Harry. "I didn't wake up," she said after
him. We must 'a looked as if we didn't see how that could be, for

after a minute she said, "I sleep sound." Harry was going to ask her more questions but I said maybe we ought to let her tell her story first to the coroner, or the sheriff, so Harry went fast as he could to Rivers' place, where there's a telephone.

COUNTY ATTORNEY. And what did Mrs. Wright do when she knew that you had gone for the coroner?

HALE. She moved from that chair to this one over here [*Pointing to a small chair in the corner.*] and just sat there with her hands held together and looking down. I got a feeling that I ought to make some conversation, so I said I had come in to see if John wanted to put in a telephone, and at that she started to laugh, and then she stopped and looked at me—scared. [*The* COUNTY ATTORNEY, *who has had his notebook out, makes a note.*] I dunno, maybe it wasn't scared. I wouldn't like to say it was. Soon Harry got back, and then Dr. Lloyd came, and you, Mr. Peters, and so I guess that's all I know that you don't.

COUNTY ATTORNEY. [*Looking around.*] I guess we'll go upstairs first—and then out to the barn and around there. [*To the* SHERIFF] You're convinced that there was nothing important here—nothing that would point to any motive.

SHERIFF. Nothing here but kitchen things. 25

[*The* COUNTY ATTORNEY, *after looking around the kitchen, opens the door of a cupboard closet. He gets up on a chair and looks on a shelf. Pulls his hand away, sticky.*]

COUNTY ATTORNEY. Here's a nice mess.

[*The women draw nearer.*]

MRS. PETERS. [*To the other woman.*] Oh, her fruit; it did freeze. [*To the* COUNTY ATTORNEY] She worried about that when it turned so cold. She said the fire'd go out and her jars would break.

SHERIFF. Well, can you beat the women! Held for murder and worryin' about her preserves.

COUNTY ATTORNEY. I guess before we're through she may have something more serious than preserves to worry about.

HALE. Well, women are used to worrying over trifles. 30

[*The two women move a little closer together.*]

COUNTY ATTORNEY. [*With the gallantry of a young politician.*] And yet, for all their worries, what would we do without the ladies? [*The women do not unbend. He goes to the sink, takes a dipperful of water from the pail and pouring it into a basin, washes his hands. Starts to wipe them on the roller towel, turns it for a cleaner place.*] Dirty towels! [*Kicks his foot against the pans under the sink.*] Not much of a housekeeper, would you say, ladies?

MRS. HALE. [*Stiffly.*] There's a great deal of work to be done on a farm.

COUNTY ATTORNEY. To be sure. And yet [*With a little bow to her*] I know there are some Dickson county farmhouses which do not have such roller towels.

[*He gives it a pull to expose its full length again.*]

MRS. HALE. Those towels get dirty awful quick. Men's hands aren't always as clean as they might be.

COUNTY ATTORNEY. Ah, loyal to your sex, I see. But you and Mrs. Wright were neighbors. I suppose you were friends, too.   35

MRS. HALE. [*Shaking her head.*] I've not seen much of her of late years. I've not been in this house—it's more than a year.

COUNTY ATTORNEY. And why was that? You didn't like her?

MRS. HALE. I liked her all well enough. Farmers' wives have their hands full, Mr. Henderson. And then—

COUNTY ATTORNEY. Yes—?

MRS. HALE. [*Looking about.*] It never seemed a very cheerful place.   40

COUNTY ATTORNEY. No—it's not cheerful. I shouldn't say she had the homemaking instinct.

MRS. HALE. Well, I don't know as Wright had, either.

COUNTY ATTORNEY. You mean that they didn't get on very well?

MRS. HALE. No, I don't mean anything. But I don't think a place'd be any cheerfuller for John Wright's being in it.

COUNTY ATTORNEY. I'd like to talk more of that a little later. I want to get the lay of things upstairs now.   45

[*He goes to the left, where three steps lead to a stair door.*]

SHERIFF. I suppose anything Mrs. Peters does'll be all right. She was to take in some clothes for her, you know, and a few little things. We left in such a hurry yesterday.

COUNTY ATTORNEY. Yes, but I would like to see what you take, Mrs. Peters, and keep an eye out for anything that might be of use to us.

MRS. PETERS. Yes, Mr. Henderson.

[*The women listen to the men's steps on the stairs, then look about the kitchen.*]

MRS. HALE. I'd hate to have men coming into my kitchen, snooping around and criticizing.

[*She arranges the pans under the sink which the* COUNTY ATTORNEY *had shoved out of place.*]

MRS. PETERS. Of course it's no more than their duty.   50

MRS. HALE. Duty's all right, but I guess that deputy sheriff that came out to make the fire might have got a little of this on. [*Gives the roller towel a pull.*] Wish I'd thought of that sooner. Seems mean to talk about her for not having things slicked up when she had to come away in such a hurry.

MRS. PETERS. [*Who has gone to a small table in the left rear corner of the room, and lifted one end of a towel that covers a pan.*] She had bread set. [*Stands still.*]

MRS. HALE. [*Eyes fixed on a loaf of bread beside the breadbox, which is on a low shelf at the other side of the room. Moves slowly toward it.*] She was going to put this in there. [*Picks up loaf, then abruptly drops it. In a manner of returning to familiar things.*] It's a shame about her fruit. I wonder if it's all gone. [*Gets up on the chair and looks.*] I think there's some here that's all right, Mrs. Peters. Yes—here; [*Holding it toward the window.*] this is cherries, too. [*Looking again.*] I declare I believe that's the only one. [*Gets down, bottle in her hand. Goes to the sink and wipes it off on the outside.*] She'll feel awful bad after all her hard work in the hot weather. I remember the afternoon I put up my cherries last summer.

[*She puts the bottle on the big kitchen table, center of the room. With a sigh, is about to sit down in the rocking-chair. Before she is seated realizes what chair it is; with a slow look at it, steps back. The chair which she has touched rocks back and forth.*]

MRS. PETERS. Well, I must get those things from the front room closet. [*She goes to the door at the right, but after looking into the other room, steps back.*] You coming with me, Mrs. Hale? You could help me carry them. [*They go in the other room; reappear,* MRS. PETERS *carrying a dress and skirt,* MRS. HALE *following with a pair of shoes.*]

MRS. PETERS. My, it's cold in there.

[*She puts the clothes on the big table, and hurries to the stove.*] 55

MRS. HALE. [*Examining her skirt.*] Wright was close. I think maybe that's why she kept so much to herself. She didn't even belong to the Ladies Aid. I suppose she felt she couldn't do her part, and then you don't enjoy things when you feel shabby. She used to wear pretty clothes and be lively, when she was Minnie Foster, one of the town girls singing in the choir. But that—oh, that was thirty years ago. This all you was to take in?

MRS. PETERS. She said she wanted an apron. Funny thing to want, for there isn't much to get you dirty in jail, goodness knows. But I suppose just to make her feel more natural. She said they was in the top drawer in this cupboard. Yes, here. And then her little shawl that always hung behind the door. [*Opens stair door and looks.*] Yes, here it is.

[*Quickly shuts door leading upstairs.*]

MRS. HALE. [*Abruptly moving toward her.*] Mrs. Peters?

MRS. PETERS. Yes, Mrs. Hale?

MRS. HALE. Do you think she did it? 60

MRS. PETERS. [*In a frightened voice.*] Oh, I don't know.

MRS. HALE. Well, I don't think she did. Asking for an apron and her little shawl. Worrying about her fruit.

MRS. PETERS. [*Starts to speak, glances up, where footsteps are heard in the room above. In a low voice.*] Mr. Peters says it looks bad for her. Mr. Henderson is awful sarcastic in a speech and he'll make fun of her sayin' she didn't wake up.

MRS. HALE. Well, I guess John Wright didn't wake when they was slipping that rope under his neck.

MRS. PETERS. No, it's strange. It must have been done awful crafty and   65
still. They say it was such a—funny way to kill a man, rigging it all
up like that.

MRS. HALE. That's just what Mr. Hale said. There was a gun in the
house. He says that's what he can't understand.

MRS. PETERS. Mr. Henderson said coming out that what was needed for
the case was a motive; something to show anger, or—sudden feeling.

MRS. HALE. [*Who is standing by the table.*] Well, I don't see any signs of
anger around here. [*She puts her hand on the dish towel which lies on the
table, stands looking down at table, one half of which is clean, the other half
messy.*] It's wiped to here. [*Makes a move as if to finish work, then turns
and looks at loaf of bread outside the breadbox. Drops towel. In that voice of
coming back to familiar things.*] Wonder how they are finding things
upstairs. I hope she had it a little more red-up up there. You know, it
seems kind of *sneaking.* Locking her up in town and then coming out
here and trying to get her own house to turn against her!

MRS. PETERS. But Mrs. Hale, the law is the law.

MRS. HALE. I s'pose 'tis. [*Unbuttoning her coat.*] Better loosen up your   70
things, Mrs. Peters. You won't feel them when you go out.

[MRS. PETERS *takes off her fur tippet, goes to hang it on hook at back of room,
stands looking at the under part of the small corner table.*]

MRS. PETERS. She was piecing a quilt.

[*She brings the large sewing basket and they look at the bright pieces.*]

MRS. HALE. It's log cabin pattern. Pretty, isn't it? I wonder if she was
goin' to quilt it or just knot it?

[*Footsteps have been heard coming down the stairs. The* SHERIFF *enters followed by* HALE *and the* COUNTY ATTORNEY.]

SHERIFF. They wonder if she was going to quilt it or just knot it!

[*The men laugh; the women look abashed.*]

COUNTY ATTORNEY. [*Rubbing his hands over the stove.*] Frank's fire didn't do
much up there, did it? Well, let's go out to the barn and get that
cleared up.

[*The men go outside.*]

MRS. HALE. [*Resentfully.*] I don't know as there's anything so strange, our   75
takin' up our time with little things while we're waiting for them to
get the evidence. [*She sits down at the big table smoothing out a block
with decision.*] I don't see as it's anything to laugh about.

MRS. PETERS. [*Apologetically.*] Of course they've got awful important
things on their minds.

[*Pulls up a chair and joins* MRS. HALE *at the table.*]

MRS. HALE. [*Examining another block.*] Mrs. Peters, look at this one. Here,
this is the one she was working on, and look at the sewing! All
the rest of it has been so nice and even. And look at this! It's all

over the place! Why, it looks as if she didn't know what she was about!

[*After she has said this they look at each other, then start to glance back at the door. After an instant* MRS. HALE *has pulled at a knot and ripped the sewing.*]

MRS. PETERS. Oh, what are you doing, Mrs. Hale?

MRS. HALE. [*mildly.*] Just pulling out a stitch or two that's not sewed very good. [*Threading a needle.*] Bad sewing always made me fidgety.

MRS. PETERS. [*Nervously.*] I don't think we ought to touch things. 80

MRS. HALE. I'll just finish up this end. [*Suddenly stopping and leaning forward.*] Mrs. Peters?

MRS. PETERS. Yes, Mrs. Hale?

MRS. HALE. What do you suppose she was so nervous about?

MRS. PETERS. Oh—I don't know. I don't know as she was nervous. I sometimes sew awful queer when I'm just tired. [MRS. HALE *starts to say something, looks at* MRS. PETERS; *then goes on sewing.*] Well, I must get these things wrapped up. They may be through sooner than we think. [*Putting apron and other things together.*] I wonder where I can find a piece of paper, and string.

MRS. HALE. In that cupboard, maybe. 85

MRS. PETERS. [*Looking in cupboard.*] Why, here's a birdcage. [*Holds it up.*] Did she have a bird, Mrs. Hale?

MRS. HALE. Why I don't know whether she did or not—I've not been here for so long. There was a man around last year selling canaries cheap, but I don't know as she took one; maybe she did. She used to sing real pretty herself.

MRS. PETERS. [*Glancing around.*] Seems funny to think of a bird here. But she must have had one, or why would she have a cage? I wonder what happened to it.

MRS. HALE. I s'pose maybe the cat got it.

MRS. PETERS. No, she didn't have a cat. She's got that feeling some 90 people have about cats—being afraid of them. My cat got in her room and she was real upset and asked me to take it out.

MRS. HALE. My sister Bessie was like that. Queer, ain't it?

MRS. PETERS. [*Examining the cage.*] Why, look at this door. It's broke. One hinge is pulled apart.

MRS. HALE. [*Looking too.*] Looks as if someone must have been rough with it.

MRS. PETERS. Why, yes.

[*She brings the cage forward and puts it on the table.*]

MRS. HALE. I wish if they're going to find any evidence they'd be about 95 it. I don't like this place.

MRS. PETERS. But I'm awful glad you came with me, Mrs. Hale. It would be lonesome for me sitting here alone.

MRS. HALE. It would, wouldn't it? [*Dropping her sewing.*] But I tell you what I do wish, Mrs. Peters. I wish I had come over sometimes when *she* was here. I—[*Looking around the room.*]—wish I had.

MRS. PETERS. But of course you were awful busy. Mrs. Hale—your house and your children.

MRS. HALE. I could've come. I stayed away because it weren't cheerful—and that's why I ought to have come. I—I've never liked this place. Maybe because it's down in a hollow and you don't see the road. I dunno what it is but it's a lonesome place and always was. I wish I had come over to see Minnie Foster sometimes. I can see now—[*Shakes her head.*]

MRS. PETERS. Well, you mustn't reproach yourself, Mrs. Hale. Somehow   100
we just don't see how it is with other folks until—something comes up.

MRS. HALE. Not having children makes less work—but it makes a quiet house, and Wright out to work all day, and no company when he did come in. Did you know John Wright, Mrs. Peters?

MRS. PETERS. Not to know him; I've seen him in town. They say he was a good man.

MRS. HALE. Yes—good; he didn't drink, and kept his word as well as most, I guess, and paid his debts. But he was a hard man, Mrs. Peters. Just to pass the time of day with him—[*Shivers.*] Like a raw wind that gets to the bone. [*Pauses, her eye falling on the cage.*] I should think she would 'a wanted a bird. But what do you suppose went with it?

MRS. PETERS. I don't know, unless it got sick and died.
[*She reaches over and swings the broken door, swings it again. Both women watch it.*]

MRS. HALE. You weren't raised round here, were you? [MRS. PETERS   105
shakes her head.] You didn't know—her?

MRS. PETERS. Not till they brought her yesterday.

MRS. HALE. She—come to think of it, she was kind of like a bird her-self—real sweet and pretty, but kind of timid and—fluttery. How—she—did—change. [*Silence; then as if struck by a happy thought and relieved to get back to every day things.*] Tell you what, Mrs. Peters, why don't you take the quilt in with you? It might take up her mind.

MRS. PETERS. Why, I think that's a real nice idea, Mrs. Hale. There couldn't possibly be any objection to it, could there? Now, just what would I take? I wonder if her patches are in here—and her things. [*They look in the sewing basket.*]

MRS. HALE. Here's some red. I expect this has got sewing things in it. [*Brings out a fancy box.*] What a pretty box. Looks like something somebody would give you. Maybe her scissors are in here. [*Opens box. Suddenly puts her hand to her nose.*] Why—[MRS. PETERS *bends nearer, then turns her face away.*] There's something wrapped up in this piece of silk.

MRS. PETERS. Why, this isn't her scissors.   110

MRS. HALE. [*Lifting the silk.*] Oh, Mrs. Peters—it's—

[MRS. PETERS *bends closer.*]

MRS. PETERS. It's the bird.

MRS. HALE. [*Jumping up.*] But, Mrs. Peters—look at it! Its neck! Look at its neck! It's all—other side *to*.

MRS. PETERS. Somebody—wrung—its—neck.

[*Their eyes meet. A look of growing comprehension, of horror. Steps are heard outside.* MRS. HALE *slips box under quilt pieces, and sinks into her chair. Enter* SHERIFF *and* COUNTY ATTORNEY. MRS. PETERS *rises.*]

COUNTY ATTORNEY. [*As one turning from serious things to little pleasantries.*]   115
Well, ladies, have you decided whether she was going to quilt it or knot it?

MRS. PETERS. We think she was going to—knot it.

COUNTY ATTORNEY. Well, that's interesting, I'm sure. [*Seeing the birdcage.*] Has the bird flown?

MRS. HALE. [*Putting more quilt pieces over the box.*] We think the—cat got it.

COUNTY ATTORNEY. [*Preoccupied.*] Is there a cat?

[MRS. HALE *glances in a quick covert way at* MRS. PETERS.]

MRS. PETERS. Well, not *now*. They're superstitious, you know. They   120
leave.

COUNTY ATTORNEY. [*To* SHERIFF PETERS, *continuing an interrupted conversation.*] No sign at all of anyone having come from the outside. Their own rope. Now let's go up again and go over it piece by piece. [*They start upstairs.*] It would have to have been someone who knew just the—

[MRS. PETERS *sits down. The two women sit there not looking at one another, but as if peering into something and at the same time holding back. When they talk now it is in the manner of feeling their way over strange ground, as if afraid of what they are saying, but as if they can not help saying it.*]

MRS. HALE. She liked the bird. She was going to bury it in that pretty box.

MRS. PETERS. [*In a whisper.*] When I was a girl—my kitten—there was a boy took a hatchet, and before my eyes—and before I could get there—[*Covers her face an instant.*] If they hadn't held me back I would have—[*Catches herself, looks upstairs where steps are heard, falters weakly.*]—hurt him.

MRS. HALE. [*With a slow look around her.*] I wonder how it would seem never to have had any children around. [*Pause.*] No, Wright wouldn't like the bird—a thing that sang. She used to sing. He killed that, too.

MRS. PETERS. [*Moving uneasily.*] We don't know who killed the bird.   125

MRS. HALE. I knew John Wright.

MRS. PETERS. It was an awful thing was done in this house that night, Mrs. Hale. Killing a man while he slept, slipping a rope around his neck that choked the life out of him.

MRS. HALE. His neck. Choked the life out of him.

[*Her hand goes out and rests on the birdcage.*]

MRS. PETERS. [*With rising voice.*] We don't know who killed him. We don't *know.*   130

MRS. HALE. [*Her own feeling not interrupted.*] If there'd been years and years of nothing, then a bird to sing to you, it would be awful—still, after the bird was still.

MRS. PETERS. [*Something within her speaking.*] I know what stillness is. When we homesteaded in Dakota, and my first baby died—after he was two years old, and me with no other then—

MRS. HALE. [*Moving.*] How soon do you suppose they'll be through, looking for the evidence?

MRS. PETERS. I know what stillness is. [*Pulling herself back.*] The law has got to punish crime, Mrs. Hale.

MRS. HALE. [*Not as if answering that.*] I wish you'd seen Minnie Foster when she wore a white dress with blue ribbons and stood up there in the choir and sang. [*A look around the room.*] Oh, I *wish* I'd come over here once in a while! That was a crime! That was a crime! Who's going to punish that?   135

MRS. PETERS. [*Looking upstairs.*] We mustn't—take on.

MRS. HALE. I might have known she needed help! I know how things can be—for women. I tell you, it's queer, Mrs. Peters. We live close together and we live far apart. We all go through the same things— it's all just a different kind of the same thing. [*Brushes her eyes; noticing the bottle of fruit, reaches out for it.*] If I was you I wouldn't tell her her fruit was gone. Tell her it *ain't.* Tell her it's all right. Take this in to prove it to her. She—she may never know whether it was broke or not.

MRS. PETERS. [*Takes the bottle, looks about for something to wrap it in; takes petticoat from the clothes brought from the other room, very nervously begins winding this around the bottle. In a false voice.*] My, it's a good thing the men couldn't hear us. Wouldn't they just laugh! Getting all stirred up over a little thing like a—dead canary. As if that could have anything to do with—with—wouldn't they *laugh!*

[*The men are heard coming down stairs.*]

MRS. HALE. [*Under her breath.*] Maybe they would—maybe they wouldn't.

COUNTY ATTORNEY. No, Peters, it's all perfectly clear except a reason for doing it. But you know juries when it comes to women. If there was some definite thing. Something to show—something to make a story about—a thing that would connect up with this strange way of doing it—

[*The women's eyes meet for an instant. Enter* HALE *from outer door.*]

HALE. Well, I've got the team around. Pretty cold out there.

COUNTY ATTORNEY. I'm going to stay here a while by myself. [*To the* SHERIFF.] You can send Frank out for me, can't you? I want to go over everything. I'm not satisfied that we can't do better.

SHERIFF. Do you want to see what Mrs. Peters is going to take in?

[*The* COUNTY ATTORNEY *goes to the table, picks up the apron, laughs.*]

COUNTY ATTORNEY. Oh, I guess they're not very dangerous things the ladies have picked out. [*Moves a few things about, disturbing the quilt pieces which cover the box. Steps back.*] No, Mrs. Peters doesn't need supervising. For that matter, a sheriff's wife is married to the law. Ever think of it that way, Mrs. Peters?

MRS. PETERS. Not—just that way.

SHERIFF. [*Chuckling.*] Married to the law. [*Moves toward the other room.*] I just want you to come in here a minute, George. We ought to take a look at these windows.

COUNTY ATTORNEY. [*Scoffingly.*] Oh, windows!

SHERIFF. We'll be right out, Mr. Hale.

[HALE *goes outside. The* SHERIFF *follows the* COUNTY ATTORNEY *into the other room. Then* MRS. HALE *rises, hands tight together, looking intensely at* MRS. PETERS, *whose eyes make a slow turn, finally meeting* MRS. HALE'S. *A moment* MRS. HALE *holds her, then her own eyes point the way to where the box is concealed. Suddenly* MRS. PETERS *throws back quilt pieces and tries to put the box in the bag she is wearing. It is too big. She opens box, starts to take bird out, cannot touch it, goes to pieces, stands there helpless. Sound of a knob turning in the other room.* MRS. HALE *snatches the box and puts it in the pocket of her big coat. Enter* COUNTY ATTORNEY *and* SHERIFF.]

COUNTY ATTORNEY. [*Facetiously.*] Well, Henry, at least we found out that she was not going to quilt it. She was going to—what is it you call it, ladies?

MRS. HALE. [*Her hand against her pocket.*] We call it—knot it, Mr. Henderson.

CURTAIN

LI-YOUNG LEE

This Room and Everything in It

Li-Young Lee (1957–   ) is a Chinese American whose father was once the personal physician to China's powerful leader, Mao Tsetung. After his father fell from favor and served two years as a political prisoner, the family fled to Indonesia, where Lee was born. The family lived in Hong Kong, Macau, and Japan before settling in

America, where Lee's father became a Presbyterian minister. Lee's relationship with his father, who died in 1980, is the subject of much of his poetry. Educated at the University of Arizona and the State University of New York, Lee has taught at several institutions, including the University of Iowa and Northwestern. He has received grants from the National Endowment for the Arts and a Guggenheim fellowship. His first book of poetry, *Rose,* was published in 1986; his second book, *The City in Which I Love You* (1990), was the 1990 Lamont Poetry Selection of the Academy of American Poets. In 1990 Lee traveled to China and Indonesia to conduct research for *The Winged Seed* (1995), a book of reminiscences.

"This Room and Everything in It" is from *The City in Which I Love You.* Lee's poem is an exercise designed to improve a memory—in this case, a moment with a loved one—by making imaginative connections. In the speaker's struggle to capture the essence of the moment, the poem seems to challenge Patricia Hampl's claims about "memory and imagination." Yet in the end, Lee agrees not only with Hampl but also with Carol Bly, who asserts in "Growing Up Expressive" that great subjects like love cannot be pinned down, for they can never be completely understood and are always evading our grasp.

> *Lie still now*   1
> *while I prepare for my future,*
> *certain hard days ahead,*
> *when I'll need what I know so clearly this moment.*

> *I am making use*   2
> *of the one thing I learned*
> *of all the things my father tried to teach me:*
> *the art of memory.*

> *I am letting this room*   3
> *and everything in it*
> *stand for my ideas about love*
> *and its difficulties.*

> *I'll let your love-cries,*   4
> *those spacious notes*
> *of a moment ago,*
> *stand for distance.*

> *Your scent,*   5
> *that scent*
> *of spice and a wound,*
> *I'll let stand for mystery.*

> *Your sunken belly*   6
> *is the daily cup*
> *of milk I drank*
> *as a boy before morning prayer.*

The sun on the face   7
of the wall
is God, the face
I can't see, my soul,

and so on, each thing   8
standing for a separate idea,
and those ideas forming the constellation
of my greater idea.
And one day, when I need
to tell myself something intelligent
about love,

I'll close my eyes   9
and recall this room and everything in it:
My body is estrangement.
This desire, perfection.
Your closed eyes my extinction.
Now I've forgotten my
idea. The book
on the windowsill, riffled by wind . . .
the even-numbered pages are
the past, the odd-
numbered pages, the future.
The sun is
God, your body is milk . . .

useless, useless . . .   10
your cries are song, my body's not me . . .
no good . . . my idea
has evaporated . . . your hair is time, your thighs are song . . .
it had something to do
with death . . . it had something
to do with love.

Appendix A: Sixteen Assignments Using The Dolphin Reader

The assignments below can be thought of as representatives of dozens of other possible assignments. If your instructor chooses to use them in their present form, notice that we have not specified length and format; check with her or him about such matters.

1. In American culture, initiation rituals tend to be informal: a driver's license, graduation, or moving away from home marks significant change in status for young people. By this time in your own life, you have most likely experienced some form of initiation and are able to comment on the role it played in your maturation. Drawing on your own experience and the readings from this unit, write an informal analysis of initiation in American culture (or, if you grew up elsewhere, in the culture of your homeland). You may wish to begin by telling your story, then show how it fits into the larger theme of initiation by connecting it with readings from the *Initiation* unit. A likely audience is a group of your peers, so you may wish to write a piece for publication in your college newspaper or literary magazine. To get started, consider the following suggestions.

- Look specifically at high school graduation as a rite of passage and compare your experience to those of Steven Foster ("Bunny Bashing") and Maya Angelou ("Graduation").
- Examine the role of work and play in initiation, drawing on the experiences and ideas of Mark Twain ("Cub-Pilot") and Rigoberta Menchú ("Life in the *Altiplano*").
- Take an anthropological approach to initiation by applying to your own experience the classic definition of a rite of passage Steven Foster describes in "Bunny Bashing" (including severance, threshold, and incorporation).
- Examine the roles of other people or the community in your initiation experience—both the positive and the negative; for your analysis, draw on the essays by Mary McCarthy ("Names"), Nathan McCall ("Makes Me Wanna Holler"), Maya Angelou ("Graduation"), and Naomi Wolf ("Promiscuities").

2. In some cultures, adults take it upon themselves to initiate the young, to teach boys to be men and girls to be women. On her tenth birthday, for example, Rigoberta Menchú's parents formally acknowledged her role within the community and explained to her what it meant to become a woman (see "Life in the *Altiplano*"). At one time it

was common for Native American elders to lead adolescent boys on a vision quest to teach them about manhood. Yet if America is truly the "sibling society" Robert Bly describes, adults routinely fail to provide guidance to young people, and adolescents are left alone to choose—however blindly—from a multitude of sex roles. To what extent do you believe young people need guidance? How should adults teach young people about becoming men or women? For this assignment, write a proposal that, by focusing on these questions, presents the problem our society faces and offers a solution.

- Remember that young people live in a society with its own established (and sometimes conflicting) notions of masculinity and femininity. Be aware of the effect on all concerned of either accepting what society offers or rejecting it.
- You may find that Robert Bly's essay ("A World of Half-Adults") is a good point of departure and will help you describe the problem you see; consider using essays such as those by Naomi Wolf ("Promiscuities"), Jennifer Brice ("My Mother's Body"), Scott Sanders ("Reasons of the Body"), Noel Perrin ("The Androgynous Man"), and Michael Norman ("Against Androgyny") to develop your solution.
- You may wish to build upon the stated or implied proposals found in essays by Naomi Wolf ("Promiscuities") and Steven Foster ("Bunny Bashing") or in the story "X" by Lois Gould.

Your essay should be appropriate for inclusion in a magazine frequently read by parents—either a specialized publication like *Parenting* or a more general one like *Reader's Digest*. Look at these magazines to get a sense of the level of knowledge writers assume the audience to have and the ways writers attempt to engage the reader's attention.

3. Perhaps because we live in a period when sex roles are changing dramatically, perceptions of masculinity and femininity have been the topic of many short articles in the press. *The New York Times*, for example, regularly publishes columns called "About Men" and "Hers," to which writers contribute essays about 1,500 words long, usually based on personal experience. Write an essay appropriate for such a column.

- For models see Noel Perrin's "The Androgynous Man," Perri Klass's "Learning the Language," Michael Norman's "Against Androgyny," Deborah Tannen's "Every Choice a Woman Makes Sends a Message," and Katha Pollitt's "The Smurfette Principle," all of which were published in *The New York Times*. Note that four of the five deal directly with sex roles and that Klass's essay deals with them indirectly by presenting the perceptions of a woman entering what has been a man's profession.

- Note that the essay may be either humorous or serious.
- The essays in the *Femininity and Masculinity* unit should give you some ideas for writing. You may want to allude to one or more of these essays in your own. If you do, be sure to give information the reader may need about the author and the source, but *only* essential information. The newspaper reader doesn't need a scholarly citation.

You may want to consider submitting your essay to *The New York Times:* you will find an address for submissions on the Op-Ed page. Information about other potential places of publication can be found in *Writer's Market.*

4. Counseling psychologists, among others, have worried that the American way of life eliminates the benefits of living in a community that recognizes us and gives us a structure in which to grow. Americans move frequently from place to place, from job to job, from school to school, even from marriage to marriage; we may have little sense of belonging to anything. Of course, part of the problem may be that we fail to *see* the communities that surround us. Most students who read this book are temporary members of one of America's typical temporary "communities": the college or university campus. Write an essay in which you consider this community *as a community.*

- Consider the smaller groups and rituals practiced almost unconsciously by insiders, but perhaps striking to outsiders. Several of the essays in *Communities* and *Insiders and Outsiders* are full of such small details. Particularly useful are Gretel Ehrlich's "Wyoming," Scott Russell Sanders's "The Common Life," and Robert Frost's poem "Mending Wall."
- Consider the frictions and discomforts people feel as they try to enter into the community without completely belonging to it. Here Cynthia Ozick's "We Are the Crazy Lady," Terry Galloway's "I'm Listening as Hard as I Can," Annie Dillard's "Singing with the Fundamentalists," and Langston Hughes's "Theme for English B" may be particularly valuable.
- Consider situations in which the community deliberately enforces its boundaries, differentiating members from nonmembers. On this matter, you might find ideas in Jane Jacobs's "The Uses of Sidewalks," Perri Klass's "Learning the Language," Martin Luther King's "Letter from Birmingham Jail," and Toni Cade Bambara's "The Hammer Man."

As you write this essay, think hard about how broadly to define the community you are describing. Is the classroom the center of the college community, or is the center elsewhere? What nonacademic activities are essential parts of community life? If you think long and hard about how the campus serves (or fails) students as a community, your essay may interest or even influence those in a position to change the way the community defines itself.

5. Political scientists often use the ancient Greek *polis*, or city-state, as a yardstick against which to measure modern communities. H. D. F. Kitto's chapter on the polis is so thorough in its description of the Greek model that after you read it, you should be in a position to do the same. Write an essay in which you compare a community you know to the Greek polis as Kitto describes it, demonstrating ways in which it is superior or inferior.

- Choose any size community you wish, but be alert to the implications of your choice. Comparing the U.S.A. to the Greek polis is possible and might lead to some interesting insights into the nature of American democracy. Comparing a given city or town to the polis is also possible and might lead to a fruitful discussion of the way that we interact with our neighbors. Comparing a family or school to a polis is a bit more far-fetched; it might be a springboard for ironic or humorous essays.
- Assume that your audience is educated enough to have some vague knowledge of what Greek democracy was like, but don't assume that they have read Kitto. You will have to provide them with a compressed picture of what a polis was.
- Make judgments. The comparison to the polis is a means to an end, not an end in itself. It is a way of organizing and validating your impressions of the community, positive or negative.

Assume that you are writing for an audience with strong social and political interests. You might visualize your audience as the members of a political organization (e.g., Young Republicans or Young Democrats) or as a political science professor for whom you are writing an assigned essay.

6. It used to be said that America was an "assimilationist" or "melting pot" culture in which minorities were proud to blend into the "mainstream." Today, there is much more emphasis on diversity, and Americans often feel themselves torn between striving to assimilate or striving to build an identity as part of a culture outside the mainstream. The tension between assimilating and asserting a separate identity is most obvious in matters of race, religion, and gender, but anyone who feels like an outsider, including the disabled, the old, the poor, and (perhaps) the very rich, faces it. Write an essay in which you discuss a particular case of someone who feels this tension.

- You'll find the tension present in "Living Under Grace" by Henry Louis Gates, Jr., and in Terry Galloway's "I'm Listening as Hard as I Can," Naomi Wolf's "Promiscuities," N. Scott Momaday's "The Way to Rainy Mountain," and Joseph Bruchac's "Turtle Meat."
- You may want to discuss your own difficulties with assimilation, or you may want to focus on the difficulties of someone else. If you focus on someone else, you will probably find an interview useful.
- Don't feel that your essay needs to take on deep grievances. Multicultural dilemmas are sometimes temporary (e.g., being the only woman in a calculus class) and sometimes even humorous (e.g., Dave Barry's "Lost in the Kitchen," which raises the question of whether men *can* assimilate with the human race).

Write your essay so that it would be publishable in a general-interest magazine like *Life* or in a magazine with a more political focus, like *The Nation* or *National Review*.

7. Randall Jarrell's "A Sad Heart at the Supermarket" suggests that the growing importance of the media in the twentieth century has radically changed what people think about and how they think about it. This is a difficult assertion to assess, but it might be possible to address it with an examination of your own life. "Follow" yourself closely through a typical hour or so of your life and make notes on ways that your thinking is affected by media that didn't exist in 1899. Then write an essay discussing the extent to which you seem to be living a life that would have been unlivable in the nineteenth century.

- Don't think of this as an open-and-shut question. You may feel that the media changes are less important than writers like Jarrell and Neil Postman ("Now . . . This") believe, so you may want to argue that the differences between the way people think now and the way they did a hundred years ago are merely superficial.
- If you are uncertain about the status of the media in the nineteenth century (e.g., how quickly could Americans learn about events in Europe or Asia?), consult such sources as the *Encyclopaedia Britannica* and the *McGraw-Hill Dictionary of Science and Technology*.
- Consider not only external events having to do with the media, but internal ones. To what extent does your mind turn naturally to subjects, ideas, or examples that would not have been available in an earlier technological era? To what extent are you thinking pretty much the same thoughts someone might have thought in 1899?

You may aim your essay at an audience particularly interested in media, such as subscribers to *Omni,* or you may aim for a more general readership, like that of *Time.*

8. As more and more of human life is lived indoors or in outdoor settings (like the carefully manicured and pest-free suburban lawn) almost as carefully controlled as the indoors, accounts of times spent closer to nature become interesting in the same way that accounts of travels to exotic countries can be interesting. Write an essay in which you discuss an encounter with the natural world.

- Your encounter need not take place in the wilderness; any step away from your customary state of civilization may produce interesting material—even a weekend camping trip in a well-developed state park.
- Try to be a good travel writer, re-creating the sights, sounds, and smells of the place, particularly those you would not experience (or notice) in a more civilized setting.
- Report, too, on the logistics of your situation. How much "civilization" did you carry with you into nature, and how reliant were you on it?

Several essays and stories in *Nature and Civilization* may stimulate your thinking for this essay, notably those by Diane Ackerman, Alice Walker, E. B. White, Harry Crews, Joseph Bruchac, and Dale Peterson.

9. At the heart of many essays in *Nature and Civilization* is the surprise of discovery that comes from peering deeply into the world of nature; having read these essays, you may make surprising discoveries of your own, particularly as to the way the essays play off or complement one another. Write an essay in which you synthesize your findings, using one of the following suggestions as a point of departure.

- You may wish to focus on the surprising similarities or vast differences between human and nonhuman animals; see, for example, essays by Diane Ackerman ("The Moon by Whale Light"), Alice Walker ("Am I Blue?"), Lewis Thomas ("Crickets, Bats, Cats, & Chaos"), and Dale Peterson ("To Snare the Nimble Marmoset").
- Rather than focusing on the creatures themselves, you may wish to study the barriers that separate human from nonhuman animals—those real or imagined, shifting or dissolving—and comment on how the writer uses this theme to make a statement about the separation of civilization from nature; see, in particular, essays by E. B. White ("Twins"), Melissa Greene ("No Rms, Jungle Vu"), and the poem by Randall Jarrell ("Field and Forest").

- You may be interested in the shocking brutality, or perhaps the surprising gentleness, found in the natural world, as revealed by Diane Ackerman ("The Moon by Whale Light"), Annie Dillard ("The Fixed"), Dale Peterson ("To Snare the Nimble Marmoset"), and Harry Crews ("Pages from the Life of a Georgia Innocent").

As you consider your audience, think of publications like *Audubon* or *Natural History* that attempt to explain the wonders of nature to a general audience. Think of ways to keep the notion of "discovery" alive in your essay by including vivid details that help your audience see the natural world you are discussing.

10. Work, however we define it, has become so "natural" to us that we have trouble asking the most fundamental of questions: why do it? The obvious explanation—that we do it in order to keep roofs overhead and food on the table—doesn't explain much. Certainly it doesn't explain what keeps the average American, unthreatened by starvation or exposure, working more than forty hours a week. Write an essay in which you try to cast some light on what keeps people working after their subsistence is assured.

- You might, like Gloria Steinem in "I Was a Playboy Bunny" or Rita Dove in her poem "The Satisfaction Coal Company," concentrate on some unpleasant form of work and describe both what it demands of the worker and what accounts for the worker's staying with the job.
- You might, like Juliet Schor ("Housewives' Hours"), and John Kenneth Galbraith ("The Higher Economic Purpose of Women"), focus on unpaid work and examine the motives of those who put in long hours doing it.
- You might, like Carol Bly ("Getting Tired") or Sally Tisdale ("Good Soldiers"), concentrate on workers who find their work satisfying for reasons that have little or nothing to do with a paycheck.

Though library research might be useful to you (as it was to Sally Tisdale when she wrote about the Salvation Army), the most promising form for this assignment is the "profile"—a portrait based on observation and interviews. If you profile yourself, observe and "interview" yourself, trying to understand your relationship to your work as an intelligent and sympathetic stranger might understand it. Profiles are commonly published in newspapers or magazines, and you should be able to make yours interesting enough to take its place in such a publication.

11. Everyone who has studied or written about media seems to agree that programming is a two-way street. That is, humans "program"

computers, television, movies, magazines and all the other media of
communication, but at the same time, humans are programmed by the
result. As every advertiser knows, the five-year-old sitting in front of
the television is drinking in ideas, values, and desires that she will
come to think of as her own. Write an essay in which you examine the
implications of this programming.

- You might, like Katha Pollitt ("The Smurfette Principle") and
  Donald Hall ("Purpose, Blame, and Fire"), concentrate on the
  effect particular programs have on children. If you take this
  route, try to go beyond the most obvious messages. Look for
  messages that might affect children precisely because they aren't
  obvious and announced, but are taken for granted as truths
  about the world.
- You might, like David Bradley ("How TV Drew Our Family Together") or Barbara Ehrenreich ("Spudding Out"), concentrate
  on the way programs affect family life.
- You might, like Gloria Steinem ("Sex, Lies, and Advertising")
  and Neil Postman ("Now . . . This"), concentrate on the way the
  media environment affects the "truth" that the reader perceives.
- If you are particularly interested in the effects of the new wave
  of technology—the Internet and the World Wide Web—you
  might compare its cultural effects to the television-era effects
  that so alarm Randall Jarrell in "A Sad Heart at the Supermarket."

Any of these options will take you beyond the role of a consumer of
the media (whose opinion may be expressed just by changing a channel). You will be analyzing the effect of programs rather than their appeal. You might imagine your essay appearing in a magazine (*TV Guide,*
for example, or *Omni*) that occasionally encourages the reader to stand
outside the program.

12. Access to a videocassette recorder makes possible a kind of research not often done for college classes. With a VCR, you can study an
individual program intensively, re-viewing scenes as a scholar rereads
sections of a book. Or you can record a set of programs for purposes of
comparison. Take advantage of this capability by writing an essay in
which you scrutinize a program or set of programs (e.g., evening sit-
coms) to show the attitudes it (or they) promote.

- Since children are more likely than adults to have their characters shaped by what they watch, you may want to focus on programming directed at them. You could study a Disney film, for
  instance, or a Saturday-morning cartoon show with its surrounding commercials. Katha Pollitt's "The Smurfette Principle"
  might give you some ideas for such an essay.

- David Bradley's "How TV Drew Our Family Together" focuses on the images of African-Americans that television brought into his home. Consider the possibility of doing a similar survey of today's images of African-Americans or any other group.
- Or you might focus on news and information sources that seem to be value-neutral. Neil Postman's "Now . . . This" can give you some ideas for such an essay. Comparing the way two networks (PBS versus CNN, for instance, or CNN versus NBC) cover the same event may produce an interesting essay on the question of whether there is such a thing as a neutral news source.

Write an essay that would appeal to readers of *TV Guide* or the entertainment section of your local newspaper.

13. When we think of education, we most often picture it taking place within a school building or on a college campus and having something to do with the people we know as "teachers." Indeed, most of us have had memorable learning experiences within such settings, and some of us could easily write essays describing a teacher we will never forget. However, teachers do not always stand up in front of classrooms, and they may even be found in quite unlikely places. Often parents, consciously or unconsciously, take on the role of educator to their children, as do friends, or even mere acquaintances we make by chance. Write an essay describing an unforgettable learning experience, focusing in particular on the person who "taught" you.

- You may wish to focus on learning within a traditional setting and the relationship you had with an inspiring (or not-so-inspiring) teacher; if so, you may find Samuel Scudder's "Learning to See," Annie Dillard's "The Fixed," or Perri Klass's "Learning the Language" useful.
- For a taste of the disillusionment that often comes from traditional school experiences—and the alternative learning that can occur in such situations—Mary McCarthy's "Names," Maya Angelou's "Graduation," and Peter Cameron's "Homework" may be helpful.
- If you are more interested in learning that takes place far removed from an academic setting, think back to the places where you learned some of your most valuable life-lessons. Here, you may find ideas in Nathan McCall's "Makes Me Wanna Holler," Karla Holloway's "The Thursday Ladies," Frank Conroy's "Think About It," or Malcolm X's "Learning to Read."

Since your essay could appeal to almost anyone, direct it toward a general-interest newsmagazine or newspaper. For example, your hometown newspaper would probably welcome a portrait of one of your favorite high school teachers; at the same time, however, essays about learning experiences are often published in national magazines like *The New York Times Magazine* or *Harper's.*

14. The *Understanding* unit contains ten essays, a poem, and a play, all concerned with ways in which people get beyond superficial knowledge and achieve a deeper or clearer comprehension of the world. This type of comprehension is, of course, one of the great goals of a college education, but it is so difficult to define and measure that it sometimes gets lost in the day-to-day business of learning and being tested on "objective" material. Write an essay in which you try to clarify the meaning of *understanding* as it applies to your college experiences. To get started, consider the following ideas.

- Going off to college often means breaking out of prescribed thinking and looking at things in a new way; sometimes, doing so leads to insight and understanding. Carol Bly's "Growing Up Expressive," William G. Perry's "Examsmanship and the Liberal Arts," and George Orwell's "Politics and the English Language" could all add to your understanding of this issue.
- One path to understanding involves the mental habit of finding meaning within—or perhaps imposing meaning upon—seemingly random things, ideas, or events. In Frank Conroy's "Think About It," Samuel Scudder's "Learning to See," Annie Dillard's "Seeing," Patricia Hampl's "Memory and Imagination," and Susan Glaspell's "Trifles," you will find moments of discovery based on this mental process.
- A strong liberal arts education is interdisciplinary, encouraging students to relate knowledge from one course to another. Think, then, about how understanding involves making unlikely connections or relating seemingly disparate things. On this matter, Linda Hogan's "Hearing Voices," Jacob Bronowski's "The Creative Mind," and Li-Young Lee's "This Room and Everything in It" may be particularly helpful.

As you think about audience, consider a group of first-year students who have recently arrived on campus. Perhaps assume you are giving a talk on the meaning of a true college education from a student's perspective, and consider blending your findings in the essays with some of your own encounters with understanding.

15. Innumerable writers report that they learned their skill partly by intensively studying the work of a writer they admire. The purpose of this assignment is to give you an opportunity to do the same. Choose one writer represented in *The Dolphin Reader* whom you particularly admire. Starting with the information provided in the *Reader,* search out additional essays or stories by the writer. Using such sources as *Contemporary Authors, The Readers' Guide to Periodical Literature,* and

computerized indexes, locate interviews with the writer and reviews of his or her work. Your reference librarian can be a great help to you with this assignment. As you prepare to write the paper, think about such questions as these:

- What is the relation between the writer's life and work?
- What constant themes unite various essays by the writer?
- What is the writer's purpose in writing?
- How does the writer establish a relationship with the reader? What is the nature of the relationship?
- What is the writer's tone? How does it vary from essay to essay or story to story?
- What are the salient features of the writer's style? Does the writer have more than one style?

The audience for your essay might be English teachers, in which case you might look at *English Journal* to get a sense of what a professional journal in the field is like. Or it might be writers or aspiring writers, in which case you might look at *Writer's Digest* or *The Writer*.

16. The editors of *The Dolphin Reader* want your help in their search for essays and stories. Write us a letter in which you recommend a selection for the next edition.

- To make the reasons for your recommendation clear, summarize the essay or story briefly and explain why you think its content would be appealing to college students.
- Quite independent of how entertaining readers might find the selection, explain how they would benefit by reading it or how others would benefit by their having read it.
- Explain what student writers can learn from the way that the essay or story is written—what lesson(s) in style, organization, etc., a fledgling writer might learn from close study of the piece.
- If the selection is to fit into one of the existing units of the reader, tell what selection it should replace and why.
- If the selection doesn't fit into any of the existing units, describe a new unit into which it might fit.
- Give adequate bibliographic information to allow us to locate and read the selection.

Send your letter to:

Professor Carolyn Perry
English Department
Westminster College
Fulton, MO 65251

Be sure to include a return address so that we can respond with thanks and comments.

Appendix B: A Sampler of Style Exercises

That we all learn to write partly by reading is obvious, but to learn to read with a writer's eye is sometimes difficult. The set of style exercises that follow are intended to help you focus your attention on some stylistic features from our collected writers. Often they ask you to imitate the writer's style. Imitation has a less-than-glorious reputation in our nation of individualists, but we have the testimony of innumerable writers that close imitation of admirable prose can be a step toward developing a style as individual as a fingerprint. The key is first to try on another writer's style and then to set it aside or adapt it to your own.

When you imitate, do so phrase by phrase, trying to match the writer's rhythms exactly. If Thoreau, known for his well-crafted sentences, gives you this:

> I dug my cellar
>> in the side of a hill
>>> sloping to the south,
>>> where a woodchuck had formerly dug his burrow
>> down through sumach and blackberry roots,
>> and the lowest strains of vegetation,
>> six feet square by seven deep,
>> to a fine sand
>>> where potatoes would not freeze
>>>> in any winter.

You might respond with this:

> She searched the drawer
>> at the bottom of the dresser
>>> stored in the attic,
>>> where grandfather had always kept his mementos,
>> down through clippings and theater tickets,
>> many layers deep and hopelessly jumbled,
>> to the dusty bottom
>>> which no hand had touched
>>>> for two generations.

The imitation is rarely much good in its own right, but the process of imitating gives you a sense of how much thought and craft goes into the writer's work.

Once you get a sense of the stylistic options available to writers, you may find style exercises everywhere you look. The eighteen collected below are part of a larger collection available in the *Instructor's Resource Manual* for this book.

1. Mark Twain, "Cub-Pilot," page 25
   Description with a Purpose

In "Cub-Pilot," as in many of his other works, Twain includes a long list of details that may seem random at first glance. Look closely, however, and you will find a strong sense of order and direction: Twin gives us a panoramic view of the small town of his boyhood, gradually but insistently leading us to the landmark that made the place memorable and serves as the central focus of the description—the Mississippi River. Re-create a place from your past—perhaps your hometown or a favorite vacation spot—by imitating the structure and layers of detail found in Twain's single sentence (given below). In organizing your sentence, lead from details of lesser importance to the focal point of the place as you remember it.

> After all these years I can picture that old time to myself now,
> > just as it was then:
> > > the white town drowsing in the sunshine of a summer's
> > > > morning;
> > > the streets empty, or pretty nearly so;
> > > one or two clerks sitting in front of the Water Street
> > > > stores,
> > > > > with their splint-bottomed chairs tilted back
> > > > > against the walls,
> > > > > > chins on breasts,
> > > > > > hats slouched over their faces,
> > > > > > > asleep
> > > > > with shingle-shavings enough around to show
> > > > > > what broke them down;
> > > a sow and a litter of pigs loafing along the sidewalk,
> > > > doing a good business in watermelon rinds and
> > > > > seeds;
> > > two or three lonely little freight piles scattered about
> > > > the "levee";
> > > a pile of "skids" on the slope of the stone-paved wharf,
> > > > and the fragrant town drunkard asleep in the
> > > > > shadow of them;
> > > two or three wood flats at the head of the wharf,
> > > > but nobody to listen to the peaceful lapping of
> > > > > the wavelets against them;
> > > the great Mississippi,
> > > > the majestic,
> > > > the magnificent Mississippi,

<blockquote>
rolling its mile-wide tide along,
shining in the sun;
the dense forest away on the other side;
the "point" above the town,
and the "point" below,
bounding the river-glimpse and turning
it into a sort of sea,
and withal a very still and
brilliant and lonely one.
</blockquote>

2. Mary McCarthy, "Names", page 40
   Using Semicolons to Create Unity

If you read much of McCarthy's writing, you will find that she loves to use semicolons to create both lengthy and unified sentences. Below is part of a paragraph from "Names" with all semicolons removed. Try to reconstruct the original, keeping in mind that semicolons are used to link ideas by bringing two closely related clauses together in one sentence. Make sure you can justify your use of semicolons, but don't be surprised if your passage is not exactly the same as your classmates' or McCarthy's.

> Names have more significance for Catholics than they do for other people. Christian names are chosen for the spiritual qualities of the saints they are taken from. Protestants used to name their children out of the Old Testament and now they name them out of novels and plays, whose heroes and heroines are perhaps the new patron saints of a secular age. But with Catholics it is different. The saint a child is named for is supposed to serve, literally, as a model or pattern to imitate. Your name is your fortune and it tells you what you are or must be. Catholic children ponder their names for a mystic meaning, like birthstones. My own, I learned, besides belonging to the Virgin and Saint Mary of Egypt, originally meant "bitter" or "star of the sea." My second name, Thérèse, could dedicate me either to Saint Theresa or to the saint called the Little Flower, Soeur Thérèse of Lisieux, on whom God was supposed to have descended in the form of a shower of roses. At Confirmation, I had added a third name (for Catholics then rename themselves, as most nuns do, yet another time, when they take orders). On the advice of a nun, I had taken "Clementina," after Saint Clement, an early pope—a step I soon regretted on account of "My Darling Clementine" and her number nine shoes.

3. Virginia Woolf, "Professions for Women," page 129
   Examination of an Extended Metaphor

In paragraph 5 of "Professions for Women," Woolf uses the metaphor of a fisherman who hooks something unimaginably large to explain the situation of the female novelist whose imagination (likened to the minnow used as bait) runs up against "something about the body, about the passions." The metaphor is complex and worth thinking about. Try to recover the words for which capitalized words are substituted below. You may wish to work with your classmates.

> The image that comes to my mind when I think of this girl is the image of a WRITER lying sunk in dreams on the verge of a deep SUBJECT with a PEN held out over the PAPER. She was letting her imagination sweep unchecked round every NOOK and cranny of the world that lies REPRESSED in the depths of our unconscious being. Now came the experience, the experience that I believe to be far commoner with women writers than with men. The AGITATION raced through the girl's CONSCIOUSNESS. Her imagination had rushed away. It had sought the SOURCES, the depths, the dark places where the STRONGEST EXPERIENCES slumber. And then there was a smash. There was an explosion. There was TURMOIL and confusion. The imagination had dashed itself against something hard.

4. Deborah Tannen, "Every Choice a Woman Makes Sends a Message," page 144
   Arranging Sentences for Emphasis

Each of the following sets of items represents one sentence from "Every Choice a Woman Makes." The core sentence of each set has been broken into parts, and these parts have been presented in random order. As you attempt to combine the sentences to reconstruct the original one, operate under this stylistic principle: Old or less important information should come first; new, surprising, or more important information should come last. Assume that Tannen's point is to show that the choices women make in presenting themselves have serious consequences; organize the sentences in a way that best emphasizes this point. If you can begin each sentence with a subordinating conjunction (as, while, when, etc.), do so; if the organization of the sentence is insignificant, mention this in your response.

1. One woman had a hair style that was a cross between Cleopatra and Plain Jane.
2. Her hair was dark brown in classic style.

1. [The second woman's] hair robbed her of bifocal vision.
2. Her hair created a barrier between her and the listeners.
3. She looked down to read her prepared paper.

1. [The third woman] spoke.
2. She frequently tossed her head.
3. Her head-tossing called attention away from her lecture.
4. Her head-tossing called attention to her hair.

1. I suddenly wondered why I was scrutinizing only the women.
2. I amused myself finding coherence in these styles.

5. Dave Barry, "Lost in the Kitchen," page 175
   Casual Style, Loose Sentences

Barry's casual style relies on frequent loose (cumulative) sentences that begin with a simple statement and then add on a series of modifying phrases and clauses that take the reader in unexpected directions. To appreciate how loose and casual the style is, combine the following short sentences (from paragraph 7) into one, without looking back at the original. Try to recapture the rambling effect of the original.

> I think most males rarely prepare food for others. They sometimes do. Then they have one specialty dish. In my case it is spaghetti. They prepare it maybe twice a year. It is a very elaborate production. They expect to be praised for it. It is as if they had developed a cure for heart disease, right there in the kitchen.

6. N. Scott Momaday, "The Way to Rainy Mountain," page 189
   A Sentence with Parallel Subparts

Combine the following sentences into one, using one colon and three semicolons (as Momaday does in paragraph 10 of "The Way to Rainy Mountain"). The exercise should help sharpen your skills at parallel sentence construction. You will, of course, have to change wording slightly to combine the sentences.

> Now I can have her only in memory. I see my grandmother in the several postures. These were peculiar to her. I see her standing at the wood stove on a winter morning. I see her turning meat in a great iron skillet. I see her sitting at the south window. She is bent above her beadwork. I see her sitting there afterwards. Her vision had failed. She looked down for a very long time into the fold of her hands. I see her going out upon a cane. She went very slowly as she did when the weight of age came upon her. I see her praying.

7. H. D. F. Kitto, "The Polis," page 194
   A Memorable Analogy

In paragraph 6 of "The Polis," Kitto introduces a memorable analogy that shows his preference for the small Greek city-state rather than modern states "so big that they have to be referred to by their initials." With the help of a classmate, fill in the blanks, then discuss the effectiveness of the analogy: Is it precise? Does it clarify Kitto's attitude? Does it change the reader's attitude?

> The modern writer is sometimes heard to speak with splendid scorn of "those petty Greek states, with their interminable quarrels." Quite so; Plataea, Sicyon, Aegina and the rest are petty, compared with modern states. The _____ itself is petty, compared with _____ but then, the atmosphere of _____ is mainly _____, and that makes a difference. We do not like

breathing ____—and the Greeks would not much have liked breathing the atmosphere of the vast modern State. They knew of one such, the Persian Empire—and thought it very suitable, for ____.

8. James Baldwin, "Fifth Avenue, Uptown," page 215
    Varying Sentences in a Passage of Contrasts

In paragraph 19, Baldwin's contrast of the Northern response to Negroes with the Southern response runs the danger of sounding mechanical and choppy, but the variety of his sentences saves him. Here are the first two sentences of the paragraph unaltered and the information for the next five in table form:

> None of this is true for the Northerner. Negroes represent nothing to him personally, except, perhaps, the dangers of carnality.

NORTH	SOUTH
Negroes are never seen.	Negroes are seen all the time.
Whites never think about Negroes.	Whites never really think about anything but Negroes.
Negroes are ignored.	Negroes are under surveillance.
Negroes suffer hideously.	Negroes suffer hideously.
Whites are not able to look on the Negro simply as a man.	Whites are not able to look on the Negro simply as a man.

Fit the tabular information into sentences built on the pattern below.

> He [phrase]. Southerners [phrase]. Northerners [phrase], whereas Southerners [phrase]. [Clause] in the North and [phrase] in the South, and [phrase] in both places. Neither the Southerner nor the Northerner [phrase].

9. C. S. Lewis, "The Inner Ring," page 281
    A Periodic Sentence

In paragraph 13 of "The Inner Ring," Lewis uses a long periodic sentence to describe the insidious approach of the hint that leads a person to become a scoundrel. Imitate his sentence, writing on a subject of your choice.

> Over a drink or a cup of coffee,
>   disguised as a triviality
>   and
>   sandwiched between two jokes,
>   from the lips of a man, or woman,
>   whom you have recently been getting to know rather
>   better

and

whom you hope to know better still—

just at the moment when you are most anxious not to appear

crude,

or

naif,

or

a prig—

THE HINT WILL COME.

10. Martin Luther King, Jr., "Letter from Birmingham Jail," page 315
 Use of Repetition and Parallelism

Martin Luther King's style, based on a tradition of pulpit eloquence, makes heavy use of parallel patterning and repetition. To gain a sense of how repetition works in such a style, fill in the blanks in the following passage and be prepared to explain how you decided what to insert.

A just law is a man-made code that squares with the moral law or the law of God.

An _____ _____ is a code that is out of harmony with the _____ _____ .

To put it in the terms of St. Thomas Aquinas:
 An unjust law is human law that is not rooted in _____ law and _____ _____ .

Any_____ that uplifts human personality is _____.

Any_____ that _____ _____ _____ is _____.

All segregation statues are _____

because _____ distorts the _____

and

_____ the personality.

It gives the segregator a false sense of superiority

and

_____ _____ _____ _____ _____ _____ _____ .

Attractive as this style is, every writer needs to distinguish occasions when such patterning is desirable (in speeches, for example) from occasions when the repetition is a detriment (the academic paper, for example.) King's is not a style for every occasion.

11. Annie Dillard, "The Fixed," page 358
 Precise Verbs and Verbals

In paragraph 8 of "The Fixed," Dillard describes a mantis laying eggs. The description uses a series of verbs and verb forms to show the abdomen's apparently separate life and intelligence. To appreciate how much can be suggested by verb forms, try to recall the words Dillard used instead of the generalized synonyms in capital letters.

> . . . I settled my nose an inch from that pulsing abdomen. It MOVED like a concertina, it MOVED like a bellows; it WENT, WORKING, over the BRIGHT, IRREGULAR surface of the egg case FEELING and TOUCHING, PUSHING and CORRECTING. It seemed to act so independently that I forgot the BREATHING brown stick at the other end. The bubble creature seemed to have two eyes, a frantic little brain, and two busy, soft hands. It looked like a hideous, harried mother PREPARING* a fat daughter for a beauty pageant, ADJUSTING* her, FUSSING over her, TOUCHING and REPAIRING and CLEANING and TOUCHING.

12. Dale Peterson, "To Snare the Nimble Marmoset," page 368
    Combining Sentences

The following kernel sentences are based on paragraph 23 of "To Snare the Nimble Marmoset." Combine them to form six to eight sentences (Peterson's original has six), focusing in particular on the following stylistic features: sentences with parallel subparts, a variety of sentence types and lengths, economy and coherence. Feel free to omit and rearrange words when necessary.

1. The whole forest was filled with the industrious sound of hammering.
2. By then it was late afternoon.
3. The light was fading.
4. I turned to watch a mother play with her baby.
5. She was nibbling on his toes.
6. She was wrestling with him.
7. She was looking into his little face with a goofy bliss.
8. In another spot three young adult females surrounded and played with an infant.
9. All four of them were hanging in a low cluster of vines and branches.
10. One of the adults was below the baby.
11. The other two were above it.
12. All three seemed to be sharing it.
13. They were tickling and kissing the infant.
14. I saw familiar expressions on their faces.
15. The expressions were absolutely familiar.
16. They were human expressions.
17. They were Madonna-like expressions of pure adoration.
18. It was astonishing!

---

*In place of *preparing* and *adjusting*, Dillard uses participles formed of two words, like *giving up* (for surrendering) or *looking over* (for examining).

13. Juliet B. Schor, "Housewives' Hours," page 469
    Short Sentences and Long

The following ideas are derived from Schor's essay. She combines them into a short paragraph of ten sentences. Without looking at her version, combine them into one ten-sentence version of the material and one five-sentence version, changing the order of information and the wording as necessary but trying to keep the content constant. Discuss the advantages and disadvantages of each version.

1. Being a mother is a highly labor-intensive job.
2. It is a demanding job.
3. Increasingly, being a father is highly labor intensive.
4. It is increasingly demanding.
5. Children need constant attention, supervision, and love.
6. That they need this attention is an article of faith.
7. Children grow older.
8. Then they also require education and moral training.
9. All these needs translate into countless hours.
10. Motherhood was always like this.
11. So one might have thought.
12. Newborn babies in the fifteenth century were helpless.
13. They were just as helpless as those in the twentieth century.
14. But three hundred years ago, parents acted very differently.
15. Children were hardly "raised" in today's sense of the term.
16. We cannot project contemporary child-rearing practices backward in time.
17. Historians of the family and of "private life" have discovered that this projection will not work.
18. The standards and norms of mothering have been dramatically upgraded.
19. So have housecleaning, laundering, cooking, and many other domestic labors.

14. Randall Jarrell, "A Sad Heart at the Supermarket," page 513
    A Two-Sentence Definition of a Way of Life

Throughout "A Sad Heart at the Supermarket," Jarrell gives thumbnail descriptions of a way of life that dismays him. The two sentences below (from paragraph 7) form one such sketch, featuring parallel predicate verbs in the first sentence and infinitives as subjects in the second. To practice Jarrell's style while thinking about the issues he raises, imitate his sentences while writing about a way of life very different from the consumer's.

Everything about the knowledgeable consumer*
> looks like
> or sounds like
> or feels like
>> money
>>> and informed money at that.

To live is
> to consume,
to understand life is
> to know what to consume:
he has learned to understand this,
> so that his life is a series of choices
>> —correct ones—
>>> among the products and services of the
>>> world.

15. Katha Pollitt, "The Smurfette Principle," page 527
    Cohesion and Coherence in a Paragraph

The following sentences can be rearranged to form paragraph 4 of Pollitt's essay. Attempt to put them in the "right" order; be prepared to explain your reasoning. What references and transitions hold the paragraph together? Compare the order you and your class prefer to Pollitt's order. How much "freedom" of order is there?

1. The message is clear.
2. In the worst cartoons—the ones that blend seamlessly into the animated cereal commercials—the remake is usually a little-sister type, a bunny in a pink dress and hair ribbons who tags along with the adventurous bears and badgers.
3. Girls exist only in relation to boys.
4. Piggy, of "Muppet Babies," is a pint-size version of Miss Piggy, the camp glamour queen of the Muppet movies.
5. Contemporary shows are either essentially all-male, like "Garfield," or are organized on what I call the Smurfette principle: a group of male buddies will be accented by a lone female, stereotypically defined.
6. April, of the wildly popular "Teen-Age Mutant Ninja Turtles," functions as a girl Friday to a quartet of male superheroes.
7. Boys are the norm, girls the variation; boys are central, girls peripheral; boys are individuals, girls types.
8. Boys define the group, its story, and its code of values.

---

*Note that we have omitted part of sentence 1.

9. Thus, Kanga, the only female in "Winnie-the-Pooh," is a mother.
10. But the Smurfette principle rules the more carefully made shows, too.

16. Linda Hogan, "Hearing Voices," page 635
    Trimming Fat

In "Hearing Voices," Linda Hogan states that she wants her writing to be simple, clear, and direct. The following passage from paragraph 10 has been revised to destroy these three qualities; your job is to restore them. To create simplicity, cut out excessive words (try reducing the passage from 130 words to no more than 80); to regain clarity and directness, replace ungainly phrases with direct ones. Remember that a carefully chosen verb can often render a whole phrase unnecessary.

It is my desire that my writing contain the quality of simplicity, be marked by clarity of expression, and contain a sense of direction. Likewise, I am of the feeling that it is not enough for me to simply engage in the process of writing, but I need to live it, to be informed by it. It has come to my attention over the past several years that I am not in possession of the same amount of courage as my work itself. The amount of wisdom in my writing is more than I have in myself. My writing plays the role of the teacher for me, leads me places I never knew I was heading. And my writing is about a new way of living, of being in the world.

17. William G. Perry, Jr., "Examsmanship and the Liberal Arts," page 660
    "If . . . Then" and Other Qualifiers

As a product of academic culture, Perry has developed a style that qualifies and limits direct statements. In paragraph 32 of "Examsmanship and the Liberal Arts," he states that "Bulling . . . expresses . . . what a pluralistic university holds dear," but he spends another sixty words qualifying and defining his terms. Try out the academic style by writing a parallel sentence on a subject other than bulling. A concrete subject like basketball or hamburgers might get interesting results.

If a liberal education should teach students "how to think,"
    not only in their own fields
    but in the fields outside their own
    —that is, to understand
        "how the other fellow orders knowledge,"
then BULLING,
        even in its purest form,

EXPRESSES an important part of
WHAT A PLURALISTIC UNIVERSITY HOLDS DEAR,
surely a more important part
than the collecting of "facts that are facts"
which schoolboys learn to do.

18. George Orwell, "Politics and the English Language," page 670
Memorable Similes and Metaphors

*The similes and metaphors Orwell uses in "Politics and the English Language"
are remarkably vivid and memorable. To test how memorable, work with other
students in an attempt to fill in the blanks in the following passages. Hints:
think about a barnyard, tea, science fiction, weather, an octopus, and a
painkiller.*

As soon as certain topics are raised, the concrete melts into the abstract
and no one seems able to think of turns of speech that are not hackneyed:
prose consists less and less of *words* chosen for the sake of their own
meaning and more and more of *phrases* ____ together like the ____ ____ a
____ ____-____ (paragraph 4).

[T]he writer knows more or less what he wants to say, but an accumulation of stale phrases chokes him like ____ ____ ____ a ____ (paragraph
12).

"When one watches some tired hack on the platform mechanically repeating the familiar phrases . . . one often has a curious feeling that one is
not watching a live human being but some kind of ____: a feeling which
suddenly becomes stronger at moments when the light catches the
speaker's spectacles and turns them into ____ ____ which seem to have
no ____ behind them" (paragraph 13).

A mass of Latin words falls upon the facts like ____ ____, blurring the outlines and covering up all the details (paragraph 16).

When there is a gap between one's real and one's declared aims, one
turns as it were instinctively to long words and exhausted idioms, like a
____ ____ out ____(paragraph 16).

Phrases like *a not unjustifiable assumption* . . . are a continuous temptation,
a ____ of ____ always at one's elbow (paragraph 17).

AUTHOR/

TITLE INDEX

725

HARRY CREWS: Harry Crews, "Pages from the Life of a Georgia Innocent," *Esquire*, July 1976. Copyright © 1976 by Harry Crews. Reprinted by permission of John Hawkins & Associates, Inc.

ANNIE DILLARD: Excerpt from *Pilgrim at Tinker Creek* by Annie Dillard. Copyright © 1974 by Annie Dillard. Reprinted by permission of HarperCollins Publishers, Inc.

RITA DOVE: "The Satisfaction Coal Company," from Rita Dove, Thomas and Beulah, Carnegie-Mellon University Press, copyright © 1986 by Rita Dove. Used by permission of the author.

BARBARA EHRENREICH: From *The Worst Years of Our Lives* by Barbara Ehrenreich. Copyright © 1990 by Barbara Ehrenreich. Reprinted by permission of Pantheon Books, a division of Random House, Inc.

GRETEL EHRLICH: "Wyoming: The Solace of Open Spaces" is reprinted by permission of the author.

STEVEN FOSTER: Reprinted by permission of Open Court Publishing Company, a division of Carus Publishing Company, Peru, IL, from *Crossroads: The Quest for Contemporary Rites of Passage*, edited by Louise Carus Mahdi, Nancy Geyer Christopher, and Michael Meade.

JOHN KENNETH GALBRAITH: "The Higher Economic Purpose of Women" from *Annals of an Abiding Liberal*. Copyright © 1979 by John Kenneth Galbraith. Reprinted by permission of Houghton Mifflin Co. All rights reserved.

TERRY GALLOWAY: "I'm Listening as Hard as I Can" is reprinted with permission from the April 1981 issue of *Texas Monthly*.

HENRY LOUIS GATES, JR.: From *Colored People* by Henry Louis Gates, Jr. Copyright © 1994 by Henry Louis Gates, Jr. Reprinted by permission of Alfred A. Knopf Inc.

SUSAN GLASPELL: "Trifles" by Susan Glaspell. Copyright ©1916 by Frank Shay; copyright 1920 by Dodd, Mead & Company, Inc. Copyright renewed 1958 by Susan Glaspell. Text revised, prompt book added and new material, copyright 1951 by Walter H. Baker Company. For production rights contact Baker's Plays, Boston, MA 02111.

ALBERT GOLDBARTH: From *A Lineage of Ragpickers, Songpluckers, Elegiasts and Jewelers: Selected Poems of Jewish Family Life 1973–1995*, by Albert Goldbarth. Reprinted by permission of Time Being Books. Copyright © 1996 by Time Being Press. All rights reserved.

LOIS GOULD: "X" from *Ms. Magazine*, May 1980, pp. 61-64. Reprinted by permission of The Charlotte Sheedy Literary Agency.

MELISSA GREENE: Excerpts from "No Rms, Jungle Vu" by Melissa Greene. Reprinted by permission of the author. First published in *The Atlantic*, December 1987.

DONALD HALL: "Purpose, Blame, and Fire," *Harper's*, May 1991. Copyright © by Donald Hall. Reprinted by permission of the author.

PATRICIA HAMPL: "Memory and Imagination," copyright © 1985 by Patricia Hampl. Reprinted by permission of The Rhonda Weyr Agency, Chapel Hill, NC.

permission of the author. "Reasons of the Body" from *Secrets of the Universe* by Scott Russell Sanders, © 1991 by Scott Russell Sanders. Reprinted by permission of Beacon Press, Boston.

DOROTHY L. SAYERS: Dorothy Sayers, "Living to Work." From *Unpopular Opinions: Twenty-One Essays*. Copyright © 1947. Reprinted by permission of the Estate of Dorothy Sayers and the Watkins/ Loomis Agency.

JULIET B. SCHOR.: Excerpt from *The Overworked American: The Unexpected Decline of Leisure* by Juliet Schor. Copyright © 1991 by BasicBooks, a Division of HarperCollins Publishers, Inc. Reprinted by permission of BasicBooks, a subsidiary of Perseus Books Group, LLC.

JANE SMILEY: Copyright © 1995 by *Harper's* Magazine. All rights reserved. Reproduced from the June issue by special permission.

GLORIA STEINEM: "I Was a Playboy Bunny" from *Outrageous Acts and Everyday Rebellions* by Gloria Steinem, © 1983 by Gloria Steinem. Reprinted by permission of Henry Holt and Company, Inc. "Sex, Lies, and Advertising," *Ms.* July/August 1990, pp. 18–28. Reprinted by permission of the author.

DEBORAH TANNEN: "Wears Jumpsuit, Sensible Shoes, Uses Husband's Last Name." By Deborah Tannen, *The New York Times*, June 20, 1993, copyright Deborah Tannen. Originally titled "Marked Women, Unmarked Men." Reprinted by permission. Material in this article is taken in part from the author's book *Talking from 9 to 5* (Avon, 1995).

LEWIS THOMAS: "Crickets, Bats, Cats, & Chaos," *Audubon*, 1992. Reprinted by permission of the Darhansoff & Verrill Agency.

SALLIE TISDALE: Sallie Tisdale, "Good Soldiers," *The New Republic*, 1/3/94, pp. 22–27. Reprinted by permission of The New Republic © 1996, The New Republic, Inc., and the author.

ALICE WALKER: "Am I Blue?" from *Living by the Word: Selected Writings 1973–1987*, copyright © 1986 by Alice Walker, reprinted by permission of Harcourt Brace & Company.

E.B. WHITE: Drafts of "Notes and Comment" by E.B. White (final draft appearing in *The New Yorker*, July 26, 1969) are reprinted by permission of the Estate of E.B. White.

WILLIAM CARLOS WILLIAMS: "Jean Beicke" by William Carlos Williams, from *Doctor Stories*. Copyright © 1938 by William Carlos Williams. Reprinted by permission of New Directions Publishing Corp.

NAOMI WOLF: From Naomi Wolf, "Promiscuities: The Secret Struggle Toward Womanhood." *Tikkun* 12/3. May/June 1997, pp. 53–57. Copyright © 1997. Reprinted by permission of *Tikkun*.

VIRGINIA WOOLF: "Professions for Women" from *The Death of the Moth and Other Essays* by Virginia Woolf, copyright 1942 by Harcourt Brace & Company and renewed 1970 by Marjorie T. Parsons, Executrix, reprinted by permission of the publisher.